THE MECHANISM OF CATASTROPHE

This edition was made possible by the generous support of

Michael and Mary Jaharis, and Angelo and Sophia Tsakopoulos

The Mechanism of Catastrophe

The Turkish Pogrom of September 6-7, 1955,
and the Destruction of the Greek Community of Istanbul

Speros Vryonis, Jr.

GREEKWORKS.COM • NEW YORK

2005

© 2005 Speros Vryonis, Jr.

Third Printing

greekworks.com
New York, NY
info@greekworks.com

Book design by Chris Frieman.

Maps by Jonathan Wyss, Topaz Maps Inc.

Jacket design by Viktor Koen.

Publishers Cataloging in Publication data

Library of Congress Control Number: 2005923077.

Vryonis, Speros.
The Mechanism of Catastrophe: The Turkish Pogrom of September 6-7, 1955, and the Destruction of the Greek Community of Istanbul
p. cm.
Includes index/bibliographical references.
1. Greece 2. Turkey 3. History 4. Politics 5. Human Rights
6. 1950s 7. Minorities 8. Cyprus
I. Title
ISBN 978-0-9747660-3-4 (cloth)

*To Dêmêtrios Kaloumenos, who lived, photographed, and described
the destruction of the Turkish pogrom of September 6-7, 1955, in Istanbul,
and in so doing suffered much on behalf of the truth.*

The marriage of time to history bred both deception and truth,
and these offspring are engaged in perpetual struggle and turmoil.
—*Dêmêtrios Kaloumenos*

Table of Contents

LIST OF ILLUSTRATIONS

1. Dêmêtrios Kaloumenos is honored by the academy of Athens on November 29, 1979, for his photographic documentation of the pogrom; sitting directly behind him is Kônstantinos Tsatsos, president of the Greek republic (courtesy of Dêmêtrios Kaloumenos).
2. Adnan Menderes (courtesy of Dêmêtrios Kaloumenos).
3. Athênagoras I, ecumenical patriarch of the Orthodox Church (courtesy of Dêmêtrios Kaloumenos).
4. Alexandros Papagos (courtesy of Dêmêtrios Kaloumenos).
5. Kônstantinôs Karamanlês (left) with Adnan Menderes (right), as F. R. Zorlu looks on; Euangelos Averôf-Tositsa is half-hidden behind Karamanlês (courtesy of the Historical Archives Service of the Greek ministry of foreign affairs).
6. Patriarch Athênagoras with Fahrettin Kerim Gökay (middle), *vali* of Istanbul, in 1954 (© Dêmêtrios Kaloumenos).
7. Rioters batter in the front of a Greek shop (*The Illustrated London News* picture library).
8. One of many youthful bands that led the rioting, driving through the streets, waving flags, and shouting slogans (*The Illustrated London News* picture library).
9. A crowd of mainly young men demonstrates in an Istanbul street, shouting anti-Greek slogans (*The Illustrated London News* picture library).
10. A portrait of Kemal Atatürk is held above a speaker (*The Illustrated London News* picture library).
11. Destruction of a Greek store (*The Illustrated London News* picture library).
12. Troops stand by an overturned car after rioters have passed (*The Illustrated London News* picture library).
13. Tanks gather in Istanbul after the proclamation of martial law (*The Illustrated London News* picture library).
14. Wreckage is strewn in a Beyoğlu street (*The Illustrated London News* picture library).
15. *The Illustrated London News* coverage of the pogrom; the subhead under the headline reports £100 million of damage.
16. Pedestrians strolling over destroyed goods, with six ruined stores in background, İstiklal Caddesi, Beyoğlu (© Dêmêtrios Kaloumenos).
17. Three destroyed Greek shops (on the left), İstiklal Caddesi (© Dêmêtrios Kaloumenos).

In dedicating this book to Dêmêtrios Kaloumenos, I wish to acknowledge his important contribution to our knowledge of the little-known pogrom of September 6-7, 1955, which inflicted massive destruction on the Greeks of Istanbul.* His contribution was twofold and resulted from both his copious photography, which was done under dangerous circumstances, and from his personal record of the events, published and unpublished. Above and beyond Kaloumenos's direct experience of the pogrom lie his keen perception and strong ethical values. A well-read man, with complete command of both Greek and Turkish, he is also highly intelligent, with great physical and moral courage, and dedicated to the truth.

Early on the evening of September 6, he quickly understood that violent and important events were in the making, and so hastened to his studio in Galata, took his camera and numerous rolls of film, and, over the next five days, shot some 1,500 photographs of damaged or destroyed Greek homes, businesses, churches, monasteries, cemeteries, schools, and print shops. These images soon made their way to the outside world. Consequently, we now have a plethora of visual documentation to illustrate the oral and written testimony of the pogrom's course and nature. In short, Kaloumenos was an extraordinary individual who understood history and politics, as well as the ethnic hatred and violence that often ensued from the former, and who, in full knowledge of the danger to him, undertook to preserve the truth.

That the pogrom of September 6-7, 1955, is virtually unknown—and has been effectively excluded from the scholarly and political discourse concerning its larger context—does not testify to its insignificance. Rather, it bespeaks the fact that, for the most part, the event has been, in turn, ignored, rationalized, excused, or denied by the Turkish government, and by the governments that have underwritten Turkey for half a century, in order to further their respective national and geopolitical interests. We are thus

*I have a short CV of Kaloumenos in manuscript form, dated July 22, 1987. The Komotênê newspaper *Chronos* carried brief biographical notes of him in April 1999. Finally, I inaugurated, with the assistance of a second interviewer, a taped interview (four reels) of Kaloumenos during his visit to the US in February 1991. This is his most detailed autobiographical account and is of considerable importance, and much of the biographical material in this preface is taken from this interview, as well as from the intense and extensive conversations I have had with him over a period of thirteen years, and from conversations with his wife, Euangelia, and daughter, Marina.

all deeply indebted to Dêmêtrios Kaloumenos for his foresight, unwavering courage, and perseverance in documenting and preserving the historical truth of the pogrom, and for his unrelenting pursuit of justice.

Kaloumenos opened his studio, Embeka, in 1948 at Maden Han 5, in Galata. His father, uncle, and brother were also professional photographers, and their studio, Lumiyer, which they had earlier established in Yüksek Kaldırım, was to be destroyed during the pogrom (see the photographic inset). Kaloumenos was not only the ecumenical patriarchate's official photographer, but served as import agent for the newspapers and magazines of Athens and Thessalonikê. Thus, his connections to the Greek press were close and constant, which was to be a significant factor in the subsequent dissemination of his photographs of the pogrom. Kaloumenos was well-prepared to document the violence against the Greek community because, in addition to his experience as a photographer and journalist, he was deeply knowledgeable—indeed a student—of the history of Istanbul and its culture.

Kaloumenos found himself at Tophane at 5:00 PM on September 6, 1955, among a group of Turkish soldiers preparing to participate in the pogrom. He observed that they were removing their uniforms and putting on civilian clothes while, nearby, people in parked trucks with official markings were arming them with crowbars and pickaxes. Sensing that something dramatic was about to take place, Kaloumenos hurried to his studio; by 6:00 PM, he was in Taksim Square prepared to photograph what he thought would be a demonstration. He caught the tail end of the speeches to the gathered mob and then witnessed the onset of violence.

From that time onward, and for many days thereafter, the patriarchal photographer busied himself with the dangerous business of photographing the destruction, although the conditions were anything but felicitous. The police and military forbade taking pictures, and so Kaloumenos had to hold the camera under his coat. Furthermore, despite the poor lighting, he could not afford to use a flash attachment, as this would have given him away. By 10:00 PM, he had boarded the ferry for Heybeliada (Chalkê), where his family had been staying for late summer vacation. On the morning of the seventh, he boarded the same boat at 6:00 AM and now went to his studio, took a second camera and ten more rolls of film, and spent most of the rest of the day photographing in Galata, Yüksek Kaldırım, Beyoğlu, Kalyoncu Kulluk, Tataula, Tarabya, and Büyükdere.

On September 8, he was joined by the correspondent from the Athens newspaper *Ethnos*, Giôrgos Karagiôrgas, who had been sent to cover the devastation suffered by the city's Greeks (and who was joined, in turn, on September 9 by Iôannês Iôannidês, the editor of *Makedonia*, the major newspaper of Thessalonikê). Thus, on the morning of the eighth, Karagiôrgas followed Kaloumenos to the large Greek cemetery of Şişli. Both men have left accounts of their experience, and of their encounter with the police, which included Karagiôrgas's escape and Kaloumenos's arrest. Karagiôrgas's description of their "voyage of discovery" in the destroyed cemetery of Şişli contains details of how they furtively (since they were followed by security police) photographed the ruins and desecrations:

> I...managed...to enter the cemetery of Şişli two hours before entrance was to be forbidden. Horror was scattered over all the little "streets" of the cemetery, over the fallen and smashed [marble] crosses, over the exhumed corpses, intermingled with the repulsive stench. To the left and in the distance, the ossuary was still burning [almost two days after the destruction]. From within the piles of bones, there arose a light, diaphanous white smoke....There were also two young Turks [police] with their wrinkled red shirts following us....
>
> Dêmêtrios Kaloumenos...loaded with his camera was constantly grumbling, "Do not indicate that you know me...stay close to me...but with a little distance between us." He was continually turning to the left and right to see who was near us. He photographed everything, even the interior of the ossuary, which was smoking with a smoke that was choking us. We issued forth once more into the cemetery. There, with a small Japanese camera, I photographed a priest who had been slashed, with a knife, on the forehead....
>
> [Throughout Istanbul] the Greeks were weeping, Dêmêtrios wept, the priests were weeping. Greeks had gathered at the [Greek] consulate...and mutely sought comfort from the consul....
>
> Our rolls had finished, time was passing, and so we decided to leave. I led and Dêmêtrios followed; we had passed the rolls inside our socks. Suddenly, three men (one of them was the young policeman who had followed us) jumped out from behind the graves and ordered us..."Police, come here!" Two of them immediately surrounded Dêmêtrios....[†]

Karagiôrgas escaped by hiding in open graves; before leaving the cemetery, he quickly gave the film to a priest with orders to get them to Kaloumenos's studio. Kaloumenos was taken in for questioning, but, as he had managed to get rid of his film, was released. The priest, meanwhile, took the rolls of film to Kaloumenos's studio, and the photos were ultimately delivered to

[†] Giôrgos Karagiôrgas, "Enas Septemvrês prin apo 26 chronia," in *Dêmosiografika. Epilegmena keimena pente dekaetiôn*, Volume 1, pp. 540-544.

Karagiôrgas, who, on the day he left Istanbul, taped them on his back to keep them from being found in his luggage. Finally, on the ninth of the month, *Makedonia* gathered further photographs from Kaloumenos, and so it was that a large body of very graphic pictures found their way into the Greek press within two weeks of the pogrom.

Kaloumenos's life became increasingly difficult because of his harassment by the security police. On June 15, 1957, he was arrested, incarcerated in the central police station at Sirkeci, and alternately interrogated and tortured by the police. As he was held incommunicado, Kaloumenos's wife did not know where he was or what had happened to him. He relates that he was subjected to bastinado four times, estimating that the beating was spread out each time over twenty to thirty minutes over a period of about fifty-six hours. In the end, the police decided that he had little to tell them. He was subsequently expelled from the country by the Turkish authorities.

One is amazed at Dêmêtrios Kaloumenos's persistent pursuit of truth, which endangered him bodily and psychologically. In these days of ready and crude compromise, such courage and willingness to persist are truly rare. On a final and personal note, without his generosity—and the direct and free access he gave me both to his extraordinary photographic archive of the pogrom and to his photographic collection on various aspects of the life, culture, and society of Istanbul's Greeks—this study would have been much diminished.

At the outset, I wish especially to acknowledge the gracious support of The Jaharis Family Foundation, without which it would have been impossible to undertake the publication of this work. The editorial and production demands of the book were such as to render publication both unusually difficult and financially onerous. Mr. and Mrs. Jaharis have long established themselves as important donors to and patrons of Hellenic and Orthodox cultural and scientific endeavors in the United States and elsewhere as well. To them, and to The Jaharis Family Foundation, I express my profound gratitude for their critical support, which not only made the publication of this book possible, but also allowed its contents to be made accessible to the American public, and to the educational and governmental institutions of the United States.

During my tenure at the Alexander S. Onassis Center at New York University, my duties often took me to various universities and cities, both in the States and abroad, which allowed me to avail myself of a number of libraries for the present work. Near at hand, in New York, I searched the collections of the Butler (now in a sad physical state) and Lehman libraries and found a number of useful books and articles there on the Menderes era (1950-1960). A term stay, as the Solomon Katz Distinguished Professor of the Humanities at the University of Washington in Seattle, gave me the chance to utilize the library's rich collections in modern Turkish history, politics, and literature. While the UCLA library was far richer in its Ottoman collections, it had a number of items from the Menderes era as well. Finally, I also visited the modern Greek collection of the University of London.

I was able to work in the British national archives (formerly, and absorbing, the public record office) at Kew Gardens, in the archives of the Greek ministry of foreign affairs and of the Greek embassy in Washington, DC, and in the national archives in Washington. From these four archives, 1,048 documents of some 4,000 pages were identified as relevant and I am most grateful to these institutions and to their staff for their generous accommodation of my requests to reproduce them.

I was also fortunate to have access to a manuscript copy (governmental) of the *Decisions* (*Kararlar*) and legal *Opinions* (*Gerekçeler*) of all the tribunals at Yassıada (1960-1961), which convicted the great majority of the 592 accused officials brought to trial. Also of interest was further access to a formal photographic album prepared by the *İrtibat Bürosu* (ministry of communications) with some 254 photographs of the various trials, from the arraignment of the more important members of the Menderes government to the hangings of Menderes, Zorlu, and Polatkan. Of equal importance was my access to some sixty files of damaged or destroyed Greek religious institutions. Although not all of the files were complete (data concerning fifty institutions were available to me), many were quite detailed, both as to description of damages and of the various materials employed, as well as to prices for materials (as officially determined by the government). These documents were an excellent source, not only for establishing the extent of damages, specific items damaged, and partial compensations, but also for verifying the damaged items for which no compensation was received by the Istanbul *vakıflar*, which undertook the assessments of the actual repair and rebuilding. Far more detailed are the archives of the Greek committee, known as the 6/7 *Eylül Hey'et*, which was the conduit to the *vakıflar* for all applications for repairs or rebuilding of the Greek community's religious institutions. These exhaustively detailed accounts (of which, again, I had access to the documentation for fifty institutions) cover the entire process of repair and rebuilding, including contractors' bids and amounts paid to contractors by the *vakıflar*.

As for sources and documentation on the trials at Yassıada, it is fortunate that the military junta that overthrew Menderes was anxious to plead its case both legally and publicly, and so released all types of records to incriminate his government. In some ways, however, this book cannot be an exhaustive treatment of the pogrom and its aftereffects, as much of the primary source material is inaccessible to scholars. This includes the *tutanaklar* (proceedings of the trial in 1960 of those responsible for the pogrom), of which there is a copy in the Turkish Grand National Assembly Library. Some evidence was destroyed by the Menderes government and his *Demokrat Parti* (DP)—or was sequestered and is, therefore, still unavailable—including the destroyed portions of the DP's central registry, from which the mass of relevant pages was ripped out and destroyed. In addition, no one has yet seen the archives of the *Kıbrıs Türktür Cemiyeti* or of other organizations (although, in this case, we have the published works of Hikmet Bil). The files of the Red Crescent, the Istanbul aid committee, and even the archives of the Turkish foreign ministry have not yet been opened. In their stead, I used the detailed reports of Greek, British, and American diplomats, all of which contained a wealth of data. Also, there was neither time nor need to undertake a full examination of the German, Austrian, Russian, French, and Italian archives. Nicole van Wees's dissertation, based on research in the Dutch archives (and kindly made accessible to me by Prof. Pavlos Hidiroglu), fills at least one of these many archival gaps. It is highly unlikely, however, that these particular governmental archives will tell us anything fundamental that is not already more than covered in the Greek, US, British, and Turkish archival materials and sources already consulted. For the assessments and compensation payments, I had access to Turkish as well as other materials—but it must be repeated in this case, as in so many others, that access to Turkey's governmental archives is crucial, as is access to the archives of other private and public Turkish institutions.

Without going into detail, I also want to mention the scholarly and memoir literature to which this study is partly indebted. The atmosphere and chaos of the night of September 6-7, 1955, are conveyed with remarkable accuracy, but witty and consummate literary artistry, by the late Aziz Nesin. A victim of successive repressive Turkish regimes himself, he understood the fundamental internal contradiction of the structure and political life of the modern Turkish state. *À propos*, he stated that there is a comic element in every tragedy, while a tragedy of lesser or greater proportions lurks in every comic episode. He managed to convey in his record of the pogrom not only the crazed psychological atmosphere that served as a constant background to its fanaticism and senseless violence, but also the sight, faces, and even smells of the violators (their old shoes and clothing, for example, which were eventually discarded and replaced with looted clothes, shoes, hats, jewelry, and watches). On a different, historical level, he referred to the pogrom as the Turkish version of the St. Bartholomew's Day massacre of Protestants by Catholics in France. Once into French parallels, in fact, he made the sardonic observation that a knowledge of French was indeed useful to understanding the violence. This was an indirect reference to the then-governor of the Banque de France (and former prime minister), Pierre Mendès France, who, after witnessing the riots (having been present for an international conference in Istanbul that night), punned, "Qui brise, Türktür" ("He who smashes is a Turk")—a clever play on the slogan, *Kıbrıs Türktür* (Cyprus is Turkish).

As was to be expected from someone who was not only a literary figure but also a physician, Hulusi Dosdoğru's analysis of the corruption of Turkish political culture was unemotional and clinical. Dosdoğru showed both Adnan Menderes and his court-martial head, General Fahrettin Aknoz, to be brutal and completely shameless figures. He justifiably accused both men of punishing the innocent for the crimes committed by Menderes, the state, and its organs of security. As a physician, his clinical logic mustered the evidence not only from his eyewitness account of what transpired in his own neighborhood (Ortaköy), but also from his systematic consultation of the archival evidence and his experience of both the Aknoz courts-martial, in which he stood accused, and the Yassıada trials. Like Nesin, Dosdoğru was not a stranger to the political repression of various Turkish governments and had spent time in prison. Unlike many others who were falsely charged in connection with the pogrom, he seems to have defended himself without the aid of lawyers. Consequently, he consulted a very wide body of legal evidence as he was writing his book. He quotes extensively from the *tutanaklar* and very extensively from the *Decision* and *Opinions* of the trial. His analysis of the role in the pogrom of the local DP chapters, and presidents and boards, is detailed and proves their guilt point by point. Of everything that has been written on the pogrom, the trials, and the role of Menderes and the DP, Dosdoğru's account is the most detailed, and it is thoroughly convincing. As a literary author, his clinical analysis is humanized by his moving descriptions of those few Greek victims that he was able to aid and comfort on the very eve of his arrest and incarceration. Unlike Nesin's account, there is no humor whatever in Dosdoğru's presentation, for he found nothing humorous in the violent crimes of Menderes and the Turkish state. His account is tightly organized and periodically punctuated by his hammered conclusions. In short, it is the most valuable of all the accounts of this crime. It is a pity that his book has not been translated (although Nesin's book was faithfully rendered into Greek and published in Athens).

Of the extensive Turkish literature on the subject, one of the more detailed and useful analyses of the Yassıada trials is that of Tekin Erer, published in Istanbul in 1965. Consisting of some 665 pages, it provides the entire structure and most of the relevant facts of these trials. Particularly revealing of many aspects of Turkish justice and of the mechanics of Turkish trials—which heavily favored the prosecution, even allowing it to attack the political ideology of the accused, and denied defense attorneys time to read all the materials essential to their defense—are the two books of the noted Istanbul lawyer Cemal Fersoy. He was part of the defense team of both Zorlu and Menderes, and he describes in detail the legal restrictions imposed by the court on his efforts to provide an effective defense for the accused. He specifically underlines the fact that he was allowed very little time for consultation with Zorlu and was not given time to consult the details of the accusations and proceedings.

Because the internal breakdown of Menderes's DP accelerated from September through December 1955, and because İsmet İnönü's attacks began to take effect, the writings of certain Turkish journalists as well as of truculent DP members—who were champing at the bit both over Menderes's refusal to place responsibility for the pogrom where it belonged and his effort to take dictatorial control of the political process—are particularly rich and informative. Many, but not all, are mentioned in the bibliography, but one can point to the work of Ahmed Hamdi Başar (published in 1960), which gives a detailed account of the DP caucus that took place prior to the special session of the Turkish parliament on September 12, 1955, which was called in order to vote for martial law (of six months' duration) in Istanbul, Izmir, and Ankara. The electric atmosphere of this caucus was occasioned by the desire of the majority of DP members of parliament to assign responsibility for the pogrom. The refusal of Menderes and his supporters to allow such a discussion led to the party's fracturing, which culminated on November 29, 1955, when dissident DP members helped the opposition to bring down the government. Başar's account is critical in its detailed description of this event, which occurred so soon after the pogrom.

The observations of the Turkish journalist Emin Karakuş, which were written much later (1977), had the full benefit of a generation's worth of hindsight as well as greater access to documentation; consequently, they fill in details on the affair of the İspat Hakkı, the fall of Menderes's government on November 29, 1955, and the DP's splintering. Karakuş also includes excurses on Namık Gedik's suicide and the book by Hikmet Bil, accusing Menderes of planning the pogrom. Meanwhile, Mahmut Dikerdem's memoir (1977, reprint 1990) was written almost from the point of view of the established order (the Turkish government and foreign ministry during Zorlu's era). Dikerdem was a younger member of the Turkish delegation to the tripartite conference in London and later played an important role in the pressing question of Turkish compensation for the victims of the pogrom. His work has been utilized very effectively in Neoklês Sarrês's book.

Particularly valuable for this study have been the works of two Greek authors. The first was the late Christoforos Chrêstidês's principal work, the *Ekthesis* on the pogrom, which was finally published in 2000, but which I used when it was still in manuscript. Chrêstidês probably finished this work in late 1957, some two years after the event, and the reason why it was not published at the time must lie in the fact that the matter of compensation (of whatever form and nature) had been legislated on February 29, 1956. His book, in any case, seems to have suffered the same fate as the *Black Book* composed by Alexander Pallês at the request of the Greek foreign ministry. Chrêstidês's *Ekthesis* is a basic source, and anyone researching the pogrom must analyze it in great detail. He had access to all kinds of materials, some of which have not appeared elsewhere, such as the partial list of the first compensations paid out to forty-odd Greek merchants in Istanbul. This list is invaluable not only because it identifies the compensated, but, above all, because it reveals in great detail the processes by which special commissions of the Turkish finance ministry reduced payments by some 81 percent of the original assessments (British citizens had their claims cut by some 80 percent).

Chrêstidês had complete command of Turkish and was also a keen observer of the Turkish political scene inasmuch as he had a Turkish client who was a member of parliament. He had sensed, and written in the Greek press, that the month of August 1955 would be critical in Greek-Turkish relations. His essay includes a detailed analysis of the extent and locations of the violence, and contains an excellent examination of the press campaign and national hysteria that preceded the pogrom. He includes a number of original documents, including the letter of a Turkish noncommissioned officer whose band of followers destroyed houses and stores in the district of Edirnekapı, and reports by Greek hierarchs on the destruction in their respective jurisdictions. Finally, his book on the Cyprus issue (published in 1967) significantly supplements the *Ekthesis*, which should be translated and enriched by supplements and notes that bring it up to date.

The second author whose rich and important work concerns the pogrom, and indeed Greek-Turkish relations more broadly, is Prof. Neoklês Sarrês. The first volume of his massive study, *Ê allê pleura*, which appeared in 1982, constitutes a masterful analysis of the events, beginning with the state of heightened political tensions in August 1955, then the pogrom itself, the Yassıada trials, and, finally, the relationship of all these events to the issue of Cyprus. Born in Turkey and formerly a member of the *Demokrat Parti* himself, Sarrês has written the first analysis in depth of the entire diplomatic complex that hopelessly doomed Greek-Turkish relations for so many decades. His study's richness resides in its successful synthesis of both Greek and Turkish sources, especially of the memoir literature on the Turkish side, and in its use of the relevant Yassıada documentation. What Sarrês has to say more generally on this complex of issues is even more significant now in light of Cyprus's entry into the European Union and the debate raging around Turkey's possible accession; his analysis also speaks to the ongoing violations (until most recently) of Greek and Cypriot airspace by the Turkish air force.

These few references by no means exhaust the works that have been of assistance to me in writing this book and the bibliography at the end includes them all. It remains for me now to express gratitude to all those who assisted me at various stages of researching and writing this book.

A great deal has already been said about Dêmêtrios Kaloumenos and his epic enterprise of photographing the consequences of the pogrom. I first became aware of this extraordinary photographic archive by reading Dr. Alexis Alexandris's book on the Greek minority of Istanbul (published in

1983). Thereafter, I decided to call on Mr. and Mrs. Kaloumenos during my next visit to Athens. Since that time, Dêmêtrios and Euangelia, as well as their daughter Marina, have been steadfast friends, inspirers, and models of moral courage, as well as informants on Istanbul during their lifetime of turbulent experiences. When I told him of my study and of its publication, Dêmêtrios responded with unexpected generosity. To Dêmêtrios Kaloumenos, to his wife Euangelia, and to their daughter Marina, I owe a great debt and I wish here merely to record it again.

I owe thanks to many others. First, I wish to thank Mr. Antônês Samaras who, as Greek foreign minister, opened the rich archives of his ministry, as well as of the Greek embassy in Washington, DC, for the benefit of this research. He was most cordial to my request and asked that his colleagues give me access to all documents that I would need. Those who expedited the matter in the ministry offices were the late Manôlês Kalamidas (a specialist with rich experience in Greek-Turkish relations) and certain others who saw to the identification and photocopying of the documents. Their advice and command of the information on the subject were of inestimable value. When the lack of photocopying equipment threatened the project, Deputy Foreign Minister Virginia Tsouderou saw to it that the necessary equipment was acquired and installed so that reproduction of the voluminous documentation could proceed unhindered. More recently, I was given timely assistance by Dr. Photini Tomai-Constantopoulou, director, and Mr. Iôannês Begos of the ministry's service of diplomatic and historical archives, for which I am grateful.

In the offices of the Greek embassy in Washington, then-Ambassador Chrêstos Zacharakês and his counselor, Charalambos Rokanas, saw to it that all relevant files were brought to me, after which I proceeded to photocopy them in the embassy. Their courtesy and promptness were and are much appreciated. Two other officials of the ministry helped me in particular. Dr. Euangelos Kofos was a graduate student in Washington at the time of the pogrom and had considerable duties in connection with the so-called *Black Book* then being prepared, while Pavlos Hidiroglu, a specialist in the history of contemporary Turkey, was a rich source of information and insights. I wish to express my warmest appreciation to these two friends and scholars. I must also mention here the kindness and generosity of Ambassador Vyrôn Theodôropoulos, who was present in Istanbul at the time of the pogrom and was responsible for authoring many of the diplomatic dispatches concerning it. He very kindly gave me a copy of an official summary and analysis of the events that he had prepared for the foreign ministry during the first months of 1956. It is one of the most incisive and important analyses of the event and I have been privileged to refer to it in the text of this book. Mr. Vasilis Portokallis also opened his personal archive to me, with its slides, newspaper articles, and, above all, the valuable correspondence of his mother, Despoina Portokallis, who has left us important accounts of the pogrom and of its dire economic consequences. Mr. Portokallis also experienced the pogrom and has left his own account of it.

I must express my thanks in particular to the directors and staffs of the respective national archives in Washington and Kew Gardens for kindly providing me with copies of numerous documents from their rich collections. In the case of the latter, I wish to express my appreciation also to my younger colleagues, Prof. Alexander Kitroeff of Haverford College (and my former colleague at the Onassis Center of New York University) and Prof. Elena Frangakis-Syrett of Queens College. These seasoned veterans and experts in British and American archives prepared and advised me on my first venture into the British collection in particular.

The well-known Greek journalist Lambros Papantoniou was a profound and endless source of information and insights into the turbulent relations of Greece and Turkey, as well as into the difficult relations among the United States, NATO, and Greece. The prolific Greek journalist Alexis Papahelas provided me with a copy of the first major report of the American consulate in Istanbul on the pogrom (No. 132, dated September 23, 1955). Wing Commander Panagiôtês Skoutelês of the Greek air force provided me with a copy of the uncirculated *Black Book*, which previously was thought to have been completely destroyed.

I am particularly indebted to Mr. Hovannes Khosdegian, who translated into English the four newspaper articles that appeared in the Parisian Armenian newspaper *Har'ach* in September 1982. The anonymous author of these articles (signed simply B. E.) was an eyewitness to the pogrom. I should also mention the help rendered me by Aram Arkun, librarian at the Armenian diocese of New York. I owe many thanks as well to Dr. Rouben Adalian, director of the Armenian Assembly in Washington, DC, for his many suggestions. At the beginning of this research, Prof. Paschalis Kitromilidis, then director of the Center for Asia Minor Studies in Athens, opened the center's archives to me and provided me with photocopies of the Chrêstidês archive, including the latter's invaluable manuscript. Access to this manuscript was, of course, critical to my research, and I wish to thank him—and the Center's staff, which assisted me in many details—most warmly. Dr. Spiro Macris, a former supreme president of the Greek American organization AHEPA, took time off from a heavy professional schedule to provide me with a considerable body of material that he had identified in AHEPA's publication series. This has proven to be of considerable interest, especially for the history of the expulsions of Greeks from Istanbul in 1964.

The Syllogos Kônstantinoupolitôn of Athens kindly arranged for me to speak on the subject of my research and to profit from the discussions, observations, and corrections offered by an attentive and well-informed audience. In particular, I wish to express my appreciation to Mr. Nikos Atzemoglou, Mr. Leônidas Koumakês, and Mr. and Mrs. Geôrgios Isaakidês, both for their hospitality and for their substantial contributions to my further knowledge of the details of the pogrom. Similarly, Dr. Liana Mystakidou has been a constant source of information—and one that I greatly value—on all things concerning modern Turkey. Particularly rewarding was the invitation of Prof. Anastasios Tamis, director of the National Centre for Hellenic Studies and Research at the University of LaTrobe in Australia, to visit and lecture there, as well as in other Australian universities and Greek communities, on the pogrom. This opened up large audiences and discussions from which I profited greatly. Further, he opened to me the use of the center's rich collection of Greek newspapers.

I had particularly valuable conversations with Prof. Marios Evriviades on the triangular relations of Greece, Turkey, and the United States. Even more specifically, Dr. Patroklos Stavrou's assistance in matters concerning Cyprus, and the patterns of Islamization and Turkification of the northern regions of the island, was important. As undersecretary to the president of Cyprus, Dr. Stavrou's knowledge of all these issues was especially valuable.

The personal discussions with my friend, Prof. Giannês Chasiôtês of the University of Thessalonikê, were of particular interest and profit. Mr. Theodôros Buyanas, a native of Istanbul who witnessed the pogrom and who knows a great deal about it as well as about many of the churches that were attacked, has been of constant help on many details. With the tragic accident that damaged the eyesight of Dêmêtrios Kaloumenos, he has taken an active role in the Kaloumenos archive, for which we must all be grateful. I also wish to thank my former student and, for years now, president of Melissa Media Associates, Inc., Aristide Caratzas, for undertaking the difficult task of transporting the Kaloumenos archive to the United States, where I could study and utilize it to good effect.

To a certain degree, the research and writing of this work also had an important family dimension, and for this I wish to express my gratitude to the members of my immediate family. My dear wife, Badri, undertook the first draft or schema of the relevant topical maps, and did so with her experience in the arts and draftsmanship. My youngest son, Nikolas, photocopied some 18,000 pages of printed sources and materials, and carefully mounted them in twenty-three thick spiral notebooks, thus rendering it possible for me to consult these materials systematically and effectively. Finally, my older son, Demetrios, served as a constant interlocutor and commentator on the organization, execution, and goals of the book, constantly stressing the importance of the principal goal, that is, to find the truth behind the violence on the night of September 6-7, 1955. Although a lawyer, he was trained in both classics and classical history, as well as in the history of Byzantium.

I must not fail to acknowledge the Herculean labors of my publishers, Peter Pappas and Dr. Stelios Vasilakis, of *greekworks.com*. Our cooperation was based on a past association in other scholarly ventures and collaborations, and in our common interest in the cultural and political ambience of Hellenism and of its associations with other peoples, religions, and cultures. Finally, my gratitude goes back to my late father and mother, and to their respective families, travelers over the globe, across six oceans and into five continents, who were living examples of the historical relations between the Hellenism of their tiny island, Kephalonia, and the rest of the world.

To all these people, and many more, I owe gratitude, whereas all the errors are my own.

Speros Vryonis, Jr.
El Dorado Hills, California

A Personal Chronicle

The origins of my interest in this subject go back to a time when I was a graduate student in the history department of Harvard University and, more specifically, to a period when—as recipient of a junior fellowship to Harvard's Byzantine center at Dumbarton Oaks in Washington, DC—I was researching my doctoral dissertation on the Byzantine "Time of Troubles" (1057-1081).[1] The dissertation, among other things, was concerned with the first appearance of the Seljuk Turks in Asia Minor, and their conquests and settlements there. This latter subject was to become the foundation and base of a life-long interest in the Turks, the Balkan peoples, and the Islamic world. My student years at Dumbarton Oaks and Harvard (1956-1960) coincided with the decolonization of the British empire, the Cold War, and the reconstruction of much of western Europe—including Greece—as well as the beginning of the Cyprus "problem."

My arrival at Dumbarton Oaks in August 1955 coincided, more or less, with the ill-fated London tripartite conference. That conference had been convened by the Eden government to encourage Turkey to join forces with Britain in order to block the drive of the Greek Cypriots to place the issue of their self-determination before the United Nations. Some days later, just before the conference's completion, the pogrom of the night of September 6-7, 1955, erupted. In a relatively few hours, forty-five Greek communities in the greater Istanbul area had been savagely attacked by extensive arson and vandalism, and the larger Greek community lay ruined in its homes, shops and businesses, churches, cemeteries, medical clinics, schools, and newspapers. The event made its way into the local Washington press and radio. For a month or so, the subject emerged at the luncheons served at

---

[1] On Dumbarton Oaks, its earlier Washington affiliation, and the center for Byzantine studies, see Walter M. Whitehill, *Dumbarton Oaks: The History of a Georgetown House and Garden, 1800-1966*, Cambridge, 1967; Ernest R. May and Angeliki E. Laiou, editors, *The Dumbarton Oaks Conversations and the United Nations 1944-1994*, Washington, 1998; Milton V. Anastos, "Dumbarton Oaks and Byzantine Studies, A Personal Account," in Angeliki E. Laiou and Henry Maguire, editors, *Byzantium: A World Civilization*, Washington, 1992, pp. 5-18; Giles Constable, *Dumbarton Oaks and the Future of Byzantine Studies*, Washington, 1978; and *Handbook of the Byzantine Collection*, Dumbarton Oaks, Washington, 1967.

the Dumbarton Oaks fellows building, which also served as the temporary lodging for three junior fellows and the occasional senior scholars invited to do research and give lectures. The atmosphere that prevailed at the institution, however, was, by and large, not only unsympathetic to the pogrom's victims, but also pro-British and even, to a certain degree, pro-Turkish. Indeed, what impressed me at the time was the indifference of the scholars there to the commission of such a massive crime.[2]

The Dumbarton Oaks library subscribed to *The New York Times*, *Washington Post*, and *Manchester Guardian*, and so I began to read the reportage in those newspapers. These reports were garbled at best, while, at worst, surprisingly uninformative and inaccurate as to the pogrom's nature; in many ways, they reflected the views of the US or British governments. The only difference was one of quantity, as the *New York Times* had much more detail, thanks to Cyrus Sulzberger's particular interests.[3] By and large, the American press tended to praise Turkey for taking serious measures in the early morning of September 7, 1955, to restore some degree of quiet to Istanbul. There was not a word on the role of the Turkish government in allowing this outburst to take place, nor was there any such suggestion. Generally, the American and British press tended to follow the official policies of their respective governments.

---

[2] Inasmuch as the Cyprus issue was and remained inextricably intertwined not only with the pogrom but with every aspect of Greek-Turkish relations, as well as with Turkish relations with the United States, Britain, NATO, and, today, the European Union, a brief glance at Turkish policy—until recently—toward the religious and communal monuments and heritage of Greek Cypriots is indeed revealing. The destruction wreaked by the Turkish army and mainland settlers in Cyprus strikingly recalls the pogrom in Istanbul. A report from the Eighties released by the Cyprus department of antiquities catalogued the following damage inflicted by Turkish forces in the occupied north of the island:

Churches seized and converted to mosques	37
Churches destroyed	17
Churches looted	29
Churches utilized by the Turkish army	11
Churches subjected to specific desecration	17
Cemeteries destroyed	2
Churches converted to stables	11
Churches converted to public toilets	2
Churches converted to storehouses	6
Churches converted to cultural and athletic centers	6.

Memorandum; for supplementary documentation, see the book, *Flagellum Dei: The Destruction of Cultural Heritage in the Turkish Occupied Part of Cyprus*, Cyprus press and information office, ministry of the interior, 1987; and Michael Jansen, "Cyprus: The Loss of a Cultural Heritage," *Modern Greek Studies Yearbook*, II, 1986, pp. 314-323.

A few weeks after the violence, at a meeting in Saint Sophia Cathedral in Washington, Archbishop Michaêl, primate of the Greek Orthodox Church of North and South America, informed the communicants of the pogrom's grim details and asked for help for the victims. I decided to attend, and what I heard was so different from the local media reports, and from the luncheon table at Dumbarton Oaks, it was as if the archbishop had referred to an entirely different event. The media, as well as many of my senior and junior colleagues, either considered the pogrom of little importance (and certainly not a moral issue) or else thought that the "troublesome" Greeks had gotten what they deserved. These first impressions of the American media and academe were to be reinforced by almost half a century of my life as a citizen of this great country and as a student, and then a professor, in several of America's finest universities. Apparently, human and democratic rights are only for the select. Today, this attitude is officially condemned, but still has a powerful and semi-covert existence.[4]

During such discussions in the hallowed halls of an august Harvard institute, what could a lowly graduate student say? I stayed two years at that rich and extraordinary institution of Dumbarton Oaks, finished my dissertation, and went to Harvard on a four-year instructorship as a member of the history department and of the late Sir Hamilton Gibb's newly founded Center for Middle Eastern Studies.[5] There, I taught courses on the Middle

---

[3] See especially the *New York Times* of September 11 and 12, 15-20, and 24; thereafter, the interest subsided and the coverage was erratic.

[4] The recent literature in the United States on the Iraq war, for example, recalls the effect of the Vietnam war on the gullibility of the American public. The disbelief of many Americans regarding the policy statements of the upper ranks of the US government has been effectively expressed in many contemporary books by American authors, some of them coming from the ranks of present and former government officials. See, indicatively, Chalmers Johnson, *The Sorrows of Empire: Militarism, Secrecy, and the End of the Republic*, New York, 2004, for a scholar's critique; and, for the chronicle of a former cabinet member, Ron Suskind, *The Price of Loyalty: George W. Bush, the White House, and the Education of Paul O'Neill*, New York, 2004.

[5] This was the era of the founding of area-studies programs in a dozen or more American universities. The purpose of these programs was twofold: teaching, studying, and researching regions of eastern Europe, the Middle East, Asia, Africa, and Latin America, on the one hand, and creating area specialists who would serve the interests of the US government, on the other hand. The lack of sufficient specialists in these areas has become marked during the course of the Afghan and Iraqi wars. See on these programs, R. D. Lambert *et al.*, *Beyond Growth: The Next Stop in Language and Area Studies*, Washington, 1984. For the background of these studies, and the politics both within and outside the universities, see: John Trumpbour, editor, *How Harvard Rules: Reason in the Service of Empire*, Boston, 1989; Morton and Phyllis Keller, *Making Harvard Modern: The Rise of America's University*, Oxford, 2000; Clark Kerr, *The Gold and the Blue: A Personal Memoir of the University of California, 1949-1967* (in two volumes, *Academic Triumphs* and *Political Turmoil*), Berkeley, 2001 and 2003. I was twice approached to

East, the Balkans, the Ottoman empire, and classical antiquity. Having finished my dissertation, I turned to preparing an ambitious book on the decline of medieval Hellenism in Asia Minor and the process of Islamization from the eleventh to the fifteenth century. Simultaneously, I spent the next four years utilizing whatever spare time I had to study classical Arabic and Turkish, as they would be necessary for any serious venture into my new research.

My two years at Dumbarton Oaks and four years at Harvard brought me into the whole arena—or, rather, arenas—of Turkish, Armenian, Greek, Israeli, and Palestinian controversies and confrontations, first through the back door of academe and then through the front door of US foreign policy in those areas. Still, when I left Harvard in 1960, the pogrom had become a distant interest pushed far back into the more remote chambers of memory. My small file of contemporary articles on the event and a few other official documents that had strayed into my hands lay neglected in my quickly growing files. Upon arriving at UCLA in the fall of 1960, I found myself in a much more stimulating academic environment. The vigorous direction of the late Gustave von Grunebaum had created a massive Center for Near Eastern Studies with such distinguished scholars as Andreas Tietze, Wolff Leslau, and, eventually, Amin Banani, Moshe Perlman, Giorgio Buccellati, and many others, who helped build a great program of undergraduate and graduate studies in which the source languages were all taught systematically and effectively, and where a great library was built in an astonishingly brief period of time.[6]

Eventually, I left UCLA to inaugurate and administer the newly founded Alexander S. Onassis Center at New York University in 1988, where I remained until 1995. There, I became immersed in the activities of the Modern Greek Studies Association, so that once more I was wrapped up in the internal politics of a small, navel-gazing organization. Because of the ongoing and accelerating tensions between Greece and Turkey, particularly over Cyprus and the Aegean, and the expansion of tensions and political difficulties throughout the Balkans, I began to turn to these areas and found my small file on the pogrom.

enter the CIA, first in the summer of 1955 while studying Russian at Harvard and a second time in early 1956 while finishing my doctorate at Dumbarton Oaks. I refused on both occasions, preferring the open career of intellectual endeavor to one of a more clandestine nature.

[6] The history of the rise to prominence and precipitous decline of UCLA's Gustave von Grunebaum Center for Near Eastern Studies is of considerable interest and deserves attention. Its decline is shrouded in the administrative "indifference" of the university's deans and administration, and was rendered complex by the internal jealousies and feuds of some of its members. Symptomatic of the former is the disappearance of the valuable von Grunebaum collection of 7,000 rare editions of historical, philological, and political studies of the Near East.

What had, early on in my academic career, astonished me was the readiness, not only of the US government and State Department, but also of academics to prostitute the truth for money, recognition, and/or political acceptance. Despite the argument that one can never know the "real truth," such moral relativism opens the door to arbitrariness, dictatorship, and the violation of any and all forms of justice. The attempts of so-called revisionists to demonstrate that there was no Holocaust or massacre of the Armenians—just to name the two most egregious examples—are enough to demonstrate that convenience is often far more powerful than truth. Often, those who attempt to assert the truth are mocked and ridiculed (both effective weapons when the media are controlled) and dismissed as troublesome at best. The truth long ago became a haphazard commodity: useful when it can be brought to bear by those in power, but disturbing to the authorities when it is contrary to what they wish it might be.[7]

The present book is not only about the larger issue of slanting and distorting history to fit various political and personal agendas, but about distortion of truth as an immoral act in and of itself. That is to say, it seeks to create a broad basis of fact, regardless of sources or political points of view, so that the pogrom of September 6-7, 1955, can finally be properly understood for what it clearly was and represented. An examination of the pogrom thus gives us prismatic views of Turkish, Greek, British, and US interests on a broader level. It is, above all, a search to ascertain basic truths, not the "truths" of political convenience.

At the practical level of the regional politics of the time, the pogrom is also a prism that refracts the internal difficulties of the ten-year Menderes government, in which are clearly discernible all the basic issues, both internal and external, that so beset and characterize Turkish society today. These issues are largely the same, albeit much more magnified, as are the current issues of US foreign policy. Turkey during the decade in which the *Demokrat Parti* ruled is a rich subject that beckons any gifted and qualified scholar.

---

[7] Speros Vryonis, Jr., "American Foreign Policy in the Ongoing Greco-Turkish Crisis as a Contributing Factor to Destabilization," UCLA *Journal of International Law and Foreign Affairs*, Volume 2, spring/summer 1997, #1, pp. 69-89.

THE GREEKS OF ISTANBUL ON THE EVE OF SEPTEMBER 6, 1955

Before proceeding to delineate the violent course of the pogrom of September 6-7, 1955, a necessarily brief collective portrait will be offered of the object of the destructive fury of this massive, government-organized, and tragic act of violence. In systematically destroying the Greek community of Istanbul in only nine to ten hours' time, what—and, more specifically, since each of these individuals had a face and a personality and a personal history, *who*—was it that the Turkish state and its accomplices set out to efface? What was the nature of this largely passive, defenseless victim? What were its demographic characteristics, its structures of self-articulation, and cultural self-identity? What were its economic bases and internal "political" structure, its relations to the Turkish government and nation, to the Greek government and nation, and to two of the world religions (Christianity, to which it belonged, and Islam, under which it functioned as a second-class confessional community)? Without some attempt to give an analytical answer to these basic questions, it is difficult to give an adequate explanation of the destruction of the Greek community, of the hatred and rage that imbued this violent act, and of the role of the Turkish state in it. Further, this attempt will, I hope, indicate the resiliency and dynamism of a much-persecuted minority that, in the few years prior to the pogrom, was on the road to a comeback and toward an economic prosperity and sociocultural flowering that would approach its experience from the 1830s to 1922. This, too, will place the phenomenon of the pogrom—with all its elements of ethnic hatred, religious fanaticism, and economic envy—within a more nearly complete background and historical environment.

First, there are a few elemental facts of history that were, and remain, deeply engraved in the historical-cultural experience of Greeks and Turks. Along with Jews, Egyptians, and Italians, the Greeks possess one of the longest, most continuous, and most extensively recorded histories in the Mediterranean basin. Because of this unbroken chronological presence—as well as the role of the ancient element of this history in the formation of Western civilization and Byzantium's contribution to the formation of the civilization of much of eastern Europe—the Greeks are extremely sensitive to their historical presence as a people. The eighteenth-century revival of classical content in western European education, literature, and the arts, as well as the establishment of Byzantium as a reputable object of research and teaching in the latter half of the nineteenth century, were equally to infuse modern Greeks with a deeper understanding of the accomplishment of their ancient and medieval predecessors, with the result that all this was reincorporated into their cultural self-consciousness in a systematic manner. Constantine the Great's conversion to Christianity and his transferal of the Roman empire's capital to the renamed city of Constantinople introduced the last elements to the cultural base of modern Greeks: Orthodox Christianity, and the rise of a Greek city, Constantinople-Byzantium, to the status of a world, and imperial, capital. This site—bounded by the Sea of Marmara, the Bosphorus, and the Golden Horn—had been settled by Greek colonists from Megara some 1,000 years before Constantine's dedication of his capital, and, as a colony, had the benefit both of rich fishing grounds and of the strategic location that enabled it to influence and grow rich from the international commerce moving in the north-south and east-west axes, both by land and sea. Constantine and his immediate successors eventually transformed this provincial Greco-Roman *polis* into a thriving metropolis and cosmopolis (and its excellent location assured its existence as an imperial capital not only from 330 to 1453, but from 1453 to 1922). By the reign of Justinian, the city was justly famed for its splendid civic and ecclesiastical monuments, its schools and letters, its wealth and leisure and pleasure. For over 1,000 years after Constantine, it was the seat of the Byzantine *basileus*, and the primary dispenser of ancient Greek and Byzantine literature and culture.

The Greek minority of the Istanbul region for the 200 years prior to the pogrom was increasingly aware of this heritage, and, although caught up in the movements of modern nationalism, could find social and economic expression in the multicultural and multiconfessional system of the Ottoman empire. It could find no ultimate political expression, however, in a traditional Islamic empire that could never admit non-Muslims to any kind of formal civic equality, let alone political parity. Thus, the modernizing Greek community of Istanbul increasingly looked to the small, newly founded Greek state for its political ideology and fulfillment.[1] In any case, the Greek minority represented the older "indigenous" or "native" inhabitants of the imperial city on the Bosphorus, and both Turks and Greeks were

---

[1] Neoklês Sarrês, in his introduction to Nikos G. Apostolidês, *Anamnêseis apo tên Kônstantinoupolê*, Athens, 1996, pp. 15 and 61.

conscious of this historical past, a fact which contributed, under Mustafa Kemal Atatürk's inspiration and command in the 1930s, to the invention and official propagation of the artificial Turkish theses of history (the *Türk Tarih Tezi*) and linguistics (the *Güneş Dil Teorisi*).[2] Turkish educational theorists were, accordingly, forced to create a new Turkish identity with a historical consciousness, albeit on a falsified historical basis, that taught Turkish students in primary, secondary, and university courses that the Turkish "race" was the mother of all races and that the Turkish language was the mother tongue of all other languages. According to these theories, the Turks, in the form of the Hittites, were the earlier inhabitants of Asia Minor, and the Greeks and their language were merely minor branches of the Turkish people and language. Thus did nationalism provide a myriad cures for historical difficulties.

In fact, as nomadic warriors, the Turks appeared on the eastern Anatolian boundaries of Byzantium in the latter half of the eleventh century, after having first passed through the Persian and Arab lands of Islam. They appeared, formally at any rate, as a nation of Islamic warriors who had come to renew the struggle between the world of Byzantine Christianity and the Islamic caliphate of Baghdad. In an ongoing and long period of 400 years of warfare, Turkish Muslim warriors succeeded in wresting Asia Minor from Byzantium and the Armenians, and large numbers of Greek and Armenian Christians were Islamized confessionally and Turkified linguistically.[3] When the early conquests of the first Ottoman rulers culminated in the capture of the Byzantine imperial capital of Constantinople on May 29, 1453, and the conquerors replaced the Byzantine empire with the long-lived Ottoman empire, the Greek, Armenian, Bulgarian, Vlach, Serbian, and Albanian Christians became the subjects of a very powerful and traditional state, which inherited the full panoply of administrative, legal, religious, and cultural paraphernalia of formal and popular Islamic culture and civilization. The millennial capital of the Byzantine, and Eastern Orthodox, empire was transformed by the political genius of its conqueror, Mehmet II. Vast destruction, pillaging, killing, enslavement, and rape had accompanied the

---

[2] Speros Vryonis, Jr., *The Turkish state in history: Clio meets the Grey Wolf*, Thessalonikê, 1991, pp. 67-88; A. F. Çöker, *Türk tarihinin ana hatları. Kemalist yönetimin resmi Tarih Tezi*, Istanbul, 1938, reprinted 1996; A. F. Çöker, *Türk tarih Kurumu. Ana hatları. Kemalist yönetimin resmi Tarih Tezi*, Istanbul, 1930, reprint, 1996; K. Steuerwald, *Untersuchungen zur türkische Sprache der Gegenwart I-III. Die türkische Sprachpolitikzeit*, 1928 (1963-1966); Özel-Özen-Puskulluoğlu, *Türk Dil Kurumu, passim.*

[3] Osman Turan, *Selçuklular zamanında Türkiye. Siyasi Tarih Alp Arslandan Osman Gazi'ye (1071-1381)*, Istanbul, 1971, *passim*; Speros Vryonis, Jr., *The Decline of Hellenism in Asia Minor and the Process of Islamization From the Eleventh Through the Fifteenth Centuries*, Berkeley, 1971; Abdülbâkı Gölpınarlı, *Mevlanadan sonra mevlevilik*, second edition, Istanbul, 1983.

city's conquest. Once this terminated, however, Mehmet, like Constantine some 1,100 years earlier, set out to recreate an unequalled imperial capital on the magical site of old Constantinople, which, in this instance furthermore, would become a great center of Islamic political and military might.

How did the Greek-speaking and Orthodox community of Constantinople survive this devastating siege? Mehmet first provided for the manumission of a significant segment of the enslaved Christians by ransoming them himself from his troops, and these he returned to Constantinople as the earliest Greek settlers (the Latins were all slain). Then he set into motion a long program of forced colonization of elements from all over his empire. On the basis of historical tax data compiled by Halil Inalcik,[4] we can safely assert that the proportion of Greek Orthodox households was roughly 23 percent

[4] Halil Inalcik, "Istanbul," *Encyclopedia of Islam*, second edition, Leiden, 1997, pp. 238-239. Inalcik's precise data are as follows:

"*Sürgüns* (forced colonists)

1459	Armenian and Greek merchants from the two Focas and Amasra
1460	Greeks from the Morea, Thasos, Lemnos, Imbros, Samothrace
1461	Greeks from Trebizond
1462	Greeks from Mytilene
1463	Greeks from Argos
1468-1474	Muslims, Greeks, Armenians from Konya, Larenda, Aksaray, Eregli
1470	Greeks from Euboea
1475	Armenians, Greeks and Latins from Kaffa."

In his publication of a comparatively early tax record of Istanbul and Galata, respectively, dated 1477, we see reflected the proportion of tax-paying households according to confession:

Istanbul	*households*	%
Muslim	8,951	60.0
Greek Orthodox	3,151	21.5
Jews	1,647	11.0
Kaffans (Latins?)	267	2.0
Armenians	372	2.6
Armenians and Greeks of Karaman	384	2.7
Gypsies	31	0.2
	14,803	

Galata	*households*	%
Muslim	535	35
Greek Orthodox	592	39
Europeans	332	22
Armenians	62	4
	1,521	
Total households	16,324."	

in Istanbul in 1477, while Muslim households made up 60 percent (and Jewish ones another 11 percent), which might be an indirect indication of the relative size of each community in the regular population, although these figures of taxable households do not include the large number of state officials and soldiers. A crucial part of Mehmet's elaborate scheme to transform the sacked town of Constantinople was the decision to make of Istanbul not only a metropolis—that is, a very large city—but also a cosmopolis, a city that would include all the disparate and useful elements of the empire, in other words, a microcosm of his multiethnic and multiconfessional state. This was, of course, a long-established tradition in the imperial capitals of the Umayyads, Abbasids, Fatimids, and even of the more restricted state of the Rum Seljuks. So it was that, on January 6, 1454, Mehmet met Gennadeios Scholarios— elected by the patriarchal synod as the first Greek Orthodox patriarch of Ottoman Istanbul—who, along with an interminable line of successors, would reconstitute the social and religious life of the Greek community as a minority within the guidelines and legal forms of the Islamic world.[5]

Thereafter, the Greeks of Istanbul remained a constant religious minority in Istanbul. In the count of males over the age of thirty in the 1833 Ottoman census, Inalcik reproduces the following figures:

Table 1: Population of Istanbul

Muslims	73,496
Greek Orthodox	50,343
Armenians	48,099
Jews	11,413

The total population of the greater Istanbul area in 1927 was 447,851 Muslims and 243,060 Christians.[6] Thus, from the very moment that Mehmet II began rebuilding and repopulating the city in the mid-fifteenth century, to the end of the Ottoman empire in 1922-1923, the Greeks of Istanbul lived the traditional life of *dhimmis*, that is, of non-Muslims officially recognized by Islam and the Islamic empires. The Greek community was, of course, no longer dominant in all areas of public life as it had been in Byzantium. As a result, while it possessed the rights to security that Islam normally provided its major non-Muslim minorities, it was also subject to the legal and fiscal limitations, and occasional outbursts of fanaticism, of an Islamic state.

---

[5] Inalcik, "Istanbul," p. 225; Speros Vryonis, Jr., "Byzantine Patriarchate and Turkish Islam," *Byzantinoslavica*, 57:1966, pp. 83-84 and *passim*.

[6] Inalcik, "Istanbul," p. 243.

Nevertheless, the period from the latter half of the seventeenth century, and especially the late eighteenth century, saw a rise in the development, size, economic activity, sociolegal organization, and educational institutions of Istanbul's Greek community. This culminated in what some have chosen to call its "golden age." All this is no doubt connected with the rise of maritime, banking, and commercial activity in Istanbul and the more general economic development of the Ottoman empire. Indeed, with the *Tanzimat* reform movement and the proposed equality of the various ethnoreligious communities of the multinational empire propounded by the *Hatt-ı Hümayûn* in 1856, the minorities were given considerable latitude of activity, which the Greek community exploited. Under these new conditions, the Ottoman administrative system began to absorb some Christians into the state apparatus, and the Greek community was slowly transformed into a Westernizing organism that adopted and adapted to the new outlook in business, education, and social organization.[7]

The organization, structure, and mentalities of this reviving Greek community in the latter half of the nineteenth century and the first two decades of the twentieth century have been the focus of a number of important studies that have analyzed its characteristics.[8] It would seem that the combination of economic growth, the articulation of the Ottoman state more generally, the concomitant expansion of the financial and economic institutions and services that this all demanded, and the modernization of the Ottoman administrative system, transformed Istanbul into a center of important economic activity and opportunity. Understandably, these new opportunities served as a stimulus to the city's growth, and so induced new immigration to Istanbul of Greeks and others from various parts of the empire, as well as from Greece itself.[9] The city became the economic center of the Balkans and of important parts of the Middle East. The problematic nature of the city's demographic statistics—whether Ottoman, Greek, or of any other community—notwithstanding, there is clear evidence that the Greek Orthodox had become a significant minority by the time of the Young Turk revolution in 1908, and that they had indeed increased in number.[10]

Two estimates, one Turkish and the other Greek, place the population

---

[7] Carter V. Findley, *Bureaucratic Reform in the Ottoman Empire: The Sublime Porte, 1789-1922*, Princeton, 1980, pp. 205-209.

[8] Kônstantinos Svôlopoulos, *Kônstantinoupolê 1856-1908: Ê akmê tou ellênismou*, Athens, 1994, for succinct summaries of much of the scholarly examination of the structure and life of the Greek community of Istanbul during this "golden age."

[9] Svôlopoulos, *Ibid.*, pp. 37-42.

[10] *Ibid.* summarizes and identifies the origins of these statistics; Paschalis M. Kitromilides and Alexis Alexandris, "Ethnic Survival, Nationalism and Forced Migration: The Historical

of the city and its immediate environs at 1,052,000 and 1,173,673, respectively.[11] According to the Ottoman surveys of 1885 and 1906, the Greeks inhabiting the city numbered 152,741 in the first case and 176,442 in the second.[12] The Greek male population is said to have numbered 58,516 in 1856, and 68,006 in 1882. Western observers place the number of the Greek minority somewhat higher. The formal Greek estimates, based largely on figures of the ecumenical patriarchate, indeed give a number that is much larger for the early twentieth century:

Table 2: Greeks in three *vilayets* (provinces)

Istanbul	235,215
Çatalca	54,787
Üsküdar	74,457
Total	*364,459*

An important difference in the bases of these surveys is that Greek nationals living in Istanbul were not counted in Ottoman statistics. In any case, whether one takes the lower figure of the Ottoman census or the figures of the patriarchate, the native Greek community plus the Greek citizens resident in Istanbul constituted a substantial minority that might have varied from 17 to 22 percent of the city's population.[13] If one were to include the Greek citizens resident in the city, the total number of Greeks therein would have varied between 214,441 and 236,442 (that is, between 20 and 22.5 percent).

Although it is difficult to trace the movement and settlement patterns of the Greeks in Istanbul during the entirety of Ottoman rule, which covered several centuries, it would seem that their general dispersal on the eve of the pogrom is already visible in the pattern of settlement in the period from 1856 to 1908. The earlier Ottoman demographic configuration, with the presence of Greeks along the land walls of the city and on the shores of the Sea of Marmara and the Golden Horn, was supplemented by Greek communities on both sides of the Bosphorus, in Hasköy, Galata, and Beyoğlu. A major movement eventually followed into the Pera-Beyoğlu district in the newer economic center of Pera. Accordingly, Greek communities were to be found along the south shore of the Golden Horn, especially at Fener, Un Kapani,

Demography in Asia Minor at the Close of the Ottoman Era," *Deltio Kentrou Mikrasiatikôn Spoudôn*, Volume V, 1984-1985, pp. 9-44.
[11] Svôlopoulos, *Ibid.*, pp. 38 and 102 (notes 51-53).
[12] *Ibid.*, p. 38.
[13] If one accepts the figure of 364,459 for Istanbul, Çatalca, and Üsküdar, then the percentage would reach 34.5 percent. See also *Ibid.*, note 55, page 103.

Cibalı, Balat, and Vlaherna. They were also strung out along much of the inside of the Byzantine land walls at Edirnekapı, Sarmaşık, the Gates of St. Romanus and Belgratkapı, and beyond the walls at Balıklı and also at Bakırköy and Yeşilköy on the Sea of Marmara. Turning east, the communities were spread out along the sea walls facing the Sea of Marmara at Samatya, Yenikapı, Kumkapı, and Altı Mermer. To the north of the Golden Horn, Greeks were settled at Hasköy, Kurtuluş, in the high hills of Beyoğlu, and to the southeast in the neighborhood of Galata, which fed on the life of the port and its complex of maritime activities.

Greek communities were also located to the north, along the beautiful hills and shores of the Bosphorus. On the European shores, they included Beşiktaş (Diplokionion), Ortaköy (Mesochôrion), Kuruçeşme (Xerokrinê), Arnavutköy (Mega Reuma), Bebek, Boyacıköy (Vafeochôrion), İstinye (Stenê), Yeni Mahalle (Neochôrion), Büyükdere (Vathyryax), Tarabya (Therapia), and Rumeli Fener (the Phanar). On the Asian side were Şile, Beykoz, Paşabahçe, Çengelköy, and Kuzguncuk (Chrysokeramon). On the Asian shores of the Sea of Marmara were the communities at Fenerbahçe, Maltepe, Üsküdar (Skoutari), and Kadıköy (Chalcedon). Finally, there were the Greeks settled on the three Princes Islands of Burgazada, Heybeliada, and Büyükada (Antigonê, Chalkê, and Prinkipo).[14] The Ottoman census of 1885, using (ten) different geographic designations, lists the number of the Greek minority living in each administrative department:[15]

Table 3: Greek communities
(Ottoman census of 1885)

1. Sultan Beyazıt	30,336
2. Fatih	24,270
3. Cerrah Paşa	20,931
4. Beşiktaş	21,222
5. Yeniköy	6,394
6. Kule Kapısı	17,589
7. Büyükdere	7,308
8. Kalınca	6,782
9. Üsküdar	10,046
10. Kadıköy	6,876

A more detailed statistic, in rounded numbers but incomplete, lists the

[14] *Ibid.*, pp. 43-44.
[15] *Ibid.*, p. 47.

following data for the early twentieth century, in two columns according to the number of families and number of unwed inhabitants.[16]

Table 4: Greek communities (early 20th century)

District	Families	Unwed inhabitants
Pera-Beyoğlu (Staurodromion)	8,000	10,000
Feriköy	279	50
Kurtuluş (Tataula)	2,000	1,000
(Wider area) [*sic*]	250	30
Galata	1,200	1,900
Fener	650	220
Muhli	170	10
Potiras	140	100
Hasköy	200	701
Cibalı	500	1,500
Kumkapı (Kontoskali)	1,230	220
Yenikapı (Vlanga)	900	500
Samatya	730	100
Samatya (again)	250	100
Altı Mermer	350	300
Belgratkapı	200	200
Sarmaşık	70	40
Topkapı	140	80
Salmatobruk	105	50
Tekfur Sarayı (Palation Kônstantinou)	80	10
Edirnekapı (Pylê Adrianoupoleôs)	160	176
Eğrikapı		NA
Pylê Kaligariôn	100	24
Balino	120	50
Tahtakapı (Xyloporta)	200	40
Balat	300	50
Beşiktaş	620	110
Ortaköy	200	100
Kuruçeşme	100	30
Arnavutköy	800	250
Bebek	70	10
Boyacıköy	220	50
İstinye	70	10
Yeniköy	415	250

[16] *Ibid.*, pp. 47-49.

The Greeks of Istanbul rose in importance because of their economic presence. Although there might have seemed to be an increase of Greeks in the lower ranks of the Ottoman administrative structure, and a number of them did reach ambassadorial rank in the Ottoman diplomatic service, the regimes of Abdul Hamid and of the Young Turks after him were ever more reluctant to appoint minorities to the administration. It was rather in the society's economic sector and in the liberal professions that the Greeks found an open horizon. Thus, there appeared a small and influential group of Greek bankers, financiers, industrialists (especially in light industry), and commercial entrepreneurs (often agents for larger European companies and firms). Further, the Greek community, which was in the forefront of modernization and of the creation of a truly urban society, was possessed of a bourgeois class that included insurance agents and realtors, lawyers, engineers, architects, and physicians. There were shopowners throughout the city, from the fancy streets of Pera to the more removed suburbs of the poorer and richer Istanbulis. In a contemporary observer's statistical report, we get a rather good idea of the thorough social stratification of the middle and lower classes of the Greek community:[17]

Table 5: Occupations of Greeks

amba (coarse wool) tailors	2,028	itinerant fruitsellers	195
asbestos-makers	160	jacket-tailors	54
bakers	2,652	latheworkers	120
blacksmiths	110	mattressmakers	897
boatowners	278	milksellers	590
builders	657	merchants	893
butchers	982	olivesellers	269
candlemakers	97	plasterers	127
cobblers	1,180	repairers	204
coffeesellers	615	retail druggists	28
doormakers	489	tailors	887
drivers (horse)	NA	tavernowners	764
dyers	141	tobacconists	348
fishmongers	395	watercarriers	1,359
furnituremakers	487	wagondrivers	1,929
greengrocers	640	winesellers	652
grocers	2,250		

[17] *Ibid.*, p. 108, note 156.

All of this evidence is a good indication that elements of Istanbul's Greek community had prospered in the expanding Ottoman economy. It also points to a vital middle class of professionals and businessmen (located throughout the greater Istanbul area, and active both in the marketplace and in their respective communities), as well as to a sector of small merchants, craftsmen, and skilled workers that existed in substantial number—some 22,477 according to the above data—so that socioeconomic stratification of the community at large was substantial and vital. It was this socioeconomic base that invigorated community life as a whole by virtue of the money that it infused into it through various corporate bodies. The economic development of the Greeks in Istanbul, and their ability to rise in the private sector, had become obvious to many Western observers by the end of the third quarter of the century. By the early twentieth century, it was to provoke a boycott of Greek businesses and merchandise by the Young Turks. Alongside the harshness of the Young Turks' ethnic policies, this was to have an immediate effect (both economic and psychological) and was to leave a toxic legacy to the future Turkish republic and to its Greek minority in the three decades from 1918 to 1947.

Two features in particular characterized the forms and content of Greek community life in Istanbul, and both were firmly based on certain older traditions and on the newer economic vitality that the Greeks had generated within the quickening Ottoman economy. These two features were, first, the growth of a whole network of corporate institutions of lesser and greater magnitude through which the community provided for an ever-expanding array of needs; and, second, the evolution of a Western-inspired system of schools and instruction that incorporated the spirit and content of modern education. Both features helped to provide for the daily needs of the community and for its future security (or so it was hoped), as well as strengthening the bonds of social and cultural solidarity.

The oldest of the great institutions was, of course, the ecumenical patriarchate, a long-lived Byzantine and Ottoman body whose status in Greek Orthodox society was guaranteed by the absolutist political structure of both empires. During the classical Ottoman period, it had served as a religious institution primarily, but also as a legal force and patron, not only of Greek and Christian education, but of some of the arts. Because of its long historical tradition, and of the attachment to it of the Greek Orthodox, it retained an important status in the Greek community of Istanbul; increasingly during the nineteenth century, however, it interacted with the growing secular, powerful, wealthy, and influential Greek middle classes. Accordingly, by the latter half of the nineteenth century, the bulk of the laity's educational and philanthropic corporate bodies took over most of the educational and charitable functions in the community at large, particularly at the local level of the many different communities. Simultaneously, however, the patriarch and the holy synod retained the Church's educational and philanthropic institutions, while strengthening those of the laity with their moral support.

Among the secular institutions, the organizations or guilds of Greek workers, which had a kind of semi-autonomy, were very important. Each guild had its own *kehayia* (steward, from the Turkish *kahya*) and treasury, and a kind of juridical right to judge the misdemeanors and behavior of its own members within its corporate body. By 1892, the guilds were administered by the Office of the Guilds under the authority of the *vali* of Istanbul.[18] Their number and importance were evident in the founding of the Hospitals of Balıklı in 1838. It was by the initiative of the 113 Greek guilds of Istanbul that a group of older Greek institutions were united and the famous Hospitals of Balıklı were created. This complex was to become the largest and best-organized medical center in the Balkans.[19] In earlier times, the guilds had played an important role in electing the ecumenical patriarchs; in fact, even in the latter part of the nineteenth century, ten representatives of the more important guilds were still participating in patriarchal elections.[20]

Alongside these older corporate entities, there were many new ones, often known as "adelfata," or brotherhoods (which, as institutional forms, were much older), and which most often were committed to education or philanthropy. Indicative of the growing concern over cultural questions in the unity of the community was the foundation of the *adelfato* of *Anastasê*, created by Fôtês Fôtiadês in 1905 to promote the vernacular form of the Greek language as the national tongue of state, education, and literature among Greeks. Of a more regional character were the numerous *filologika salonia* (literary salons), the most famous of which was the Hellenic Philological Society of Constantinople (founded in 1861). In its efforts to disseminate knowledge to the Orthodox of the Ottoman empire, it published scholarly studies, sponsored lectures and reading rooms, held scholarly and literary competitions, and created a library and laboratory. By the end of the third quarter of the nineteenth century, it had established seventy-five branch chapters in Istanbul and had spread into other towns of the empire.

The movement for the legal establishment of institutions that promoted Greek culture resulted in three times as many cultural associations as existed

---

[18] *Ibid.*, pp. 82-84.
[19] *Ibid.*, p. 108, note 155.
[20] *Ibid.*, p. 84.

in Athens.[21] There were similar associations that concerned themselves with athletics, music, philately, and the arts, as well as with social welfare for those Greeks unable to provide for themselves or their families.[22] The most spectacular of the latter entities were the aforementioned Hospitals of Balıklı. Their reputation had spread by 1910, not only to the Balkans but to the Middle East as well. A brief glance at the number of patients that they treated from 1866 to 1906 will give some idea of their growth.

Table 6: Patients at Balıklı hospitals

1866	2,470
1884	3,877
1901	5,565
1906	6,365

The orphanage that functioned in Istanbul from 1853 to 1909 and then moved to the island of Büyükada was also important. Education became ever more important, not only because it laid a common base for self-identity and therefore social cohesion, but also as a way to maintain the economic and social capacities of the community's future generations. The community's wealthy and middle classes saw to it that the necessary funds for financing community schools were forthcoming. Both the Ottoman and Greek governments also participated in the financial support of community schools (the former insisting that Ottoman Turkish be taught to students), as did Greek foundations and the wealthy who lived abroad. The available statistics indicate a general growth in the numbers of schools, teachers, and students.

Table 7: Patriarchal statistics for greater Istanbul[23]

Year	Schools	Teachers	Students
1870	104	245	9,730
1902	185	612	19,132
1907	277	no data	29,929

This brief sketch of the crucial areas of the Greek minority's life depicts a vital community in which all its social strata contributed both to the orientation and financing of the institutions necessary to a satisfactory

---

[21] *Ibid.*, pp. 84-88.
[22] Kôstas Stamatopoulos, *Ê teleutaia analampê: Ê kônstantinoupolitikê Rômiosynê sta chronia 1948-1955*, Athens, 1996, p. 155.
[23] *Ibid.*, pp. 55-56.

communal life. The decline and ultimate dissolution of the Ottoman empire, and the initial successes of the Greek army in western Asia Minor, encouraged further immigration of Greeks to Istanbul and seemed finally to establish the economic dominance of the Greeks over the city's life. British reports placed the Greek population of the Istanbul area at roughly 300,000 at the onset of the First World War in 1914, a number that swelled to about 400,000 in 1922.[24] This was accompanied by increased Greek influence on the city's economy. The military victories of the Turkish nationalist armies in Anatolia, however, eventually led to the return of Istanbul to the new Turkish state, with dire consequences for the city's Christian minorities, but especially for the large Greek community now living there. When the Allied commission departed from Istanbul on October 2, 1922, the flight of tens of thousands of Greeks from the city was already under way. The Turkish army entered the city a year later, on October 6, and the fate of its Greeks was sealed, both immediately and for the longer term. The demographic decline of Istanbul's Greeks was almost precipitous between 1922-1924, as the numbers of those who departed indicate.

Table 8: Greeks leaving Istanbul (1922-1924)

60,000	Greek citizens
40,000	Non-expellable Greeks
35,000	Greeks who had entered Istanbul after 1918
20,000	Greeks from Istanbul's suburbs
155,000	*Total (approximate)*[25]

When the Turkish army returned to the city, a series of measures followed, some enacted by law, others applied informally, that removed some 5,000 employees from various businesses, coerced Greek businessmen to sell their businesses for very little, and brought Turkish businessmen into the economy of the city and country while removing a substantial part of the Greek element. At the same time, the local Greek press was terrorized and the government began to apply the law against "cursing Turkism" to both the Greek press and Greek individuals. Indeed, one journalist was hanged, a newspaper closed, and its offices physically destroyed. The Turkish "Citizens, Speak Turkish Society" began the general harassment of Greeks who dared to speak their own language. Greek teachers were arbitrarily disqualified

---

[24] Alexis Alexandris, *The Greek minority of Istanbul and Greek-Turkish relations 1918-1974,* Athens, 1983, p. 96, note 4.

[25] *Ibid.,* p. 104 and *passim.*

as "unfit" to teach and were removed from the Greek schools in an effort to exercise tighter control over them and, in fact, to undermine them. In the end, the state did close down a number of schools, which proved to be catastrophic for Greek communal education, which entered a period of rapid decline in both numbers of students and teachers. A brief glance at the figures of students attending Greek schools from 1920 to 1928 speaks volumes on the deleterious effects of Turkish control and interference:

Table 9: Decline of students in Greek schools

Period	Number of students in Greek community schools
1920-1921	24,296
1923-1924	15,766
1925	8,515
1928	5,923[26]

The largest and most important Greek cultural institution, the Hellenic Philological Society of Constantinople, was closed by the Turkish government, which then proceeded—in violation of the Lausanne agreements on the respective Greek and Turkish minorities of Turkey and Greece—to confiscate its very important library (and to give its books to various Turkish institutions) and archives. (Incredibly, the archives remain inaccessible to Greek scholars even today.) Meanwhile, the government sequestered the properties and capital of the large number of Greek charitable and cultural institutions, and denied them full control of their resources, so that the community's institutional life atrophied while the community itself struggled to survive.[27]

This accelerating centralizing activity by the Turkish government culminated in a 1935 law that put all religious and community institutions under the strict control of the state and specifically froze their wealth, including whatever part of it was dedicated to philanthropy and culture. In providing for the governmental appointment of a solitary administrator (the *tek mütevelli*) for each of the many foundations or incorporated bodies, the law removed the initiative, and the decisionmaking power in allocating funds, from the respective *ephoreia* (a legal body's governing board). Previously, this domain of the purse and of decisionmaking had been the prerogative of each organization through its elected representatives, and so the law eliminated

[26] *Ibid.*, pp. 131-135.
[27] *Ibid.*, pp. 100 and 143, has given a well-structured account of the economic, institutional, and cultural constriction of the Greek community by the measures of the Turkish government.

a previously acknowledged right of the Greek minority. Although the law
was not fully implemented in the case of the Greek community, it had a
very negative effect on communal activities and life, as the Greeks could no
longer elect the governing boards of their organizations.[28] Under these new
conditions (and subsequent to them and many other policies of the Turkish
government), and after its substantial demographic decline following on these
powerful state pressures, one not only sees the Greek community shrinking,
but also the clear Turkish supremacy now in Istanbul's daily life. Even after
the initial departure of about 155,000 Greeks from the city and its environs
by 1924, the demographic reduction of the Greeks continued apace:

Table 10: Population of greater Istanbul (Turkish statistics)[29]

Year	Istanbul/ Environs	Muslims	Greeks	Armenians	Jews
1924	1,065,866	656,281	297,788	73,407	56,390
1927	806,993		100,214 + 26,419 Greek citizens		
1934			111,200		

These figures help to explain the economic, social, and cultural decline of the
Greek community throughout the two decades of the interwar period.

***

Having looked cursorily at the ups and downs of the Greek community of
Istanbul during its "golden age" and then during the disastrous aftermath of
the Greek-Turkish War, which resulted in its precipitous decline from 1923
to 1947, it is appropriate to pass on to the temporary and rather remarkable
revival of the community in the eight years prior to the pogrom. The measures
imposed by the Turkish government on Greek Istanbulis from 1923 to 1947
were in effect punitive, and they succeeded in undermining the social,
political, and economic underpinnings of the community's extraordinary
flourishing prior to the Turkish republic's establishment.

These anti-minority measures were aimed at the systematic dissolution
of the Greek community in particular. We have already had a glimpse of the
community's demographic decline, the forced divestiture of its businesses,
and the subversion of the principle of independent legal entities, whether

[28] *Ibid.*, pp. 201-203.
[29] *Ibid.*, pp. 142-143.

guilds, philanthropies, or cultural, educational, and athletic associations. Replacing the locally elected *ephoreies* of these institutions with government-controlled administrators sapped and circumscribed the community's ability to decide on its activities and economic life. Concurrently, the numbers of schools, teachers, and students fell dramatically. Finally, labor battalions vitiated the healthy male population, while the *varlık vergisi* "legally" stole a major portion of the community's wealth, enabling Muslim Turks to "buy" the businesses and real estate for a pittance. (I will describe both these labor battalions and the *varlık vergisi* in the next chapter.)

Ironically, it was the establishment of the *Demokrat Parti* of Adnan Menderes and Mahmud Celal Bayar, its ensuing competition with the Republican People's Party (RPP), and its final victory in taking control of government, which initially led to a remarkable loosening of the asphyxiating conditions and circumstances of political life, and simultaneously to an open economic policy of easy money and development for all Turkish citizens. The political competition of the two parties allowed the removal of the severe and punitive controls on the minority communities of Istanbul, and permitted them to take part in economic development. Inasmuch as the votes and related support of the minorities were important to both Menderes and İsmet İnönü (head of the Republican People's Party founded by Mustafa Kemal Atatürk), both tried to cultivate them.

İnönü introduced a measure that removed a 5-percent tax on minority institutions, while Menderes provided easy loans for businesses, thus making capital accessible more generally, from which minority businessmen profited. Also, the dissolution of the *tek mütevelli* system in the last years of the İnönü government and legislation passed in 1950 unleashed the various Greek institutions from state control and allowed the establishment of an entirely new group of incorporated institutions in the Greek community. At the same time, the 1950s marked the influx of American private capital and government aid into Turkey, which served as a strong tonic to the stagnant Turkish economy. And while the Turkish government often saw to it that Greek businessmen were excluded from participating in many direct American investments, the economic opportunities generated therefrom were quickly seized upon by those Greeks who had managed to survive the crippling effects of the previous quarter of a century of economic coercion by the Turkish government. By 1950-1951, Greek businessmen, great and small, were part of the dynamic new developments in the Turkish economy and, within a few short but intense years of activity, their input in the Greek community's institutional life was to have a remarkable effect. By 1955, they had become very important to the economic life of Turkey's largest city.

It was precisely this development, of course, that was to intensify the already substantial hostility of both the government and Turkish Muslims at the time, but that was not at all obvious earlier in the decade.[30]

In fact, in 1950, the Greeks found themselves in unusually thriving circumstances. Absolutely crucial to this progress had been the law of May 31, 1949, which restored autonomy to the *ephoreies* of the corporate bodies of the community at large as well as of the approximately 45 discrete Greek communities. (The confusion as to the exact number of communities emerges from the sources themselves, and from the likelihood that, as some communities waned, they were merged administratively with others.) This restoration of rights gave the community as a whole its voice back in all its projects and finances. Thus it began successfully to take the initiative again, which it had not done for some twenty-five years, and it also attempted to create a larger organ that could coordinate and unite the efforts of all the separate communities. Atop the total of 106 Greek communities and various foundations (based on legal charters) sat two much larger legal entities: the *kentrikes ephoreies* (central boards of trustees) of the three populous regions of Staurodromion (Beyoğlu), Galata, and Chalcedon (Kadıköy); and the *ephoreies* of the *meizona idrymata* (the greater foundations), those large foundations that functioned not merely for a particular community but for all of the communities, including the Hospitals of Balıklı; the orphanage at Prinkipo (Büyükada); the patriarchal *Megalê tou Genous Scholê* (Great School of the Nation); the Iôakeimeion school for girls; and the Zappeion school for girls.[31] The famous theological school of Chalkê (Heybeliada) was under the patriarchate's direct supervision.

Following İnönü's 1949 legislation, Menderes legislated his own more liberal right to legal association, and the minorities of Istanbul immediately availed themselves of it. Nevertheless, his government also began to initiate efforts, seemingly disparate in the beginning but intended to test the waters and to lay down legal precedents, to circumscribe the rights of minorities to profit from the new law. The first and most important test case occurred when the community in Galata attempted to reclaim the rights to its property, only to be opposed by the faction of Papaeftim Karachisaridês, whose associate had been appointed *tek mütevelli* and who now succeeded in taking and keeping the Church of the Panagia Kaphatiane and all its related properties. This raised the issue of property titles; and the problem was a general one for all the Greek communities, whose *ephoreies* had lost control of their respective

[30] Stamatopoulos, *Ê teleutaia analampê*, pp. 21-60.
[31] *Ibid.*, pp. 22-25.

properties. The government administrators often refused to relinquish the titles to the property that had been sequestered and removed from community administration in the preceding period, and this led to long and expensive court proceedings. Often the communities succeeded in retrieving only a part of their possessions.[32]

At the same time, the Turkish government began working on a measure, called the "General Regulations," to deal with all minority issues. The person appointed head of this process was Nuri Birgi, general secretary of the foreign ministry, who would eventually play an important and quite sinister role in the Menderes government's increasing hostility to minorities, and to the Greek minority especially. (Birgi wrote the Turkish *White Book* that advanced Turkish claims to Cyprus, in preparation for the London tripartite conference in the late summer of 1955.) Characteristically, this was long kept secret, and the ongoing work on the "General Regulations" was carried on without any consultation with the representatives of the minority communities. It only became known toward the middle of 1955, when the Cyprus crisis was already raging and preparations for the pogrom were under way.[33]

The improving economic base of the Greek community and of its enterprises was equal in importance to, and a presupposition for, revitalizing the institutions of community life. Given the loss of some two-thirds of the community's demographic base, and the tragic and diminished condition of its properties and revenues, securing a better economic base was of utmost importance. The new economic and political conditions provided the appropriate atmosphere for the economic upswing of the Greek community. Under the stimulative conditions of the early Fifties, the Greeks made rapid strides and soon regained some of the real estate and capital that they had lost because of the *varlık vergisi* in the 1940s. This was a period of internal economic expansion for Turkey more generally, when the foundations were laid for an expanding class of Turkish entrepreneurs and smaller businessmen. For the time, the Turkish state tolerated a simultaneous business recovery of the Greeks, but, unfortunately for the latter, the transfer of the country's wealth to the hands of ethnic Turkish businessmen had long been a major policy of the Turkish government. Thus, the rebirth of Greek business fortunes and prosperity was to be temporary, and would not be tolerated for long. The old law of 1932 "on trades/professions"(see the next chapter), which had been so restrictive, remained on the books and on occasion was used at the expense of the Greeks.[34]

[32] *Ibid.*, pp. 26-28.
[33] *Ibid.*, pp. 29-30.
[34] *Ibid.*, pp. 55-60.

The significant participation of the Greeks in the economy of the Menderes era (primarily in the private sector, for government policy discouraged public employment of minorities) affected a wide spectrum of local Greek society. Statistics from 1950 reveal a substantial body of craftsmen, petty traders, and salaried employees:

Table 11: Greek employment (1950)

1,674	Fishermen, hunters, foresters, farmers
18	Metal industry, mining, quarries
8,732	Craftsmen
36	Employees in electric, gas, water, and sewage services
1,055	Employed in construction
5,872	Involved in commerce, banks, insurance, and as real estate agents
526	Working in transport, storage, refrigeration
4,418	Self-employed
22,331	*Total*

The total number of 22,331 was a healthy economic sign of people in the Greek community working, investing, and accumulating—and, of course, consuming. Larger businesses and operations were to be seen in the food-processing and provisions industry. The Greeks were still prominent in the areas of fisheries, maritime supplies, real estate, confectioneries, and winemaking. They also began to reappear in the heart of the business district, along İstiklal Caddesi in Beyoğlu, and by the time of the pogrom had regained their dominant position there, having once again bought more than half of the shops in this fashionable neighborhood. At the time of the September 1955 events, there were more than 4,500 shops owned by Greeks in greater Istanbul.[35]

The assembly for the election of the *ephoreies* of the greater foundations on December 26, 1954, inaugurated an innovation by appointing a seven-man committee to draw up a rule that would regulate all procedures for elections of the *ephoreies* in all the Greek communities and would further expand the activities of the central organ to the supervision of each community. Henceforth, the assembly would no longer be limited to financial audits. The

---

[35] *Ibid.*, pp. 61-105.

sudden change in the political atmosphere and the intensified attacks on the patriarch and the Greeks of Istanbul intervened, however, and the proposed changes were never implemented.[36]

In education, we see the same general pattern of precipitous decline in the three decades following the founding of the Turkish state, and then a substantial recovery that coincides with the new political and economic conditions of the late 1940s and early 1950s. The patriarchal statistics of 1907 record 237 schools (108 in the *sancak* of Istanbul, 71 in the *sancak* of Çatalca, and 58 in the district of Üsküdar) with 29,929 students. The shrinking number of schools and teachers in the 1920s and 1930s reflected a dramatic shrinkage in the population of Greek students in a much smaller number of schools. By 1945-1946, the condition of education and of educational institutions in the Greek communities had declined pitifully: there were now only 3,172 students in attendance, of which only 572 were in the *gymnasia* (secondary schools). The communities turned their immediate attention to this lamentable situation and, by 1954-1955, the student population had doubled to 6,495 (1,145 in *gymnasia*), while, a year later, the number rose slightly to 6,597 (1,209 in *gymnasia*). Although there was a marked improvement in educational quality, its state was still pitifully low: schoolbooks were so few that they were passed down from one class to another, while there was great need for both new texts and new teaching methods. Further difficulty faced the communities in replacing older teachers with new ones.[37]

The improvement in social-welfare services was more marked, however. The Greeks of Istanbul had an ancient tradition of urban life and, with it, very substantial experience in the sphere of orphanages, homes for the aged, soup kitchens, and the like. As is obvious from a brief survey of these community services in the so-called golden age of Istanbul's Greeks, they were both substantial and impressive until the change in government and state ideologies undermined their financial and administrative foundations between the 1920s and the 1940s. Many institutions were forced to close or to retrench substantially because of the community's hardships and governmental measures. A well-documented example of this prior flourishing and then subsequent shrinkage and partial disappearance in the 1920s and 1930s is that of the Hospitals of Balıklı.

Founded in the latter part of the eighteenth century and reconstituted in 1838, the Balıklı hospitals underwent an extraordinary and robust

[36] *Ibid.*, pp. 52-54.
[37] *Ibid.*, pp. 107-152.

development through the nineteenth century until they attained prestigious
status by the century's end. After the new measures taken by the Turkish
republic, however, the Balıklı hospitals lost their most distinguished staff and
property, and were finally reduced to a derelict state by their *tek mütevelli*,
Istamat Zihni Özdamar. When the buildings of the medical complex were
returned to the Greeks in 1946, they had been denuded of everything,
down to their furniture. Turned over to a Greek lawyer in 1947, the first
elected *ephoreia* took the grounds and barren buildings in hand in 1950.
Immediately, the *ephoreia* began the revitalization of the hospitals as the
Greek community responded to the institution's financial needs. Within five
years, it had rebuilt the Zervoukeios Pathology Clinic, the Syngros Wing,
the Maurokordateios Clinic, and the men's section of the Charitonideios
Psychological Clinic. There were repairs to and rebuilding of a number
of other clinics, laboratories, and areas attached to the complex. Located
on some forty-two acres, it disposed of 650 beds by 1952. By 1954-1955,
it had thirty-nine physicians, forty-five nurses, a chemist, a pharmacist, a
dietician, and 100 additional staff. Corresponding to this investment in
and rebuilding of the hospitals, the number of patients housed or treated
increased from 1,436 to 2,417 in 1954, of whom 247 were Muslim Turks. In
that same year, 6,269 patients were examined and treated in the outpatient
clinic. The complex of hospitals came to include clinics of pathology, surgery,
ophthalmology, tuberculosis, gynecology, neurology, and orthopedics. The
outpatient clinics contained other departments as well.

The Hospitals of Balıklı remained the best-endowed and most developed
of all the Greek institutions; at the time of the pogrom, their value was
estimated at $12 million. Another important institution was the orphanage
of Prinkipo (Büyükada), while a widespread institutional entity was that
of the *philoptochos adelphotês* (brotherhood caring for the poor), which,
despite its name, was usually staffed and run by the women of the various
communities. Established in some eighteen communities by 1950, among
their principal duties was running the *syssitia* (soup kitchens) for the aged,
poor, and students. In 1950, they gave hot meals daily to about 1,400 old
persons and students. Their capacity and food schedules were as follows:[38]

Table 12: Greek soup kitchens

1. Panagia Staurodromiou (Beyoğlu)	200 neighborhood students 5 days weekly

[38] *Ibid.*, pp. 153-176. See also Christoforos Chrêstidês, *Ekthesis*, pp. 27-36; the manuscript
of this important document is in the Chrêstidês archive of the Center for Asia Minor Studies
in Athens.

2. St. Constantine Staurodromiou (Beyoğlu) 175, including students, daily

3. Holy Trinity Staurodromiou (Beyoğlu)   236 students daily

4. Tataula (Kurtuluş)   90 daily

5. Feriköy   47 students and poor

6. Galata   no information

7. Kontoskali (Kumkapı)   34

8. St. Constantine Psamatheia   the communities of Yedikule, Samatya,
(Samatya)   Belgratkapı, Altı Mermer, Kazlıçeşme

9. Tzimbali (Cibalı)   100

10. Mouchlion (Muhli)   80 students

11. St. George, Edirnekapı   20 poor

12. Chalcedon (Kadiköy)   70 students and 30 poor families daily

13. Skoutari (Üsküdar)   no information

14. Mesochôrion (Ortaköy)   no information

15. Vafeochôrion (Boyacıköy)   22 students and 13 poor aged daily

16. Neochôrion (Yeniköy)   38 students and 38 poor families daily

17. Therapia (Tarabya)   25 students

18. Makrochôrion (Bakırköy)   no information

In the 1940s, certain communities began to add medical clinics to the philanthropy offered to the needy. On the church grounds of the Holy Trinity in Beyoğlu were outpatient clinics with all types of specializations: in 1953, these communal clinics treated 1,255 children; 1,853 in the pathology clinics; 260 in gynecology; 250 in surgery; 145 in urology; 1,066 in ophthalmology; 370 in dermatology; 382 in neurology-psychiatry; 260 in otolaryngology; 399 in dentistry; 273 in radiology; and 72 in the tuberculosis clinic. The community clinic of Tataula treated and examined some 2,000 Greeks and Turks in 1950-1951. Finally, the communities' social services included daycare centers for children of working parents.

What is also very impressive was the fact that despite the hostile milieu in which the Greek minority lived, and the severe economic restrictions placed upon it for most of the first half of the twentieth century, its older tradition of cultural activity survived, especially in its devotion to Greek theater, which, even in the most dismal times of the 1920s through the 1940s, still instructed and entertained the community. Cultural associations thus also experienced a last flowering in the ten years or so prior to the pogrom. The arrival of a new patriarch, Athênagoras, from the United States, who brought his long and fruitful experience in organizing Greek American children and youth so that they would not abandon their Greek American communities, was put to good use in the much more difficult circumstances and environment of Istanbul. Together with the rebounding Greek communities, he supported the twenty-five bodies that dominated the cultural scene of the Greeks (ten of these founded only after 1946). These bodies sponsored theater, literary salons, music, and the arts. The largest of these, the *Ellênikê Enôsis* of Istanbul with some 1,200 members, was a small version of the older and dynamic Hellenic Philological Society. The organizations most in evidence, however, were the fifteen amateur theater groups, one of which was sponsored by the *Ellênikê Enôsis* and another by the Athletic Club of Tataula. Athletic associations and competitions have been an intimate part of the Greek diaspora, from Istanbul to Canada and Australia, and they have always attracted both male and female youth. Greek teams and athletes were notable not only on the local Istanbul scene but nationally in Turkish sport as a whole, having produced champion or competing teams in soccer, basketball, volleyball, and wrestling. Finally, there was the ever-present Greek press. With limited circulation and resources, however, it could not compete with the press in Athens and Thessalonikê.

The remarkable aspect of the Greek community's vitality was not so much that it produced cultural and social phenomena of world or national renown, but rather that it survived within the matrix of these political, social, cultural, and welfare institutions that it had to battle to save and to reconstitute, and which, thanks to the economic revival of Turkey after the Second World War, it was able to finance. What is also remarkable was that within a period of only some eight years, its initiative and dynamic character was able to pull it from the brink of dissolution, revive it, and give it new life.

But not for long. It was this vibrant and progressive community that the pogrom, so carefully planned and implemented by the government and by the ruling *Demokrat Parti*, destroyed thoroughly and finally, as we will see shortly.

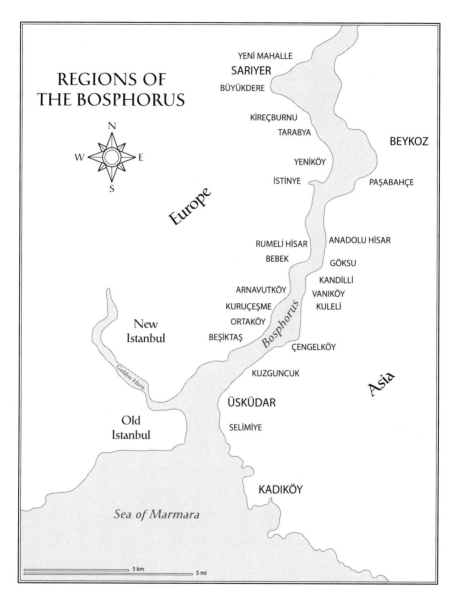

REGIONS OF
THE BOSPHORUS

N
W — E
S

YENİ MAHALLE
SARIYER
BÜYÜKDERE

KİREÇBURNU
TARABYA

BEYKOZ

YENİKÖY

İSTİNYE

PAŞABAHÇE

Europe

RUMELİ HİSAR
BEBEK

ANADOLU HİSAR

GÖKSU

KANDİLLİ
ARNAVUTKÖY
KURUÇEŞME
ORTAKÖY
BEŞİKTAŞ

VANIKÖY
KULELİ

New
Istanbul

Bosphorus

ÇENGELKÖY

Golden Horn

KUZGUNCUK

ÜSKÜDAR

Old
Istanbul

SELİMİYE

Asia

KADIKÖY

Sea of Marmara

5 km
5 mi

CHAPTER ONE

BACKGROUND AND INSTITUTIONS OF THE POGROM

W e are very much concerned these days, often merely *pro forma*, with the central constitutional issues of democratic society: human rights, respect for minorities, and the rights to cultural—indeed multicultural—identity within a state. The United States Department of State, the United Nations, Human Rights Watch, Amnesty International, the European Union, and a host of governmental and non-governmental organizations continually monitor these crucial matters and prepare annual reports that they disseminate globally to an ever-increasing segment of world opinion that is sensitive to them. The governments that are directly affected keenly follow these reports, as well as the unceasing development and codification of human-rights law and practice internationally. Most governments also attempt to influence these reports in efforts to obtain favorable treatment in the relevant findings, or even to block them, if they believe that circulation of the information contained therein will have negative effects on internal or external policies. Regarding the United States, the countless examples of political expediency in dealing with such reports in the cases of allies that have had violent records of violating political and human rights are well-known, and offer a sobering spectacle of the political hypocrisy and rationalization that very often not only ignores such violations but actually rewards them.

When treating the subject of the Turkish pogrom that destroyed the Greek community of Istanbul in a matter of some nine hours on the night of September 6-7, 1955, we are dealing with a period when today's sensitivity to suppression of human rights and political freedoms was as yet a luxury enjoyed by few nations. Furthermore, it was a period of intense anticommunism in America, of a McCarthyism that diverted the country from its internal enforcement of civil and political rights at a time when segregation, both legal and cultural, was defended by a significant portion of an American electorate that accepted even the most flagrant violations of these rights within its own borders.

In most discussions that have, in one form or another, touched upon the pogrom of 1955, there has been considerable effort, not always successful, to explain away this violent act—and the thorough material and psychological destruction of the Greek community in which it resulted—as the outcome of the rising tensions over Cyprus between Greece, on the one hand, and Turkey and Britain, on the other.[1] Others have seen the pogrom as the consequence of the relative economic affluence of the Greek minority of Istanbul in contrast to the relatively penurious underclass of the city that, jealous of its more prosperous Christian fellow citizens, spilled out into the streets in a paroxysmic and "spontaneous" rage, and looted the Greeks' property. Indeed, the court at Yassıada, which sat in judgment of the principal figures of Adnan Menderes's government in 1960-1961 and ultimately found them guilty, concluded that the pogrom was a crime against *property* and not against human beings.[2] Still others have argued that the violence was a spontaneous outpouring of feeling by citizens of Turkish Muslim origins outraged by the explosion of a dynamite fuse within the complex of the Turkish consulate in Thessalonikê, Greece, which includes the house in which Mustafa Kemal Atatürk was supposedly born.[3] Since, according to this argument, the political cult of Atatürk is a central reference point in Turkish national and ethnic pride—with any attack on his house constituting an affront to the Turkish nation—it was only natural that the attempt to damage the house of the "father" of modern Turkey would result in violent, and simultaneous, reactions by Turks in Istanbul, Izmir, and Ankara, and the consequent

---

[1] This is the general thrust of many, but not all, Turkish writings on the subject, as, for example, Fahir H. Armaoğlu, *Kıbrıs meselesi 1954-1959: Türk hükümeti ve kamu oyunun davranışları*, Ankara, 1963, pp. 155-174; and Hulusi M. Dosdoğru, *6/7 Eylül olayları*, Istanbul, 1993, pp. 9-10. The two accounts are written from a diametrically opposed point of view.

[2] The decision of the Yassıada military court refers to Greeks living in Istanbul as wealthy ("mal ve mülk sahibi olan"), *Yüksek adalet divanı kararları, Yassıada, 1960-1961*, Esas no. 1960/3, "6/7 Eylül olayları davası karar gerekçesi," p. 6, from the stencil manuscript. Cemal O. Fersoy, *Bir devre adını veren başbakan Adnan Menderes*, Istanbul, 1971, p. 357, gives the law and article (Law 64, Article 517) of the Turkish penal code on the basis of which Adnan Menderes, Fatin Rüştü Zorlu, and Kemal Hadımlı were condemned and punished: "Anyone who causes destruction or breaks or who causes the loss of real or movable property in any manner" will be subject to the above law. See also Dosdoğru, *6/7 Eylül olayları*, pp. 361-362, and Hulusi Turgut, *Menderes, Zorlu Polatkan'dan yaptırılmayan*, Istanbul, 1982, p. 49. Neoklês Sarrês, *Ê allê pleura: Diplomatikê chronographia tou diamelismou tês Kyprou me vasê tourkikes pêges*, Volume II, Part I, Athens, 1982, pp. 268-272, reasonably explains why the trial turned the pogrom into a "crime against property" and declined to charge the defendants with a crime against human beings, although this was implicit in the major trial charging Menderes and his government with violating the Turkish constitution.

[3] Cemal Fersoy, *Devlet ve hizmet adam Fatin Rüştü Zorlu*, Istanbul, 1979, pp. 219-222, in particular, was insistent on this while denying any governmental responsibility. Through Fersoy, who was his lawyer, Zorlu insisted that this was a spontaneous national and emotional agitation, p. 237, "O gün 200-300 bin kişi bir millî heyecan içinde sallanırken."

destruction of everything Greek. Finally, there was the official accusation by the Menderes government that the crimes were actually organized and carried out by communists. In fact, forty-five to fifty-five leftists were arrested and jailed in Harbiye prison on September 8, 1955, charged with organizing and executing, in those few hours, the physical destruction of the Greek community over a vast area that reached from the Black Sea to the Sea of Marmara.[4] According to many observers, this "solution" was suggested to the Turkish government by Allen Dulles, the director of the Central Intelligence Agency, who had been attending an international congress on criminology in Istanbul at the time.[5] In reality, Istanbul's "active" communists were few in number, without effective organization and funds, and could never have perpetrated any such vast undertaking in a country in which the state controlled all political movements, strikes, and demonstrations—indeed every aspect of the country's political life—to an asphyxiating degree.

More generally, there has been a tendency to look at the crescendo of Greek-Turkish crises as something in the very nature of things, and of the political life of the Balkans and the Middle East, and thus to be viewed as inescapable and fated. This type of reasoning, of course, conveniently avoids placing "fault," or even a degree of fault, in one or another party; hence, not only are all parties guilty but they are equally so, or—since these confrontations are ostensibly "rooted" in "age-old hatreds" and therefore inevitable—no one is at fault. In the event, moral issues are irrelevant since what matters solely is political interest or concern. This has been, and remains, the view of the US State Department and British Foreign Office.

Unfortunately, the historical evidence is quite different. Whereas it is true that the Cyprus issue eventually became the pivot on which Greek and Turkish national interests and activities turned, this was not the case for some two and a half years following the onset of the drive for self-determination by the Greek Cypriots. Britain's concern was manifest, however, as the anti-colonial agitation obviously affected its control of the island. It was Greece's

---

[4] For a detailed treatment of the arrested leftists, see Dosdoğru, *6/7 Eylül olayları*, pp. 24-91; Aziz Nesin, *Salkım salkım asılacak adamlar*, Istanbul, 1987, *passim*; Hasan İzzetin Dinamo, *6-7 Eylül kasırgası*, Istanbul, 1971, pp. 9-62 and 89-96; Sarrês, *Ê allê pleura*, II-A, pp. 138 and 144; and Armaoğlu, *Kıbrıs meselesi*, p. 155, who stated that the accusation that communists intentionally deformed and then led astray the events of September 6-7, 1955, was indeed a false and trumped-up charge.

[5] Nesin, *Ibid.*, pp. 110-111; Alexandris, *The Greek minority*, Athens, 1983, pp. 260 and 265, refers to Köprülü's interview with *Cumhuriyet*, October 21, 1960. Although they detained them for a considerable period in Harbiye prison, the courts-martial set up by General Fahrettin Aknoz were finally forced to release the leftists as there was no evidence whatever against them. Indeed, the Menderes government cooked up the entire scheme, which backfired.

attempt to place the issue before the UN that constituted the turning-point that would lead to Turkey's decision to make serious claims on Cyprus. Prior to that, the Turkish government had shown little interest in Cyprus; in fact, its foreign minister, Mehmet Fuat Köprülü, had declared that Cyprus was not a Turkish issue.[6] Subsequently, however, something changed radically in the priorities and considerations of Menderes's government. It has been pointed out by British scholar Robert Holland that this sudden change in Turkey's interest in Cyprus was in significant part a reaction to the external dynamic of British imperial concern over, and fear of, the success of Greek Cypriots in bringing their cause before a world tribunal in which they might find allies.[7] As such, the crisis leading to the pogrom was not fated by an ostensibly long history of territorial truncation of the once-extensive Ottoman empire that modern Turkey felt obliged to reverse.

Along this more general line of reasoning, one must examine the modern Turkish state's effort to create—which is to say force—a homogeneity of its disparate constituent elements in consonance with presumably Western theories of nation, state, and nationalism, first given a racial basis by Ziya Gökalp and his theories of innate racial cultural qualities and virtues.[8] Anyone familiar with the history of modern Turkey is aware of Atatürk's studied re-creation of modern Turkish political institutions; Atatürk not only created the modern Turkish state, but the prototype of the modern Turkish citizen, based on certain European models combined with Gökalp's racist theories. Atatürk secularized the state, closed religious schools, undermined the dervish orders, Latinized the alphabet to isolate Turks from their rich Ottoman heritage,[9] and invented a new history and "new" language for the new Turkish citizen. Alongside the hat law (outlawing the fez and compelling the wearing of Western hats), legislation stipulated the Turkification of names, spoken language, and education of this ostensibly new citizen.[10]

---

[6] Dosdoğru, *6/7 Eylül olayları*, p. 10.

[7] See Robert Holland, "Greek-Turkish relations, Istanbul and British rule in Cyprus 1954-59: Some excerpts from the British Public Archives," *Deltio Kentrou Mikrasiatikôn Spoudôn*, 10, 1993-1994, pp. 328-365.

[8] Ziya Gökalp, *The principles of Turkism*, translated and annotated by R. Devereux, Leiden, 1968, *passim* and p. 102. Gökalp's racism was not strictly biological, as he specifically dismissed predetermination "by blood" of ethnic culture and non-material characteristics. It was rather what he called "Ethical Turkism": "Every great nation has demonstrated superiority in some particular field of civilization. The ancient Greeks excelled in aesthetics, the Romans in law, the Israelites and Arabs in religion, the French in literature, the Anglo-Saxons in economics, the Germans in music and metaphysics. The Turks have excelled in morals. Turkish history, from its beginning, is an exhibition of moral virtues." This "moral superiority," which Gökalp believed to be exclusive to Turks, related to "Turkish moral ambients [*sic*]…patriotic morals, professional morals, family [sexual] morals, personal morals and international morals."

The years of peace between the two world wars were thus the period of concentrated gestation that created the modern Turkish state, society, citizen, and culture, with Turkification considered to be the highest good. Yet, the problem of the ethnic minorities was not completely eliminated. A serious reminder of this fact was the dramatic rebellion of the very large Kurdish minority of eastern Turkey in 1925, which brought about the suspension of civil government in the area and its replacement with martial law until 1929.[11] Kurdish demands for political independence, or autonomy, and preservation of their ethnic culture began to reappear in the 1950s; by the late 1980s-1990s, they had become a matter of grave concern for the Turkish state and army. The response in both these striking cases of the survival of ethnic minorities was brutal military repression and a campaign of state terrorism, which aimed immediately and ultimately at destroying the Kurds as a coherent ethnic community that could make demands on the Turkish state. This violent attempt at "resolving" the problem posed by the substantial Kurdish minority in Turkey resulted, in the 1990s, in the destruction of approximately 4,000 Kurdish villages, extensive murder and displacement of Kurds, and the creation of a wasteland of great geographical extent.[12] The Turkish military's ultimately futile insistence on destroying Kurdish cultural identity and rights to education, language, culture, and press and media, and the impact of a scorched-earth policy, martial law, and roaming death squads within the Turkish state and society resulted in the worst systematic oppression ever of a large Muslim minority within a domain of modern Islam—unsurpassed even by Pakistan's attempt to crush its own Muslim minority in what finally became Bangladesh.

Greeks, Armenians, and Jews are the principal non-Muslim minorities that remain in Turkey. Their numbers, however, have diminished drastically because of the historical developments that led to the creation of modern Turkey, and the practices, theories, and mentalities that sought to obliterate

[9] Bernard Lewis, *The Emergence of Modern Turkey*, second edition, Oxford, 1968, pp. 239-293.

[10] For the introduction of the new racial theories of world/Turkish history and linguistics created by Atatürk in order to form a new youth and nation, see Speros Vryonis, Jr., *The Turkish state in history: Clio meets the Grey Wolf*, Thessalonikê, 1991, pp. 11-88; A. F. Çöker, *Türk tarihinin ana hatları. Kemalist yönetimin resmi Tarih Tezi*, Istanbul, 1938, reprinted 1996; Geoffrey Lewis, *The Turkish language reform: A catastrophic success*, Oxford, 2002.

[11] Lewis, *Modern Turkey*, pp. 266-268; David McDowall, *A modern history of the Kurds*, London, 1997, pp. 119-213 and 395-444.

[12] Speros Vryonis, Jr., "American Foreign Policy in the Ongoing Greco-Turkish Crisis as a Contributing Factor to Destabilization," UCLA *Journal of International Law and Foreign Affairs*, Volume II, Number 1, 1997, pp. 73-75; Eric Rouleau, "Turkey: Beyond Ataturk," *Foreign Policy*, June 1996, pp. 70-75.

ethnic identities, first in the crumbling Ottoman state and then in its modern Turkish successor. The Turkish state's record of behavior toward these now-tiny ethnic minorities, located primarily in the region around and in Istanbul, has been one of grudging and limited acceptance, heavily vitiated by calculated acts of state terror and repression, aided and abetted by significant portions of the area's dominant Muslim population. Indeed, extremist segments of the latter remain a constant threat to the minorities, carrying out their own more violent acts against their non-Muslim co-citizens, often with the indifference or even active but unspoken complicity of state authorities.[13]

Thus, the record of Turkey's treatment of its minorities in the eighty-two years since the end of the Greek-Turkish war and the establishment of the modern Turkish state in 1923 has a definite and substantive history and tradition. Having made this generalization, one should nonetheless pause to examine some details of the relations between the modern Turkish state and its Greek minority, for without considering the pre-1955 history of these relations, a crucial explanatory element regarding the pogrom of 1955 is sorely lacking. Indeed, the pogrom of 1955 fits clearly into the original policy of the Turkish state, not only in regard to its few remaining non-Muslim minorities, but, more generally, regarding the nationalist, racist, and repressive policies of the Young Turks during the last agonizing years of the Ottoman empire.

THE *AMELE TABURLARI* AND THE *VARLIK VERGİSİ*

To understand and interpret the 1955 pogrom, we must examine the complex web of causes, policies, and government actions that defined Turkey's official policy of Turkification.[14] To begin with, legislation passed by the Turkish parliament in 1932 (law #2007) and thereafter barred entry to a large number of professions and trades to the so-called *établis* ("established ones" or "settlers," a euphemism for Greek citizens of Istanbul who were allowed to remain in the city following the treaty of Lausanne in 1923).[15] A series of

[13] See what follows below. Stamatopoulos, *Ê teleutaia analampê*, pp. 21-60; Alexandris, *The Greek minority*, p. 105.

[14] As in footnote 10 above.

[15] The rights of, and provisions for, the Greek communities of Istanbul, Imvros, and Tenedos, as well as for the Turkish Muslim minority in Greek Thrace, are clearly set forth in the treaty of Lausanne. For a convenient and readily accessible translation of the relevant articles (37-45), see Lois Whitman, "The Greeks of Turkey," *Helsinki Watch*, pp. 51-54. The treaty's contents are remarkably "modern" in regard both to minority and citizens' rights. By and large, the gross violations of the treaty have resulted from the destruction of the Greek communities of Istanbul, Imvros, and Tenedos, which have almost completely disappeared, while the Turkish Muslim community of Greek Thrace has grown demographically and its schools, religious institutions, and businesses continue to function, in contrast to the Greeks who once lived in

some thirty-one laws during the period between the two world wars severely crippled and, finally, paralyzed the community as a result of these efforts to reduce its political, legal, economic, and cultural presence. The laws against the *établis*, for example, forbade them from some thirty trades, including those of tailor, itinerant merchant, photographer, carpenter, and doorman, as well as from professions of more "elevated" social and economic status such as medicine, law, insurance, and real estate. Some 10,000 Greek *établis* were thus deprived of their livelihoods and forced to abandon their homes and businesses in Istanbul and emigrate, penniless, to Greece (at the expense of the Greek state).[16] It is noteworthy that, alongside this more general xenophobia, a certain antisemitism was soon manifest in Turkish government policy at the same time that it was mushrooming in Nazi Germany.[17] The law on language in turn placed the Greek minority under constraint not to speak Greek in public and subjected it to "correction" by its ethnically Turkish co-citizens, who were in fact legally enjoined to vigilance against and public rectification of these infractions, which were all liable to punishment.

Even more serious, however, were the discriminatory, intimidating, and economically ruinous laws passed by the Turkish government during the Second World War. The first, in 1941, led to the forced conscription into labor battalions (*amele taburları*) of all Christian and Jewish males between the ages of eighteen and forty-five. Many of these men died from the heavy labor they were compelled to do (particularly in road-building).[18] This discriminatory mobilization, and the hardships imposed, led not only to the death of many conscripts but to the terrorizing of their communities. The labor battalions were finally disbanded for reasons not immediately apparent.[19]

Just a few months later, however, in 1942, the government of Şükrü Saraçoğlu passed legislation that was not only highly discriminatory against non-Muslim minorities but actually punitive. It thus set the foundation for

Turkey. (In Turkish, by the way, "établi" was rendered as *etabli*.)

[16] Alexandris, *The Greek minority*, pp. 184-185; Syllogos Imvriôn-Kônstantinoupolitôn-Tenediôn and Anatôlikothrakôn Thrakês, *Oi paraviaseis tês Synthêkês tês Lôzanês*, second edition, Komotênê, 1993, pp. 19-28.

[17] Faik Ökte, *The tragedy of the Turkish capital tax*, London, 1987, pp. 38-39, "a new class of tax payers, the Dönme Class (D) (of Jewish converts to Islam) was instituted, which was taxed at rates double those for Muslims (M)…." Also, Alexandris, *The Greek minority*, pp. 215-216.

[18] Nikos G. Apostolidês, *Anamnêseis apo tên Kônstantinoupolê*, Athens; 1996, pp. 210-213, was among the Greeks sentenced to hard labor in Anatolia, although he had faithfully performed his military service in the Turkish army during 1935-1936. He estimates that the number of Greeks conscripted into the labor battalions at 20,000, and refers to them as "twenty generations."

[19] Alexandris, *The Greek minority*, pp. 213-214, speaks of very large groups containing 5,000 men each by the end of 1941, pp. 207-233; Lewis, *Modern Turkey*, pp. 297-302.

the economic ruin of these ethnic communities, their psychological disarray, and the state's effective appropriation of a major portion of their liquid wealth and real estate—and, ultimately, the transfer of the relevant businesses and commercial institutions to the hands of Muslims. This entire process of what was in fact the state expropriation of the property of the non-Muslim minorities was facilitated by a number of officials and police, who determined and enforced the taxation levied on minority businesses and individuals. These officers of the government often "failed" to announce the public auctions that transacted the liquidation of goods, buildings, businesses, and factories; as a result, favored Turkish businessmen in effect looted this wealth as "insider" beneficiaries of the processes of tax assessment, enforcement and collection, and public auction.[20]

This legislation, known in Turkish as the *varlık vergisi* (capital tax), succeeded the discriminatory legal regime of labor battalions and once more placed the minorities under dire threat of imposed, harsh labor, this time in an even less fortunate geographical and climatic region—Aşkale, in northeastern Turkey, known as the Turkish Siberia—but added to this punishment a destructive financial component. Though legislated by the Turkish parliament on the initiative and under the close supervision of Prime Minister Saraçoğlu, it was essentially administered by Istanbul's *defterdar* (or director of finances), Faik Ökte, since it was in that city that the majority of non-Muslim minorities and their business affairs were located. Ökte not only administered the property evaluation required by the new law, but (despite his feeble claims to the contrary) also enforced the resulting taxation and sanctions with a savage ferocity that sent off thousands to the snowbound camps of Aşkale for default. He further exempted lower-income Muslims from paying their assessments in contrast to his actions regarding their very numerous minority co-citizens, who were shipped off to camps under stringent conditions.[21]

---

[20] The fundamental source to date is the memorandum of Faik Ökte, *Varlık vergisi faciası*, Istanbul, 1951. The reference here is to the English translation by Cox, *The Turkish capital tax*, *passim*. Rıdvan Akar, *Varlık vergisi kanunu. Tek parti rejiminde azınlık karşıtı politika örneği*, Istanbul, 1992, includes a great deal of new statistical material and should be consulted. Alexandris, *The Greek minority*, pp. 207-233, is a very good analysis that incorporates British and Greek archival materials. Apostolidês, *Anamnêseis*, pp. 214-218, briefly relates his own more felicitous experiences. Stamatopoulos, *Teleutaia analampê*, pp. 97, 154, 170, and 230, describes the deleterious effects of this discriminatory tax on the Greek community and on its educational, religious, cultural, and economic institutions. Syllogos Imvriôn, *Paraviaseis*, pp. 28-30; Edward Clark, "The Turkish Varlik Vergisi Reconsidered," *Middle East Studies*, Volume 8, 1972, pp. 204-206.

[21] It is curious to read Ökte's memoir, published some nine years after the events, as it is a weird mixture of repentance but also of pride in his ruthless application of the law. The memoir

According to Ökte's memoirs,[22] the principal features of the *varlık vergisi* were that it was originally conceived as a tax on capital earnings and windfall profits at a time when wartime conditions favored businessmen and large landowners. The fiscal qualifications for either category was an annual income of 2,300 Turkish liras (TL) or property that exceeded the value of TL5,000; but this tax was ultimately imposed on all wage-earners outside of the public sector, even peddlers. The *varlık vergisi*'s levies were to be paid within fifteen days of the law's promulgation, with a grace period of another fifteen days (to be paid off with interest). Those who defaulted were to be sent to Aşkale's camps, where they were to labor for two liras a day (one lira to be applied to the tax debt), with responsibility for their own food, clothing, and medical care (to the degree that it was available). It has been estimated that, at this rate of compensation, many defaulters would have had to work for 250 years to pay off the exorbitant taxes levied.[23] Furthermore, defaulters' property, as well as that of all ascending and descending relatives, was then to be sold off at public auction as necessary to pay off the tax liability.

In other words, according to Ökte's memoirs, despite being sent to a labor camp—and thus ostensibly beginning the process of paying off one's "debt"—one still lost one's property (in addition to one's freedom). Servitude was therefore, not a compensation for default but an *additional*, and particularly egregious, punishment. There was to be no appeal against assessments of property value or tax payments. If a defaulter was serving in the Turkish armed forces, he was to finish his military service and then be dispatched to a labor camp. The compilation of tax lists, as well as catalogues of names and sums, all took place under strictest secrecy.

At the time the law was passed (November 12, 1942), there was no modern system of income tax in Turkey (although the *varlık vergisi* was

---

is at the same time an extremely important source for understanding the mentality behind this legislation, as well as the processes it set in motion. Finally, it constitutes a kind of cathartic confession. Ökte writes (*The Turkish capital tax*, p. 38) of his colleague in this matter, Adalan, that: "Thus far he had tried to find a middle ground between [*sic*] Kırdar and [Suat Hayri] Ürgüplü. [But] now he began to talk the Premier's language, exhibiting an exaggerated zeal comparable to that of Ürgüplü [a member of the Republican People's Party who insisted on a merciless application of the *varlık vergisi*]. We had all become excessively over-zealous." He continues (p. 39): "At a stroke our system began to be permeated by Hitler's hysterical racist attitudes. We had all lost our cool-headedness and our sense of proportion, which are such important qualities for a finance expert. This state of mind influenced all of us during the enforcement of the tax." He relates that he managed to find "relief" from the heavy labor of mercilessly assessing and collecting the tax "by going hunting."

[22] *Ibid.*, *passim.*
[23] Alexandris, *The Greek minority*, p. 222.

conceived primarily as a tax on capital, it was also, in part at least, levied as tax on income). As a result, there was no appropriate state service for evaluating, assessing, and collecting such a national tax. Statistical data, and alphabetical catalogues of individuals and businesses, were lacking, and reference to Istanbul banks, the ledgers of the ruling Republican People's Party (RPP, or *Cumhuriyet Halk Partisi* in Turkish), or the records of the security services could not (and did not) meet the sudden, new need for pertinent information. How, then, did Faik Ökte and his colleagues arrive at their evaluations and assessments? As a typical bureaucrat, Ökte comments (always at a loss) on the absence of the necessary infrastructure and data, adding that despite it all, he and his colleagues came up with what were essentially "guesstimates" for the prime minister when the latter was drafting the *varlık vergisi* for submission to parliament: "But we had no official tax-rolls. The only lists we had were rough estimates presented to Ankara to enable the Ministry of Finance to formulate an opinion about the taxable wealth in Istanbul."[24]

Once the bill was passed and Ökte had to proceed to enforcing the law as chief of Istanbul's fiscal administration, he still had no statistical basis by which he could exact the taxes demanded:

> The tax assessors had very limited resources. With no data whatsoever in their possession for thousands of tax-payers, they felt at a loss. Their efforts to collect information from members of the business community and from the Revenue Department failed to bear fruit. In effect, the assessment commission had to rely solely on its own resourceful imagination. A group of young employees in the Finance Department took it upon themselves to fix the tax rates by using their imagination, totally disregarding the individual's ability to pay or the true state of his financial standing.[25]

Whereas the statistics, institutions, and information necessary for imposing the tax were almost completely lacking, the general directions from Saraçoğlu, Suat Hayri Ürgüplü (the RPP's representative on the Istanbul tax-assessment board), and Ökte were clear and emphatic that this was to be a tax that would be applied in a completely discriminatory manner, and punitively, against the non-Muslim minorities. Among the very first instructions that Ökte gave to his subordinates was to ensure a segregation that would mark the entire spirit and philosophy of the *varlık vergisi*: "I had asked every single local board for lists of all those liable to wealth tax, *stressing* [italics added] that there should be separate lists for the Muslim Turks and the non-Muslim

[24] Ökte, *The Turkish capital tax*, p. 26.
[25] *Ibid.*, p. 33.

Greeks, Armenians and Jews."[26] Indeed, this part of the work was carried out with great diligence: "The assessment was especially careful to separate the Turkish from the Greek, Armenian and Jewish taxpayers."[27] This Ottoman legacy of discriminatory taxation according to confession, in which non-Muslims were generally more heavily taxed than Muslims—now transformed by the further imposition of a modern nationalistic bias—led Ökte and his colleague, Şevket Adalan, to formulate the following solution regarding the respective tax rates of Muslims and non-Muslims (the terms used by Ökte at this point):

> While the finance inspectors were busy classifying the tax lists forwarded by the local assessment boards, Adalan and I searched for a formula to tax those who had hitherto been liable to profits tax and who constituted 80% of the entire taxable population. We finally agreed to divide them into two categories—the Muslim Turks and the non-Muslim Greeks, Armenians, and Jews. Relying on Article 34 of the Profits Tax Law No. 2395, we managed, while remaining within the letter of the law, to impose a token tax on Muslims and [to] tax minorities at a rate two or three times over that of their Turkish co-citizens.[28]

From these few references to Ökte's memoir, we see clearly the thinking and, more important, the actions of significant elements of the Turkish state regarding the respective roles of Christians, Jews, and Muslims in modern Turkish society, which clearly betray the vigorous survival of old Ottoman Islamic state theory and mentalities, but now vigorously reinforced by a Turkish nationalism that could never fully reject its historical past. In the event, even Ökte and Adalan were surprised by Ankara's reception to their tax-assessment and -collection scheme:

> But Ankara thought differently. When Şevket Adalan took the tax assessment lists for Istanbul to the capital, the Turkish government, while approving our proposed system of classification (Muslims/non-Muslims) set new tax rates for the Greeks, Armenians, and Jews. Instead of being two or three times more, as we suggested, non-Muslim taxes were to be five to ten times the amounts levied on Muslim Turks with corresponding estimated wealth....
>
> What appeared so glaring in the new assessment lists was

---

[26] *Ibid.*, p. 26. This reveals that the classic Ottoman Muslim system of differentiated taxation always enforced on non-Muslims was still alive in the mindset of both modern Turkish citizens and the bureaucracy.

[27] *Ibid.*, p. 32.

[28] *Ibid.*, p. 34.

the difference between the tax rates imposed on Muslim Turks on
the one hand and the Greek, Armenian, and Jewish minorities on
the other.[29]

But the greatest surprise that Adalan brought from Ankara
was the order to include private salary earners and peddlers in the
Capital Tax. Both my colleagues and I [had] envisaged the Varlık
tax as a tax on capital....such a tax could not have been collected
from salary earners who were themselves victims of the inflationary
conditions and had already witnessed a dramatic drop in their
standard of living. According to instructions from Ankara, we had
the power to exempt sections of the salary-earning group from the
tax. As a result, Adalan and I agreed to exempt all the Muslim
Turkish salary earners and concentrate solely on the non-Muslims.
Our suggestion met with the approval of Ankara.[30]

During the limited and feeble debate over the bill in the Turkish assembly,
it was further made clear, in a classic example of scapegoating, that Prime
Minister Saraçoğlu had exploited economic necessity to create legislation
with which to bludgeon Turkey's minorities. As Ökte commented:

The following week the draft Bill was approved by the Republican
Party Assembly Group and by the Grand National Assembly.
Some criticism is said to have been voiced among the deputies
during the secret party session, but in the Assembly the debate
was low-key. On both occasions Premier Saraçoğlu defended the
Bill and, as at least fifty deputies have since told me, singled out
the non-Muslim minorities as the hoarders and war profiteers.
The impression given by the Premier that the tax measure was waged
solely against the minorities was certainly very strong.[31]

The anti-Jewish and anti-Greek animus of the law appears again in the
manner of taxing foreign residents and Dönmes (descendants of Jewish
converts to Islam in Turkey). Preexisting law prohibited discriminatory
taxation of foreign residents based on religious affiliation. Furthermore,
consulates and embassies intervened on behalf of their citizens, if not always
effectively.[32] In the event, the Turkish authorities excluded Turkish Jews who
were also citizens of Axis countries from the benefits of consular intervention
that applied to non-Turkish Jews with such citizenship. Similarly, Turkey
completely ignored the Greek residents settled in Istanbul (the largest

[29] *Ibid.*, pp. 34-35.
[30] *Ibid.*, p. 35.
[31] *Ibid.*, p. 23; for the antisemitic measures against the Dönmes, see pp. 38-39.
[32] *Ibid.*, pp. 56-57.

number of foreign nationals in the city) and subjected them to the full range of discriminatory taxation, as Greece was then occupied by the Axis and was therefore in no position to protect its citizens.[33]

According to Ökte, the total number of individuals from Istanbul assessed in the *varlık vergisi* was 62,575 for a total sum of TL349,989,922. He also writes that those who could not pay were sent to the labor camps in Aşkale. At the same time, Ökte and his colleagues charged with the tax collection decided to exempt Muslim wage-earners from exile and forced labor.[34] The effect on the Greek community was devastating.[35] British diplomatic observers had foreseen that Turkey would exploit wartime conditions and the ensuing economic difficulties to strike at its non-Muslim minorities; they thus considered the strident tones of Saraçoğlu and the Turkish press at the time as a sure reflection of this fact.[36] According to the memorandum of a British diplomat in Turkey, the taxes to be collected were TL344 million in Istanbul, TL27 million in Izmir, and TL16 million in Ankara.

Although these figures differ somewhat from those given by Ökte, they are not far off. And of the approximately TL445 million assessed, the confessional/ethnic breakdown of the tax burden was highly and undeniably discriminatory. Total tax revenues in 1935 in Turkey had been TL16,188,767, while that of the religious minorities had been roughly TL300,000 (or 1.7 percent of the total). Yet with the *varlık vergisi*, non-Muslims were assessed some TL233 million (or 52 percent of the total), whereas Muslims— who constituted close to 98 percent of the population—were assessed only TL132.5 million (approximately 29 percent of the total). Foreign residents were assessed TL79.5 million (19 percent).[37] Lira for lira, the inequity of the law was monstrous and had as its goal the economic and social destruction of Turkey's minorities and their communities.[38] The British analysis cited above not only saw through the vast fiscal discrimination of this clearly confiscatory measure, but actually estimated the percentages of the *total capital* of each group that the tax sought to appropriate:

---

[33] Alexandris, *The Greek minority*, pp. 220-221 and 225-226.

[34] Ökte, *The Turkish capital tax*, pp. 48 and 70-77.

[35] The chapter in Alexandris, *The Greek minority*, pp. 207-233, is based not only on Ökte's memoir, but is enriched with significant materials from the British and Greek archives.

[36] Alexandris, *The Greek minority*, pp. 214-215.

[37] Clark, "The Turkish Varlik Vergisi," pp. 208-209, as referenced in *Ibid.*, p. 217.

[38] The recent book by Turkish journalist Rıdvan Akar, *Varlık vergisi kanunu*, raises the figures of those sent off to the camps to some 4,000-5,000, and places them in the tax bracket of TL40,000. He attributes the primary motivations for the *varlık vergisi* to both the Turkish state's desire to destroy the non-Muslim minorities and the influence of Nazi antisemitism.

Table 13: Estimates of appropriated capital under the *varlık vergisi*

Armenian firms	232% of total capital
Jewish firms	184% of total capital
Greek firms	159% of total capital
Muslim Turks	4.9% of total capital[39]

As can be seen, the *varlık vergisi* was even more anti-Armenian and antisemitic than anti-Greek. Nevertheless, Greek nationals residing in Istanbul were the only foreigners to suffer confiscation of their property and its subsequent sale at public auction. Some 3,000 Greek nationals had their taxes set at a total of TL8,705,412. Britain's commercial counselor in Ankara wrote to the Foreign Office in London that, "The Turks are determined to eliminate the Greeks from Turkish national life, whether they form part of the Greek minority or are Hellenic Greeks [Greek nationals] who played a large part in the commercial and cultural life of Istanbul."[40]

[39] Alexandris, *The Greek minority*, pp. 217 ff. The same was obvious in the discriminatory taxation of "low-income non-Muslims," as their Muslim counterparts paid no tax at all.

[40] For some of the many discriminatory tax figures published, see *Ibid.*, p. 226:

Taxes Assessed (in TLs)

Profession	Greeks	Muslims
Importers	10,000/75,000	1,000/10,000
Exporters	60,000/400,000	5,000/25,000
Merchants	15,000/1,000,000	1,500/100,000
Industrialists	75,000/262,500	500/35,000
Grocers	6,000/150,000	500/10,000
Shopkeepers	12,000/160,000	500/15,000
Agents	10,000/120,000	1,000/10,000
Merchant tailors	15,000/75,000	1,500/17,000
Furniture merchants	6,000/140,000	1,200/3,000

On p. 218, Alexandris reproduces the following figures from the records of the British Foreign Office, which illustrate a conscious policy of over-taxation of Jews and Greeks, and minimal taxation of Muslims:

Auto Spare Parts	Estimated Capital (in TLs)	Taxed On (in TLs)
Ototürk (Jewish)	65,000	150,000
Christos Amand (Greek)	25,000	75,000
Bedri Tok (Muslim)	60,000	2,000
N. Bozkurt (Muslim)	60,000	10,000
Wool Merchants		
Eskenazi (Jewish)	20,900	90,000
Eskenazi Fils (Jewish)	70,000	120,000

The patterns of aggression against Turkey's non-Muslim communities prior to the pogrom of September 6-7, 1955—and the Turkish government's decision to destroy these communities—are quite clear, therefore. They constitute a powerful inheritance from the Ottoman empire and the Young Turks, and a dual heritage for which both Kemalism and Turkish modernization made room. Most studies of the *varlık vergisi* agree that, in the end, it did not serve any practical purpose; indeed, later scholarship that emphasizes the legitimate economic concerns of the Turkish state has concluded that its primary intention was the economic impoverishment of the non-Muslim communities.[41]

THE INSTITUTIONAL BACKGROUND TO THE POGROM

This long-term evolution in Turkey's treatment of its non-Muslim minorities forms a kind of matrix within which the Cyprus conflict was fitted, as what

Soursaki (Jewish)	229,379	750,000
H. Eren (Muslim)	500,000	30,000
M. Yucat (Muslim)	300,000	20,000
Shipowners		
Barsılay & Benjamin	19,300	
(Jewish)	(5 ships)	2,000,000
Kalkavanzade	21,550	
(Muslim)	(5 ships)	60,000
General Merchants		
I. Modiano (Jewish)	97,000	2,000,000
Vehbi Koç (Muslim)	2,000,000	60,000
Restaurants in Pera		
K. Pavloich (Greek)		15,000
Abdullah Rest. (Muslim)		5,000
Nain Rest. (Muslim)		3,000
Commission Agents		
L. V. Stelianides (Greek)		10,000
F. Verdi (Muslim)		4,500
EN Barlo (Muslim)		5,000
(Both Muslim businesses were far larger than the Greek one.)		
Real Estate		
M. Rizzo (Greek)	73,000	25,000
Agopian (Armenian)	176,000	100,000
S. Karamanoğlu (Muslim)	1,000,000	20,000

[41] The destruction of the wealth of many Jews (both those with Turkish and foreign citizenship) has been purposely ignored by Stanford Shaw, *Jews of the Ottoman Empire and the Turkish Republic*, New York, 1991, *passim*; see the very critical review by Bernard Wasserstein, *Times Literary Supplement*, January 7, 1994, pp. 4-5, of yet another of Shaw's books, *Turkey's Role in Rescuing Turkish and European Jewry from Nazi Persecution (1933-1945)*, in which Shaw puts forth even greater exaggerations.

began as a Greek-British dispute over the island's future gradually evolved into a trilateral issue that increasingly included Turkey. Current research based on an ever-widening basis of new documentation has come back to the role of the British government in inducing a fundamental change in the Turkish government's disinterested status in the dispute. Reference has already been made to Turkish foreign minister Mehmet Fuat Köprülü's official statement that the Cyprus issue involved only Greece and Britain and not Turkey. Obviously, as time passed, the Menderes government radically altered its stand; the replacement of Köprülü with Fatin Rüştü Zorlu as minister of foreign affairs brought in someone who, as a product of the foreign service, supported a much more aggressive Cyprus policy that agreed with the new policy of Menderes himself.[42] Menderes's relations with his former foreign minister—both of them very active politicians and among the founders of the *Demokrat Parti* (DP)—became further strained given their growing alienation over Cyprus and following the pogrom of September 6-7, 1955. (In the extraordinary meeting of the Grand National Assembly, Turkey's parliament, held on September 12, 1955, Köprülü declared that the government had known ahead of time about the riots.) In 1959, Köprülü formally removed his son Orhan from the DP's rolls and inscribed him on the list of the opposition Republican People's Party. The culmination came during the Yassıada trials of 1960-1961, however, when Köprülü openly condemned Menderes as the pogrom's instigator and organizer. Clearly, along with its other consequences, the pogrom also had a catastrophic effect on the DP's future disarray and final dissolution.[43]

This radical reorientation of the Menderes government's foreign policy, which actually preceded Köprülü's replacement as foreign minister, was to bring other modifications in the DP's command structure. Most notable was the temporary suspension of the authority and initiatives of Fahrettin Kerim Gökay, the *vali* (governor) of Istanbul. Menderes placed his minister of the interior, Namık Gedik, in charge of Istanbul's security, and Gedik was actually to control and execute the pogrom. What led Menderes to this radical alteration of policy from non-involvement in the Greek-British imbroglio to

[42] The reasoning of the High Court's Decision at Yassıada, *Yassıada Trials, Esas* no. 1960/3, "6/7 Eylül olayları davası kararı gerekçesi," p. 2, from the stencil manuscript. See also the relevant section of the present study below.
[43] Emrullah Nutku, *Demokrat Parti neden çöktü ve politika'da yıtırdığım yıllar 1946-1958 siyasi anılarım*, Istanbul, 1979, pp. 282-291. Samet Ağaoğlu, *Arkadaşım Menderes*, Istanbul, 1967, pp. 123-155. Emin Karakuş, *40 yıllık bu gazeteci gözü ile işte*, Ankara, Istanbul, 1977, pp. 289-294. Rıfkı Salim Burçak, *Yassıada ve öncesi*, Ankara, 1976, *passim*. William Hale, *Turkish Politics and the Military*, New York, 1994, pp. 94-95 and 126-131. Cem Eroğul, *Demokrat Parti (tarih ve ideolojisi)*, Ankara, 1970, pp. 126-131. Metin Toker, *İsmet Paşalı 10 yıl 1954-1957*, I, 1966, pp. 103-120.

direct and aggressive participation in 1954 and 1955? An immediate factor seems to have been Great Britain's weakening position on the Cyprus issue, and the corresponding British need for vigorous support from the Turkish side. A second consideration was very probably the stiffening opposition to Menderes's internal policies. In regard to the latter, a number of Turkish analysts as well as the Yassıada proceedings attributed the change in policy to Menderes's need to divert the attention and passions of the public to Cyprus so as to distract it from socioeconomic matters. Ahmet Hamdi Başar, a former member of both parliament and the DP, wrote the following during the 1960 tribunals:

> From the first day it had become clear that the events of September 6-7 had been organized by those who governed. Only they had not reckoned that the results could be so horrendous. What was the purpose of this clever exploitation of the masses supposedly over the Cyprus issue?...It is clear from these rebellious events this was exploited so as to strengthen the powers of Menderes and to enforce his dictatorship with its resort to violent measures in the realm of internal policy.[44]

From the outset, Greek analysts have pointed an accusatory finger at Britain's role in provoking Turkish intervention on the Cyprus issue during the years 1954-1955. Although there was not much proof originally to substantiate such a charge, the evidence is somewhat more compelling today regarding a prominent, if not dominant, role for British policy in dragging the Menderes government into a "violent" intervention during the London tripartite conference in late August to early September 1955, much to the shock of the Greeks. In the beginning, the available proof was circumstantial.[45] Subsequent research and publications, however, have shed some light on the British effort.

The published memoirs of the seasoned Turkish diplomat, Mahmut Dikerdem, are explicit on the matter. As a member of the mission that then-acting foreign minister Zorlu took with him to the conference, Dikerdem was in a position to give a revealing account of the Turkish side—and, in

---

[44] Ahmet Hamdi Başar, *Yaşadığımız devrin iç yüzü*, Ankara, 1960, p. 90. Sarrês, *É allê pleura*, Volume II, Part I, p. 111, gives a Greek translation of the Turkish text. Christoforos Chrêstidês, *Kypriako kai ellênotourkika: Poreia mias ethnikês chreôkopias 1953-1967*, Athens, 1967, pp. 164-165.

[45] From the remarks in the perceptive report of the Greek diplomat and former Greek consul in Istanbul, Vyrôn Theodôropoulos, *Sêmeiôma*, p. 20, still in manuscript form, which he was kind enough to provide to me. See also the comments of Chrêstidês, *Kypriako kai ellênotourkika*, p. 190.

particular, of British behavior and of the British attitude in getting a more vigorous Turkish reaction on Cyprus.[46] He emphasizes British efforts to secure a strong stance from Turkey on the issue, which would basically bolster the faltering British position. Further, he remarks that after Zorlu had read his lengthy and detailed catalogue of demands on Cyprus to the assembled conferees, Harold Macmillan terminated the day's discussions and hastened to congratulate Zorlu on strengthening Turkish policy on Cyprus and articulating Turkish demands.[47]

In a cryptogram sent to Ankara on August 28, Zorlu informed his government that even at this late hour (that is, before his speech to the conference), the British were still uneasy over the prospect that the Turkish mission would not make any strong claims in opposition to those of the Greek representatives.[48] By the first half of 1954, the British government was uneasy over the possibility that Turkey would not support Britain on Cyprus.[49] On July 15, 1954, a member of the Foreign Office suggested that Britain actively court Turkey:

> I am informed that the Turkish Foreign Minister has given an official promise that his government will not actively oppose Greece's effort to secure a favorable decision from the United Nations Organization's General Assembly on the question of the unity of Cyprus and Greece....She [Turkey]will rather maintain a neutral attitude. Moreover, should the question take an active turn during the General Assembly discussion the Turkish delegates will try to suggest [a] means of settlement capable of easing the tension....You may think it wise to give the Turks further encouragement to keep them up to the mark. It would, of course, severely damage our position in the United Nations if the Turks were to adopt a neutral attitude in the question of considering Cyprus on the Assembly agenda.[50]

By October 1954, it seems that British efforts had largely succeeded in persuading the Menderes government to reverse its official position of "neutrality" in the Greek-British dispute over Cyprus. Under prodding by

---

[46] Sarrês, *Ê allê pleura*, Volume II, Part I, pp. 79-81, utilizes the rich memoir of Mahmut Dikerdem, *Ortadoğuda devrim yılları. Bir Büyükelçinin anıları*, Istanbul, 1977, reprint, 1990, pp. 127-129, to very good effect on this point. See also Fersoy, *Zorlu*, pp. 262-274.

[47] Sarrês, *Ê allê pleura*, Volume II, Part I, pp. 89-91.

[48] Chrêstidês, *Kypriako kai ellênotourkika*, p. 165. This is reported in Fersoy, *Zorlu*, pp. 278-284, and Dosdoğru, *6/7 Eylül olayları*, pp. 329 ff.

[49] On March 29, 1954, the Foreign Office notified the British ambassador in Ankara in this matter. For all that follows, see Holland, "Greek-Turkish relations," pp. 328-365.

[50] This document was first published in *Ibid.*, p. 328 and note 3.

British ambassador James Bowker, Ankara had quietly reoriented its position in a series of secret instructions to its embassies abroad and, although remaining outwardly neutral on Cyprus, had nevertheless responded favorably to the British ambassador. British efforts to elicit a more determined Turkish stand on matters, and thus to buttress their case, were transformed by the start of the armed campaign of EOKA (*Ethnikê Organôsis Kypriôn Agônistôn* in Greek, or National Organization of Cypriot Fighters) against British rule at the beginning of April 1955. This, in turn, set in motion a hysterical outpouring from the Turkish press, along with the activities of Fazıl Küçük and Faiz Kaymak, and their efforts to exert pressure on the Turkish government. The British consul in Istanbul wrote to the Foreign Office on April 19, 1955, that the renewed violence had persuaded Ankara to display much greater concern for Cyprus, and that this marked a decisive turn in the Menderes government's policy toward more active involvement in the issue:

> The strong Turkish press reaction to the recent outbreaks of terrorism in Cyprus has continued but there is now an increasing tendency to criticize the Cyprus [British] government for its handling of the situation.
>
> This tendency has not been helped by the wild and exaggerated statement made on his arrival here by Fazil Kucuk, the Secretary-General of the Cyprus National Turkish Union....Several Turkish newspapers, including the largest in the country, Hurriyet, which has always maintained a close interest in Cyprus, have sent correspondents to the island to follow the situation and most of their reports have been extremely critical of the supposedly ineffectual way in which the Cyprus authorities have handled the Greek terrorism.
>
> A fairly large section of the press is taking the line that British policy aims to set Turks and Greeks on the island at each others' throats so that the problem can be shown to the world as merely a private quarrel between the two communities....
>
> Even moderate press comment here has adopted a less favorable line than hitherto towards British policy....Although no cases of Greek terrorism directed against the Turks have been reported here, most of the press has referred to the dangerous position in which the Cypriot Turks find themselves....Throughout this violent and often garbled reaction the constant theme, of course, has been repeated emphasis that Turkey will never in any circumstance agree to the island being ceded to Greece and that she will take the necessary action in the event of any move in this direction by Britain....So far in all this the Turkish government

has remained aloof and has made no official pronouncement....[51]

Soon thereafter, Turkey made a formal request to the Foreign Office "for immediate access to British thinking and decisions over Cyprus." About a month later, on May 15, 1955, Britain consented grudgingly, as it not only needed a more aggressive Turkish policy but realized that Turkey now understood that the British position in Cyprus was weakening before both EOKA's campaign and the Greek government's success in bringing the issue before the United Nations.

> This is a disturbing but natural development. The Turks are (a) naturally rattled by the recent disorders in Cyprus and afraid that we shall be bundled out....[They are] taking advantage of their position as our only and essential supporter to raise their price in terms of having an increased say in Cyprus affairs. So far, the Turkish government has been restrained but they may not remain so.
>
> Apart from restoring order in Cyprus, a need which this development underlines, we can only do our best to appease the Turks by giving them full information about our intentions, whilst continuing to make clear that we, not they, rule the island.[52]

Britain's inability to maintain order in Cyprus was increasingly apparent in the course of 1954 and during the first half of 1955; indeed, in concert with British efforts to obtain more direct Turkish participation, the Foreign Office thought that this failure would provoke a Turkish reaction that would lead to further British loss of control. In his incisive and perceptive study of this neglected aspect of the Cyprus issue, Robert Holland concluded that: "Although officials and ministers in London were always aware of the danger that Turkey's own claims could easily escalate if incautious encouragements were given, the logic of their own tactical embarrassment progressively forced their hands into yielding that 'consultation' with Ankara which some warned was bound to be the thin end of a very dangerous wedge."[53]

The decision by Foreign Secretary Harold Macmillan and Prime Minister Anthony Eden to accept Adnan Menderes's proposal of "collusion" in advance of the London conference sealed the fate of the gathering, which, in turn, became tied to the pogrom of September 6-7.[54] In fact, the Turkish mission under Zorlu's leadership arrived in London fully prepared to announce Turkey's

---

[51] *Ibid.*, pp. 330-331, for the full text of this report of the British diplomatic service in Turkey to its home office.
[52] *Ibid.*, pp. 331-332.
[53] *Ibid.*, p. 332.
[54] *Ibid.*, pp. 332-333.

new Cyprus policy, and to do so in all its expansive and aggressive detail.[55]

Already, in a Foreign Office memorandum a year before the pogrom (September 14, 1954), at a time when British apprehension had been conveyed to Turkey, an English official had stated that, "A few riots in Ankara would do us nicely."[56] Holland summarizes the total effect of all this succinctly and logically: "It had also became obvious that the Greek community in Istanbul was a hostage to the Cyprus dispute. The anti-Greek riots in Istanbul which broke out on September 6 [1955] did not therefore come as a complete shock to those involved in the *higher reaches* [stress added] of the dispute."[57]

Naturally, the full details of Britain's policy of encouraging Turkey's aggressive behavior are not forthcoming. However, the facts that have come to light are sufficient to suggest that, by the early fall of 1954, the British government may have made vague, informal references on the desirability of some demonstration in Istanbul as a political barometer of public, and violent, Turkish sentiment on the subject of Cyprus. Holland's perceptive book on Cyprus gives proof that there was a direct connection between British and Turkish policy over the issue at this stage—as well as a British connection to Turkish behavior at the London tripartite conference.

It is against this background that a marked change occurs in Turkey's position on Cyprus and Greece, a change increasingly characterized by the Menderes government's rapidly intensifying efforts to formulate an aggressive policy over Cyprus. The accelerating, and open, development of this policy was carried out both on official and quasi-official (that is, semi-covert) levels. In August 1955, these two institutional levels of action were to peak, and to inflame Turkish nationalist passions to such a degree that events at the London conference would combine with the successful plot of the Turkish government to explode dynamite on its consular grounds in Thessalonikê to culminate in the devastating Turkish pogrom that destroyed the Greek community of Istanbul on the night of September 6-7, 1955. It is clear that governmental institutions and quasi-official organizations shifted their attention in 1954-1955 from the Turkish minority in Greek Thrace and Cyprus to the hostage Greek community of Istanbul. The subsequent attacks on the Greek community reached a point of hysteria in the summer of 1955, and they were characterized by a series of dangerous and ominous

---

[55] For all these details, see Dikerdem, *Ortadoğuda*, pp. 121-139. This work has been carefully utilized by Sarrês, *Ê allê pleura*, Volume II, Part I, pp. 79-128.

[56] Holland, "Greek-Turkish relations," p. 333 and note 1.

[57] *Ibid.*, p. 333. Holland concludes, "There is, however, good reason to believe that demonstrations on a very much smaller scale had been planned earlier to coincide more or less with the end of the London Conference on Cyprus."

episodes in which the government itself, along with student and irredentist organizations (all approved and controlled by the government), were the principal instigators.

With the government's approval, the National Federation of Turkish Students and the National Union of Turkish Students were founded in 1952. They afforded Menderes vehicles for political action and pressure that were legally not a part of the state apparatus but were, nevertheless, under strict government control.[58] The two groups were to take active part in "popular" demonstrations that were ostensibly unconnected to the government, but which the latter now encouraged and approved, since it had decided that it needed them. In conformity with the new direction in Turkish policy on Cyprus in 1954, the two organizations' role became to attack, through demonstrations and demands, the Greek minority in Istanbul, as well as the ecumenical patriarchate residing in the city.[59]

Other organizations joined the fray, including the Society for Relief of Refugees from Western Thrace, which had been established in 1953, and the Committee for the Defense of Turkish Rights in Cyprus, which proved to be particularly active and was reorganized as the *Kıbrıs Türktür Cemiyeti* (KTC or Cyprus Is Turkish Assocation).[60] It was *Kıbrıs Türktür Cemiyeti* that was to figure most prominently in arousing Turkish interest in Cyprus, and it was an organization in which Menderes was to centralize much, but not all, of the plans and schemes for an energetic policy in asserting Turkish claims on the island. Its creation marked a significant transition from a passive stage during which the Turkish government had maintained a formal neutrality on Cyprus (according to Köprülü) to one in which the government had decided to prepare public opinion for a more direct policy. Thus, the government began to gather in the reins of existing organizations and somehow to connect them to the newly founded KTC as the central clearing-house for a reoriented foreign policy.

Kıbrıs Türktür Cemiyeti's founder, Hikmet Bil, was to have a relatively close and much-discussed relationship with the Turkish prime minister during late 1954 and throughout much of 1955, that is, during the crucial phase in the change of Turkish policy on Cyprus and in the transformation of

---

[58] Theodôropoulos, *Sêmeiôma*, p. 2; Chrêstidês, *Ekthesis*, pp. 122-123.

[59] Armaoğlu, *Kıbrıs meselesi*, pp. 125 and 134.

[60] Alexandris, *The Greek minority*, p. 253; the Journalists' Union of the Athens Daily Newspapers, *The anti-Greek riots of September 6-7, 1955, at Constantinople and Smyrna*, Athens, 1956, pp. 61-62; Chrêstidês, *Ekthesis*, pp. 116-122. According to Theodôropoulos, *Sêmeiôma*, p. 3, in contrast to Alexandris, it was the Union for Education and Aid of the Turks of Cyprus that was incorporated into the *Kıbrıs Türktür Cemiyeti*.

public opinion. But Bil's importance, which initially hinged on his personal connection with Menderes and his position as vice-president (although the sources also refer to him as president or general president) of the KTC, had an additional and very great significance: As an editorial writer for the newspaper *Hürriyet*, Bil bound a notable part of the Turkish press to the new Cyprus policy and to the government's efforts to incite a certain segment of public opinion on the issue. The Turkish press was nothing short of incendiary in an atmosphere that increasingly became electric and menacing to Istanbul's Greek minority. Bil's arrest almost immediately after the pogrom, and his imprisonment in Harbiye prison on order of Menderes, is one of the supreme ironies in his personal history.[61] Embittered by his experience, Bil later wrote a book in which he accused Menderes of encouraging him to found and run the KTC, and of contributing to it financially and then utilizing it for his purposes. Hesitating to shut the organization down during the beginning of the London tripartite conference, Menderes finally ordered it to be shut down, and Bil to be arrested, the day after the pogrom. The police confiscated the group's papers and archives, which obviously contained documentation that would have posed a threat to Menderes and his government should their involvement with the organization become public—which it did much later through Bil's memoir.

According to this memoir, the National Union of Turkish Students called a meeting on August 24, 1954, to which representatives of the Turkish press were invited. Haldun Simavi (of the family that owned *Hürriyet*) chaired the meeting; after four hours of discussion, it was decided to found an organization that would concern itself with Cyprus similar to the Greek American group, AHEPA. (Clearly, there was no understanding here of AHEPA as an ethnic American *fraternal* association whose purpose was only secondarily political.) A committee was formed comprising Husamettin Canöztürk (president of the National Federation of Turkish Students), Orhan Birgit (a lawyer and journalist who would later become a minister in a government of Bülent Ecevit), Ahmet Emin Yalman (editor-in-chief of the newspaper *Vatan*), Ziya Somer (professor), Nevzat Yalın (Cypriot lawyer), Kamil Önal (journalist), and Hikmet Bil himself. This committee took the name of the *Kıbrıs Türktür Komitesi* and elected Bil as its president. Its title, the Cyprus Is Turkish Committee, was adopted in opposition to the Greek word—and slogan and battle-cry of the Greek Cypriots—*Enôsis* (or "Union,"

---

[61] Hikmet Bil, *Kıbrıs olayı ve iç yüzü*, Istanbul, 1976, pp. 83-102, for what follows, as well as Theodôropoulos, *Sêmeiôma*, pp. 3-5; Chrêstidês, *Ekthesis*, pp. 122-125 and 134-139, who translated Bil's interview in the January 7, 1956, issue of *Akis*.

the implication being union with Greece).

The new organization's first job was to prepare a brochure explaining why Cyprus was Turkish and justifying Turkish claims on the island on historical, geographical, strategic, and other grounds. After producing and circulating the Turkish version, English, French, Spanish, Italian, German, and Arabic editions were produced and sent throughout the world. At the same time, the committee began feverishly to organize and provide material assistance to chapters throughout Istanbul and all of Turkey. Within a year's time, the group seems to have acquired a sufficient treasury. As a follow-up to the brochure, it published a "pankart" (placard) that displayed Cyprus within a large Turkish flag. "We sent tens of thousands of 'Pankarts' to our own great city [Istanbul] and even to the village coffee shops," Bil wrote. "Chauffeurs decorated their cars with it. Thereafter they [the placards] were seen in practically all the store windows of Istanbul....We labored thus energetically and lovingly so that our days mixed with the nights."[62]

Although the government initially ignored the organization, Menderes very quickly realized that it could be a convenient tool in forging his new policy, and he soon approached its leaders, inviting them to a meeting on August 29 in the offices of the Istanbul *vali*. The gathering, which lasted approximately an hour and a half, also included Köprülü (still foreign minister), Zorlu (at the time a minister to the prime minister), and the minister Mükerrem Sarol. Köprülü, with his usual witty and acerbic tongue, opened the reception by asking Bil, "Friend, inasmuch as there is the State, what is there left for you to say?" Menderes interrupted the "Professor," however, and attempted to encourage the visitors by saying that the Cyprus question was a matter for all of them. He then asked about the nature of their organization. He eventually urged them to organize it properly (that is, legally); thus, after a slight rearrangement—and renaming—as the *Kıbrıs Türktür Cemiyeti*, the Menderes government became a "silent" partner of the group, and used it in a manner that was to play an important role, particularly in turning the Cyprus issue into a national Turkish issue. In fact, both Bil and his association proved to be dispensable after they had accomplished their tasks, as is evident from Menderes's conversations with Zorlu before the pogrom's outbreak and indeed from the prime minister's actions immediately following, when he had Bil and Birgit arrested, and the KTC outlawed. To the degree that blame for the pogrom could be placed on Bil, the officers, and the organization of the KTC, to that degree Menderes could hide his own involvement. In the end, however, although its role in whipping up Turkish fanaticism should have

[62] Bil, *Kıbrıs olayı*, pp. 85-86.

been reckoned a secondary cause of the pogrom, not one officer of the group was jailed by the Yassıada court.[63] Prominent journalists were intimately connected to the organization (Bil, Yalman, Birgit, Önal); indeed, Yalman, from an old and prestigious Istanbul Dönme family, served as Menderes's go-between with the group.[64] Despite the KTC's numerous local chapters (eighteen in Istanbul and 118 in Anatolia), the average Turk's access to the Cyprus issue was through the press, which, unfortunately, completely poisoned the atmosphere around the problem with hatred of and hysteria toward the Greek minority. A less sentimental but more instrumental factor in the destruction of the Greek community— although far more hidden (in part because they destroyed their records in Istanbul)—were the local offices of the DP (in Istanbul and elsewhere). These were excellently positioned to prepare, lead, and carry out the pogrom, and to identify Greeks, their homes, businesses, churches, cultural organizations, charitable institutions, schools, newspaper offices, cemeteries, and the like, as well as to draw up neighborhood catalogues that would enable the pogromists to concentrate on the Greek minority without mistaking its property for that of Turkish Muslims or of other groups.[65]

The very highest echelons of the government itself were, of course, of great importance in both planning and executing the pogrom: from the prime minister, Adnan Menderes, to the minister of foreign affairs, Fatin Rüştü Zorlu, to the minister of the interior, Namık Gedik, to the former foreign minister, Mehmet Fuat Köprülü, and minister of defense, Ethem Menderes, to other important cabinet members and officials such as the *vali* of Istanbul, Fahrettin Kerim Gökay.[66] The generals who overthrew Menderes in the coup of May 27, 1960, and who subsequently tried almost the entire Menderes government at Yassıada, went to great pains to observe all the necessary and formal legalities in the tribunals in which the 592 individuals were charged. Although the brief time allowed for the defense was a glaring defect—as was the political badgering of the accused by judges and prosecutors—the legal documentation, testimony, and other materials that emerged from this massive trial constitute incredibly rich sources for reconstructing a critical

---

[63] Sarrês, *Ê allê pleura*, volume II, Part I, p. 245, note 213. According to Bil, *Kıbrıs olayı*, p. 89, the organization's membership rose to 200,000. For the realities, see my discussion on the role of the local DP branch offices.

[64] Chrêstidês, *Ekthesis*, p. 136.

[65] On the important but half-hidden role of the local Istanbul offices of the DP, see Hasan İzzetin Dinamo, *6-7 Eylül kasırgası*, Istanbul, 1971, p. 43. This text is also cited in Sarrês, *Ê allê pleura*, Volume II, Part I, pp. 154-155.

[66] Rasih Nuri Ileri, *27 Mayıs Menderes'in dramı*, Istanbul, 1986, pp. 21-25.

turning-point in the political, social, and economic history of modern Turkey,
and in the latter's relations with Greece, Britain, and the United States.[67]
Thus, the court proceedings and their testimony are not only important, but
seem to reveal the nature of the Menderes government and of its faults, and
to confirm that the pogrom was organized by Menderes and a number of
his senior officials (see Chapter 6 for the details and political background of
the trials).

Indeed, the overwhelming majority of Turkish sources and observers
testify that the actual responsibility for organizing and executing this highly
complex and skillfully orchestrated violence fell on none other than Prime
Minister Menderes, Foreign Minister Zorlu, Interior Minister Gedik (who was
not tried as he committed suicide beforehand), and the *vali* of Izmir, Kemal
Hadımlı. In addition to the pogrom, the court hearings disposed of eighteen
other cases of malfeasance.[68] Menderes, and those in his government who

[67] For a succinct but incomplete evaluation of the Yassıada court trials, see Walter Weiker,
The Turkish Revolution 1960-1961: Aspects of Military Politics, Washington, 1963, especially
Chapter 2, pp. 24-47; also Hale, *Turkish Politics and the Military*, pp. 94 ff, and Ali Fuad
Başgil, *La révolution militaire de 1960 en Turquie*, Paris, 1963. For the trials themselves, there is
a plethora of materials. First there are the *tutanaklar* (proceedings), *iddianameler* (indictments),
and *kararnameler* (decisions), with their *gerekçe* (opinion or reasoning of the court). Dosdoğru,
6/7 Eylül olayları, pp. 7-12, gives a short but very useful *précis* of these for the 1960-1961
trials, and, *en passant*, he deals with some of the courts-martial that the military governor of
Istanbul, Fahrettin Aknoz, set in motion in 1955-1956, pp. 24-91, especially in regard to the
bogus trials against the leftists charged with the pogrom. In Part Two of his book, Dosdoğru
(pp. 93-308) presents detailed testimony from the accused and witnesses, then his own letter
to the prosecuting attorney, the decision and the logic behind it (pp. 309-367), and, finally, the
coverage given the trials by the Turkish press (pp. 369-86). There is also the massive body of
documentation and records of the trials, preserved in their original stenciled form. For further
materials now published—including memoirs of some of the lawyers who defended a number
of the more prominent accused, of those actually tried, and of interested observers—consult
the footnotes in the rest of this study. The Turkish and foreign press are also of interest.

[68] Tekin Erer, *Yassıada ve sonrası*, Istanbul, 1965, pp. 565-615, for the results of the trials;
Türgüt, *Menderes/Zorlu/Polatkan*, pp. 41-217. Of particular interest is Dosdoğru's most
recent book. As one of the leftists arrested and charged with the pogrom, he pays particular
attention to their tribulations. Sarrês's book, *Ê allê pleura*, Volume II, Part I, to which I also
frequently refer, is both skillfully crafted and highly analytical; further, it is the first major work
to incorporate the rich Turkish literature of memoirs and accounts of the era. The Turkish
literature on the subject is obviously considerable (it is increasing with each passing year as
the immediacy of the event and the freshness of the wounds in Turkish society recede into
the distant background), and it is absolutely essential. Among the authors, listed below, were
individuals who were tried in 1960-1961, interested observers, or those involved directly as
lawyers in the proceedings: Enver Durmuş, Cemal Fersoy, Hikmet Bil, Hasan Dinamo, Aziz
Nesin, Abdurrahman Dilipak, Rasih İleri, Emin Karakuş, Mithat Perin, Mükerrem Sarol,
Ahmet Başar, Turhan Dilligil, Semih Günver, Haydar Tunçkanat, Nusret Kirişçioğlu, Samet
Ağaoğlu, Fahir Armaoğlu, Şevket Aydemir, Ali Birand, Rıfkı Burçak, Piraye Cerrahoğlu,

were directly involved (including those who were acquitted at Yassıada), knew well in advance of the pogrom's outbreak in the late afternoon of September 6, 1955, what was to transpire since they had planned and organized the events through the government's extensive network of command. This extended down from the prime minister himself and his ministers through the municipal offices of the *vali* of Istanbul and the heads of the police, armed forces, and departments of communication and transportation, down into the local party headquarters of Istanbul and Izmir, as well as into the provinces or regional towns such as Eskişehir and Bursa. The DP's local officials had close relations with the local police, as well as with the leaders and organizers of the labor unions. All these levels of party-government control appear in the sources, and they also appear as acting in consonance with a centralized and well-organized plan. The student groups and the KTC were much more limited, and their principal role was to raise the political temperature over the Cyprus issue, which was indeed raised to a red-hot pitch. But the enormous undertaking of destroying in some nine hours the individual and communal property, institutions, and society of 85,000 Greeks scattered over a huge area of about 45 square kilometers from the Black Sea to the Sea of Marmara called for numbers (many tens of thousands), organization, and equipment that were far beyond the power of these lesser groups, especially because the large Greek minority did not live in one segregated ghetto, or even in a few, but was scattered throughout some twenty-nine neighborhoods among which transportation was extremely difficult.[69]

To return to the KTC, however, and to its temporary but very important role in preparing the pogrom, varying estimates of its membership were very high, between 180,000 and 200,000 (although it is hard to confirm these figures). Further, during the course of the riots, various observers spoke of 100,000 to 200,000 pogromists at any given point in the events. That it was truly a mass phenomenon cannot be doubted, and its magnitude is further indicated by the approximately 3,500 arrests immediately afterward, as well as by the 5,000 persons who appeared or were mentioned in the military trials ordered by General Fahrettin Aknoz in late 1955 and early 1956 after the declaration of martial law on September 12, 1955. At this point, perhaps a more general discussion of the structure of the KTC's branch organizations in Istanbul will help somewhat to fill in this vacuum regarding the size, extent, and nature of the society.[70]

Mahmut Dikerdem, Hulusi Dosdoğru, Tekin Erer, Cem Erogül, Adnan Menderes, Emrullah Nutku, Metin Toker, Hulusi Turgut, Ahmet Yalman.

[69] Chrêstidês, *Ekthesis*, pp. 27-36.

[70] The questions of numbers of participants in and the extent of the pogrom will be discussed below.

THE *KIBRIS TÜRKTÜR CEMİYETİ*

The degree of integration of many of the previously mentioned quasi-official (that is, student and other) organizations into the central office of the *Kıbrıs Türktür Cemiyeti* has already been made clear. The participation of labor unions has also been implied, but a little more should be said here about their important, indeed essential, presence in the pogrom itself, as well as in the administrative structure of the KTC. By way of a short preface, it should be stressed that many Turkish labor unions had a purely governmental existence, that is, their leaders were not only appointed by the government but were essentially DP operatives and agents. Whereas they catered to the interests of workers, their policies were essentially those of the government and of the ruling political party. Thus, the relation of the DP government to the labor unions was characterized by an identity of interests. The labor unions' participation in the pogrom was absolutely crucial. The first hint of their role in preparing for, organizing, and executing the riots emerges from a confidential telegram from the American consulate in Istanbul to the secretary of state on September 13, 1955, about a week after the events: "Leading Istanbul trade unionists say all union headquarters Istanbul closed last night and doors sealed by martial law authorities. No reason given them for closure. Ministry Labor official understands headquarters will be searched for 'Communist material' and will presumably be opened after search. Ministry official says unions still legal and not otherwise affected by this measure."[71] It is most likely that what the government feared, especially because of the tumultuous DP parliamentary group meeting in Ankara prior to the discussion of the pogrom (but also as a result of the more general discussion and criticism that followed in parliament), was precisely the leak of incriminating evidence that might flush Menderes and his colleagues out into the open political arena.

Another confidential dispatch from the US embassy in Ankara, dated December 1, 1955, is much more informative regarding the relation of the labor unions to the government and the DP:

> The police chief alleges that it was through the unions that the various tools of destruction were collected. As further evidence of the unions' ties to the [Cyprus Is Turkish] Association, one of the Istanbul Consulate General's contacts in the Textile Union reported that at some time before the riot, his union and unnamed others had helped make some banners and displays which were

---

[71] National Archives, Foreign Office Dispatch No. 180, American Consul General Istanbul to Department of State, Sept. 13, 1955.

later shipped to the "Cyprus is Turkish Association" in Cyprus. It is not meant that the unions were responsible for the riot, but only that some of their leaders were involved and allowed the unions to be used as a tool.

Few foreign observers seemed to have paid much attention to the Cyprus is Turkish Association prior to the riots. Now that its offices have been closed and its leaders arrested, *an investigation is quite difficult* [stress added, to emphasize Menderes's efforts to close all access to incriminating evidence]....According to the Istanbul police chief, the Association had a central executive of 8 members and within Istanbul 13 district executive committees. The total membership of the executive committees was 84 persons, which included four or five students from the Istanbul University branch of the National Union of Turkish Students. Also on the executive committees were *four or five labor union officials* [stress added]. Neither the police chief nor any other informed person has ventured to guess on the Association's total membership....

It is believed that the riots in Izmir and Istanbul developed quite differently *in respect to their being mass affairs* [stress added] largely because of a different relationship between the Association and the labor unions in the two cities. The Izmir branch seems to have lost its contact with the unions and the working class of the city when the head of the Egi Federation [a local union] dropped out about September 1...but the Embassy does know that several prominent labor union leaders appeared to have been active in the affairs of the Association up until September 6.[72]

The government's general policy of preventing access to the minutes and records of Istanbul's labor unions was repeated when the KTC's and DP's official minutes and records were also impounded (during the Yassıada trials, it was revealed that all the substantive sections of the official minutes of the DP had been destroyed).[73] The same undoubtedly occurred with the records of the DP's local branches in Istanbul, although we are not suitably informed about this. This destruction of documentation has obviously precluded any definitive conclusions about the *degree* to which the Menderes government penetrated the principal institutions and organizations that figured so prominently in the pogrom of September 6-7, 1955. Yet evidence of a critical nature on this matter was available to the American ambassador and to his consular staff, although it was either ignored or overlooked. In any case, it was

[72] National Archives, Foreign Office Dispatch No. 228, American Ambassador to Department of State, December 1, 1955.
[73] Yassıada Trials, *Esas* no. 1960/3, *6/7 Eylül olayları*, stenciled text, p. 25.

not brought to bear on the ambassador's important report to Washington a mere three months after the pogrom. Had it been, it would have substantially altered his account (as will be seen below).

Particularly revealing as to the thorough penetration of the central KTC office and of its Istanbul branches by Menderes and the DP was the reportage by Turkish journalist Hüseyın Cahit Yalçın in his article, "Başkanın mesuliyeti" ("The Prime Minister's Responsibility"), which appeared a little less than a month after the pogrom (and which is discussed in more detail below). As much of the information on the pogrom came out of Turkey in the form of confidential and highly influential reports from the various foreign missions in the country, the initial and "formal" impressions that were formed outside of Turkey tended to see the violent disturbances of September 6-7 as having been initiated by non-governmental groups, forces, and individuals. The Turkish government very quickly—and in part inspired, according to certain observers, by Allen Dulles—decided to reinforce these impressions by blaming Turkey's communists. Soon, the mass of the Turkish press began to parrot the government's view, as did Aknoz's military tribunals in response to government directions.[74]

Of course, Yassıada gives a final, convincing, and decisive answer to the government's allegation of communist violence, and even the Aknoz courts-martial had already found the standard communist accusation a road that led nowhere. Nonetheless, some archival documentation in Turkey as well as in various other national archives gives the definite impression that the Turkish government was either not responsible for the pogrom, or else had merely called for a very limited demonstration, to support the London tripartite conference, which then got out of hand. This view has had an altogether unjustified and long afterlife.

A typical and highly representative example of this "school" of reasoning is the important, twenty-one-page, confidential report sent by the US ambassador to Turkey, Avra Warren, to the State Department on December 1, 1955; it represents the sum total of US analysis of the pogrom and of its entire complex of issues. The report is doubly valuable since it ferrets out much that was previously concealed, while, at the same time, being fundamentally in error about the political impetus behind the pogrom and its ultimate purpose as far as the Menderes government was concerned. Further, this erroneous interpretation seems to fit in with US foreign policy during the Cold War and constitutes important testimony of what proved to be an unswerving

---

[74] Dosdoğru, *6/7 Eylül olayları*, pp. 313-314, on Yalçın and his criticism of Menderes's role in the pogrom.

course in that part of the world that, as such, represented an alignment with British views on the region. But one must let the ambassador's report speak for itself:

> The [Turkish] Government has attempted to blame the Communists for the riot. The small number of Communists and the care with which the Turkish secret police have observed their activities in the past tends to severely restrict the likelihood of Communists having been the prime organizers without the Government's learning of it....
>
> On the basis of information received, the Embassy's opinion is that the riot was organized wholly against Greeks. However in Istanbul the Association [KTC] brought too many people into the melee and the leaders lost control over the mobs. It was then that the city's depressed, irresponsible element took over to complete the destruction and carry out the looting. Prime Minister Menderes estimated that this uprooted element in Istanbul numbers about 300,000 or 1/5 of the total population![75]

Implicit in this report is the American ambassador's belief that a much smaller, controlled demonstration had been planned and that the intentions of the organizers were for a very limited protest. (The ambassador does not specify, of course, who the original planners were—although he implies that it was the government—nor does he say much regarding the mechanisms by which "the leaders lost control" over this supposedly smaller government demonstration.) His report argues in detail that the Turkish government was not responsible for the pogrom, thereby unwittingly implying that this US ally was politically incompetent as far as controlling its internal affairs or the imagined "communist threat" against it—an inconsistency that was amply pointed out by Turkish diplomats and authors. Thus, Warren reasoned: "Some responsible leaders of the religious minority communities, as well as some foreign observers, accuse the [Turkish] Government, or at least some of its officials, of having knowingly allowed and encouraged the riot to take place. For many reasons the Embassy does not believe this is true." This view is then justified by what "the Embassy" considers to have been the Turkish government's serious mistakes:

> (1) They [Turkish government officials] did not keep themselves fully enough informed as to what sort of anti-Greek demonstration they admit unofficially as having known was planned;

[75] National Archives, Foreign Office Dispatch No. 228, American Ambassador to Department of State, December 1, 1955.

(2) They misjudged the temper of the people in regard to popular sentiment against Greece and against their current economic hardships; and

(3) They did not recognize until too late that the demonstration was a serious threat to public security. The efforts of the police and army to restore law and order also seemed to have revealed certain unfavorable conditions:

(a) The police force of Istanbul and Izmir, and perhaps other urban centers, are neither manned nor equipped to handle civil disturbances;

(b) Neither the police nor the army are properly trained to control unruly crowds;

(c) The procedure for coordinating police and army units during periods of emergency is clumsy and confused.[76]

This report, which seems so reasonable and logical on the surface, either willfully refused to see—or simply distorted—the mechanics both of the pogrom's organization and its execution, since it does not present any substantive evidence for its claims that:

• The Turkish government had not intended any thorough destruction of the Greek community, or its property, houses, schools, churches, and businesses.

• The Turkish government had only intended to stage a demonstration of very limited scope.

• The great numbers that finally took control of the demonstration were responsible for transforming it into a "massive"—the word used in the ambassador's report—and spontaneous intervention by Istanbul's 300,000-strong underclass.

• The city's police, as well as the army, were poorly trained for containing rioters.

• The procedure for coordinating army and police during emergencies was clumsy and confused.

• Menderes had not sufficiently attended to the economic and social problems of Istanbul's underclass.

Warren's evaluation of the events essentially exonerated the Menderes government from direct responsibility in this vast and "hysterical" riot, and such arguments were repeated in many similar reports to the Foreign Office and even to the Greek foreign ministry by the corresponding ambassadors

---

[76] *Ibid.*

and consuls.[77] Consequently, a closer examination is necessary of the flow in the chain of command among Menderes, his immediate colleagues in the cabinet, the ministries and parliament, the DP's central and branch offices (especially those in Istanbul and its environs), the DP's central and local officials, and, finally, the KTC's central organization, its eighteen local branches in Istanbul, and some of its 118 branches in Turkey and Cyprus. Indeed, by concentrating on this last link in the chain of command, one can shed more light on Ambassador Warren's argument, as well as on the intentions of the Menderes government.

We have already referred to the association of student organizations, unions, journalists, and the KTC, a private group that, after its initial contact with Menderes and some of his ministers, became a quasi-governmental entity through government subvention and protection. Thus, the relation of the central board of the organization with the highest echelons of the Menderes government is apparent and by now well-known. Much less attention has been paid, however, to the creation of the KTC's eighteen or so Istanbul branches, the processes of this political initiative, and the relations between these branches and the DP's local Istanbul neighborhood or ward offices.

One of the many merits of Hulusi M. Dosdoğru's book on the pogrom is its incisive understanding of the politics of the local branches of both the DP and KTC. He also cites the extended analysis of the pogrom ("The Prime Minister's Responsibility") written by Hüseyın Cahit Yalçın and published in the Turkish newspaper *Ulus* on January 5, 1956. In presenting this material, Dosdoğru writes:

> Putting aside what has been written in the world press, and simply casting an eye on the various published accounts in the *Ulus* daily newspaper, the following facts emerge in the lead article of the editor-in-chief, Hüseyın Cahit Yalçın....
>
> In the first days after the events, it was particularly desired [by the government] that the [*Kıbrıs Türktür*] *Cemiyeti* and the communists be charged [with the pogrom].
>
> However, among the plunderers and destroyers there were seen to be presidents of the local *Demokrat Parti*, the *Kıbrıs*

---

[77] Dosdoğru, *6/7 Eylül olayları*, added the following subtitle on the inside title page of his book: "6/7 Eylül 1955 in karası topluma sürülemez!"—"The events of September 6-7 cannot blacken the people!"—precisely to forewarn the reader as to his view that the pogrom's perpetrators were the government and the DP, and not an agitated Turkish people. He also indicates some influence from Allen Dulles in persuading the Turkish government to blame the episode on the communists.

Türktür Cemiyeti chairman, and other organizers [who were later] examined and, having been found innocent, were released.... The founding committee of [KTC] had been received by Menderes and, as F. Köprülü, M. Sarol, and F. R. Zorlu were well disposed, the members of the organization perceived that the kind reception and treatment were beyond their hopes. At that time, these individuals found themselves near the Prime Minister and each one had become a director....[78]

The KTC's two principal officers, Orhan Birgit and Hikmet Bil, were not DP members, and so their organization did not begin as a DP operation. Nonetheless, their contact and agreement to cooperate with Menderes on the Cyprus issue, and the subsequent acceptance of financial support, led to a very different organization, and to a fundamental change in it. The prime minister's office absorbed it at the central level, whereas, through its cooptation by the local Istanbul DP leadership, it fell into that leadership's control at the branch level. The very person designated by Menderes as the KTC's liaison, the distinguished journalist, Ahmet Emin Yalman, was editor of the paper *Vatan*, while Sedat Bayur was a member both of the Local Administrative Council and the Local General Assembly. Menderes placed both men on the *Cemiyet's* administrative council, whereas the organization's secretary-general, Kamil Önal, took a position in the state's national security bureau and was also a member of the DP's Zühtüpaşa chapter in Kadıköy. Hüseyın Yalçın's catalogue of local DP members and officials who became leaders in the *Cemiyet's* newly founded local chapters is eloquent testimony to the process by which the DP absorbed these branches, having already coopted the KTC's central office and primary officers.

> Serafim Sağlamel, who was chief of the Kadıköy branch of the *Kıbrıs Türktür Cemiyeti*, had been president of the *Demokrat Parti's* Zühtüpaşa chapter. This arch-destroyer [*kirişcibaşı*], was close to the fallen President [Mahmud Celal Bayar] and to the fallen Prime Minister [Menderes]. For in order to found this branch of the *Cemiyet*, he had to have written consent of the *Demokrat Parti Merkezi* [central office]. The Administrative Council of this branch [of the *Cemiyet*] was formed from the members of the Zühtüpaşa Chapter Administrative Council. The Paşabahçe, Beykoz, Küçük Çekmece Branch Officers were registered in the name of the *Demokrat Parti*. Of these, only the Büyük Çekmece Branch belonged to the Republican People's Party. Similarly, the president of the Beykoz Chapter, Seyfi Lobat, and others of the

[78] *Ibid.*, pp. 314-315.

Chapter Council formed the *Kıbrıs Türktür Cemiyeti*'s Beykoz Branch and Administrative Council. Hasan Türkay, president of the Paşabahçe *Demokrat Parti* Chapter and alternate member of the Local General Council, and member of the *Demokrat Parti* Workers' Committee, was sent to Cyprus by the government and there he separated the workers from the old unions and joined them to the workers' union in Turkey.

The president of the Florya Branch of the *Kıbrıs Türktür Cemiyeti*, and a member of the *Demokrat Parti* close to the fallen President and to the fallen Prime Minister, was Mustafa Polatkan. All the members of this Branch were also members of the *Demokrat Parti*.

The Mecidiyeköy, Fener, Karagümrük *Kıbrıs Türktür Cemiyeti* Branches were all founded by members of the *Demokrat Parti*. The Pendik Branch of the *Kıbrıs Türktür Cemiyeti* was founded shortly after the 6/7 September Events by Sabri Taşkin, a member of the *Demokrat Parti* Local Administrative Council and of the Municipal Assembly.

Haşim Pekşen, a member of the *Demokrat Parti*'s Şehir Assembly founded the *Kıbrıs Türktür Cemiyeti*'s Yenikapı Branch.

That the members of the *Demokrat Parti* created the foundation of the *Kıbrıs Türktür Cemiyeti* was demonstrated openly by the events. It is also evident that it was the *Kıbrıs Türktür Cemiyeti* that, prior to the Events of September 6-7, marked in a special way the doors of the houses, stores, churches, and other [structures] that were to be destroyed. Just as before the Saint Bartholomew Night Massacres, it had been necessary, in Paris, for the Catholics to mark secretly the doors of the Protestant houses....[79]

Yalçın's reconstruction and analysis demonstrate the pattern of cooptation of the small central organization founded by Hikmet Bil and his original colleagues once they accepted Menderes's support: total incorporation into the DP's apparatus. The KTC's rapid spread in European and Anatolian Turkey, as well as in Istanbul, is thus due to the vast DP network throughout the country, a task far beyond the manpower and financial resources of Bil and Önal, who were busy traveling, the one to England, the other to Cyprus. The KTC's growth and "power," then, are those of Menderes and of his partisan network. Thus the *Kıbrıs Türktür Cemiyeti* was a cover for the government and its covert policies on Cyprus, among other things. Neither Yalçın nor Dosdoğru think that, from the original organization, either Orhan Birgit or Hikmet

[79] *Ibid.*, pp. 315-317.

Bil took part in marking the houses and businesses of the Greeks before the pogrom. Also, the memoirs of both Bil and Birgit reflect some confusion on these matters. Neither was a DP member, and they might not have been fully informed. In reality, the *Kıbrıs Türktür Cemiyeti* had disappeared, having become just another element of the DP's local organization, although it retained its name and some figurehead officials. As simply another part of the DP's local network, it had served its purpose once the pogrom was over. As Yalçın/Dosdoğru say: "After the Events of September 6-7, viewing the members of the *Kıbrıs Türktür Cemiyeti* Administrative Council and of the Branches with an indifferent eye, and on the supposed grounds of too many other matters of concern, Menderes offered to the *Cemiyet's* vice-president, Hikmet Bil, the office of Turkish cultural attaché in Lebanon as a bribe for his silence, and, according to Orhan Birgit's explanation, a similar position was offered to him by the Prime Minister, but he refused to accept it."[80]

THE *DEMOKRAT PARTİ* AND THE POGROM

Of the KTC's eighteen branches in the Istanbul area, ten were in effect controlled and run by local DP officials and members. One "belonged" to the Republican People's Party, and we have no specific information on the others. The vision of a tightly and efficiently organized network of DP offices and institutions bespeaks a rather agile and supple provincial structure, tightly integrated and coordinated with the party's head, who thus managed to entangle political, media, and labor organizations in his party's tentacles. The head of the party, who was also head of the government, thus operated on all levels of Turkish society, and amassed support that was at the same time a rich reservoir of manpower, finance, propaganda, and other resources for controlling and implementing policy. Thus, to argue, as Ambassador Warren did in his report of December 1, that the demonstrations "got out of control" reveals a critical inability in intelligence-gathering and analysis by US diplomats in Turkey.[81] We shall see, when discussing the pogrom itself, that each subgroup of pogromists, often forty to fifty, had leaders, with specific orders on what was (or was not) to be done, and on destroying everything Greek. Further, there is ample evidence, and specific examples that demonstrate, how effectively the DP network could mobilize large numbers of demonstrators, thugs, and others. Also, there is ample, indeed copious evidence that the riots could have been prevented, or halted, at any given time

---

[80] *Ibid.*, p. 317.
[81] National Archives, Foreign Office Dispatch No. 228, American Ambassador to Department of State, December 1, 1955; Chrêstidês, *Ekthesis*, p. 47.

in their duration, as indeed occurred when martial law was declared, and the army and police finally intervened *after* the property of the Greek minority was destroyed under the very eyes of the previously passive police and armed forces. By contrast, the Turkish contingents that were sent to guard the patriarchate and the Greek consulate had no trouble whatever in repelling the attackers. It is from a person called to testify by the head prosecutor of the Yassıada trials that one of the most telling examples emerges of the ability of local organizations, the labor unions, and indeed important DP members, to recruit large numbers of people from the provinces, simply and effectively, for the demonstrations in Istanbul. Following is the deposition of the lawyer, Halim Said Kaylı:

> Witness Halim Said Kaylı.
> Presently exercising profession of law at Eskişehir
> Interrogator: Do you know the accused?
> Witness: I know them from a distance.
> I: Are there any obstacles to your giving testimony?
> W: There is none. [The witness is made to swear the oath.]
> I: Give us whatever knowledge you have in regard to the concocted nature of the events of 6-7 September. You have said that workers were sent from Eskişehir to Istanbul, to Ankara and so forth…many more to Istanbul. Can you explain, if you know [about this]?
> W: I followed and evaluated, step by step, all the movements of the government during those days.
> I: Are you registered in a [political] party?
> W: Yes.
> I: With which party?
> W: At that time I was registered with the *Köylü* [Villager] Party.
> I: And now?
> W: Today I am neutral. After the elections, we, the colleagues, having met and having discussed the municipal elections, we took the decision not to participate in the election.
> On the 3rd or 4th of September, commencing with the beginning of September, Eskişehir lived through very lively days. For, September 2 is the day of the liberation of Eskişehir [during the Greek-Turkish war of 1919-1922]. A great importance is given to it. The *Demokrat Parti*, with its entire establishment, came to celebrate this day. That year [from the DP], there came Polatkan [it is unclear if the reference here is to Hasan Polatkan], Abidin Potuoğlu, Hicri Seven. Even Kemal Zeytinoğlu, who was unable to come, sent a telegram. On that day, there was to be the opening

of an industrial market. They sent the great mass of workers to the site of the ceremony. On that day, a rumor circulated [that] Polatkan had invited the workers to Istanbul....Such a secret rumor arose. And so we said, let us investigate who is behind this. So I dropped in on the police station at the Firewood Market. A policeman was there. I asked him, "Were you here yesterday? Today you are here. What is going on," I said. He replied: "By God, two days duty fell on me," he said. So we charged one of our worker comrades concerning this matter. The latter went to the train station. Afterward, he brought us the information. A train full of workers was going to Istanbul. They were hanging about in rags. Our colleague arrived and explained to us this circumstance. But, our comrade said, he could not ascertain why the train that was going [to Istanbul] was full of workers. But on the 5th or 6th of September, the torrent broke out violently. The two rivers overflowed into one. During this period, there were annoyances. There were people in the "torrent" who were not to be found in their houses. On the following day, the events of 6-7 September having taken place, naturally so-and-so had participated in the pillaging that took place during the events [in Istanbul], and some plunderers were arrested in Eskişehir. I know myself that two of them were sent to jail. And so we deliberated about this.

I: In saying "we," what do you mean?

W: The *Köylü* Party's Provincial Administrative Board.

I: What are their names?

W: On the Board at that time were Dr. Sami [*sic*], Ibrahim Yetim, Hasan Ekici, and a number of other colleagues. We were saying that the government had created this movement. A week or ten days later, I went to Istanbul. On the returning train, I encountered a police colleague.

I: What is his name?

W: I do not know his name. On the train, he said to me: "They [the government] carried out this deed. And now they are banishing us to the east." They were sending them to such places as Bitlis and Muş. According to the form [date?] of the event [in Istanbul], on the 3rd or 4th the director of the sugar factory, the director of the State Railways, and the municipal Mayor [all of Eskişehir]...

I: What are their names? Their names...

W: The mayor of the municipality [of Eskişehir] is Galip [*sic*]. After the mayor Galip had visited [the local] head of the *Demokrat Parti* several times in the morning and afternoon, he went to the *vilayet* [provincial] office. It was the 4th or 5th of September. At that time, we ascertained that the workers [from Eskişehir] had been sent off [to Istanbul]. There is a catalogue of officials, in the office of Security, who go out [of the city]. According to what our colleague had said, an important section of the police workforce had been sent to Istanbul and it was also explained that members of the Security had been summoned to Istanbul from neighboring *vilayets* as well. The confirmation of this is basically simple. There are catalogues [of those] in military service. If one examines them, it will emerge who of these Security forces remained [in Eskişehir] and who were sent off to Istanbul. Independently of this, it is possible to examine the third-class tickets sold at the Eskişehir station of the State Railways on that day and to compare the number of tickets sold on other days.

I: Do the factories list the workers, who are on the move, on registers?

W: The factories have registers. Certainly they contain the names of overzealous partisans [of the DP]. If one should examine them, it will be seen who had been sent, on leave, at the time of the events [in Istanbul].

I: According to your estimate, how many workers, on leave, went to Istanbul?

W: I estimate them at 400-500. And among them were leaders of partisan [party] chapters.

At this point, Fatin Rüştü Zorlu's lawyer, Ertuğrul Akça, asked:

A: The police having been sent to Istanbul for the purpose of security or, if not, [if they were sent] with the thought of pillaging, as in the opinion of the witness, what else is he able to tell us?

W: There is in the *Demokrat Parti* a body called the *değnekçi grubu.* Their duty is to destroy peace, to produce confusion, and to stir up disorder in their immediate surroundings. It is their duty to act as emcees during ceremonies. They always contrive new tasks for these types of men, for a policeman who works in his own provincial police station does not accept to execute a job in his own district, where he is known, so it is natural that he is transferred to another district.[82]

Halim Said Kaylı's testimony sheds light on the pogrom's planning because it presents a specific example of synchronized action by a high official of the central government. According to Kaylı, just a few days before the pogrom, a certain Polatkan, a member of the DP, apparently "invited"

---

[82] I have translated the Turkish into English on the basis of the Turkish text reproduced in Dosdoğru, *6/7 Eylül olayları,* pp. 274-277.

substantial numbers of workers to come to Istanbul at the time of the pogrom. Further, we see that the local DP coordinated the mobilization and organization of these workers. Second, the mayor of Eskişehir, Galip, took all his orders from the head of the local DP, and indeed visited the latter several times on the matter. There were additional meetings with the local heads of the state railways to arrange the transport of workers to Istanbul, and the "leaders" of the local DP branches were sent off to the city as well. Finally, a major portion of the security officers (police) was sent off to the city and, after the pogrom, some were transferred to distant eastern Anatolia. And what was the role of the local police and security officials? Simply, to arrange the orderly boarding of hundreds of local workers on trains and then to help, along with the local DP leaders, to organize and direct the workers in their assigned destruction and looting. Kaylı sketched the local DP's role in bold relief. In effect, it ruled and controlled the city of Eskişehir: the mayor, director of state railways, and head of security all took their orders from the party's local head. The same was true of the workers and unions.

In answering questions about the purpose of sending Eskişehir's police to Istanbul, Kaylı is brief but to the point. They were not sent to help restore order (the riots had not yet occurred, so Ertuğrul Akça's question on that point is nonsensical). They were sent to Istanbul to assist the Eskişehir DP-chapter leaders to arrange their contingent of union men or laborers, and to coordinate their destruction and looting, along with other numerous groups, which were waiting ahead. Kaylı then explains to Akça that there was a special body in the DP called the *değnekçi grubu*, which, as "foremen" (literally carriers of the cane or baton, or "beaters"), specialized in disturbing the peace and, generally, acts of violence. His explanation regarding their identity was simple: they were the security police. Thus, these *değnekçiler*-security police were also part and parcel of the DP's illegal violence, which they carried out outside their own provinces since the fact that they were known locally made it difficult for them to engage in such acts in their own areas. Nonetheless, when they had finished wreaking their violence and illegality in a strange province, they were not sent home (to Eskişehir in this case), but far away to the eastern provinces (Muş, Bitlis, etc.), where their faces and previous misdeeds were unknown. The word, *değnekçi*, by the way, originally referred to a guild official. Apparently, however, in Menderes's Turkey, an institution originally connected to the organization of guild labor came to denote either a specialized sort of security policeman or someone connected to the labor unions, who, in both cases, was the willing instrument of the *Demokrat Parti*.

And what of the number of workers from the local factories recruited by the DP for the pogrom? Kaylı estimates them at between 400 and 500.[83] Further, he remarks that similar operations were carried out elsewhere in the neighboring *vilayets*. There is no mention of any of the numerous chapters of the KTC in this testimony. Still, sending 400-500 laborers from local factories and unions from one city alone in a region close to Istanbul, which was obviously near many other towns, is valuable testimony of the ability of local DP cadres, not only to command the area's civil government and transport, but also to control the security apparatus.[84] Their control over the workers was just as strong, and the latter could be manipulated almost at will.

What of the actual numbers of those that participated in the pogrom, and of their social and geographical origin? This is a complex and important question. However, on the bases of sources available today, we can only yield general and vague answers. Most numerical estimates are general, and the full geographical or regional identity of the groups is yet to be determined. Should the forty-nine filing cabinets of materials and records assembled for the Yassıada trials ever be opened, a great deal more will be forthcoming in regard to the numbers, organizations, leaders, and social and geographical origins of the participants in the events of September 6-7, 1955. Despite these obstacles, it is important to have some idea of the magnitude of the numbers participating in the events, not only because this will help to explain the vast extent of the destruction of the Greek community, but because it will serve as an indication of the ability, or lack thereof, of its organizers, the DP, to carry out such an enterprise.[85]

One must begin with the scant information concerning the numerous participants, who lived in many communities and neighborhoods over a vast area of the city and its sprawling suburbs. The sources that seek to absolve the Menderes government of the pogrom put emphasis on the poverty of Istanbul's underclass and on the latter's envy of the rich more generally. Menderes himself stated that this element played a crucial role, and that there

---

[83] *Ibid.*, p. 276.

[84] Bil, *Kıbrıs olayı*, p. 89, boasts that a large meeting of the *Kıbrıs Türktür Cemiyeti* was held on September 9, 1954, in the city of Eskişehir. He makes no mention of the participation of the city's factory workers in the pogrom, although they are mentioned as having taken part in substantial numbers. It seems that the meeting of which Bil boasts as having had many attendees is to be explained by the fact that it was all in the hands of the local DP officers who in effect controlled the city's political life and its participation in the pogrom a year later.

[85] Although the most compelling reason for opening the Yassıada—and all other relevant— files is, of course, to bequeath some justice to the pogrom's victims, for a nation that seeks to become part of a democratic, and transparent, Europe, historical honesty also requires that the materials be released. In any case, the relevant portions of the DP central registers concerning the events will still be missing, as they were all destroyed.

were 300,000 "uprooted" persons living in Istanbul, that is, one-fifth of the city's entire population.[86] An anonymous Armenian observer of the pogrom, "B. E.," who seems to have followed the pogromists very closely in a number of the central and critical neighborhoods of Istanbul, relates that there were "at least one hundred thousand who 'worked,' shouting, and yelling, and cursing [in the district of Taksim-Tünel]....In five or six hours the heart of Istanbul was subjected to wartime destruction at the hands of more than 200,000 and fanatic demonstrators...." He finally gives an overall number for the entire episode of "300,000 Muslims."[87]

Cemal Fersoy, Zorlu's lawyer at Yassıada, also stated that those who were active in the pogrom numbered 300,000.[88] In his own defense against charges of conspiracy in the events, Zorlu indirectly validated the large numbers by asking, "What does this legal decision [the indictment] mean? How could I have moved these thousands of men in such a destructive riot, [all the way from] London?"[89] The Istanbul police's estimate, which must be the closest to the number of *organized* pogromists (as opposed to those who participated outside any organized and controlled bodies), set the number at 100,000.[90] This was reported in Ambassador Warren's December 1 dispatch to the State Department and repeated elsewhere. Frederic Sondern, Jr., an editor of *Reader's Digest* attending the same international conference as Allen Dulles, was very impressed with the size of the demonstrations. Describing the masses proceeding down İstiklal Caddesi and their thorough destruction of the Greek shops, he wrote: "The crowd was moving tightly packed now, moving like a relentless stream of lava....By nine o'clock, just two hours after the center of the city had erupted, at least 50,000 frenzied Turks had formed a hundred other lava streams, pouring down avenues and streets, tearing and smashing as they went."[91] Yet another journalist, the Belgian A. Rockaerts, reported that, "Ten to fifteen thousand persons assembled, as by magic, in one and the same place. The same thing occurred simultaneously in all the suburbs."[92] Noel Barber, a journalist who was also in Istanbul, described the

[86] National Archives, Foreign Office Dispatch No. 228, American Ambassador to Department of State, December 1, 1955.

[87] B. E., "A Historical Night," translated by H. Khosdeghian, p. 14.

[88] Fersoy, *Zorlu*, p. 237; Bil, *Kıbrıs olayı*, p. 89, claimed 200,000 members for his organization, but that seems highly unlikely.

[89] Cemal Fersoy, *Menderes*, p. 358.

[90] National Archives, Foreign Office Dispatch, No. 228, American Ambassador to Department of State, December 1, 1955. It is also the figure given by *Makedonia*, the Greek newspaper of Thessalonikê, in its long and detailed description of the pogrom, September 9, 1955.

[91] Frederic Sondern, Jr., "Istanbul's Night of Terror: An Eyewitness Account of One of the Most Destructive Riots of Modern Times," *Reader's Digest*, May 1956, pp. 186 and 188.

[92] Journalists' Union, *Anti-Greek Riots*, pp. 21-22.

rioters similarly as "a well organized mob of 20,000."[93]

A particularly specific and detailed account is to be found in the reports by the journalists writing in *Milliyet*. Especially relevant is their brief account of the large group that destroyed Greek establishments in the Sirkeci area.[94] Some 5,000 well-organized men were transported across the Galata Bridge by taxis and trucks and, having been delivered to their destination, spread out to effect their destruction, thereafter reuniting to march on to a further rendezvous with another large group. The efficient transport of this body of 5,000 from its starting-base on the other side of the Golden Horn, its division into larger and smaller groups to effect the destruction of the neighborhood, and then its orderly reunification into the original large group of 5,000, all reflects more than just this body's organizational structure. It is also clear evidence of exact coordination, tactics, and mobilization. The extrapolation from this one episode onto the entire night's violence—which entailed coordinating the so-called three waves of attackers (to be dealt with in a subsequent section) as well as the entire operation itself, and included the original gathering of men in the provinces as well as Istanbul, transportation to the Istanbul area, mobility within the city and its suburbs through provided means (trucks, cars, cabs, trains, boats), and obedience of the larger mass and much smaller bodies to their respective leaders (i.e., local DP officials, *değnekçiler*-security police, military commissioned and noncommissioned officers, labor leaders, and police, all of whose individual organizations and institutions answered to the central organs of the Menderes government and the national DP)—reveals an extraordinary degree of planning and a preexisting institutional network thoroughly penetrated by the DP and, therefore, the government.

There can be no doubt, although we cannot be sure of exact numbers, that the formally organized pogromists were very many indeed, as both the general figures and impressions, as well as the police report, support each other on this. A second fact tends to confirm this statement. Any attack on the Greek community, especially one perpetrated within a matter of a few hours, demanded large numbers of participants, for the destruction was not only extensive but thorough. Furthermore, most general accounts, both of those present and those who later studied the matter from a distance, concur as to the simultaneity of the attacks throughout the entire area, which, of course, would not have been possible without large numbers or planning. Ertuğrul

[93] Barber, *Daily Mail*, September 14, 1955. A Swiss journalist spoke of the pogrom as a "beast with 20,000 legs," Chrêstidês, *Ekthesis*, pp. 65-66.

[94] *Milliyet*, September 7 (or 8?). Iôannês Iôannidês, the editor of *Makedonia*, who went to Istanbul to report on the pogrom, stated that there were some 4,000 taxis and trucks that helped move about the large numbers of pogromists, *Makedonia*, September 14, 1955.

Ünal wrote in *Milliyet*: "The disturbances began, independently, at 7:30 PM, and, separately, in Bankalar Caddesi, Karaköy, Fermeneciler, Perşembe Pazarı, and in other neighborhoods."[95] His colleague, Bedirhan Çınar, reporting on the region of Gedikpaşa, wrote: "The people, angered by the event in Thessalonikê, moved in collected groups and like an avalanche crushed Kumkapı, Gedikpaşa and Çarşıkapı districts....In this period thousands of people descended to Gedikpaşa and Kumkapı."[96] The disturbances began on the Bosphorus at about 7:00 PM, at Sirkeci at 8:00 PM, at Taksim after 6:00 PM, and along İstiklal Caddesi somewhat later. In the latter case, the rioters left Harbiye, Dolmabahçe, and Tarlabaşı, after having carried out their destruction there, and united with the rioters from Taksim in order to carry out the heavy work ahead of them on İstiklal Caddesi.

There were, however, the very small groups, of between ten and forty, to which was entrusted the actual labor of destroying the Greeks' property and then throwing it out on the streets. The organization and actual functioning of these small, basic units, of which there must have been thousands moving about in those few hours of September 6-7, are of some importance, and should be analyzed. "B. E." early on identified the essence and size of these units:

> The demonstration was raging in all its destruction; thousands of people in orderly groups of 30 or 40 were led by a person showing them which store, which church, which restaurants, to loot, to destroy. I followed them from a distance, this group or that one....
>
> I found that the secret police personnel were leading the groups of 20 to 30 persons armed with steel bars, pickaxes, and wooden clubs. The group followed its leader who carried an address list and showed them which store or firm belonged to an infidel....I admit that exemplary discipline shone through this chaos, because everyone blindly followed his leader."[97]

The last detail in the description of "B. E.," the discipline, is, of course, important because it is another fact that contradicts the arguments of all those who, in describing the riots as a "spontaneous" outburst of Turkish ethnic passions, wished to exonerate the Menderes government, and Turkey more generally. Both the discipline as well as the effectiveness of these smaller "forces de frappe" are revealed in a letter, dated September 10, 1955, of such a unit leader. The author, Salih Kırmızı, had served as a noncommissioned officer in the Turkish contingent during the Korean War, and he addressed his

[95] *Milliyet*, September 7 (or 8?), 1955.
[96] *Ibid.*
[97] B. E./Khosdegian, "A Historical Night," p. 6.

correspondence to his former commander in Korea, Captain Cevat Şevkili. Among other things, this letter, written only three days after the pogrom in which Kırmızı had taken a very active and energetic role himself, reveals relevant details:

> My dear, big brother and commanding officer,
>   ...Before all else, my Captain, let me give you certain information concerning our beloved Istanbul. Though I am sure that you will have been informed by the radio and the newspapers as to the news, I think that you will be more convinced if you are informed as to these matters by a letter from a source who participated in the event. On Wednesday [actually Tuesday and Wednesday]...the announcement on the radio concerning the throwing of the bomb into the house of Atatürk[98] aroused the entirety of the youth, and every corner of Istanbul filled up and spilled over with a mass of people. These masses, rushing out into every neighborhood, with clubs, pickaxes, shovels, and iron crowbars in hand, burned and destroyed the stores, and above all the houses of the Greeks, and destroyed their possessions. Among all these masses, I also had a team. I wrapped a Turkish flag around my neck, I wore a hat of felt, holding an iron crowbar in one hand and a knife in the other. We [a larger group that included his own smaller one] destroyed all the Greek houses in Edirnekapı. My band alone, which consisted of some 10 to 15 persons at most, destroyed 23 Greek houses, 21 Greek taxis, 3 stores, 1 coffee house, a barber shop, and 5 tailors' establishments. Oh, my captain, we destroyed and smashed more than 20 refrigerators, 25 radios, sewing machines, silk garments, easy chairs, and all the valuable furniture, and then we left....Finally at night, between 2:30 and 3:00 AM martial law was proclaimed and each one of us returned to his home.
>   My address in Istanbul is M. Salih Kırmızı, Tekir Saray Caddesi, Limoncu Hüseyin Sokak #3, Edirnekapı, Istanbul
>   Your devoted "brother,"
>   Noncommissioned officer M. Salih Kırmızı.[99]

In this case, the leader of the small group that "worked" the Edirnekapı district was not necessarily a security officer (although he might have been that as well) but a noncommissioned officer in the Turkish army. The presence (to which other documents allude) of both commissioned and noncommissioned

---

[98] As was shown by both official Greek and Turkish reports, the dynamite was placed by the Turks themselves as the signal for unleashing the pogrom.

[99] Chrêstidês, *Ekthesis*, pp. 74-77. This letter is referred to in an official document in the Greek archives, but I was unable to find the Turkish original. However, Chrêstidês identified both the military men in question as well as their current addresses at that time.

army officers as leaders—*değnekçiler*—of these smaller groups raises a larger problem, however, which is hardly mentioned in these documents and concerns the Turkish secret or security police. Known today as MIT (*Milli İstihbarat Teşkilatı*, or National Intelligence Service), they were then known as MAH (*Milli Amele Hizmeti*, or National Affairs Service), and the suspicion is that all security police involved in the riots as group leaders were MAH agents.[100] Thus, it is they who appear with the lists or catalogues of all the Greeks, i.e., a large part of the non-Muslim inhabitants of the city. They might also have been the sources of the discriminatory tax lists for the *varlık vergisi* in the previous decade. In any case, security police and MAH, whether one or separate entities, were in effect under the ultimate control of DP head Menderes. In the pogrom, they acted in accordance with the detailed plans in whose creation the local DP presidents had played such an important role. Many leaders of the student organizations, the KTC, and the labor unions must have also been in this huge network of security police via the *Demokrat Parti*.

In attempting to summarize the disparate and insufficient sources regarding the numbers of participants, and the general and tactical *modus operandi* of larger and smaller groups, in the violence of September 6-7, the figure that seems to be somewhat more reasonable than all others is about 100,000 organized demonstrators, as it emerges from a police and security source. In addition, if some 5,000 demonstrators were transported to Sirkeci, it is reasonable to assume that since there were at least forty-five Greek communities or groups spread out over a very large area, 100,000 demonstrators would be necessary for such a task in such a short period. As such, the frequent reference to "thousands" of participants in the Greek, Turkish, and European press (many of whose correspondents witnessed the events and read translations of the news reports the next day), as well as in the legal proceedings and memoirs written afterward, is not merely a hackneyed exaggeration but, rather, reflects the realities.

It is clear that what was decisive for the pogrom's success was the ability of the DP network to mobilize such large numbers of demonstrators, to bring them to Istanbul, and, once there, to coordinate them. The KTC was just one of many organizations through which the DP acted, and it was certainly not the most important. By virtue of Menderes's power, the party infiltrated all government services; indeed, his death sentence by the Yassıada tribunal for violating the Turkish constitution was directly related to the fact that the *Demokrat Parti*'s penetration and domination of the state, especially after September 6-7, veered into authoritarian rule. In at least three other cases,

---

[100] *Anatolê*, August 1997, pp. 8-10, "Septemvriana '55. Parlar, Gizli Devlet," *passim*.

he was tried for acts of violence carried out essentially through the *Demokrat Parti* organization.[101]

From where, however, did the organizers recruit the mass of pogromists who changed the face of Istanbul in one short night? A major recruiting-ground was Istanbul itself (with its immediate suburbs), the country's most populous city, with approximately 1.5 million inhabitants. The large number of groups headquartered in the city provided a ready and organized system of local recruitment. The largest among them, and easily accessible through their leadership (which was usually appointed by the government), were the labor unions. The Istanbul *İşçi Sendikaları Birliği* (Union of Workers' Syndicates) totaled about 180,000 members. The *Devlet Demir Yolları Vagon Atölyesi Sendikası* (Union of State Railway Factory Workers) had about 3,000 members. The *Türkiye Deniz İşçileri Sendikalısının Federasyonu* (Syndicalist Union of Turkish Maritime Workers), the Istanbul *Deniz ve Maden Eşya İşçileri Sendikası* (Union of Maritime Workers and Miners), and the *Hereke Kumaş Fabrikası İşçi Sendikası* (Union of Hereke Textile Workers) created a massive reservoir for DP recruitment. Labor unions also existed in provincial cities such as Eskişehir from which, as we have already seen, workers were sent to participate in the general looting in Istanbul.[102]

The representation of the city's various neighborhoods, through the aggressive recruiting of its political partisans by local DP chapters, was very important to the mass violence.[103] Members of groups such as the KTC were able to bring their own members, while the student groups and ethnic Turkish regional organizations (from areas such as Bulgaria, Greek Thrace, and Cyprus)[104] cooperated as well.[105] The report of the US consul in Istanbul noted that "recruits in each neighborhood swelled the ranks and remained to finish the destruction while the main bands proceed[ed] to other targets."[106]

There were, additionally, people who looted whatever was left from the initial looting, but it is difficult to determine the proportion of destruction that this "follow-up" wave represented. In Istanbul, there were poor neighborhoods, neighborhoods of *gecekondus* (squatters' huts), and

---

[101] For these, one should consult the stenciled minutes/proceedings of the Yassıada trials.

[102] Armaoğlu, *Kıbrıs meselesi*, pp. 140 and 156-157.

[103] Dinamo, *6/7 Eylül kasırgası*, p. 43.

[104] Theodôropoulos, *Sêmeiôma*, p. 12.

[105] Paulos Palaiologos, *Diagramma ektheseôs*, pp. 3-4; the Palaiologos *Diagramma ektheseôs* is in the Chrêstidês archive of the Center for Asia Minor Studies in Athens. Also, National Archives, Foreign Service Dispatch No. 180, American Ambassador to Department of State, September 13, 1955.

[106] National Archives, Foreign Service Dispatch No. 116, American Consul General to Department of State, September 14, 1955.

neighborhoods of recent refugee arrivals who participated in the riots. It appears from the evidence that some of them participated in an organized manner, with their own leaders,[107] while others probably joined in randomly after most of the destruction was over. The districts beyond Şişli and Kasimpaşa, all indigent, certainly were involved.[108]

Although the numbers recruited in Istanbul were definitely large, there is evidence that the government, through local DP branches, recruited heavily as well in the European and more western parts of Anatolia, and perhaps even in Greek Thrace and Bulgaria, where large Turkish minority populations were within reach of the respective Turkish consular offices. There are references to participants[109] from parts of Anatolia such as Pendik, sent by boat; some 200-300 sent by thirty or forty boats from Asia Minor to sack the island of Büyükada (Prinkipo);[110] and people from Maltepe and Yalova. As for Anatolia more generally, Halim Said Kaylı testified that recruitment had also occurred in the *vilayets* adjacent to that of Eskişehir.[111]

The recruitment from Turkey's European provinces is equally apparent from the assembly-points in villages and towns of Thrace from which some men came.[112] These latter participated in the disturbances under their own group leaders.[113] In addition, the issue of the political complicity of some members of the Turkish communities in Greece and Bulgaria, and of the collusion of the Turkish consuls in those countries, emerges from several incidents. One is the participation of Oktay Engin, an ethnic Turk from Greek Thrace, and of the Turkish consular officials and staff of Komotênê in the Thessalonikê explosion conspiracy. Another is the case of the fifteen ethnic Turks from Bulgaria, who were arrested by the Turkish police in Edirne for looting during the pogrom as they tried to return to Bulgaria. (The fact that they were richly attired in new suits, with their pockets stuffed with jewelry, might have tipped off the police.)

The demonstrators seem to have been representative of most of Turkish and Istanbul society as far as social origins were concerned. They were Muslims, and most were Turks (although there were Kurds and Roma involved as well).[114] There were impoverished Turkish immigrants from

---

[107] Karakuş, *40 yıllık*, p. 279.

[108] Palaiologos, *Diagramma*, p. 3.

[109] Sarrês, *É allê pleura*, Volume II, Part I, p. 250, note 220.

[110] Chrêstidês, *Ekthesis*, p. 85.

[111] See note 82 above; Megas A. Reumiôtês, *É syrriknosê tou ellênismou*, Volume I, Part I, Komotênê, 1984, p. 23; Palaiologos, *Diagramma*, p. 3; Greek ministry of foreign affairs, *Report to the Vice President of the Greek Government*, Athens, September 10, 1955.

[112] Palaiologos, *Diagramma*, p. 20; Alexandris, *The Greek minority*, p. 264.

[113] Karakuş, *40 yıllık*, p. 279.

[114] Reumiôtês, *É syrriknosê*, I, p. 23, speaks of people from Anatolia; Chrêstidês, *Ekthesis*,

Greek Thrace and Bulgaria, *gecekondu* residents, and vagabonds, in short the wretched of Istanbul.[115] Involved in the disturbances were local and provincial workers,[116] *hamals* (porters),[117] dockworkers,[118] owners of small-oared ferryboats,[119] security police and *değnekçiler*,[120] noncommissioned and commissioned officers of the armed forces (in civilian clothes),[121] military and naval cadets,[122] lawyers,[123] members and leaders of the DP's local branches,[124] as well as members of other parties, union leaders, and officers and members of the *Kıbrıs Türktür Cemiyeti*,[125] students and student organizations. Women were not absent either, some applauding and urging on the rioters from the comfort of their balconies, others actually participating in the destruction and looting.[126] Muslim religious leaders were also present.[127] "Criminals," too, were noted[128]—as was one head of a bank.[129]

p. 42, mentions the participation of Kurds and Lazes; Palaiologos, *Diagramma*, p. 3, speaks of inhabitants of Şişli and *gecekondus*; Theodôropoulos, *Sêmeiôma*, p. 13, of the poor from the district of Kasımpaşa who took part; Alexandris, *The Greek minority*, pp. 257 and 264; Chrêstidês, *Ekthesis*, pp. 42-43, speaks of Kurds and villagers.

[115] Alexandris, *Ibid.*, p. 257.

[116] National Archives, Foreign Service Dispatch No. 116, American Consul General of Istanbul to Department of State, September 14, 1955.

[117] Chrêstidês, *Ekthesis*, p. 48. National Archives, Foreign Service Dispatch No. 116, American Consul General of Istanbul to the Department of State, September 14, 1955, mentions villagers, *hamals*, and vagrants.

[118] Chrêstidês, *Ibid.*, p. 48.

[119] *Ibid.*

[120] See footnotes 80 and 94 above.

[121] The prime example is that of the noncommissioned officer M. Salıh Kırmızı; see note 99 above. The dropped identity card in a destroyed Greek shop identified a Turkish army officer.

[122] Cadets from the naval and military academies on Heybeliada and at Kuleli took a leading role in destroying Greek houses, businesses, and churches at Üsküdar and Heybeliada (Chalkê); Reumiôtês, *É syrriknosê*, I, pp. 51 and 63.

[123] *Proinê*, February 1989, "Unknown Details from the pogrom in Constantinople (of 1955)," reported the murder of the lawyer Murşid Zülker, a student at the law school of Istanbul University at the time of the pogrom. The report goes on to recount his participation in the pogrom, his bloody deeds, and his service in MAH, the predecessor of today's MIT in Turkey; Theodôropoulos, *Sêmeiôma*, p. 12.

[124] See notes 76 and 77 above.

[125] Yassıada Trials, *Esas* no. 1960/3, *6/7 Eylül olayları*, from the stenciled manuscript, pp. 3 and 22-26; Theodôropoulos, *Sêmeiôma*, pp. 7-8 and 12; National Archives, Foreign Office Dispatch No. 228, American Ambassador, December 1, 1955.

[126] There are several references to the participation of women, who were shown in newspaper photographs actively swinging timbers to break open the doors and gates of Greek stores. Nesin, *Asılacak adamlar*, pp. 22-23; Theodôropoulos, *Sêmeiôma*, p. 12.

[127] Palaiologos, *Diagramma*, pp. 4 and 15.

[128] *Ibid.*, p. 4.

[129] Chrêstidês, *Ekthesis*, p. 87, footnote 1, the director of the local branch of the İş Bankaşı

Further analysis and investigation would undoubtedly reveal much more detailed social stratification in this massive outbreak of violence. The current evidence, however, is sufficient to confirm two points: that the state, and the *Demokrat Parti* that controlled it, planned and executed the pogrom; and that segments of all the social groups mentioned above participated willingly in it and, according to the subsequent statements of their representatives, approved of its effects, with some even expressing the desire to bring these effects to a "logical" conclusion with more lethal demonstrations.[130]

THE PSYCHOLOGICAL BACKGROUND TO THE POGROM, AND ITS INTENSIFICATION

After his decision to initiate a new policy regarding Cyprus, Adnan Menderes turned to marshaling public opinion and support. Time and money were dedicated to a critical agenda of orchestrating student organizations, groups that supported Turkish minorities abroad, and the press, as well as artificially stimulating rumors. His general tactic was to replace the respective focus of many of these organizations with one that concentrated on his new policy. With other organizations, however, such as *Kıbrıs Türktür Cemiyeti*, the focus was, *ab initio*, on a more aggressive Turkish policy in Cyprus. In all cases, Menderes wished to mask the government, at least in the beginning, by using these various organizations. Thus, though it did not formally appear at the outset of this new phase in the Cyprus issue, the government controlled the direction, politics, and movement of these organizations from behind the scenes. The objects of these organizations' violent agendas were Greece and the Greeks of Cyprus, but very soon this Hellenophobic animus rapidly pushed both Cypriot and Greek Hellenism to the background and thrust Istanbul's Greek community to the foreground of increasingly strident and aggressive attacks.[131]

The ease with which this animus was transferred from Greeks abroad to the Greeks inhabiting Turkey's largest city is sorrowful testimony to the

---

received the seaborne pogromists and took charge of the work destroying Greek houses, businesses, and churches on the island of Büyükada (Prinkipo).

[130] Zorlu expressed his satisfaction that the pogrom had greatly helped him in the London conference, whereas Bayar said that both he and all his colleagues thought that the pogrom had been a "good thing."

[131] Yassıada Trials, *Esas* no. 1960/3, *6/7 Eylül olayları*, stenciled text, p. 4, mentions the psychological manipulation of the Turkish people by Menderes, Zorlu, and Bayar; Theodôropoulos, *Sêmeiôma*, pp. 5-9; Chrêstidês, *Ekthesis*, pp. 109-112, on the psychological atmosphere, which prepared the way for the pogrom, also pp. 151-171; Palaiologos, *Diagramma*, pp. 1-3; Armaoğlu, *Kıbrıs meselesi*, pp. 127-131.

continuity of hatred, suspicion, and envy with which a significant segment of the Turkish people viewed the Greek minority among them. The actions of the Turkish government during the interwar period and especially during the Second World War, when Greece was occupied by the Nazis and could not effectively support the Greek minority in the face of legal and economic persecution, are further testimony of a sad heritage. From 1944 (and the repeal of the *varlık vergisi*) to 1954 (and the reversal of Turkish policy on Cyprus) and 1955 (the year of the pogrom), very little time had passed so as to weaken this traditional attitude to the Greek minority. Now, the government's decision to work through irredentist and nationalist organizations transformed the very powerful and continuous hatred and envy of the Greek minority into a national hysteria. On this important point, there is a consensus of opinion, with some serious exceptions, among Greek, British, and Turkish analysts. Moreover, the chief prosecutor at Yassıada was emphatic on this aspect of the psychological climate that paved the way for the pogrom.[132]

The Turkish state's need for foreign-policy support from Turkish public opinion, the continuity of a discriminatory attitude and behavior toward Istanbul's Greek minority, and the various Turkish organizations active on behalf of Turkish minorities in Greece and Cyprus, all came together and generated, during a relatively brief period (late 1954 to late spring of 1955), a nationalistic, religious, racist, and political atmosphere that achieved two goals: it created the appropriate atmosphere for the pogrom; and, given this electrified atmosphere, it allowed the increasingly open emergence of the Turkish government on the Cyprus issue. All this was to lead to the failed London conference among Greece, Turkey, and Great Britain in late August and early September of 1955.

The founding of the *Kıbrıs Türktür Cemiyeti* under prime-ministerial patronage at the end of August 1954 points to Menderes's critical decision to abandon his position of studied neutrality in the diplomatic battle raging between Greece and Great Britain over the issue of Cyprus. Regarding this new policy, Menderes originally hid behind various, and ostensibly "non-governmental," organizations. The government tried to maintain the fiction that, within the context of a democratic polity, it did not interfere in the "independent" life of such "civil" groups. This, of course, was a pretext of rather thin fabrication that deluded neither the Turkish organizations nor the external political world. British pressure on the Turkish government to take an aggressive stand on Cyprus had already begun to bear fruit, and indeed there is a suspicion that the Turkish press, especially *Vatan* and *Hürriyet* (as

---

[132] Yassıada Trials, *Esas* no. 1960/3, *passim*.

the latter's circulation had suddenly skyrocketed), enjoyed British subsidies. Bil and Yalman began to travel to London (the former to Cyprus as well), and Bil also assisted in mounting a demonstration of 5,000 Turks living in London at the time of the London conference. Both Yalman and Bil were thus on the scene in London at that critical time, as well as before.[133]

The stages in this transformation of Turkish public opinion and the groundswell of public support for Menderes's change to a more direct policy on Cyprus have been clearly analyzed in a number of studies. Nevertheless, it is necessary at this point to sketch the salient events and stages of this groundswell and general activities that not only gave Menderes his needed public support, but also succeeded in transforming the Turkish view of the Greek minority, which, increasingly, became hopelessly entrapped and without any effective support or defense from any quarter whatsoever. Through its basic representatives—Ecumenical Patriarch Athênagoras and Alexandros Chatzopoulos, the Greek member of the Turkish parliament— and through part of its local press (especially the fearless stance of the editor of Istanbul's Greek-language newspaper, *Embros*), the Greek minority tried repeatedly to assure Turks that they were not involved in the Cyprus issue and that they, in fact, sided with Turkey on this matter. They also tried to refute the charges (all of them unfounded), which were beginning to appear in a type of reckless Turkish journalism, of the supposed political treachery of the Greek minority and of its Church, but all to no avail. These charges, which issued out of a seemingly inexhaustible font of ethnic hatred, were to consume the entire Turkish press.[134]

Thus, the anti-Greek demonstrations of the student and other organizations were, in a sense, preceded by the vituperation of the Turkish press from the very beginning of 1954. During the year, rallies and demonstrations gradually increased in tempo and stridency, and finally peaked in what came to be a river of emotion that would overflow into and, ultimately, flood and destroy the Greek community of Istanbul and, with

---

[133] Bil, *Kıbrıs olayı*, pp. 98-99. National Archives, Foreign Service Dispatch No. 334, American Consul General Istanbul to Department of State, February 28, 1956, for the courts-martial instituted in Istanbul and a detailed account of the *Kıbrıs Türktür Cemiyeti*. On the suspicions that the British subsidized the two newspapers, see Ypourgeion Proedrias Kyvernêseôs, No. 1670/A 10459, and the Greek ministry of foreign affairs, October 26, 1955, which includes the report of the Greek *chargé d'affaires*, Ankara, No. 1213, October 17, 1955.

[134] Although much of this has been sketched out, there is still need for a detailed analysis of the role of the Turkish press from 1954 to 1955, and of the various organizations that began to attack the Greek minority, and so influenced Turkish opinion at that critical political juncture of the Cyprus issue. Alexandris, *The Greek minority*, pp. 252-254; Armaoğlu, *Kıbrıs meselesi*, *passim*; Chrêstidês, *Ekthesis*, *passim*.

it, a major share of the city's economic life and institutions. On April 21, 1954, the National Federation of Turkish Students carried out an officially sanctioned "Day of Cyprus" celebration in Istanbul.[135] In late summer, the Committee for the Defense of Turkish Rights in Cyprus demanded that the "Greek" (although he was, and remains, the ecumenical) patriarch discipline all Greek Orthodox hierarchs who had involved themselves in the Cyprus issue. This was picked up by the Turkish press, which, among other things, demanded that the patriarch restrict the political activities of Makarios, the archbishop of Cyprus (who, however, was in fact independent of patriarchal authority as he was the head of an autonomous, and therefore independent, Church). This led eventually to articles in the Turkish press that demanded the removal of the "Greek" patriarch from Istanbul and Turkey. This led to a further, and false, embellishment of the supposedly treacherous conduct of patriarch, holy synod, and the entire Greek community over the Cyprus affair. This was, finally, tied in with the charge (again false) that all of the above entities were participating in a secret fundraising drive to send money to EOKA, the organization fighting for Greek Cypriot self-determination.[136]

Before continuing any further, however, some clarification is needed here about EOKA itself. The organization was, of course, a liberation group; as such, it used armed violence to achieve its goals. Nonetheless, the historical record makes it very clear that EOKA's first acts of violence were aimed at the British and local colonial constabulary in Cyprus, which included *Greek* Cypriots. According to Robert Holland, whose scholarship on this issue is both recent and very careful, EOKA's first attacks were directed against British troops and, above all, local police stations, which had *not* yet openly recruited Turkish Cypriots. Furthermore, these attacks entailed a series of explosions intended to secure the weapons stored at these stations. It is evident from Holland's book that the turning-point in EOKA's armed campaign against Turkish Cypriots came *after* the pogrom of September 6-7, 1955. Indeed, it needs to be said again that the Greek minority of Istanbul feared the consequences for it of the Cypriot imbroglio. The manufactured "reports" that were to be spread throughout Turkey alleging attacks against Turks in Cyprus and Thessalonikê were all part of a purposely created rumor mill in which Hikmet Bil, among others, played his role. This is not to deny or mitigate EOKA's violence. It is simply to attempt to reestablish the historical chronology, which makes it clear that EOKA's turn against Turkish Cypriot constabularies and villagers was

---

[135] Theodôropoulos, *Sêmeiôma*, p. 3.
[136] Alexandris, *The Greek minority*, pp. 253-254; Chrêstidês, *Ekthesis*, pp. 116 ff; Armaoğlu, *Kıbrıs meselesi*, p. 124.

largely a post-pogrom phenomenon.

The organization, legal incorporation, and *sub rosa* encouragement by Menderes and his colleagues of the *Kıbrıs Türktür Cemiyeti* in late August to early September of 1954 is rightly considered by many to mark a significant institutionalization of anti-Greek activities by the Turkish government and the second phase of the formation and mobilization of public opinion on Cyprus. It is at this point that the KTC becomes a new factor in Turkish politics. At the concluding session of the organization's first general meeting, the governing board proceeded to an open and systematic confrontation with Istanbul's Greek minority. The members of the new society invited Alexandros Chatzopoulos to join its governing council. It demanded that the patriarch admonish all Orthodox hierarchs to refrain from involvement in the politics of Cyprus. It further demanded that all the organizations of the Greek community in Istanbul issue printed statements that they took the side of Turkey in the Cyprus issue.[137] With these demands, the government, through the KTC, began to tighten the two separate jaws of a political and ethnic vise that now increasingly threatened to crush the Greek minority. On the one hand was the political friction between Greece and Turkey over Cyprus, while, on the other, was the tradition of hatred, suspicion, and jealousy that many Turks—and many members of the Turkish government—inherited and harbored in their respective political outlooks.

Many of these attitudes were in evidence in the formal manifesto issued on October 17, 1954, at the annual meeting of the Organization for the Welfare of the Refugees from Western Thrace: "Since the Turks of Western [i.e., Greek] Thrace have remained as non-exchangeables [in Western Thrace] by virtue of the Treaty of Lausanne, as counterparts of the Greeks of Istanbul, they must be found to be in the same situation *from every point of view* [stress added] as the Greeks of Istanbul. This being the case, it is obligatory that equality shall be secured, and that the Turks of Western Thrace be raised to the level of the Greeks of Istanbul, or that the Greeks of Istanbul come down to the level of the Turks of Western Thrace."[138] The organization's statement, including the explicit threat to bring "the Greeks of Istanbul...down to the level of the Turks of Western Thrace," was repeated and expanded by the Turkish press. The latter insisted that though the Greeks of Istanbul had been allowed to prosper so that they remained in the city, the Turks of Western

---

[137] Theodôropoulos, *Sêmeiôma*, p. 3; Armaoğlu, *Kıbrıs meselesi*, p. 124; Robert Holland, *Britain and the revolt of Cyprus, 1954-1959*, Oxford, 1998, *passim*, especially Chapter 3, pp. 55-82; and François Crouzer, *Le conflit de Chypre, 1946-1959*, Brussels, 1973, Volume II, pp. 688-690.

[138] Chrêstidês, *Ekthesis*, pp. 120-121.

Thrace had become so poor that they had to abandon the region and come to Turkey. Thus, the Turkish press was led to a different conclusion from that in the statement above, namely, that the Greeks *should* be removed from Istanbul. Unfortunately, both the Organization for the Welfare of the Refugees from Western Thrace and the Turkish press had very selective memories. They chose to ignore the three decades of incessant and growing discrimination against Istanbul's Greek community, which had been restricted in the trades and professions it could exercise—indeed, had been financially destroyed through the wartime measures that had plundered Greek businesses, estates, and wealth—and had its men conscripted into the harsh labor battalions of Asia Minor, in which many perished.

On August 30, 1954, the day of national celebration of the decisive victory of the Turkish over the Greek forces in Asia Minor in 1922, the National Federation of Turkish Students attacked the Greek stores of Istanbul that had failed to place Turkish flags outside their shops. After an oral admonition of displeasure with these actions, the *vali* of Istanbul let the matter pass, however.[139] In the event, despite the ups and downs in the continuing struggle between Britain and Greece in the United Nations over Cypriot self-determination, the intensity of demonstrations by students and regional organizations, and the stridency of the Turkish press, continued to increase. Throughout the winter of 1954-1955, this unrelenting pressure raised the temperature of Turkish internal political life and, in so doing, reduced the Greek minority of Istanbul to frightful despair.[140] From June 30, 1955, when Great Britain invited Greece and Turkey to a conference in London to propose its own settlement of the Cyprus issue, to the time that Turkey and Greece accepted the invitation (July 2 and 8, respectively), the Turkish press and various Turkish organizations pulled out all the stops in a frenetic effort to rouse Turkish popular feelings and therefore complete the general task that they had set for themselves since the latter half of 1954. The appointment of a new foreign minister, Zorlu, who had very different views from his predecessor regarding Cyprus, fit in with the general turn of events.

Indeed, Zorlu was crucial in the further evolution of the events that led to the London conference, to its failure, and to the pogrom's timing. After his appointment, on July 27, 1955, as acting foreign minister and Turkey's representative to the London conference, he established a small committee of experts to study the Cyprus problem. The committee included Nuri Birgi (general secretary of the ministry of foreign affairs), who composed Turkey's

---

[139] Theodôropoulos, *Sêmeiôma*, p. 3.
[140] See note 131 above.

White Book on Cyprus; Rüştü Erdelhun (second-in-command of the Turkish general staff); Settar İksel (Turkish ambassador to Athens); Orhan Eralp (general director of the ministry of foreign affairs); and Mahmut Dikerdem.[141]

Meanwhile, the press stepped up the frequency and intensity of its attacks on the Greek community, and the various organizations intensified their political activity in the same general direction.[142] In June, *Türk Sesi*, a newspaper in which the government often aired its views, proposed amending the treaty of Lausanne (1923) so that the Greek *établis* in Istanbul, whose status was regulated by the treaty, could be expelled from Turkey.[143] In general, the subject of removing the patriarchate from Turkey, and a broad attack on the institution, had already become a set piece for the better part of a year and now began to appear in profusion.

This was to continue into August 1955, as the tripartite conference loomed on the horizon. With Zorlu's appointment, a new and more aggressive leadership infused Turkish policies toward Cyprus, Greece, and Great Britain with a vigorous and efficacious spirit.[144] In this penultimate and intense stage of "manufacturing consent," the government, acting discreetly through the student and regional organizations, fully applied the tactics of disseminating false news and manufacturing rumors so as to raise to the level of hysteria the pitch of public fervor and anger against Istanbul's Greek minority.[145]

A critical factor in this campaign of disinformation was the generation and diffusion of the false rumor, essentially manufactured by Fazıl Küçük, that the Greek Cypriots planned to massacre the Turkish Cypriots on August 28, 1955. Given the transformation of the Greeks of Istanbul into a helpless and hostage community, the rumor of a purported Greek plan (in fact, false)

---

[141] For a detailed account, see Sarrês, *Ê allê pleura*, Volume II, Part I, pp. 51-71; Dikerdem, *Ortadoğuda devrim*, pp. 121-159, especially p. 125. Sarrês, pp. 81-83, gives a detailed exposition of the new Turkish position on Cyprus as presented in London and in the Turkish *White Book*. Also, Armaoğlu, *Kıbrıs meselesi*, pp. 27-28; Burçak, *Yassıada ve öncesi*, pp. 124-125, like many other observers who wanted a more aggressive Turkish policy on Cyprus, warmly welcomed the replacement of Köprülü with Zorlu as foreign minister, and his evaluation of the two men represents the thought of all those who wanted Cyprus for Turkey. Whether Zorlu's "abilities" served his country well in the end or not remains in question.

[142] Palaiologos, *Diagramma*, pp. 20-22, gives a representative sampling of the specific issues and tone of the Turkish press; for other references, see footnote 137 above.

[143] Theodôropoulos, *Sêmeiôma*, pp. 4-5.

[144] Such was the opinion also of Nüsret Kirişçioğlu, *Yassıada Kumandanına cevap*, p. 149: "Köprülü, a man with no clear idea, was an incompetent minister....We almost lost Cyprus because of him. Finally, the late Fatin Rüştü Zorlu was elected to the Assembly and we were saved....We were saved but the blessed Fatin Rüştü Zorlu was not able to save his neck from the hands of the clever Fuat Köprülü...."

[145] Sarrês, *Ê alle pleura*, Volume II, Part I, *passim*.

to massacre the Turkish minority of Cyprus required no daring conceptual leap on the part of belligerent Turks to consider the Greeks of their (mutual) city as future targets to be destroyed. Early on in its genesis, this rumor was exploited by Hikmet Bil, who issued a secret circular to the KTC's branch offices on August 16. Here, one can do no better than to quote from the transcript of the court-martial proceedings in February 1956 against him and other members of the society:

> While Kamil Önal was making these trips and confusing opinion by boastings ignominious to his own country, Hikmet Bil took upon himself to send an urgent and secret circular directive to the organizations. In this circular, dated August 16, 1955, Hikmet Bil refers to a letter dated August 13, 1955, sent by the Cyprus is Turkish Party President General [*sic*] Dr. Fazıl Küçük to the central headquarters [of the society] in which the latter said that particularly recently the Island [i.e., Cypriot] Greeks had become intolerable and unfortunately the situation is becoming worse. If one can believe the news being spread around Nicosia, they [the Greek Cypriots] are getting ready for a general massacre [of the Turkish Cypriots] in the near future.

Dr. Fazıl Küçük added the following sentence in this letter:

> My request of you is that as soon as possible you inform all branches of this situation and that we get them to take action. It seems to me that meetings in the mother country would be very useful. Because these [Cypriot Greeks] will hold a general meeting August 28. Either on that day or after conclusion of the Tripartite Conference they will want to attack us. As is known, they are armed and we have nothing.

Bil added his own order to the society's many branches, attaching it to the end of Küçük's message: "As might be suitable, with whatever additional observations that the headquarters wishes to make, please notify all organizations that our branches should choose whatever action they see fit, particularly with the view that London and Athens should be intimidated by the manly voices arising in the mother country."[146] It is of no little interest to observe at this point the enormity of the transmogrification of Küçük's letter

---

[146] National Archives, Dispatch No. 306, American Consul General of Istanbul to the Department of State, February 20, 1956. The memorandum is discussed in Armaoğlu, *Kıbrıs meselesi*, pp. 127-130. Dosdoğru, *6/7 Eylül olayları*, p. 220, quotes the text from the third trial at Yassıada. It is interesting that Chrêstidês, *Ekthesis*, pp. 152-153, translates from the Turkish newspaper *Tercüman*, August 19, 1955, a message by Faiz Kaymak in Ankara stating that the Turks of Cyprus are being threatened with destruction and asking for assistance from Turkey.

at Bil's hands, his transformation of a general fear of an "attack" on Turkish Cypriots into a specific plan, and finally the *carte blanche* to respond given to the KTC's branches, without prior approval of the society's governing board but undoubtedly with covert approval from on high (as we shall see later). One of the military tribunals set up by General Aknoz that later charged Bil accused him of incitement to violence, as argued below by Major General Namık Arguç:

> This circular that gives the branches a complete freedom in the matter of actions to be taken in the mother country as a counter to the activity of the Greeks who had announced they were preparing for a massacre will go down in our political history as a masterpiece of presumption on the part of the Cyprus Is Turkish Society President General who took upon himself the defense of the Cyprus problem. Whereas in a matter this important it would not be a question for the central executive committee or even a congress, nor a general assembly. First the line the government would follow in such a case should be established to the last detail and then a circular might be sent to branches. Noting good intentions and common sense of the executive committee of the branches, it was necessary that the President take into consideration that they could fall into error or that each branch would consider the question from a different angle and that therefore a complication would arise. Later, during the explanation of the roles played by the Kadıköy and Sarıyer branch presidents Serafim Sağlamel and Osman Tan, it will become clear how this very urgent and secret circular was understood and particularly how the directive regarding the "intimidation from the manly voice" was applied.

Bil was charged—along with other members of the KTC, and with officials and members of DP branch offices—with a variety of offenses, including the KTC circular, burning Greek newspapers, and drafting a KTC statement on the day of the pogrom. His colleague, Kamil Önal, was accused of making various statements to the press, burning Greek newspapers, a demonstration in Taksim, and destroying evidence.[147] (It should be added, in regard to these military tribunals functioning under the martial-law regime legislated on September 12, 1955, that they were clearly kangaroo courts. Hikmet Bil and his co-defendants were used as scapegoats by Menderes to deflect guilt from himself and his government. Still, the KTC did commit the acts of violence during the

---

[147] National Archives, Dispatch No. 306, American Consul General of Istanbul to the Department of State, February 20, 1956.

pogrom of which its leaders were accused. While Menderes bore the moral responsibility for the crime, his confederates were the actual perpetrators.)

Bil's secret circular to the KTC's branches helped considerably to inflame Turkish public opinion, but also to provoke acts of violence against the Greek minority, not only during the riots but, as we shall see, in the sporadic violence against Greeks that broke out even before the pogrom. Furthermore, his circular and its effects were tied to the violence of the local DP branch officers who were also officers of the KTC's local branches. Finally, Bil transformed the general anxiety of a segment of Turkish Cypriots—and the general, non-specific information passed on to him by Fazıl Küçük and Faiz Kaymak—into a definitive, planned, general massacre of Turkish Cypriots by their Greek neighbors on August 28. There is no evidence whatsoever that such a massacre was ever planned, and it was certainly never attempted either by EOKA or the Greek Cypriot leaders at the time. Nevertheless, through the circular and in an article that was published in *Hürriyet* on August 18, Bil gave the rumor of the massacre its final form, which, as such, was passed off to the Turkish people as a whole. Only two days after receiving the copy of Küçük's letter, he wrote in his newspaper that: "One can say today that the Greeks of Cyprus are fully armed. As for the Turks, they do not have weapons even for display....In this manner there has arisen today a paradoxical situation in Cyprus. According to special information that has been transmitted to us from Cyprus, the Greeks of the island will organize a major demonstration on the twenty-eighth of the present month, and they will attack the Turks. From all this, the Greeks have also given a name to this day: They have named it 'The day of the general massacre'...."[148] Accordingly, from August 18, by virtue of both the circular and the article in *Hürriyet*, the rumor of the massacre became an established "fact," and was now adopted by individuals and groups devoted to creating an atmosphere of hysterical chauvinism and passionate hatred of the Greek minority.

On the day Bil's article appeared, the KTC's Bandırma branch telephoned the offices of the newspaper *Tercüman*, which published the branch's decision to send 1,000 KTC members to defend Turkish Cypriots, all to go before August 28. One day later, on August 19, *Hürriyet* published the declaration of Hüsamettin Canöztürk (general director of the National Federation of Turkish Students) and of the president of the Union of Turkish Students, according to which, "The Greeks cannot proceed to general massacre in Cyprus because they would reflect carefully on the consequences of such an act."[149] On the

---

[148] Chrêstidês, *Ekthesis*, p. 153
[149] *Ibid.*, p. 154.

twentieth of the same month, the journalist Doğan Can published an interview with Bil in *Yeni Sabah* in which the Greek minority of Istanbul was depicted as hostages who would have to pay for the purported massacre of Turkish Cypriots, specifically on August 28 or 30: "I asked the General President of the organization KTC to inform me as to what his own opinion is in regard to the decision which the Greeks of Cyprus have taken in connection with the twenty-eighth of August, in which they have announced that that day will be the day of the general massacre of the Turks. To this question, Hikmet Bil gave me the following answer: 'The answer to such a question is the following: In Istanbul, there are many Greeks.'"[150] On August 20, *Tercüman* published a second news item from Bandırma, according to which Menderes himself had replied to the local KTC office's offer to send 1,000 volunteers to defend Turkish Cypriots: "I esteem your patriotic sentiments. At the same time that I express to you my respect, please remain certain that the Government is ever alert and that it shall not hesitate to take the required measures."[151] The following day, *Yeni Sabah* published a second statement by Faiz Kaymak: "The innocent and unarmed Turks fear that at any moment they will be massacred by the terrorists. We desire that Turkey provide every aid and that it ensure the lives and the property of the Turks of Cyprus."[152]

The Turkish government, aware of the sources of this rumor-become-"fact," did nothing to squelch it. On the contrary, the government validated it by giving it credence and, ultimately, used it to justify its new Cyprus policy. Given the fact that Menderes's liaison with the KTC was his close confidant, Ahmet Emin Yalman (who was on the KTC's governing board); that Bil and his organization had been handpicked by Menderes himself as the man and group to arouse Turkish national passions; and that, finally, the organization itself was financed by the government, it is clear that Menderes knew well what the organization was about in spreading such rumors, first covertly, and then openly through the Turkish press. Finally, such a rumor-become-fact would please both Eden and Macmillan at the London conference, during which time the pogrom had been calculated to erupt.[153]

On August 24, Prime Minister Menderes held a banquet at the *Liman Lokantası* (Harbor Restaurant) in honor of Foreign Minister Zorlu and of the members of his mission who were to depart for London to represent Turkey at the tripartite conference. Among the guests were various other ministers,

---

[150] *Ibid.*, p. 155.
[151] *Ibid.*, p. 155.
[152] *Ibid.*, p. 156.
[153] Sarrês, *Ê allê pleura*, Volume II, Part I, pp. 74-77, gives a brief survey of the virulence of the Turkish press.

members of parliament, businessmen, and newspaper editors.[154] Menderes would seize the occasion to make a strong public statement on Turkey's new policy on Cyprus. The process of transforming his previous, more circumspect policy *vis-à-vis* Greek claims in Cyprus and the issue of self-determination had ended as a result of the Turkish response to the British prodding of the preceding year. The intensified encouragement and support, often covert, of student and political organizations now gave way to a trumpeting of Turkey's overriding interest in Cyprus because of the former's "historical rights" in the matter and because the Turkish minority was supposedly threatened by massacre. The timing was excellent, as the new Turkish team of foreign-ministry specialists and officials were preparing for the trip to the London conference after having prepared and published the *White Book* that set forth Turkey's claims, indeed demands, which not only startled the Greek side, but made the British apprehensive at the Pandora's Box-like results that they had provoked, with a number of Foreign Office staff unsure as to what they had unleashed exactly. The Greek scholar, Neoklês Sarrês, has described the Turkish appearance at the conference as the "Turkish Premiere." The time and place were appropriate for Menderes's speech to the assembled banqueters. The speech formally announced Turkey's new policy and outlined the demands to be made in London. It also included the timeworn clichés about his opposition to Cypriot self-determination, the plight of Turks in Greek Thrace, the war between Greeks and Turks in Asia Minor, the old (and long-settled) "Cretan Question," and related subjects of random relevance. He gave his sharpest attention and force to Cyprus, however, still building on Bil's fabrications:

> I wish to observe that our recently published diplomatic note to the British Government does not constitute the full and complete content of the actual importance and significance of this diplomatic note. In this diplomatic note, we expressed the malaise which we feel over the danger to which our fellow Turks in Cyprus are exposed.
>
> The stance that the terrorists have taken on the question of Cyprus, and all that which is being said in regard to our subject, have plunged us into justified uneasiness. This malaise refers in part certainly also to the future. Among all these things, the major source of our malaise is constituted by all those things that are reported, somber events that will unfold in Cyprus from one day

---

[154] Sarrês, *Ibid.*, has an informative account of the meeting as well as of the perception of the coming London gathering from the pen of a more junior member of the diplomatic mission, Mahmut Dikerdem, as presented in the latter's memoirs, *Ortadoğuda devrim*, pp. 121-159.

to another. We do not wish to consider these things certain, nor are we able to accept that it is possible that the matter may take such a turn. Nevertheless, those men announce uninterruptedly, with a terrorist air, that August 28 shall be a day of general massacre of our fellow Turks in Cyprus. We are certain that the British Government, based upon its legal rights, shall carry out its obligations thoroughly. It is said that the excitation of the Greek population of the island...has reached a peak. Consequently, a sudden undertaking, a criminal initiative devoid of all conscience, could provoke results of which the consequences would be inescapable and incurable....The local officials, it is possible, will be unprepared for this. And our population there will probably be found to be unarmed and unable to move against a majority which is extremely excited and armed. This does not mean, however, that these people, I mean the Turks, will remain, not even for a moment, undefended.[155]

This speech combined many of the weapons of political complaint from the traditional Turkish armory of diplomatic war on Greece. Nevertheless, it was based primarily on the fabricated Greek Cypriot plan to massacre Turkish Cypriots, combined with a new diplomatic offensive to wrest the previously existing advantage from the Greek side and transfer it to the Turkish side. This offensive would ultimately lead to the split of the *Demokrat Parti*, the pogrom of September 6-7, 1955, the destruction of the Greek community of Istanbul, and the poisoning of all hopes for some kind of rational and peaceful accommodation of two neighbors fated to live side by side. For Turkey and its people, the speech was the opening salvo in the dictatorialization of Menderes's government; it also led to the decades-long presence and interference of the military caste in Turkish society, politics, culture, education, and the economy that was inaugurated by the overthrow of Menderes's government by the military coup of May 27, 1960. For Menderes was to be destroyed in the end by his very success in subverting the structure of democratic government through the party structure of the *Demokrat Parti*, which, at the same time, was increasingly subjected to his personal authority.

In his extraordinary and astute account of the pogrom, Christoforos Chrêstidês, the most perceptive Greek observer of Turkish social and political evolution, and of the relations of Greece and Turkey in particular, describes his increasing apprehension over the disintegration of these relations. An attorney by profession, Chrêstidês was in and out of Istanbul for consultation with a

---

[155] Chrêstidês, *Ekthesis*, pp. 157-158, where it is translated into Greek.

Turkish client in the city; consequently, he was present in it during part of the month of August. Chrêstidês became so alarmed at the rapid deterioration of Turkish-Greek relations that he tried to warn the concerned parties to try to head off the looming crisis before August 28, since he thought the course of events would take a dramatic turn, with irreparable harm, thereafter. By the time he composed his *Exposition* (which remained unpublished until 2000), the apprehension expressed in it had become a deadly reality. He wrote:

> From mid-August…the tone of the Turkish press was transformed and its language became shrill as the press was diverted into a language of undisguised curses and threats, with the clear purpose of laying the psychological foundation for the persecution that was to be unleashed.
>
> During this period there multiplied manifold the provocative petty manifestations of chauvinistic touchiness and religious fanaticism in the daily behavior of the Turks toward the Greeks: A kind of quarrelsome criticism was increasingly addressed to Greeks who were speaking Greek in public vehicles of transportation, petty squabbles were transformed into, and reported to the police stations, as attacks on the Turkish nation.…By the evening of the twenty-eighth of August, these episodes began to take on a frightening form and magnitude of preliminary, physically violent clashes: At 9 PM, bands of Turks having crossed the Bosphorus from Beykoz on the Asian shores to the opposite side to Yeniköy [Neochôri],[156] they attacked, under the "tolerant" eyes of the police, and destroyed the church of the Dormition of the Theotokos. At approximately the same time, other bands destroyed the narthex of the church of the Taxiarchs in İstinye [Stenê]; simultaneously, they inflicted lesser damages on the houses of the Greeks by throwing rocks. In the district of Fener, the *Megalê tou Genous Scholê* was attacked with stones…and its windows were smashed. The inside of the Patriarchal complex was also stoned.[157]

The transition from violent words to violent deeds was so striking that, on August 29, Patriarch Athênagoras and the local Greek press took note. The expression of their fears and anxieties evoked little response from the Turkish government. The *vali* of Istanbul, Kerim Gökay, conveyed to the patriarch a "confidential" message that the patriarch should not, under any circumstances, go out from the patriarchal residence "for a number of days

---

[156] Dosdoğru, *6/7 Eylül olayları*, p. 316, on Seyfi Lobut; Chrêstidês, *Ibid.*, p. 111; Yassıada Trials, *Esas* no. 1960/3, *6/7 Eylül olayları*, stenciled text, p. 36, refers to Kaptan as the *Beykoz'daki Parti Başkanı.*

[157] Chrêstidês, *Ibid.*, pp. 110-111; Reumiôtês, *Syrriknosê*, Volume I, p. 13.

because of the danger that existed."[158] During the last week of August, the KTC printed some 15,000-20,000 posters on Cyprus that were disseminated throughout the city. Their inflammatory slogans included: "Four Turks have been hanged in Crete"; "In an old mosque of Thessalonikê, 150 Turks were burned to death"; and "The Turks are going to be massacred in Cyprus."

The press was relentless after August 24, following Menderes's speech. As it became evident that the Turks of Cyprus were not going to be massacred after all, popular mania was now fully concentrated on the victims-to-be, the Greek minority. The ecumenical patriarchate in particular was increasingly the focus of the newspapers' virulence. On August 28, *Yeni Sabah* demanded that the patriarchate submit its financial records to Turkish authorities. Three days later, in an open letter to the patriarch that appeared in *Ulus*, the journalist Nurettin Artan attacked the patriarch's purported fundraising, supposedly in response to a request by Archbishop Makarios forwarded via the patriarch of Alexandria, who had stopped in Istanbul on the way to Moscow. This open letter proceeded to charge that all local (Istanbul) Greeks who had contributed funds had been promised Greek citizenship. There was, of course, no basis for any of these accusations. Artan further charged that pro-Cyprus demonstrations had taken place at the patriarchal theological academy on Chalkê.[159]

In the September 1 issue of the newspaper *Dünya*, another journalist, Muzaffer Akalın, exhorted the Turkish government to stop closing its eyes to the flagrant and illegal activities of the head of the "Greek" Church.[160] The tone of M. Nermi's article in *Yeni İstanbul* was much more militant, taking what had become the characteristic and daily Turkish diet of fanaticism and accusing the Greeks and the Church of spreading this poisonous fare. Pompously referring to the "ease" with which "we" (i.e., the Turks) could easily squelch the "second Byzantine dream" of the Greeks, he went on to excoriate Greeks for their medieval hatreds:

> From the day when the greatest enemy of Turkey, General Alexander Papagos [the aging former general who had been pushed into the Greek premiership by the State Department], in cooperation with the Orthodox Church, which is ever given to inflammatory undertakings, began utilizing as weapons the ancient hatreds and the old opposition of Islam and Infidel (long forgotten), everything has fundamentally changed. We must take the most serious of measures in order to safeguard our national

[158] Chrêstidês, *Ibid.*, p. 111.
[159] *Ibid.*, p. 161.
[160] *Ibid.*, p. 162.

lands, not with superficial friendships, but with our own power.

This in particular underlines what would appear in the course of the pogrom: the depth of the inherited, historical hatred of much of Turkish Islam for anything not Muslim, one of the strongest, though not the only, driving force in the frenzy of the pogromists, based on old, anti-Kemalist, religious passion.

On September 3, in *Hürriyet,* Bil came back to the charge that the patriarch was fundraising on behalf of Archbishop Makarios and the Greek Cypriots. He explained:

> The Patriarchate has many lands in different parts of the world. Among these are charges and monasteries called "Stavropegai" [*sic*] which are very rich in land holdings from which the Patriarchate collects income through his representatives in various lands....Thereby, the Patriarch Athênagoras, instead of sending money to Cyprus from Istanbul, has ceded to Makarios his incomes in Cyprus. It is in this manner that the Phanar gives assistance to Cyprus. We call upon Mr. Athênagoras, not only to prove false this charge, but to prove the opposite. Is he able to give an accounting of the Patriarchal properties in Cyprus? Did he collect even a dime from his properties in Cyprus?...[161]

Much has been said about whether or not the pogrom was carried out in accordance with a carefully worked-out plan, or whether it was a simultaneous and spontaneous eruption of an agitated and economically impoverished mob. The accumulation and weight of evidence by many contemporary eyewitnesses, some government officials, most diplomatic observers, and much of the press led to the conclusion that in fact the pogrom had been planned beforehand. In his five years in office, Menderes had fashioned a party structure that embraced the far reaches of the Turkish state, geographically and administratively, and which, at the same time, thoroughly penetrated the society and its institutions. It was basically through this elaborate and supple party structure and its tough, often "physical," ward bosses, or local presidents, that the head of the government, who was also head of the *Demokrat Parti,* secured power from the top down and the bottom up. Menderes relied heavily on the local DP leaders to marshal the population and control situations of every kind. He found it increasingly convenient to function in crises through the paralegal activities of the local DP branches and their well-organized gangs of toughs and experienced thugs.[162]

---

[161] *Ibid.,* pp. 162-163.
[162] Dosdoğru, *6/7 Eylül olayları,* p. 342: "Bu süretle hareketin bir merkezden evvelçe verilen talimata uygun olarak idare edildiği müsahede olunmuş ve D.P. iktidarının bu kabil işlerde

In many ways, Menderes's speech at the *Liman Lokantası* is a key event. Previously, he and Zorlu had planned the Turkish counterattack at the London conference in an effort to affirm Turkish interests in Cyprus. Zorlu needed a strong demonstration to convince the British and others (mostly Greece) that Turkey was committed to a long-term and dominant position in Cyprus. Both men were, it seems, strongly committed to a vigorous public demonstration to convince all of the concerned parties of this proposition. Zorlu would thus win points with the British in the negotiations ahead, while Menderes no doubt felt that the faltering economic policies of his government, and the rising discontent and strength of the opposition, would be lessened, and to some degree forgotten or deferred, by a successful Cyprus policy that would include a demonstration against the Greek minority.

The initial violence and destruction of Greek churches and property by the hoodlums of Mehmet Kaptan, president of the DP's Beykoz chapter, and other local DP chieftains in Yeniköy, Tarabya, and Fener on the night of August 28 were not chance occurrences. They were planned, synchronized, and took place under the permissive eye of the police. On the same day, Menderes had received a telegram from Zorlu in London informing him that the British were "ambivalent as to the degree to which we shall persevere in the matter of our rights over Cyprus."[163] The second phrase worthy of note in this message read: "We respectfully request that you give the order that would be most useful for those of the countries that are interested in this matter."[164]

Zorlu himself, along with his later defenders, chose to explain this vague telegram as a putative instruction for Menderes to give to foreign ambassadors in support of Turkey's position in Cyprus. The Yassıada prosecution, however, gave this ciphered telegram quite a different meaning, choosing to interpret it as asking Menderes to enact a much more "persuasive" policy—that is, to give the signal for the pogrom, which had already been planned. Soon after the pogrom, when the DP became seriously divided over responsibility for it, Zorlu asserted that "this affair" had helped him to push Turkish claims on Cyprus in London.[165] Perhaps the most telling testimony at Yassıada on

---

parti teşkilatına müracaat eylediğini....İzmir, Topkapı, Geyikli, Kayseri, *Demokrat İzmir* [newspaper] gibi olaylar açıkça göstermiştir. Topkapı olayı bir günde tertip ve ihzar edilmiş, beş altı bin partili kısa bir müddet içinde bir noktaya (Topkapı, Kayseri, *Demokrat İzmir* dosyaları) yığılmıştır."

[163] *Ibid.*, p. 324, "...ancak bizim, haklarımızda ne dereceye kadar ısrar edeceğimiz tereddüt sahibi oldukları anlaşılmaktadır...."

[164] *Ibid.*, p. 324, "...tarafı devletlerinden bu hususta ilgililere verilecek emrin pek faydalı olacağını saygılarımızla arz ederiz...."

[165] Fersoy, *Menderes*, p. 343: "Recently, a week or ten days ago, according to what we learned from Turan Güneş: During a recent break in the [parliament] this subject [the pogrom]

this matter was that of Hikmet Bil, who, along with many others, stated that Zorlu had communicated to Menderes that he wanted a much more aggressive policy in Turkey itself, and that the prime minister in turn informed Bil that Zorlu "wanted us to be active."[166] It was the opinion of the prosecution at Yassıada that the telegram of August 28 referred specifically to the planning of the pogrom some nine days before the event. But it must have been planned even before then, as the primary disturbances already began to break out on the night of August 28, and they were led by local DP bosses and approved by the police—which means that Zorlu's telegram to Menderes was a further refinement in the scheduling of the pogrom.

THE INCIDENT AT THE TURKISH CONSULATE

It is particularly important to set the two chronological points in the transition from agitation, and fanning the flames of hatred, to the final stages leading to the pogrom. At what point did Menderes and his colleagues make the decision to launch the attack on the Greek minority of Istanbul, and thus to begin mobilizing the government's and the DP's forces? And at what time on the very early evening of September 6 did the first acts of destruction begin? The answer to the first question is especially important in regard to the testimony of Hikmet Bil, who asserted that the plan for the pogrom was born the night before, September 5, at a meeting in Florya that included Menderes, President Mahmud Celal Bayar, and Interior Minister Gedik, while Zorlu was deeply engaged in the negotiations in London.[167] Accepting Bil's account, however, raises insurmountable difficulties of interpretation.

The second chronological issue, the actual hour of the pogrom's outbreak, has an important relationship to the responsibility of Menderes, Bayar, Köprülü, and Gedik, all of whom were gathered at the train station of Haydarpaşa and the first three of whom were en route to Ankara. They were to abandon the train only later, at Sapanca, to return to an Istanbul well on the way to vast destruction. The basic question, therefore, is why Turkey's leaders abandoned its greatest and most beautiful city to a destruction they knew was pending. Those who defended them would assert that they had

became a subject of discussion of the [DP] Parliamentary Group and during this discussion Fatin Rüştü Zorlu said to those about him: 'Let us not exaggerate this affair. This affair greatly strengthened our position in the London Conference.'" He was defending the pogrom.
[166] Dosdoğru, *6/7 Eylül olayları*, p. 324. Köprülü had already admitted during the extraordinary session of parliament on September 12, 1955, that the government knew about the pogrom before its outbreak.
[167] Bil, *Kıbrıs olayı*, p. 111; Yassıada Trials, *Esas* no. 1960/3, *6/7 Eylül olayları*, stenciled text, p. 5: "Bu hususta sanık Menderes ile Fetin Rüştü Zorlu arasında mutabakata varılmıştır."

left the city before the violence began. Thus, the hour the violence actually began is important. If the government's leaders were still in Istanbul when the destruction commenced, then their defense, for example, that they were unaware of the planned events or did not think that they would "get out of hand" would make even less sense.[168]

Most observers testify, as we have already seen, to the pogrom's size and efficiency, and so have presumed the need for a longer period (certainly much longer than that which Bil claimed) in order to gather and coordinate the human and other resources necessary for the attack.[169] Bil's statement that the pogrom was planned on the evening of September 5 would have meant an unprecedented logistical feat in organizing such a massive movement of pogromists within twenty-four hours; it would not only have required mobilizing thousands of demonstrators but forewarning the security police and military authorities not to intervene.[170] Further, if the attack was coordinated with the London conference of August 29 to September 7, and if indeed, as seems clear, Zorlu was one of its main planners (some attribute the very conception of the pogrom to him), then the plot most certainly could not have been hatched as late as September 5.[171]

As one moves backward in time from the date of the attack itself, telltale details "stretch" the preparation back in time to such an extent that long-term planning is even more evident. The fuses for the explosion to be detonated in the consular complex of Thessaloníkê were sent from Turkey very probably via Oktay Engin on September 3.[172] Thus, the plans for the incident that was meant to signal the pogrom's eruption were already in place when the authorities in Ankara secretly sent the fuses to Greece. Following the string of events connected with the bomb plot, the evidence shows clearly that the wife of the Turkish consul-general in Thessaloníkê had stayed behind to "tidy things up" before departing for Turkey to join her husband, who had already departed. In so doing, she telephoned a local Greek photographer, a certain Kyriakidês, to come and photograph the interior of the consular complex—and in particular the house that is supposed to be Atatürk's birthplace, which is within the

---

[168] This is especially the case with a number of the American diplomatic reports to the State Department immediately after the pogrom that have been cited above in the previous discussion.

[169] See the Greek, British, and American diplomatic reports, all of which are in agreement on this, as are those of other foreign observers and of most Turkish commentators.

[170] Bil, *Kıbrıs olayı*, p. 103.

[171] Yassıada Trials, *Esas* no. 1960/3, 6/7 *Eylül olayları*, stenciled text, pp. 4-6; Sarrês, *Ê allê pleura*, Volume II, Part I, pp. 210-211.

[172] Yassıada Trials, *Ibid.*, pp. 48-52.

complex. The photographer came, photographed, and, on September 4, the consul's wife returned to Turkey with the photographs as "souvenirs" of her stay in Thessalonikê. The photograph of Atatürk's house that Kyriakidês had taken, however, was to appear in the sensational second edition of the Istanbul *Ekspres* published in the afternoon (4:00 PM) of September 6, as the signal for the attack on the Greek community. The photograph was identical to the one that Kyriakidês had given the consul's wife, but it had been crudely falsified to imply a huge explosion at the house. It was, of course, a forgery: its intention was to show major structural damage to a building that had only suffered the breaking of a very small number of windowpanes.[173] Clearly, we are dealing with an elaborate, albeit foolishly executed, conspiracy to blame the explosion on the Greeks, and so to electrify further the anti-Greek atmosphere in Istanbul. All this came out not only in the efficient investigation of the Greek police, but also in the proceedings at Yassıada.

As the plot was of a complex nature, it required time to prepare and send the explosives. The first device did not go off and was almost immediately recovered by the Greek police. So the date of September 5 did not really take into account this part of the planning for the pogrom. The dynamite plot had to be organized some days before September 5, the actual date of the explosion (the dynamite had been brought to Greece from Turkey by a Turkish agent, and it was subsequently ignited by the consulate's Turkish doorman). It is possibly true, as the prosecution at Yassıada asserted, that the decision for the pogrom might have been passed on to the DP branch heads on the morning of September 6,[174] but this might also have been a matter of a final detail regarding the exact hour. The grand plan already existed, however, since only in this manner can one explain the extraordinary coordination needed to bring non-Istanbulis to the scene by land and sea, and then incorporate them into the larger body of the attack. The witness Kaylı testified that Polatkan and his DP colleagues had arrived in Eskişehir on September 2. Subsequently, the local heads of the *Demokrat Parti* arranged for factory workers and local security police to be sent to Istanbul via the state railways. This larger plan to recruit pogromists was carried out in other Anatolian and European provinces of Turkey as well.[175]

---

[173] Chrêstidês, *Ekthesis*, pp. 165-171; Dêmêtrios Kaloumenos, *To istoriko tôn gegonotôn* (manuscript), pp. 14-17, gives a very precise and logical account, and is based on the typed memorandum of the secretary-general of the ministry of Northern Greece issued to the press in Thessalonikê on September 16, 1955.

[174] Yassıada Trials, *Esas* no. 1960/3, 6/7 *Eylül olayları*, stenciled text, p. 9, assumes this close coordination for, among other things, "üç şehirde de hazırlanmış olan parti teşkilatına gereken emir ve talimat verilmiştir."

[175] This episode is discussed above.

When the KTC petitioned Ankara's *vali*, Kemal Aygun, to grant its request for the establishment of a local office, he urged it "to wait a few days" upon signing the permit.[176] A "few days" later, the attacks took place in the three cities, and the petitioners remarked that they subsequently understood that the *vali* himself had been involved in the plans for the pogrom, since he had known when they would occur. Indeed the *valis* of the other two cities, Gökay in Istanbul and Hadımlı in Izmir, also knew about the plans, and Hadımlı was in fact found guilty of participating in the violence.

The conspiracy extended to a wider circle of higher officials beyond and parallel to the *vali* of Istanbul. Patriarch Athênagoras's testimony is revealing in this and other respects. He attempted to resist the summons to testify at Yassıada, for experience had taught him to be suspicious of any Turkish authority, but to no avail. He was, in the end, forced to testify (and did so in Greek through two interpreters). Upon examination, he declared that he did not know if the pogrom had been planned or not, and, if the former, he did not know who the organizers might have been. However, he did indicate that Gökay had called less than two hours before the outbreak of violence—that is, at 5:00 PM, according to him—and told him that the patriarchate had been secured days before. When asked how many days before it had been secured, the patriarch replied two weeks before the attacks, which would have placed it at some time around August 24, which further indicates that both Gökay and Athênagoras had known of the pending violence.[177]

The preliminary acts of violence organized by the DP's local branches on August 28 indicate that many groups of pogromists were already well-prepared, possibly spurred on by Hikmet Bil's secret August 16 circular (as indicated previously, the KTC and DP were largely indistinguishable in Istanbul). The telephone calls and Zorlu's telegram from London also point to an effort on Menderes's part to calibrate all these movements, as well as the exact moment of the pogrom's eruption. The patriarch's testimony indicates that the *vali* and Turkish security forces had decided to secure the patriarchate against violence by August 24. This coincides with the date that Menderes summoned the press to the official dinner at the *Liman Lokantası*. Instead of squelching the manufactured rumors of the purported massacre of Turkish Cypriots on August 28, Menderes embraced the rumor and gave it the authority and official status of the Turkish state. According to the Yassıada prosecutors, Zorlu originated the idea of an attack against the Greek minority (his subsequent behavior is consonant with such an assertion), and witnesses

---

[176] Yassıada Trials, *Esas* no. 1960/3, 6/7 *Eylül olayları*, stenciled text, p. 8.
[177] Dosdoğru, *6/7 Eylül olayları*, pp. 6-7; Sarrês, *Ê allê pleura*, Volume II, Part I, pp. 192-193.

testified that he had met with Menderes and agreed on the violence. All this would have had to transpire before the banquet of August 24, however, and Zorlu's departure for London on the following day. It is difficult to say how long before August 24 these discussions took place, but it should be remembered that the remark of the Foreign Office staffer referred to earlier—namely, "that a few riots would do us nicely"—was made in 1954.[178]

The actual looting and destruction—when extrapolated from the movements of Menderes and Bayar from Florya on the night of September 6 through the old city of Istanbul, across the bridge over the Golden Horn to Kabataş, where they took the ferryboat to Üsküdar, and from there to the station at Haydarpaşa—must have taken place between 7:00 and 8:00 PM.[179] The train that they were to board for Ankara was to be delayed by an important telephone call from London, so that it would not depart until 8:20 PM.

The September 7 issue of *Milliyet* published a timeline of the events that transpired on September 6-7; given the considerable detail of the reportage, it is of some interest to follow the rough chronology of the events as the newspaper's reporters observed them:

> 6:05 PM Destruction of Greek stores on İstiklal Caddesi begins.
> 6-7 PM All Greek stores on İstiklal Caddesi have been destroyed.
> By 7:30 PM Destruction and looting have enveloped the districts of Karaköy, Tarlabaşı, Fermeneciler, Eminönü, Sirkeci.[180]

This brief excerpt from a larger timeline enables us to review some of the testimony at Yassıada, at which secret security reports became available. The testimony of Ethem Yetkiner, the general director of security on the scene revealed that when he had left his home at about 6 PM, he saw a part of the band, on İstiklal Caddesi, which was returning from the aborted attempt to attack the Greek consulate, where the assembled police had easily dispersed the rioters.[181] He then wired *Vali* Gökay but also the interior minister (who was in overall charge of Istanbul that night), who was en route to Haydarpaşa to help send off the president and prime minister, who were setting out for

---

[178] See Theodôropoulos, *Sêmeiôma*, p. 8; National Archives, Dispatch No. 230, American Consul General of Istanbul to the Department of State, December 14, 1955. As mentioned above, Patriarch Athênagoras stated at Yassıada that the pogrom had been prepared beforehand although he refused to name the organizer(s): Dosdoğru, *6/7 Eylül olayları,* "6/7 Eylül olaylarının mürettep olduğu, tertipçilerinin kim olduğu hakkında herhangi bir bilgim yoktur," p. 191; and Holland, *Greek-Turkish relations*, p. 333.

[179] Dosdoğru, *6/7 Eylül olayları*, p. 330.

[180] *Milliyet*, September 7, 1955; Dêmêtrios Kaloumenos, *Ê staurôsis tou Christianismou*, 1963, p. 23, reproduces the calendar of events from *Milliyet*.

[181] Sarrês, *Ê allê pleura*, Volume II, Part I; Dosdoğru, *6/7 Eylül olayları*, pp. 330-331.

Ankara in the very midst of the destruction now consuming the city. It is noteworthy that, according to Yetkiner, the destruction had begun even earlier, at 5:00 PM in some districts.

Alaettin Eriş related to Hayrettin Sümer that he had kept both Gökay and Gedik (by now both back in the offices of the *vali*) informed "second by second" of these events, and further that he had also continually updated both Menderes and Bayar at the train station, until their train's departure.[182] He stated his opinion that had the prime minister and president desired to do so, they could have halted the violence and avoided the disaster that finally ensued.

Nadi Üp was to testify at Yassıada that the destruction had indeed begun as early as 5:00 PM and that the president and prime minister had been kept informed.[183] The route of Menderes and Bayar by car from Florya went through areas where, by 7:30 PM, the pogrom was well under way, and so they actually saw parts of it. The court witnesses that revealed the constant flow of information about the destruction to the *vali*, as well as to Bayar and Menderes at Haydarpaşa station, indicate that the two supreme heads of the state were in full possession of the knowledge of the destruction of major portions of the country's largest city.[184] In any case, since they had been involved in the conspiracy, they already knew what was occurring. Above and beyond these facts, however, the train's delay was occasioned by Zorlu's famous telephone call to Menderes, which the latter took in the train station itself. Zorlu called to discuss the final formal statement of the Turkish mission to the London conference. We know something of this conversation from the memoirs of Mahmut Dikerdem. After Zorlu's introductory comments, Menderes interrupted him, told him about the attack on the Greek community, now in full swing, and ordered Zorlu to return to Turkey immediately, asking him the rhetorical question, "What are you now seeking in London?" The planned pogrom now superseded the Turkish presentation of the country's claims on Cyprus.[185]

---

[182] Dosdoğru, *Ibid.*, p. 331.

[183] *Ibid.*; Sarrês, *Ê allê pleura*, Volume II, Part I, p. 222.

[184] Chrêstidês, *Kypriako kai ellênotourkika*, Volume I, p. 156; Chrêstidês, *Ekthesis*, p. 139.

[185] Dikerdem, *Ortadoğuda devrim yılları*, p. 133: "Ortak bildiri taslağını Başbakan'a okumaya hazırlanırken Menderes, Fatin Bey'in sözünü kesmiş, İstanbul'da Rum azınlığa karşı başlayan saldırı olaylarını anlatmış, kendisinin Ankara'ya hareket etmekte olduğunu bildirerek: 'Londra'da artık ne arıyorsunuz? Hemen geri gelin emrini vermişti.'"

THE POGROM

From the preceding chapter, it is clear that the pogrom was organized carefully, broadly, and surreptitiously. Accordingly, there was a centralized plan that coordinated the grand strategy and attack, and called for extensive marshaling and transport of human forces from Asia Minor and Thrace, as well as their direction and positioning so that the forty square kilometers to be attacked would be effectively penetrated. The state commanded the entire network of transportation that included railways, buses and cabs, and the vessels plying the city's European and Asian shores. Once brought to Istanbul to join those already living there, the "imported" pogromists had to be fed, perhaps bedded down for a night or two, and finally assembled at strategic points (two of which proved to be Taksim and Tophane); they then had to be provided with the crowbars, acetylene torches, clubs, spades, pickaxes, dynamite, and gasoline (for the planned arson) that would be the tools of their destruction. (In the case of police and soldiers, they also had to be outfitted in civilian clothes). Lists of churches, schools, houses, cultural and social organizations, and businesses had to be drawn up for each neighborhood and turned over to the leader of each group, and many of these buildings had to be marked to distinguish them from "non-Greek" structures (reprising, to quote Hüseyın Yalçın, the centuries-old method of the Saint Bartholomew's Day massacre). The *vali* of Istanbul, local DP heads, and the heads of the security, police, and intelligence services all had to be carefully and confidentially apprised of the coming enterprise. The Greek minority was to have no warning whatever of its impending doom. There is some indirect evidence of previous warning in a few cases, but it was so isolated and sporadic that it was ignored. Although it was observed that large numbers of poorly dressed provincials had been brought into the city during the last two or three days before the pogrom, it was not sufficiently suspicious to occasion alarm among the Greeks, despite the electric atmosphere of those days.

THE OUTSET
Although the security police's secret files, made accessible to the *Yüksek Adalet Divanı* (High Court of Justice) that tried Menderes and his government

at Yassıada in 1960-1961, were extensive, they were never made widely available. As for the minutes of the proceedings, the *tutanaklar*, they have been accessible to very few in complete form. At the same time, there is a large, and continually growing, body of sources that constitutes a sufficient basis for attempting a kind of history of the pogrom itself, namely:[1]

(1) First, the diplomatic reports of the British, American, and Greek officials from Istanbul and Ankara, which reveal much, though by no means all, of what transpired in Istanbul during September 1955 and thereafter. Many, albeit not all, of these documents have been declassified. In addition, there are the ambassadorial reports of reactions in the Turkish parliament, especially during its extraordinary session of September 12, 1955.

(2) Next, there are the reports of the Greek, Turkish, and world press.[2]

(3) Perhaps most crucial, however, are the decisions, reasoning, and sentences of the High Court of Justice. They have been used notably by Hulusi M. Dosdoğru and Neoklês Sarrês with interesting results. Indeed, Dosdoğru has published extensive parts of them in his study. Nonetheless, access to the transcripts of this body of material is still essential.[3]

(4) Increasingly, Greek and Turkish memoirs are now appearing in print, especially as the immediate political relevance of the Menderes period recedes into the background.

(5) Finally, a substantial and relevant body of photographic material appeared in the Turkish and Greek press over the years. From the Greek side, the photographic archive of Dêmêtrios Kaloumenos is of substantial archival importance.[4]

---

[1] For references to the files of the security police and detailed records of the nineteen trials, see Dosdoğru, *6/7 Eylül olayları*, pp. 6-8, 32-34, 330, 341-343, etc.

[2] For the extended international press coverage of the pogrom, see the Greek Ypourgeion Proedrias Kyvernêseôs, Genikê Dieuthynsis Typou (Exôterikon Tmêma), *Ektakton Deltion #1*, November 15, 1955. The corresponding collection on the reportage of the Turkish press has not yet been found.

[3] For the transcript of the third trial, which contains the material from the trial on the pogrom, *Yüksek Adalet Divanı Kararları*, İkinci Bölüm, *Esas* no. 1960/3, pp. 1-52. A substantial part of the transcript is to be found in Dosdoğru, *6/7 Eylül olayları*, pp. 319-367. For discussions of parts of the trial, Fersoy's books, *Zorlu* and *Menderes* (*passim*), are of interest. A special insert of the newspaper *Hayat* of September 15, 1961, published the court decisions and sentences.

[4] The Turkish press published a considerable number of photographs, both of the damage inflicted by the rioters and of the rioters "in action." From the Greek side, the pictures taken by Dêmêtrios Kaloumenos were the principal source, not only of photographic documentation but of much that was published in the Greek press. For his work, see above all his volume, *Ê staurôsis tou Christianismou. Ê istorikê alêtheia tôn gegonotôn tês 6ês-7ês Septemvriou 1955 eis tên Kônstantinoupolin*, Athens, 1966; the text is accompanied by over 400 photographs.

A good deal has already been said about the timing of the pogrom in conjunction with the role of Menderes and his immediate entourage in its planning. We now return to the question of timing in regard to this tragedy's general unfolding. From a variety of sources, one realizes that the ostensible outbreak of Istanbul's destruction on the evening of September 6, 1955, tends to vary, from 4:00 PM to 8:00 PM. This is to be explained by a variety of factors, including:

(1) the possibility that the violence began at different places at different times;

(2) the faulty memories of those reporting on the matter at later dates;

(3) an assumption by some that since Menderes had in fact organized it, the event should have begun at the same time everywhere;

(4) the fact that many who reported the beginning of the violence did so in terms that reflected the time that they first observed it, although it had begun earlier in other places, as is evident from the third trial at Yassıada.[5]

By 6:00 PM, the police had already dispersed the attack on the Greek consulate; shortly thereafter, Ethem Yetkiner, general director of security, walking from his house at 6:00 PM, saw the destroyed Greek pastry shop Haylayf as well as that of the Park Oteli, and duly informed Interior Minister Gedik, while the *vali* of Istanbul, Gökay, asked for military reinforcements (which were not forthcoming).[6]

Contrary to most reports that the pogrom broke out simultaneously in Izmir and Istanbul at 7:00 PM,[7] it seems to have broken out in both cities somewhat earlier, at 5:30 PM.[8] Certainly, the data from the secret security reports that were revealed at Yassıada are closer to the truth. Security officials monitored the evolving situation minute by minute; furthermore, such records were vital and essential, as they went to superiors and, ultimately, to Menderes, before he reached Haydarpaşa station, during his wait there, and throughout the course of his journey to Sapanca en route back to Ankara.

Many observers who witnessed the destruction reported that it had begun anywhere from 7:00 to 8:00 PM. An example is the American consular

---

[5] Yassıada Trials, *Esas* no. 1960/3, pp. 9-11. At the third trial, the witness Nadi Üp mentioned 4:00 PM as the time when the pogrom began, with the destruction following through the next hour until 5:00 PM.

[6] *Ibid.*, pp. 11-12. İnönü, leader of the opposition at the time, in his speech before the extraordinary session of the Turkish parliament on September 12, 1955, also stated that the destruction began between five and six in the afternoon, National Archives, Foreign Office Dispatch No. 100, American Embassy, Ankara, September 13, 1955.

[7] National Archives, Foreign Office Dispatch No. 116, American Consul General, Istanbul, September 14, 1955; Journalists' Union, *Anti-Greek Riots*, pp. 21 and 25.

[8] Yassıada Trials, *Esas* no. 1960/3, p. 20.

official who reported on September 8 that, "About seven or so the mob split into two sections...in an orgy of vandalism...."[9] The important report of British consular official Michael Stewart, addressed to Foreign Secretary Harold Macmillan on September 22, relates: "This Embassy's first intimation of the rioting was the sound of breaking glass and shouting at about eight o'clock at an open-air night club immediately below the Embassy garden wall which faces the Golden Horn."[10] Obviously, the embassy was distant from other centers of activities where the violence had already broken out, and so this report indicates at what time the embassy first became aware of events, not when they first occurred.

Many of these reports focused on Istanbul's most important district, Beyoğlu (or, as it was better known, Pera), from Taksim to Galatasaray, along İstiklal Caddesi. As a result, they reflected the violence that had occurred on that important commercial thoroughfare and not necessarily anywhere else or at any other time. In what is still, more generally, one of the most thoughtful and convincing accounts, the Greek consul in Istanbul (present on the scene but no longer consul) reported in January 1956 that the destruction of the Greek stores on İstiklal Caddesi began at 7:00 PM.[11] Dêmêtrios Kaloumenos, however, who is an invaluable witness because he was present at the outbreak and systematically photographed the consequences, records that the first Greek store was looted at about 6:05 PM and that the destruction spread from Taksim throughout İstiklal Caddesi from 6:00 to 7:00 PM.[12] This is confirmed by the pogrom's timeline published in the Turkish press, which indicated that the first Greek store was ransacked at about 5:30, and that the rest of the Greek stores between Taksim and Tünel were attacked mostly between six and seven o'clock in the evening.[13]

The reports of Turkish security forces, as well as those of Greece, Britain,

[9] National Archives, Foreign Office Dispatch No. 116, American Embassy, Ankara, September 14, 1955.

[10] The National Archives, Public Record Office (hereinafter cited as TNA:PRO), FO 371/117711, no. 193, Istanbul, 9/22/55; *Makedonia*, 9/9/55, set the hour at 9:30 PM.

[11] Theodôropoulos, *Sêmeiôma*, pp. 9-10. The American consular report from Istanbul seems to agree (National Archives, Foreign Office Dispatch No. 116, American Consul General, Istanbul, September 14, 1955). The report sent by Dêmêtrios Chronopoulos to the Greek deputy premier, Panagiôtês Kanellopoulos, sets the time at 8:00 PM (*Ios fakellos*, 35,000-40,000, *Tourkia*, 4, 1955, *Gamma* 4, *Epeisodia genika*, 9/10/55). But the special report of the Greek citizen, Iôannês Spetsiôtês, who was in Tarlabaşı during the events, places it at 6:50 PM in that area (Greek Foreign Ministry, A2 Dept, Political Affairs Section: *Tourkia* 4, 9/20/55). Journalists' Union, *Anti-Greek Riots*, pp. 21 and 25, also puts the simultaneous outbreaks in Izmir and Istanbul at 7:00 PM.

[12] Kaloumenos, *Ê staurôsis*, p. 23.

[13] *Milliyet*, September 7, 1955.

and the us, note the seeming simultaneity of the events in Istanbul with the destruction in Izmir and the disorders in Ankara. The same seems to hold true for the attacks on Istanbul Greeks throughout the city's greater area itself, whether in the new city, the European shores of the Bosphorus, the islands, or the old city and its neighborhoods. Indeed, the tools, methods, and organization of the violence were identical from one place to another.[14] They were in a sense uniform. It is also clear that both during and after the Greek—and many Jewish and Armenian—properties were being destroyed on İstiklal Caddesi, the same ruin, arson, and violence were being carried out elsewhere. Although Greek consular reports indicate that a raging destruction had become generalized in the greater Istanbul area by 9:00 PM, in actuality, pogromist bands had been at work in many areas simultaneously or almost simultaneously.[15]

Milliyet reported that a trail of destruction was evident by 7:30 in Karaköy, along the major thoroughfares of Fermeneciler and Perşembe Pazarı, all the way to Tünel,[16] while Kaloumenos also noted the attacks along Tarlabaşı.[17] Soon, they had spread into Sirkeci and Eminönü. *Milliyet* reporter Mücahit Beşer wrote: "From 7:00 [PM], the Rumeli side of the Bosphorus presented a view of terror."[18]

In the oral accounts recently published by Greeks who experienced different phases of the violence in various parts of the city, we can see how rapidly the pogrom manifested itself in the far-flung areas of Istanbul and its suburbs. One must, of course, be careful in using these accounts, as memory is notoriously imprecise and even inaccurate. Nevertheless, these fifty eyewitness accounts tell us much that is of interest. The destruction of Greek houses, businesses, and religious and other institutions were observed to have broken out at about the following times in the following areas:

Table 14: Time when the pogrom struck throughout Istanbul

Areas	Approximate time
Yedikule, Samatya	7:00 PM
Beyoğlu	7:00 PM
Kurtuluş	When night fell
Sıraselviler	7:00 PM

[14] One need only refer to the various sources, many of which are cited above.
[15] Theodôropoulos, *Sêmeiôma*, pp. 9-10.
[16] *Milliyet*, September 9, 1955.
[17] Kaloumenos, *Ê staurôsis*, p. 23.
[18] *Milliyet*, September 9, 1955.

Yeşilköy (Agios Stefanos)	7:00 PM
Edirnekapı	8:30 PM
Bakırköy (Makrochôri)	7:00 PM
Büyükada (Prinkipo)	7:30 PM
Center of Istanbul	7:00 PM
Kalyoncu Kulluk	9:00 PM
Aksaray	11:00 PM
Çengelköy	Midnight
Kuzguncuk	After midnight[19]

The onset of destruction in many areas of new Istanbul, the European side of the Bosphorus, the islands, and old Istanbul and its neighborhoods, indicates indeed a kind of simultaneity throughout the general area. Obviously, in some areas, such as in the Asian parts of the Bosphorus, the onset was much later. The sum total of the evidence, however, clearly points to a preplanned and carefully worked out strategy that was to work grimly and efficiently.

In addition to the large number of sources that refer, extensively, to the careful organization of transport to bring the pogromists to Istanbul through a vast network of boats, trains, municipal and military trucks, and some 4,000 taxis, there are extensive eyewitness accounts of the timely and efficient provision of crowbars, axes, pickaxes, acetylene torches, wooden timbers, dynamite, and large amounts of stones in carts. The offices of state security, the city's *vali*, the local DP chapters, and the government-controlled unions provided both rank-and-file manpower and two leaders for each small unit, and they also arranged for each unit to have detailed catalogues of anything Greek. Both the unions and the *Kıbrıs Türktür Cemiyeti* played an important role in marking the Greek establishments and dwellings, and in ensuring that Turkish property was distinguishable from that of the Greek, Jewish, and Armenian minorities. There is also a general indication in the sources that pogromists were instructed to concentrate on destroying Greek property and institutions, but not to proceed to murders and massacres. There is no mention of any firearms having been issued to them. Nevertheless, the highly intimidating slogan chanted throughout the night of violence was, *Evvela Mal, Sonra Can* ("First Your Property, Then Your Lives"). In the event, over thirty Greeks lost their lives, many were severely beaten, and a substantial

---

[19] Pênelopê Tsoukatou, *Septemvriana. Ê nychta tôn krystallôn tou Ellênismou tês Polês*, interview nos. 15, 16, 17, 18, 33, 39, 40, 41, 42, 47, 49, 50.

number of girls, women, and boys were raped.[20] By and large, the police, soldiers, and firemen did not respond to the Greek pleas for protection and intervention, although there were exceptions, which were notable precisely because of their rarity. There are many accounts, not only of official inactivity and the failure of the municipal and national institutions to protect the Greek minority, but also of the constant assistance that police and soldiers gave to the pogromists in their labor of destruction. Particularly prominent was the active involvement of the municipal night-watchmen in "directing traffic," as it were, and leading groups that did not know the various neighborhoods to the targeted dwellings, institutions, and businesses, and to entrances that could be easily breached. These "watchmen" also participated in the looting. Most contemporary observers were highly impressed by the pogrom's disciplined and organized nature. Finally, many local residents and gangs joined the groups that were brought from outside in destroying and looting their neighbors' properties.

All observers of the events have left us a broad, more or less incisive, clear, and often frightful image, or images, of their nature and progress. Initially, on September 6, us and British diplomatic reports did not fully grasp the extent and organizational nature of the occurrence, and most failed or refused to believe that it had anything to do with the highest officials of the Turkish government. The first telegram sent to the secretary of state from the us consul in Istanbul at 5:36 PM, Washington time, reported the following scant information:

> Extensive mobs roaming through Istanbul tonight destroying property. Demonstrations, which are rapidly increasing in violence, were set off by reports published in evening papers that Ataturk's birthplace in Salonika had been attacked there today. Destruction extensive and situation appears completely out of hand with no evidence of police or military attempts to control. I personally witnessed looting of many shops while police stood idly by or cheered the mob. Attacks were first restricted to Greek property but destruction has now become indiscriminate.
>
> As of 10 PM no fires reported but danger of disastrous fire seriously threatens....Have requested police protection....[21]

The consul's second telegraph was sent to the State Department some twenty-two hours later, at about 8:00 PM, Istanbul time, and was somewhat

---

[20] Chrêstidês, *Ekthesis*, pp. 70-71; Tsoukatou, *Septemvriana*, 15, p. 100; Megas Reumiôtês, *Syrriknosê*, pp. 90-91.
[21] National Archives, telegram, unnumbered, Control 2678, 9/6/55.

more extensive, but still fell far short of understanding the pogrom's nature. Nevertheless, from his accumulated reports and information, us consul Arthur Richards had now grasped the wide extent of the destruction, suspected that it was organized, and realized, once more, that the government and police displayed a crucial indifference to the violence.

> Out of the welter of exaggerated and conflicting stories concerning the events of the last 24 hours in Istanbul, the following facts seem clearly to emerge:
>
> 1. Over a period of some weeks the Istanbul press coverage and comment on the Cyprus issue was increasingly inflammatory....These articles, supported by irresponsible public statements by senior government officials, increased intensity of feeling which was (1) pro-Nationalist, (2) anti-Greek, and, (3) opposed to residents of Greek descent even though of Turkish nationality.
>
> 2. There was apparent organization to encourage claims to Turkish sovereignty over Cyprus....For example tens of thousands of printed Turkish flags with the map of Cyprus superimposed... recently appeared throughout the city. As of last night these posters were more valuable than passports or any other identification, and any person not possessing and prominently displaying one was subject to immediate attack.
>
> 3. The published stories in last evening's press regarding the explosion at the Turkish Consulate at Salonika, which explosion was widely reported to have damaged Ataturk's birthplace, inspired student gangs to frenzy.
>
> 4. Once these gangs had congregated and passion had been aroused by fiery speeches, it was a short step to attacks on property owned by persons of Greek descent.
>
> 5. In the absence of any effective police opposition, these attacks were immediately joined in by great numbers of rabble of the lowest classes who gave vent to unreasoning nationalism and at the same time delighted in vindictive vandalism. Many observers commented on the exceptional number of poorly dressed persons and of men wearing typical village dress who were swarming through the streets....
>
> 7. Although the first evidence of trouble was observed by members of the [consular] staff early in the evening, and although by 9 PM destruction and looting were widespread, no effective police action was taken until midnight....
>
> 8. The government's apparent indifference or ineptitude as displayed in its handling of the shameful events of the past 24

hours can hardly be exaggerated....It is difficult to anticipate what may happen tonight....

Istanbul has witnessed a sad display of violence brought to white heat by propaganda and uncontrolled by effective security measures. The city has suffered destruction which is grim and extensive. It will take days to clear up the mess; weeks to rehabilitate the city; and years for Turkey to live down the events of the past 24 hours.[22]

The longest official American analysis, however, was the one previously cited in Chapter 1 and sent by US ambassador Avra Warren to the State Department some three months after the facts, on December 1, 1955. The first conclusion of this lengthy report was that:

It seems there is no doubt but that the riots during their anti-Greek phase were organized....The Embassy has received no confirmed evidence of the allegation made by the Prime Minister and some other government officials that the riots were organized by Communists....The Embassy believes over-emotionalism among irresponsible elements of the popular Cyprus is Turkish Association was responsible.

The report then proceeds to protect the Menderes government against the charges, made by many, of its responsibility: "Some responsible leaders of the religious minority communities, as well as some foreign observers, accuse the Government, or at least some of its officials, of having knowingly allowed and encouraged the riot to take place." Warren chose instead to accuse the Turkish government of innocent carelessness and incompetence. The ambassador then undertakes to illustrate his interpretation by examining the events in both Izmir and Istanbul:

In Istanbul the main part of the riots had its inception in Taksim Square at about 7:00 PM, when a large crowd of youth began to assemble....After partially listening to one or two speeches, the demonstration began to break up into separate large groups with cores of about 20 to 30 activists. Some of the groups moved into Istiklal Caddesi and the surrounding residential and shopping area called "Pera"....The remaining groups in Taksim moved out toward Kurtulush, Shishli, and Dolap, where they attacked and destroyed Greek-owned houses and shops. At about the same time other groups that came from various places began to attack the Greek-owned shops and houses in the various little villages along

---

[22] National Archives, telegram, unnumbered, Control 3411, 9/7/55.

the Bosphorus on the European side. It is almost impossible to fix any time table, but by 9:00 PM it seemed that separate groups had started rioting in almost every section of the city, up and down the Bosphorus clear to the Black Sea, and out on the Princes Islands in the Sea of Marmara. The Greek population is spread out all over Istanbul and almost without exception there was some rioting in every section of the city and its environs—that is, the spots of rioting were spread out over an area of almost fifteen miles by ten miles wide!

Warren goes on to discuss the destruction of Armenian and Jewish properties. One thousand stores, 150 homes, three churches, and four schools belonging to the Armenian community were targeted, while the Jewish community had 500 shops and twenty-five homes vandalized, and one synagogue damaged. He adds that "intense" rioting continued from about 8:00 PM until after midnight, but that even after martial law was imposed, the destruction did not cease until late Wednesday morning, September 7.

Naturally, Warren pays particular attention to the troublesome question of placing responsibility for the pogrom. Immediately after the riots, suspicion was rife that "some group had deliberately organized the riots," and even Menderes was reported to have agreed on this point. Through his superiors in Washington, however, Warren had denied that Menderes and his government could have been responsible for organizing such an event: "The Embassy....does not agree with some people who believe that this riot could have occurred only with the consent and knowledge of the government....It is expected that normally one of Turkey's security organizations would have discovered the preparations."[23] The ambassador then places the blame for the riots on the KTC and on the laxity of Turkish security officials, who presumably believed that this was such a patriotic society that its conduct did not call for close scrutiny. Furthermore, he further justified the failure of the military commander of Istanbul to respond to the *vali's* call for military reinforcements on the grounds that the former feared for his career and so refused to respond to the civil authority's demand for military assistance! All in all, although Warren's report is extremely detailed, and contains much useful corroborating evidence for much of the events' flow, it is clear that he failed—or did not want—to see the forest for the trees.

By contrast, the British *chargé* in Istanbul, Michael Stewart, was an acute observer of the Turkish scene and far more perceptive than the US ambassador

---

[23] National Archives, Foreign Office Dispatch No. 228, American Embassy, December 1, 1955; see also National Archives, telegram, No. 406, Control 8145, 9/15/55.

in Ankara. We see clearly from his report that he immediately dismissed the KTC as the probable vehicle and mechanism for the massive attack on Greek Istanbulis on the obvious grounds that it did not possess the organization, funds, or—most important—ultimate *authority* to undertake such a massive act of violence. Instead, Stewart saw seriously the possibility that the local DP was intimately involved in implementing the pogrom:

> Another possibility is the local organization of the Demokrat Parti itself. There is fairly reliable evidence that local Demokrat Parti representatives were amongst the leaders of the rioting in various parts of Istanbul, notably in the Marmara Islands, and it has been argued that only the Demokrat Parti had the political organization in the country capable of demonstrations on the scale that occurred. This is true, but I myself do not believe that the Parti, as distinct from individual members, can be held to be consciously responsible for more than the opening stages.

After having reported the involvement of the DP's local chapters in the events, Steward shied away from taking the final step of blaming the DP as a whole—let alone its leader, Menderes—for what transpired. Still, he was on the right track. As was customary in the home offices of the Foreign Office, his report was subjected to the critical comments of a number of officials; these remarks, written in as addenda to the report itself, are of some interest. The question was whether Stewart's report should be printed for internal circulation within the appropriate quarters of the ministry. Two addenda in particular indicate the importance that was attached to Stewart's report. One comments, in a clear hand: "Print....A grim story which bears out the Greek Ambassador's allegation to me yesterday that Menderes knew all about the business. Not for the first time, a sponsored riot got out of hand (cf. anti-Pakistan riot at Kabul recently). Certainly this should be printed...and anyway why must [we] be so tender to the American gullibility?" The second added note is of equal interest: "The Turkish government almost certainly knew and approved of the intention to stage a demonstration...." A final and short postscript in this document states: "The question of due diligence being exercised [*sic*] by the Turkish authorities is much affected by the possibility that the Government connived at the riots—a new factor and one which if provable renders them liable for the consequences."[24]

If one compares this report, and the comments on it from the specialists in the Foreign Office, with Ambassador Warren's long report, one discerns that "American gullibility" to which the British commentator above referred.

[24] TNA:PRO, FO 371/117711, No. 193, 9/22/55.

Of particular interest on that note is the astute report drawn up in January 1956 by the former Greek consul in Istanbul, Vyrôn Theodôropoulos. In the following excerpt, he takes up the events taking place from 5:00 PM on September 6:

> 5:00 PM The gathering at Taksim listens to various speakers as they deliver fiery speeches attacking Greece and Greeks.
> 6:30 PM The gathering is transformed into a demonstration of which one group reaches the Greek consulate and it is dispersed by the immediate appearance of police forces who have blocked off all approaches to the Consulate.
> 7:00 PM There commences the smashing of shop windows and steel shutters of the Greek shops in Taksim Square and İstiklal Caddesi. Almost simultaneously, violent acts commence in the remaining [quarters] of the city, and within two hours this state has become widespread in a huge triangle from the eastern edge of Boğaz-Sarıyer-Yeni Mahalle to Propontis-San Stefano [Yeşilköy] and the Isles.
> The synchronization of these demonstrations acquires an even greater significance when one comprehends the tactics of arson and destruction that were followed. One can, in effect, distinguish, more or less exactly, three waves of attacks: (a) The first wave had the task of breaking down the doors and shutters of the stores and, of course, of the dwellings, in order to prepare the way for the second [wave]. (b) The second was the wave of pillaging and theft of everything that could be moved away. (c) The third wave had as its mission the complete destruction of whatever remained.[25]

He also remarks on the open use of trucks from various official offices, which supplied the pogromists with the standard set of tools to implement destruction; specifically, Theodôropoulos comments on the trucks stationed at Sıraselviler Boulevard. According to his report, the destruction in various districts often came from outside: "And in each district was to be found the 'representative' of the district, for the most part the official night watch, and it was these local elements that would guide the attackers to the Christian homes and stores."[26] Thus one of the first security measures after martial law was declared in the early hours of September 7 was the army's blockade of all roads leading into and out of the city, so that no more looters could enter and those who had looted and destroyed inside the city could not escape: "Thus

---

[25] Theodôropoulos, *Sêmeiôma*, pp. 9-10; other sources indicate a similar division of labor.
[26] *Ibid.*, p. 11.

it was that many who had entered the city from Eastern Thrace and who had participated in the pillaging were arrested at the gates as they were attempting to leave with their booty."[27]

Like Michael Stewart, Theodôropoulos moves from the highest government level to lower levels and points his finger at the role of the local offices and officials of the DP when discussing the moral responsibility for the events: "At the lower levels, at any rate, it was asserted that many local leaders of the Demokrat Parti were actively engaged as the leaders of the bands of attackers, given the fact that the Parti disposed of a complete organization, offices, and local chapters in every district, even in the smaller ones. It is logical to suppose that the organizational mechanism of the Parti played a role in the execution of the plan."[28] Evidently, the two diplomats from Greece and Great Britain saw what had happened much more clearly than the US ambassador did.[29]

THE PRESS

Istanbul's Turkish press had the advantage of on-the-spot observation and reporting, although this was often hindered by the martial-law censorship. All the relevant reports of the Istanbul press were accompanied by considerable photographic evidence and material.[30] At this point, it would be well to quote the series of short articles published in *Milliyet* by a number of its staff writers shortly after the pogrom.

6-7 September 1955
(general description by Fahir Ersin)

5:30 PM

Taksim Square presents a crowded picture. A Greek grocery store opposite the Şehir Club: one of the groups admonishes, "Hang the flag." Since he did not put out the [Turkish] flag, with the first kick they brought down the shutters. Then they proceeded to stone and club the store. After five minutes, the store was turned into a

[27] *Ibid.*, p. 12. The Turkish government attempted to put the blame for the pogrom on such "exotic" elements and indeed arrested some 2,525 people on September 7 (Chrêstidês, *Ekthesis*, p. 43). Much of the looted wealth and property were traced as far away as Edirne in European Turkey and Eskişehir at the northwestern edge of the Anatolian plateau.

[28] Theodôropoulos, *Sêmeiôma*, p. 13. This fact comes out clearly in a number of the cases brought against Menderes and his government at Yassıada.

[29] The long analysis of Chrêstidês, *Ekthesis*, is also very rich in detail.

[30] The photographic coverage in much of the Turkish press is very rewarding in terms of the details and sociology of the pogrom. For an exhibit of much of this material in Istanbul in the fall of 1996, see the monthly Greek newspaper *Politês*, November 1996.

ruin. After that, they proceeded to destroy the Ankara Grocery.

One group smashed the Park Hotel pastry shop, another group went to Güney Park and another to Haylayf [High Life].

The youth, joining with other groups coming from Harbiye, Dolmabahçe, and Tarlabaşı like some torrent, began to flow into İstiklal Caddesi. All vehicles halted as the street was crammed full and not a person passed out of this torrent. Someone wanted to hang out a [Turkish] flag at Vili's [store] in order to save the store. But who would believe this banner? After that, they entered İnci, Franguli, and Baylan pastry shop[s], Smart, Motolo, Silvio, Osep, Daryo, and finally the Saray cinema, Atlantic, Orman, and, with the blows of pickaxe and shovel, they scattered restaurants, beer shops, bar, wineshop, haberdasher, perfumery, in short, whatever store, rubble, lumber they encountered.

Shortly thereafter, they went and emptied outside all the Greek shops on left and right of İstiklal Caddesi. The street took on the appearance of a confused, disorganized department store. There were to be seen, trodden underfoot, pastries and sweets alongside electric vacuum cleaners and refrigerators, clothes, shirts, and ties of Silvio and Osep, together with remainders of a grocery, sunken in mud and filth. Streetcars, taxis, cars, went clanging with refrigerators, motorboats, and sewing machines tied to their back ends.

The First Episodes in Karaköy
by Ertuğrul Ünal

These events in Bankalar Caddesi, Karaköy, Fermeneciler, Perşembe Pazarı and in their neighborhoods, beginning at 7:30 [PM], commenced as separate events. This series of events smashed the store windows of large stores...and destroyed their goods, one by one. The events flowing out of Ziyapaşa Caddesi and other streets progressed abruptly. The youths and the common groups passing through the Greek shops in these streets, their hands with iron bars and clubs, suddenly filled Karaköy. One column [of pogromists] followed the street of the tram and arrived in front of the Selanik Bank, smashing the windows of three stores, destroying telephones, radios, and the auto parts inside.

Thereafter the events centered along the front side of Tünel, with Fermeneciler, Perşembe Pazarı, and the Greek establishments there smashed and pulled down in a short time, and the merchandise inside destroyed.

Continuing their destructive movements, a portion of these groups attached, with rope, refrigerators, motorboats, typewriters, [and] bales of cloth to the backs of automobiles and trams, and these were dragged about.

At ten minutes to ten, moving by truck to the Karaköy side of the bridge, infantry with bayonets and naval contingents cut off communication with Istanbul. This measure was taken with a view to preventing merchandise from being taken away, as well as looting. Every vehicle [on the streets] was stopped, one by one, and searched, and then permission to move on was given.

The First Fire

This broke out in Karaköy at 10:10 [PM]. The store of Vasil Devletoğlu, which sells chemical materials and is contiguous to the Karaköy post office, suddenly caught fire. In a short time, the maritime fire department and that of Beyoğlu arrived and put the fire under control. At that time, one group of demonstrators made an effort to take a boat at the [Galata] Bridge in order to go to the islands, but, as there were no boats, their efforts remained without results. They broke the windows and destroyed the merchandise of well-known establishments, including Yani Keşişoğlu, Nas Mumas, Vasil Devletoğlu, E. V. Keçecıoğlu, Alvitte.

After this, the events beginning from Eminönü reached into Küçükpazar and Tahmis Street and eventually attained Sultanhamam and Mahmutpaşa. We did not expect destruction in this district…but in a very short time all Greek stores had their windows smashed and their goods destroyed.

At about 11 [PM], one group attempted to pass from Yeşildirek to Çağaloğlu. Only along Ankara Boulevard, motorized [military?] contingents had taken positions and [the group] were prevented from doing so.

70 Churches Burned

Important events took place in Kumkapı, Samatya, Yedikule, and the environs and in particular churches were burned. In this district, nearly 70 churches were burned [the numbers are all wrong]. At this time, since many Greeks live in this area, there were episodes and the Greek houses were stoned.

The incidents began later in Kadıköy. The situation there was the same.

The "Business" in Sirkeci
by Veli Sezai Balcı

The sky became dark. At that time it was 8:00 [PM]. More than 5,000 youths passed over the Galata Bridge. Arriving at Eminönü Square, they split up into two groups. One group marched toward Bahçekapı and Sirkeci, and the other toward Tahtakale and Sultanhamam.

With the Turkish flags in their hands, wherever they would come across pictures and busts of Atatürk, Cyprus maps and plans, they would exclaim: "Dear Atatürk did not die; The vile people who wish to betray him shall not go unpunished; Cyprus is Turkish and shall remain Turkish." Saying such words, after marching, the group began to destroy the Greek stores in front of them: the Zenith clock store and the Bi Ba Bo. Before them, they began to destroy all, small or large, no matter, and they were leveled with the earth. Large refrigerators, ice boxes, motors, motorcycles, bicycles, sewing machines, no matter how heavy, they flew into the air like rubber balls. Going ahead, the group grew large and arrived at Sirkeci Square. From there, one group went to Babıali and the other group to Defterdarlık. The situation was all the same. With all the taxis that belonged to the Turks, innumerable trucks, buses, private cars decked with banners, they shuttled back and forth in the streets. Those in them, each one singing with his mouth [sic] our national marches, at one and the same time, while at the same time young people exhorted others. Along the Sirkeci tram street, there is no Greek store that has not been touched by them. There, this group turned back and, uniting with the first group and after having put their hands [to the shops] on the streets nearby, they went along Babıali Street to Çemberlitaş.

The most important aspect of the event was that one group from each district arose and oversaw the situation. On finishing their "work," they scattered with government military vehicles. At this place [time?], we can say with pride that in no place was there a fire [he might mean Sirkeci].

In Gedikpaşa
by Bedirhan Çınar

With the anger coming out of the Selanik episode [the "explosion" at the Turkish consulate] and the gathering of people having been set into motion, a veritable avalanche crushed the districts of Kumkapı, Gedikpaşa, and Çarşıkapı.

On Çarşıkapı Boulevard, the more than 80 stores belonging to the Greeks were completely destroyed. At that time, a number of looters wished to loot goods....[T]housands of people went down to Kumkapı and, having destroyed very many shops, restaurants, and wineshops, they burned the Greek church at Kumkapı.

Meanwhile, a regrettable incident occurred in Kumkapı. There were two Greek families living in one house and as they did not want to place a Turkish flag outside it, and as the anger of the Turks exceeded all bounds, the latter entered the house and all the goods were thrown out on the street. All the Greek houses, 100 to 150 of them, found in those districts suffered the same result. But no looting was carried out. And in no form was the smallest object mistreated and no persons were touched.

On the other hand, military units had come to these districts against the contingency that they might be looted, and made their preparations. In Çarşıkapı, in a shop adjacent to the Ekspres paint shop, a fire broke out as a result of a short-circuit. When it became apparent, some people extinguished it.

In the interval, thousands of people assembled and an exciting event took place. Two young men endangered their lives by ascending to the fourth floor of a building, thus saving our flag.

In Boğaz (Bosphorus)
by Mücahit Beşer

From 7:00 [PM], the Rumeli side of the Bosphorus presented a view of terror. Arriving in an angry state, small groups, in thousands of people, put their hands to the stores, houses, institutions, casinos belonging to the Greeks and, with iron crowbars and clubs, smashed them. Even the smallest item in thousands of shops and stores was scattered into nothing. They drag[ged] along merchandise in places, they move[d] it from one place to another, tearing it to pieces with their hands and cutting it into pieces with knives. And so these groups, with their flags, portraits of Atatürk, and clubs, shouting, "Long live Turkey," "Cursed be the red Makarios," went from place to place and destroyed all the places that belonged to Greeks.

The local police remained ineffective against the mass of the crowd's intensity and were unable to interfere [this is the reporter's explanation]. Later, with the arrival of gendarmes and police, and even later of military units, this finally changed.

At the hour of nine, they had already blocked off the Bridge [probably the Galata Bridge], and of all those structures belonging to the Greeks that had not been previously destroyed, not one remained undestroyed. Groups were seen hurling rocks at some houses, breaking their windows and breaking their doors into pieces. At that time a very large crowd, despite the precautions taken by the Security Police, set fire to the house of the Patriarch [actually, the metropolitan] in Tarabya. And like a swollen torrent, the crowd grew and expanded until it had spread throughout. It is impossible to express in writing these events. Every place and thing had sunk into turmoil. Some groups, attacking the churches in the neighborhood, burned them. The Security Forces, military units, and fire department were scattered, so it was not possible to find them.

At 10:00 [PM] on both sides of the Bosphorus, as it were, the neighborhoods looked as if they had been struck by some kind of disaster. In Arnavutköy, Sarıyer, Yeniköy and their environs especially, all drinking casinos and stores were destroyed. The Lido casino in Ortaköy was destroyed, and not one item survived. In many districts, the flames of the fires rose high. These groups also burned a number of churches there. Those groups that assembled in the square, so long as the head of some forces did not appear, struck, smashed, and burned.

Efforts at Retaliation by the Greeks of Arnavutköy

After midnight, more than 500 Greeks from Arnavutköy attacked the Turkish quarter by way of retaliation. Because of this, the Turkish families appealed to the Security Forces to help by striking them [the Greeks]. Because of this, a group of gendarmes and police intervened and scattered the excited body of Greek men. Because of this failed Greek excess, the enraged group of our youth attacked the Greek stores in Arnavutköy and demolished them. At the same time, they threw six Greek automobiles into the Bosphorus.

During these episodes, 29 of our compatriots were wounded.[31]

Although there are some factual errors in the various accounts of the *Milliyet* coverage, it is nevertheless an attempt to give a coherent picture of the pogromists' general movements throughout the city, and to indicate which actions were carried out by large groups and which by smaller ones.[32] It seems that the further from the center of Istanbul that these accounts moved, the more likely they were to make mistakes, as in the numbers of churches destroyed on the edges and outskirts of the old city. Nevertheless, in tracing movements of larger groups, such as those over the Galata Bridge to Eminönü and Sirkeci, one gets a clearer picture of the organization and discipline of these large bodies. This reportage, obviously available within the first week of the events, would have been sufficient to dispel the erroneous idea that this was a spontaneously generated disturbance carried out by leaderless mobs.

The accounts by Western observers are in some ways the most colorful. A Belgian journalist from the *Gazette de Liège* who witnessed the pogrom later described it to a correspondent for the Greek paper *Ethnos* as follows: "Ten to fifteen thousand persons assembled, as if by magic in one and the same place. The same thing occurred in all the suburbs. The Turkish authorities can congratulate themselves on having created the impression abroad that merely a few incidents took place in the center of Istanbul and Smyrna, whereas the Greeks even in the smallest suburb suffered the same damages as in the center of the city."[33]

One of the most dramatic eyewitness accounts was that of Saladin Volkman, a Canadian who found himself in Istanbul on the night of September 6 because of his work as president of a philanthropic organization:

---

[31] *Milliyet*, 9/9/55.
[32] Two or three days after the pogrom, *Hürriyet* not only gave data on the destruction but also on those arrested under martial law, preparatory to the courts-martial.
[33] Quoted in Journalists' Union, *Anti-Greek riots*, pp. 21-22.

I have never seen such an evil in my life. I found myself in Istanbul just a few days ago as a tourist, and I had intended to stay about one month. But, as you can see, I have left, sickened and troubled with Turkey and have made the decision never to return. This evil commenced Tuesday evening while I was staying at the Hilton Hotel. Suddenly I heard wild voices and shouting outside in the streets. As I stood in the hotel door, I saw groups of wild men moving in a threatening manner with knives, clubs, and crowbars in their hands toward the central boulevard of the city [İstiklal Caddesi]. I followed the raging mob out of curiosity. Without realizing it, I found myself among hateful men that were smashing store windows of Greek stores and who were setting fires and stealing. They were striking women, old men, and small children with a madness that betrayed a dark soul. For a moment, I imagined that I was inside a group of people gone insane. I attempted to return to the hotel, but it was impossible to extricate myself from the multitude of these insane people who had flooded the streets and were overturning cars, destroying stores, and grabbing and scattering the latters' contents onto the streets. I stopped at a corner and awaited the intervention of the police or the army in order to restore order, but I had at the beginning failed to notice that among the multitude of destroyers there were both many police and many soldiers, who were either assisting the demonstrators to destroy the stores and burn the churches, or who were laughing animal-like. This anarchy prevailed for many hours. Two things impressed me: The primitive instinct of the entire mob and the fact that had the police and army so desired, they could have avoided the evil, but it is undeniable that they did not wish to do so.[34]

This graphic image of violence in a world gone mad very much resembles the macabre pogrom scenes in the account of the Turkish writer, Aziz Nesin, who would later recount his experiences during the events.

The reporter of the *Allgemeine Zeitung* of Basel, who evidently knew Turkey well, contrasted the behavior of Turks and their government on the night of September 6-7 with their frequent boasts of culture and "civilization":

The Night of Terror in Constantinople

Various Turks of officialdom, with whom I have had the opportunity to speak, clearly show how difficult it now is for them to share the opinion of the newspaper *Zafer* of

---

[34] The text is taken from the Greek version in Chrêstidês, *Ekthesis*, pp. 45-46.

August 26, according to which the countries that are friendly to Turkey will be forced, finally, to accept that the actual center of civilization in the eastern Mediterranean is to be found in Turkey.

Forty-two days earlier, the president of the Turkish Republic, Celal Bayar, stated: "We are near the end of our pursuits. Very soon, there will come a day during which, and before all the world, Turkey will take its place among the more civilized nations." This morning the president, in a blacked-out car, passed the mounds of material and ethical ruins underneath which there wept the non-Muslim children of his land, the Greeks, Armenians, and Jews.

Like a beast with 20,000 legs, the mass of the Turkish people attacked the goods of their own greatest commercial city....

The students had, much earlier, prepared catalogues containing the names of the future victims of the hatred of the Turkish people.

This hatred spilled out on the night of September 6, in every region of the city, simultaneously, either by coincidence or by premeditated planning at a much earlier date, as the vandal masses poured out into the streets.[35]

The best known of the Western reports, however, is that of Frederic Sondern, Jr., who was also in Istanbul on the fateful night. His short description, published in one of America's most widely read magazines at the time, *The Reader's Digest*, played a very important role in forming public opinion, and has left a long-term imprint on American perceptions of that part of the world.

Istanbul's Night of Terror

Above [Taksim] square, on the terrace behind the memorial to Kemal Ataturk... stood a colonel of police. Some university students were staging an anti-Greek demonstration and special police details were on hand to prevent any major disturbance....The colonel was watchful but unworried....Then the colonel noticed a new activity: news vendors were hawking the late editions of the evening press and knots of people were gathering around them....

He sent an aide to buy a paper. One glance told him that there was trouble ahead: Greek Terrorists Defile Ataturk's Birthplace, the headline screamed....The colonel reached for a field telephone, but even as he began barking orders he knew he was too late.

Five main streets converge on Taksim Square, and mobs in solid phalanxes were already pouring down each one, jamming into the place: "Kill the Greeks!" the

---

[35] Ypourgeion Proedrias Kyvernêseôs, *Ektakton Deltion #1*, November 1955, pp. 12-13.

staccato shouts filled the square.

In one corner stood a shanty used to store the tools of a street-car repair gang. The door was torn off and some fifty angry men armed themselves with crowbars, pickaxes, sledge hammers, sections of rail. Backed by a crowd of several hundred they made for the Avenue of Independence [İstiklal Caddesi]. When police tried to block the entrance the mob simply bowled them over.

Along the one-mile length of the Istiklal [*sic*] Caddesi are some 400 shops, most of them operated by Christian Turks of Greek extraction. As soon as the trouble began, most merchants locked their doors, pulled down their heavy iron shutters and fled. They saved their lives, but they could not save their stores....

The crowd was tightly packed now, moving like a relentless stream of lava. Suddenly several hundred rioters surged into a side street leading to the beautiful Greek Orthodox Church of the Holy Trinity, the city's largest Christian place of worship....

Meanwhile in the rest of Istanbul, a city of 1,500,000 people, the frenzy was spreading. In the coffeehouses, on street corners, the orators were at work. "A night of reckoning has come," shouted one. "Cleanse the fatherland of the infidel!" shrieked another. The ancient cry was echoing from one end of Istanbul to the other.

By nine o'clock, just two hours after the city had erupted, at least 50,000 frenzied Turks had formed a hundred other lava streams pouring down avenues and streets, tearing and smashing as they went. At ten o'clock, eight sheets of flame shot up into the sky in different parts of the city. Torches flung into the kerosene drenched interiors of Istanbul's largest churches set them ablaze. This was the signal for gangs to go to work on other Christian places of worship....

One group of several hundred men descended on the big Greek Orthodox cemeteries of Shishli with torches and tools....

Forty square miles of densely populated metropolitan and suburban area were out of police control. And now a new sentiment appeared in the crowds. "Down with the rich" they chanted as they overturned parked cars and set fire to them.

Istanbul was a city gone mad, and, as usual in such craziness, villainy and valor, tragedy and humor were side by side.[36]

THE YASSIADA *GEREKÇE*

A brief examination at this point of the trials at Yassıada that condemned Menderes and his government for their roles in the destruction of Greek property and institutions—again from the point of view of the general image and motive forces behind the actual events—would constitute a

---

[36] Sondern, "Istanbul's Night of Terror," pp. 185-188.

partial corrective to the general images projected by diplomats, journalists, and historians already mentioned above. Following is the opening of *The Reasoning and the Decision in the Trial Concerning "The Events of September 6-7"*; it is the *gerekçe*, or rationale, of the Yassıada tribunals:

The Cyprus problem and controversy having been in process and at a time when the event had reached its limits, and the individuals [below] having united in an association that had as its objective the partial removal, by way of racism, of their civil rights, which the constitution guarantees to the citizens of Greek origin, and the latter being in a sensitive condition because of the Cyprus events, these individuals [below] are accused of the intention to set into motion a plot and movement of demonstrations to destroy the property of the Greek co-citizens of the Turks:

1. The former, now fallen, President of the Republic Celal Bayar

2. The former, now fallen, Prime Minister Adnan Menderes

3. The former, now fallen, Minister of Foreign Affairs Fatin Rüştü Zorlu

4. The former Minister of State Fuat Köprülü.

The [following persons] have not been shown to have shared in the "association" together with those accused whose names appear inscribed above, but they nevertheless took no measures to prevent the demonstrations from attaining their actions and movement, which had as their purpose destruction, and they undertook to put no preparations in place at that time, and so they are accused of participating internally in the crime by reason of the fact that they permitted and indulged demonstrations that were both extensive and destructive:

5. The former *Vali* of Istanbul Kerim Gökay

6. The former Director of Security Alaettin Eriş

7. The former *Vali* of Izmir Kemal Hadımlı.

The following are accused of having knowledge of the purposes of the accused Celal Bayar, Adnan Menderes, Fatin Rüştü Zorlu, and Fuat Köprülü, and, in order to assure this, they made provisions by bringing the bomb from Turkey to Greece, and having hurled it at the house of Atatürk in Thessalonikê are accused of planning and exploding the bomb:

8. The former Consul General of Thessalonikê Mehmet Ali Belin

9. The former Deputy Consul General of Thessalonikê Mehmet Ali Tekinalp

10. Oktay Engin, at that time a Greek citizen and student

11. The *kavas* [doorman] of the Consulate in Thessalonikê, Hasan Uçar.

On the basis of the decrees of the High Investigatory Council dated 21/9/1960 and 2/10/1960, and with paragraph 4.68 joined to laws 64, 65, 141 of the Turkish Republic, and according to the 173rd paragraph, the following decision was rendered before the Supreme Judicial Council at an open session of the accused and their attorneys.

It is necessary to discuss broadly, from the point of verification of the penal side, and before entering the matter of the analysis of the assembled evidence and argument, the situation that led to the "Events" [pogrom]: to wit, the Cyprus matter and controversy, which were the cause of the crime and the main factor in reality.[37]

After having discussed this Cyprus background, the court's *gerekçe* turns to marshaling its evidence and testimony, with specific reference to the report of the chief of national security presented to General Fahrettin Aknoz (who convened the 1955 courts-martial) on September 9, 1955, in which one clue to the "tertip," or contrived nature, of the demonstrations was that the (unnamed) plotters were accused of "having commenced demonstrations and actions almost simultaneously in neighborhoods far distant from one another in a city which has very poor transportation and communication."[38] The *gerekçe* then abandons the wording of the security chief's report and speaks in its own voice:

> In a determined manner, stores and institutions were attacked, causing the state to pay TL35 million for damages and destruction… and only after midnight did the military units formally intervene in order to restrain the destruction, and looting begun at Nişantaş between five and six PM and thereafter spread to Beyoğlu. Such witnesses as Nevzat Emrealp [a government official] and [Orhan] Eyuboğlu gave testimony that the destruction began at 7:30 PM. Thus it is clear that between the beginning of the demonstrations and the destructive phase not much time elapsed, and at the most beginning at about 8 PM, the destruction occurred in a generalized form at this time, according to the Martial Law Authority on 3/13/1956. Menderes and his retinue were still at Haydarpaşa.[39]

In this report, the Yassıada prosecution cited testimony that Menderes, other officials, and the head of the military units in Istanbul were apprised of

---

[37] Yassıada Trials, *Esas* no. 1960/3, pp. 1-2.
[38] *Ibid.*, p. 9.
[39] *Ibid.*

the situation by Ethem Yetkiner, the general director of security. The *gerekçe* states, "That those who were connected with the government and whose duty it was to do so gave news, in fact, without doubt, gave the news on the flow, form, and movement of the destruction."[40]

The *gerekçe* then indicates that Yetkiner reported by wireless on all the demonstrations and destruction that he witnessed to both Istanbul's *vali* and to the security authorities in Haydarpaşa. The latter, in turn, informed Celal Bayar, Adnan Menderes, and Namık Gedik of all that was occurring. In addition, the violence that had begun as early as 5:00 PM (as reported by Nabi Üp) and was widespread by 7:00 PM had also been reported to the party waiting at Haydarpaşa. Further, and despite the fact that *Vali* Gökay had already asked for military reinforcements after the pogrom had begun:

> Bayar and Menderes set out [by train for Ankara at 8:20 PM], underlining the fact that the damage and destruction had been part of the plan and conspiracy. According to Orhan Eyuboğlu [deputy director of security at the time], when he asked for strong reinforcements from his Director, since some windows had been broken and [the rioters] wished to attack the Zappeion Lycée, he [Eyuboğlu] informed the General Director of Security, Ethem Yetkiner, that they should disperse the mob. The latter replied: "Do not display such force over a few windows." The latter's answer is thus also a further indication that the affair had been planned.[41]

After the departure of Bayar and Menderes, Gedik returned to the *vilayet*'s offices in Istanbul and reviewed the accumulating reports on the ongoing attacks. When he was told that the demonstrations had taken a very dangerous turn, he replied: "This is a national fervor, take no violent action." The *gerekçe* then comments: "In saying this, he did not hesitate to give inspiration and an order, having thus given permission for continuing the attack and destruction that essentially was appropriate in thought and deed to a party chief."[42] The *gerekçe* concludes this section by asserting that, among other things, Turkey had become, by these actions, a lawless state.

In another, particularly important section, the *gerekçe* took up the crucial question of what it termed, "The Role of the Party Organization and Members of the Demokrat Parti," where, in five terse pages, it pointed to the ties among the DP, its local chapters, and the execution of the pogrom.[43] The High Court's *gerekçe* was composed five years after the events, and obviously represented,

---

[40] *Ibid.*, p. 11.
[41] *Ibid.*, pp. 12-13.
[42] *Ibid.*, pp. 13-14.
[43] *Ibid.*, pp. 22-26.

to a large degree, a political and judicial rationale for the armed forces' violent overthrow of Adnan Menderes and his government. Eventually, of course, Menderes, Fatin Rüştü Zorlu, and Hasan Polatkan were hanged, and a large number of government officials and DP members of parliament were condemned. Nevertheless, the detailed arguments of the Yassıada prosecutors were heavily based on the written sources and reports of the Menderes government's *own* national security agency, as well as on witnesses who were part of Menderes's government at the time. The responsibility of Menderes, Zorlu, Celal Bayar, Mehmet Fuat Köprülü, and Namık Gedik, as well as of the heads of the army and police stationed in Istanbul, is clear and proven. Indeed, Menderes often substituted his local party structure for the local governmental authorities, thus ruling through the party as opposed to the government— something for which he was also tried in a separate, major trial.

EYEWITNESS ACCOUNTS: TAKSİM AND İSTİKLAL CADDESİ
There is no complete description of the course of the pogrom's destruction, but there are numerous descriptions of both general and specific destruction throughout much of the city, its suburbs, and outlying districts. Christoforos Chrêstidês's *Ekthesis* was an early overall effort made over three decades ago to bring the evidence together. There are lists (usually only partial) of individuals, shops, dwellings, and churches that suffered damage and/or destruction. What follows is an effort, based on Chrêstidês's work, to bring together information that documents the process of destruction throughout much, but not all, of the area, which, for our purposes, breaks down into five general geographical regions: new city, old city, the European and Asian sides of the Bosphorus, and the Princes Islands.

Table 15: Greek communities at the time of the pogrom

	Families	Churches	Schools	Soup kitchens	Assoc.	Clinics
New city (6 communities)						
	12,649	12	14	5	various	4
Old city (17 communities)						
	1,831+	24	11	6	various	2
European shore (11 communities)						
	962	15	7	6	various	
Asian shore (7 communities)						
	NA	13	7	1	various	1
Princes Islands (4 communities)						
	NA	11	4*		various	

*plus the theological seminary

THE NEW CITY

In Bakırköy (Makrochôri) and Yeşilköy (San Stefano), finally, there were 2 communities, 609 families, 2 churches, 2 schools, and other associations.[44] The pogrom would wreak massive destruction on the shops and businesses of the Greeks of the new city and especially in its center. The heart of the region, some two miles long between the shore of Karaköy in the south at the entrance to the Golden Horn to Harbiye to the north, and about one and a half miles from the Bosphorus at Dolmabahçe to Feriköy to the northwest, was Istanbul's economic center, and the economic heart of its Greeks. The principal thoroughfare, İstiklal Caddesi, stretches out northward from Tünel (which is just to the north of the historic Genoese Tower) to its intersection with Yeni Çarşı Caddesi, at which point it turns northeast in front of the famous Galatasaray school, and for the next half mile runs straight until it reaches Taksim Square, the site of the Independence Monument. This center gives way in the south to the regions of Tünel, Galata, and Karaköy. To the southeast and east are the districts of Tophane, Fındıklı, Cihangir, and Galatasaray. Northeast of Taksim are the neighborhoods of Maçka and Harbiye. Due north and northwest of Taksim are the districts of Pangaltı, Osmanbey, and Şişli. West of and parallel to İstiklal Caddesi is Tarlabaşı, to its north are Kurtuluş and Feriköy, and further west are Kasımpaşa and Tepebaşı.

Three independent sources confirm that large numbers of organized pogromists began to descend on Taksim Square in the late afternoon to early evening of September 6. Fahir Ersin writes in *Milliyet* that demonstrators from Harbiye, Dolmabahçe, and Tarlabaşı quickly joined the demonstrators already on İstiklal Caddesi.[45] Saladin Volkman viewed the spectacle of the rushing human torrent along Cumhuriyet Caddesi from the door of the Hilton Hotel. Fred Sondern noted the massive "phalanxes" marching into Taksim Square along five boulevards. Those coming from Dolmabahçe ascended along Yeni Dolmabahçe Sokak probably via Gümüşsuyu. A third column must have taken Tarlabaşı and İstiklal Caddesi, respectively. Those whose starting-point was somewhere to the north of Taksim obviously proceeded along Cumhuriyet Caddesi. The fifth may have ascended Sıraselviler to Taksim. The anonymous Armenian observer, B. E., who lived in the neighborhood of Pangaltı a little less than a mile from Taksim, was startled by the noise of demonstrators in his neighborhood and decided to go to Taksim to see what was happening.

About half an hour later [8:00 PM], I had just finished dinner,

---

[44] Chrêstidês, *Ekthesis*, pp. 27-36; he underestimates somewhat the numbers of families and churches, but his estimates of damaged schools is confirmed by other sources.
[45] *Milliyet*, 9/9/55.

when the shouting of an angry mob exploded, and I ran to the window. I saw a band of about forty people one hundred meters away, armed with iron bars, breaking windows and doors of all houses not flying the Turkish flag. I barely made it to hang a flag from our windows. And the protesters yelled, "there is a flag," and passed by. Our house was not attacked, while all the houses on our street were attacked, except a few inhabited by Turks, as well as ours. Who had given the order?...

At 20:30, we heard sirens of cars in the distance. I concluded that danger had passed and decided to go out. My grandmother, God bless her soul, who had lived through the Hamidian massacres of 1895-1896 and who lived through tragedy, pleaded and begged me to be extremely careful....I went out and witnessed the historic event of September 6. The wide road from Pangaltı was filled with buses and cars proceeding toward Pera and honking all the while. Small flags were flying all over them....Where were the security forces? Where do they [the pogromists] come from? They shouted, "Down with Europe!" "Down with Britain!" "On to Selanik or Athens!" On my way to Taksim Square, I began to see stores being looted. Protesters divided in groups attacked and broke down the doors of stores belonging to Greeks, to Armenians. They entered inside and threw out everything in the street. They shouted, "We do not need merchandise of infidels!" I slowly began to understand; the security forces did not intervene, therefore the government was well aware of what was going on. I noticed that each group had a leader, whom all protesters—all of them wearing caps—followed in *absolute* [stress added] obedience. None were from the neighborhood."[46]

---

[46] B. E./Khosdegian, "A Historical Night," III, pp. 5-6. B. E.'s reference to the Hamidian massacres concerns the reign of the Ottoman sultan Abdul Hamid II, and particularly the years 1894-1896 and thereafter. It was during his sultanate that the Ottoman empire used massacres as a response to its minority "problems"—specifically and foremost in regard to the Armenian minority. In the mid-1890s, this "solution" was effected in the towns of Sassoon, Zeitoun, and Van, and more generally in the six provinces of Sivas, Harput, Diyarbekir, Erzerum, Bitlis, and Van (as well as in the imperial capital of Istanbul), where Ottoman troops and Kurdish irregulars killed between 200,000 and 250,000 Armenians, destroyed 2,500 Armenian settlements (in both villages and towns) and 645 churches and monasteries, converted 328 Armenian churches into mosques, and rendered desolate some 540,000 Armenians. For the documentation of these statistics, and for the massacre of Armenians by Abdul Hamid more generally, see Vahakn N. Dadrian, *The History of the Armenian Genocide: Ethnic Conflict from the Balkans to Anatolia to the Caucasus*, Providence, 1995, pp. 179-184, with special attention to the nature and reliability of the primary sources, pp. 152-156.

It is obvious that B. E. had entered Taksim only after some time had elapsed, having had to proceed through Cumhuriyet Caddesi, swollen by now with vast throngs of demonstrators. (Volkman had noted that its density was such that he could not disengage himself from the crowd, and was swept along by it.) B. E. writes that he took the decision to go to Taksim at about 8:30 PM, and that by the time he arrived there, the cyclone of destruction had moved farther down İstiklal Caddesi and into the side streets:

> When I reached Taksim Square, there were no secrets: all the stores overlooking the square that did not have the flag were looted. No merchandise was left. The demonstration was raging in all its destruction; thousands of people in orderly groups of thirty or forty were led by a person showing them which stores, which church, which restaurant, to loot, to destroy. I followed from a distance this group or that one. The stretch from Taksim to Tünel on Independence Boulevard [İstiklal Caddesi] was the hardest hit area; at that time, those were minority-owned stores. None of those stores belonging to Greeks, Armenians, Jews, and to a small number of Europeans living in Istanbul, had the flag flying. One cannot but admire the unity of the Turkish people, their ability to keep a secret, and their discipline when they deal with minorities. It had long been decided certainly by the government to fly the flag on properties owned by Muslims or Turks in order to avoid destruction. The interesting thing is that all the Turks were aware of this secret ordinance, and no one belonging to the minorities knew it....
>
> Events became more interesting as I continued my tour. I checked the state of the stores of Beyoğlu owned by Turks doing business with Europe. All were guarded by one or two armed soldiers. The flying flags were not deemed enough.
>
> I found that the secret police were leading the groups of twenty or thirty persons armed with steel bars, pickaxes, and clubs. The group followed its leader, who carried an address list and showed them which store, restaurant, or firm belonged to an infidel. From Taksim to the Tünel, a crowd of at least 100,000 "worked," shouting, and yelling, and cursing....In a second, doors and windows were pried open and merchandise flew out on the street. I admit that exemplary discipline shone through this chaos, because everyone followed his leader.[47]

At this point, however, Fahir Ersen identifies a number of Greek

---

[47] *Ibid.*, p. 6.

establishments in Taksim Square and on İstiklal Caddesi and its environs
that were either damaged or destroyed.[48] Sondern remarks that soon after
the mob had destroyed much of Taksim, they turned down İstiklal Caddesi,
but that "suddenly several hundred rioters surged into a side street leading
to the beautiful Greek Orthodox Church of the Holy Trinity...." He then
continues:

> For a moment their pace slowed down....Then the mob pushed
> forward. Within seconds the doors buckled, and the crowd
> streamed inside....
>
> Again there was a pause while the rioters gawked at the
> unfamiliar scene—the great ancient ikons, the crucifix, the fine
> altar. Suddenly one screamed, "Tear down the Greek blasphemies!"
> Two young men with axes jumped onto the altar and the rioters
> went berserk. Massive oak benches were ripped apart like paper;
> thick stone slabs were shattered. One group pushed into the vestry
> and smashed priceless vessels. They ripped magnificent cloths and
> robes and hammered candlesticks and chalices into junk. Another
> squad appeared with cans of kerosene.[49]

When B. E. arrives, after the attack on the Holy Trinity is over and the
vandals have moved on, he finds a solitary soldier "guarding" the desecrated
church:

> I saw, right across from the Esayan High School and adjacent
> to the Greek Lyceum for Girls, the *Hagia Triada* [Holy Trinity]
> church still burning. I went closer to the entrance. There was an
> armed soldier on guard. I did not understand, nor did he, why he
> was standing there, since the church already had been set ablaze.
> I wanted to go inside. He did not object. I am sure he did not
> even think that I could be an Armenian infidel. In all my life I
> never witnessed such a scene: the precious paintings had melted
> from the heat. Mary the Mother of God with the Child Jesus
> in her arms seemed to be crying....Water was dripping from
> everywhere...the firefighters had come, extinguished the blaze
> partially and left without putting out the flames....I could not see
> any of the precious items of the church. Probably they were looted.
> I came back to the guard, who asked me: "Brother, can you hold
> my rifle for a moment?" I held it. He went inside the church and
> tried to take down the crystal chandelier still hanging from the
> ceiling. "He is going to be crushed," I thought. He did not succeed.

---

[48] *Milliyet*, 9/9/55.
[49] Sondern, "*Istanbul's Night of Terror*," pp. 187-188.

Frustrated, he picked up stones and pieces of wood littering the floor and threw them towards the altar, where half of the picture of Christ's head was still hanging. Then with the satisfaction of a person having performed his duty, he came and took back the rifle, and mounted guard.[50]

It is difficult to explain the vandals' attitude toward Christian religious art as anything else but an automatic reflection of their basic attitude toward the religion of the Greek minority, to be demonstrated over and over again during that awful night.

B. E. continued along İstiklal Caddesi toward the end of the boulevard, at Tünel, recording his impressions generally without much attention to details.

I proceeded towards Tünel. The street was filled with protestors given to industrious work. Once in a while a "Dikkat" ("Attention," in Turkish) dominated the shouts. People looked up and moved a bit to the right or to the left and down flew on the street a refrigerator, a radio, or a sewing machine from the upper floors of buildings. The street was filled with goods. Those who could not get inside were busy destroying with unimaginable rage anything that was tossed out, tearing fabrics into pieces, and shouting "this country does not need merchandise of infidels"....I thought about the merchants who waited for so much time to bring the goods into the country, and now, in a second everything was destroyed. They were destroying the wealth of their own country.

I suddenly remembered about several Armenian and Jewish friends who owned stores in the area. I went first to my Armenian friend's place; the door shutter was still intact; his Turkish employee was standing at the front. I witnessed an interesting episode here. The neighboring stores belonging one to a Greek and the other to a Jew were looted and destroyed to pieces. The leader of the attacking group had in his hands a list of addresses. Suddenly he turned toward me; we recognized each other. He knew I was an Armenian, and I knew he was one of the secret police chiefs of Istanbul....He faked not to have seen me, or better not to have recognized me, and he led his group to another store which shared the fate of the others....

Next I went to my Jewish friend's store, about one hundred meters further ahead. I saw my friend sitting on the floor and crying like a child. He said he tried to stop them, but the gang threw him out of the store. And when I got there, they were busily

---

[50] B. E./Khosdegian, "A Historical Night," III, pp. 6-7.

carrying on the destruction, always repeating the same refrain: "We do not want infidels' merchandise in our country." My friend was crying, he begged them to leave untouched at least a portion of the merchandise. At this, someone came up to him and said: "Do not be afraid, we won't touch you today, we have not received orders to kill." This sentence still resounds in my ears, word by word.[51]

B. E. observed that a few Turkish stores were also looted inadvertently.[52]

Hürriyet reported a detail that chronologically seems contradictory. It stated that the demonstration proceeded as far as Tepebaşı without incident, but that a Greek pharmacy belonging to a certain Koutsouradês on Asmalı Mescit Street was stoned and destroyed at 7:30 PM after the owner refused to raise a Turkish flag.[53] *France Soir* reporter Rose Thibaut lived in an apartment on Taksim Square and was, naturally, present early on in the events. Emerging from her apartment building, she followed the scene from Taksim to Tünel.

> I witnessed a crazed crowd of about 500 demonstrators attacking the large luxurious department store belonging to a Greek. Within a half hour…the demonstrators had smashed the display windows of the store into bits and pieces while the twenty-five employees, terrified, retreated to the back of the store. I traversed the famed İstiklal Boulevard, the once familiar Grand Boulevard of Pera, along the length of which [to an extent of two kilometers] are arrayed the most beautiful stores of the city, the majority of which belong to the minorities: Greeks, Armenians, and Jews. From all these stores, which only two hours earlier I had seen shining in the neon lights, nothing remained.[54]

A further detailed scene is reported by the German reporter of the *Erlangen Tagblatt*:

> I saw a Turk who was bringing out of a shop hundreds of bottles of alcoholic beverages, which he then smashed on the foundations of the store to the accompaniment of the shouts of the mob. Gold watches from a jewelry store were stomped on in the street into a shapeless pile…six pieces of furniture were thrown out the window of the first floor. As soon as they hit the ground, a large number of men and women strike the furniture with clubs. They

---

[51] *Ibid.*, pp. 7-8.
[52] *Ibid.*, p. 11.
[53] Chrêstidês, *Ekthesis*, p. 47, who takes the *Hürriyet* text from the indictment of the court-martial set up by General Aknoz. The text probably means that this was the first act of destruction in Tepebaşı, and not more generally.
[54] *Ibid.*, pp. 52-53.

tear the mattresses to shreds. Immediately across from my house, they attack the store of a Greek grocer. From my solarium, I see how they hurl out of the display windows butter, cheese, eggs, and fruit, and these too are trod underfoot by the shrieking mob.[55]

All this is also witnessed from the first floor by the storeowner and his wife, who is holding their infant.

The jeweler Vassilis Portokallis (now living in Chicago) had a shop on İstiklal Caddesi (Pasaj Kristaki), and was also a witness to the events.

At age 27, I had a modern *atelier* on the third floor of the Stoa Chrêstakê in which I made "genuine" and "imitation" European jewelry, which for the most part I sold in the store of my uncle Leandros Williams, whose shop was on the corner of İstiklal Caddesi and Stoa Chrêstakê, opposite the pistachio and fruit store of Mustafa and Niazi....

At about 7:45 PM, we began to hear a hubbub of the daily sort common to the Stoa, which houses the beerhalls and the stores that sold sheep entrails, shrimps, lobsters, fried mussels, etc. We reckoned that this was one of the customary arguments brought on by the misunderstandings that the aromatic ouzo occasions. Suddenly, the voices seemed to become angrier and louder.[56]

Accordingly, Portokallis sent his assistant to investigate; on his return, the latter breathlessly cried out that, "The university students are smashing the windows and the shops. Come down and let us get out in time."[57] Once outside, they saw throngs of men led by a youth, who indicated the addresses of the stores, most of which were closed at the time. The mob came nearer as it approached the restaurant Degustation, next to which was the shop of Portokallis's uncle. The young Portokallis went to stand in front of his uncle's store to protect it, whereupon his neighbor, the pistachio-seller Mustafa, came over to him. He was a Muslim Albanian, but he lived with a Greek woman. He took Portokallis away and brought him across the street, from where he could safely view what was about to happen to his uncle's store.

I watched as the demonstrators filled their pockets with the imitation jewelry, cosmetics, and women's scarves....In a few minutes, the shop was completely empty, with smashed remains about and my uncle's hat hanging on the wall....Presently, I ran to

[55] *Ibid.*, p. 54. See also Knudsen, quoted by Chrêstidês on p. 59; then Chrêstidês quotes *Hürriyet* of 9/7/55.

[56] Tsoukatou, *Septemvriana*, #3, pp. 69-70.

[57] *Ibid.*, p. 69.

Aynalı Çeşme Street, where Uncle Williams lived....[O]n the way
I passed by the Balık Pazarı [the famous Fish Market] and saw the
Nea Agora and Artemis destroyed. At that moment I saw a man
carrying away a lamb on his shoulder from the nearby butcher
shop, while holding a head of *kaseri* [cheese]. Others who were
better organized came with pickup trucks, on which they loaded
the merchandise from the two largest grocers of Pera....

I returned once more to Pera, going toward Santa Maria
next to which was the most luxurious store of Kourtelês, which
sold women's clothing and undergarments....On my way, I saw
destroyed the shops of my friends Tsitourês, Veletsos, Kontaxês and
others....I passed in front of TAE [the Greek airline office]...it was
completely denuded, only walls and ceiling. Further on, I passed by
the smoldering church of the Holy Trinity.[58]

Lilika Kônstantinidês and her husband owned Kristal, a large store that
sold crystal, glassware, and kitchenware in Babuk Pazarı on Teatro Street.
They had closed their shop for the evening at 7:00 PM, and made their way
to their dwelling on Sıraselviler. En route, they ran into the demonstrators.
Upon arriving at their home, their Turkish employee informed them that
the vandalism had already begun, and since the same was occurring on
Sıraselviler, her husband returned to the store. He managed to get back before
the mob arrived. He unlocked the door, hoisted the Turkish flag, threw off
the rope ladder so that rioters could not reach the store's upper shelves, turned
off the electricity, and returned home, giving whatever money he had in the
store to his wife. He then came back to the neighborhood where his shop was
to see what would happen:

In a little while, a group of fifteen to twenty people passed by,
pulled down the flag and tore it to shreds...and, with tools they
had brought from Anatolia for this occasion, cut up the shutters of
the store, entered through the smashed windows, began to smash
everything in the store, and soon departed. Then a second group
came shortly thereafter, again made up of some fifteen to twenty
persons, entered through the window, and began to smash.

My husband was watching from across the street as twenty
years of labor was reduced to ruins.

A Turkish neighbor tapped him on the back and said to him:
"Leave. You cannot do anything, you will simply become sick."
And so he departed.

---

[58] *Ibid.*, pp. 69-70; *Hürriyet*, 9/7/55, in Chrêstidês, *Ekthesis*, p. 56, relates that those houses of
prostitution run by Greeks were damaged and the prostitutes thrown out on the streets naked.

One can imagine in what state he returned home. We sat in the dark, saying nothing. Outside the world was coming to an end. It was then that he said to me: "We must leave, for it is the third time that they destroy me. The first time was military service, which in fact was not military service but captivity in Anatolia for a year and a half. The second time was the tax on my estate [the *varlık vergisi*], which was confiscatory so that they might take our business. And now this; it's frightful."[59]

In the end, her husband went to Athens and bought property there; by April 1957, the couple had left Istanbul. Kônstantinidês concluded: "We were among the first to depart. Later began the mass departure. In this manner did the city empty. Thus died Pera, which was a small European city and our pride, and became the worst province of Turkey."[60]

The Greek dentist Anestês Chatzêandreou had a similar experience. Although Chatzêandreou lived in Yeşilköy, his clinic was in Beyoğlu. He spent the evening of September 6 with his wife, first visiting his sister, who also lived in Yeşilköy, and then at his home. The pogrom struck the neighborhood that night, and the couple had a difficult time getting back to their house. After a certain hour, they could see the fires of Beyoğlu lighting up the sky; the next day, he went to his office with a heavy heart.

> As soon as I saw the sight of destruction of twenty years of labors, I repeatedly felt that I would faint. I managed with great effort to stand upright on my feet for half an hour and then I felt a deathly silence all about me. Before entering my clinic, I gazed about me and saw that the street was full of smashed objects of every type: furniture, vessels, windows, clothes, etc., and I shuddered. Then, as I walked forward, I found the iron door of the clinic smashed and the doors of the two rooms from the hall also smashed. All the machines, furniture, medical tools of the clinic and waiting rooms destroyed...the office and the headlight and lighting fixtures destroyed...as well as my framed diplomas from the university and the *Megalê tou Genous Scholê* smashed...missing also were the gold dentures prepared for my patients, as was a suit, two pairs of shoes, a gold pocket watch (a memento from my father)....I departed with my soul mortally wounded.[61]

Chatzêandreou eventually fell into a depression and left Turkey forever two years later.

[59] Tsoukatou, *Septemvriana*, #16, p. 102.
[60] *Ibid.*, p. 102.
[61] *Ibid.*, #28, pp. 137-138.

Leônidas Koumakês records the experience of his father, who left his home on Enli Yokuşu and Kalyoncu Kulluk to go to his shop in Beyoğlu, which he closed at 7:00 PM on September 6, only to be accosted physically by five demonstrators who beat him badly. It was only the passing of a car with a screaming siren that momentarily distracted his attackers and allowed the badly hurt Koumakês to melt into the crowd in the ensuing confusion. It took him two hours to struggle back to his nearby home.[62]

From these isolated case histories of individuals on and about İstiklal Caddesi, we get a picture of a carefully prepared agenda of physical violence. The Greek newspaper *Makedonia* kept tabs on the number and names of destroyed Greek establishments and, less than two weeks after the pogrom, listed the names and owners of 113 Greek shops destroyed on İstiklal Caddesi.[63] British *chargé* Michael Stewart reported great damage inflicted on the Greek business community on that thoroughfare:

> The most concentrated damage was inflicted on the Rue de Pera [İstiklal Caddesi], the main shopping centre of Istanbul. In this street 250 shops and restaurants were wrecked more or less completely. Shops of other minority communities and foreigners suffered with the Greeks. Only 97 shops—all belonging to Moslem Turks—escaped. The shops wrecked included most of the better class clothing, jewellery, and glass and china shops and shops selling household appliances. Elsewhere damage mainly fell on small retailers and craftsmen....
>
> Apart from these cases practically no damage has been done to major industrial establishments. Much of Istanbul's light industry, however, is still carried on by the small craftsmen, many of them Greeks and these trades have suffered severely. The private foundry industry consisting of thirty small workshops owned by Greeks has been practically destroyed and all the machinery and moulds stolen. A hundred and fifty workers are unemployed. There are about two thousand Greek shoemakers in Istanbul and most of these have had their premises destroyed. Many small printing shops have been broken up and the machinery smashed, throwing about four hundred workers out of work. At the same time the demand for chairs and tables for catering establishments and also for domestic furniture is exceptionally high as thousands of people are endeavoring to restore homes wrecked by the rioters. Prices for furniture have been raised and the Turkish carpenters who

[62] Leônidas Koumakês, *The Miracle: A True Story*, Athens, 1995, pp. 183-185.
[63] *Makedonia*, 9/15/55. The issue of 9/13/55 lists the churches by name, that is, seventeen churches, one *agiasma*, and "many other churches."

produce the inferior grades of domestic furniture are enjoying a period of unprecedented prosperity.

The figures of unemployment can only be approximate as most of them relate to small-scale industries and one-man businesses. To those already given must be added about two thousand seven hundred waiters and other restaurant staff said to have been thrown out of work by the destruction of places of entertainment. Much of this unemployment will only be temporary, but many small craftsmen whose imported tools and machines have been destroyed will have great difficulty in resuming business.[64]

One can close this section on the destruction of İstiklal Caddesi by returning to the description in Aziz Nesin's mournful account. After having deposited his drinking friend, Mansour, now suffering from a heart condition, at the latter's home in Koska (a district that was still being looted and vandalized in the early morning hours of September 7), Nesin sets out on foot for Beyoğlu, across the Golden Horn. Thus, he witnesses the tragic spectacle of the main business boulevard on the morning of the seventh, while the first efforts are being made by street cleaners to clear the streets and sidewalks (subsequently memorialized in many photographs).

> I walked through Beyoğlu on foot. As I have said previously, most of İstiklal Caddesi had risen in elevation twenty to thirty centimeters from the foodstuffs and fabric that had been thrown out on the street. But what really attracted my attention was the discarded old shoes. Most of the shoes had been pressed down at the heel at the back end of the shoe [a Turkish way of wearing them], there were shoes that were torn and ragged and with holes, boots, army shoes, light peasant shoes, *çarıks* [peasant footwear], buttoned boots, boots without shoelaces, rubber shoes, etc. Their very sight was repulsive, and they stank so much that in passing by them I had to hold my breath.[65]

Nesin first thought that these countless pairs of discarded shoes were the result of the madness and violence of the pogrom, in the enthusiasm of which they had come off because of the rioters' violent exertions. But as he thought more about the matter, he realized that the vandals had taken advantage of the opportunity to walk away, literally, with this immediately applicable booty, thus ridding themselves of their old, tattered footwear. After all, Nesin

---

[64] TNA:PRO, FO 371/117712, no. 202E, 10/5/55.
[65] Aziz Nesin, *Asılacak adamlar*, p. 28.

concluded, it is easier to walk away with a pair of shoes than to try and wear a refrigerator.[66]

EYEWITNESS ACCOUNTS: THE NEW CITY

Beyond the attacks on Beyoğlu and İstiklal Caddesi, however, there is the broader—and difficult—issue of simultaneity. To what degree, in other words, were the attacks synchronized, as separate but closely interrelated actions over a wide area of Istanbul and its suburbs, and to what degree were they, on the contrary, a phenomenon that was spread from the business center to other areas by the same groups of attackers.[67] Whereas the central massive meeting at and attack on Taksim Square and İstiklal Caddesi were of such magnitude that Taksim seems to have been a major terminal of very large groups from areas to the north, east, west, and south (e.g., Dolmabahçe, Pangaltı, Tepebaşı)—as well as for large numbers of provincials mustered for the occasion—after the initial violence around Taksim, many groups proceeded down İstiklal Caddesi and its smaller side streets. At the same time, many of these groups spread out into neighborhoods and districts to the north of Taksim.[68] Ultimately, many of the large original groups reappeared actively in other regions of Beyoğlu. Thus, it is possible that a major segment of the people originally assembled at Taksim attacked central Beyoğlu.

On the other hand, according to a number of sources,[69] attacks on Greek and other minority property in such distant neighborhoods as Yedikule, Samatya (in the old city), Bakırköy (Makrochôri), and Yeşilköy were already underway at about 7:00 PM, or at the same time that the torrent of demonstrators had become active in Taksim and İstiklal Caddesi. This evidence points, clearly, to a simultaneous outbreak of violence over a very large area.[70] Although US ambassador Warren's report indicated that the massive group at Taksim split into two separate groups moving off into two different directions, it merely described the breakdown of these two larger groups into smaller sub-groups. The same larger group could carry out attacks

[66] *Ibid.*, p.29; see also the Chronopoulos report to the Greek foreign ministry, on the discarded shoes of the demonstrators, Ypourgeion Exôterikôn, *Ios fakellos*, 35,000-40,000, *Tourkia* 4, 1955, G4, *Epeisodia genika*, 9/10/44.

[67] Since I have not been able to see the complete text of the security-police report to the martial-law authorities of General Fahrettin Aknoz on September 9, 1955, I have necessarily reconstructed events from the various other reports to which I have had access, such as, for example, Chrêstidês, Dosdoğru, the decisions of the Yassıada trials, and the British and US diplomatic reports.

[68] National Archives, Foreign Office Dispatch No. 228, American Embassy, December 1, 1955.

[69] See above.

[70] See above.

in different districts by splitting up. One report even spells out the process by which larger groups split into smaller groups of fifteen to fifty persons, which then could and did reunite with the larger groups containing as many as 5,000 individuals, which, in turn, were united with other larger groups as they moved from one district to the other.

Ertuğrul Ünal, in *Milliyet*, remarked both on the separation of the various groups attacking property and on the movement of the same groups in a manner which answers our question. We have already seen from the testimony of such eyewitnesses that at the same time that minority establishments were being destroyed in Beyoğlu, other groups were attacking Greek houses and shops in Pangaltı, Sıraselviler, Kumkapı, Bakırköy, and Yeşilköy. Since Beyoğlu was the center of the greatest destruction, it would be profitable to attempt a brief survey leading out of İstiklal Caddesi/Taksim in all directions, eastward to the Bosphorus at Dolmabahçe, south to the Golden Horn, westward to Tepebaşı, and north/northwest to Meşrutiyet, Tarlabaşı, Kalyoncu Kulluk, Kurtuluş, Şişli, Feriköy, Dolapdere, Osmanbey, and Maçka.

Returning once more to Aziz Nesin's nocturnal wanderings, he first becomes aware of the violence and destructive nature of the demonstrations while he and his drinking companion are at the İzmir restaurant in Tepebaşı, across from the old Public Theater (now long destroyed), north of İstiklal Caddesi:

> As we were talking, we heard the cries, "Cyprus is Turkish and Shall Remain Turkish," at times rising and at times falling in volume, but they never ceased shouting it, like some musical background, like a choir. But we paid no attention…darkness had fallen and we assumed eventually the demonstration would be dissolved.…
>
> What time was it? Maybe ten, but it could also have been twelve.…One part of the glass door of the restaurant İzmir slammed open against the wall, and a young man wrapped in a Turkish flag that waved in the wind entered like a typhoon. A group followed, about ten or fifteen entered with him, the remainder stayed outside on the street. One of them had one hand stretched out in front (holding the staff of the flag within which the young man was wrapped), and his other hand behind him, directing the group. They entered the restaurant step by step…there were [now] about forty or fifty, and behind them were still others. What kind of people were these men…dressed in tatters, their hair disheveled, ragged. And with their voices hoarse, they howled.…
>
> The customers of the restaurant got out in a hurry.…
>
> The restaurant-owner had gotten on top of an empty table

at the back and had made a kind of shield from a huge framed photograph of Atatürk. He hid behind his "shield" and, at small intervals, he would raise his head a little above the picture and, whining, plead: "This is not a Greek restaurant." He swore this upon everything sacred and holy...and then he would again hide his head behind his "shield"...then he would say that he was a Turk and a Muslim....

You [Nesin is now addressing his reader], how many photographs of Atatürk can a small shop have?...two, three? No, yet more! The owner of the restaurant...addressing himself to the waiters, ordered:

"Quickly, bring photographs of Atatürk!...the [rest] of the mob was now rapidly advancing into the restaurant....[E]ventually, the owner held two pictures of Atatürk in his hands and all the waiters had in their hands, in turn, the remaining photos of the restaurant. These were photographs with huge gilt frames, carved, wooden, rectangular, oval, encased in glass, some without frames, of varying sizes and of great variety: Atatürk in military or civil dress, with boots, with a hat or fez...that is to say the owner was a man of foresight....

I do not know whether or not the owner was a Turk and Muslim, but he spoke the Turkish of Istanbul without any accent...and as the owner protested, "I am a Turk and Muslim and I am with you," each time he did so, there would reverberate the crashing noise of the smashing of windows, plates, everything.[71]

Nesin manages to help his sick companion get out of his chair, and the two make their way out of the restaurant and into the street through the enraged mob, all to the tune of smashing sounds and the general destruction of that night. Nesin recognizes the leader of this particular group as a drifter whom he had gotten to know in prison during one of Nesin's many political incarcerations by various Turkish governments. Once outside the restaurant, the two companions realize that all hell has broken loose in Istanbul. They have a difficult time crossing the street because of the terrible traffic and congestion of sidewalks and streets, and also because the street here, too, is full of cheese, marmalade, olive oil, dried fruits, canned food, foodstuffs, honey, salami, sausages, pastries, chocolates, sandwiches, and beverages. All this has been pressed by the passing traffic and pedestrians into a muddy slime. As the two men carefully make their way across a street, they notice a fat, middle-aged woman walking in front, who turns and looks at them with

[71] Nesin, *Asılacak adamlar*, pp. 18-20.

apprehension: "She held a long-haired fur in her arms and was also chanting, 'Cyprus is Turkish and Shall Remain Turkish.' Who knows where she had gotten this fur while crying out, 'Cyprus is Turkish and Shall Remain Turkish.' Lowering her voice, she turned off from the street to one of the darker alleys and disappeared." Later, Nesin muses about the seeming incongruity of demonstrating for a Turkish Cyprus while stealing an expensive fur. He comments that the middle-aged woman had elaborated a new variant on the "patriotic" slogan on Cyprus: "The fur is mine and shall remain mine."

Nesin's acerbic humor asserts itself again later. He observes a vagabond-demonstrator who has stolen a bottle of *raki* from a Migros store (a Swiss concession, many of which were wagons) belonging to a minority merchant. The demonstrator is drunk and, either because of his inebriated state or because of a cynicism born of a difficult and penniless life, he, too, parodies the familiar slogan: "Migros is Turkish and Shall Remain Turkish."[72]

B. E. also passed through Tepebaşı during the height of the violence: "First I reached Galatasaray, then turned right towards the British consulate sitting in the middle of a vast garden and surrounded by high walls....Along the boulevard were numerous stores owned by Greeks. They were destroyed, without exception, and on the corner the beautiful men's fashion center looked as if it had been under heavy bombardment and was completely destroyed."[73] He also went to the Russian consulate, just east of İstiklal Caddesi, where he witnessed the looting of the nearby "Syrian Market" and saw the "fierce looting....Inside that huge building were large and luxurious stores owned by Jews. That night all those stores were looted and destroyed."[74] (The British consul reported that vandalism near the consulate was first noted at 8:00 PM in an open-air theater.[75])

The most comprehensive description of the violence in this area that I have examined so far is the testimony of the Greek sailor, Ioannês G. Spetsiôtês, who had gone to Istanbul to bring back his son, Constantine, whom he first saw during Easter week of 1955. He then stayed three months with his son after the latter had finished his military service in the Turkish army. About a little more than two weeks before the pogrom, he had returned to Istanbul to bring his son to Greece. The arranged date of departure happened to be September 6; understandably, their departure was delayed until September 8, after which Spetsiôtês was immediately deposed by the

[72] *Ibid.*, p. 24.
[73] B. E./Khosdegian, "A Historical Night," III, p. 9; for examples of destruction on Hamalbaşı Boulevard, Tsoukatou, *Septemvriana*, pp. 157-158.
[74] B. E./Khosdegian, "A Historical Night," III, p. 12.
[75] TNA:PRO, FO 371/117711, no. 193, 9/22/55.

Greek foreign ministry.

> During my stay in Istanbul I happened to be an eyewitness to the
> sorrowful events. Specifically, those things which I witnessed are
> as follows. On the evening of 9/6/55, I was in the neighborhood
> of Tarlabaşı. I saw Turkish trucks going up and down the streets,
> stopping in front of houses, and the people in the trucks yelling
> out to those in the houses to come out, to raise the Turkish
> flag, and cry out, "Long live Turkey"....When the occupants of
> the houses did not comply, the men in the trucks entered the
> dwellings and then destroyed their windows, and threw out their
> belongings and clothes, leaving them in their pajamas. While all
> this was going on, the police would clap their hands in approval
> and they made no effort whatever to interfere so as to restore
> order. Quite the opposite, when the demonstrators could not find
> the doors of entry into the dwellings and stores, the police would
> inform them where they could enter. By way of example, in the
> case of the church of the Euangelistria, they were not able to break
> down the door in front, so the police showed them the back door,
> which they broke and entered. After they had looted the church,
> they set fire to it. They took away the priestly vestments and
> stoles and, tying them to the back of their trucks, dragged them
> around the streets. They also took away the communion chalices
> and transformed them into bells of the type that garbage men
> use on the streets. They also took away the bells of the church.
> In the large commercial stores, they would enter and would put
> on clothing and take whatever they wanted and load their trucks.
> As for the remainder of the clothes and fabrics, they would cut
> them up into small pieces so as to destroy everything completely.
> As for the shoe stores, they would put as many of the shoes in
> their trucks as they wanted, and wore new shoes, and left their
> own old shoes in exchange. All the new shoes that remained, they
> threw into the streets. The pastry and other shops, they destroyed
> completely, both the merchandise and the furniture. Generally,
> in all stores, they scattered the goods into the streets, which were
> filled with discarded beans, sugar, rice, etc.[76]

Spetsiôtês adds that, on the following day (September 7), he saw Turks
beat an Armenian almost to death in front of his own family before police
intervened.[77]

---

[76] Ypourgeion Exôterikôn, no. 40300, *Tourkia 4, Epeisodia genika*, protocol no. 2757/29/3,
9/20/55.
[77] Noel Barber records the vicissitudes of an elderly Greek widow, seventy years of age, who

The nearby street of Kalyoncu Kulluk was also the scene of attacks on Greek dwellings and stores.[78] The apartment of the Koumakês family, whose father had been severely beaten outside his shop, was located at the edge of that street and Teatro Street. It was bombarded by rocks. Unexpectedly, however, the attackers were redirected from further violence by the appearance of the wife of the priest, Papa Eftim, on her own balcony across the street. She literally ordered the attackers to desist and told them that the apartment was occupied by Turks. The Kristal store owned by the Kônstantinidêses, however, which happened to be in the same building as the Koumakês apartment, was completely destroyed.[79] The destruction was similarly complete along Meşrutiyet Boulevard, which, according to *Makedonia*, had 27 vandalized or destroyed Greek stores.[80]

Shifting our focus to the districts immediately to the southeast of İstiklal Caddesi, specifically, to Kumbaracı Caddesi, we observe a continuation of the large group that was destroying the former boulevard. Kumbaracı Caddesi intersects İstiklal Caddesi from the southeast, as it ascends and joins it at the site of the Galatasaray school. The following description comes from the voluntary memorandum prepared by Reverend Walter B. Wiley, pastor of the Dutch Chapel near the school; it was forwarded to Washington by American consul Arthur Richards, who welcomed the report as an "impartial eyewitness account...of interest and value."

> About eight PM cars with banners...came down through Istiklal Cad. With shouts of "Cyprus is Turkish" and "Long live the Turks." Soon gangs of men and boys came along from the direction of Galata Saray shouting and talking. They surged down Kumbaraci Sok. and demolished a Greek Bookstore [*sic*] and another shop or two nearby. Crowds began to gather on the avenue above to watch. Then the attacking mob came back and threw stones through the plate glass windows at Lebon's on the

lived in Tarlabaşı. "Mrs. Argyropoulos was alone in her home when eight demonstrators broke in and entered and systematically threw every single stick of furniture into the streets, including her piano and bed, from the apartment windows. Then they took all the clothes from her wardrobe and burned them, and threw the food from the pantry on top of the floor." TNA:PRO, FO 371/11772, 9/21/55, simply a copy of his article that appeared in the *Daily Mail*, 9/14/55.

[78] Tsoukatou, *Septemvriana*, #16, pp. 101-102. On the northern side of the Golden Horn, a little more than a mile away in the small Greek community of Hasköy, the demonstrators wrecked the church of Saint Paraskeue and looted the Greek houses, Tsoukatou, *Septemvriana*, #31, p. 143; Palaiologos, *Diagramma*, p. 15.

[79] Tsoukatou, *Septemvriana*, #45, pp. 103-105.

[80] *Makedonia*, 9/17/55.

corner. From there they surged down the street and attacked the French-American Bookstore, breaking the windows and door, and then pulling the books out all over the street. Then they came back and began to demolish Lebon's sweetshop. Before the night was over Lebon's was completely cleared out.

The cloth shops at the south end of the Swedish consulate property were next in turn. One of them was a new one, recently opened by the widow of the former owner of the electrical shop there. Yards and yards of expensive material were pulled into the street while they tried tugs-of-war to tear it to pieces. Ends were tied to the rear bumper of cars driving through and dragged around the streets as long streamers.

A silver shop across the street from us was broken into, the iron shutters or curtain battered with sticks and rocks and then with long board rams until they buckled and then torn out from the sides. The showcases inside were smashed with sticks and stones, and then the silverware from the cases and shelves swept onto the floor and kicked around. Then everything was thrown out through the broken storefront onto the street, stamped upon, battered with sticks, banged against a car that stood just at one side, and then dropped in the street. Up to this point there was very little if any stealing. The store's night-watchman came and threw the battered silverware back into the store, and prevented odd prowlers from going in. Many paraders in the street carried framed pictures or busts of Ataturk or Celal Bayar in their arms. People on the sidewalk watching clapped and shouted as the marauders went from shop to shop. Flags were displayed from shops everywhere and many paraded in the streets.

Then about 9:30 came our turn. The mob concentrated on the Palavidis Shoe Store, occupying the two floors below us. The Turkish flag was prominently displayed on the staff on the outside. The building there is supported by two iron posts, allowing for a small arcade around the glass door and windows. At night prettily designed wire cages fence off the space between the posts. These they tore from their fastenings and threw into the street. Then with stones and clubs and long heavy boards they proceeded to shatter the plate glass windows and door. Surging into the store, they dragged the men's haberdashery and women's scarfs [sic] into the street and pulled it [sic] to pieces. Then they went through the store pulling boxes of shoes from the counters and shelves, smashing everything that would break. The crew of men serving the store with Mr. Palavidis, all Greeks, retreated to the second floor, and then as the crowed surged up the stairway, locked themselves in his office at the front. In the next fifteen minutes all of them disappeared. When the crowd tried to batter in the office door Mr. Palavidis opened it and stepped out, calling "Long live the Turks." He grabbed someone and kissed him on both cheeks, and they let the half dozen men go out. On the way, seeing men put on shoes and two or three raincoats apiece, he lost control of himself and tried to pull them away. A fist fight threatened, which brought him to himself, and they left, abandoning everything. This morning no coats are left....

About eleven, while the mob was demolishing shop after shop all around us, I called the American consulate to report what we supposed was a fairly local disturbance. While I was talking, the janitor rushed in to say that the store under us was afire....[W]hile we were calling, a hose and ladder and then a pump, which were in the street, came to us and got busy. The fire was out in five minutes....

The little bookstore across the street which belongs to a White Russian woman who...had become a Moslem Turkish citizen, was pried open and the books scattered over the street. A large car parked in front of it was battered as much as sticks and clubs and stones could do it, and then overturned. Many coming by took their whack at it. Later when the cloth shops across from the Swedish Consulate were smashed and the goods pulled out into the street, and there seemed little left to do, another car parked at that point was beaten up and overturned. We saw a third one in like condition a block up the street.[81]

Richards singled out one bit of information in the pastor's report that he considered most significant: "Mr. Palavidis told me that he had been told by the Chief of Police, with whom he supposes he was on the closest of good terms, on Thursday ten days ago that something like this was to happen, and advised him to stay in the country with his family."[82] The analysis at this point has attempted to follow, and sketch in detail, the violence in central Beyoğlu from Taksim in the north, to Tünel, Galata, and Karaköy in the south, and from Tepebaşı in the west to the regions of Tophane, Cihangir, and Dolmabahçe in the south. In the course of his peregrinations, B. E. proceeded from central Beyoğlu to Tünel and Yüksek Kaldırım. "In Yuksek Kaldirim," he commented, "I saw looted stores of the

---

[81] National Archives, Foreign Office Dispatch No. 108, American Consul General, Istanbul September 14, 1955.
[82] *Ibid.*

poor and middle class Jews who had nothing to do with Cyprus."[83] The bookstores of Patriarcheas and Sergiadês in Tünel appear in the first list of stores that submitted requests for compensation.[84] The testimony of the Greek businessman, Athênodôros Tsoukatos, on the disastrous fate of his businesses is revealing:

> With the compensation that I received for twenty-six years of bookkeeping services for the brothers D. and K. Plakas at the "Ekselsiyor," I bought an old store at Yüksek Kaldırım, which I razed to the ground and built a modern three-storey store. In this store, which I named Eifel, I sold radios, refrigerators, lighting fixtures, and other goods. I bought these wholesale directly from the importers....
>
> My business was doing very well and, as my capital had increased greatly by the end of the second year, I opened a second store at Tünel in Pera, the Great Ekselsiyor, which sold clothing, men's overcoats, women's clothing, jackets, trousers, etc.
>
> In this store, I also had partners and the company was known as Büyük Ekselsiyor A. Cukatos ve Ortakları K. S. The customers at the Eifel in Galata also became customers of the new store and business was very good. Unfortunately, this did not last long. In 1955 occurred the lamentable events of September 6-7, as a result of which the store was destroyed, along with all of its merchandise, valued at over 300,000 lira at the time.
>
> The Eifel store was also destroyed, and I was accordingly completely destroyed. This latter store remained standing but was completely empty.
>
> As if this were not enough, there also came the audit of the tax authorities. Because of the general destruction of both stores, the account ledgers were also destroyed. Because of this, my accounts were audited without the benefit of ledgers. As all my merchandise was destroyed, I obviously could not have made a profit. Nevertheless, the tax authorities forced me to pay taxes on profits of 100,000 lira.
>
> I was then forced to sell my building at Yüksek Kaldırım, the Eifel, to pay the taxes. This, too, was not enough, and the furniture from my home, even my bed, was confiscated.
>
> Thus, I remained without work for awhile. I was forced to seek employment in my profession of bookkeeper. For a considerable period, I kept the books of many merchants whom I had known, and at the end, before I was expelled from Turkey, I kept the books

---

[83] B. E./Khosdegian, "A Historical Night," III, p. 10.
[84] *Makedonia*, 9/17/55.

of a Turkish shipowner.

On September 9, 1955, the *epoptês* (overseer) of the ecclesiastical district of Galata-Ortaköy (Mesochôrion), Bishop Gregory of Daphnousia, submitted a written report to Patriarch Athênagoras and the patriarchal synod on the damages to the Greek churches, schools, and shops of the community of Galata:

> *Community of Galata. The Church of Christos Soter*
> Not even the hand or pen of a painter, even of the most capable, could properly describe the vandalism, the religious pillaging and the complete destruction of this church. Nothing from the church has been left standing. All the holy vestments and gospels were either stolen or destroyed and the sacred vessels have been scattered. The great icons and the chandeliers were thrown down, together with the pews, candelabra, and lecterns. The holy pulpit and episcopal throne were torn down and destroyed. The glass of all the windows was smashed by rocks hurled from outside. It was impossible to save anything of the holy objects. Such were the mania and madness of the barbarians that they came back twice and, despite the proclamation of martial law, completed the labor of pillaging and destruction so that now there are in evidence only the bare columns of the holy church and nothing else....
>
> After the desecration of the holy church and its complete destruction, to the degree that it appeared to have been bombed from the inside, they [the vandals] broke into the offices of the church's governing board, sacked it, and broke open the safe containing the church's money.
>
> Then they ascended to the cells of the priest, of the *neokoros* [subdeacon], of the *Philoptochos* Society, and finally of the bishop, destroying everything, howling all sorts of coarse blasphemies and insults against our holy religion and our people. They threatened to strangle our bishop, whom they encountered on the way.
>
> *The Holy Church of Saint Nicholas*
> At that same time, 7:30 PM, yet another wild mob, consisting of about 300 individuals, attacked the holy church of St. Nicholas, breaking down its doors with iron crowbars and then entering unrestrained, cursing our people and the church with unmentionable words.
>
> There, they desecrated and destroyed everything so that the holy icons and all other things were smashed to bits, but as they were in a hurry to depart, they left the pulpit and the episcopal throne alone....

The Church of St. John of the Chians
Herein they carried out the same labors of destruction and
arson....

The School of Galata
At the same moment, yet another barbaric mob attacked the
beautiful marble school of Galata, where it destroyed the student
desks, the kitchen, the gymnasium, offices, and the rooms of the
director.

The Stores
Practically all the stores of the Greeks were destroyed, not only
those of the Greeks of Galata but of all of them, which had
constituted a real ornament of the city. Such were the arson and
destruction that one imagined that it was a day in some war. In
the midst of the city, the streets were choking with ruins and with
shredded objects from the stores, scattered in disorderly manner
so that one could pass through the streets and alleys of Galata only
with great difficulty. Storeowners and other Christians wailed and
wept before all the monasteries [*sic*] and stores, lamenting their
unspeakable disaster.[85]

The correspondent from the *Basler Nachrichten* described the spectacle,
on the morning of September 7, of the street that led up to Tünel and
connected it with the port: "It [the street] had been transformed into a pile
of ruins. Watches, cameras, fabric, automobile tires, destroyed refrigerators,
radios, and countless shoes, parts of furniture and chairs, torn dresses, and
an abundance of smashed windows covered the streets."[86] Ertuğrul, writing
in *Milliyet*, confirms all this. By 7:30, the streets of Bankalar (now Voyvoda),
Fermeneceler, Perşembe Pazarı and other neighborhoods witnessed massive
destruction of Greek and other minority property. Practically all the Greek
stores were damaged or destroyed, and, at some point, the first fires broke out
in Karaköy.[87]

The neighborhoods of Tophane, Cihangir, Kabataş, Dolmabahçe, and
Beşiktaş form a rough triangle that is bounded in the west by the Boulevard
Defterdar Yokuşu-Sıraselviler that runs south to north from Tophane to
Taksim Square, a distance of three-quarters of a mile. From Taksim to

---

[85] Greek Embassy, Washington, no. 4311/B/29, 10/21/55. Ypourgeion Exôterikôn, Dept.
of Churches protocol no. 42741 AR 3q, 10/14/55: "Report on the destructions of Galata
Constantinople."
[86] *Basler Nachrichten*, 9/12/55, reproduced in Ypourgeion Proedrias Kyvernêseos, Genikê
Dieuthynsis Typou (Exoterikon Tmêma), *Ektakton Deltion #1*, November 15, 1955, p. 9.
[87] *Milliyet*, 9/19/55.

Dolmabahçe is also about three-quarters of a mile, and the longest leg of this geographical triangle begins at Tophane on the Bosphorus and follows the shoreline a mile to Dolmabahçe and for a small distance to just beyond Beşiktaş to the northeast.

At 5:00 PM on the evening of September 6, Dêmêtrios Kaloumenos found himself at Tophane near Galata, where he saw soldiers removing their military uniforms and putting on civilian clothing, as they were being equipped with crowbars.[88] *Hürriyet* reported demonstrators smashing windows and entering the Greek stores in Tarlabaşı and Yenişehir at that time, while, "at 20:15, the windows of the Greek stores were being smashed in Cihangir."[89] A teacher of the *Megalê tou Genous Scholê* who has remained anonymous, had gone with her husband to visit the principal, who lived in Cihangir, as did his two visitors:

> We passed a pleasant evening there and left before dark, as we decided to return home, which was located on Akarsu Yokuşu near Sıraselviler Boulevard. When we exited from the apartment building in which the principal lived, we were approached by a man who was standing there…from the Security…and speaking to us in broken Greek, he told us not to speak Greek because some demonstrations would take place. Presently, we encountered a group of wild men holding clubs and timbers. Many of them had shaven heads. We immediately moved to a different street, but in this latter street we encountered yet others. And these latter were smashing up a store maniacally. With great difficulty, we reached our house, for no matter which street we chose, we would always encounter raging mobs. At home, we found our mother in a state of terror for she did not know which room would be safer for our four-month-old daughter.
>
> For the [demonstrators] had already passed by and destroyed the three Greek stores there, two groceries and a cleaning establishment, and they had not left windows, doors, or display windows in place.
>
> Across the street was an apartment building where the doorman had removed the sign "Nenopoulos Apartments" and was trying to repel a group that insisted on entering. It was in this building that Iakôvos, the metropolitan of Ikonion, lived. Finally, Tahir Efendi [the doorman] managed to persuade the demonstrators that no priest dwelled there, despite their insistence.…
>
> Considerable time passed before Mr. Panagiôtês, the owner

---

[88] Communicated to the author by Dêmêtrios Kaloumenos.
[89] Quoted by Chrêstidês, *Ekthesis*, p. 58.

of the cleaning establishment, arrived. He wanted to remain to protect the clothes of his customers still in the shop. A policeman and a night-watchman were striking him in the back, telling him to get out, that they would guard the clothes....[F]inally, they persuaded him, and he left. At that moment, these two emptied his store right in front of our eyes.

All night, the Turks who lived on the downward slopes toward Fındıklı were hauling away the merchandise of the two (other) stores by the sackful: rice, sugar, soap, beer, olive oil, and all the rest. By morning, the stores across the street were empty....

Note: On New Year's Eve of the same year, a large wooden house behind our apartment building, which was at the beginning of the road leading down to the port [Tophane] on the right side, had burned down. An entire family lived in each of its rooms. The people who had emptied the Greek stores were members of these families.

In the spring of the following year, the other large house nearby and below Ege Bahçe also burned down. Many Turkish families lived in it also. All of them believe that this [burning] was divine justice [for their stealing the previous September].

Underneath the apartment in which we lived was the shoe store of Alaettin....On the evening of September 6, our mother saw him getting into a truck full of men, as his wife called out to him, "Where are you going?" He signaled for her to be silent. After a few days, we saw his wife wearing luxurious clothes and a fur.[90]

With reference to a few specific incidents, this anonymous narrator has depicted in broad strokes the intensity and widespread nature of the violence in Cihangir. Lilika Kônstantinidês confirms the extent of the destruction of Greek property on Sıraselviler: "When my husband left [to go to their store], the great evil in our neighborhood commenced. The shop windows of the Greeks, Armenians, and Jews were smashed. How strong they were! How easily they removed refrigerators and destroyed them as if they were nothing. Destruction!"[91]

The demonstrators approached the Park Hotel, in full view of Kabataş, having destroyed its pastry shop, and almost proceeded to attack the hotel itself.[92] Bishop Gregory reported on the events at Beşiktaş:

Here, the groups of demonstrators came to the portals of the

---

[90] Tsoukatou, *Septemvriana*, #9, pp. 85-86. This display of newly found wealth is commented on by a number of observers.

[91] *Ibid.*, #16, p. 101.

[92] Chrêstidês, *Ekthesis*, pp. 6-7.

church [of the Panagia] and attempted to open them with iron crowbars. Fortunately, however, a Turkish merchant with some associates confronted them with shouts and repeated requests, and stopped them, and thus the beautiful church of the community of Diplokionion [Beşiktaş] was saved by a miracle. Having been unable to invade this holy church, they turned against the school and the cultural society, in which they destroyed everything. They burned the houses and shops of Neofytos and Euangelidês, members of the community board. Then they opened and destroyed the shops of the marketplace and some Christian houses.[93]

Although there is, at present, less information on the pogrom's consequences in Tophane, Cihangir, Kabataş, and Beşiktaş, there is sufficient evidence to indicate its thoroughness and the widespread destruction.

North of Taksim at a distance of about a mile lies the district of Osmanbey, in which the pogrom was carried out in the by-now familiar pattern, but commenced somewhat later, perhaps a little before 8:30 PM. A fairly detailed and balanced account of its course in the area was recorded by the eyewitness Iôannês Raptês. He was at the home of a friend when the bell rang and the local Turkish grocer hurriedly advised Raptês to park his car inside the nearby garage, which Raptês promptly did:

I ran to the window and saw crazed men in tattered clothes, holding crowbars, clubs, and rocks, breaking the windows of the Greek stores on Osmanbey Street…crying out, "Cyprus is Ours," "Raise flags on the windows," and other such things.

In the blink of an eye, the doors and display windows of the stores were destroyed, and the surface of the street was filled with merchandise. Meanwhile, other Turks, unable to transport the refrigerators outside of the stores, merely destroyed them with axes and crowbars. They destroyed everything, leaving nothing behind.

The destructive mania of the mob went to the extreme of "skinning" the walls and erasing all writing from them. Many of these vandals, since they had nothing more to destroy, would manifest their rage by smashing the already broken part of windows and display windows….

When they had carried out their work and begun to withdraw, another group that had already finished its labors in its district immediately replaced them, and checked to see if the previous

---

[93] Greek Embassy, Washington, no. 4311/B/29, 10/21/55. Ypourgeion Exôterikôn, Dept. of Churches, protocol no. 42741 AK 3a, 10/14/55: "Report on the destructions of Galata Constantinople."

group had left anything still undestroyed...and then followed
with new blows and looting.

Then, and thereafter, the directors—who were the
real leaders—of the destruction would pass by in cars with
photographs of Kemal Atatürk, and the mobs would continue
their cumbersome labors. Each appearance of such an automobile
was received with greetings and applause....

The groups of vandals succeeded one another and the streets
were filled with destroyed pianos, bicycles, and fabrics. We are not
talking about a mob, but about organized companies of vandals.
Merchandise worth millions of dollars was destroyed. And the
police? During the demonstrations, we saw only one soldier and
one policeman, standing by passively....[94]

Demonstrators were equally active in Şişli. An anonymous witness, who
lived in the area, gave a brief account of events:

In 1955, we lived in Şişli, exactly in its center, opposite the
mosque....My father-in-law had a barber shop for many years in
Şişli. They smashed and robbed it. He came home and told us that
at four in the afternoon they were smashing the store windows
in Pangaltı. As it became night, people became uneasy....Our
apartment was on the ground floor and below it was a clothing
store. The first [group] that came by broke our windows and the
store's display windows. The second [group] removed the iron
shutters from the stores and the third entered them, robbed them,
and was ready to set fire to them. But the Turks who lived in our
apartment building saved us....

On the third day, we learned that the Metamorphosis
cemetery was burning and that they had broken open the graves.
We went there because members of our family were buried there.
The church was burned, looted, and the bones thrown out,
smashed, and burned. We all wept.[95]

The cruel fate of the cemetery at Şişli and of its graves and tombs, as well
as of the Church of the Metamorphosis and its ossuary, constitutes one of
the clearest reflections of the religious hatred of the pogromists and of the
significant role this sentiment played in the events. Noel Barber witnessed the
ruined state of the cemetery soon after and, in a secret telegram hidden in his

[94] *Makedonia*, 9/9/55; see Palaiologos, *Diagramma*, p. 6, for Ferıdiye and Parmakkapı, and
Chrêstidês, *Ekthesis*, p. 56, for Yenişehir.
[95] Tsoukatou, *Septemvriana*, #14, p. 97; see also the testimony of Vasilis Portokallis in *Ibid.*,
#3, p. 71, who also went to this cemetery to see the grave of his father on 9/7/55, and then
gave way to uncontrolled weeping.

shoe so that it could be smuggled out of Turkey, described his horror in very few words:

> Finally I went to the funeral at Chichli [*sic*] of an old friend who had been battered to death in her bed.
> *Tombs Wrecked*
> At first I could not believe what I saw. Every single tombstone had been uprooted and smashed, every mausoleum pried open, the contents of every coffin spilled into the streets, where still they lay.
> Bulldozers could not have done a more thorough job. In the Church itself the crosses had been torn down, the altar had been desecrated in a way I would prefer not to describe, and the priceless windows smashed.[96]

Those who had attacked the cemetery, church, and ossuary came from the nearby area of Mecidiyeköy; they destroyed 525 marble graves and burned the church. They removed the coffin of the recently deceased Nikolaos Êliaskos from its mausoleum and pierced the corpse with a sharp iron that was later found still in the body, whereas the upper body bore knife wounds and lacerations. The body was not located for some days, but was finally found and reburied. The graves of the Negropontês, Kopasês, Zarifês, Sideridês, and Skylitzês familes were destroyed, and human excrement was left on many graves.[97]

The December 1 report of Ambassador Warren remarked generally on the attacks on Greek houses and businesses north of Taksim after the general assembly at Taksim Square, when one of the two large groups split off from the main body and began to descend İstiklal Caddesi: "The remaining groups in Taksim moved out toward Kurtulush, Shishli, and Dolap[dere] where they attacked and destroyed Greek owned houses and shops."[98] British *chargé* Stewart reported that, "The Greek residential area of Kurtulush in new Istanbul is badly damaged."[99] *Hürriyet* reported not only Greek houses but also Greek stores being attacked, and damage wreaked on the local church.[100] There are two dramatic accounts of individuals who lived through the pogrom in

---

[96] TNA:PRO, FO 371/117712, 9/21/55, contains the report, for the *Daily Mail*, smuggled out of Turkey by Noel Barber.

[97] Chrêstidês, *Ekthesis*, pp. 64-65; Megas Reumiôtês, *Syrriknosê*, p. 74, who also refers to eating the flesh of the recently deceased.

[98] National Archives, Foreign Office Dispatch No. 228, American Embassy, Ankara, December 1, 1955.

[99] TNA:PRO, F0 371/117711, no. 193, 9/22/55.

[100] *Hürriyet*, 9/7/55, in Chrêstidês, *Ekthesis*, p. 59. The church that was burned was Saint Athanasios. There is passing reference to destruction in this area in the above-cited testimony of Spetsiôtês, Ypourgeion Exôterikôn, *Tourkia* 4, *Epeisodia genika*, protocol no. 2757/29/3, no.

Kurtuluş. The first, Anna Dêmêtriou Doptoglou, was thirteen years of age and lived with her family in an apartment on Kurtuluş Boulevard. Her father, born in Niğde in southeastern Anatolia, had served seven years in the Turkish army.

> Frightened, we gathered in one corner of the house and now heard clearly the voices, together with the noise as they smashed the windows....They were howling and singing marching songs....
>
> They were men with wild faces, very different, resembling wild beasts. With crowbars, stones, or timbers, they attacked the display windows of the stores and broke whatever they found in front of them.
>
> A little further up from our apartment building, there was a clothing store. After they had entered and stolen as much as they could, they tied the rest to the bumpers of two cars, one of which was going up and the other down, so that the clothes were shred into long narrow strips....
>
> At the corner across from the [Greek] bakery of Psilakês, a large, modern grocery had recently opened. They destroyed it completely, leaving only the walls. After they stole and smashed, they flung the rest onto the street, including the refrigerators.
>
> From the other side of the house we saw flames. The churches were burning. We saw the Holy Trinity of Taksim and Saint Demetrios in Kurtuluş....
>
> The houses below the church of St. Demetrios were pillaged and many girls were raped.[101]

The second eyewitness account is rather long and is signed anonymously by "Enas Tataulianos"—that is, a "Tataulian," a resident of Tataula, which was the Greek name for Kurtuluş. He begins by explaining that it is very difficult to remember things that happened thirty-seven years ago when he was a child of seven. On the other hand, he relates, there are certain things that so deeply impress themselves in the mind that one never forgets them. Having lost his mother, he lived with his aunt near Büyük Akarca Street. The tense atmosphere that had enveloped Istanbul in early September had induced widespread anxiety among the city's minorities, and so his widowed aunt had decided that they should go to stay with her older married daughter, who lived near the Church of St. Demetrios in Kurtuluş. Her daughter's house had a massive wooden door and windows on the ground floor that were protected by iron bars. When night came, they began to hear the yelling

40300, 9/20/55. Yet a third church was destroyed, Saint Demetrios, and the Greek cemetery desecrated.
[101] Tsoukatou, *Septemvriana*, #8, pp. 83-84.

of the mob, and then the latter attacking the Church of Saint Demetrios. The family barred the door with furniture and whatever else they could find.

They then moved to a back room of an upper floor, where they tied sheets together in case they had to escape if the front door were knocked down. After the demonstrators had looted and wrecked the Church of Saint Demetrios, they went further downhill, to attack the Church of Saint Athanasios. Because their leaders knew which houses were Greek, they stopped at the house of the young Tataulian and his family, and began trying to open the front door. Angered by their failure to do so, however, they began throwing rocks at all the windows and breaking them:

> In the meantime, as the rocks fell into the living room, they broke the windows but also the furniture and the family glassware....So the mob turned once more to the church....After awhile, we saw enormous flames rising from the church, and they lighted all the neighborhood and were visible until morning....Later [days later], the representatives of the Patriarchate and the government came to examine the damage to the two churches (we then had enough courage to follow them and so to see with our own eyes the damage inflicted by the barbaric mob). I remember very well the image of the burned church of Saint Athanasios, of which only the stone walls remained.[102]

EYEWITNESS ACCOUNTS: THE OLD CITY

This survey of the pogrom throughout new Istanbul gives a picture of a well-organized and vast attack on the Greeks (of both Turkish and Greek citizenship), and on their community's economic, religious, and cultural life. Next, we shall examine the course of attacks in old Istanbul, south of the Golden Horn. A large area, old Istanbul was the site of the original Byzantine city and, therefore, also the heart of Ottoman Istanbul. Connected to Karaköy, Galata, and Beyoğlu by the Atatürk and Galata Bridges, old Istanbul in 1955 was still dotted with Greek communities in Cibalı, Fener, Balat, Balino, and Tahtakapı, along the southern shore of the Golden Horn, with shops and offices stretching out to the coastal regions of Eminönü and Sirkeci as well. Greeks still lived along almost the entire length of the old Byzantine walls that formed a long band along the western edge of the old city: at Tekfur Sarayı and Eğrikapı in Ayvansaray at the walls' northern edge, as well as along Edirnekapı, Topkapı, Silivrikapı, Belgratkapı, and at the southern end of the walls at Yedikule. Istanbul's Greek communities stretched out along the

---

[102] *Ibid.*, #17, pp. 103-106.

southern shore of old Istanbul on the Sea of Marmara from Samatya, Yenikapı, and Kumkapı. Their residences and shops were also scattered from the shores of the Golden Horn into Sirkeci-Eminönü, and around and in Mısır Çarşı, Sultanhamam, Ayasofya, Vefa, Kapak Cami, Gedikpaşa, the Valide mosque, Beyazıt, Aksaray, Muhli, Potiras, and Altı Mermer. Despite the extent of the Greek presence in the old city, the numbers were much smaller than in the new one, as many Greeks had, over the course of the nineteenth and early twentieth centuries, moved out. Nevertheless, the pogrom did not overlook them, and severe destruction ensued here as well.

In his report quoted previously, *Milliyet*'s Veli Sezai Balcı remarked on the violence and complete destruction in Sirkeci, Eminönü, Bahçekapı, Babıali, and Çemberlitaş. *Hürriyet* reported on the same events in a shorter form but somewhat differently:

> An atmosphere akin to the wrath of God fell on Beyazıt and along the entire area from Tahtakale-Sultanhamam. With iron bars tied to wooden beams, the shutters of the windows in the aforementioned areas were destroyed. One saw scattered in the street fabric and other merchandise...and the goods brought out of the stores were parceled out to passersby.
>
> On the other hand, a different group of demonstrators proceeded from Şişhane toward Karaköy and finally across the Galata Bridge to Sirkeci, where in the blink of an eye they destroyed all shops that had not raised a flag....They also destroyed the stores of the Greeks in Eminönü.[103]

Ertogrul Ünal's report, quoted above, says of the pogromists that in a very brief period of time they destroyed the windows and goods of all the Greek shops in Küçükpazar, Tahmis Street, Sultanhamam, and Mahmut Paşa. Nikos Atzemoglou relates that on September 7, he and his father went to examine their store in Eminönü, which sold dried fruit, only to find that "nothing had been left...."[104] On searching the ruins left behind, they soon found two identity cards: one was that of an army officer, while the other was of a member of the Millet Party. (The Millet Party had splintered off from the DP, and there is no further information that, as a group, it participated in the pogrom.) Yet another witness, Nikos Apostolidês, walked to the dried-fruit market next to Mısır Çarşı on Hassırlar Street to check on his father-in-law's shop: "The entire street [was covered] with mud to a height of at least twenty centimeters, which had been kneaded [like dough] with raisins, dried figs,

---

[103] *Hürriyet*, in Chrêstidês, *Ekthesis*, pp. 69-70.
[104] Nikos Atzemoglou, *Mnêmes + Theseis*, Athens, 1999, p. 71.

THE OLD CITY

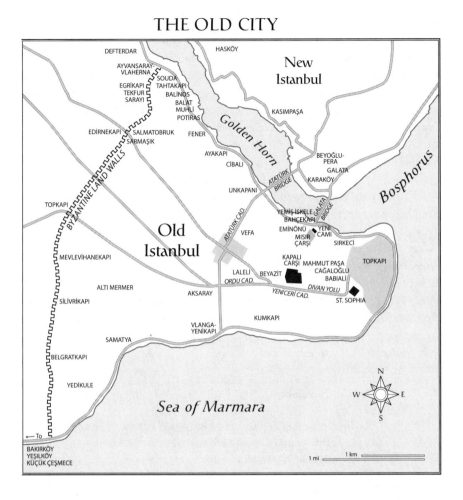

almonds, hazelnuts, etc. The store was empty, all the merchandise out on the streets and his [the father-in-law's] cash box had been smashed."[105]

The destruction along the Sirkeci-Eminönü-Un Kapani boulevards and districts (between Sarayburnu and the Atatürk Bridge) was also being carried out by separate groups along the southern shore of the Golden Horn westward to the areas of Cibalı, Ayakapı, Fener, Balat-Balino, Tahtakapı (Xyloporta or Lonca) to Ayvansaray (Vlacherna), where the land walls meet the Golden Horn. In Cibalı, the rioters largely destroyed the Church of Saint Nicholas, the community school, and the *parekklêsion* and *agiasma* of Saint Charalambos, and they damaged and looted the Greek houses there.[106]

The Fener district was especially and heavily attacked, but the demonstrators were easily driven away from the ecumenical patriarchate by the assembled Turkish troops and police provided earlier by *Vali* Gökay. Nevertheless, even there, some windows were smashed. There was considerable damage inflicted on the *Megalê tou Genous Scholê* and on the Iôakeimeion Girls' School.[107] The churches of Panagia Mouchliotissa and Saint George Potiras (Antiphonetes) were badly damaged.[108] The *metochion* (dependent) church of the patriarchate of Jerusalem, Saint George, came in for its share of destruction as well. Similarly, the Greek houses of the district were vandalized. One eyewitness, Sotêrios Misaêlidês, described what he experienced that night:

> The night of September 6, 1955, will always remain engraved in my memory.
> We lived near the *Megalê tou Genous Scholê*, in Fanari [Fener]. I was a painter and worked at home. I painted icons for the church, but I also did whatever passed into my hands or was ordered.
> That night, we heard a noise from the other side of the Golden Horn, and it began to come close. We understood that it was the Turks who were shouting so we locked ourselves in the house. They finally reached our door and tried to break it down. However, it was made of strong wood and they could not have entered had not our [Turkish] neighbors helped them. Thus they entered through the back door, and we ran out into the

---

[105] Apostolidês, *Anamnêseis*, pp. 237-238; more generally, Megas Reumiôtês, *Syrriknosê*, p. 54. On the significant presence of Greek merchants in Eminönü, Mısır Çarsı, on Tahmis Street, etc., see Melpô Kesisoglou-Karystinou, *Enoria tês Agias Kônstantinoupoleôs Tzimbali*, Athens, 1998, pp. 270-275.

[106] Kesisoglou-Karystinou, *Tzimbali*, pp. 115, 122, and 157.

[107] National Archives, Foreign Office Dispatch No. 132, American Consul General, Istanbul, September 27, 1955.

[108] Tsoukatou, *Septemvriana*, #21, p. 115.

streets. They smashed everything with pickaxes, and took away whatever they wanted.

We went on, to another neighborhood where my father-in-law lived. But the Turks had previously passed by there and had destroyed everything. We returned to our house weeping over our fate. Our life in this city came to an end that night. We picked up our things and departed. No one showed concern over us."[109]

Of equal interest is the eyewitness account of I. Meletiadês, a graduate of the *Megalê tou Genous Scholê*. On September 7, he decided to go see what had happened to his *alma mater* on the previous night. Having examined the destruction in Beyoğlu, he crossed over to Fener, but on reaching the school was forbidden by soldiers from entering since they were now "guarding" it, although it had already been seriously damaged. He next went to the house of a friend in Fener, who took him to see the heavily damaged Church of the Antiphonetes: "So we went…to the church of the *Antiphonetes*. What a sight and horror! You could barely enter it. All the pews were destroyed and scattered on the ground. The large metal candelabra were bent in two. The chandeliers were severed from their supports and had fallen and were scattered about. Candles and other items were thrown down. There was no longer any *iconostasis* or icons. You gazed upon a sight devoid of all hope….What a disgrace!"[110] The Maraslês school, between Ayakapı and the patriarchate, was also severely damaged.[111]

One last tragic detail about the actual physical violence against many Greeks that often characterized the attacks on their houses and stores comes out of the eyewitness account of the anonymous T. I. P. S., and it concerns the then well-known Greek teacher, Alexandros Iatropoulos:

> [A] barbaric and most painful event…related to me by [my] parents, refers to the teacher Alexandros Iatropoulos of blessed memory. That fateful evening…he had gone to visit the family of Nicholas Muratoglou, a well-known wholesale lumber merchant, in the neighborhood of Kiremit on Köroglu Sokak, up on the heights of Fener and next door to the house of my parents.
>
> At sunset, Iatropoulos…[112] left in order to return home, about 100 meters *away*. The unfortunate man did not manage to go more than ten steps before he was suddenly "besieged" by a

---

[109] *Ibid.*, #46, p. 175, taken from the archives of the Syllogos Kônstantinoupolitôn, Athens.

[110] *Ibid.*, #21, p. 115.

[111] Megas Reumiôtês, *Syrriknosê*, p. 54.

[112] Iatropoulos was principle of the Iôakeimeion School for Girls in Fener, Stamatopoulos, *Analampê*, p. 304.

raging and shouting crowd armed with every type of destructive instrument, with clubs and crowbars. They attacked him, grabbed him under his arms, and dragged him on the ground, while others struck him on the head....

The concussions he suffered to his head from the merciless blows...brought about his death after some time."[113]

The evidence is that all of the Greek houses in Fener were attacked.[114] The neighboring Greek community in Balat underwent heavy attack that destroyed forty Greek shops on Balatyan, Vodina, Leblebiciler, Köprübaşı, İskele, and Lapçıncılar Streets. The stores included butcher shops, greengrocers, groceries, charcuteries, dairy shops, a restaurant, clock-repair shop, bar, tavern (i.e., an establishment that served food in addition to drink), shoe stores, a doctor's clinic, blacksmiths, a tailor, paint store, stationer, wine bottler, storage facilities, a wine shop, cafe, candlemaker's shop, hardware store, soap factory, and coopers' shops. H. H., another anonymous witness who was an official of the Balat community and had access to its ledgers, gives the names of the owners and the addresses of the businesses.[115] This catalogue of destroyed shops may well have been taken from the official list of requests for compensation from the appropriate governmental offices. H. H.'s eyewitness testimony also mentions that, "Aside from the aforementioned looted and destroyed Greek stores, there were also destroyed fifty Greek houses, our three Greek churches, and the sexton of the Church of Panagia of Balino, Koutroulês, was hurt, as were many others." He then names the three churches: the Sinaitic *metochion* of Saint John, with the *agiasma* of Saint Menas; Panagia of Balino, with its *agiasma* of Saint Basil; and the Church of the Taxiarchs, with its *agiasma* of Saint Nicholas.[116] He fails, however, to mention the major damages to the local Greek school of Balat.[117] As for the actual compensation itself, H. H. repeats what was a common refrain in many contemporary references: "The Turkish state gave as payment for the damages not quite 10 percent of our actual losses."[118] As a former member of

---

[113] Tsoukatou, *Septemvriana*, #47, pp. 179-180.

[114] Megas Reumiôtês, *Syrriknosê*, p. 54.

[115] Tsoukatou, *Septemvriana*, #26, pp. 127-130.

[116] H. H. also says that after martial law was declared on September 7, he went to the Turkish authorities and accused a local Turk, Talat Bey, of having organized the destruction of the Greek stores in Balat and the latter was arrested. For the destruction of the church of Saints Taxiarchs, National Archives, Foreign Office Dispatch No. 132, American Consul General, Istanbul, September 27, 1955.

[117] National Archives, Foreign Office Dispatch No. 132, American Consul General, Istanbul, September 27, 1955.

[118] Tsoukatou, *Septemvriana*, #26, p. 130.

the *Demokrat Parti* for many years, H. H. found this very little indeed.

In Tahtakapı (Xyloporta-Lonca), immediately to the west of Balat-Balino, both the Church of Saint Demetrios Kanavos and the Greek school suffered major damage.[119] Between the regions of Tahtakapı and Ayvansaray was the important Church of Panagia Vlachernôn. The anonymous T. I. P. S. was taken by the priest Karampodos on the Sunday after the pogrom to view the ruins of the church: "The sight that greeted us can hardly be described. The narthex no longer existed. The interior of the church was leveled to the ground. There was neither *iconostasis* nor pulpit, nor episcopal throne, nor pews, nor lecterns nor icons nor holy altar. Everything was in smithereens. It was impossible to walk there. Father Anthimos and the good sexton, Kyr Stratos, told us what happened, still terrified."[120] Tahtakapı abuts on the region of Ayvansaray (Vlacherna) and on the corner that is formed by the northernmost reaches of the Byzantine land walls and the westernmost part of the Golden Horn. From here south to their terminus just beyond Yedikule at the Sea of Marmara is a distance of about three and a half miles, along much of which Istanbul's Greeks lived, with their houses, businesses, and churches.

Two weeks after the pogrom, when many details were becoming clear, the anonymous reporter (W. E.) of a newspaper in Bern, Switzerland, published a perceptive article on the subject and made special reference to the areas of the land walls, and to the ferocity of the attacks on the Greek churches and houses:

> In regard to the destroyed churches, there are no exact figures. Some churches were burned even after the declaration of martial law....Vandalism manifested itself everywhere and in the same manner. In the old city, between the surviving Patriarchate and Yedikule, one sees only the blackened walls of the churches as though they had been bombed. In the beginning it was believed that private dwellings had not been harmed. But here also the counting/examinations showed great destruction. The house-by-house examination of the Greek dwellings (besides the houses of the other minorities) revealed vast damage. We (ourselves) saw houses where contents had been completely destroyed, even the staircases...had been torn down.[121]

The dispatch goes on to give an estimate of damaged and destroyed houses in

---

[119] *Ibid.*

[120] *Ibid.*, #47, p. 179.

[121] Ypourgeion Proedrias Kyvernêseos, Genikê Dieuthynsis Typou (Exôterikon Tmêma), *Ektakton Deltion #1*, November 15, 1955, p. 22.

that large area of 1,500 Greek dwellings.[122]

The northernmost region of Aksaray-Vlaherna had a small Greek community, all of whose houses, along with the Church of Panagia tes Soudas, were badly damaged.[123] Demonstrators also wrecked and looted the Church of Panagia Chantzirgiotissa at Tekfur Sarayı in Ayvansaray.[124] In Eğrikapı, the Greek houses were attacked by mobs led by two equestrian leaders who had lists of addresses.[125] In the Greek community of Edirnekapı, the mob looted, wrecked, and partly burned the churches of Saint George, the Dormition of the Theotokos, and another church with the same name. They also destroyed twenty-one of the twenty-five Greek dwellings.[126] Not far off, in Salmatobruk, the demonstrators wrecked the Church of the Dormition of the Theotokos and looted thirty-nine of the forty Greek homes.[127] Just to the east and south of Salmatobruk, the rioters looted thirteen of the fifteen houses at Sarmaşık and wrecked the Church of Saint Demetrios.[128]

In Chapter 1, I quoted from the letter of the noncommissioned army officer, Salih Kırmızı, who led a small group of demonstrators in and around Edirnekapı. Here, I will only quote from his conclusion: "We did not encounter anyone in the houses, neither man nor woman....I imagined I was in Korea....And indeed this affair was much worse, for we smashed whatever we found before us. I think that we [his group] wreaked the greatest damage...."[129] Kırmızı's letter is indeed of great interest, especially because he was assigned to a marginal area that had far fewer shops, wealth, and Greeks than any quarter of new Istanbul. But he was assigned to lead this small group not only because he was a noncommissioned officer out of work (as emerges from the letter), but also because he was identified as a resident of the neighborhood he helped to destroy.

In conjunction with his activities and self-revelatory letter, let us look at a Greek eyewitness account in Edirnekapı, that of Mrs. Despoina Isaakidou:

[122] *Ibid.*

[123] Megas Reumiôtês, *Syrriknosê*, p. 58; National Archives, Foreign Office Dispatch No. 132, American Consul General, Istanbul, September 27, 1955; Chrêstidês, *Ekthesis*, p. 29, lists twenty-seven Greek families in the community of Eğrikapı in 1955. He refers to the church of Panagia tes Soudas as the Dormition of the Theotokos.

[124] National Archives, Foreign Office Dispatch No. 132, American Consul General, Istanbul, September 27, 1955.

[125] According to Megas Reumiôtês, *Syrriknosê*, p. 58, Roma from Sulukapı and Turkish refugees from Bulgaria carried out the attacks.

[126] National Archives, Foreign Office Dispatch No. 132, American Consul General, Istanbul, September 27, 1955; Megas Reumiôtês, *Syrriknosê*, pp. 54 and 58.

[127] *Ibid.*

[128] *Ibid.*

[129] Chrêstidês, *Ekthesis*, pp. 76-77.

My experience was very shocking, and until I die I shall remember those moments with great bitterness. I shall never forget the night of September 6.

Our house was located in the yard of the church of Saint George...at the Edirne Gate. We were three children, one still in mother's arms. My father, after countless struggles, managed to open a small tavern that attracted many Turks. One of these latter was an old friend of my father. He came, then, at five in the afternoon to my father's shop and told him: "Take whatever money you have and run to your home so as to be close to your wife and children."

My father asked him why, but he would not tell him, but simply repeated to hurry....Father came home and we all sat down to eat.

At 8:30, we heard shouting outside the house. Two trucks had halted, and from the first poured out tens of men clad in rags. The second truck was full of clubs and crowbars. Thinking that the family that lived in the churchyard was the priest's family, they started climbing over the metal fence, which was two and a half meters high. They fell upon our house. They smashed the door, the windows, and the glass.

I remember my eleven-year-old brother asking mother what was happening. She replied, "Tomorrow, they may massacre us." He then ran and jumped from a window four meters from the ground. He fell into the yard like a cluster of grapes. My father searched for him all night but found him only the next day, badly bruised, bloodied, and shocked.

During the course of the looting, a Turko-Cretan family came from across the street and gathered us in their house to protect us....

After having passed the night in their house, next afternoon my mother decided to go to our house to get clean clothes for the baby.

I hung by her, clutching her dress. I jumped out to go with her. We entered the yard and saw three soldiers guarding our house, of which only the bare walls remained. My mother asked them if she could get a few things and at first they refused. After she persisted, and they had whispered among themselves, they let us enter. Then I heard the heavy door from the yard shut behind us. One soldier remained outside the house, while the second said to the third: "You rape the mother and I'll rape the child."

I was a child of eight years that September. I did not know or understand the meaning of what they had said. I thought they had arranged to kill us, and I began to shout, "Not my mother. She has an infant to raise."

Then, like a *deus ex machina*, the Turkish friend of my father, who had tried the previous evening to return to our house but found the roads blocked, appeared. He ran into the yard and shouted at the soldiers: "What else do you want? You've burned down their livelihood [the shop], you've blackened their souls. Leave their honor alone...." He was so furious that he grabbed both of them and threw them out of the house. Thus we were saved....

From that time on, I never lived with my younger brother again. He was only two years old, but he had experienced such conditions that when we returned home he refused to come, and he went to live with my aunt....We have been deprived of him.[130]

Several years ago, Mrs. Isaakidou became aware of Salih Kırmızı's letter, and identified Kırmızı as a neighbor living close to her family's house. She had never known who had wrecked and looted their home in Edirnekapı.

In the small isolated islets of Greek Istanbulis and their churches, the Church of Saint Nicholas in Topkapı (62 families) was destroyed;[131] the Church of the Koimesis of the Theotokos in Altı Mermer (Ex Marmarôn) was burned and completely destroyed, and its community of seventeen families suffered the customary looting;[132] and the Church of the Birth of the Theotokos in the small and declining community of Belgratkapı (about sixteen families) was burned and completely destroyed.[133] Much more information is available on the destruction visited upon the ecclesiastical-monastic-cemetery complex of the Zoodochos Pege at Balıklı outside the land walls. This site in the region between the Belgrade and Silivri Gates had a long history going back to the fifth and sixth centuries CE, and it remained an important spiritual center for Greeks and Orthodox Christians for the better part of fourteen centuries. Rebuilt again and again, its form when much of it was destroyed on the night of September 6-7 resulted from its rebuilding in 1834. Of particular importance in its continuity was the belief of the faithful

---

[130] Tsoukatou, *Septemvriana*, #33, pp. 147-148.

[131] The patriarchal statistics of 1955 give the number of sixty families, whereas the patriarchal statistics of 1949 indicated that there were sixty-seven. On the destruction of the church, see Chrêstidês, *Ekthesis*, p. 78; also National Archives, Foreign Office Dispatch No. 132, American Consul General, Istanbul, September 9, 1955, and Stamatopoulos, *Analampê*, pp. 290-291.

[132] Chrêstidês, *Ekthesis*, pp. 29 and 78; National Archives, Foreign Office Dispatch No. 132, American Consul General, Istanbul, September 27, 1955.

[133] Chrêstidês, *Ekthesis*, pp. 28 and 78-79; Stamatopoulos, *Analampê*, p. 291. It had forty-six families in 1949.

that the water from its spring was possessed of miraculous curative powers, corresponding to its name, which means Life-Giving Spring in Greek. Indeed, this is the subject of the majority of icons painted and dedicated to the cult of the *Zôodochos Pêgê*. When the looters entered the complex on the night of September 6, they badly beat the monastery's abbot, a ninety-year-old monk, and a novice monk. After a savage beating, the elderly monk was killed and his body hidden. The bishop was beaten at three different times on the night of the pogrom. The third and last beating was administered successively by a number of military officers after he had been placed under the "protection" of four policemen on the way to the hospital. (This episode will be dealt with in detail in the next chapter.)

The destruction and arson of the church, monastery, and cemetery of Zoodochos Pege match in their extent and viciousness the destruction of the other great cemetery of the Greek minority at Şişli, with the same gross patterns of behavior and religious fanaticism. Zoodochos Pege's bishop-abbot later made a deposition on the attack on the monastery and on the severe beatings suffered by him and his two sacerdotal colleagues. The entire operation was controlled by the police and the local watchman, who seemed to be in contact with the Turkish authorities that had entered the Armenian cemetery nearby. The arson, looting, and destruction of the church and monastery were matched by the mass desecration of the cemetery, the burning of its ossuary, and the scattering of the bones found within the latter building. Particularly sacred were the cemetery's eleven patriarchal graves, of which seven were smashed and opened, and the bodies desecrated. Similarly, the graves of the great benefactors of Istanbul's Greek community were savagely wrecked and desecrated.[134]

Some distance outside the land walls, on the shore of the Sea of Marmara, were the two communities of Bakırköy and Yeşilköy.[135] The diplomatic and other reports record that the outbreaks in both were more or less simultaneous with the outbreaks in Beyoğlu and other places.[136] The reports on the fate of these two communities are sparse but, if reliable, would indicate that the

[134] Chrêstidês, *Ekthesis*, pp. 79-95; for details, and especially for the extensive quotes from the testimony of Bishop Pamphilos, Megas Reumiôtês, *Syrriknosê*, pp. 69-72.

[135] The patriarchal statistics for 1955 show a population of 490 and 119 families, respectively, Chrêstidês, *Ekthesis*, pp. 35-36. The testimony of Peter Sarantês, a resident of Bakırköy, gives the figure of 898 families who "lived in the village" in 1955; Sarantês further extrapolates 3,592 individuals from the number of families (see Tsoukatou, *Septemvriana*, #39, p. 162). His larger figures may be due to the influx of those who had summer homes there.

[136] National Archives, Foreign Office Dispatch No. 108, American Consul General, Istanbul, September 14, 1955. Greek Embassy #3846/B/29, 9/19/55, was sent by the foreign ministry (9/15, protocol no. 38596/T4, *Epeisodia genika*) to Washington.

fate of the Greeks of Yeşilköy was somewhat harsher than that of those in Bakırköy. In his eyewitness account, Petros Sarantês relates that he was on İstiklal Caddesi in Beyoglu when the second edition of the Istanbul *Ekspres* began to circulate, announcing the explosion of the "bomb" in the Turkish consular complex of Thessalonikê. This and the sight of the many "strange faces" in Beyoğlu caused Sarantês to return early to Bakırköy, where he thought he would feel more secure from possible demonstrations:

> But I was proven to be in error as to the matter of safety. About seven in the evening, bands of demonstrators, each with its own leader, had come to our village [area] in trucks, from their "huts" in the neighboring environs of Zeytinburnu. Most were refugees from Bulgaria.
>
> Their first target was the village church, Saint George. They were unable, however, to break down the iron door and enter. It is one of the few churches in Istanbul that was saved. [Sarantês's memory is actually wrong here, as the church was in fact damaged.][137]
>
> Continuing their labor, the vandals, under the leadership of a young newspaper-seller, then went off to the Greek dwellings. They looted and wrecked about ten of them. I think that our house was the first since it was the nearest to the church. It was an old wooden, two-storey house with a very large garden. They smashed the door, wrecked, and then looted it.
>
> My parents and I exited from the back door into the garden and passed the night up in the trees....
>
> Some days later the *muhtar* [head official] visited us...to express his sorrow. A month later, he gave me a remuneration that was merely symbolic. I think it was just enough to repair one broken window....
>
> The street and sidewalks were completely littered with broken windows, fabric, suits, refrigerators, furniture, mattresses, and many of the demonstrators' old clothes and shoes, exchanged for new ones from the stores.[138]

Although there is some inconsistency in Sarantes's testimony, the

---

[137] Tsoukatou, *Septemvriana*, #39, p. 161. The inference from the list of damaged churches in Chrêstidês, *Ekthesis*, p. 93, is that this is one of those churches. Obviously, Sarantês is in error on this point, as there is an entire file on the detailed petition by the community for compensation for the damage done to this church. The application was addressed to the Turkish department of *vakıfs*, which approved all the repairs listed in the petition. This issue will be examined in depth in a later chapter.

[138] Tsoukatou, *Septemvriana*, #39, pp. 161-162.

overall picture is still consonant with the patterns of destruction elsewhere in Istanbul.

For Yeşilköy, we again rely on one eyewitness account for some details of the violence there. The dentist Anestês Chatzêandreou was born in Yeşilköy, and his widowed mother and sister still lived there in the paternal house. He also had a summerhouse and clinic in Yeşilköy. With the rapid and threatening deterioration of the political atmosphere, Chatzêandreou decided to come home in the early afternoon of September 6 from his office in Beyoğlu, in order to comfort his wife, who was in the seventh month of her pregnancy with their second child. After dinner at 6:30, they decided to go to the home of his sister and mother. At about 8:00 PM, they heard loud, angry shouting. On going outside, Chatzêandreou had his first view of what was to transpire:

> I saw a raging mob of Turks, about twenty-five to thirty of them, holding iron crowbars, shafts, clubs, and they were smashing the stores and doors of the houses right and left, smashing the glass panes and display windows while shouting: "Death to the *Gavurs* [Infidels]"; "Massacre the Greek Traitors"; "Cursed be the Greeks."
>
> A little farther up, they halted at a club, the Rene Park, which belonged to a Greek with a mother of Arab descent, who had taken care to close the establishment....
>
> My wife and daughter locked themselves in the house, and I followed the frightful scene while hidden and unseen. They attacked without restraint, and began to strike, cursing crudely, smashing and destroying doors, walls, furniture, tools, worktables, and whatever else in the store that was useful, and violently taking away whatever they could. The destruction was complete....
>
> At 10:10 PM, we cautiously went out and the first thing we saw was a vast brightness to the east, exactly over Istanbul's Greek area, Pera, a sign of the arson used by the Turks to cover the orgy of stealing and looting....
>
> Immediately, I decided that we should proceed to our summer house some 1,200 meters away, located in the center of this suburb....
>
> Approaching our house, I saw, with fear, the mob of fanatic Turks destroying...the Greek shops in the center....[139]

Returning to the southern reaches of the land walls of old Istanbul, and following the entire shoreline of the Sea of Marmara eastward to Kumkapı, the attacks are marked by the same, perhaps even more, rage. The first of these

[139] *Ibid.*, #28, pp. 136-137.

regions includes the Yedikule and Samatya neighborhoods.

In 1955, Yedikule (Eptapyrgion-Psamatheia) is recorded to have had 304 Greek families, five churches, and a number of other institutions.[140] The diplomatic reports and other sources seem to confirm that the attacks on Greeks institutions and properties were particularly vicious in this area.[141] Three of the five churches were completely destroyed and burned: Saint George Kiparissas, Saint Menas, and Saints Constantine and Helen.[142] Saint Nicholas also seems to have suffered extensive damage. There is an eyewitness account of the desecration of the Church of Saints Constantine and Helen from Gedikoulianê Iôannidou-Môysidou, who was a local housewife:

> The beautiful Yedikule and Samatya, a little Paris, in a very brief period were reduced to dust.
>
> I was an inhabitant of this district and lived exactly opposite from the church of Saint Constantine. At 7:00 PM, I heard them tearing down doors, windows, and throwing rocks and boulders....
>
> I went out to gather the wash to iron, and the wild beasts attacked me...like wild wolves.
>
> Earlier, they had marked all the Greek houses with the letter X, which meant "here, a Christian." They had no difficulty in finding us, for everything had been planned ahead of time.
>
> They brought from Anatolia all the barbarians, whom they had instructed on how to smash and destroy, how to steal....
>
> As we looked out the window, they charged into the house and began to hit and curse us in the coarsest language...and they pushed us away as though we were garbage....
>
> They poured gasoline around the church and set fire to it and, like a torch, our church became ashes. They took the holy [communion] chalice and urinated in it, crying out to us, "Come, so that the priest may give you to drink."
>
> There was nothing that we could say or do. They took the wooden litter [*kouvoukli*] for the *Epitaphios* [the embroidered brocade depicting the dead body of Christ] just as is it was, [set it] on fire, and threw it into our house, to burn us alive. They showed respect neither to old men nor old women, nor to children, nor

---

[140] Chrêstidês, *Ekthesis*, p. 29; the patriarchal statistics of 1951-1952 show a Greek community of 577 families in the Yedikule-Samatya region, Stamatopoulos, *Analampê*, p. 290.

[141] *Makedonia*, 9/11/55; TNA:PRO, FO 371/117711, Istanbul, 9/22/55.

[142] Chrêstidês, *Ekthesis*, p. 78. One should consult the photographic evidence in Kaloumenos, *Ê staurôsis, passim*. Chrêstidês states that two other churches survived, the Theia Analepsis and Saint Nicholas. But the final patriarchal catalogue of damaged and destroyed churches adds the churches of Saint Paraskeue and Saint Menas (National Archives, Foreign Office Dispatch No. 132, American Consul General, Istanbul, September 27, 1955). This needs to be clarified.

to my father lying ill in bed, whom they beat into a state of vegetation....

They attached iron nails to their hands in order to shred and tear whatever they found. The refrigerators, furniture, all of it, they threw out the window down into the street, to those waiting with pickaxes to smash these objects so that we could no longer use them.

The food that we had in the kitchen (legumes, olive oil, flour, etc.) they poured on the floor and doused with gasoline so as to make inedible.

The entire street filled with tattered clothes. Everything came to a halt...trucks and buses. You could not cross the street....

The next day was the *laikê* (farmers') market in Samatya. You should see the Turkish women wearing furs and stockings with holes, and the Turkish men with pajamas and neckties, as they had all come out to shop.

When we went to see our store...a great catastrophe! They had said they would reimburse us for the damages down to the last dime. Unfortunately, none of this happened. And even if a few received compensation for damages, this was not enough to buy a candle for the church. They burned all our churches and monasteries....

In addition, we also lost our father [who had been beaten] and mother. May God punish them and, however much they persecute us, may we to that degree prosper.

We sold everything for a piece of bread and came here [to Greece] so that we may die here without their tyrannizing and cursing us.[143]

Moving eastward along the Sea of Marmara, we come to Langa (Vlanga), around Yenikapı, and Kumkapı (Kontoskali). In Langa, the community's church, Saints Theodoroi, was destroyed, along with 120 of the 220 Greek dwellings, forcing ninety-five Greek families to seek refuge and security in Beyoğlu.[144] In Kumkapı, the destruction was equally massive. Two churches,

---

[143] Tsoukatou, *Septemvriana*, #15, pp. 99-100; see also Atzemoglou, *Mnêmes*, for the testimony of Marika Kontopoulou, a teacher who lived in the district of Yedikule, p. 73: "I witnessed, terrified, as they stoned our neighborhood church of Saint Constantine. Presently, they poured gasoline all around the church and set fire to it." She describes the "invasion" of her house and the destruction on the streets on the morning of the seventh. Tsoukatou, *Septemvriana*, #4, p. 76: "When the church of Saint Constantine of Samatya was burning and the fire engines came to put out the fire, they [the Turks] punctured their tires." Kontopoulou further states that when she came into her kitchen, she found the soldiers, ostensibly there to protect her dwelling, "...in the act of stealing everything they found of value."

[144] Chrêstidês, *Ekthesis*, pp. 73-74 and 78. Many Turks from Silivri came to participate and thus to settle old scores with the local Greek inhabitants (National Archives, Foreign Office

Panagia Elpis and Saint Kyriake, were wrecked and looted, the school was destroyed, and so many businesses and homes were wrecked that they could not be rebuilt.[145] As we have already seen above in Bedirhan Çınar's reportage in *Milliyet*, Kumkapı, Gedikpaşa, and Çarşıpaşa suffered large-scale destruction.[146] The US consular report of September 14 paid particular attention to the violence of the attacks in these more central regions of old Istanbul:

> As of this hour [7:00 PM] the same vindictive destruction broke out all along the Bosphorus...in Uskudar and Kadikoy on the Asian side, on the Princes Islands and in inland suburbs....In old Istanbul the riots swept rapidly from St. Sophia, around the Bazaar, over near the city walls....Mobs proceeded from one neighborhood to another, sometimes uniting with groups coming from the opposite direction. Recruits in each neighborhood swelled the ranks and remained to finish the destruction while the main bands proceeded to other targets....For example, in some areas of old Istanbul where Greeks have depots [storage areas] on the third or fourth floor of buildings, where there is no indication on the street of their name or location, the marauders proceeded directly to the place and dumped whatever they could find in the street.[147]

The neighborhoods and streets of Vefa, Aksaray, Koska, and Laleli witnessed devastating attacks. The church and *agiasma* of the Theotokos of Vefa were destroyed.[148] Aksaray, north of Kumkapı, was also attacked. When Aziz Nesin crossed the Golden Horn by boat from Karaköy, he helped his companion walk to his apartment in Koska, south of Ordu Boulevard and near Laleli mosque.

> Sometime between 4:00 and 5:00 AM, we were barely able to squeeze into a small boat and pass over to the other side. After walking, we arrived at Aksaray. And in Aksaray, Koska, and Laleli, the looting was still going on....The hatred of the mob had not yet

Dispatch No. 132, American Consul General, Istanbul, September 27, 1955).
[145] Chrêstidês, *Ekthesis*, pp. 73-74 and 78-79; National Archives, Foreign Office Dispatch No. 132, American Consul General, Istanbul, September 27, 1955. The Greek consul of Istanbul, on 12/8/55, forwarded a patriarchal communication asking why the ministry had blocked a petition of the community of Kontoskalion for funds from Athens College to rebuild its school, which was completely demolished by the pogrom (no. E. P. 2083). The patriarchal note reads: "Let it be said, in addition, that the pious flock of this parish underwent terrible destruction, both in their shops and their homes, during the night of the events, with the result that they are unable, naturally, to carry this new financial burden."
[146] *Milliyet*, 9/9/55.
[147] National Archives, Foreign Office Dispatch No. 116, American Consul General, Istanbul, September 14, 1955.
[148] Kesisoglu-Karystinou, *Tzimbali*, p. 214; Chrêstidês, *Ekthesis*, p. 79.

subsided. As we ascended toward Koska, the things that we saw
were frightful. In front of our eyes, they smashed the iron shutters
of a store and entered. It sold coffee, tea, and candies....Whatever
they found inside, they threw out. There must have been an
internal passage to the upper floor. As we witnessed the windows
[of the upper floor] being broken, we saw them throw down a
sewing machine, refrigerators, and other objects. Suddenly one
heard a pained outcry. The sewing machine had fallen on one of
the mob who was waiting outside the store.[149]

Despite the declaration of martial law at about 2:00 AM, the destruction
of Greek property in old Istanbul was still going on at about five or six o'clock
in the morning. For Nesin and his companion to get to Koska, they had to
cross Ordu Caddesi (a continuation of Divan Yolu), which means that they
found themselves in the midst of the destructive advance of the groups that
had rampaged among the shops and homes around Saint Sophia and the
bazaar, and in Gedikpaşa, Kumkapı, and Langa.

Here is another eyewitness account, this time from Maria Iordanidou,
who lived in Aksaray and suffered the destruction of her own house:

When "the Events" occurred, my house was transformed
into a mountain of broken furniture and objects, with the
result that I did not even have a pair of shoes to walk to my
mother's. Everything was in pieces—refrigerators, pressure
cooker—broken, you would think, by hand. The clothes were
in shreds.

I lived with my family in Aksaray. The mob entered the house
at 11:00 PM, after having broken down the door, although we had
raised a Turkish flag. They took down the flag and began to attack
the house with axes, until 4:00 AM. We managed to flee before the
mob entered the house, after we had seen them attack the house
of the neighbors. We left all our possessions there, and I did not
even manage to take my jewelry.

The next day, the army came and guarded the mountains of
smashed and destroyed property....

Even though Aksaray was my neighborhood, my home,
after "the Events" we were forced to move, not only to another
house but to another neighborhood. And this because our Turkish
neighbors, whom we saw and to whom we said "Good morning"
every day, did not help us at all in this difficult moment![150]

---

[149] Nesin, *Asılacak adamlar*, p. 28.
[150] Tsoukatou, *Septemvriana*, #42, p. 167.

EYEWITNESS ACCOUNTS: THE EUROPEAN SHORE OF THE BOSPHORUS

The Greek communities on the European shore of the Bosphorus stretched northward for most of the thirty-mile coastline from Beşiktaş. Greeks were found, therefore, in Yeni Mahalle, Büyükdere, Tarabya, Yeniköy, İstinye, Boyacıköy, Bebek, Arnavutköy, Kuruçeşme, and Ortaköy.[151] As *Milliyet* reporter Mücahit Beşer wrote, it was "impossible…to express" what occurred in writing as, "Every place and thing had sunk into turmoil. Some groups, attacking the churches in the neighborhood burned them."[152] The report of the metropolitan of Derkon, whose ecclesiastical jurisdiction covered Yeni Mahalle, Büyükdere, and Tarabya, reflects the fury of the onslaught and the elevated pitch of religious fanaticism among many of the participants:

> The frightful tabulation of arson and destruction alone is as follows….
> The building of the Holy Metropolitanate in Tarabya was burned to the ground. As a result, its rich archives…its rich library, with all the holy vestments, the *iconostasis*, the furniture and the other objects were reduced to ashes….[153]
> The wrecked and looted churches included:
> Saint Paraskeue, Tarabya
> *Agiasma* of Saint Kyriake, Tarabya
> Cemetery of Saints Constantine and Helen, Tarabya
> Chapel of the Metropolitanate, Tarabya
> Church of Saint Paraskeue, Büyükdere
> Church of Saint John, Yeni Mahalle.[154]

Yeni Mahalle, Sarıyer, Büyükdere, Kireçburnu, and Tarabya had some 3,000 Greek inhabitants at the time, and the pogromists passed through most of these communities, wrecking homes, shops, churches and other institutions.[155] The following eyewitness account is from someone whose family's shop was in Eminönü but who had their summer house in Büyükdere:

> Our family—that is, my parents, my twenty-year-old sister and I—spent our summers at Büyükdere, on the Bosphorus. I was fourteen years old. Our house was located on the main street. I

---

[151] On these, see Chrêstidês, *Ekthesis*, pp. 32-35, for a few basic statistics.

[152] *Milliyet*, 9/9/55.

[153] The Greek text is quoted in Chrêstidês, *Ekthesis*, pp. 92-93.

[154] *Ibid.*, p. 93.

[155] *Ibid.*, pp. 92-93. The court-martial charged Osman Tan, a president of the *Kıbrıs Türktür Cemiyeti* local chapter in Sarıyer, with participating in these events (Megas Reumiôtês, *Syrriknosê*, pp. 49-51 and 73).

recall that a little before night fell, many cars and trucks full of people began to pass by, shouting slogans for Cyprus and against Archbishop Makarios. On the balcony across from our house a Turkish neighbor, a lady, hung out the Turkish flag. A little later, as soon as night had fallen and most of the stores had closed, a truck stopped and about thirty ragged men with crowbars and clubs poured out. They were joined by certain locals, most of whom I knew. One of the leaders wrapped himself in a Turkish flag, cried out "Yallah" [by God], and fell upon the display windows of the Greek grocery located exactly opposite us....In a few seconds, they had knocked down everything inside the store. They threw out cheeses, olive oil, butter, and sausages, as well as the refrigerators. The same action was repeated in the neighboring butcher shop and in all the Greek shops. Not one Turkish store suffered any damages. Further away, they reached the church of the village [area], Saint Paraskeue, which they destroyed completely, along with its *agiasma*....The sexton who lived in the courtyard leaped out terror-stricken. They took hold of him and hitched him to the funeral coach, in place of the horse...and, whipping him, they ordered him to pull the coach down to the sea. There, they threw him into the water....Then I heard voices from passing cars, shouting, "the Patriarchate is burning" (meaning the Metropolitanate building in nearby Therapeia [Tarabya]). Indeed, although it was night, the sky reddened from the fire....

The next morning, I went out to see what had happened. Everything was destroyed. The church was in pitiful condition. The funeral coach was still in the sea. I encountered some Turks who were familiar to me and that I had observed destroying the Greek stores the previous night. And they, as though nothing had happened, greeted me with the word "geçmiş" [may it pass].[156]

Tarabya, the ecclesiastical seat of the metropolitan of Derkon and home to 144 Greek families, as was noted above,[157] suffered the destruction of the metropolitanate building, its church, and its *agiasma*. Homes and stores were also looted and wrecked, of course.[158] It seems that among the demonstrators that participated in the attacks in Tarabya and surrounding areas were workers from the glass factory of Paşabahçe on the eastern side of the Bosphorus. An anonymous witness recorded the following:

---

[156] Atzemoglou, *Mnêmes*, pp. 70-71.
[157] Chrêstidês, *Ekthesis*, pp. 36-37.
[158] Tsoukatou, *Septemvriana*, #6, p. 79; Megas Reumiôtês, *Syrriknosê*, p. 50; Chrêstidês, *Ekthesis*, pp. 92-93; TNA:PRO, FO 371/117712, 9/14/55.

At that time, Iôsêf Sklavounos worked at the glass factory of Paşabahçe. He was the only "mastoras" [master craftsman] who remained of those [Greek workers] who came from the fertilizer factory of Drapetsona in Piraeus [in 1943] to teach the Turks glassmaking.

That night [September 6], he worked on the night shift from six until morning.

When he went to the factory, most of his colleagues were absent but the foreman tried to explain their absence....It seems that he had been informed that they would be going to wreck the villages [areas] of Yeniköy, Tarabya, Büyükdere, and Yeni Mahalle on the other [European] side of the Bosphorus. After midnight, these workers began to return, all of them dirty and angry.

When his shift ended, *mastoras* Iôsêf's foreman asked him to wait so that they could leave together. When they left the factory, which was located near the seashore, he saw a crowd watching a fire raging in Tarabya. It was the Metropolitanate building of Derkon, which was still burning.[159]

The interest here, naturally, is in the recruitment of factory workers in the violence for the opposite side of the Bosphorus. It also coincides with the fact that the president of the local chapter of the *Demokrat Parti* of nearby Beykoz, just to the north of Paşabahçe, led a contingent (in all probability of factory workers again) across the Bosphorus to attack Greek property in Yeniköy, where it looted many houses and damaged the Church of Saint Nicholas, whose seventy-five-year-old priest was stripped and tied naked to an automobile and dragged through the streets.[160]

Another eyewitness, a foreign architect living with his family in Tarabya, recounted his experience two days after the event, on September 8, 1955. He was in Beyoğlu when the demonstrations started, and begins his testimony by conveying the powerful impression that the night of September 6-7 left on him:

> I wish to state first of all...that that which imbued us with painful emotions from all this entire incredible story of beastly violence was that this mob was no blind rabble marching only to spread catastrophe. Rather it was, from beginning until the end, an excellently organized undertaking directed against the Greeks.
>
> It certainly had predetermined and objective goals, with a plan of action, responsible leaders, orderly movements, and formal

[159] Tsoukatou, *Septemvriana*, #11, pp. 89-90.
[160] Chrêstidês, *Ekthesis*, p. 94; TNA:PRO, FO 371/117712, 9/14/55; National Archives, Foreign Office Dispatch No. 116, American Consul General, Istanbul, September 14, 1955.

catalogues....The state officials, that is the police and army, not only did not move against the attackers, but quite the opposite, with their passivity and inaction, reinforced and placed...the terrorists under their protection.

When, at about 7:00 PM, the architect and his wife saw countless poorly dressed people—who were under the leadership, however, of people who were well-dressed—appearing in Beyoğlu, they began to fear the outbreak of violence and so departed for their apartment in Tarabya. By 9:00 PM, they noticed that Tarabya had filled with the same strange mix of people they had already seen in Beyoğlu:

> The groups having united, at about 9:00 PM they carried out a massive demonstration on the central thoroughfares, while in the small side streets the demonstrators parked their cars with the obvious goal of surrounding the apartments when the attacks were carried out....
>
> Before 11:00...the mob became agitated. Until then, the demonstrations had been sporadic. Now monotonous screams were being repeated as the streets of Istanbul were shattered by cries that reached to the heavens. Suddenly, we heard the loud noise of windows being smashed, and in a few minutes the noise of wrecked shutters....Amazed, we looked on as the mob, in a crazed state, invaded the stores, smashing whatever they found before them and then throwing it out in the street. Before we could recover from this sight, we saw the first flames shooting up from the stores to a height of eight to ten meters, which indicated that the terrorists had used gasoline....
>
> From minute to minute, the flames thickened and the reflection from the sky, uniting at various points, illuminated the raging hordes and imbued us with feelings of horror for we feared...that perhaps our turn might come....Then the leaders of the demonstration...in the midst of the screams and roars of the mob, which was "dancing"...about the burning stores, cried out, "Now destroy the churches of the Infidels"!

The demonstrators immediately turned on the church of the metropolitanate, which was near the architect's apartment.

> As my wife wept and began to pray, I continued to observe from my window as thousands of crazed men were running, armed with knives or steel rods. Very quickly they reached the Metropolitanate. Terrorists, dressed in workers' clothing, arrived with heavy sledgehammers, broke down the entrance door, and the mob rushed

in. Inside the church, everything was destroyed. One could hear the blasphemies and laughter of the mob…and soon after, they brought containers of gasoline and the church was burned….

After the day had dawned, we saw the entrance of the first army units, as the demonstrators peacefully withdrew.[161]

It is impossible not to notice the word—"terrorist"—that this particular witness used to describe the pogromists.

At İstinye, south of Yeniköy, the demonstrators wrecked and looted the Church of the Taxiarchs,[162] as they did the Church of the Euangelismos[163] and most of the Greek property in Boyacıköy,[164] and the Church of Saint Charalambos in Bebek.[165] Arnavutköy was a flourishing Greek community— called Mega Reuma (Big Creek) in Greek—at the time, with churches, 250 students in the local Greek grammar school, and cultural, drama, music, and athletic organizations.[166] The demonstrators arrived there at about 7:00 PM on the night of the sixth, as the Greeks, who had noticed ominous signs earlier, had begun to return to their homes. By 8:00 PM, demonstrators began forming into smaller groups; by 9:00 PM, they were wrecking various stores. During the destruction, they taunted the Greeks, "Until 12:00, we smash; after 12:00, we kill."

They destroyed the contents of the stores and, as always, threw much of them into the streets so that Arnavutköy's main thoroughfare was impassible until the next morning.[167] After wrecking the garage of Avraam Dadai, they threw several automobiles into the sea. They then turned to the Church of the Taxiarchs. At that time, they were painting it so there was scaffolding in place that enabled the demonstrators to ascend to the high campanile and enter the church from there. Once inside, they opened the heavy front doors, and the mob streamed in. At about midnight, they began to strike the church bell and profane the Christian symbols. Some demonstrators donned the priestly robes, paraded the cross in the streets, forcibly impaled icons on the sharp iron fence staves around the church garden, and stomped on the

---

[161] *Makedonia*, 9/9/55.

[162] Chrêstidês, *Ekthesis*, p. 94.

[163] National Archives, Foreign Office Dispatch No. 116, American Consul General, Istanbul, September 14, 1955.

[164] Chrêstidês, *Ekthesis*, p. 94.

[165] *Ibid*; Megas Reumiôtês, *Syrriknosê*, p. 50.

[166] Megas Reumiôtês, *Syrriknosê*, p. 43, gives a thumbnail sketch of all this. Metropolitan Êlioupoleôs Gennadius, *Istoria tou Megalou Reumatos*, Istanbul, 1949, on the community's history prior to the pogrom.

[167] Megas Reumiôtês, *Syrriknosê*, p. 47, gives a representative but incomplete catalogue of the Greek storeowners who suffered damages.

communion vessels. Finally, they removed the sarcophagus of a dead woman, Maria Mousourê, from the church crypt. They then wrecked the chapel of Saint Paraskeue in the churchyard.

The various groups turned to the Greek houses next, shouting, "You shall die, *gavurs.*" One group attacked the quarter of Saint Kyriake and, having wrecked it, reunited with the other group that was ascending the hill of the cemetery of the Prophet Elias, attacking Greek houses en route. At the cemetery, they smashed the crosses and marble graves, disinterred the dead, and, according to many reports, "played soccer with the skulls of the dead."[168]

The demonstrators also destroyed the Church of Saint Demetrios in Kuruçeşme, a suburb of Ortaköy.[169] The official report of Metropolitan Gregory, overseer of Ortaköy's religious community, summarized the destruction in his jurisdiction:

> This holy church [of Saint Phokas] suffered the same fate, more or less....The priest, terrified by the size of the mob and by its outcries, hid under the sacred altar, thinking that they would desist from it [the altar of the sanctuary]. The mob, however, upon entering the church, began to destroy it and, in so doing, reached the holy sanctuary, smashing and overturning everything. They discovered the priest hidden there under the holy altar. The priest, on seeing the crowd, suffered a nervous breakdown.
>
> The candle stall was broken and looted of its cash. The cells of the priest and the neophyte were destroyed. They did the same to the Cultural Association of the school and to the offices of the *Philoptochos* Society, robbing the latter's treasury.
>
> The catastrophe of this community...is adjudged to be even more tragic because both houses and stores of the Greeks were pillaged, and they themselves were cast out from their houses in the night, half naked, and deprived of their "daily bread."
>
> And of the many houses of this community, only twenty remained unlooted.[170]

[168] *Ibid.*, pp. 47-50; Tsoukatou, *Septemvriana*, #4, p. 76, on a recently deceased Greek being disinterred and paraded about the streets by Turkish demonstrators who wished to mock the Greeks' religion. V. Portokallis states that when the bus he was on entered Arnavutköy, the demonstrators stopped it, took off three Greeks, and threw them into the sea, in *Ibid.*, p. 71.

[169] Chrêstidês, *Ekthesis*, p. 95. During an attack on the church, the pogromists raped the thirty-eight-year-old wife of the sexton. Dosdoğru, *6/7 Eylül olayları*, pp. 24-29, describes the destroyed apartments, shops (especially in the marketplace), and cars of the Greeks in Ortaköy, where he had his apartment and the office of his medical practice.

[170] Chrêstidês, *Ekthesis*, p. 32. The patriarchal statistics for early 1955 list 180 Greek families living in Ortaköy. Accordingly, the information of the metropolitan that only twenty houses were not looted is revealing as to the destructive nature of the pogrom in Ortaköy.

The Christians have beseeched me continually to refer this
matter to the Church and to Your Most Divine Holiness, so that
the appropriate measures be taken, as they [the community] are
threatened with starvation.[171]

The evidence from these eight Greek communities spanning the entire
European shore of the Bosphorus clearly reveals two things: the extensive
destruction of Greek property and the fact that the pogrom of September
6-7, 1955, was the last and decisive episode in the ethnic cleansing of
Greek society—with all its requisite religious, cultural, and educational
institutions—in Istanbul and, more generally, Turkey.

EYEWITNESS ACCOUNTS: THE ASIAN SHORE OF THE BOSPHORUS

The patriarchal statistics for the Asian side of the Bosphorus list seven
communities from south to north: Kadıköy (Chalcedon); Üsküdar (Skoutari
or Chrysoupolis); Kuzguncuk (Chrysokeramon); Çengelköy; Kandilli;
Paşabahçe; and Beykoz (see Appendix A for a more detailed breakdown).[172]
All indications are that the more southerly centers (Kadıköy, Üsküdar,
Kuzguncuk, and Çengelköy) contained some 90 percent of the Greeks on the
city's Asian shore.

In Beykoz, although the Church of Saint Paraskeue was attacked,
the intervention of military units limited the damage to the narthex.[173]
In Paşabahçe, according to *Hürriyet*, the Greeks' stores were razed to the
ground[174] and the narthex of the Church of Saints Constantine and Helen
was damaged.[175] At Anadolu Hisar, the demonstrators burned the local
agiasma,[176] whereas, in Göksu, the chapel of the Panagia and the *agiasma*
were looted and wrecked.[177] In Kandilli, all the Greek homes, the community
school, and the Church of the Metamorphosis were seriously damaged.[178]
Details regarding the demonstrators in Kandilli and the man who organized

---

[171] See the report of the hierarch Gregory, dated 9/9/55, addressed formally to Patriarch
Athênagoras, and then sent by the foreign ministry to the Greek embassy in Washington, and
received there on October 21, 1955, #4311/ B.29, protocol no. 42741 EK/3a.

[172] Chrêstidês, *Ekthesis*, p. 34. Unfortunately, the numbers of Greek families usually given
have been omitted. *Makedonia* gives the following figures for the year 1951/1952: Kadıköy,
700; Üsküdar, 152; Kuzguncuk, 200; Çengelköy, 120; Kandilli, 30; Paşabahçe, 25; and
Beykoz, 15. These figures are taken from Stamatopoulos, *Analampê*, p. 291.

[173] Chrêstidês, *Ekthesis*, p. 87.

[174] *Hürriyet*, quoted by Chrêstidês, *Ekthesis*, pp. 87 and 89.

[175] Chrêstidês, *Ekthesis*, pp. 89 and 90.

[176] *Ibid.*, p. 59.

[177] *Ibid.*, p. 90.

[178] *Ibid.*, pp. 88 and 90.

them came from a military officer of Greek origin posted in a garrison on the Asian side of the Bosphorus:

> At that time, I was doing my military service as a reserve second lieutenant....
>
> At Kandilli, we were placed in a two-storey house that belonged to the cantor Athanasês Athanasatos, which was exactly across the street from the grammar school in the Eugenidês Ekpaideutêria, and across from the church of Christ the Savior. The Turkish inhabitants, on being notified that a *gavur* was in charge of the soldiers, were fearful lest I gather information from the Greek inhabitants and accuse those who had wrecked the church, the school, and many homes. They met immediately and, under the leadership of a captain whose first name was Kiami and whose last name I could not learn, they condemned me in writing to the general in charge of the base at Selimiye, accusing me of dereliction of duty and of frequenting Greek houses where banquets took place. They charged me with drinking *raki*, wine, and other alcoholic beverages. The house in which these events supposedly occurred belonged to [someone] I did not even know.
>
> On the basis of this accusation, they called me back to my unit, where I remained in solitary confinement for twenty days.

After twenty days, the officer was found to be innocent of the charges:

> I asked that they give me the last names of those who had signed the document, as well as the last name of Captain Kiami. But they gave me nothing. At this time, certain people who had wreaked the destruction in Kandilli were jailed. Kiami ran hither and yon trying to save them, coming regularly to my unit; finally, those arrested were acquitted, as happened with all the barbarian attackers. Later, I learned from a Turk from Kandilli that Kiami had organized the attacks in the area.
>
> Let it be noted that the [Turkish] officers in my unit were gratified to see this destruction, and one of them expressed the hope that [Greek] revenge would be taken on the Turks of Western Thrace, so that he could avenge himself by destroying the houses of the Greeks in Üsküdar, where he lived.[179]

In Vaniköy, demonstrators broke into the summerhouse of Dr. Nikolaos Fakatselês, a former deputy of the Turkish parliament and a member of the Popular Party. Locking his front door, he and his family went to the upper floor. When the demonstrators broke down the door and started to climb

---

[179] Tsoukatou, *Septemvriana*, #13, pp. 95-96.

the stairs, Fakatselês grabbed his hunting rifle, forcing an impasse for about an hour. When the demonstrators decided to rush him, he fired and wounded one of them in the hand, whereupon the group dispersed and abandoned the house.[180]

An anonymous eyewitness in Çengelköy left an account that gives a few details on the violence there. The demonstrators were brought into the area by the ferryboat, Üsküdar #72, at about 11:00 PM on an unscheduled run:

> A large group disembarked and asked where the Greeks resided. They [the locals] showed them the three Greek shops and the destruction commenced.
>
> They began with the butcher shop of Leonidas Kotês. They smashed the icebox, meat machine, his office, and threw out all the meat into the street. The few inhabitants of the village [area] took no notice, and neither did Kotês....In the morning, he saw his livelihood scattered in the streets and the cats and dogs, sated, lying around....
>
> Above this store was the clinic of Dr. Alexis Meliopoulos. Here, they [the locals] did not allow the demonstrators in, as they loved him especially and also needed him....He had saved many and helped others by giving them free medicine.

The head of the local police put a halt to any further violence, probably because martial law had been declared at that point. While the flames of the burning metropolitanate in Tarabya could still be seen from Çengelköy, however, the soldiers brought in, to guard the area and its inhabitants, actually *continued* the destruction. They broke the windows of the local church with the butts of their rifles, "[a]nd in Saint Kyriake, they placed explosives, despite the fact that it was being guarded, and when they [the explosives] went off, the house and shop across the street were damaged." (When the Üsküdar #72 sank about a year and a half later, with about 400 passengers, on its daily run in the bay of Izmit, many Turks at the time believed it was divine retribution.)[181]

Çengelköy apparently underwent two separate attacks on the night of September 6-7. The first was the one described above by the demonstrators unloaded from Üsküdar #72, who did not stay long, however, although some may have lingered behind. The second attack came from the cadets of the Kuleli officers' training school in Çengelköy, at about midnight.[182] Both attacks emerge from the testimony of eyewitness Maria Andreou Kanakês, who

---

[180] Chrêstidês, *Ekthesis*, p. 88.
[181] Tsoukatou, *Septemvriana*, #11, pp. 89-90.
[182] The timing is implied by *Ibid.*, #40, p. 163.

owned a three-storey summer house in which she and her family were staying that night. She, her husband, two children, and aged mother lived on the first floor, while the second and third floors were rented to Turkish families.

> Because of the humidity, we went to bed early.
>
> Very soon, my older son knocked on the door and said: "Get up, something is happening at Arnavutköy."
>
> We paid no attention and sent him off to sleep.
>
> A little while later he returned and, again, angrily said: "Get up immediately, they're breaking tables, chairs in the casino at the dock. Don't you hear it?"
>
> Immediately, we arose and saw the destruction that was taking place. The entire neighborhood had awakened. Aside from two Greek families, all the families [in the neighborhood] were Turkish.
>
> One of the Turkish ladies who rented from us told us: "The same is going to happen here. Try to save yourselves."[183]

The husband hurriedly took his sick mother-in-law from her bed and carried her to a room on the other side of the house. No sooner had he removed her from her bedroom than a huge rock was thrown through the window, landing exactly on top of her bed. Eventually, the other members of the family made their way through the basement to the apartment of the Turkish woman on the second floor.

> We now heard the noise from our own apartment rising from the smashing of china, furniture, and other objects. Our stored foodstuffs they threw out into the street, and our neighbors seized them like mad dogs and carried them off to their houses. They slashed the mattresses with knives, throwing the stuffing out on the street....
>
> About 11:30, the demonstrators began to withdraw. Thus, my husband and I went back to our apartment by the same way we had left.
>
> It was a horror!...Nothing remained upright; everything had been destroyed and smashed.

The only thing that had remained intact was her wardrobe, where her personal jewelry remained untouched. This apparent miracle partially alleviated their fear and despair. But this respite was short-lived:

> At exactly 12:00 midnight, martial law was declared. We both made the sign of the cross and said: "We're saved!"
>
> Unfortunately, however, we did not expect a second attack

---

[183] *Ibid.*, #2, p. 65.

to occur, more destructive than the first, after martial law was declared.

And we saw the military cadets, howling and advancing toward our house. Like crazy people, we sought refuge again in our shelter.

Our neighbor, Hamdi, who was on duty at the [Officers'] School that fateful night, gave them the order: "Loot the house of Kanakês, and take whatever those who preceded you left behind."[184]

On September 7, Mr. Kanakês went to the officer in charge of the base at Selimiye to report the destruction and Hamdi's role in it. The matter was investigated and an order was issued for his arrest. Hamdi committed suicide, however, rather than face police custody and the subsequent shame of a trial.

In Kuzguncuk, the churches of Saint Panteleimon and Saint George were damaged.[185] Two eyewitness accounts indicate that, because of a coincidence, the damage there was not as extensive as elsewhere. One observer remarks that at about 9:00 PM, he heard shouting, smashing, and store windows being broken on Kuzguncuk's main thoroughfare. On investigating from his residence, he saw not only the destruction in Kuzguncuk, but also "…fires on all the opposite shores of the city of Istanbul."[186] By midnight, the fury had diminished in Kuzguncuk:

> Our neighborhood had survived without damage, thanks to a neighborhood friend, Ali Rıza, the assistant director of the civil police. Ali Rıza was a Turk from Crete and he…stood at the crossroad of our neighborhood's central street and refused to allow the demonstrators to pass. Thus, thanks to the Turko-Cretan, the Greek homes of our neighborhood were saved from disaster….
>
> Meanwhile, a boat from Istanbul full of demonstrators arrived at Kuzguncuk toward midnight. The village's [area's] *muhtar* and an officer threatened to shoot the ship's captain if he dared to land. Finally, the ship left and unloaded at Çengelköy, where the demonstrators were reinforced by the cadets from the military school of Kuleli and did great damage….
>
> There were three [Greek] groceries [in Kuzguncuk]. These they destroyed. They poured gasoline into the grain sacks to render them useless.[187]

---

[184] *Ibid.*, #2, pp. 65-67; for an example of raw physical violence, #50, p. 189, in Çengelköy.
[185] Chrêstidês, *Ekthesis*, p. 90.
[186] Tsoukatou, *Septemvriana*, #1, p. 57.
[187] *Ibid.*, pp. 57-58.

The demonstrations broke out in Üsküdar early (at about the same time as they had broken out in much of Istanbul),[188] and the Church of the Prophet Elias was destroyed,[189] along with the *agiasma* and private property.[190] It was Kadıköy, however, that suffered the most widespread destruction of all the Greek communities on the Asian side of the Bosphorus. Kadıköy was also the largest Greek community on the Asian side,[191] with five churches and three grammar schools in and nearby the area, as well as a medical clinic and various associations.[192] The Church of the Holy Trinity and the metropolitan's residence were looted and wrecked. There is some disagreement in the sources as to the fate of the Church of St. Ignatios in the cemetery.[193] The churches of Saint John Chrysostom,[194] Saint George at Yeldeğirmeni,[195] and St. John Prodromos at Kalamış were also looted and destroyed. Regarding the latter, there is the testimony of Peter Tsoukatos, who was nine years old at the time and staying with his aunt in Kalamış.

> What I very much remember…that night, and I shall never forget it, were the images I saw, from the window of the house in Kalamış, of the Turkish mob passing by, holding clubs and lighted torches, howling, and moving toward the center….
>
> On the morning of September 7, we learned that the goal of the looters we had seen the previous night had been to destroy everything Greek or Christian in the area. The church of Saint John of Kalamış did not escape their rage, as it was consumed by fire, and many summerhouses were looted and destroyed. I recall that the priest of the area was beaten mercilessly.[196]

EYEWITNESS ACCOUNTS: THE PRINCES ISLANDS

While the course of attacks on the eastern side of the Bosphorus followed the patterns already observed, the role of ferries was particularly important

---

[188] National Archives, Foreign Office Dispatch No. 116, American Consul General, Istanbul, September 14, 1955.

[189] Chrêstidês, *Ekthesis*, p. 90.

[190] *Ibid.*, p. 88.

[191] The statistics presented by *Makedonia* for 1951/1952 state that some 700 Greek families lived in and around Kadıköy; Stamatopoulos, *Analampê*, p. 291.

[192] Chrêstidês, *Ekthesis*, pp. 33-34.

[193] *Ibid.*, p. 90, but the comprehensive patriarchal catalogue lists it as damaged, National Archives, Foreign Office Dispatch No. 132, American Consul General, Istanbul, September 27, 1955.

[194] National Archives, Foreign Office Dispatch No. 132, American Consul General, Istanbul, September 27, 1955.

[195] Chrêstidês, *Ekthesis*, p. 80; see also Tsoukatou, *Septemvriana*, #1, p. 58.

[196] Tsoukatou, *Septemvriana*, #37, p. 157.

in transporting outside elements to the area. This was to be even more the case with the Princes Islands, which made up their own metropolitanate with fourteen churches, one monastery, three grammar schools, the famous theological school at Chalkê (the functioning of which has been prohibited since 1971 by the Turkish government), and other local organizations. While all four islands were included in the pogrom's master plan, the Turkish authorities on the island of Kınalıada (Prôtê) in effect refused to allow the ferry-borne demonstrators to land and attack the Greek community.[197] The island's assistant director of rural police, along with only three other police officers, turned back the "armada" of destruction.[198] As to the second island, Burgazada (Antigonê), the available sources are contradictory as to whether or not local authorities barred demonstrators from landing, or Greek property was destroyed.[199]

As for both Heybeliada (Chalkê) and Büyükada (Prinkipo), however, the sources are unambivalent, indicating a coordinated, ferry-borne attack supported by local elements and police. On Heybeliada, the vandals were assisted, again, by cadets from the local naval academy.[200] They attacked the Greek shops in the marketplace, as well as the churches of Saint George of Kremnou, Saint Nicholas, and Saint Spyridon.[201] While they attacked the theological school, its director and students hid and cut off its electricity. So, while doors and windows were destroyed, no one dared to enter it in complete darkness.[202] The brief eyewitness account of Kônstantinos Katsaros gives a few notable details:

> On the night of September 6, the Turks began the organized attack on everything belonging to Christians.
>
> The first group determined what should be destroyed, the second implemented destruction of inanimate objects. The third group undertook the [destruction] of the animate. Fortunately, this [latter] group did not complete its…task.
>
> That night, my father gave us instructions as to how we

---

[197] Chrêstidês, *Ekthesis*, pp. 85-86.

[198] Megas Reumiôtês, *Syrriknosê*, p. 67.

[199] Chrêstidês, *Ekthesis*, p. 85, says that the authorities did not allow them to land. Megas Reumiôtês, *Syrriknosê*, asserts that they did allow them to disembark and that there were attacks on the local church and on the Greek restaurants, shops, and houses. National Archives, Foreign Office Dispatch No. 132, American Consul General, September 27, 1955, does not list the church of Burgazada in its patriarchal catalogue of damaged churches. The patriarchal catalogue has, however, failed to list churches that were damaged in certain other cases.

[200] Megas Reumiôtês, *Syrriknosê*, p. 63.

[201] Chrêstidês, *Ekthesis*, p. 86.

[202] *Ibid.*, p. 56; Megas Reumiôtês, *Syrriknosê*, p. 63.

would defend ourselves should our house be attacked....[203]

The barbarians succeeded in disembarking at Chalkê. They destroyed the church of Saint Nicholas, they even threw its bell into the sea.

They tried to burn the Theological School, together with its very valuable library....

In Chalkê, a monk who made small crosses out of cane was murdered. Many Greek houses and Greek institutions have been destroyed, as also the church to which I referred.[204]

Somewhat more detailed is the course of the pogrom on the fourth isle, Büyükada (Prinkipo), where the damage inflicted was extensive. It has been noted by other chroniclers that the events in Prinkipo were described in the session of the Turkish parliament convened to solve the crisis following the pogrom. It was the parliament's Greek representative, Alexandros Chatzopoulos, who spoke of events on Büyükada on that occasion:[205] "At around midnight, five to ten boats arrived in Prinkipo, where their passengers disembarked. There were between 200 and 300...individuals. They consulted with the [local] police and then destroyed Prinkipo. They departed without having encountered any resistance. Had it decided to do so, would not the police have been able to capture the four or five local boats and arrest the demonstrators like rats in a trap?"[206]

Damage was inflicted on the churches of Saint Demetrios and the Panagia, the monastery of Christos Soter (Christ the Savior), and the grammar school. Kônstantia Geôrgiadou Vezanê fills in certain relevant details:

In August 1955, the atmosphere in Istanbul had become unbearable. One understood that something would break out. Many groups of "kourelades" [people wearing tattered clothes] came to Prinkipo in light seacraft and large fishing boats....

The Ministry of Education sent Turkish teachers every summer to spend their vacation at our school, requiring both the school principal and the [Greek] community to afford them a pleasant stay to the degree possible. Thus, the Turkish teachers were enthusiastic over this hospitality and had a good time with the Greek teachers....

In August of '55, this all vanished. Whenever they would pass, they would not even greet or smile at us, and they left in

---

[203] I leave out here the interesting details regarding the nature and variety of this family's reactions to the mortal threat it faced, putting it aside for discussion with other such examples later.

[204] Tsoukatou, *Septemvriana*, #35, p. 151.

[205] Chrêstidês, *Ekthesis*, pp. 86-87.

[206] *Ibid.*, p. 87.

mid-August without so much as bidding us farewell or a simple "thank you," as they had in the past.

In the small Turkish quarters [of the island], they cursed the Greeks without cause, and every so often, in order to spread fear, would repeat, "katliam olacak" ["a massacre will take place"]. Because of all this, the Greek teachers left the school and went to stay in the houses of relatives. Only my father, who was the school's principal, stayed behind, alone.

In Prinkipo, we only had one Turkish teacher, a retired general from a family of paşas, who was very rich and had fought at Dumlu Pınar with Atatürk. His name was Fahrettin. We asked ourselves why he, who was so rich and great in age and status, still worked? It was very simple. He wished to keep tabs on, and be informed about, Greek community affairs, and thus report to the ministry. He displayed affection and friendship to the principal and said, "A hand that you cannot bite, you must kiss." Fahrettin Bey came to my father and told him: "Come and stay at my house because there is going to be a massacre...."[207]

But the principal refused and insisted on guarding his school by himself. At night, the demonstrators' noise was audible, and the Turkish houses were brightly lighted and decorated with Turkish flags. The radios blared out marching and military music. The principal was busy lighting the school and raising the Turkish flag when he suddenly smelled smoke. He ran into the classrooms and saw piles of timbers, paper, and rags, all doused with gasoline, burning. Grabbing the fire extinguishers, he managed to put out the fires.

Then he saw the altar of the church of Saint Demetrios burning brightly. Across from the church there lived a relative of Fahrettin, who was also a general. The latter cried out to the [arsonists]. "What evil did you ever see from the Saint? If his church should burn, all the neighborhood, and you together with it, shall burn." They then called the fire department, which came very unwillingly, without any haste in extinguishing the fire, which finally died out, [but] only after destroying the altar, and burning many icons and holy treasures. There was very great damage...."

Kônstantia Vezanê's house was located across from the police station. From her balcony, she heard shouts and noted that they came from about fifty wild men armed with clubs and crowbars. The officers at the police station had forced them to line up in orderly fashion and sing the national anthem and a marching song, and, as though blessing their weapons, wished them success:

[207] Tsoukatou, *Septemvriana*, #12, pp. 91-92.

> In charge of the gang was the director of the [local] Labor Bank (*İş
> Bankası*). They charged toward our house....
>   But the terrorists attacked the house across the street...[of
> a great Greek benefactor] and, with the ugliest blasphemies and
> curses, hurled rocks and boulders at the house, which was closed.
> Also across from us...lived the president of the Academy of Fine
> Arts. He came out and told the attackers, pointing to our house:
> "It is there that Greeks live, on both the upper and lower floors."

The attack was thereafter focused on Vezanê's house, which was damaged
by the flying rocks and boulders. But, as the rioters were unable to break
down the door, they went off to attack other houses.[208] Next day, Vezanê's
husband went to Karaköy to see what had happened to his office in the
famous *Havyar Hanı* (the Caviar Building), which was opened by its Turkish
employees and the entire complex ruined. He found his office, papers, and
furniture completely destroyed.[209]

A second witness, I. Meletiadês, who experienced the nightlong attack as
a guest of his family, was an Athenian policeman. Although born in Istanbul
and a graduate of the *Megalê tou Genous Scholê*, he had emigrated to Athens
and made his career and family there. On the night of the pogrom, he secured
his family within the house, far from the pelted rocks (in the morning, he
counted and photographed the sixty-four rocks that had smashed through
the windows and damaged the house). Thereafter, he decided to go to the
market and see what had occurred there.

> I went down to the island's marketplace to see what had happened
> there. What to look at first! They had ruined all the stores/
> restaurants by the shore. All their contents were thrown into the
> sea. Refrigerators, tables, chairs, plates, glassware, and whatever
> else the store disposed of, was all hurled into the sea.

He then went to see what had befallen Beyoğlu and Fener, as well
as his *alma mater*, the *Megalê tou Genous Scholê*, and the ruined community
of Balat.[210]

This chapter has attempted to trace and document the physical
destruction wreaked by the pogrom of September 6-7, 1955. The result is not
complete because much of the evidence is not yet accessible. Nevertheless,
the extant sources allow a specific focus on many neighborhoods and even
streets within five broad geographical areas. As a result, one is often able to

---

[208] *Ibid.*
[209] *Ibid.*, #12, p. 93.
[210] *Ibid.*, #21, p. 114; see also #24 and #43, pp. 123 and 169.

follow the movements of various groups of demonstrators from area to area. Frequently, one can easily observe the successive waves of attacks in the same neighborhood or street, as well as the attackers' highly disciplined organization and coordination. The fact that there were often waves of attacks in one street or area assured destruction that was both homogeneous and thorough. The refusal, save on very rare occasions, of police and soldiery to intervene is also characteristically uniform. Not only did the authorities encourage and often assist the pogromists, but they frequently aided and abetted the looting, thus committing the actual crimes they had been sworn to prevent. In addition to the uniformity of planning and destruction throughout greater Istanbul, the weapons and implements of destruction issued by the demonstrators were also uniform.

Many of the slogans and curses reveal an attitude of people who readily desire the physical and psychological destruction of their victims. This furor was chauvinistic, religious, fanatical, vandalistic, and voracious. Worst of all, it represented a massive and well-organized *official* attack on Greek Istanbulis in which the organs of *government* directed and oversaw the violence against its own citizens.

Finally, the purpose of the extensive description of the pogrom in this chapter has been to give "life" to the forensic nature of the analysis in the next chapters and, therefore, to animate an almost static picture of a series of events that were continually in motion over a comparatively large area. Drawing upon a large number of varied sources, we saw how the same events were perceived, interpreted, and, above all, experienced by politicians, diplomats, bureaucrats, police, religious leaders, shopkeepers, businessmen, bank presidents, workers, trade-unionists, writers, physicians, and journalists who were Turks, Greeks, Armenians, or Jews, and who were also parents or children. Not only do these accounts help to flesh out the pogrom as it occurred in many neighborhoods of the far-flung city of Istanbul, but they serve as an index of the psychological state of both victims and victimizers. They also convey more than the picture of the pogrom; they convey its conditions: the odors of burning merchandise, foodstuffs, chemicals, fabric, and metal, as well as the din of explosions, crumbling structures, crazed crowds shouting, and crackling infernos of destroyed churches that lit up the midnight skies on both sides of the Bosphorus. As this chapter has, of necessity, *depicted* events, rather than analyzed them—and since the experiences of the enormous range of eyewitnesses cited here were either similar or even identical—there has been an unavoidable repetition of elements, and even of sentiments. Indeed, in order to give the most complete picture, it has been necessary to include as much testimonial documentation as possible, even at the risk of apparent repetition or, even worse, of seemingly gratuitous descriptions of the violence perpetrated during the events described. Editing out even more material (than was already done as a natural part of reconstructing the narrative) would have seriously marred the historical tableau of this massive event. The attitudes of both victims and victimizers have been recorded, but it stands to reason that the accounts of the latter are expressed in very different terms, and spirit, from the testimonies of the former.[211]

[211] An effort has been made in this chapter—and throughout this study—not only to trace the broader outlines but to search out, where possible, the pogrom's constituent elements and smallest details. It has been a difficult task, as many source materials have not been accessible; indeed, after half a century, many have been lost. No historical analysis can be better than its sources.

Moreover, the sources at the basis of this narrative are incomplete and those that I have managed to recover are of varying value and, so, of unequal reliability. It is to be hoped that the passage of time will lead to the uncovering and study of additional material, which will clearly enrich and correct the present analysis. Of sources contemporary with the events described herein, I was fortunate to have access to the archives of the Greek ministry of foreign affairs, the Greek embassy in Washington, DC, the British public record office, and the national archives in Washington, DC. They were obviously of value by virtue of their contemporaneity and because they reflected the general understanding and policy of the respective governments. All too often, however, these archives included consular and ambassadorial reports that did not contain the critical materials on the basis of which these reports made their evaluations. In other cases, they included only parts of these important documents and data. On occasion, however, they did contain crucial data and information on the pogrom.

As for "anonymous" sources—that is, written or oral testimony for which the witness has reason to fear the consequences of revealing his or her identity—the psychological atmosphere that prevailed before, during, and long after the pogrom was decisive in this matter. Greeks, Armenians, and Jews then, and even today, often fear criticizing or testifying publicly to specific acts that have violated their person or human and civil rights. The fear of reprisal, both physical and political (and often violent), was fully justified. This comes out in the reports of the Greek consuls, and in much of the anonymous testimony itself. Thus, although anonymous reports are to be approached skeptically in the abstract, there were concrete reasons *in the event* for witnesses to fear the consequences of eponymous denunciations. For the most part, in any case, these anonymous reports are confirmed by a variety of other data that in and of themselves point to the pogrom's operating principles: destroy and violate. The total of the anonymous data thus confirms the more specific data, or is consonant with it.

Given the incomplete nature of the accessible sources—as well as the errors and mistakes in some of them—is the picture drawn of the pogrom in this chapter reliable? Using such a range of disparate—that is, Greek, Turkish, British, and US—sources in this difficult effort to give a valid picture of the events of September 6-7, 1955, has created a sufficient source matrix to answer the question affirmatively. The intersection of sources creates a general framework of agreement, with many identifiable specifics, which allows one to reconstruct a relatively accurate model of the pogrom with some degree of confidence. It is clear from this analysis that all the documents are talking about the same historical event, which was carefully planned, efficiently realized, and satisfied the original intentions and goals of its instigators. The planned and coordinated nature of this pogrom is confirmed by this methodology. One can clearly see its institutional execution, and its extension into all Greek communities, businesses, and ecclesiastical institutions is chronicled in rather amazing detail. Practically all the sources agree as to the violence at the outset, the large numbers of organized participants, the successive and differentiated waves of attacks, and, in many cases, the studied refusal of the police or military to intervene in the violence.

That which one hopes to obtain from as-yet-inaccessible sources is depth in detail and additional specific identification of persons and groups who either inflicted or suffered violence. Generally, it can be said that the pogrom was undeniably a massive attack whose great destruction was carried out with cruel efficiency.

Of the legal documents, the most important ones utilized in this chapter were the legal opinions, decisions, and punishment issuing out of court trial no. 3 (*Esas* no. 3) of the nineteen trials at Yassıada that condemned the Menderes government and the DP deputies of the Turkish parliament. However, what was not available was the body of material known as the *tutanaklar*, that is, the complete records of the legal proceedings themselves. This is a massive body of evidence based on some forty-nine files consisting in part of the data from the security police. One would hope to find in this material specific information on what actually occurred in the different neighborhoods. The richness of this material is indicated by Dosdoğru's book, which quotes, *in toto*, some of the interrogations and witness responses during the course of the trial. Many of the records and minutes of various Greek communities, in which discussions on damages and petitions for remuneration are recorded, might perhaps be lost, too. There are also the records of the ecumenical patriarchate, as well as of the Greek archdiocese of North and South America. These are practically inaccessible.

The reports of the Greek, Turkish, and international press have been useful in adding detail to the pogrom, although, again, one must always check for accuracy. The narratives of Greek and, especially, of Turkish origin are increasingly being published and made available, and these include the accounts of individuals who were present during the pogrom and were involved in it. There is also the report of the World Council of Churches, which is of considerable interest, not only for the details of the destruction, but also because of the organization's clash with the Foreign Office over the matter.

Finally, and significantly, substantial parts of the relevant Turkish documents emanating from the Istanbul *vakıflar* and Committee for Repair were accessible. This documentation is extensive and detailed in the specific matters, both of the destruction of Greek Orthodox ecclesiastical establishments and of the partial compensation for their rehabilitation.

CHAPTER THREE

MORAL AND MATERIAL DAMAGES, AND THE ECONOMICS AND POLITICS OF COMPENSATION

An effort was made in Chapter 1 to put the pogrom in its historical, institutional, and political context. In Chapter 2, the events were traced to the five geographical areas in which they transpired and, within each of these broader areas and where the sources permitted, located in their specific streets and/or neighborhoods. This chapter will examine the pogrom's damages, both moral and material, while the efforts of various organizations or individuals to put a financial value on them will be treated in the following chapter.

The pogrom's intent was twofold: first, it was a planned and successful effort to destroy the forty-five Greek communities spread out over the vast area of greater Istanbul and its environs; second, it served certain domestic and foreign policies of the Menderes regime. Domestically, Menderes's economic policies had, to a certain degree, proved to be a failure, leading to inflation and, consequently, to hardship on a large part of the Turkish population. Further, the rapid centralization of authority in Menderes himself, and his increasing use of the *Demokrat Parti* as an instrument of personal governance, produced an acerbic reaction from İnönü and the Republican People's Party, as well as from much of the press that was not aligned with the government. In foreign affairs, his open change of policy on the Cyprus issue in 1954-1955 transformed the status of the Greeks of Istanbul from that of a hostage to the Turkish minority of Greek Thrace to that of a sacrificial offering to Turkey's policy on Cyprus.

The term, "pogrom," implies government-inspired and -organized violence against an ethnic minority or social group within the territory of a state. Greek sources and media were already using it almost immediately after the events of September 6-7.[1] The massive body of Greek and Turkish

---

[1] The term, "pogrom," began to appear in the Greek press immediately after the events of September 6-7. On September 8, the newspaper *Ethnos* wrote that, "This destruction

sources leaves no doubt as to the fact that the violence directed primarily, but not exclusively, against Greeks on that fateful September night was indeed a pogrom. For the Greeks, it was the Pogrom (capitalized). These and very many other European and American sources indicate, very clearly, that leading members of the Turkish government—including Menderes, Zorlu, and Gedik—were among the principal planners, whereas certain diplomats, chiefs of security, police, and the army (stationed in the Istanbul area) presided over the riots in close cooperation with the presidents of the DP's local chapters.[2] What is not clear, of course, is *why* Menderes and Zorlu would have given the green light for this attack at a time when Istanbul was hosting five separate international conferences. In a kind of historical irony, these congresses included those of the International Police Conference and International Monetary Fund. The city was filled with reporters, as well as with important economists and financiers from the four corners of the earth. As a consequence, the pogrom was one of the best-covered events in postwar Europe.

There is copious testimony—from Greek, Turkish, and other sources (British and American archives are full of documentation and analyses of the events' larger significance)—to the fact that the enormous injury to Istanbul's Greeks was both moral and material. Indeed, this was openly acknowledged by both Prime Ministers Menderes and Alexandros Papagos of Greece. Although the material damage inflicted was enormous, and beyond the Turkish government's desire or means to pay compensation, the violation of the morale, psychological well-being, and simple faith of the Greek victims in what they regarded and thought of as their native city was even more brutal and devastating. It is far easier, in fact, to demonstrate, with fairly indicative numbers, the material destruction and subsequent failure of the Turkish government to render just financial compensation. It is far more difficult to reveal the extent and effect of the moral and political crimes that the government inflicted on the victims with—this must, unfortunately, be said—the complicity of a significant part of Istanbul's citizens.

The humiliation of Istanbul's Greeks was profound. It was a humiliation felt equally, however, by the Greek government and people, which, although ostensibly allied to Britain and the United States, were forced to endure the

constitutes an actual pogrom like those that were carried out in tsarist Russia with the cooperation of the Police in order to annihilate the Jews." On September 10, *Makedonia* carried a half-inch headline in capital letters that read, "The pogrom was based on a prearranged plan. The vandalism had been methodically prearranged ahead of time." In the same issue, the newspaper carried an article entitled, "The Barbarities Recall the Annihilation of the Jews by the Hitlerites."

[2] For references to the documentation, see Chapter 1.

trauma of this premeditated attack on their brothers and sisters in Istanbul under the cover of those two countries' official Cold War foreign policies. This sense of profound—and unprovoked—violation was articulated in the terse language of the spiritual leader of Istanbul's forty-five Greek communities, Patriarch Athênagoras, in his memorandum of November 15, 1955, addressed to the Turkish prime minister and delivered to Menderes some days later:

> Excellency:
> In accordance with the decision of the Holy Synod of the Patriarchate we had in our telegram dated September 11, 1955, expressed the profound affliction felt by us in the face of the great disaster experienced by our churches and the Greek Orthodox Community as a result of the regrettable events which occurred in the course of the night of September 6-7....
>
> Mobs moving under guidance organized according to a specific plan and program, upon a given signal went into action at night, at different points of the town simultaneously, and equipped with different kinds of transportation means and tools of destruction with awe-inspiring violence, engaged in an attack on our race before the very eyes of officers charged with the preservation of public order.
>
> Indeed, the very foundations of a civilization which is the heritage of centuries, the property of entire mankind, has been gravely attacked. The sacred things of our religion have been defiled, seventy of our churches and houses of worship destroyed and most of them set on fire....
>
> Our sacred objects of religion were desecrated, flouted, and plundered. The graves of our dead, including those of the Patriarchs, were broken open. Newly buried corpses were torn to pieces, the bones of the dead removed from their resting places, scattered around and set on fire.
>
> Our clergymen were everywhere persecuted; when found they were manhandled, threatened with killing, and one of them was actually put to death.
>
> The immunity of private dwellings was violated, virgins were ravished and even the sick and the old as well as children, were maltreated. All of us, without any defence, spent moments of agony, and in vain sought and waited for protection on the part of those responsible for order and tranquility. The guaranteed rights of ownership...were trampled upon and hundreds of dwellings were either completely or partially destroyed. The property therein was destroyed or plundered. Precious belongings and savings

which represented the yield of long labor were usurped and many families were deprived of their livelihood and thus plunged into need and poverty.

Damage was wreaked on school buildings and heavy losses were inflicted on school teachers. Worse than the damage done to the establishments, is the offence done to the noble notion of learning and culture....

The fact now is that although the followers of our church formerly lived in a complete sense of security and reliance on the law, and although during the dreadful night in question they fully relied on the legitimate organs of the Government and thus gave full evidence of their law-abiding attitude, after the abominable assault on the fundamentals of their sacred beliefs, on their religion and honor, on the inviolability of their family life and on other gifts of welfare, their sense of being free citizens has been shaken to its very foundations. Seeing themselves all of a sudden deprived of all rights of protection, they are living today in a climate of uncertainty, oppressed by concern.[3]

Although the memorandum's language is terse, the patriarch draws a powerful image of the moral violence inflicted by the Turkish state. The law was violated, and it is implied that the Turkish government was the violator. This was to become widely acknowledged later, but the Menderes government could not afford to admit it as it would obviously have been self-incriminating. However, Athênagoras does remark that those who were responsible for securing Turkish citizens' rights refused to do so. Ultimately, the state bears this responsibility. He speaks with controlled pathos but with uncontained passion and sadness of the violation of family, of personal security and well-being, of the sacred and holy, of learning and culture, of the respect for human labor and its achievements. For him, the pogrom represents "the human being who has become monster," to quote Aziz Nesin.[4] He underscores the obligations of a genuinely democratic state to protect the freedoms and rights of its citizens and to respect the ethics and morality of a generally acknowledged civilization. In this respect, Nesin's vivid descriptions and vignettes in his chronicle of the events[5] stand in stark contradiction to the hollow declamations of Celal Bayar, who, on the one hand, vaunted Turkish civilization—which, he said, had reached a European level—while, on the other hand, gave his "moral" approval to the pogrom's violence. This contrast

---

[3] The English text of the patriarchal memorandum is contained in National Archives, Foreign Office Dispatch No. 210, American Embassy, November 25, 1955.

[4] The description is in *Asılacak adamlar*, p. 27, "insan canavar olmuştur."

[5] *Ibid.*, pp. 16-31.

was immediately apparent on the evening of September 7, when Turkish state radio broadcast Menderes's official version surrounding the pogrom:

> The criminal attack undertaken against the house of our dear Atatürk and our consulate in Salonika, added to the deep emotion created over a period of months in public opinion by the developments in connection with the question of Cyprus, and also influenced by the situation in part premeditated and criminal and in part involuntary and unreasoning, has provoked demonstrations on the part of large masses which have continued...in Istanbul until late last night. We have to state with the deepest regret that in the course of those movements, shops and stores belonging to our fellow citizens of Greek origins have been entered and great damage done.
>
> It may be said that last night Istanbul and the country were in reality exposed to a Communist plot and to a serious blow.
>
> This thoughtless and criminal attempt against the high interests of this country has not only destroyed a part of the national wealth but has also inflicted losses that will be difficult to make good on a part of the Turkish citizenry [i.e., the Greek minority] all of whose rights are guaranteed by the constitution....It goes without saying that it is a requirement of the very concept of a state urgently to make good and to indemnify the losses which have been suffered by these citizens.
>
> The actual participants and the authors of this very painful occurrence...as well as those who organized and provoked it, shall be punished without fail and delay.[6]

THE TURKISH REACTION

The guile, evasions, and falsehoods in this statement, regarding both the role of the government in the pogrom and the pogrom itself, are evident. They would become more so during the next five years, as Menderes's administration continued to employ violence against both Turkey's citizens and its opposition parties. Indeed, he was finally hanged for violating the Turkish constitution. His language in the radio address above is a convenient concoction of "high theory" of democratic governance—and, therefore, of citizens' rights and security—and an epic and crude disregard for the truth, let alone for any ethic of democratic government. Menderes realized, indeed stated, that the damage to the minority community entailed a moral

---

[6] National Archives, Foreign Office Dispatch No. 351, American Embassy, September 8, 1955.

violation. Yet, as we shall see, he blocked all discussion of moral responsibility in the extraordinary session of the Turkish parliament held on September 12. Nonetheless, he did speak to the state's obligation to render moral restitution to the violated rights of the Greek minority, who were, after all, Turkish citizens. *Pro forma*, at least, he was in agreement with the moral claims of the Greek patriarch.

The contradiction between Menderes's statements and deeds was to become striking during the preparations for the September 12 parliamentary session. It was customary for the principal parties to caucus before important debates or votes in the national assembly. Thus, the *Demokrat Parti* Assembly Group met for lunch at the home of Refik Koraltan, the parliament's speaker, in order to discuss the approval of the martial-law bill that Menderes was to propose for Istanbul, Izmir, and Ankara. It seems that the shock of the pogrom weighed heavily on the minds of a growing number of DP deputies, as the temporary martial law had led to the arrest for looting and vandalism of a small number of communists and a very large number of (non-communist) individuals (over 3,000). The organized nature of the violence, and the studied "failure" of police and soldiery to halt it, began to cast suspicion on the government.

Unexpectedly for Bayar, Menderes, Köprülü, Zorlu, Gedik, and other members or supporters of the government, the first speaker to address the DP group proposed that before proceeding to a discussion of the martial-law legislation, the group should discuss, *in camera*, the pogrom itself, and examine the events of September 6-7. The majority approved, or rather favored this reordering of the luncheon agenda, but the government's partisans opposed it and insisted that discussion be limited to the pending measure concerning martial law. Thereupon, Hulusi Köymen, the group's chairman and government supporter, sensing the meeting's unfavorable turn for Menderes, thought to quash it by asking for an open show of support for reordering the agenda. He requested all those favoring the change to stand: the large majority stood. Köymen immediately called a fifteen-minute recess.

During this intermission, Menderes, Köprülü, Koraltan, and other government supporters consulted hurriedly. When the meeting reconvened, Köymen simply announced that there would be no vote on the matter, so the large majority left and the remaining ninety members then voted to discuss martial law only. Shortly thereafter and prior to the parliamentary session, Namık Gedik offered his resignation as interior minister and as a member of the DP. This was undoubtedly called for by Menderes and his ministers, as Gedik had been empowered to replace Gökay as *de facto* governor of the Istanbul region, and had implemented the policy of nonintervention by the security police and army on September 6-7. In fact, for many members of the DP group, the fear of discovery of the government's role was a factor in what would eventually become a schism in the party.[7]

Although he had suppressed the questioning within his own party, Menderes still had to face the opposition Republican People's Party in parliament. Representatives of the US embassy in Ankara followed the proceedings of the assembly's afternoon session, as did a full array of Soviet diplomats. A significant number of Turkish ministers (with the conspicuous absence of the suddenly resigned Gedik) helped to fill an overflowing audience. The interest concentrated on two questions. One was the officially stated purpose of the meeting, which was to ratify the proposed martial-law legislation. The other, which was not an official part of the agenda, was the political survival of Menderes and his government in the face of the question of responsibility for the pogrom.

The leader of the opposition, chief of the RPP, and former prime minister, İsmet İnönü, at the very beginning of his attack on Menderes's parliamentary agenda, expressed the opposition's frustration over Menderes's "failure" to allow a discussion "of the incidents which are given as reasons for the declaration of the state of siege."[8] İnönü remarked that the material losses of citizens from the events of September 6-7 were so great that "our nation has lost a very important part of her national wealth." But the major loss, although undoubtedly great, was not this destruction of material wealth. "In the September 6-7 incident it is really from the moral aspect that our losses are very heavy."

For İnönü and the opposition, as well as for those members of the DP who had attempted to discuss the matter of responsibility for the pogrom, this issue in part overshadowed the priority of approving martial law. İnönü stated that agitations, even those leading to lesser losses, are to be expected, as they are normal in society. But the state is obliged to intervene to protect its citizens and their rights: "The saddest part of the September 6-7 incidents is that the attackers are seen not as people who have lost themselves under the stress of high emotion [a reference to Menderes's explanation of a 'national psychosis' that took hold of government officials and pogromists], but as people who did their work in comfort and ease and almost without any

---

[7] See Başar, *Yaşadığımız devri*, pp. 96-98. He remarks that Menderes's actions and government were to be burdened with this crime, and that Menderes burdened the Turkish state with the material damages inflicted, to the extent of TL100 million.

[8] National Archives, Foreign Dispatch No. 100, American Embassy, September 13, 1955; all references to the parliamentary session are taken from this detailed American report unless otherwise noted.

obstacle in front of them." He continues in this basic manner, in concise language, asserting that the very concept of the inalienability of the rights of the citizen, and of the moral obligation of the law and the state to protect these rights, was grievously attacked on September 6-7: "The activities were aimed at turning this country into a state of hell and at dishonoring the Turkish nation among civilized countries."

Although İnönü supported the maintenance of martial law in Istanbul, he asserted that it was not necessary in the other two cities and so opposed its imposition there. At the same time, he insisted on a detailed examination of the facts surrounding the pogrom and the declaration of martial law: "Every phase of the events remains obscure....We definitely expect that the honorable soldiers who are responsible for the state of siege will fully enlighten the Grand National Assembly and our great nation as the facts become known. It is the only way by which our great nation can be cleansed regardless of how bitter or shameful the facts may be." İnönü had gone to the heart of the matter: the enormous economic destruction, although devastating, was secondary to the attack on the moral fiber of Turkish society. It was for him a matter of moral and civic destruction, and of the corruption of the Turkish state, which had immorally attacked the "honor of the innocent citizen," that is, Turkish citizens of Greek origin.

Having restricted the DP during its assembly-group meeting in the morning, Menderes was now able to resist the opposition, particularly on the points raised by İnönü. First, he clearly set the agenda of the parliamentary session by restricting the matter on which the body was to vote to the continuation of the state of siege, which he succeeded in getting extended to Ankara and Izmir as well, thus easing his adaptation to the changed political atmosphere in this moment of national crisis. The matter of responsibility for the pogrom, and therefore of its origins, could not be passed over in complete silence, however. His own party had in effect thrown it in his face, and the opposition went a good bit further. So Menderes covered himself with a few remarks on the subject, beginning with a defense of the inactivity of the government, police, and army in the face of the large-scale violence, arson, and looting of Istanbul. He attributed this inertia to a national "psychosis which...reduced the police forces in the beginning to such an inaction that it must be admitted that we have suffered a national catastrophe."

Having delivered himself of this justification of the police, he then urged parliament not to concern itself with searching for the pogrom's causes and course. "To go into details on the course of the incidents and to discuss measures would involve the inconvenience of divulging the steps that we propose to take and of prejudicing the facts when they are not yet clarified and crystallized. I am therefore of the opinion that the discussion of the incidents in this Assembly should be terminated at this stage and that it would be advisable to pass to a vote." As in his own party's morning meeting, Menderes acted to forestall any significant discussion of the pogrom's organization and origins, let alone assignment of responsibility. He assured the assembly that the question of the pogrom had been placed before the courts, and that the government supported these courts, "in order that the truth may be brought to light. The Grand National Assembly may await the results with confidence."

In his remarks, Menderes did not state the obvious: these courts were, initially, military courts, which the assembly knew and which was the reason that Inönü did not wish to see them extended to Ankara and Izmir. Nor does Menderes say anything about their procedures, which everyone understood were thoroughly oblivious to the rights of citizens. The subsequent description of these actual procedures depict them as anything but exemplary, and the testimony of Hulusi Dosdoğru is razor-sharp in its observations and ironic descriptions of their improprieties and illegalities.

Having avoided the dangers of a full-blown assembly discussion, Menderes proceeded to pay lip service to the virtues of the genuine state that renders justice to its citizens. In so doing, he attempted to answer Inönü's charges about the rights of innocent citizens and the moral obligation of the state to protect them and itself:

> Furthermore, dear esteemed colleagues, I must state that those who have suffered from these events have for the most part been our Greek fellow countrymen. Among those who have suffered are also Turks and Armenians. When I say that we are accepting as a duty the rectification of the wrongs they have suffered and to compensate them of [*sic*] their losses, whatever they may be, all of you without exception support my declaration. At the same time that we shall make good the material losses we shall rectify the moral side of the matter....

So, once more, Menderes affirmed that the pogrom inflicted not only material damage but perpetrated a moral violation. And how does he propose to right this moral violence, not only against the Greeks, but also against the Turks and Armenians and, finally, the Turkish state and society? He suggests that he will do this "by unmasking the true nature of the affair and by proving in the eyes of the whole world that this incident is not a Turkish act." By the time of parliament's extraordinary session, Menderes and his collaborators were caught up in a desperate struggle literally to save their necks. The cover of political morality and the protection of Turkish citizens' security was obviously a thin veil that could not long hide the grim realities of the Turkish state.

THE GREEK REACTION

The general outrage of the Greek victims themselves was and still is obvious from the very night of the events until today. It was most graphically expressed, as we have already seen in the various eyewitness accounts in Chapter 2. However, one of the earliest and bluntest Greek governmental protests was that of Foreign Minister Stefanos Stefanopoulos, which was sent to the Turkish foreign ministry on September 9. It was short, direct, and threatening in tone. Stefanopoulos came quickly to the main point: political responsibility for the pogrom. This is an important document in the history of Greek-Turkish relations as it set the stage for the diplomatic battle that, after the events of September 6-7, 1955, led into an endless and increasingly complex vortex of Greek-Turkish hostility and enmity.[9] Stefanopoulos warned the Turkish government that:

> The Greek Government has become aware of the violent anti-Greek demonstrations, the unprovoked attacks against the Greek citizens and Greek minority of Constantinople, against the Greek military officers serving NATO, of the destroyed Orthodox Churches, of the Greek consulate building in Smyrna, of houses and buildings belonging to Greek citizens and to the Greek minority of Constantinople. The Greek Government desires to express its most vigorous displeasure as well as the exasperation of the Greek people with these unprecedented events. We fear that they shall have a serious effect in the evolution of relations between the two countries.
>
> The Greek Government strongly protests in the face of these attacks and the consequent great destruction as well as at the manifestation of hostility at the expense of an ally. The Greek Government also protests the stance of the Turkish authorities which, according to the precise reports that have reached us, was clearly passive, in many cases beyond the tolerant observation of riots. These grievous events were of such intensity and form that they endanger the relations between the two countries....
>
> Unfortunately, the impression has been created that there no longer exist, on the Turkish side, the very presuppositions for the

---

[9] Ypourgeion Exôterikôn, Dispatch No. 38901 to Washington, September 13, 1955; the following quotes and references are to this document. Its force and open condemnation of the Turkish government for its responsibility for the pogrom were particularly offensive to Zorlu, for obvious reasons.

preservation of the bonds of friendship that serve the common interests of both countries and the more general proposition of peace.

The Greek Government can in no way accept the view that one is dealing here with deeds of only local significance effected by irresponsible parties. The fact that the attacks took place in all the towns where Greek officials and Greek minorities existed and that all these events took place simultaneously in very many places of these towns which were far distant from one another proves, clearly, that the attacks had been planned beforehand and had been appropriately organized.

And, finally, the fact that these movements evolved in an organized manner and under directives demonstrates at the very least that the Turkish Government did not display the necessary attention and that it did not take clearly the necessary measures, nor did it intervene immediately to restrain these acts after they had commenced.

Despite the justified exasperation of the Greek Government and the Greek people, they kept comparatively calm and they avoided any deed that might have worsened the new tension in their mutual relations.

In the face of this recently created situation, the Greek Government cannot limit itself to a mere expression of stern protest, for it is, at the same time, obliged to call to the attention of the Turkish Government the broader political consequences which will possibly be provoked by the anti-Greek manifestations.

Stefanopoulos

This document was sent on the very day of the special parliamentary session in Ankara. It shows clearly that the Greek government had evaluated the events quite accurately and had no qualms in describing the nature or reality of the destruction, or in charging the Turkish government with the political and moral responsibility for what had occurred. The effect of the memorandum on the Turkish foreign ministry was substantial. Indeed, Zorlu was able to hold back the response until it was sufficiently polemical and combative. Furthermore, Zorlu seems to have refused to accept the communication formally.

On September 12, the American consul in Istanbul sent the State Department an English translation of the shortened, earlier report of the Greek consul on the identified damages to the Greeks. In this document, Agis Kapsambelês, the Greek consul, described the threefold aims of the violence as "[t]he destruction of the financial status of the Greeks; the destruction of the community and religious life; and, the destruction of their morale."[10]

Because of the outrage that the violence aroused throughout Greece, Prime Minister Alexandros Papagos was obliged to address the nation on September 17. As he had been fully apprised by this time of the discussions that had earlier taken place in the Turkish parliament, he also took this opportunity to note Menderes's remarks in the assembly:

> It is with great emotion that I am addressing the Greek people today, mainly to extol the coolness, wisdom, and self-control with which they reacted as a civilized people, to blows affecting the Nation's soul.
>
> I deeply share the Greek people's indignation on account of the tragic events of Turkey against our holy Orthodox Church and our brothers in Turkey.
>
> The destruction of property, plundering and offences against all that is Greek, including the Smyrna Consulate-General and the NATO Greek echelon, which took place simultaneously at different points in Turkey, deeply offends our national feeling and points to the existence of responsible persons. In view of our sincere adherence to the friendship and alliance with Turkey, we expected a different treatment, and that is why reparation should be complete and absolute.
>
> The Greek Government has expressed, through a protest to the Turkish Government, the Greek people's resentment and has formulated complete requests for the moral restoration of national dignity, the material compensation of the victims and the ensuring of positive guarantees for the future of Greek-Turkish relations.
>
> From the speech of the Prime Minister, M. Menderes, before the Turkish National Assembly, we noted what he said about Greek-Turkish friendship, the sanctions to be imposed against the persons responsible for the tragic events and the payment of indemnities to those who sustained material losses.
>
> Further, however, to the good will expressed by words with a view to healing certain wounds, the promise about fair compensations must materialize. But still further, the question of our heavily wounded national dignity remains open.
>
> The satisfaction of those requests is the prerequisite for the continuation of our good relations with neighbor Turkey. When our above justified expectations will have been met, we will be able to talk again about a Greek-Turkish friendship.[11]

---

[10] National Archives, Foreign Dispatch No. 106, American Consul General, Istanbul, September 12, 1955.

[11] TNA:PRO, No. 1014/38/55, Foreign Office, 371/117711, 198335, undated; the English

THE AMERICAN REACTION

From all these exchanges, between the Greek and Turkish governments, between the DP and the RPP, between the two factions within the DP, and between Athênagoras and Menderes, it seems that everyone agreed on two points: the heavy material destruction and, what was even more serious, the moral violation of the Greeks in greater Istanbul. Further, the political significance of the violence, and of the damage caused by it, was inherent in all of these exchanges, speeches, and memoranda. The repercussions on international politics, however, were manifested on September 18, the day after Papagos's address to the Greek nation, when the US secretary of state issued a common statement to the Greek and Turkish governments that would end up encouraging the Turkish side and discouraging the Greek side in their confrontation following the pogrom. This statement also constitutes a landmark in the genesis of anti-American sentiment in Greece, which had felt its ties to the US to be close and warm from the time of its independence in the early nineteenth century. In the short preface to his hortatory advice to Greece and Turkey, John Foster Dulles briefly, almost insignificantly, passes over the recent disturbances in Istanbul. They are regrettable, he remarks, because they occur at a time of Cold War, when the United States has need of Greece and Turkey in the struggle against the Soviet bloc. He continues in this vein:

> I have followed with concern the dangerous deterioration of Greek-Turkish relations caused by the Cyprus Question. Regardless of the causes of this disagreement, which are complex and numerous, I believe that the unity of the North Atlantic community, which is the basis of our common security, must be restored without delay....
>
> I cannot believe that in the face of this record of common achievement, any problem will long disrupt the course of Greek-Turkish friendship. Nor can I believe that the unhappy events of the past two weeks will reverse policies of cooperation which were initiated twenty-five years ago....
>
> I urge you therefore to make every effort to assure that the effectiveness of your partnership is not impaired by present disagreements.

This common note to the Greek and Turkish governments only twelve days after the devastating attacks on the Greeks of Istanbul, in which the suspicion of responsibility hung over Menderes, obviously came as a relief

translation is that of the Foreign Office.

to the latter and as a direct provocation to the Greek government and people. To most Greeks, Dulles's attitude of so-called impartiality toward both the victimizer and the victim appeared as the height of cynicism and political convenience. Moreover, the average Greek considered it an injustice to a faithful ally that had made great sacrifices and sustained substantial destruction in both the Second World War and in the Civil War against the communists.[12]

Why would Dulles have sent such an inflammatory message, which reeked of political expediency, since both the Greek *and* Turkish governments had agreed that the pogrom had unjustifiably caused moral and material harm? The customary, and intelligent, habit of the special departments in the Foreign Office of commenting on the margins of documents sent to them is helpful in this case (as in so many others). Attached to a Foreign Office copy of Dulles's message are the remarks of J. A. Thomson of the Southern Department:

> This message has produced a lively resentment among the Greeks. But it no doubt will do good in the long run. It is satisfactory that Mr. Dulles has reversed the earlier line of the State Department which blamed the Turks and favored the Greeks.
>
> The [British] Secretary of State has sent a message to Mr. Dulles expressing his appreciation of his appeal....

Thomson's statement that Dulles's note would "do good in the long run," despite the "lively resentment" produced in Greece, was obviously the result of wishful thinking and an inability to foresee just how long "the long run" would prove to be. It was clearly occasioned by Macmillan's intense involvement in the Cyprus issue and by the British stance on the matter, as recently expressed in the tripartite conference. Of further interest is Thomson's remark that the State Department had initially blamed Turkey for the pogrom. With his salvational view of his own labors, however, Dulles saw only one goal: marshaling NATO against the Soviet bloc at any cost. For him, "lesser" issues did not deserve any moral consideration.

Prime Minister Papagos lost no time in replying to what he considered to be a provocation and insult to Greece.

> With the unreserved frankness which has always marked the close and friendly relations of Greece with America, I have to inform you of the following:

---

[12] Greek Embassy, Washington, No. 3841/B/29, September 28, 1955, for the text; it also includes the version sent to Menderes and the English version of Papagos's reply to Dulles. Dulles's text is also reproduced in TNA:PRO, No. 371/477, No. 1983351.

Your observation in regard to the restoration of the unity of the North Atlantic Community, which is the basis of our common security, finds us in agreement, and we are fully conscious of our mission and objective in the Mediterranean area where Greece has repeatedly undergone great sacrifices.

Nor do we forget all we owe to the United States of America, which has enabled us to fulfill the requirements of our national interest as well as those of the general interest of the free world. However, morality and justice must not be overlooked. These two factors constitute the most important asset at the disposal of the democratic world and greatly affect the Greek people which is sensitive to all matters touching its national honor.[13]

What emerges from the Dulles note, and from the letters of Papagos and Menderes in response to it, is a commonplace of political life. In 1955, political morality was important only when it coincided with "greater" issues such as the Cold War. Dulles increasingly catered to what the Foreign Office considered to be its interests over Cyprus. And, since Turkey and Britain had come together on this matter, at least at the apex of this development (that is, at the tripartite conference), Dulles considered Britain's political and colonial designs to have priority over Greek demands for justice, honor, or political morality. Material damages, however, can come and then go once they are settled. Moral damages have a remarkable staying power and political longevity.

Finally, it is noteworthy that Dulles's note flew in the face of the analysis of the US's own consulate in Istanbul. On September 14, four days before Dulles sent his note to Menderes and Papagos, US consul Katherine Bracken sent a report to Washington, in which she discussed Menderes's "national-psychosis" theory of the pogrom. In her opinion, the violence had other motivations:

It appears, however, that the following factors played a part in whipping up the tempers of the mobs to the point of uncontrolled fury reached that night:

(1) Excessive nationalism and a fear of latent Greek irredentism which has been inflamed by the Cyprus issue.

(2) Vindictiveness against the Greeks, and vengeance against them for a community life around churches and schools that Turks do not have. These feelings are also tinged with envy of the generally higher standard of living of the Greeks. This was associated with anti-Christianism. In many parts of town the cries

---

[13] Greek Embassy, Washington, No. 3841/B/29, September 18, 1955; see also the report of the British embassy in Athens, TNA:PRO No. 371/117711, No. 198335, for the reaction in Greece. Attached also is Papagos's text of September 17 and Menderes's reply to Dulles.

of "gavur" (infidel) and "Rumlar haram" (Religion wise Greeks are
tabu) were heard.

(3) A display of resentment against the pressure of rising
costs of living, and especially continued shortages of coffee, tea
and sugar which form basic items of diet for lower middle and
lower classes.

Furthermore, just two and a half weeks after Dulles's note on October
5, Bracken sent another report to the State Department, in which she
analyzed the character of public opinion in Turkey in regard to the Greeks
and the country's other minorities more generally. Entitled, "Tendency
Toward Resentment of Minority Elements as a Result of the September 6
Disorders," it was unusually astute, not only about the psychological state
of the minorities, but also about the sentiments of different segments of the
Turkish Muslim majority.

> An atmosphere of tension and uneasiness resulting from the
> September 6 disorders is still evident in Istanbul. Martial Law and
> a midnight curfew has [sic] brought a period of calm. Underneath
> the surface however, there is considerable resentment, anxiety,
> frustration and shock at work on the morale of the various
> elements. At this point the net result appears to be a widening
> of the social breach created by the violence exhibited against the
> minorities during the destruction of September 6.
>
> Minorities generally, as well as some of the French and
> British Levantine families, have lost faith in the development of
> Turkey toward a democracy that would preclude a repetition of
> the outbreaks of discrimination against non-Moslem elements
> which have occurred sporadically during the last several centuries.
> Among middle class and richer minority elements a determination
> is increasingly evident to liquidate capital investments in Turkey
> and to emigrate to some place they consider offers more security.
> The Government has recognized this tendency and has imposed
> an administrative freeze on transfers of property in Istanbul.
>
> Among the Turks, those who are the well educated, who
> have traveled abroad and who have continuing contacts with
> foreigners are still humiliated by the outbreak. The humiliation
> tends to evidence itself more and more in open expressions of
> disillusion, dissatisfaction and loss of confidence in the Menderes
> government. There have also been reported isolated instances of
> Moslem Turks who have abandoned factory investment. Among
> Turks who do not associate with foreigners, there are dangerous
> expressions of "Turkey for the Moslem Turks." This is indicated by

continued statements of resentment against non-Moslem elements in Istanbul, of complaint against the minorities for the problems they have created for the Turkish government, and of justification for the destruction of September 6 on the grounds that "they got just what they deserved."

This openly expressed rejection of the minorities as an assimilable part of Turkish life has obtained such currency that CUMHURIYET [Kemalist, left-liberal newspaper] on September 29, editorially warned Turkish public opinion to be alert and not let "enmity toward the minority elements" disrupt the development of the country...."[14]

On September 29, eleven days after Dulles's note, the Turkish embassy in Athens transmitted a letter from Menderes to Papagos. In it, Menderes attempted to persuade Papagos of his government's sincerity in wishing to make good the moral damages. After noting that his government had expressed its profound regret publicly and officially, and that he had personally proclaimed the value he attached to the Greek-Turkish alliance in the September 12 parliamentary session, he stated that he understood that these gestures had not been considered sufficient to satisfy the dignity and honor of the Greek nation. He agreed, he wrote to Papagos, and perhaps a good opening to future cooperation would be an official ceremony that would restore honor to the Greek flag, to the Greek consulate in Izmir, and to the Greek military contingent serving NATO in the same city.[15] Papagos replied on October 3, and thanked Menderes for his message, which he valued as constituting the first step in restoring Greek-Turkish friendship. At the same time, however, he noted that the matter of reconstruction following the vast devastation was still outstanding and had to be effected quickly. Nevertheless, Papagos concluded, so long as its national honor and legal rights were observed, Greece looked forward to relations with other entities.[16]

A number of large religious institutions worldwide became involved in the effort to inform the US and British governments of the violence and destruction to Greek religious institutions in Istanbul and of the plight of their communicants. These bodies included the National Council of Churches of Christ in the United States, the World Council of Churches

---

[14] National Archives, Foreign Office Dispatch No. 116, American Consul General, Istanbul, September 14, 1955, for the first report; for "Tendency Toward Resentment of Minority Elements as a Result of the September 6 Disorders," National Archives, Foreign Dispatch No. 148, American Consul General, Istanbul, October 5, 1955.

[15] Greek Embassy, Washington, No. 4206/B/29, received in Washington on October 4, 1955.

[16] *Ibid.*

(WCC) in Geneva, and the Church of England. In general, these religious bodies reacted vigorously to the Istanbul atrocities and organized to relieve the suffering. Each had its own separate department of international affairs, and soon the Foreign Office and State Department found themselves carefully responding to the inquiries and, in particular, to the plans for action of the three ecclesiastical bodies. As they will receive separate treatment below, it will be sufficient here to refer to only one such case, the statement adopted by the General Board of the National Council of Churches of Christ in the United States on October 15 and addressed to Dulles in an accompanying letter dated October 12, 1955. Dulles's correspondent was Eugene Carson Blake, president of the council, who closed his letter to the secretary by thanking him for "this opportunity to amplify our concern for the plight of the Greek minority in Turkey."[17]

The council's statement declared that after investigating the matter, it had confirmed that the destruction of Christian churches as well as the property of Greek Christians had been massive, and that people had been injured and even killed.

> Such an outburst of terror cannot be overlooked on grounds of extenuating circumstances....It was therefore timely and appropriate that the Commission of the Church on international affairs brought to the attention of the Secretary of State the reports...concerning the destructions [sic] and possible measures for assistance.
>
> The National Council...expresses profound shock and deep sorrow that such inhumanity of man to man can occur anywhere....
>
> The General Board of the National Council...authorizes its officers and the officers of its Department of International Affairs to continue to exercise their best efforts to arouse concern for the plight of the Greek minority in Turkey by all proper means, including the representations to the Secretary of State and to the United States Delegation to the United Nations.

Although Dulles did not deem it fit to reply, he ordered that the State Department "answer the pointed and aggressive note of president Blake." The answer was duly succinct: "The Department of State was shocked by this unexpected outburst of violence resulting in the wanton destruction of property, and was particularly grieved at the widespread destruction of religious shrines....We deplored not only the moral and physical damage

[17] National Archives, Foreign Office Dispatch No. 104, American Embassy, Athens, October 12, 1955.

involved, but the threat to friendly relations and treaty alliances between the two countries...."

The reference is, most probably, to Dulles's neutered position, in which he blamed both the Greek and Turkish governments equally for disturbing NATO.[18] Dulles's letter does not touch upon the question of morality. At a formal level, both the US and (especially) the British governments were loath to broach the moral questions, sweeping them under the carpet of the political needs of the "Free World." As we shall see later, the Foreign Office's Southern Department was particularly peeved by the intrusion of the World Council of Churches and the archbishop of Canterbury. Finally, one should note, even if only in passing, the formal protests of the Orthodox patriarchates of Moscow, Sofia, Belgrade, and Bucharest in support of the ecumenical patriarchate of Constantinople, albeit under the political bidding of the Soviet government, which nevertheless, for once, coincided with the desires of the Soviet-bloc patriarchs themselves.

A last point in the issue of moral damages was the insistence of the Greek government, throughout its heated discussions with the Turkish government, on severe punishment, not only of those who actually carried out the destruction but of those who conceived and planned it.[19] As we have seen, Menderes expressed his determination to identify and punish those responsible basically through military courts. These courts, however, never even discussed the possibility of governmental responsibility for the events, and so the Greek side had to await the "revelations" of the third Yassıada trial in 1960-1961. *Quis custodiet ipsos custodes?* Who will guard the guardians? The Greek government insisted on placing responsibility, and punishing all who were truly guilty, for a practical reason. It hoped to preclude the repetition of such violence at the expense of the Greek or any other minority. Unfortunately, the persecution of the Greek community continued. In 1964, there was a mass expulsion of the remaining Greeks of Istanbul; today, the Greek *établis* and Greek-minority population as a whole left in the city constitute less than 1 percent of the former Greek population, with much of its property lost.

The entire issue of moral damages essentially flows out of violations of the law, which in turn flow out of the violations of the constitution that embodies every democratic state's principles of law and governance. In theory, at least, a democratic government exists to secure the rights of its citizens, in consonance

---

[18] The State Department reply is included in the document cited above.

[19] Ypourgeion Exôterikôn, No. 48645/T4, Ep, telegram of ministry, November 8, 1955, to Greek embassy in Ankara, instructing the embassy to raise the issue of punishing the guilty.

with its constitutional mandate. When the state intentionally abridges or attacks these rights, or when it fails to protect its citizens when other citizens attack them, then it is, of course, guilty of violating its own constitutional legality. Historically, the modern Turkish state has been the principal violator of its citizens' rights. Until recently, its laws were often legislated in order to give a "legal" basis to these violations.

In the case of the pogrom of September 6-7, 1955, the state conspired to attack the Greek communities of Istanbul, and did so with approximately 100,000 Turkish citizens who committed the actual acts of destruction. It has to be admitted that this large body of vandals participated willingly in the violent and illegal acts that traumatized—and, in fact, effectively destroyed— these communities. Nonetheless, the *constitutional violence by the Turkish state itself* is reflected in the fact that many of the nineteen trials at Yassıada, and many charges in those proceedings, were derogated to or subsumed under the more important trial that accused Menderes and his government of violating the Turkish constitution (as opposed to just, or even primarily, inciting and causing material damage).[20]

Since it was proven that the pogrom resulted from conspiracy, and that the ruling *Demokrat Parti* prepared it and recruited the participants, the state was responsible for the criminal acts of each participant and organizer. Accordingly, all the crimes committed by the pogromists were done so not only under the state's authority but at its request. Consequently, thousands of individual criminal acts perpetrated during September 6-7 were also crimes of the Menderes government. Thus, in investigating these crimes and their destructive and moral aftereffects, we are examining both the perpetrators and those who conceived and planned them, that is, the government.

When the Menderes government imposed martial law on September 7, subsequently railroaded it through parliament, and had General Fahrettin Aknoz arrest thousands of people (many of whom, such as the communists, were innocent), it was in effect prosecuting the willing executors of its own premeditated violence. Dêmêtrios Kaloumenos recounted a conversation he had with a Turkish soldier the day after the pogrom. He asked the soldier why he was guarding a "house-store" (a residential building with a store on the ground floor) that had been destroyed. The soldier answered: "I don't know. Yesterday, they ordered me to change from my military uniform to civilian clothes, and then to proceed to the destruction of this house-store. Today,

---

[20] See *Decisions* and *Opinions* of the nineteen trials at Yassıada. Although extensively quoted in the work of Dosdoğru for the events of September 6-7, 1955, one must consult the transcripts of all nineteen trials.

they told me to change from my civilian clothes into my military uniform and guard the house-store."[21] Each criminal act carried out by the mobs was also one in which the government took part: vandalism, theft, sale of stolen goods, arson, destruction of buildings, libraries, clinics, schools, churches, and cemeteries, as well as physical attacks on individuals, including kidnapping, rape, and murder.[22] Today, in addition to their criminal nature, these offenses would also certainly fall into the category of hate or racially inspired crimes. Still, as reprehensible as the events of September 6-7 were, they were already being justified in Turkey soon after their occurrence.

A telling example of the confusion and turmoil within government ranks as to whether the pogrom was a crime or merely an enthusiastic national outpouring of youth is to be found in Mükerrem Sarol's own reaction during the night of the events. Sarol was a government minister (without portfolio) and close to Menderes. On the night of September 6, he was in his office in Ankara chatting with a friend:

> The phone rang and on the other end of the line, the alarmed and agitated voice of İhsan Doruk spoke to me.
>
> "Mercy, Mükerrem Bey...a very harsh disaster has fallen on...Istanbul. The city has filled with thousands of raging men. They have smashed the display windows, they have poured out into the streets the merchandise, and the buildings are being destroyed. Whence they came and from where they emerged is unknown. This group of people, with tools in their hands, are filling İstiklal Caddesi, they have leveled every store to the ground. *The security of life and property has vanished* [stress added]. I have with me Muzaffer Paşa, commandant of the air force, who was able with great difficulty to escape from the danger of the maddened crowd and managed to reach my house. As an eyewitness of the experience, I now put him on the phone."
>
> In the background, I heard the voice of Muzaffer Paşa. Though he was a cool-headed soldier his voice was agitated:
>
> "The sight I saw was terrible...thousands of men, rage projecting from their eyes, attacked shops, dwellings, display windows, and the merchandise inside them, and no matter what else, they tore and destroyed....*There were no police, no security, there was indeed nothing at all* [stress added]....There was raging

---

[21] Dêmêtrios Kaloumenos, oral interview (the soldier's photograph appears in his book, as well as in this volume).

[22] In this respect, the replacement of due process by martial law suited Menderes from every point of view.

desire and no control, for Istanbul had been seized....If measures
are delayed, I fear that the road is open to irreparable damage."[23]

To İhsan Doruk (an unidentified official) and Muzaffer Paşa, all law and
order had vanished, as had the security forces, and the state had ceded its
sovereignty over life and property to the pogromists.

Sarol then attempted to get through to Kerim Gökay, Istanbul's *vali*,
to get a more accurate reading and evaluation of the seeming chaos and
lawlessness:

> "*Vali Bey efendi*, what is happening in Istanbul? According to my
> various phone communications, the city is in a raging state. The
> flood of the *başıbozuks* [irregular bodies of Ottoman armies], it
> is said, has burned and destroyed Istanbul. This is unbelievable,
> what is the essence of the matter? If it is said to be true, why do
> you sit peacefully in your office?"
>
> The *Vali*, who did not answer my question, said directly: "His
> excellency, the Minister of the Interior is here. Let me put him on
> the phone and you will see."
>
> Gedik was on the other end of the phone. Thus I now
> transmitted the information to the appropriate minister, my
> colleague, according to which Istanbul was enveloped by disaster.
> For it was explained to me in telephone communication...that
> the disturbances were fraught with serious consequences. For, I
> said, if this looting spread over all Istanbul it would be a tragedy
> for the country.
>
> Gedik answered in an annoyed but quiet voice: "They
> exaggerate! The situation is not like that! In Salonika, they hurled
> a bomb at the house of Atatürk. The radio announced it at noon.
> Some reporters put it in large headlines and this aroused the
> people. Those things that were explained to you are mistaken due
> to the misleading....[break in text] These events are the protests of
> our compatriots. Indeed they are much more, and they should be
> likened to a national rebellion."
>
> "Namıkcık," I said, "what kind of a national rebellion is
> this. They smashed windows, they poured the merchandise out
> into the streets and they looted everything. How can you call
> this a national rebellion? I think that because you sit around in
> the *Vilayet* office, you are very little informed of these events.
> This is not a national rising, but simply a rebellion, simply a
> national disaster. As a minister, how could you abandon the city
> to the hands of brigands? If the police are not sufficient, demand

---

[23] Mükerrem Sarol, *Bilinmeyen Menderes*, Istanbul, 1983, vol. 1, pp. 444-445.

assistance from the army. Certainly, you must do something!" Namık [Gedik] replied: "The commander of the army, Vedat Paşa, is by my side. He says that the necessary precautions have been taken!"
"Mercy, Namıkcık, what kind of precaution is this? You have abandoned enormous Istanbul to the hands of looters. How can the state stand by idly as a spectator to this vile disgrace?"...[24]

Hulusi Dosdoğru wrote that, although the whole world knew that the pogrom had been a conspiracy by the government, the latter obviously kept that fact a secret from the Turkish people, which gave the *Demokrat Parti* its support again in the belief that the violence was a spontaneous, national outbreak. About the Greek minority, which had also supported Menderes, Dosdoğru wrote that "it suffered carnage and destruction, the bones of their dead were exhumed from their graves, their churches and schools were burned and destroyed, their priests were circumcised, and their virgins were raped." Further, he saw it as ironic that the state had planned such destruction and then had to pay dearly from its treasury for the ruins.[25]

PHYSICAL VIOLENCE, AND THE ISSUE OF THE NUMBER OF DEAD AND RAPED
It would seem that there was no mass murder. There is no evidence that pogromists, with the exception of police and soldiers, were issued firearms, although, as indicated previously, they were uniformly issued clubs, planks with nails, axes, iron rods, gasoline, dynamite, and even knives. There is evidence in the sources, however, of the ever-present danger of events spiraling out of control and leading to a massacre. The pogromists' rage against the Greeks and other minorities, and even against foreigners, was intense and widespread. According to one eyewitness, this rage was not sated with massive destruction of property: "What we did to them was nothing [said one demonstrator]. We should have killed them so that the Greek and Armenian languages would be completely destroyed."[26] And, as mentioned in Chapter 2, one of the oft-repeated chants during the chaos was *Evvela Mal, Sonra Can* ("First Your Property, Then Your Life").[27] Nevertheless, there are

[24] *Ibid.*, p. 446.
[25] Dosdoğru, *6/7 Eylül olayarı*, p. 11.
[26] Ypourgeion Exôterikôn, No. 2757/29/3. T4, Ep, sent by KYP (the Greek Central Intelligence Service) to the foreign ministry on September 20 and received on September 21, 1955.
[27] Theodôropoulos, *Sêmeiôma*, p. 13. For references to religious insults, see National Archives, Foreign Office Dispatch No. 116, American Consul General, Istanbul, September 14, 1955; Paulos Palaiologos, *Diagramma*, p. 35; Leônidas Koumakês in Tsoukatou, *Septemvriana*, p. 183.

also specific references to orders given to the organized bands and groups of demonstrators *to refrain* from taking human life. The Greek consul-general of Istanbul, in his report to Athens, noted that despite the massive size of the demonstration and its consequent destruction, the demonstrators carried out the latter "while avoiding bloodshed as far as possible."[28] His view was confirmed by Výrôn Theodôropoulos, who stated that the pogromists had been given orders *not* to kill.[29] Osman Tan, president of the DP's Bosphorus chapter, testified (in the military trials presided by General Aknoz in 1956) that on witnessing a physical assault on Theodore Enotiadês, a Greek priest, he cried out to the attackers: "Boys! Smash, devastate, but do not take the life of anyone."[30]

In the poverty-stricken neighborhood of Belgratkapı, the pogromists had, at one point, finished with their destruction and were sitting by idly, awaiting further instructions. One of the less submissive Greeks asked the band why, if they were finished in Belgratkapı, did they not go elsewhere. One of the vandals answered: "We do not move on yet as another order may come to kill you."[31] Alexandros Chatzopoulos, the Greek member of the Turkish national assembly, stated that, although his aged and ailing father had been beaten in his mother's presence, generally, "in all the houses that they invaded," the demonstrators immediately announced: "Do not be afraid. We shall not massacre you. For there is a specific order on that matter. We shall only destroy your houses!"[32] The American consular report of December 1, 1955, stated that "only one person is fairly certain to have died during the riots."[33] Similarly, and much earlier, the British consul in Istanbul reported that: "One Greek priest lost his life in the riots. He is believed to have burned to death when the Greek Orthodox church at Balıklı was set on fire."[34] Taken as a whole, all this evidence clearly points to an organized attack against property, in which the demonstrators desisted, for the most part, from taking human life. However, they were not ordered to desist from any other depredation

---

[28] National Archives, Foreign Office Dispatch No. 106, American Consul General, Istanbul, September 12, 1955.

[29] Theodôropoulos, *Sêmeiôma*, pp. 10 and 13.

[30] Chrêstidês, *Ekthesis*, p. 108.

[31] *Ibid.*, p. 108.

[32] The testimony is quoted from the court-martial proceedings, *Ibid.*, p. 108.

[33] National Archives, Foreign Office Dispatch No. 228, American Embassy, Ankara, December 1, 1955. This was to prove incorrect on two counts: first, the court-martial proceedings were communicated to the Turkish government and, second, numerous Greek sources indicated that murders were indeed committed and were being tried in the military tribunals.

[34] TNA:PRO, Istanbul, No. 1491/87/55, September 22, 1955; again, the number of only one death is in error, for the reasons stated in the previous footnote.

(except from attacking Muslim Turks and their property).

Still, the American and British consular reports have greatly oversimplified the matter of killing. On closer examination of the evidence, it seems that more than one individual died. There were deaths of Greeks that occurred during the riots and even afterward as a result of the physical violence.[35] Indeed, the specific evidence points to the deaths of at least thirty Greeks, and perhaps more, for it is possible that a number of deaths went unrecorded as a result of the ensuing chaos. Certain evidence indicates that there was a definite effort by the Aknoz martial-law regime to tone down and suppress much of the news, especially in the Turkish and local Greek press.

I have used five sources (see Appendix B) for a catalogue of the dead, all of which, however, are vague on details (and obviously lead to issues of victim identification or, just to give one example, double-counting of the same victim). Nonetheless, the fact is that the assessment by diplomats of only one known death seems way off the mark.

It also appears that many people over a wide area were severely beaten, that rape was a consistent form of violation, and that there were even cases of forced circumcision.[36] In a confidential report to the Greek government, the journalist Paulos Palaiologos, who had been sent on a special mission to investigate the pogrom, described the violence: "The demonstrators avoided the use of firearms, for the order of the pogrom's organizers was that demonstrators not shed blood. Thus, they were restricted to using their hands

---

[35] Lois Whitman (Helsinki Watch), *The Greeks of Turkey*, p. 50, lists fifteen deaths, while sixteen are given in the reports of Senator Homer Capehart and journalist Noel Barber. Atzemoglou, *Mnêmes*, pp. 61-63, adds the name of a seventeenth. Yelda, *Azaltırken*, pp. 17-18, adds that it is possible that some deaths were not even reported, as in the case of the three charred bodies in a sack in Beşiktaş. Megas Reumiôtês, *Syrriknosê*, pp. 84-85, refers to three bodies found in ruins of stores, and to two bodies washed up on the shores of the Bosphorus. Koumakês, *Miracle*, pp. 54-55, speaks of over twenty people dead.

All recent catalogues of purported deaths and/or murders during the pogrom are based on the specific investigation by Helsinki Watch, whose substantive report on the human- and civil-rights violations of the Greeks of Turkey was published in 1992. The report lists fifteen such deaths, of which four are anonymous (and questionable); and while the site of death is noted in all cases, the exact (or approximate) time of death is given in only eight. What is important for the present analysis, however, is that the report often gives its sources for the deaths, including six cases (with names and dates) cited in contemporary Turkish newspaper accounts and two cases referred to in the subsequent debates in the Turkish parliament. To date, unfortunately, there is still no official Turkish governmental or police report on the violence of September 6-7, 1955.

[36] See, below, the conclusions of the Aknoz court-martial proceedings on the numbers tried for such crimes; Chrêstidês, *Kypriako*, p. 157.

to repulse, beat, and strike."[37] According to the first reports of the events, hundreds of Greeks required first aid for treatment of wounds and blows sustained from the attacks.[38]

Far and away the great majority of beatings must have gone unreported, although the confidential files of the Turkish police and security forces might contain these data. Furthermore, while large-scale destruction of shops, churches, and homes were, by their nature, both notable and easy to detect, a five-minute beating of an individual involved a much smaller scale and certainly a quick and transient one. Still, the evidence is clear that there were numerous assaults. While the few cases reported dealt primarily with Greek clergy and schoolteachers, a contemporary observer asserted that although Greek clergy were specifically targeted for assault, "the lion's share of the beatings fell on the common people...."[39] Most official documents, however, focus on the attacks on the Greek clergy. In many neighborhoods, the pogromists actively sought out hierarchs, priests, deacons, and sextons.[40] The patriarch had complained bitterly to Menderes concerning this fact in his memorandum of November 15. Apparently, next to looting and destroying the material possessions of Istanbul's Greeks, the mobs took particular pleasure in beating and humiliating their spiritual representatives. The frightful attacks on the three clergymen at Zoodochos Pege (Balıklı) monastery mentioned briefly in Chapter 2 is the best-documented episode. The victims were Gerasimos, bishop of Pamphilos and abbot of the monastery, ninety-year-old monk Chrysanthos Mantas, and novice Euangelos Mastorakês. After having survived a hellish night subsequent to his many beatings, Gerasimos was taken to a hospital, where he recounted his story the next day.

Although the great gate of the walled monastery had been shut and barred, rioters led by three policemen managed to climb a utility pole, leap onto the refectory roof, pass onto the roof of the offices, and jump down into the courtyard. Once inside the courtyard, the gate was opened and the crowd rushed in, screaming, ringing the monastery's bells, and smashing windows. The bishop, completely defenseless, waited in his cell.

The demonstrators first set about looting the two storehouse rooms below

[37] Paulos Palaiologos, *Diagramma*, pp. 6 and 24; Chrêstidês, *Kypriako*, p. 156, reports that they were lightly wounded.

[38] See Greek Embassy, Washington, No. 4266/B/29, dated October 17, 1955, which received on that date the detailed report entitled, "Concerning the Events of September 6," sent by the foreign ministry on October 11 of that year. It states that, "hundreds of Greeks were beaten in the very worst manner possible."

[39] Megas Reumiôtês, *Syrriknosê*, p. 84.

[40] National Archives, American Consul General, Istanbul, Dispatch No. 210, November 25, 1955; also, see above footnote 33 as to the erroneous nature of the earlier reports.

the episcopal offices (one for the monastery's supply of candles, the other for food). They then broke into the offices and, waving their clubs, ordered Gerasimos to emerge from his cell while some set about destroying the furniture and others the refectory. Demanding that he turn over a Turkish flag to them, they raised it over the monastery. As they smashed the furniture, they hurled the broken pieces at the bishop himself and then threw a container of water on him. During the chaos, meanwhile, the lights suddenly went out; the vandals then turned on the terrified bishop and began to beat him furiously about the head, which resulted in the hemorrhaging of his right eye, nose, and forehead. Having succeeded in breaking into the fortress-like monastic enclosure and initiating its destruction, this first wave left the monastery, although not before kicking the bishop into a state of numbness atop the accumulated rubble. When the bishop recovered, he hoped that the monastery's trials had passed and that it would now be left alone. Unfortunately, roughly an hour later, a second attack followed, with a far greater number of attackers, which, for that reason, proved to be far more destructive.

This new wave attacked with crazy yells and patriotic songs, accompanied by clapping and ringing of the monastery's bells. Then began the general arson of the monastery and church, and the desecration of the patriarchal mausoleums. Quickly thereafter, the episcopal office filled with thick smoke, with the bishop trapped in the room. As the stairs leading to the office were rapidly being consumed by flames, he jumped out of a window that was about four meters from the ground. Shortly, however, he was discovered and brought back to endure the rioters' mockery. In the general confusion, he managed once more to escape into the area of the patriarchal tombs, but was rediscovered, beaten by metal rods, and accused of hiding artillery! By this time, a policeman had intervened and Gerasimos was led away from the monastery and his assailants, although his suffering still did not end. Four policemen accompanied him to the police station, but they were not about to shield him from further assault. "From this point on, a new tragedy began," Gerasimos recounted. "Every four or five paces, a certain man in military uniform…between…two policemen…began to kick me and the nearby soldiers refused to intervene."[41]

The fate of his other two colleagues, especially that of the aged monk, Chrysanthos Mantas, was also tragic. After the novice, Euangelos Mastorakês, was found hiding under the bed in his cell, he was subjected to systematic beating and taunting. En route to the hospital, he was robbed of his money and gold watch. The elderly archimandrite Chrysanthos suffered a much

---

[41] The essence of the bishop's suffering is recounted in Chrêstidês, *Ekthesis*, pp. 80-84.

worse end, however. Mastorakês saw him last at about 2:00 to 2:30 AM, when he set off for the hospital. It was thought at first that the old monk had been burned alive when the monastic residence partially collapsed in the fire. But his remains were not found there.[42] He was killed, and his body flung into a well. The bishop also seems to have died, later, from his many wounds.[43]

The metropolitan of Helioupolis, a well-known scholar and historian of Orthodoxy, was confronted by the pogromists in the suburb of Arnavutköy (Mega Reuma). They broke into his apartment to loot and destroy, and then beat him badly, pulling out his beard and hair and leaving him drenched in blood.[44] The metropolitan of Derkon was attacked and trampled underfoot, being badly beaten about the face and body.[45] The metropolitan of Chalcedon (Kadıköy) was beaten and dragged, half-naked, into the streets. A policeman took him under his protection, as the mob continued to cry out: "It's good you suffered these things. They should let us crush you underfoot like *pestil* [dried fruit pressed into thin layers]."[46]

In his report to the patriarch on the destruction in Galata, Beşiktaş, and Palaion Banion, the bishop of Daphnousia detailed the desecration of the church of the Birth of the Virgin: "The tragedy of the destruction and desecration attained [is of] a more frightful and unusual character as a result of the beating of the old priest, the archimandrite Sôkratês Papanikolas, who, having been beaten, was dragged out [of the church] to the tramlines. After the desecration, some Christians, fearful and terrorized, transferred him to his home, half-dead."[47]

Noel Barber, the reporter from the *Daily Mail*, arrived on September

---

[42] *Ibid.*, p. 84. These episodes and the three men's fate were much discussed among local Greeks and eventually entered their folklore. See Tsoukatou, *Septemvriana*, p. 75, who repeats the following oral tradition: "As soon as martial law was declared, they turned the bishop over to some soldiers to take him to a hospital, for he had been beaten. On the road, they said to him: 'You have two eyes, and that is too many,' so they plucked out one of his eyes. But look, you know all that. Let us turn to the story of my father." The growth of legend in this brief narrative is obvious. In fact, the bishop seems to have died from his wounds, but later.

[43] Atzemoglou, *Mnêmes*, p. 60. For these episodes, see also National Archives, Foreign Office Dispatch No. 106, American Consul General, Istanbul, September 12, 1955; Ypourgeion Exôterikôn., Istanbul, No. 116, September 9, 1955; Ypourgeion Exôterikôn, Ekkl., Athens to Washington, No. 38665, September 11, 1955; Megas Reumiôtês, *Syrriknosê*, p. 69.

[44] National Archives, Foreign Office Dispatch No. 106, American Consul General, Istanbul, September 12, 1955; Paulos Palaiologos, *Diagramma*, p. 24; the next day he was seen running about the streets of Arnavutköy shouting madly, "Exchange, Exchange [of populations]!" Megas Reumiôtês, *Syrriknosê*, pp. 82 and 84.

[45] *Ibid.*, plus Chrêstidês, *Ekthesis*, pp. 92-93; Greek Embassy, Washington, No. 3745/B/29, September 9, 1955, sent from the foreign ministry in Athens, No. 38683, on the same day.

[46] Chrêstidês, *Ekthesis*, pp. 90-91; see also Paulos Palaiologos, *Diagramma*, p. 24.

[47] Greek Embassy, Washington, No. 4311/B/29, October 21, 1955.

8 and made an extensive effort to review the vast extent of destruction. He spoke to many who had experienced the violence. Turkish censorship made sure that none of his dispatches ever left the Turkish post office, and he was able to file his reports only on reaching Athens on September 13. His reportage is authoritative, often specific, and reliable inasmuch as the physical remains of the ruins could not be censored. Somewhat more difficult is the matter of checking his oral sources, for they were compiled after the fact, not at the time of the events. Still, many, if not all, of the details from his oral accounts are broadly corroborated by independent observers.

> The church of Yedikule was utterly smashed, and one priest was dragged from bed, the hair torn from his head and the beard literally torn from his chin.
>
> Another old Greek priest, in a house belonging to this church, and who was too ill to be moved was left in bed, and the house was set on fire and he was burned alive....
>
> At the church of Yeniköy, a lovely spot on the edge of the Bosphorus, a priest of 75 was taken out into the street, stripped of every stitch of clothing, tied behind a car and dragged through the streets.
>
> At the church of Yenimahalle one priest was stripped and driven nude tied to the top of a lorry.
>
> They tried to tear the hair of another priest, but failing that they scalped him, as they did many others.[48]

Among those physically accosted was the deacon of Tarabya, who "received a severe beating and while unconscious was placed in a coffin and thrown into the sea....He was saved by an unidentified man who threw himself into the sea, took him out and nursed him during the night."[49]

---

[48] *Daily Mail*, September 14, 1955. Some of these episodes were reported independently of Noel Barber. For the incidents in Yeni Mahalle and Yedikule, see Tsoukatou, *Septemvriana*, pp. 60 and 75. The former incident was recounted by Symeôn Vafeiadês, a member of the patriarchal committee appointed to determine the damages to churches, while the latter one was related by the son of the very priest who suffered the mistreatment described on p. 75. The son signed his testimony anonymously as "Enas Kônstantinoupolitês" (A Constantinopolitan); he did not name his father's church because, as he said, "we still own land there." He described how he finally secreted his father out of Yedikule: "[I] placed a turban on and about his head so that the few remaining patches of beard would be hidden, and placing a cap on his head and employing whatever other camouflage, with the fear of God...I took him to the isle of Antigonê where we were spending the summer." He adds "that the demonstrators hung the priest of Vlanga upside down." Tsoukatou, *Septemvriana*, p. 60.

[49] The dispatch of Greek consul Kapsambelês, as reported in National Archives, Foreign Office Dispatch No. 106, American Consul General, Istanbul, September 12, 1955. It is difficult to evaluate this report inasmuch as Kapsambelês and all diplomatic officials were prohibited from

The religious hatred behind this physical violence against Orthodox ecclesiastics was not restricted to them but included Orthodox communicants. The pogromists repeatedly yelled out a variety of pejoratives, including: *gavur* (infidel); *Kahrolsun, gavurdur* (Damn him, he's an infidel); *Rum haram* (the Greek is illicit); *Yıkın, kırın, gavurdur* (Destroy, smash, he's an infidel); and *ihtar geçesi* (night of warning), which was completed by the phrase, *Dün şeker bayramı, bugün kurban bayramı* (Yesterday was the holiday of sugar, today is the holiday of sacrifice).[50] In destroying Greek merchandise, the rioters often yelled out, "We do not need infidel goods."[51] So it was that the local Greek masses bore the brunt of the attacks. The Greek government estimated that some hundreds of Greeks were assaulted that night.[52] We are, accordingly, looking at mass assaults in which the police intervened only when it seemed that the attack might lead to the victim's death, which nevertheless occurred in a number of cases.

Fred Sondern writes of a particular incident in which a Greek storeowner and his wife were present when the demonstrators appeared: "The owners of the store, an elderly Greek-Turk and his wife, had pulled down their shutters but had stayed in the shop. The old man had courage: 'You filth,' he shouted as the first rioters broke in, 'my family lived in Istanbul for six generations. We are as good Turks as you.' He was silenced with a blow of a club. In a few minutes the store was a shambles."[53] Reference has already been made to the frightful clubbing by demonstrators of the teacher Alexandros Iatropoulos.[54] The author, Leônidas Koumakês, himself born in Istanbul and present in the city that night, records the experience of his father, who had been forewarned by a Turkish friend and neighbor to stay home the next day. The elder Koumakês had ignored his friend's warning, however, and was closing his shop the following evening when he heard strange noises:

> He hurriedly turned off the lights and slipped out of the shop. That instant he was approached by five people who had detached

naming their sources out of fear of compromising them.

[50] See footnote 26 above, and also Koumakês, *Miracle*, p. 65. For "gavur" and "Rum haram," see National Archives, Foreign Office Dispatch No. 116, American Consul General, Istanbul, September 14, 1955; for "ihtar geçesi" and "Dün şeker bayram, bugün kurban bayram," see Paulos Palaiologos, *Diagramma*, p. 35; and for "Kahrolsun, gavurdur" and "Yıkın, kırın, gavurdur," see Leônidas Koumakês in Tsoukatou, *Septemvriana*, p. 183.

[51] B. E./Khosdegian, "A Historical Night," II, "The demonstrators shouted, 'we do not need the merchandise of infidels'"; also, footnote 38 above.

[52] Greek Embassy, Washington, No. 45871/T4, Ep, October 11, 1955; also, footnote 38 above.

[53] Sondern, "Istanbul's Night of Terror," p. 186.

[54] Tsoukatou, *Septemvriana*, pp. 179-180.

themselves from the mainstream of the mob. They closed in on him menacingly....

"Hey, *gavur*, why don't you hoist a Turkish flag in your shop, eh," asked one of them. That was the signal. The five of them fell on him immediately, punching and kicking him.

My father, dizzy from the pummeling, tried, hopelessly, to protect himself with some defensive punches. But his situation was not good at all.

Fortunately, a noisy ambulance passing by distracted his attackers and, "bleeding badly and still dizzy from the blows, he ran for his life as fast as he could, pulling in the last ounce of his strength."[55]

The same author records the vicious attack on Apostolos Nikolaidês, whose shop was in Galata. Hearing that there would be demonstrations over the purported Greek bombing in Thessalonikê, he closed his shop early and crossed over to his home at Kuzguncuk, in the district of Yeni Mahalle. There, he and his family witnessed and heard the destruction of Greek businesses, churches, and dwellings. Although it seemed to be over by midnight, a new wave of rioters appeared on the scene and eventually reached Nikolaidês's home. The leader of this particular mob, a certain Kemal who was well-known to Nikolaidês since the latter had often helped him, placed the Greek in a dilemma as to how to avert pending disaster. He hesitated over whether to lock the door or to try and reason with his acquaintance. Taking a Turkish flag with him, he decided to reason with him. Thus, armed with the flag, he descended the steps of his house and appeared suddenly before the assembled crowd. He stated that he was loyal to Turkey and that he had actually served in the Turkish armed forces on three different occasions. The suddenness of their intended victim's appearance before them, with the Turkish flag and military service, temporarily silenced the crowd, but, after this temporary hesitation, they attacked him nonetheless. He was hit from behind, struck forcefully in the back of the head by a mace, and collapsed, unconscious. The victim's fifteen-year-old son screamed loudly, "Brother Kemal, you're murdering my father,"[56] which finally succeeded in turning away the mob. The family decided that night that they would abandon their home early in the morning, taking with them only what they could wear (so as not to attract attention), and never return. Despite two subsequent surgeries, Nikolaidês never recovered and suffered partial amnesia for the rest of his life.

In her seventh month of pregnancy, Gedikoulianê Iôannidou-Môysidou

---

[55] Koumakês, *Miracle*, p. 49.
[56] *Ibid.*, pp. 63-65.

was witness to a whole skein of crimes. A group of demonstrators broke into her house, and destroyed it and its supply of foodstuffs. This smaller group was part of a larger one that burned the church in the area (described in the previous chapter) and then proceeded to raping young girls. According to Iôannidou-Môysidou, "They destroyed young girls in the most vulgar manner. They removed their clothes and when they resisted, they scarred their faces [with a knife] and bit their breasts."[57] The matter of ascertaining the extent—and, especially, specific cases—of sexual violence is extremely difficult because, with both Greeks and Turks, one is dealing with shame cultures and not with medical or clinical case files. In both societies, virginity and sexual abstinence were prerequisites of social and family values and honor, to say nothing of marriage. Rape was considered an extreme violation of both personal and family honor. In regard to the pogrom, Christoforos Chrêstidês remarked, "they did not keep statistics for women who were raped for easily comprehensible reasons."[58] Theodôropoulos also noted this reality: "There were quite a few incidents of rape...but for reasons that are easily understood, the victims remained silent."[59] In his final report on the pogrom, the us ambassador utilized the report of Istanbul's chief of police, who "...gave no figures for the number of injured, but did say that no case of rape was reported."[60] According to unofficial sources, however, Warren then said that there were several thousand injured (mostly "rioters") and between forty and fifty cases of rape (and, according to him, only one death). The us diplomat admitted that the Istanbul police chief's estimates were "slightly on the low side."

Certainly, in the case of both murders and rapes, the estimates are all too low, as both the direct and indirect evidence indicates. The patriarch had informed Menderes of the rapes of virgins and on yet another occasion had warned, "our children are poised for flight [from Turkey]. Especially the girls, for they are overcome by the fear of being raped."[61] That rape of Greek girls and women of all ages had occurred was well-known to both Greek and Turkish officials, and there even appear to have been cases of the rape of boys, at least in the Greek sources. The Turkish security authorities were informed of many rapes, as well as of the pending danger of further rapes during the pogrom itself. Thus, the claim by Istanbul's chief of police that "no case of rape was reported" is inexplicable. Indeed, no less a representative of Turkish

[57] Tsoukatou, *Septemvriana*, pp. 99-100.
[58] Chrêstidês, *Kypriako*, p. 157.
[59] Theodôropoulos, *Sêmeiôma*, p. 15.
[60] National Archives, Foreign Office Dispatch No. 228, Ankara, December 1, 1955.
[61] Paulos Palaiologos, *Diagramma*, pp. 23-24.

authority than a retired military judge, General Arif Onat, in his testimony at Yassıada, spoke of rape in *specific* rather than general terms: "After a while [during the pogrom], Judge Şevki Mutlugil telephoned from Selimiye: 'Over here there are young girls, women, and children and the reputation of their chastity and honor is at stake.'"[62] A Greek foreign-ministry report noted that rapes of girls and boys took place in a number of areas.[63] In a conversation between two members of the Turkish communist party who were among the many communists jailed for supposedly engineering the pogrom, Hasan Dinamo records the comments of his comrade, Conga.

> That night [September 6-7], each of us was asleep in our dwellings with his wife and children....We heard the news of the destruction of Istanbul in our neighborhood and of the labors that the *Demokrat Parti* had carried out. The [DP] party members of each district went to Beyoğlu, Samatya, Yedikule, Heybeli, and Büyükada and began to carry out the plans they had made on that morning. Thereafter, speaking out loudly of how they raped Greek girls in their houses, of how they circumcised a priest, they now suddenly change their tune as they understand that these acts constitute a crime. So now they attempt to blame some socialist dealers in used shoes for the crime.[64] [Conga sold used shoes, and was arrested for possession of "stolen" goods.]

As indicated above, rapes occurred in a number of neighborhoods, and many, but not all, were carried out in the very houses that were attacked by the pogromists.[65] One of the most frequently mentioned cases of rape, however, involved the Working Girls' Hostel on the island of Büyükada (Prinkipo). Greek consul Kapsambelês, in an earlier report, wrote: "It is reported that girls living in the Girls' Home at Prinkipo were abducted and

[62] Nutku, *Demokrat Parti*, p. 394. For a Greek translation of this particular text, see Sarrês, *Ê allê pleura*, II, 1, p. 196. There is also reference to the Aknoz tribunals and the charges of rape in Alexandris, *The Greek minority*, p. 260, who notes his source as the report in *Cumhuriyet*.

[63] Greek Embassy, Washington, Dispatch No. 3745, September 10, 1955.

[64] Dinamo, *6-7 Eylül kasırgası*, pp. 43-44. Conga had previously explained how he struggled to make a living by buying and selling used shoes. He complained to Dinamo that "Menderes and Bayar, in order to save their own asses, said that, because seven pairs of old shoes had remained in the hands of a cobbler in Tahtakale, Turkey has collapsed." This is a reference to the mass arrests ordered on September 7 of all those holding suspiciously acquired goods. He refers to the local DP members as "bıçkınlar," toughs.

[65] For references, see National Archives, Foreign Office Dispatch No. 106, September 12, 1955; No. 210, November 25, 1955; No. 228, December 1, 1955; Ypourgeion Exôterikôn, Dispatch No. 116, September 9, 1955, and, especially, No. 1410, September 10, 1955; Theodôropoulos, *Sêmeiôma*, p. 15; Chrêstidês, *Ekthesis*, pp. 70-71 and 95; Megas Reumiôtês, *Syrriknosê*, pp. 43 and 90-91; Koumakês, *Miracle*, pp. 54-55.

raped. Scores of other girls in the districts of Kumkapı, Samatya, Yedikule, and Üsküdar have had the same fate and are at present under treatment at the Balıklı Hospital."[66] Considering the geographical reach of the attacks, the question thus arises again about the extent of rape—that is, the number of rapes. When the US consul wrote the US ambassador about the pogrom's overall consequences, he sought lists and numbers not only from Istanbul's chief of police, but also from the ecumenical patriarchate and the Greek consul-general in the city. In one of his ongoing reports to Washington, the American consul wrote that, "The surgeon of the Greek Hospital of Balikli reported to the Greek consul that 60 Greek girls had been assaulted in various parts of Istanbul."[67] One observer estimated as many as 2,000 rapes, but he admits that this number was calculated on the basis of rumors circulating about the city, and thus seems unlikely.[68] Absent any hard evidence (at this point, at least), the most reasonable estimate is probably that of Kapsambelês, who placed the number of rapes at about 200.[69]

Cases of rape appeared basically, but not exclusively, in old Istanbul, and they seem to have been indiscriminate, ranging from small girls to old women.[70] In Kuruçeşme, a suburb of Ortaköy, demonstrators raped the thirty-eight-year-old wife of the sexton of the church of St. Phokas.[71] An eighty-year-old woman was also raped in Ortaköy.[72] Among those listed

---

[66] National Archives, Foreign Office Dispatch No. 106, Washington, September 12, 1955; see also Ypourgeion Exôterikôn, Dispatch No. 116, September 9, 1955, and No. 1410, September 11, 1955; Greek Embassy, Washington, Dispatch No. 3745, September 10,1955. The final report by the US ambassador on the pogrom's consequences seems to refer to this matter, but is somewhat confused. On the other hand, the report of the Greek consul in Istanbul is the product of a hands-on diplomat who had consulted with the chief surgeon of the Balıklı hospital, thus eliciting the figure of sixty rape victims being treated in the hospital itself. The US ambassador wrote, in contrast: "An often heard report that all the girls in an unwed boarding school were attacked seems to be an unsubstantiated rumor" (National Archives, Foreign Office Dispatch No. 228, Washington, December 1, 1955). Not only was he in error, but it was a hostel for working girls, not for unwed mothers, and certainly not "a boarding school."

[67] TNA:PRO, Dispatch No. 1491, 87/58, September 22, 1955. In an earlier dispatch, Kapsambelês reported that there were many girls at the Balıklı Hospital being treated for rape, National Archives, Foreign Office Dispatch No. 106, Washington, September 12, 1955.

[68] Megas Reumiôtês, Syrriknosê, pp. 90-91.

[69] The general estimate given also by Koumakês, Miracle, pp. 70-71.

[70] Chrêstidês, Ekthesis, pp. 70-71; the Journalists' Union, The anti-Greek Riots, p. 13.

[71] Chrêstidês, Ekthesis, p. 95.

[72] Megas Reumiôtês, Syrriknosê, p. 90, who does not report his source. Koumakês, Miracle, p. 54, lists her as eighty years of age, and adds that she was left in bad condition in the streets overnight; the next day she was taken to the hospital where it became evident that she had lost her rationality.

in the records as murder victims (see Appendix B) were Eve Yolma and Theopoula Papadopoulou. The former, aged sixteen, was dragged out of the Working Girls' Hostel, raped, and then murdered. The latter, from Üsküdar, was also first raped and then murdered.[73] In Belgratkapı, demonstrators raped the three daughters of a local gardener.[74] In Kurtuluş, two girls whose mother had died awaited the return of their father, who was at work on the Bosphorus when the demonstrators broke into their house. After destroying it, they raped the two girls.[75] Koumakês also recounts the rape of an eight- (according to others, six-) year-old at Propodes (Yenişehir) by a porter (*hamal*) who was called "Gorilla."[76] A detailed account of this alleged crime appeared in two Greek newspapers, *Ethnos* and *Makedonia*. *Ethnos* described it as a public rape:

> A little girl six years of age.
> At Yenişehir at 7:00 PM and in the middle of the street the mob encircled a little girl six years of age and handed her over to the half-crazy porter who goes by the name "Gorilla." He raped her repeatedly while the mob howled:
> "The Greeks suffer such things. Kill her, kill her, the Greek dog."[77]

It is difficult to believe such a story at first glance. However, given the widely attested rage of the pogromists, and the crazed nature of so many of their acts and crimes, the matter of a public rape is believable. In the same lurid prose style, *Ethnos* described another rape, in Ortaköy again, of the widow of a certain Koutsou.

> As the mob was raging in Ortaköy, a woman dressed in black appeared and the mob descended upon her....[T]he little woman panicked and tried to leave but someone recognized her:
> "She is the widow of Koutsou," and they fell upon her.
> In the beginning, the woman tried to defend herself but the beasts, the Turks, threw her on the ground, turned her over, tore her clothing, and then raped her serially, each in his turn until finally they abandoned her hemorrhaging on the filthy sidewalk. She remained sprawled out on the ground all night groaning loudly, and tried to drag herself home. But she could not, and she

---

[73] Atzemoglou, *Mnêmes*, p. 62.

[74] *Makedonia*, September 14, 1955; *Ibid.*, #78, pp. 54-55.

[75] Koumakês, *Miracle*, p. 54; again, he does not give his source, but was well-informed on the pogrom.

[76] *Ibid.*, pp. 54-55

[77] *Ethnos*, September 13, 1955.

called out to the Christians to help her, but the Christians were hidden, as the mob waited to trample them underfoot. Only on the following day, when the mob of Satans had withdrawn, did the first Greeks dare to appear in the streets and try to help her but she had lost her mind. Today, she is being treated in the filthy Turkish hospital of the region.[78]

Two other women, Zênovia Charitonidou and Asêmenia Parantônopoulou, were reported to have been raped and to have died as a result.[79] An unnamed twenty-year old girl was abducted from the Working Girls' Hostel and was also raped and then killed.[80]

Despite the lack of medical records from hospitals, or the false claim of Istanbul's chief of police that no rape was reported, there is sufficient evidence to assume that rape was committed to such an extent as to constitute moral damage to the community and provoke widespread fear of what might happen to Greek girls and women in the future. The information given by the Greek surgeon of the Balıklı Hospitals to the Greek consul that at least sixty Greek girls had been raped throughout the city is significant; given the additional cases of unreported rapes, the Greek consul's estimate of 200 rapes is, as already stated, in the realm of probability.[81]

While mention has been made of reports of young Greek males being raped, there are very few details. More attention was given in some sources to the incidents of forced circumcision. Perpetrated, as it was, in the streets, it was both a religious and social outrage, as well as a physical maiming. (Circumcision has never been considered acceptable, either as religious rite or medical practice, among Greek Christians; quite the opposite, it is highly undesirable.) A brief mention was made of such a violent circumcision in the episode related above by the communist peddler Conga. But can it be confirmed?

For one thing, it is mentioned in other Turkish sources as well, but nowhere as extensively as in Nesin's book, who informs his readers that, on encountering a Greek male, demonstrators would hesitate to harm him, or otherwise do anything harmful or illegal, "For the Greeks look like us Turks." Nesin then continues:

And, a man who was fearful of being beaten, lynched or cut into

[78] *Ibid.*; see the similar texts in *Makedonia*, September 14, 1955, and Megas Reumiôtês, *Syrriknosê*, pp. 90-91.
[79] Koumakês, *Miracle*, p. 55; he does not name his source.
[80] *Ibid.*, p. 55; Koumakês says that she died on the island of Prôtê (Kınalıada).
[81] "There is information according to which tens of women of Greek origin were kidnapped and, after having been raped, were returned...," in *Ethnos*, September 10, 1955.

pieces, would imply and try to prove that he was both a Turk and a Muslim:

"By God I am a Turk, by God I am a Muslim!"

"Pull it out and let us see," they would reply.

The poor man would peel off his trousers and show his "Muslimness" and his "Turkishness." And what was the proof of his "Muslimness" and "Turkishness"? That he had been circumcised. If the man was circumcised, he was saved; if not, he was "burned." Indeed, having lied, he could not be saved from a beating. For one of those aggressive young men would draw his knife and circumcise him in the middle of the street and amid the chaos. A difference of two or three centimeters does not justify such a commotion. That night, many men, shouting and screaming, were Islamized forcefully by the cruel knife. Among those circumcised, there was also a priest."[82]

Can we believe Nesin or is he indulging in literary license? The fact is that he was not writing fiction here; on the contrary, this book was part of the ongoing autobiography of his life, which was marked by repeated imprisonment by a succession of Turkish governments. In this case, he had been arrested along with other communists for supposedly organizing the violence. The particular circumstances of the forced circumcisions seemed so ridiculous to him that he felt the need to cite documentary evidence, and he referred to the proceedings of the later Yassıada trials, which mentioned the case of a certain professional magician who was accidentally caught by rioters in the street: "As he was bearded, they [the rioters] thought that he was a priest who was running away, and so they seized him and ordered him to 'pull it out.' The magician, imploring and entreating, finally showed that he was circumcised and so was saved."[83]

That circumcision was used as proof of religious and ethnic identity is confirmed by yet another official document, this time in Greek. It is the petition of Iôannês Poulopoulos, a Greek from Thessalonikê who happened to be caught up in the violence; on November 25, 1955, he applied, through the Greek ministry of Northern Greece, for compensation of damages he had suffered on the night of September 6. On the occasion, he was going to visit friends in the region of Yüksek Kaldırım when,

> many Turks attacked me, of these who had also begun to loot and destroy the Greek stores. After they had beaten and treated me savagely, they took off all my clothes to see whether I was a

[82] Nesin, *Asılacak adamlar*, pp. 25-26.
[83] *Ibid.*, p. 26.

Muslim or a Turk, and then they robbed me, taking my wallet and 600 Turkish liras....They also grabbed a raincoat from me that I had bought that day for 135 Turkish liras. Also, a complete set of china and glass that was with me and that cost 85 Turkish liras.[84]

Taken together, these three accounts—two by Turkish eyewitnesses—are sufficient to establish the specific method for distinguishing between Christian and Muslim males. What of Nesin's charge that many Christian males were forcefully circumcised, however? In this case, we have the formal testimony of Iôannês Spetsiotês, from his deposition to the Greek foreign ministry on September 11, 1955: "They caught an Armenian priest and after they had cut him and circumcised him, they beat him savagely, and so he died a few hours later."[85]

A dramatic example of this phenomenon was published in *Makedonia* and *Ethnos*. Iôannês Iôannidês, the editor of the former newspaper, had made an extensive exploratory trip to Istanbul immediately after the events, as had Giôrgos Karagiôrgas, a feature writer from the latter. Both were not only extremely well-informed, but they published materials from formal and quasi-formal reports and lists that have not seen the light of day even fifty years later. The following account must have come from a formal report since it was published in identical language in *Ethnos* on September 13 and *Makedonia* on September 14.

Circumcision

So, soon as the signal to attack was given in Vafeochôri [Boyacıköy], waves of the mob entered the church to destroy it. But at that moment, the archdeacon appeared inside the church and he attempted to prevent them. The Turks began to beat him and to try to take off his clerical robes. The archdeacon resisted but, after a while, submitted. His mother, however, had heard the yelling, hollering, and shouts, and began to worry. So she ran to the church. The mob surrounded her and began to beat her while her son, further away, firmly bound, with his arms behind him and also bound, was placed on a chair. Thus seated, the mob moved him to the exit door. They now left a drifter to dry-shave him. When he had finished shaving him, he took him to the base of the campanile and circumcised him. They then abandoned him in a state of complete exhaustion and hemorrhaging. The archdeacon is now being treated in a hospital.[86]

[84] Ypourgeion Exôterikôn, No. 51922/Tourk. 4, Ep., December 12, 1955; Poulopoulos also asked to be reimbursed for a new suit.
[85] Ypourgeion Exôterikôn, Dispatch No. 48, September 20, 1955.
[86] *Makedonia*, September 14, 1955; *Ethnos*, September 13, 1955.

As some of these acts were carried out in the open, not hidden away (indeed, group participation was often a part of it), it was impossible that not a single policeman witnessed or reported such heinous crimes. This observation dovetails with the repeated refusal of many police and soldiers (but not all) to intervene and halt a crime in process or, at least, report it.

THE PREMEDITATED ATTACK ON THE GREEK HOME

While this survey of violence to persons is necessarily dependent on incomplete and random sources, crimes against institutions and property are better documented. Unlike crimes against the person, theft, looting, arson, and bombings were also well-photographed, and Turkish documentation often describes them both in general and specific detail. Moreover, the physical ruins of destroyed property often remained as gaping wounds in the city for as long as five or six years afterward. I was a personal observer of such cases during a stay in Istanbul in the late summer of 1959.[87]

The attack on Greek property was also a violent attack on Greek institutions, including churches, monasteries, cemeteries, schools, hospitals, clinics, libraries, and cultural, theatrical, and athletic institutions. These devastating attacks looked not only to the material enrichment of the looters, but also to the desire to extinguish the tenacious Greek communities that had weathered repeated state, ethnic, and religious violence and/or discrimination over long periods of time. In this case, the Greek communities actually faced the most extensive, and intensively organized, effort of this sort in the 500 years since Constantinople's fall to the Ottomans.

As with most societies, the most basic and well-knit Greek institution was that of the family and home. Its creation, maintenance, and enhancement were the prerequisites and focal point for the activities, directions, and goals of each member, in terms of both the household's internal and external relations. The household (*noikokyrio* in Greek) constituted the central bastion of the Greek family in Istanbul; in particular, it designed strategies for the family's security and economic well-being. The dowry system looked particularly to the needs and outfitting of the *noikokyrio*.[88] Accordingly, the

---

[87] I was in Turkey on a grant to improve my facility in spoken Turkish.

[88] *Noikokyrio* derives from two or three words that have been in use, orthographically or semantically, among the Greeks for almost three millennia. The root word is *oikos/oikia*, which specifically denotes a house or dwelling, or the household more generally. The ending, *kyrio*, derives from *kyrios* in ancient Greek, which means master. The letter "n," with which the modern Greek "noikokyrio" begins, is either a shortening of the preposition "en" or a later addition to the word, *oikos*. The modern *noikokyrês* is thus the ancient *oikodespotês*.

Without going into detail, *oikonomia* and *oikonomikos* (from which come "economy" and

attacks on Greek dwellings had important economic and social consequences in the minds of the pogrom's organizers in addition to any economic benefit they provided to many participants. From the point of view of uprooting this sturdy religious and ethnic minority from Istanbul, the Greek dwellings constituted a primary consideration, both in the pogrom's organization and in its destructive violence.

While the attack on Greek homes was well-organized and extensive, it does not seem to have reached the level of thoroughness of the destruction of Greek businesses. To date, there is no accessible evidence as to the exact number of Greek dwellings that sustained attack. The applications of Greek *établis* seem to have been claims for general payment of damages and did not specify destroyed items in all cases. It was reported that, immediately after the violence, Istanbul's police chief dispatched officers to the city's neighborhoods to ascertain the damage and that this quick survey produced an informal figure of 1,004 homes attacked.[89] Patriarch Athênagoras appointed his own mixed committee, made up of clergy and laity, to examine the damages to churches and other institutions.[90] Also, the two reports to the patriarch, mentioned in the previous chapter, by the bishop of Daphnousia and the metropolitan of Derkon, refer to the attacks on Greek dwellings but give no numbers.[91] There is evidence that, early on, the *Ellênikê Enôsis* had prepared a detailed report on the extensive damages to its community, but this report has never surfaced, although the Greek consul in Istanbul utilized it in preparing his reports.[92] Indeed, the Greek consulate began to gather information very soon after the events, and it kept records of Greek citizens as they reported

"economic") refer, in ancient Greek texts, to management of the household, as defined, for example, by Xenophon in his dialogue, *Oikonomikos*. The household (*oikos* or *oikia*), Xenophon says, has three goals: acquisition of wealth or property; biological reproduction; and assurance to the aging spouses of security through the offspring they have raised. It is also important to note that, for Xenophon, husband and wife are equal partners in managing their household, as they each bring their respective wealth to the common enterprise.

In the event, the concept of the *noikokyrio*—so important and continually developing through ancient, Byzantine, and Ottoman times—retained its internal economic and familial vitality for the Greeks over the centuries. Indeed, in the case of the Greeks of the Ottoman and modern Turkish states, their minority status tended to enhance the significance of this institution in contradistinction to those of Islamic society, and to reinforce the self-governing and economically self-sufficient nature of their households.

[89] Various documents refer to this figure as the official report of the Istanbul chief of police, National Archives, Foreign Office Dispatch No. 228, American Embassy, Ankara, December 1, 1955.

[90] See Tsoukatou, *Septemvriana*, p. 63.

[91] Greek Embassy, Washington, No. 4311/B/29, October 21, 1955; Chrêstidês, *Ekthesis*, pp. 92-93.

[92] Greek Embassy, Washington, Dispatch No. 39941, September 21, 1955.

damages they had suffered; still, damages to dwellings does not appear as a separate entry in each claim of the approximately 1,070 Greek citizens who applied for compensation.[93] In the event, the earliest estimate of the number of houses destroyed, looted, and/or damaged was the one given by the Greek consul to the American consulate in Istanbul, which recorded damages in round numbers: 600 homes of Greek *établis* and 1,500 of the Greek minority in Turkey, or a total of 2,100 dwellings.[94]

This number is more than double that of the first unofficial report of Istanbul's police chief. The US consul sent on to the State Department a report of restricted distribution, dated November 15, 1955, that had been composed by the WCC. This report was based on the data of the council's factfinding mission sent to Istanbul, which had been dispatched to investigate the state of the Greek church and Greek communities. The mission reported to its headquarters in Geneva that 2,000 Greek homes had been destroyed— that is, "utterly ruined"—so much so that 1,000 dwellings were now "without doors and without glass in their windows, no blankets for the beds and winter rapidly approach[ing]." The report also stated that, "Many people have no clothes other than those they stand up in."[95] The WCC's figure was quite close to that of the Greek consul, as was the estimate of a German newspaper, which also reported some 2,000 homes vandalized.[96] The Greek paper *Kathimerini*, however, gave a smaller estimate of 600 damaged homes of Greek *établis*, and 1,100 homes vandalized of Greeks who were Turkish citizens.[97] Kaloumenos and Atzemoglou, meanwhile, reported somewhat higher numbers: 2,600 and 2,640, respectively.[98] Theodôropoulos gives no figures on the number of damaged dwellings, but he does supply the sum of TL3,036,980 as the total compensation asked for by the 1,070 Greek *établis*.[99] The largest figure for damaged and/or destroyed dwellings was put forward by the Greek foreign ministry on October 11, 1955, in what was the longest and most systematic formal Greek analysis of the pogrom. This report was sent to all Greek embassies, Greece's representatives to NATO and the UN, and many consulates,

---

[93] Chrêstidês, *Ekthesis*, p. 188; National Archives, Foreign Office Dispatch No. 228, American Embassy, Ankara, December 1, 1955; *Ethnos*, September 9, 1955.

[94] National Archives, Foreign Office Dispatch No. 106, American Consul General, Istanbul, September 12, 1955.

[95] *Ibid.*, Dispatch No. 210, November 25, 1955.

[96] *Kölnische Rundschau*, September 10, 1955.

[97] *Kathimerini*, September 13, 1955.

[98] Kaloumenos, *To istoriko tôn gegonotôn*, p. 7; Atzemoglou, *Mnêmes*, p. 69. See also, Apostolidês, *Anamnêseis*, p. 238, who also gives 2,600; and Eleônora Maurophrydê, "Ê nychta tôn krystallôn," *Nemesis*, August, 1998, p. 17.

[99] Theodôropoulos, *Sêmeiôma*, p. 21.

and stated: "There were destroyed, completely, 1,000 Greek dwellings, and those which were partially destroyed and pillaged amount to 2,500."[100] While the total of 3,500 damaged or destroyed dwellings is considerably larger than the other estimates, what is clear from all of the above is the extent to which the destruction and vandalism constituted a social and economic disaster for the Greeks of Istanbul.

The specter of poverty, hunger, and suffering that resulted from the attacks on homes, and the thorough destruction of their contents, constitutes a constant, recurring theme in a variety of historical sources. Iôannidês, who wrote some of the most perceptive and descriptive accounts that we have, reported the following to his readers:

> In the outlying districts, the houses of the Greeks were destroyed. The Turks would enter the houses, smashing everything. They would begin with the windows, tables, chairs, lamps, kitchen furnishings, and end by destroying the furnishings and contents of the chest-trunks. The girls' dowries were destroyed piece by piece with scissors.[101]

Iôannidês also reported that demonstrators had destroyed the clothing in twenty-one of the twenty-five Greek houses in Edirnekapı, which, in some ways, was confirmed by the letter of Sergeant Salih Kırmızı quoted in Chapter 1, which detailed the destruction wrought within five or six hours by his group.[102]

A series of letters by Despoina Portokallis of Yeniköy (Neochôri), written in a minuscule but careful hand, present an often detailed account of destroyed communities, all based on personal experience and on oral accounts gathered locally. In one letter, she recounts her "tours," as she called them, on foot and tram to survey the destruction. "From…Kontoskali [Kumkapı] to San Stefano [Yeşilköy], there was great destruction," she writes. "From Kontoskali to Vlanga, Samatya, Yedikule, Fener, Balat, they entered the homes of the Greeks and destroyed them all, even to the point of shredding and burning all their mattresses." She concludes that "50,000 are without shirt and mattress" and that many of these "have lost their homes."[103] In another letter, she describes the wretched condition in which many Greeks, destroyed

---

[100] Greek Embassy, Washington, No. 4266/B/29, received on October 17, 1955.

[101] *Makedonia*, September 18, 1955.

[102] Chrêstidês, *Ekthesis*, pp. 74-77; the original Turkish letter is mentioned in the archives of the Greek foreign ministry. For the destruction of clothing in Edirnekapı, see *Makedonia*, September 11, 1955.

[103] Letter from Despoina Portokallis to Tatiana, September 20, 1955. Despoina's first letter, dated September 8, 1955, was also written to her friend, Tatiana, a physician then living in

financially by the violence, found themselves: "The people are naked, for [the pogromists] stole their clothing. They have neither mattresses nor blankets. The Church and the organizations are collecting clothes that they apportion to the 'refugees.'" The Greek homes in Despoina's own neighborhood of Yeniköy were also attacked and looted.[104]

In the previous chapter, we discussed the frequency and repetitive nature of the attacks. The region swarmed with countless bands, many of which were scheduled to succeed one another so as to carry out different functions within the general program of vandalism. This is above all evident in the case of the stores that were set upon. In these instances, observers have noted a tripartite division of labor, with a corresponding division into three separate waves of destruction. In a number of specific cases, we see two or more waves, although, as far as the attacks on Greek dwellings were concerned, it is not always clear whether this was by design or chance. In Chapter 2, we examined the two-wave attack on Maria Andreou Kanakê's apartment in Çengelköy. Just when she and her family had emerged from their hiding-place, thinking that their agony was over after the first attack at about 11:00 PM, the cadets from Kuleli launched a second attack on her apartment. Having lost everything, the family finally abandoned its home.

It is, again, a letter by Despoina Portokallis that gives us some insight into how frequent and numerous such attacks on the same house or apartment could be:

> I went to see Dora. It was tragic there, as I found them to be refugees. All the houses were without windowpanes in that region, and the church and school were in ruins. In many houses, not only the lamps were missing but also other items. As for doors, they were mere holes as the doors did not exist. They had nailed planks from smashed furniture across the doorless openings. Many people remained without clothes, mattresses, and they all fled from such houses, which are uninhabitable. The people are leaving, leaving. Dora lived in her own house in Mevlihanekapı. She had given birth and was in the hospital. They burned her house. She weeps for her [lost] dowry....[S]he saved nothing but her TL5,000....
>
> Turks lived on the floor above [the apartment of Dora's mother- and brother-in-law]...and [they] opened the door to the

Indiana. I owe many thanks to Despoina's son, Vasilis Portokallis of Chicago, for providing me with copies of these very informative and valuable letters.
[104] Letter from Despoina Portokallis to Tatiana, October 17, 1955; for the destruction of dwellings in Despoina's own neighborhood, see Chrêstidês, *Ekthesis*, p. 94.

apartment. The mother [Dora's mother-in-law] gave TL100 to the
first looters who entered, and, while they wreaked destruction,
they didn't bother anyone. Then a second group came, and she
gave them eighty Turkish liras. The second group stayed outside
the apartment and guarded them. Then there came a third "herd"
and they came to a disagreement with the earlier group at the
door. The third group wanted to enter. The earlier group told them
that the apartment was occupied by Turks. But the latecomers
understood that the earlier group had taken money. In the midst
of the dispute, a policeman arrived and separated them, and he
then entered the apartment to ascertain the truth of the matter.
The mother showed him a photograph of her son as a military
officer. The policeman was convinced and turned to leave when
he spotted an icon on the wall, with a candle burning underneath,
and he brought it down and smashed it....He called in the third
group of demonstrators. They told the old woman, "Leave, we
shall not harm you...and they took her out to the garden."

This third group stole money from her late husband's wallet, but the
elderly woman managed to save TL1,000 that had gone unnoticed. She then
opened a chest containing her grandchildren's clothes as well as her astrakhan
coat, and ran into the garden to hide them. Meanwhile, fourth and even fifth
waves of looters appeared, but found nothing left in the house to loot except
for a huge, hardwood table that could be neither moved nor broken. The next
morning, Dora's mother-in-law went out into the street to recover a shredded
mattress. She gathered the cotton strewn about from it, as well as a partially
destroyed couch from her apartment, refilled the latter with the gathered
cotton and thus was able to provide two mattresses for her family to sleep on:
one for her and her son, the other for Dora and her husband.[105]

In the end, while definitive sources are lacking for precisely determining
the number of Greek dwellings destroyed, damaged, or looted, the general
magnitude seems apparent. Further, the basic documentation presents a
clear picture of the dynamics and motives for, as well as the specific details
of, the large-scale destruction of Greek dwellings. It allows us, therefore, to
identify the neighborhoods in which these numerous attacks took place.
There is indeed a vague and general consensus that they occurred essentially
in old Istanbul and that new Istanbul was relatively free of attacks. Inasmuch

---

[105] Letter from Despoina Portokallis to Tatiana, October 17, 1955. Despoina noticed as well
that, in her own neighborhood in Yeniköy, the attacks not only took place in three waves, but
that the first attackers consisted of strangers, the second of her neighbors, and the third of the
local children to whom no one dared make any objections, Despoina Portokallis to Tatiana,
September 8, 1955.

as a general canvassing of the available sources was carried out in Chapter 2, it suffices here to address the question by tabulating the various totals of these attacks according to the five general areas that have concerned us: old Istanbul, the European and Asian shores of the Bosphorus, the Princes Islands, and new Istanbul.

In old Istanbul and its suburbs, there is clear reference to a widespread and violent attack on Greek dwellings in the following neighborhoods (in alphabetical order):[106] Aksaray; Altı Mermer; Ayvansaray; Bakırköy; Balat; Belgratkapı; Cibalı; Edirnekapı; Eğrikapı; Fener; Kumkapı; Langa; Muhli; Salmatobruk; Samatya; Sarmaşık; Yedikule; Yenikapı; Yeşilköy; and along the land walls. In addition, these sources lead us to understand that attacks most probably occurred in the following neighborhoods as well: Balino; Gedikpaşa; Koska; Laleli; Potiras; Tahtakapı; Topkapı (near the land walls); and Vefa. In a number of cases, numerical estimates of attacked dwellings are given. One foreign journalist, who was present and personally examined the destruction in old Istanbul, estimated the number of damaged dwellings at 1,500.[107] Rough estimates also emerge from a careful examination of the sources regarding the damage in old Istanbul, but, again, one must approach these figures with caution:[108] Altı Mermer, 16 houses looted; Ayvansaray, all homes destroyed; Bakırköy, at least 10 homes looted; Balat, 50 homes destroyed; Belgratkapı, 15 houses ruined; Edirnekapı, 23 of 25 homes destroyed; Kumkapı, all Greek homes destroyed (100-150 houses, according to *Vatan*), or 405 households damaged (according to Chrêstidês); Salmatobruk, 39 of 40 dwellings looted; and Sarmaşık, 13 of 15 homes damaged. For Langa, we have two different estimates again. The first indicates 120 of 220 dwellings ruined, with 95 Greek families abandoning the area, and the second calculates only 60 surviving homes out of 260.

The patriarchal statistics, just prior to the pogrom, recorded 1,774 Greek families in old Istanbul, but unfortunately these figures excluded Cibalı and the central part of the old city.[109] Perhaps the estimate of the Swiss reporter from Bern that some 1,500 Greek dwellings were attacked in old Istanbul is not far off the mark.

---

[106] For the enumeration and description of these attacks, according to neighborhoods, see Chapter 2, where also the sources are cited in the footnotes for all five regions of greater Istanbul.

[107] Chrêstidês, *Ekthesis*, p. 71; *Der Bund*, Bern, September 21, 1955; see also Ypourgeion Proedrias Kyvernêseôs, *Ektakton Deltion #1*.

[108] For the references, one should, again, consult the relevant sections of Chapter 2.

[109] According to Kesisoglou-Karystinou, *Tzimbali*, p. 95, there were some sixty families resident there in 1950.

The attacks on the European side of the Bosphorus included Arnavutköy, Boyacıköy, Büyükdere, Kireçburnu, Ortaköy, Sarıyer, Tarabya, and Yeniköy. The thorough nature of these attacks is revealed in the report on Arnavutköy and Ortaköy. As to the latter, the report remarks, "...of the many houses of this community, only twenty remained unpillaged."[110] The 1955 patriarchal census registered 180 Greek families for Ortaköy. The much larger Greek community of Arnavutköy (with some 567 families as of an earlier patriarchal census) suffered equally. The Turkish press gave a general description of the attacks on Greek homes up and down the European Bosphorus, which was confirmed by us consular reports.[111] The majority of these communities seem to have suffered.[112] The number of Greek families living on the western side of the Bosphorus was probably about 1,755, or even more.[113] Accordingly, one must assume that between 875 and 1,000 dwellings were attacked and damaged.

As for the Anatolian shore of the Bosphorus, the evidence is scanty. Attacks on Greek residences are mentioned in Çengelköy, Kadıköy, Kalamış, Kandilli, Kuzguncuk, Üsküdar, and Vaniköy. The only neighborhood in which a specific number is given is that of Kandilli, which only had 30 Greek dwellings, all of which were attacked.[114] The damage must have been considerable in Çengelköy (120 families), Kadıköy (700), Kuzguncuk (200), and Üsküdar (152).[115]

The numbers of houses attacked on the islands of Heybeliada and Büyükada must have been comparatively much smaller since the Greek communities themselves were located in considerably less-inhabited areas. Nevertheless, Greek homes were subjected to the same methods and styles of attack, although there are, at present, no statistics available as to numbers and amount of damage.

The great majority of Greeks was to be found north of the Golden Horn and west of the Bosphorus in "new" Istanbul. The patriarchate estimated 12,649 Greek families living in this area in 1955, specifically: Beyoğlu, 7,700 families; Kurtuluş (Tataula), 1,975; Galata, 1,250; Feriköy, 1,289; Kurtuluş (Euangelistria), 375; and Hasköy, 60 (see Appendix A). With one rare

[110] Chrêstidês, *Ekthesis*, p. 32; Greek Embassy, Washington, No. 4311/b/29, October 21, 1955.
[111] See the relevant footnotes in Chapter 2.
[112] Chrêstidês, *Ekthesis*, p. 94; the patriarchal catalogue of 1955 lists 220 Greek families as living in Yeniköy.
[113] The statistics come from the patriarchal catalogue of 1955; for İstinye (Stenê) and Arnavutköy (Mega Reuma), which had 26 and 567 families, respectively, see Stamatopoulos, *Analampê*, p. 290 (patriarchal catalogue of 1949).
[114] Stamatopoulos, *Analampê*, p. 291.
[115] The statistics of Greek families are for 1951-1952 in *Ibid.*, p. 291.

exception, figures on damaged homes are reported in only one case (at least in the documents I have been able to consult). The destruction and burning of Greek stores and shops was much more spectacular and so attracted more attention. But the general impression one gets from the reports is that the damage to Greek homes was far more extensive in new Istanbul than has been formerly accepted. *Vatan* reported in front-page headlines: "Destruction and looting of Greek stores and some of their dwellings occurred in the districts of Beyoğlu, Pangaltı, Yüksek Kaldırım, Eminönü, Karaköy, Sirkeci, and Kumkapı."[116] Further, there are specific references to Greek dwellings being attacked and looted north of the Golden Horn in Beşiktaş, Beyoğlu, Cihangir, Dolapdere, Hasköy, Kasımpaşa, Kurtuluş (Tataula and Euangelistria), Maçka, Mevlihanekapı, Pangaltı, Şişli, Sıraselviler, Tarlabaşı, Kalyoncu Kulluk, and Yüksek Kaldırım. Specific numbers, however, are given only for Kasımpaşa, where it is reported that 20 Greek houses were burned.[117]

There seems to have been very heavy damage to Greek homes in Kurtuluş, Şişli, along Sıraselviler Boulevard, in Cihangir, Beşiktaş, Tarlabaşı, and along Kalyoncu Kulluk Boulevard; until further documentation is available, however, it is hard to come up with figures. Nevertheless, given the large numbers of Greek families living in new Istanbul, the damage must have been extensive. According to the patriarchal census of 1955, some 1,975 Greek families lived in Kurtuluş (Tataula), which was heavily attacked, with serious damage to Greek homes, as confirmed by specific reference in British and American diplomatic reports. Consequently, despite the lack of specific figures for new Istanbul, the estimate of roughly 1,500 damaged dwellings in old Istanbul, along with the vandalism wreaked in Kurtuluş, Tarlabaşı, Cihangir, Sıraselviler, and on both sides of the Bosphorus, would seem to justify the higher overall figure of the Greek foreign ministry as to the number of damaged Greek dwellings after the violence: namely, 1,000 homes completely destroyed and about 2,500 homes partially damaged, for a total of 3,500 vandalized homes.

What was the condition of families after suffering the destruction, looting, and violation of their homes? How did they react? It is obviously one thing to have one's house broken into and ransacked when one is absent during the attack. But to witness it—and in many cases to witness the beating, rape, and other violence against members of one's household as the police stand idly by (and often participate)—is a different kind of horror altogether. As a result, the first and foremost consequence of the night of

---

[116] *Vatan*, September 7, 1955.
[117] For all the references, see Chapter 2.

September 6-7, 1955, was precisely the terrorization of its victims: namely, shock, outrage, and, ultimately, fear. The sweat, labor, and hopes of a family's entire life were wiped out in a few hours at most, and often much quicker. One's *noikokyrio* disappeared with a perverse suddenness; financially, the family was plunged into extremes of poverty, hunger, and homelessness, with the clothes on people's back often being their only remaining possessions. The moral values of the family were completely, intentionally violated in almost every respect: the sanctity of the home, the union of husband and wife, the sexual inviolability of young girls and boys, the right to one's religion, property, and dignity.

THE ECONOMIC CONSEQUENCES

On the practical level of everyday life, the ability to secure the basic necessities of physical existence were partly or completely denied to many Greek families, especially in the poorer or even middle-class neighborhoods. In the first two weeks following the pogrom, the Greek consulate reported a rush of applications for emigration to Greece. The situation was so serious, in fact, that a primary concern of the Greek diplomatic service in Turkey became to slow this movement lest the community be emptied; the patriarch and his clerics were also disturbed by this threat of community diminution. In addition, even the Turkish press noted the sudden flight of hundreds of families from old Istanbul to what they believed was the greater security of the new city. Thus began the final forced retreat of the Greek communities from their historic cradle in the old city. The threat of departure of the Greeks from Istanbul as a whole was such that the Greek consul began to plan for stabilizing the situation and turning the attention of the Greeks from flight to reconstruction.

The economic wounds were so deep, however, that it was very difficult to do so. Indeed, some recalled the persecutions of the *varlık vergisi* and the forced conscription into the labor battalions during the Second World War. The conditions of life immediately after the events, especially for those whose homes were damaged, were atrocious. There was a strong sense of insecurity as political temperatures rose, and the pogrom sharpened the hatred of the victims. Security was in the hands of the same police and many of the same soldiers who had permitted and assisted the violence. The violated homes were open, as doors and windows had been destroyed, and their insides were searing wounds, unhealed, with shattered windowpanes, smoke and the odor of burning, devoid of furniture, appliances, or even of eating and cooking utensils, refrigerators and stoves gone, with foodstocks looted, destroyed, or made inedible by gasoline, and wardrobes standing completely empty: nothing to eat, nothing to wear, and almost nothing on which to sleep. Even toilets had been destroyed. (Meanwhile, Turkish men and women often paraded in the clothes and jewelry stolen from their neighbors.)

Still, very many had no choice but to return to their ruined abodes, and to try and survive in these unlivable circumstances. It was the beginning of autumn and the weather was changing, and these ruined dwellings were open to the mercy of the elements, allowing conditions to develop that ranged from discomfort to danger to a family's health. Although some people, as we saw, saved or reconstituted mattresses from the cotton pile lying on the streets from burned or shredded mattresses, most blankets, sheets, and pillows had either been stolen or destroyed. In general, the description of families being thrown out on the street half-naked is not an exaggeration.

Hunger very soon became a real problem, alongside lack of clothing and warm abodes, for the more unfortunate victims. The soup kitchens that had provided a daily meal for children and the elderly had been destroyed on the night of September 6-7. Beyond the soup kitchens, however, the pogrom had seriously disrupted the entire food industry and distribution system. As we shall see, there was large-scale destruction of the retail food industry. Groceries and other shops were destroyed, shelves emptied, and much of the food thrown out on the streets. Further, as has been recounted, upon entering the Greek homes, the pogromists destroyed foodstocks and refrigerators, or stole for themselves the food and refrigerators they desired. The trucks engaged in hauling away the looted property were in evidence throughout, and the smaller boats at the Galata docks were busy hauling away foodstuffs from both sides of the Golden Horn.[118]

Ethnos's correspondent, Karagiôrgas, commented on the severe problems created by the destruction of Greek homes and businesses: "Goods of indeterminable value have been reduced to dust. Already, the results of the horrible destruction are being felt. More specifically, one observes the scarcity of foodstuffs and various raw materials whereas the problem of unemployment has become very acute....It is characteristic of the situation that a Turkish official observed 'that the disturbances have destroyed the economy of the land!'"[119]

[118] "It was customary for the small steam boats that carried merchandise to the villages of the Propontis to dock at the pier of the Golden Horn. But on the morning after the Pogrom, not one of these boats was to be found in its place. For they had loaded cheeses, olive oil, grains, and whatever else they could and had departed." Tsoukatou, *Septemvriana*, p. 59.

[119] Karagiôrgas, *Ethnos*, September 10 or 11, 1955; see also the comments of a British diplomat in Istanbul, TNA:PRO, Istanbul, Dispatch No. 193, September 22, 1955.

The reporter from the *Basler Nachrichten* remarked on the consequences for the participants of the various conferences in the city at the time: "There is nothing to eat. For the restaurants and stores are either destroyed or empty. In the streets, people are shoving one another in front of the bakeries so that they might at least buy bread....Today, eggs are already being sold at double price, and the cost of cigarettes has risen 10 percent....All have begun to understand that in the future Greeks, Turks, Jews, and Armenians will live in Turkey under conditions of great privation, with a continuous inflation of goods and a general worsening of the level of life, all this after the 'Night of Terror' on the Bosphorus."[120] Another Swiss reporter, also in Istanbul to cover the international meetings, elaborated: "At about 8:00 AM, there begins a slowly moving traffic. Before the Post Office, foreign travelers have formed lines in order to telegraph their families that they are well. Other lines formed at the few bakeries that were not destroyed. Much food and clothing have disappeared completely. Taxi drivers refused to carry passengers for fear of their tires. Replacing tires, already difficult before the events, is now impossible....There is nothing left in the stores to destroy."[121]

Foreign reporters based their comments on the scarcity of goods and the sudden rise in prices on their observations in the heart of the busiest section of Istanbul. In the poorer neighborhoods of old Istanbul, the situation was equally dire. *Kathimerini*'s correspondent summarized it pithily: "The poor neighborhoods around and near the Patriarchate have been destroyed....Today, Greek families are without roofs over their heads, and have been deprived of even the most basic clothing and even of a crust of bread. Their jobs, too, have been destroyed."[122] Despoina Portokallis observed these same conditions on her "tours" of the destruction: She speaks of long lines at the few surviving bakeries, destroyed dwellings, and rising prices, as the value of the Turkish lira fell against the dollar. Furthermore, the suffering was compounded by the loss of jobs for some 8,600 Greeks, as the establishments in which they had worked had been destroyed. This figure comes from the report composed by British *chargé* Michael Stewart, who, however, attempted to "balance" the image of damage done by stating that much of Turkey's heavy industry was unaffected. His estimates of Greek job losses were as follows:

[120] *Basler Nachrichten*, September 12, 1955; for the Greek translation, see Ypourgeion Proedrias Kyvernêseôs, *Ektakton Deltion #1*.
[121] *Neue Zürcher Zeitung*, September 12, 1955.
[122] *Kathimerini*, September 20, 1955.

Table 16: Greek job losses following the pogrom

Household appliances	100
Textile mills	350
Rubber-goods factories	400
Leather factories	100
Chocolate factories	500
Foundries	150
Shoemakers	2,000
Printers	400
Furniture-makers	2,000
Restaurant workers	2,700
Total	**8,700**

Stewart acknowledged that these economic consequences raised new problems:

> "The riots have left the Turkish authorities a considerable social problem with many poor people at least temporarily out of work and many of them homeless or with literally no more than a roof over their heads. So far it cannot be said that they have been very active in discharging that responsibility [to the jobless and homeless]....It does not appear...that anything very effective has been done to implement these [government] promises [of action], and the rapid restoration of so many places of business is mainly due to the energy and tenacity of the owners themselves."[123]

In other words, the beginning of the recovery was due largely to the business-owners who simply managed with less—which is why it had very little effect on their former employees. Indeed, this small-scale recovery was largely the result of the strenuous and difficult efforts of the businesspeople, community leaders, and Greek consulate. We get a glimpse of these communities and their fate some months later from Paulos Palaiologos, who went to Istanbul in January 1956 before the Turkish parliament had even enacted the compensation law, which, although passed in February, would not begin to pay out reparations for a long time. From a rather remarkable series of articles written for the Greek newspaper, *To Vēma*, one—entitled, "Under the roof of the Church the Greeks give rest to the victims"—was particularly poignant. By the time this article appeared, the Greeks had lived

---

[123] TNA:PRO, Istanbul, Dispatch No. 202E, October 5, 1955.

under these new conditions for four months of bitterness, fear, apprehension, anger, and suffering. During that time, the climate of hatred had not abated, Istanbul was under asphyxiating martial law, the economy was at a low point, and many Greeks were inhabiting ravaged homes. As for their churches (a subject that will be discussed in greater detail in Chapter 5), most were hopeless ruins.

Palaiologos, as in all his articles in this series, adopted a quiet tone and focused on practical considerations. First, he spoke of the humble manner in which the Greeks and the patriarchate began to make destroyed churches function with the poorest means. In one church, they constructed a little *iconostasis* of paper, found an *antimension* (altar cloth), and were given an old icon by a parishioner.

> Religion once more became the force that gathers together, lightens the pain, and maintains continuity. And so the believers gather about the church's ruins. And so the starting-point for a reconstruction arises from the ruins....
>
> They did not even have clothes....[T]hey have a long way to go to obtain the *noikokyria* they once had, but they now have a spoon for their soup, a windowpane to protect them from the chill winds, and a mattress on which to sleep. For they had nothing left to them, neither bed nor stove, nor even a brazier with which the poor are wont to warm themselves....The middle class suffered especially. The Patriarch wrote to each affluent family to adopt one that was needy. There were soup kitchens for the children in the courtyard of every church, with elders in charge. They would bring plates, forks, saltshakers, chairs, and tablecloths from their homes...for they did not wish to allow the little eaters [children] to gaze upon the poverty induced by destruction. Further, they try to restore the dowries...for the invaders took all these away."[124]

In January 1956, the Turkish state had done very little to alleviate the community's conditions, which were exacerbated in particular by the extensive destruction of Greek businesses, which not only suddenly precipitated mass unemployment but threatened the very economic basis of all Greek institutions in the region. One must, accordingly, turn again to the extent of damage to Greek businesses and to the general economic activity and employment of the Greeks themselves.

There is as yet no comprehensive list available of all the businesses that were attacked and the damages suffered by each. There are, however, partial lists and various estimates of damage. We have seen that such information

[124] Paulos Palaiologos in *To Vēma*, September 8, 1956.

was gathered early on by a variety of institutions, both Turkish and Greek. Often, the reports of foreign missions in Turkey relied on one or both of these types of sources. In some cases, representatives of foreign governments had to catalogue damages claimed by their own nationals. Both the nature and extent of the damage were such that both the victims and the Turkish government began to tabulate lists; soon, various Turkish ministries and foreign governments became involved in this endeavor.

The actual Greek communities themselves—the neighborhoods in as well as the very streets on which Greek establishments were attacked—provide a rich and varied basis of information for examining the numbers and types of Greek businesses damaged or destroyed. Again, as indicated previously, the region that was documented best and in considerable detail was new Istanbul, which is natural as it was the economic center of the larger metropolitan region and contained the preponderant majority of the ethnic Greek population. Although the number of Greeks settled—and, therefore, the number of Greek shops—was smaller in old Istanbul, there were still local centers of economic activity and life there, too, especially along the southern shores of the Golden Horn and in areas of the northern shores of the Sea of Marmara. (The eastern part of this peninsula, exclusive of Sarayburnu, was witness to a vigorous economic life that produced for and sold to the inhabitants of both the old and new city.) Thus, although the Greeks of old Istanbul were a tiny minority, the attacks on their shops and dwellings were well-organized and caused great destruction. (For a list of all the neighborhoods attacked in the greater Istanbul area, see Appendix C.) Finally, a quick examination of the geographical range of the violence indicates that, with some exceptions, it was concentrated on the same streets and areas. An analysis of the attacks on the churches in Chapter 5 will reveal the same geographic pattern. This "coincidence" of attacks speaks to their efficient and ruthless organization.

Again, it should be kept in mind that Jewish and Armenian stores were looted also, although the attacks against these minorities' properties were not so systematic and widespread as was the destruction of Greek establishments. The disparate eyewitness accounts (Turkish, Greek, American, Armenian, and European) are unanimous as to the thorough destruction of Greek shops and offices on İstiklal Caddesi and Taksim.[125] The Turkish journalist (and biographer of İsmet İnönü), Metin Toker, described his "stroll" and drive through the destroyed city on the fateful night:

> I shall remember the condition of Beyoğlu that night until the end

---

[125] Nesin, *Asılacak adamlar, passim*; B. E./Khosdegian, *passim*; Tsoukatou, *Septemvriana*, pp. 69-73.

of my life. Every street was filled with fabric and goods thrown
out on the street. Refrigerators, radios, washing machines were
in the middle of the street. After [the rioters destroyed], they
concocted an ostentatious description [of the event], attaching it
to "a noble national agitation." But there was no noble principle
in this movement. Beginning from Taksim, it was not possible to
enter the street [İstiklal Caddesi]. I got out of the car and began to
walk along the street to Erdal. And we walked on top of clothes up
to Tünel. At the same time, alongside of us, strange people with
cudgels and resembling robbers were, on the one hand, smashing
this and that and, on the other hand, waging a merciless war on
wealth....

　　　We visited yet other places in the city. In every place, the
situation was the same and mixed in…were notable women who
had become looters, returning to their homes with the booty
under their armpits. Perhaps Istanbul lived through its most
tragic night. Every place was on fire. Government and state had
disappeared. No one knew what to do. Inscriptions against the
Greeks were written on the walls.[126]

Michael Stewart's evaluation of the attacks on the Greek stores was
perceptive, as usual:

The Greek community is essentially a commercial one controlling
a large proportion of the business of Istanbul. It is particularly
strongly entrenched in the import and export business and in the
retail and catering trades. The riots were a systematic attack on
the property of the Greek community. Greek institutions such as
Churches and Schools and Greek shops were the main targets of
the rioters, being both the most conspicuous and the easiest to
destroy and pillage. Few churches and schools, and practically no
Greek shops escaped damages.[127]

While the thoroughness and frenzy of the destruction were, as we
have seen, the product of several waves of coordinated attackers, the
different attitudes and interests of the participants tended to intensify and
amplify the destruction. *Milliyet* has categorized these participants into six
types: provocateurs; guides and leaders; destroyers; looters; demonstrators
participating out of national consciousness; and the curious, who were
neutral.[128] In the event, the damage was staggering. The semi-official Turkish

---

[126] Toker, *İsmet Paşalı*, I, p. 105.
[127] TNA:PRO, Ankara, Dispatch No. 202E, October 5, 1955.
[128] *Milliyet*, September 9 and 20, 1955.

journal, *Ayın Tarihi*, reprinted, among many other articles from the Turkish press, a column from the newspaper *Zafer*:

> Let us look at the damages. The waste of our wealth from the destruction is calculated in the neighborhood of one billion [Turkish lira]....
>
> A city of 1,500,000 cannot live without a market. Indeed, a large city means a marketplace. Today, Istanbul is a city without a market.
>
> During the National Struggle [the Turkish war of independence], western Anatolia was left without markets and, from that time until today, Istanbul provided these markets....
>
> Let us talk of building new markets and filling them with goods.[129]

Thus, Istanbul's markets, in which Greek merchants played a significant role, included within their network not only Turkey's largest city, but much of western Anatolia as well. Greek and Turkish authors pointed to the economic magnitude and significance of the Istanbul marketplace because they understood the meaning of its partial destruction. The Menderes regime's unfortunate economic policies had already resulted in inflation, shortages of foreign exchange, restraints on imports, and hardship for the lower and middle classes. All of this was accompanied by grim corruption in the upper echelons of government. The pogrom not only brought immediate shortages in food and a variety of other goods, but also accelerated the Turkish lira's fall in value. Western commentators and journalists paid particular attention to the conjunction of the pogrom's economic consequences with a more general economic crisis, all of which created an atmosphere of doubt regarding Turkish political and economic stability. The looming specter of government inability to compensate the pogrom's victims intensified the lack of confidence in Menderes, not only locally but also abroad. This distrust also affected a number of Turkish politicians, who felt that compensation was beyond the government's ability.

What was the actual number of Greek businesses attacked and/or destroyed? The final, precise number has not appeared as yet in the available documentation. Rather, what we have is a series of basic, usually round, numbers that vary over time according to the source and compiler's ability to record or even venture a rough estimate. The various representatives of the Turkish bureaucracy and government, for example, displayed a general tendency to minimize—and eventually hide—the actual number, for both

---

[129] *Ayın Tarihi*, September, 1955, no. 262, p. 86.

financial and political reasons. In the case of damage to businesses owned by British nationals, the consular reports are sufficient—as to both numbers attacked and damages claimed and finally paid—to allow the analyst a certain insight into the entire matter. In the case of Greek nationals who were claimants, although the full 1,070 cases have not been published, Christoforos Chrêstidês has catalogued the respective names, fields of economic enterprise, damages claimed, and amounts paid of a limited number—but this number has increased substantially now that more evidence is available. Accordingly, the evidence coming from foreign nationals and their applications affords us an excellent window into the policies and procedures of the Turkish government and its bureaucracy.

The most practical approach to the issue of the number of Greek stores damaged (both of Greek nationals and Turkish nationals of ethnic Greek origin) should begin with gathering and analyzing the varying numbers already reported by the available sources. More than one document refers to the fact that no definitive registry of damaged homes and businesses has been published or made available. Thus, in most cases, we are faced with general numbers. In the statistics gathered from such general sources, an effort has been made to do four things in this study (tabulated elsewhere in the book): a) identify each specific reference; b) identify further, where possible, the source on which the report relies; c) give the figures; and d) list the various institutions or individuals that suffered the damages. In any case, until the files of the special aid committee, the Red Crescent, the Istanbul chamber of commerce, and the Turkish foreign and finance ministries are made available, we shall never know the exact numbers. The procedures for filing for damages were cumbersome, and the work of vetting claims proceeded very slowly. While the turgid nature of Turkish administrative procedures worked to the obvious advantage of the Turkish government, it just as obviously disadvantaged the victims. Furthermore, the government, relevant ministries, and the aid committee began with the intent to award minimal compensation—indeed, in many cases to give no more than a token reimbursement that merely acknowledged the victim's suffering. From the other side, there were comments by some Greek diplomats that some estimates of damage were overstated precisely because of the fear that the Turkish government would utilize the requested claims as a basis for reckoning a much lower compensation. In fact, both the government and its officials began at a later point to disqualify certain kinds of claims. In addition, the Turkish economy suffered from ongoing inflation and much of the destroyed merchandise was difficult to recoup since foreign exchange was a scarce commodity. Although the government's formula allowed for a yearly adjustment for inflation, it was in truth not enough to make up for the economic reality. The first estimates of damaged businesses were made by the chief of the Istanbul police and the region's *vali*, as well as by the Istanbul chamber of commerce. We learn from local Greek sources that very soon after the declaration of martial law on September 7, the Turkish police began to visit Greek and other stores to record the damages sustained and to verify the state of the store and its lack of merchandise. This was, however, a hastily executed exercise whose principal aim must have been to make a merely statistical assessment of damaged shops, homes, and religious and other institutions. It was far from complete, as we shall see. Actually, many categories of damages—and types of violence—had already been completely excluded from this criminal survey. As mentioned earlier, the police chief stated that no cases of rape had been reported,[130] and he failed to mention the massive destruction of the two greatest Greek cemeteries at Şişli and Balıklı. An even more truncated report was issued by Istanbul's chamber of commerce. Other estimates included those of the special clergy-laity committee appointed by the patriarch to compose the catalogue of damaged churches and other ecclesiastical institutions. Symeôn Vafeiadês, an inhabitant of Kuzguncuk who had his own business at Gemiş, was a member of this committee and left a bare record of its membership and tasks.[131] Kapsambelês, the Greek consul-general, immediately requested funds from Athens in order to support the claimants, as well as those Greeks who were beginning to flee Istanbul for Greece. While he maintained close contact with the holy synod, it seems that his earliest reports on damages relied on the catalogue drawn up by the *Ellênikê Enôsis*.[132] The Greek government sent representatives to Istanbul several times to investigate the damages to the Greeks living there.[133] Early on, the Turkish foreign ministry notified the foreign consulates in Istanbul that foreign nationals were to request compensation from the government through their respective consulates, with requests addressed to the ministry. Thus, British, Italian, French, Swedish, and Greek nationals soon directed their claims to their respective consular authorities. With the exception of the

---

[130] This was originally accepted by the British and American diplomatic authorities, but not by the Greek authorities or the court-martial command or other Turkish authorities.

[131] Tsoukatou, *Septemvriana*, pp. 61-64 and 128-129.

[132] This emerges from the report of the Greek official in Ankara, Greek Embassy, Washington, No. 3991/T/Ep., September 26, 1955; Geôrgiadês's dispatch is dated September 21, 1955.

[133] See Geôrgios Kavounidês's *ekthesis*, Greek Embassy, Washington No. 4266/B/29, October 17 (and 11), 1955, and also the *Ekthesis* of Chrêstidês; the former has now been published in Tsoukatou, *Septemvriana*, pp. 221-252.

Greek nationals, the claims of foreign citizens living in Turkey were relatively small. Thus, in contrast to the Greek case, we have an almost complete dossier for British subjects who suffered damage to their properties.

We shall deal with the aid committee in some detail later, but suffice it to say here that it was a hastily constituted group with meager funds for dealing with the emergency confronting the Turkish government. It served basically as an inexpensive token of the government's "good faith" regarding compensation for the victims. Inasmuch as this required legislation, and ensuing appropriations, the committee was more of a quick solution that could not have a lasting effect on the fundamental problem. Still, no matter how hastily it had been created and convoked, it had to deal with significant numbers of applicants: this fact is important in examining the extent of victims in need of financial assistance. The aid committee set October 15 as the deadline for applications for remuneration. By that date, the committee reported that 4,450 Turkish citizens had applied. In addition, the committee committed sixty Turkish liras (less than ten dollars in real value) to each of 2,736 destitute ethnic Greeks who were also Turkish citizens. Finally, by November 15, some 1,300 foreign nationals had applied to the foreign ministry for damages. Specifically, the statistics that emerge from the committee's activities break down as follows:

Table 17: Applications for aid following the pogrom

Turkish nationals	4,450
Destitute ethnic Greeks (also Turkish nationals)	2,736
Total Turkish nationals	**7,186**
Foreign nationals	
Greek	1,070
Italian	126
British	50
French	30
American	10
Various others (This item is left blank in the document, but extrapolated here.)	14
Total foreign nationals	**1,300**
Total claimants	**8,486**

Sums claimed (in Turkish liras)

Greeks	27,014,479
Italians	3,300,000
British	< 2,000,000
French	1,691,000
Swedes	30,000
Americans	10,000
Total	**< 34,045,479**
Turkish citizens	**69,578,744**

In addition, there was the approximate amount of TL35 million that the patriarch had indicated was the sum of damages to Greek religious institutions, as well as the other smaller sums the aid committee was expected to give the 2,736 destitute Greek inhabitants of Istanbul. The total of the two items for foreign nationals and Turkish citizens was some TL103,624,223. Consequently, one readily sees that the TL8.5 million originally collected for the aid committee were insignificant by comparison. Thus, when the committee began its work on September 20, 1955, it realized that its resources amounted to only 6.25 percent of the total compensation claimed by thousands of victims for their losses. And so the committee announced policies that made the patriarch realize that the group could not begin to provide the vast funds needed to rebuild the wrecked churches and ecclesiastical institutions. A significant report from the American embassy in Ankara to the State Department, dated December 1, more than a month after the deadline for the submission of claims to the aid committee, stated the following.

> The Committee, recognizing it did not have sufficient funds to cover all claims in full, made some procedural decisions. Among these was its decision to ignore all losses of cash money, gold, luxuries, and items with intrinsic value such as rugs and antiques....The Committee agreed to pay in general only a percentage of each loss, depending on the degree of assistance each person must have in order to get re-established. When explaining these decisions, the chairman of the Istanbul Committee accented [*sic*] the Committee's purpose was to give "aid," not to pay compensation except for approved claims for less than TL10,000 which would be paid in full. Victims who claimed less than TL10,000 were required to sign a quit claim receipt acknowledging

payment in full for all losses suffered in the riots, before [getting] any compensation. Approximately TL2,000,000 was expended in settlement of 2,250 such claims.[134]

The attempts to catalogue the destruction

The figures of 7,186 claims from Turkish nationals (the majority of whom were Greek, Armenian, and Jewish) and 1,300 from foreign nationals (of whom the vast majority, 1,070, were Greek) are significant in that they tend to give a numerical magnitude that is helpful in the effort to quantify the destruction of Greek businesses. The reported figures range from the lowest estimate of the Istanbul chamber of commerce of 862 damaged minority stores.[135] A still lower estimate of 400 was given by *The New York Times*, but that figure is hardly credible[136] given that the hasty report of the Istanbul chief of police gives a total number of businesses destroyed in Istanbul as 4,359.[137] The American embassy's analysis stated that about 3,000 of these establishments were Greek. The police report asserts that some 10 percent of the destroyed stores were owned by Muslim Turks, and goes on to allot the damaged stores by ethnic group, all of which, however, were made up of Turkish nationals.

Table 18: Businesses destroyed, according to the Istanbul police

Group	Out of a total of 4,359
Turkish (10%)	436
Greek (59%)	2,572
Armenian (17%)	741
Jewish (12%)	523
Various others (1%)	44

The percentages only add up to 99%, so the actual numbers are off by 43 businesses.

According to these statistics, the number of Greek minority stores damaged reached the figure of 2,572. But if one adds the 1,070 stores that were owned by Greek nationals, then the total number of Greek minority and Greek nationals' stores comes to 3,642.[138]

---

[134] National Archives, No. 228, American Embassy, Ankara, December 1, 1955.

[135] Karakuş, *40 yıllık*, p. 280; Armaoğlu, *Kıbrıs meselesi*, p. 172.

[136] *The New York Times*, September 17, 1955.

[137] The figures vary in the following reports: National Archives, Foreign Office Dispatch No. 228, American Embassy, Ankara, December 1, 1955; Chrêstidês, *Kypriako*, p. 157; and *Ekthesis*, pp. 183-184.

[138] Chrêstidês, *Ekthesis*, p. 210, on the 1,070 shops of Greek nationals.

According to these figures, the estimate of 2,500 damaged Greek shops in the report by Geôrgios Kavounidês—which was prepared for the Greek foreign ministry a month after the violence—is far too low, as is the number provided in the pamphlet of the Greek journalists' union.[139] Iôannidês, *Makedonia*'s editor, followed the Greek applications for compensation very closely, and obviously had access to the lists and catalogues drawn up during the first days after the violence. He even published a number of these "first-draft" catalogues for the important business streets of İstiklal Caddesi, Meşrutiyet Caddesi, and elsewhere. Based on his study of these initial lists, he estimated the total of all Greek stores attacked to have been 2,529.[140] Two days after the first estimate, however, after gathering more information, he more than doubled his estimates to between 5,000 and 7,000 businesses.[141] It is interesting to note that during the caucus of the DP members of parliament on September 12, Menderes himself placed the rough numbers of damages to Greek property as including 5,000 Greek businesses and 7,000 dwellings.[142] The early estimates of Kapsambelês and Theodôros A. Geôrgiadês, *chargé* of the Greek embassy in Ankara, set the figure for damaged Greek stores at 4,000 and 4,100, respectively, and both of them had utilized the data provided by the *Ellênikê Enôsis*.[143] It would seem, at this stage of study and available documentation, that 4,000-4,500 would be reasonable for the number of damaged Greek businesses.[144] Before proceeding to a presentation of statistics on the material damages and the institutions that suffered them, a quick review of specific numbers for certain areas and streets would be useful.

In his second article mentioned above, Iôannidês began to gather the rapidly accumulating data regarding the destruction of the Greek community.[145] In that particular piece, in fact, he randomly named some fifty-five businesses and owners in Beyoğlu, Taksim, Galata, and "beyond the bridge" (the old city). It is interesting that he lists "the automobile store of N. Katalos," whom he describes as the "president of the *Ellênikê Enôsis*." Iôannidês certainly must have had contact with him and so was able to obtain information of the catalogue drawn up by the *Enôsis*. But it was only in his

---

[139] Greek Embassy, Washington, No. 4266/B/29, October 17, 1955; Journalists' Union, pp. 17-18.

[140] *Makedonia*, September 9, 1955.

[141] *Makedonia*, September 11, 1955.

[142] Karakuş, *40 yıllık*, p, 287.

[143] National Archives, Foreign Office Dispatch No. 106, American Consul General, Istanbul, September 12, 1955; Greek Embassy, Washington, No. 3991/T.4Ep, September, 26, 1955 (Geôrgiadês had sent it on September 21).

[144] For the variety of estimates, see the more general statistical table.

[145] *Makedonia*, September 11, 1955.

later reportage (September 11) that he came out with two detailed lists of businesses and owners. He also reproduced *in toto* the summary of the local Greek newspaper *Embros* on the types of businesses destroyed:

The destruction in all [economic] sectors was horrible and beyond reckoning.

Grocery Stores

The majority of the grocery stores owned by Greeks suffered the wrath of the mob and were turned into ruins. Today, they really do not exist.…The destruction was vast and for a long time many types of their goods will be absent from the windows of the grocery stores.

Women's Goods

They underwent full and irremediable destruction in a night. The most beautiful of these stores have been transformed into ashes.

Imported Goods

The stores that sell refrigerators, radios, machines, and appliances have sustained such damage that the businesses cannot be revived. Commercial houses such as those of Philco, Archimedes, and others have been turned into complete ruins and it shall be very difficult for them to renew their activities.

Barbershops

Practically all Greek beauty parlors and barbershops have been heavily damaged after this sector had developed into a proper industry.

Bakeries

These also were unable to avoid the disaster, as so many of them belonged to Greeks.

Flour Mills

The flour mill of Papagiannopoulos in Beşiktaş sustained very heavy damage.

Chocolate Factories

Practically all the chocolate factories were heavily damaged… particularly regarding the products that have to be imported. It is now problematic as to whether these factories can function again as it is very difficult to import cocoa.…

Pasta Factories

Although they also sustained heavy damages, they are in a position to reopen.

Dried Fruits

All the Greek stores that deal in dried fruits in the region of Hasırcılar were heavily damaged.

Dyes

The dye stores of the district of Galata are in a wretched state. And it is questionable whether they can function normally once more. Generally, the future of commerce appears very difficult.[146]

Iôannidês's first systematic list of damages (along İstiklal Caddesi, Meşrutiyet Caddesi, the Food Market, Pasaj Evropa, Yüksek Kaldırım, Bankalar Caddesi, Perşembe Pazarı, and Galata) was much more specific and detailed. Here, he had access to the first (but obviously not the last) detailed catalogue of destruction. It seems worthwhile to reproduce this list at this point of the narrative although it would appear that only about half of the total damages, or even less, had been reported at the time of the list's compilation. It should be added that Iôannidês does not identify his sources here.

The first catalogue made of destroyed Greek stores on the terrible night of the sixth of September contains the following stores on İstiklal Caddesi:

1. Grocery and glass store Ankara of the Brothers Kyrkos (one of the largest of this type of store)
2. Luxury barbershop Lux
3. Cafe Eptalofos of Giannês
4. Tripe shop of Aristeidês Lenos
5. Pastry shop Şehir of Giannês Tsoulês
6. Luxury barbershop Ferdinan
7. Butcher shop of Miltiadês Giolmas
8. Stationery store of Paulos Pyrovolidês
9. The well-known restaurant of Iordanês
10. Offices of TAE (the Greek airline)
11. Shoe store Imren of Kônstantinos Athênaios
12. Women's jewelry store of Stefos
13. Shoe store Kapitan of Kapetanidês
14. The well-known and largest photo studio Şehir of Dêmêtrios Hatzêparas
15. Sausage-and-beer bar Santral of Geôrgios Iôsêfidês
16. Pastry shop Senlen of Iôsêf Koungounês
17. Fabric store Stad of Theodôros
18. Pharmacy of Charalambous Karakas
19. Sausage and beer bars Osman and Pınar of Nikos Papadopoulos
20. Cinema Lux of the Tsangopoulos Brothers and K. Lekas
21. Cinema Saray of K. Lekas (shareholder)
22. The large tennis club Luxemburg of K. Lekas
23. Shoe store of K. Zôtos

---

[146] *Makedonia*, September 17, 1955.

24. Fabric store of Stelios
25. Coffee store of Giannês
26. Pastry shop Gloria of N. Semikopoulos
27. Pastry shop İnci of Loukas and Lefterês
28. Pastry shop Kervan of Dêm. Palavidês
29. Pastry shop Baylan of Lenas and Kyritsês
30. Pastry shop Haylayf
31. The famous jewelry shop of Frangoulês
32. Eyeglass store Zeis of A. Anestidês and G. Letas
33. Clothing store San of Kyriakos Gerardos
34. The well-known coffee store Moca of Lefas
35. Luxury barbershop of Stauridês
36. The famous florist G. Sapountzakês
37. Refrigerators and appliances Nektar of Manikas
38. Pastry shop Everest of Iasôn Karidopoulos
39. Pastry shop Lozan of Rôssopoulos
40. Pastry shop Rönesans of Iôakeim Euangelidês
41. Sausage and dairy shop of Leventês
42. Beyoğlu Merrousat (furniture, bedlinens, curtains, etc.) of Makelaridês
43. Sausage and sandwich shop Pacific
44. Foto Stil of Kleovoulos and Takês
45. Clothing store of Moutevelês
46. Women's fabrics Dekor of Stauros, Kôtsos and Zacharias
47. Furrier Pars of Vasileiadês
48. Women's clothing Ledi of Xenakês
49. Furrier Eskimo of K. Doikos and P. Vougidês
50. Watch shop Syma of Papatheodôrou
51. Linen shop Beyas of Charilaos
52. Haberdashery and threads of Molokotos
53. Biblo items and crystal of Angelidês
54. La Zenes (women's purses and gloves) of Karystinos
55. Shoes of Glinidês
56. Women's hats of Elenê Pamfila
57. Goldsmith Pagônês
58. Stationery store of the Tsitouras Brothers
59. Rekor of Dêmêtrios and Theodôros Fornaros
60. The large store of women's goods, threads, and yarns Elisi of Giôrgos and Êlias Euthys
61. Elmas (lace, threads, etc.) of Euang. Kônstantinidês and Dêmos Kaloumenos
62. Women's fabrics Ipekis of Kalêvrousês

63. Stationery shop of Kottakês
64. Clothes and shoe store of Kosmas Amiralês and Platonidês
65. Women's hats Margrit of G. Dapyllas
66. Threads and notions of Mastorakês
67. Threads and notions of Batsês
68. Corset store Rosito
69. Children's clothing Pazar de Bebe of Tzimos
70. Two crystal and glass shops
71. Linen shop of Zachariadês
72. The well-known florist K. Sapountzakês
73. Glass and cooking utensils Pazar du Levan of Zachariadês
74. Yarns and notions Iplik of Plêmmyridês
75. Pharmacy of Vasileiadês
76. Yarns and notions Elit of N. Tsariôtês
77. Shoes Oliondor
78. Shoe store of Patsikakês
79. Shoe store Altin Chimbe of Diogenês
80. Luxury pastry shop Lebon of Litopoulos
81. Florist shop of Fôtês
82. Women's clothing store of Palavidês
83. Trenchcoats and *prêt-à-porter* Ekselsiyor of Athênodôros Tsoukatos and Co.
84. Trenchcoats and *prêt-à-porter* Yeni Ekselsiyor of S. Petinas, D. Pyroglou, and I. Zaarants
85. Clothing store Rex of M. Iôannidês
86. Eyeglasses and optics of Markos Salahas
87. Bookstore of Samouchos
88. Photo shop of Markos Kaloumenos
89. Goldsmith Antôniadês
90. Butcher shop of Mêltos Kyrousês
91. Bookstore of Sergiadês, Chatzopoulos Pasaj, İstiklal Caddesi
92. Threads, buttons, and notions of Mauridês
93. Papadopoulos
94. Livadas
95. N. Kônstantinidês
96. Stamatês
97. Plêtas
98. Petros
99. Kôtsos
100. Patterns for women's clothing of Themês

101. Women's hats Georges Antoine of A. Valsamakês
102. Women's hats Mod Mairie of Eudoxia
103. White goods and cotton shop of Chatzopoulos
104. Louvre (furniture, curtains, etc.) of P. Iôannidês
105. Tailor's workshop of Chr. Stylianos
106. Furs of Sôtêrakês
107. Raincoats of Millas
108. Furniture, curtains, etc., of Antôniadês
109. Workshop of embroidery and *plissé* of Kornêlios and
     Kosmas, Panagia Church Pasaj and İstiklal Caddesi
110. Gelincik bridalwear of D. Pitoglou
111. Wedding attire of Charês
112. Tailor shop of Choliadês
113. Drugstore of Vasileiadês

On Meşrutiyet Caddesi
The destroyed stores on Meşrutiyet Caddesi of Pera are:

114. Pastry shop Kibar of Iônas and Sons
115. Cleaners Izador of Prodromos
116. Musical organs of Lorentzos
117. Shoe store of Kapetanidês
118. Refrigerators and radios Lorens of Paulas
119. Women's hats Arês of D. Desirês
120. Barbershop and drugstore Moderno of Lambidês
     Papachatzês
121. Travel agency Türk Turizm of Kônstantinidês
122. Restaurant of Ananias
123. Beer hall Hala of M. Stamatiadês
124. Cafe Lala of M. Stamatiadês
125. Jewelry store of G. Zacharatos
126. Modern (lampshades, etc.) of Marangopoulos
127. Pastry shop Şehir of Achilleas
128. Restaurant Izmir of Fenerlês
129. Furniture workshop Stil of Themês
130. Workshop of advertising lights Neon of Agathoklês
     Dêmêtriadês
131. Funeral parlor of Angelidês
132. Cleaners Amerikan of Danoulakês
133. Pastry shop of K. Poulios
134. Antiquities dealer S. Toukitidês
135. Furniture workshop of Delêgiannês
136. Shoe store of Mytilênaios
137. Shoe workshop of Menegakês
138. Furniture workshop of the Bagias Brothers

139. Furniture workshop of Tsirigôtês
140. Store of bath fixtures (bathtubs, basins, etc.) of Palaiologos.

In the Food Market area

141. Haberdashery of Paulos
142. Grocery and sausage shop "Dendrinou"
143. Barbershop of Stefos
144. Biblo glass store of Stelios
145. Kristal glass and kitchenware shop of the Brothers Panagês and Petros Kônstantinidês
146. Ermês grocery of the Brothers Katanos
147. Butter and cheese shop of Eftas
148. Butter and cheese shop of K. Chatzakos
149. Poultry shop of Alexês Sôtêriadês
150. Butchershop of Naoum
151. Greengrocery of Antônês
152. Sausage shop of the Brothers Giannês, Geôrgios, and Nikos Kazas
153. Grocery of Anastasios Theocharês
154. Butter shop of Th. Tsitsilidês
155. Sausage shop of Kônstantinos Tselovits
156. Poultry shop of Stelios and Iakôvos
157. Restaurant of Euthymiadês
158. Butcher and poultry shop of G. Koukoularês
159. Nea Agora grocery of the Brothers Katanos
160. Sausage shop of George Benentatos
161. Store for refrigerators, automobiles, and Philco appliances of the Brothers Katanos Company
162. Butcher, poultry shop, and greengrocery of the Brothers Katanos
163. Grocery of Antônios Feringos and Co.
164. Wine store of the Brothers Frangakês
165. Artemis grocery of Kanakês, Vafeiadês, and Stratos
166. Bakery of Lambros
167. Tavern of Andreas
168. Grocery of Chr. Theofanidês
169. Butchershop of Manthos
170. Tavern and wine store of Kôtsaras
171. Butchershop of Manthos [repetition of #169?]
172. Building-materials store of Tsamopoulos
173. Glass shop of Lazaros
174. Bakery of Psylakês
175. Bakery of Gavrilês

176. Barbershop of Paparafeios
177. Barbershop of F. Chrysanthidês
178. Radio store of V. Oikonomidês
179. Grocery store of Giannês and Grêgorês
180. Dairy store of Charalambos Kokkinidês
181. Pastry shop of Thanasês
On Pasaj Evropa
182. Barbershop of Siôtês
183. Perfume shop of Akestoridês
184. Shoe repair of Dêmatos
185. Store of *plissé* and threads of Alekos
186. Women's purses of Pantelês
187. Thread shop of Kalfaoglou
188. Shoe-dye shop of Katinarês
189. Goldsmith store of Michalês
190. Tailorshop of N. Pagônês
In the region of Skalakia [Yüksek Kaldırım]
191. Men's hats, G. Roussos
192. Pastry shop of S. Skanidês
193. Bookstore of G. Patriarcheas
194. Purses and trunks, Ê. Solômos
195. Hat shop of Defadês
196. Bookstore of Venetia Apostolidou
197. Electrical goods store of Kôstas
198. Bakery of Th. Giannoutas
199. Purse shop of Polyvios
200. Snacks and sausage shop of Nikos
201. Print shop of Fourtounas
202. Printing shop of Mainas
203. Bookstore of Koutsoukês
204. Purse shop of Bartalidês
205. Coffee store of D. Papadês
206. Grocery store of E. Latsês
207. Shop for musical instruments of the Brothers G. and P. Papageôrgiou
208. Radio factory of V. Ouzounoglou
209. Radio store of G. Terzakês
210. Radiologist Ê. Vafeiadês
211. Alaska sausage shop of Stelios
212. Confectionery of Vasilês Symas
213. Eifel radios of A. Tsoukatos
214. Neon light-bulb store of D. Dokas
215. Bookstore of K. Patriarchaias

216. Electrical appliances of Theodôros
217. Haberdashery of Stauros
218. Thread shop of Alitzoglou
219. Haberdashery of Menelaos
220. Print shop of Kallotsês
221. Radio store of Plakas
Bankalar Caddesi
222. Electrical appliances of Spinokias
223. Modern pastry shop
224. Archimedes of Papadopoulos, the largest store of imported refrigerators, radios, drilling machinery, etc.
225. Electrical appliances of V. Zarvavatsakês
226. Electrical appliances of A. Mêtakidês
227. Electrical appliances of D. Mêtakidês
228. Electrical appliances of St. Iôsêfidês
229. Electrical appliances of I. Farasoglou
230. Electrical appliances of Dekavalas
231. Electrical appliances of St. Marasoglou
232. Electrical appliances of A. Voutsinas
233. Electrical appliances of G. Genêdounias
234. Ariel motorcycles of Dromidês
235. Fluorescent lamps of K. Koulouthrês
236. Electrical motors of K. Drakopoulos
237. Motors and electrical appliances of Iôannidês
238. Electrical appliances of Theofanês Mêtakidês
239. Electrical appliances of V. Mêtakidês
240. Children's bicycles of M. Mytarakês
241. Electrical appliances of F. Paraschos
242. Electrical appliances of S. Sigalas
243. Electrical appliances of K. Anastasiadês
244. Motorcycles "N.S.U."
245. Radiospor radios of E. Eleutheriadês
246. Electrical appliances G. Makrinas
247. Radios "EAR" of Dedekas
Perşembe Pazarı
248. Building materials of O. Isaakidês and I. Kontopoulos
249. Ironworks of I. Demirtzioglou
250. Building materials of A. Hatzêandrou and Geôrgos
251. Building materials of N. Daskalosoglou
252. Building materials of I. Ketsetzioglou
253. Building materials of Chr. Ketsetzioglou
254. Lead materials of Avraam Tsoukouroglou and Dêmêtros
255. Building materials of I. Kapisizoglou and Th. Dermosonoglou

256. Materials for insulation of G. Eugenidês
257. Building materials of Loukas Ketsetzioglou
258. Building materials of D. Kapisizoglou and L. Dermosonoglou
259. Paint store of N. Kokkinos
260. Building materials of A. Tsakyrês and Co.
261. Locks, etc., of Th. Geôrgiadês
262. Paint store of Ch. Êliadês
263. Building materials of Kyriakos Marosoglou and Co.
264. Locks, ironwork, tools, of A. Pilafidês
265. Screws and ironwork of Kyriakos Kyriakidês
266. Electrical appliances of M. Michaêlidês
267. Restaurant of G. and A. Kolaros
268. Copper materials of G. Zôrzos
269. Ironwork, tools, etc., of Iôakeim Pilafidês
270. Building materials of K. Tseklioglou
271. Canvas goods (for furniture) of K. Zervoudakês
272. Stationery store of Brothers Tsitourês
273. Porcelain (bathtubs, etc.) of M. Filippidês
274. Paint store of St. Mistiloglou
275. Porcelain (bathtubs, etc.) of K. Kourtoulmous
276. Lumber store of G. Nikolaidês
277. Furnishings (canvas) of A. Kallinikos and Brothers
278. Maritime (naval) goods of Archimêdês Stauropoulos
279. Maritime appliances of Serafeim Paschalidês
280. Maritime appliances of G. Chrêstidês
281. Paint store of V. Devletoglou
282. Machines, kitchen appliances of Filipoutsês Brothers
283. Ironwork and machines of Savvas Aslanoglou
284. Electrical appliances of Michaêl Krimêzas
285. Ironworks of Aristeidês Karamanos
286. Ironworks of L. Vasileiadês
287. Glasspanes of G. Charalambidês
288. Kerosene lamps of Chr. Paulidês
289. Glasspanes of S. Kiosef
290. Foodstuffs and sausage shop of Stelios
291. Tailorshop of G. Lolês
292. Lathe workshop of K. Piperidês
293. Lathe workshop of A. Nizamakês
294. Pattern design of Sarantês
295. Lathe workshop of G. Topidês
296. Lathe workshop of K. Pervanelês
297. Lathe workshop of Miltiadês Chrêstidês

298. Pattern design of V. Topouzoglou
Galata
299. Royal pastry shop
300. Royal chocolate factory of the Ethnopouloi Brothers
301. Baylan pastry shop of Kiritsês and Lenas
302. Kafes Express of Ch. and A. Lenas (pastry shop)
303. Mabel pastry shop of Michalês and Charalambos
304. Hats of A. Rousos
305. Hats of D. Rousos
306. Men's clothing and hats of G. Groumberg
307. Hats of Ch. Orelês
308. Hats of A. Porichês
309. Men's clothing of Lambropoulos
310. Watches of Kyriakos
311. Eyeglasses of Polatos
312. Watches of Pantzirês and Savvaidês
313. Watches of Martinos
314. Watches of Lagopoulos
315. Kamelia pastry shop of Charalambidês
316. Cumhuriyet pastry shop
317. Amerikan Pazari shoe store of Nikos
318. Shoe store of O. Marinos
319. Leather goods of K. Gizês
320. Tobacco shop of N. Chatzêgrêgorês
321. Tobacco shop of G. Chatzêgrêgorês
322. Watches of Karamalengos
323. Pastry shop of G. Papanikêtas
324. Barbershop of Nimos
325. Coffee store of Enkara
326. Lathe workshop of Athênaios
327. Maritime appliances of Zervoudakês
328. Perfume shop of Anastasês Eminönü
329. In Eminönü, there survived only the familiar *Havyar Hanı* caviar shops.[147]

While Iôannidês's catalogue, which he dug out of the first lists collected by the Greeks, is very informative, it must be far from complete. In regard to the shops on İstiklal Caddesi, for example, Greek merchants and professionals had a dominant presence in what was then the economic heart of the city. According to one estimate, there were some 400 shops on this boulevard and, by the mid-1950s, the Greeks had made a strong economic comeback in

---

[147] *Ibid.* and *Makedonia*, September 21, 1955.

its life, with more than half of the stores on the boulevard on the eve of the pogrom. In his detailed identification of the Greek stores on İstiklal Caddesi (in Tepebaşı, Tarlabaşı, and Galata), Kôstas Stamatopoulos has identified and largely located more than 467. Inasmuch as this is a representative sample, he dispenses with many categories of stores, as well as with many more "tens" of such stores in each category. Thus, the 113 stores on the avenue mentioned in Iôannidês's list is certainly incomplete. To take another source, the British diplomatic report of October 5, 1955, includes the following information: "The most concentrated damage was inflicted on the Rue de Pera [İstiklal Caddesi], the main shopping centre of Istanbul. In this street 250 shops were wrecked more or less completely. Shops of other minority communities and foreigners suffered with the Greeks. Only 97 shops—all belonging to Moslem Turks—escaped."[148]

The text is somewhat ambiguous when one does not read the paragraphs that precede it, which speak about the vast damages to Greek property. Thus, it is not quite clear in the quoted lines above whether the author means to say that the 250 shops wrecked included those of all non-Muslim Turks or only Greek losses. The number of businesses and offices was greater than this document allows in any case, for it speaks only of shops and not of professional offices. The second, third, and fourth floors of many buildings on İstiklal Caddesi housed offices of physicians, dentists, realtors, and other professionals. If, in fact, one accepts the estimate of 400 businesses on the boulevard, the calculation of the British report—that is, 250 damaged stores and 97 Turkish stores that escaped destruction—amounts to only 347. That leaves 53 stores unaccounted for. The percentages established for the proportions of Greek, Armenian, Jewish, and Turkish Muslim stores by Istanbul's police chief, however, were 59, 17, 12, and 10, respectively. As no Muslim stores were attacked on İstiklal Caddesi, then the 250 stores damaged should, with an adjustment for the absence of damaged Turkish shops, equal the following number of establishment: Greeks, 157.5; Armenians, 52.5; and Jewish, 40. Clearly, Iôannidês's early catalogue listing 328 damaged Greek shops (on this and other streets) is deficient, at least according to this particular calculation. If in effect, as seems unlikely, the British figure of 250 damaged shops is intended to refer to Greek shops alone, then Iôannidês's report is further deficient. As such, it serves as a guide until further concrete evidence is forthcoming. There is good reason to believe that the number of businesses on İstiklal Caddesi was greater than 400.

There is another piece of evidence that documents the economic strength

---

[148] TNA:PRO, No. RG10344/70, October 5, 1955.

of Greeks at the time of the pogrom. Five years before the violence, in 1950, the Turkish government had surveyed the economic life of the city's Greek minority. As this economic census was tabulated several years before the pogrom, the economic growth and expansion of the entire Greek community of Istanbul during the subsequent five-year period was, if anything, even more dynamic. As such, this census casts an important light on the significance of the Greek community in Istanbul's development. The figures are as follows:

Table 19: Census of employment in Greek community, 1950

1,647	fishermen, hunters, foresters, farmers
18	metalworks, mines, stone quarries
8,732	artisans and small industry
36	employees in electric, gas, water, and sewer services
1,055	building enterprises
5,872	commerce, banks, insurance, real estate
526	laborers in transport, storage, refrigeration
4,418	workers in private business[149]

The categories of artisans and small industry; builder-contractors; and commerce, banking, insurance, and real estate add up to a large number: 15,659. The majority of people employed in those sectors must have had offices, workshops, and stores.[150] Thus, the number of all such businesses seems to have been much greater than indicated by the various estimates. Furthermore, these statistics do not include the Greek nationals resident in Istanbul, 1,070 of whom applied for compensation after the riots. One estimate placed the percentage of damaged Greek shops at 90 percent of all Greek shops.[151] Thus, the number of damaged stores may well have been far above the 4,000-4,500 (which purportedly included enterprises of both the Greek minority and Greek nationals).

A striking exception to the general scarcity of data is the Greek community of Balat, which lies on the southern shore of the Golden Horn. A catalogue was compiled for this area, and it appears to be a formal listing of shopowners and shops, with the actual addresses of the businesses (although

[149] Stamatopoulos, *Analampê*, pp. 64-65.

[150] *Ibid., passim.*

[151] National Archives, American Embassy, Ankara to Washington, No. 128, December 1, 1955, gives this information on the basis of a "Greek community estimate." It is close to the figure given by Kapsambelês, Ypourgeion Exôterikôn, No. 1410, September 10, 1955, who states that, "Nearly 100 percent of Greek shops are complete losses in the whole area of Greater Istanbul." His estimates of the numbers of damaged Greek shops are, he says, "a fair estimate of the situation," but he admits that they "have not been checked…in their entirety."

figures on damages claimed and paid are lacking). This list is anonymously signed by "H. H.," who was a former member of the *Demokrat Parti* and resident of Balat; judging from his occasional footnotes, he was also someone who seems to have known the shopowners in his area personally. He adds a brief, informative introduction to the list after informing the reader that he was baptized in Balat, and served as treasurer and then as president (1966-1968) of the Balat Greek community. Thus, he not only knew everyone, but had access to the community's records, which undoubtedly explains the origin of his list. He relates that Balat had three Greek churches, three mosques, four synagogues, and one Armenian church. Before the pogrom, 250 Greek families lived in Balat, which later declined to fifteen. Obviously, as evidenced by the number of synagogues, many Jewish families also lived in the area, as well as a few Armenian ones. H. H. went on to describe Balat in the following manner:

> As regards the market of Balat, it was very rich in merchandise. Here is an example. It was a district with eight bakeries, ten butcher shops, ten fish stores, fifteen groceries, ten taverns, two summer cinemas, and one for the winter, many sewing and notions shops, fifteen shoe stores, and many other stores with different goods.
>
> For this reason, many inhabitants of Fener, Muhli, Antifônêtês, Cibalı, Salmatobruk, Edirnekapı, Lonca, Tahtakapı, and even Hasköy (Pikridion) across the Golden Horn, all shopped in Balat's market.
>
> The Turks thus gave great attention and value to Balat and would say: "Bağdata giden gelirmiş, Balat'a gelen gitmezmiş." (Whoever goes to Baghdad can then depart, but whoever goes to Balat cannot depart.)

H. H. then proceeds to list what he refers to as the "destroyed and looted stores of Balat."

Name [of owner]	Type of store	Street number
Balatyan Caddesi [Balatyan Boulevard]		
1. Giannês Karagiannês	butcher shop	130
2. Fôtês Troumpoulas	butcher shop	128
3. Giannês Kioseoglou	greengrocery	126
4. Theodore and Grêgorios Michaêlidês	greengrocery	120
5. Panagiôtidês Brothers	butcher shops	118
6. Nikolaos Aivatoglou	commercial-grocery [?]	91
7. Geôrgios Chourmouziadês	sausage store	89
8. Petros-Fôtês Brothers	grocery	103

| 9. Siderês Liaze | dairy store | 72 |

Balat Vodina Caddesi [Balat Vodina Boulevard]

10. Ananias and Iakôvos Tachmintzoglou	restaurant	173
11. Michalês Serafeimidês	watchmaker, repairs	165
12. Vasileios Oxousoglou	grocery	157
13. Alekos and Kôtsos Mitselês	grocery	139
14. Galimitês Rodokanakês	shoe store	127
15. Antônios and Nikolaos Mangos	grocery	226
16. Paulos Orfanidês	grocery	228
17. Alexandros Chatzopoulos	doctor's clinic	174
18. Geôrgios Rossos Tsalikidês	smithy	125
19. Alekos Alexandridês	tailor's shop	122
20. Manôlês Melitaios and Êraklês Poulês	tailor's shop	116

Balat Leblebiciler Caddesi [Leblebiciler Boulevard]

21. Theofilos Trouboulas	butcher shop	2
22. Geôrgios Sachinoglou and Tasos Karabinês	paint shop	4
23. Asterês Christodoulidês	alcoholic-beverage store	6
24. Christodoulos Christodoulidês	tavern Agora	8
25. Petros Chatzêpetros	barber shop	10
26. Andreas Benlisoy	stationery	16
27. Dêmêtrios Gourlakês	smithy	7
28. Kôtsos Arzoumanidês	shoe store	23
29. Kosmas Liaze	dairy store	42
30. Kônstantinos Stamatiadês	winery	58

Balat Köprübaşı Sokak [Köprübaşı Street]

31. Takês Tsokonas	butcher shop	102
32. Sergios Christodoulidês	warehouse	98
33. Vasileios Skenteridês	cafe	96
34. Asterês Christodoulidês and Manôlês Anastasiadês	candle factory	94
35. Michalês Tsouroukoglou	construction materials, lumber, cement	88
36. Dêmêtrios and Leftherês Karaxês	soap factory	(no number)
37. Giannês Papamanôlakês	grocery	32

Balat İskelesi Caddesi [Balat İskelesi Boulevard]

38. Petros Prasman	cooperage	18
39. Euthymios Tsivitzoglou	cooperage	15

Balat Lapıncılar Caddesi [Balat Lapıncılar Boulevard]

40.Manôlês Chrysopoulos   cobbler's shop   73

H. H. remarks that after martial law was declared on September 7, 2,057 looters were arrested and that the compensation for damages paid by the Turkish government was a little less than 10 percent of the total value lost by Greek businesses.[152] As we do not know what the total of the claims was, we cannot determine what the claimants received. In any case, the policies of remuneration will be discussed further in a subsequent chapter.

A much briefer and incomplete list was compiled for the Greek community of Arnavutköy on the Bosphorus. On it appear only the names of a restricted number of storeowners whose shops suffered damages. For the record, the names are: Karamêtsos; Papadopoulos; Tsolakoglou; Oikonomou; Dedes; Margietês; Fanariôtês; Tzonker; Mêtsakês; Krassas; Kyrilopoulos; Dourmetakês; Kyros; Nikolaidês; Papageôrgiou; Famianos; Slabidês; Amazopoulos; Diamantidês; Kanakorês; Soropidês; Raktivan; Skoulidês; Vlysidês; and Lazaras.[153]

As was seen in the previous chapter, the attacks on the European side of the Bosphorus seem to have inflicted damage on practically every Greek store. The testimony of Dosdoğru as to the marketplace of Ortaköy, of *Milliyet* for the entire western shore of the Bosphorus, of the American diplomatic report on the damages in the area, of the Greek metropolitan of Derkon, of the eyewitness Atzemoglou, of foreign and other Greek eyewitnesses, and of Portokallis, all confirm one another. The same is true for the Greek stores in the old city. It seems that the vast majority were severely damaged and looted, and some were burned. The sources indicate complete or severe damage to all Greek stores in Sirkeci and Eminönü, along Hasırcılar Street, around and in the Mısır Çarşı, along Ankara, Çağaloğlu, and Babıali Boulevards. On Çarşıkapı Street alone, some eighty Greek shops were destroyed, and Greek stores were attacked around Beyazıt, Ayasofya, Laleli, Vefa, Koska, and Aksaray more generally. The damages were extensive along Gedikpaşa Boulevard and in Kumkapı, Samatya, Yedikule, and Yenikapı. Whatever had existed of Greek shops along the land walls were ruined, as in the case of Edirnekapı and its destruction by Kırmızı's small band. The business establishments on the southwest shores of the Golden Horn were also devastated.

Thus, in concluding this part of the assessment of damage, I propose a conservative estimate of some 4,000-4,500 businesses, including professional

---

[152] Tsoukatou, *Septemvriana*, pp. 127-131.
[153] Megas Reumiôtês, *Syrriknosê*, pp. 29-34.

and commercial offices, destroyed or badly damaged—with their goods looted or destroyed in practically every case. This is a conservative estimate inasmuch as the figures are far from complete, and the Turkish government statistics of 1950 indicate a much larger number of craftsmen, merchants, businessmen, and professionals than could have been accommodated in much lower estimates. Obviously, the future recovery and availability of the official damage figures to which the aid committee and the Turkish foreign and finance ministries had access will without a doubt change some of what has been stated here.

In any case, Greek minority businessmen did not wait for the Turkish government to act, but immediately took the initiative in responding to the crisis that faced them and their families and community. In a broadcast within days of the violence, Radio Ankara announced that sixteen of the largest Greek enterprises had decided to rebuild, joined by hundreds of Greek shopowners. All they asked for, according to *Makedonia*, were the following:

> 1. That the second installment of the tax payment for the present fiscal year be postponed. The relevant deadline for payment falls on September 30.
>
> 2. That the commercial debts that have matured [amounting to tens of millions of Turkish liras] not be called in.
>
> 3. That merchants and professionals who have suffered significant damages be granted open credit.
>
> 4. That the amount of damages suffered be established quickly.
>
> 5. That the prices of building materials be kept at levels of normal profit, so that rebuilding is facilitated.
>
> 6. That sufficient imports of windowpanes and crystal are secured.
>
> 7. That the compensation that is set be paid to the victims in a timely manner.[154]

While we have examined the extent of the damages to homes, businesses, and to Istanbul and the Turkish economy as a whole, the damages suffered by the Greek Orthodox Church has been mentioned only in passing, as this issue will be dealt with in Chapter 5, for reasons that, I think, will become apparent in that chapter. Table 20, which attempts to gather together all the disparate reports on damages to homes, businesses, schools, and other institutions is intended as a beginning. More than anything, it is a symbolic mustering of the evidence, such as it is, and its intention is merely to serve

---

[154] *Makedonia*, September 16, 1955; *Aksiyon*, September 10, 1955.

as a convenient capsule of this partial evidence. At this juncture, there is no point in dealing separately with damages to schools, cultural and athletic organizations, clinics, soup kitchens, libraries, or other institutions or groups, as the information is clearly insufficient. Wherever mentioned, such entities are simply noted in the table that follows.

The monetary value of all that was destroyed, damaged, or stolen is, of course, every bit as difficult to ascertain as any of the data related to the pogrom. The truth is that the real value of the total losses will probably never be known. First and foremost, the ongoing processes by which this massive array of damages was evaluated varied with the different—and, obviously, conflicting—interests of the Turkish government, the victims, the political interests of various other states, and the passing of time. Moreover, no effort was made to place a value on physical injuries incurred in crimes against the person. Additionally, the Greek state insisted tenaciously that an essential part of the compensation it claimed on behalf of its citizens included establishing the guilt of those who had conceived and planned the pogrom as well as those who had carried it out.

THE POLITICS OF COMPENSATION

As the Cyprus issue became increasingly heated and complex, it, too, influenced Turkey and Greece on this matter, and led to the intense concern and involvement of both Great Britain and the United States. The precipitous decline of the Turkish economy and the rapid devaluation of the lira also became primary, motivating factors in evaluating damages and paying compensation. Indeed, the fall in the lira's value was to become critical as far as the realistic evaluation of damages was concerned. Finally, the nature of Turkey's system of justice and the turgidity of its bureaucracy added the last variables to the final equation of assessing compensation.

Against such an ensnarled network of factors, compensation became the victim of contending Turkish, Greek, British, and US policies. Presidents, prime ministers, and ministers formulated these various policies, and the corresponding ministries and diplomatic offices executed them. Accordingly, the Turkish and Greek prime ministers competed to curry favor both with Great Britain (over Cyprus) and the United States (over NATO, the Cold War, and the Soviet bloc). This confrontation on the world and regional stages was further complicated for Menderes by the spirited attack against him and his government by İsmet İnönü and the RPP, as well as by the deep internal fissures in his own party.

The evolution of Turkish compensation policy continued to 1960, and

Table 20: Reports and their sources

1. 9/12 Kapsambelês report, in dispatch #106 (Istanbul to Washington, DC), National Archives
   2,100 dwellings; 4,000 stores

2. 11/30 aid committee report, in dispatch #883 (Ankara to Washington, DC), National Archives
   7,186 claimants (1,300 foreigners)

3. 12/1 dispatch #228 (Ankara to Washington, DC), National Archives, in Chrêstidês, *Ekthesis*, p. 185
   1,004 dwellings (80% Greek, 9% Armenian, 5% Turkish, 3% Jewish, 2% other); 4,359 stores (59% Greek, 17% Armenian, 12% Jewish, 10% Turkish, 1% other); 81 houses of worship (75 Greek, 3 Armenian, 1 synagogue, 2 others); 41 schools (36 Greek, 4 Armenian, 1 other)

4. 11/7-11/14 World Council of Churches Istanbul mission, in 11/25 dispatch #210 (Istanbul to Washington, DC), National Archives
   2,000 dwellings; 4,000 Greek stores; 71 Greek churches; 2 Greek cemeteries

5. Istanbul *vali*, in Chrêstidês, *Kypriako*, p. 157
   1,004 dwellings; 4,348 stores; 110 restaurants/cafes; 27 pharmacies/laboratories; 21 factories; 18 bakeries; 12 hotels; 71 churches; 2 cemeteries; 26 schools; 5 athletic or cultural organizations; 11 clinics

6. Apostolidês, p. 238
   2,600 dwellings; 4,340 stores; 110 restaurants/cafes; 27 pharmacies/laboratories; 21 factories; 73 churches; 26 schools; 3 newspapers

7. Geôrgiadês/*Ellênikê Enôsis*, in 9/26 (9/21) dispatch #3991/T/Ep., Greek embassy (Washington, DC)
   2,100 dwellings; 4,100 stores

8. 10/11 Kavounidês *ekthesis*, in 10/17 dispatch #4266/B/29 (Athens to Washington, DC), Greek embassy (Washington, DC)
   3,500 dwellings; 2,500 minority stores

9. Patriarchate, in Greek press attaché, London, further cited in dispatch # FO371/117711198335.9/22/55 (Istanbul to London), National Archives: Public Record Office
   3,000 dwellings; 1,000 stores; 72 churches; 2 cemeteries; 31 schools; 5 newspapers

10. 10/5 dispatch #202E (Ankara to London), National Archives: Public Record Office
    32 Greek schools; 8 Armenian schools

11. Istanbul *vali*, in Alexandris, p. 259
    1,004 dwellings; 4,348 stores; 110 restaurants/cafes; 27 pharmacies/laboratories; 21 factories; 73 churches; 2 cemeteries; 26 schools; 5 athletic or cultural organizations

12. Journalists' Union, pp. 17-18
    1,300 dwellings; 2,300 stores; 71 churches; 2 monasteries; 2 cemeteries; 3 newspapers

13. Kaloumenos, *Istoriko*, p. 7 (ms.)
    2,600 dwellings; 4,340 stores; 27 pharmacies/laboratories; 21 factories; 73 churches; 8 *agiasmata*; 5 athletic or cultural organizations; 3 newspapers

14. *40 Chronia: Ta gegonota tês 6ês-7ês Septemvriou. Êmera mnêmês,* pp. 8-10
    2,600 dwellings; 4,300 stores; 110 restaurants/cafes; 36 schools; 3 newspapers

15. Atzemoglou, p. 69
    2,740 dwellings; 4,348 stores; 73 churches

16. Maurophrydê, p. 71
    2,600 dwellings; 4,340 stores; 110 restaurants/cafes; 27 pharmacies/laboratories; 21 factories; 73 churches; 26 schools; 3 newspapers

17. *Hürriyet,* 9/17, in Armaoğlu, p. 172,
    862 stores

18. Karakuş, pp. 280 and 287
    862 stores (Istanbul Chamber of Commerce); 7,000 dwellings and 4,000 stores (Menderes)

19. Yelda, p. 22
    5 or 6 dwellings; 22 stores; 73 churches and 1 synagogue; 2 monasteries; 16 *agiasmata*; 2 cemeteries

20. 9/27 dispatch #132 (Istanbul to Washington, DC), National Archives
    61 churches (4 Catholic); 5 monasteries; 2 cemeteries; 36 schools; 7 newspapers

21. *Makedonia,* 9/9
    2,529 stores

22. *Makedonia,* 9/11
    5,000-7,000 stores

23. *Ethnos,* 9/9
    5,000 stores

24. *Ethnos,* 9/9 or 9/10
    10,000 stores

25. *Milliyet,* 9/20
    Thousands of stores

26. *New York Times,* 9/17
    400 stores

27. *Newsweek* magazine, 9/19
    4,000 stores

28. *Time* magazine, 9/19
    4,000 stores

29. *Daily Mail* (London), 9/14
    2,000 stores

30. *Kölnische Rundschau,* 9/10
    4,500 stores

31. *Combat, Figaro, Libération* (not the current Paris daily), 9/9
    Thousands of stores

32. *Ottawa Citizen,* 9/24
    5,000 stores

33. 9/27 Patriarchate, in dispatch #139 (Istanbul to Washington, DC), National Archives
    61 churches (1 Greek Catholic); 4 monasteries; 2 cemeteries; 36 schools; 4 newspapers

followed a downward spiral in terms of actual values assessed and paid. In the first phase of this process, in the immediate aftermath of the violence, we have only broad and general figures issuing from a number of sources. The first estimates of damages are thus general but not to be completely disregarded, as they are based on at least two lists: that of the *Ellênikê Enôsis*, which was placed at the disposal of the Greek consul in Istanbul, and that of the city's chief of police, which we know was examined by Menderes himself early on. Furthermore, the observations of the city's banks and chamber of commerce are not to be completely ignored; the data emanating from these, and perhaps other, sources are reflected in these early damage reports.

Much of this early information was gathered by the Greek consulate in Istanbul, communicated to the foreign ministry in Athens, and from there disseminated to the various key Greek missions in other parts of the world and, in particular, the US ambassador in Athens and the Greek representative to NATO. Theodôros Geôrgiadês, counselor to the Greek embassy in Ankara, sent a secret report to the ministry in Athens on September 15, 1955, remarking that it was now clear that the disturbances of September 6-7 had been planned long beforehand and had been well-organized, and that they had not been instigated by the explosion at the Turkish consulate in Thessalonikê: "The Royal Greek General Consulate in Constantinople reports, on the basis of information gathered by the *Ellênikê Enôsis*, that 4,100 Greek stores and 2,100 dwellings, of the value of 1,050,000,000 Turkish liras, were destroyed. On first glance these figures would seem to be exaggerated."[155] His report ends by underlining not only the great material devastation (although damages to churches and other communal institutions were not included in his evaluation), but, more important, the destruction of Greek morale. He assumed this to be even more serious as it might prove to be decisive for the community's future in Turkey.

Geôrgiadês's report was based on Kapsambelês's earlier memorandum to Athens (9/10/55), in which the latter had given the following general statistics in a document written in English and intended for Arthur Richards, the American consul. In his note, he summarized the statistics for damaged Greek shops and dwellings but omitted any mention of churches, schools, cemeteries, or other institutions.[156]

---

[155] Greek Embassy, Washington, No. 39941/T.4 Ep., September 21, 1955.
[156] Ypourgeion Exôterikôn, Dispatch No. 1410, September 10, 1955.

Table 21: Survey of destroyed Greek property

	Shops	Homes	Value (TL)
Owned by Greek nationals	1,100	600	300 million
Owned by Turkish nationals of Greek origin (Greek minority)	3,000	1,500	750 million

In another memorandum, Dêmêtrios Chronopoulos wrote of his special mission to survey the damages to the property of the Greeks in Istanbul. He reports the following to Defense Minister Panagiôtês Kanellopoulos:

> Taking into account the dreadful economic crisis that troubled Turkey prior to the Pogrom in Constantinople, one can only describe as ironic the announcement of the Turkish President Mr. Bayar that "the victims of the destruction shall be compensated." According to the more cautious evaluations, the amount of damages is close to $500,000,000.00. And, it is impossible for the Turkish Government to pay out even a portion of this. I am, further, informed that private insurance does not exist in Turkey as a result of which insurance is provided by the State. Under such circumstances there is no possibility that the victims will be compensated.[157]

The Greek foreign minister's extensive and well-structured report of October 11, 1955, directed to all major Greek missions in Europe and the United States, is also instructive. It is a carefully integrated analysis of the official Greek position on the events of September 6-7, as well as on the matters of damages, assessments, and the politics of compensation.

> ...In formal declarations, the Turkish tax administration has raised the minimum figure for damages to the businesses of Constantinople [Istanbul] to TL2,000,000,000. Other evaluations, based on first accounts, raise the figure of total damages to $300,000,000. The exact sum of material damages will be learned later, however, after the evaluation and reckoning of all the damages, and only if, necessarily, Turkish censorship will allow this.
>
> ...But on the basis of what measure will the moral damages at the expense of Greece and the Greek name—damages that are greater and more painful—be reckoned and computed?[158]

[157] Ypourgeion Exôterikôn (no number), Athens, September 10, 1955. Le Soir, September 8, 1955, reported on estimated damages by a local insurance agent, however, but it may be that the Greek document is referring to personal insurance. Stamatopoulos, Analampê, p. 64, refers to Greek insurance agents in Istanbul during the early 1950s, but names only one, a Mr. Moschopoulos.

[158] Greek Embassy, Washington, No. 43871/T.4 Ep., October 11, 1955. Later, the reports

What is noteworthy here is that the large figure of TL2 billion is an early but *official* estimate by the Turkish tax authorities, at a time when divulging such information was less guarded.[159]

Arthur Richards filed a number of memos in which he referred to evaluations of damages. In the first one (9/7/55), he wrote that while the monetary losses were difficult to reckon, they nevertheless ran "into many millions [of] dollars."[160] Five days later (9/12/55), he reported the damage to Greeks shops and dwellings as amounting to TL1,050,100,000. He states that these figures were considered "a fair estimate of the situation."[161] Two days later, he filed his first detailed report on the pogrom, at the end of which he reported that the "first estimates of damages was in the neighborhood of three hundred million liras. As further investigation has been published, foreign banks have raised the estimates to one billion liras."[162] On September 29, Richards submitted a memorandum on the "Implications of the Istanbul Disturbances of September 6, 1955," and on their dire economic significance for Turkey's already faltering economy. He writes that three weeks after the violence, the "estimated damages range up to one billion liras."[163] Finally, on October 18, he states that the damages "run into hundreds of millions of liras."[164] Accordingly, we see that the high estimates of damages forty-two days after the pogrom are largely consistent in Richards's reports, which were based on a variety of sources.

Michael Stewart's reports introduce some changes in the estimates, which, according to Stewart, were expressed to him by the press attaché of the Greek consulate as coming from the Greek consul himself. Stewart's memorandum of September 22 states that, "A thousand shops and business premises owned by Greek nationals were destroyed; the owners assess the damage at TL300

of Noel Barber and Senator Homer Capehart, respectively, placed the damages at £100 million and between $500 million to $3 billion.

[159] Kaloumenos, *To istoriko tôn gegonotôn*, p. 7. For other references to high figures of damages, see Sarrês, *Ê allê pleura*, II A, p. 140; Alexandris, *The Greek minority*, p. 259; and Ahmet Emin Yalman, *Yakın tarihte gördülkerim ve geçirdiklerim*, Istanbul, 1970, vol. IV, p. 324.

[160] National Archives, Foreign Office Dispatch No. 3009, American Consul General, Istanbul, September 7, 1955.

[161] National Archives, American Consul General, Istanbul, Dispatch No. 106, September 12, 1955; this obviously derived from Kapsambelês's report (footnote 151 above), as Richards's phraseology in this part reproduces Kapsambelês's document.

[162] National Archives, Dispatch No. 116, September 14, 1955; in his report of September 19, 1955, Dispatch No. 200, he reports that the estimate of TL1 billion still holds.

[163] National Archives, Foreign Office Dispatch No. 138, American Consul General, Istanbul, September 29, 1955.

[164] National Archives, American Consul General, Istanbul, Dispatch No. 153, October 18, 1955.

million; but the Greek Consul believes that TL100 million would be more accurate. Another 3,000 premises owned by Greeks with Turkish nationality were destroyed, damage being assessed at TL250,000,000."[165] (Stewart gave no figures for the number of Greek dwellings damaged.)

It appears here that the original claims submitted by both Greek citizens and Turkish citizens of Greek origin, as reflected in the original Kapsambelês memorandum, have been cut to only a third of the original claims. Moreover, Stewart does not give the corresponding figures of claims for destroyed Greek homes, which means that he did not have before him the original document that Kapsambelês had sent to the US consul. There is thus the problem of what exactly the Greek press attaché reported to Stewart, for such cuts are not mentioned in any of Kapsambelês's relevant documents, although, as we have already seen, Geôrgiadês found the claims too high. If, in effect, the Greek consul had cut these original submissions for damages, it was possibly because of the realities of the situation on compensation as they had evolved by that time: the growing fear that Turkey could not pay them and that, by the time payments were made, their community's conditions would have deteriorated so badly that the Greeks would lose heart in their struggle to reestablish themselves economically in such a hostile environment.

By October 5, Stewart had had time to reflect on the "economic and commercial effects of the damages during the anti-Greek riots of September 6…,"and he addressed a detailed and reasoned memorandum to the British foreign ministry that included, among many other crucial details, the matter of damages:

> No reliable estimate of the amount of damages has yet been forthcoming and the correct figure will probably never be known. Various estimates have appeared in the press varying from 3 hundred million to 2 thousand million Turkish liras. According to the Greek Consulate one thousand shops and business premises belonging to Greek citizens and three thousand belonging to Greeks of Turkish nationality are destroyed. The Greek Consulate estimates total damages at about 350,000,000 liras. This estimate excludes damage to residential property and to schools and churches. Much of the latter cannot be evaluated in commercial terms since it includes the loss of precious relics, icons, etc. which can never be replaced. The estimate also excludes damage suffered by other communities. The Secretary-General of the Istanbul Chamber of Commerce, on the other hand, told the Commercial Secretary of Istanbul that the total commercial damages did

[165] TNA:PRO, Istanbul, No. RG10344/50, September 22, 1955.

not amount to more than TL150,000,000. His estimate should be taken with reserve, since, as will appear, he has a motive for minimizing the amount of damage.

Stewart gives as an example of the extensive losses the cases of Philco, Norge, and Hotpoint, which suffered stock damages estimated at TL2 million, as well as of three chocolate factories that sustained damages valued at TL800,000.

Aside from his remarks on the effort of the secretary-general of Istanbul's chamber of commerce to minimize damage claims—in itself an indication of the road that both Turks and Greeks were to follow—Stewart also comments on Menderes's interim measure designed to find a ready source of cash in order to deal with compensations at a much lower level of valuation.

> So far as commercial and private losses are concerned, it is now clear that the Government hopes to meet most if not all of the cost of compensation by contributions exacted from banks and private business....Although contributions are nominally voluntary, in fact the firms have little option but to comply and the amount of their donations is fixed by the [Aid] Committee....The minority communities, who were the main sufferers in the riots, are not exempt though no firm which actually suffered in the riots is being laid under contribution....
>
> The Committee's collections are unlikely to be commensurate with the damage inflicted by the riots....When interviewed by the [British embassy's] Commercial Secretary at Istanbul, the Secretary-General of the Istanbul Chamber of Commerce virtually admitted that the object of the Claims Committee was to scale down demands for compensation to as small a figure as possible. He admitted that the donations collected by the Aid Committee were unlikely to be sufficient for claims to be paid in full, but said that the Prime Minister had hinted that the Government might be prepared to add something to the total collected. Altogether there is little likelihood that the compensation finally paid will account for more than a small proportion of the losses suffered. The minority communities will clearly have to rely on their own energies and resources to restore their futures.[166]

Stewart's report to Harold Macmillan turned out to be prophetic. The policy proposed by the secretary-general of Istanbul's chamber of commerce—one of small and partial compensation—became the guiding force for the entire structure of payment to the victims. After this initial

---

[166] TNA:PRO, Ankara, Dispatch No. 202E, October 5, 1955, for all the above quotes from Stewart's text.

phase of generally admitting the enormity of the damages, the politics of partial and incomplete compensation were enforced and the process dragged out over more than two years (and, in some cases, to as late as 1959-1960). While this turn in Turkish policy produced an immediate and energetic reaction from the Greek side, the reaction from the British was semi-secretive and guarded. Although British citizens represented a very small proportion of claimants, the British archives reveal a carefully hidden but active reaction on the part of their government—albeit not in their defense. The written comments on the margins of the reports to the Foreign Office indicate that the British government was well-informed regarding the mounting evidence coming from Greek consular reports that the Turkish government was responsible both for the "bomb" in Thessalonikê and for organizing the pogrom. Nevertheless, these comments urged caution and silence on the issue of damages to British citizens so as not to endanger British interests in Cyprus or the "good will" of the Turkish government.

It is worth noting that even the very low damage estimate by the Istanbul chamber of commerce's secretary-general—which was less than a tenth of the initial official estimates of Turkey's tax authorities—placed the damages at a much higher level than was to be admitted later by Menderes or recognized by his compensation policies. In the end, the Turkish government not only lowered the damage estimates of most applicants; it refused to pay even the amounts that it itself had judged to be proper, and instead paid an insignificant proportion of the claims that it had previously determined to be justified.

The magnitude of the destruction, its organized ferocity, and, most of all, the brazen nature of the attacks on Istanbul's Greeks were such that the shock and political impact were immediate, both domestically and internationally. Menderes hastened within the first week of the events to assure his nation and the world that the victims would be compensated, and even made special mention of the principal victims, the Greeks. He was quick to assuage Greek demands not only that damages be paid but that the guilty parties be punished. As time passed, however, Turkey's prime minister attempted to isolate both the event and its handling as a matter of personal honor. This was a curious political maneuver given Foreign Minister Köprülü's confession that the government had had prior knowledge of the demonstrations, and the vast body of circumstantial and incriminatory evidence against Menderes. Even in its September 12 session, Menderes had urged parliament not to insist on affixing responsibility as matters were still being "investigated" by the courts-martial. In the end, of course, both military and civil courts acquitted all the accused either on the ground of "insufficient" evidence or of strong—and therefore, presumably, understandable—"patriotic" sentiment that had motivated the pogromists to destroy the Greek community consequent to the national ire aroused by Cyprus. It is interesting, in this light, to read Avra Warren's accounts after the acquittals were made known. Contrary to Greek charges that justice had not been done, the us ambassador saw the acquittals as a vindication of Turkish justice. The British, by contrast, were much more clearheaded regarding Menderes's strategy and ultimate purpose. On November 18, in its analysis of the reports coming out of the British embassy in Ankara, the Foreign Office noted that:

> Basically the Greeks are trying to tie the Turks down to a formal Exchange of Notes confirming the Turkish undertaking to pay compensation. Mr. Menderes is being evasive but has said that he is handling the question personally and that the whole matter could satisfactorily be cleared up at the latest by March 31, 1956. Meanwhile the Greek Government have sent two Greek civil servants to Istanbul to look into the position. These have returned with a report that recipients of compensation are being asked to sign receipts for sums of which they have not received more than a fifth.[167]

While this document anticipates our narrative somewhat, the point here is that international opinion, incessant Greek pressure, the concern of us diplomats, and the more silent insistence of the British government, forced Menderes to take some immediate action to show his "good faith" in the matter of compensation. His first step was thus to reassure international opinion about Turkey's commitment to compensate foreign citizens whose properties had been attacked. To that end, the Turkish foreign ministry issued a formal, if ambiguous, communiqué on September 14, 1955, that stated the following:

> It has been ascertained that certain persons and establishments of foreign nationalities have suffered losses in the course of the unfortunate incidents that occurred at Istanbul and Izmir on the night of September 6-7.
>
> In order that the appropriate Turkish authorities may consider the measures to be taken with a view to compensation the interested parties are requested to inform the Ministry of Foreign Affairs through their Embassies or Legations of the nature and extent of the losses that they suffered.[168]

---

[167] TNA:PRO, No. RG10344/112, 12, 1955; also Ypourgeion Exôterikôn, Ankara, No. 3476, November 12, 1955.

[168] National Archives, Foreign Office Dispatch No. 405, American Embassy, Ankara, September 15, 1955; for the Greek list, Ypourgeion Exôterikôn, Ankara-Athens, Dispatch No. 2796, September 16, 1955.

With the exception of the Greek nationals (who were by far the largest group living in Turkey), the foreign nationals were few in number and the damage to their properties was consequently small; as a result, the September 14 announcement did not affect the vast majority of pogrom victims, many in dire need of immediate assistance. So it was that some sporadic and ineffective attempts were then made to give assistance through the efforts of the Committee of the Chambers of Commerce in Turkey, the Turkish Red Crescent, and the ministry of education. The same day of the foreign-ministry announcement, the US consul confirmed the state of affairs: "No Government Machinery [*sic*] for assistance to victims has yet been established. There have been set up, however, local committees which have assembled some 800,000 liras for distribution to victims. The Turkish Red Crescent Society is also assisting, principally with funds to help tide over the unemployed workers of destroyed establishments until the owner is [*sic*] able to reopen for business."[169] By September 20, after a meeting with his advisors, Menderes announced that a fundraising drive would begin to raise more significant funds from private sources, which would be entrusted to what was to be known as the Aid Committee, which, according to the US consulate, "invited all who suffered loss to file declarations of damages which will be investigated...."[170] The banks, chambers of commerce, and other organizations had already "contributed" about TL1 million, while the education ministry had proposed initial aid of TL150,000 for rudimentary repairs of minority schools.[171]

The memorandum according to which the newly created aid committee was to function announced September 26 to October 15, 1955, as the period for applying to the committee. Applications had to specify the kind of damages, estimates of such, the account number of the particular business, and the tax office to which it belonged. Claimants who failed to meet the deadline were automatically disqualified from consideration. Professional organizations (that is, chambers of commerce and commercial organizations, the finance office, and the income-tax office) were to investigate all damage claims: "Damages verified from these sources will be paid as far as the possibilities available to the Committee permit."[172] As of late September,

[169] National Archives, Istanbul to Ankara, Dispatch No. 116, September 14, 1955.

[170] National Archives, Foreign Office Dispatch No. 200, American Consul General, Istanbul, September 19, 1955.

[171] National Archives, Foreign Office Dispatch No. 450, American Embassy, Ankara, September 21, 1955, lists the sum as TL110,000.

[172] National Archives, Foreign Office Dispatch No. 127, American Consul General, Istanbul, September 23, 1955.

the committee had managed to raise TL2,013,000 to add to the sum of TL1.4 million with which it had been established.

Menderes had three concerns regarding the aid committee. The first was to create an organization that would raise private funds at a time when the Turkish government had no resources earmarked for compensation. (In truth, the legislation enabling such fundraising would not be enacted until February 29, 1956, and the actual dispersal of these funds would not begin until 1957.) It has been noted already, however, that the source of the aid-committee funds was forced levies assessed on the private sector. The second goal was to provide an agency to which claims could be submitted, for Turkish citizens as well as for foreign nationals, since the former had been excluded from the earlier directive of September 14, 1955, although, even in the latter case, the earlier directive had provided no funds for compensation. Accordingly, this new committee was mandated to raise the funds with which to address the claims of both Turkish citizens and foreign nationals. Menderes's final objective (which, however, was not included in the formal announcement of the compensation process) was to use this new committee as the instrument for radically paring and reducing damage claims and payments—a motivation that did not escape the notice of either Turkish or foreign observers. In fact, US consul Katherine Bracken closed her brief report on these compensation procedures with the comment that although only TL3,413,000 were available to the committee to discharge its obligations to thousands of victims, "The extent of destruction in Istanbul alone continues to be estimated as totalling up to one billion Turkish liras." She concludes, "It is generally believed that applications for assistance from the Aid Committee will not reflect the total losses because of a prevailing conviction that anything like adequate compensation is unlikely if not impossible."[173] The very declaration that claims were to be paid from privately raised funds rather than by the Turkish government sounded the alarms locally and internationally. Both the Greek government and Greek minority understood the economic difficulties of the Turkish state and now were worried that Menderes's scheme was to reduce the claims and (in turn) payments even more, so that the wealth of Istanbul's Greeks would, in the end, be substantially diminished. The reliance on private donations (levies) was a clear sign of the Turkish state's inability to meet its obligations.

According to US ambassador Warren, the aid committee was chaired by Halis Kayner of the İş Bankası, who was assisted by a number of important civic leaders, including Turks, Greeks, Armenians, and Jews. The total funds

[173] *Ibid.*

ostensibly raised by the committee fluctuated according to the date of the report. Warren gave an amount of TL8.5 million.[174] Other later reports put the sum variously at TL9 million and TL9.5 million.[175] As for the broader liability of the Turkish state, Menderes rejected the idea that it had any in his two meetings with the Greek ambassador to Ankara, Iôannês Kallergês. Although this issue will be considered later, as part of Menderes's more general stance on the politics of compensation, it would be appropriate at this point to look at Kallergês's report to his government.

> In these meetings Mr. Menderes had repeatedly informed me that though there was no legal obligation whatever, either in international or national law, obligating the Turkish government to pay compensations for the damages of September 6, nevertheless he himself announced, from September 7, formally and repeatedly in his public announcements that all damages would be corrected fully and rapidly. He reasoned that inasmuch as the compensation of victims does not stem from any legal obligation but only from his just and ethical decision that the damages should be righted, it is necessary that all initiatives in this matter should be left to him....For him it is a matter of honor and thus any doubt whatever expressed would be a personal insult. It was obvious from all the above that foreign intervention or undertaking in the face of third parties would not be acceptable to him....For he did not wish it to appear that he was proceeding to compensate while giving in to foreign pressures.[176]

The matter of the legality of compensations, and whether they constituted a legal obligation of the state under the particular circumstances surrounding the pogrom, was to exercise the Foreign Office and would act, for a period of time, as a restraint on the applications of British subjects for compensation.

What was the magnitude of the claims that went to the aid committee? When one examines the figures, the first fact that emerges is the monumental reduction of the assessments of damage. The US ambassador asserted that such a cut was warranted and "more realistic," but was it? Greek consular officials were also aware that, in terms of the hard realities, one could not hope to restore damaged, destroyed, or stolen property as it had once been; still, they aimed at "realistic" assessments that they believed the Turkish government was able and willing to pay. The sorry condition of the Turkish economy was

---

[174] National Archives, Dispatch No. 883, November 30, 1955.
[175] Theodôropoulos, *Sêmeiôma*, p. 22, who lists TL9.5 million; Chrêstidês, *Ekthesis*, p. 197, gives the same for the total sum.
[176] Ypourgeion Exôterikôn, Ankara to Athens, Dispatch No. 3476, November 11, 1955.

widely discussed and businessmen were well aware of it. As was noted above, the aid committee's formula was compensation "as far as the possibilities available to the Committee permit."

Although the figures concerning the claims submitted are incomplete, they are sufficient for the history of the pogrom's aftermath. Avra Warren gathered considerable statistics from the aid committee on the damage claims submitted to the Turkish foreign ministry from foreign governments. In a dispatch to the State Department of November 30, 1955, he included the following data:

Table 22: Number of claimants for compensation

	Number of claimants	Damages sought (in TL)	Date of submission
Greek nationals	1,070	27,014,479	11/3
Italians	126	3,300,000	11/15
British	50	2,000,000 [£1,488,813.16]	11/15
French	30	1,691,000	10/5
Swedes	10	30,000	
Americans	NA	10,000	
Total	**1,296**	**34,035,479** [33,524,292.16][177]	

As can be seen, Greek citizens constituted far and away the largest group of foreign nationals applying for damages (82.5 percent). Both the number of Greek claimants and the value of their claims are confirmed by a number of sources. The two principal reports are those of Vyrôn Theodôropoulos and Christoforos Chrêstidês:

[177] National Archives, American Embassy, Ankara, Dispatch No. 883, November 30, 1955; TNA:PRO, Ankara, No.1492/12, March 4, 1956, gives a more nearly precise figure for the claims of British citizens, as does also TNA:PRO, No. RK 10111/12, Dispatch No. 360, October 26, 1955. The former reports that the British claims amounted to £1,488,813.16. Stewart, in TNA:PRO, Ankara, No. RK1011/25, December 20, 1955, reported: "The Italian Chancellor told me on November 25, that his Ambassador had had an assurance from Monsieur Zorlu, the Minister of Foreign Affairs, that all foreign claims would be met, subject of course to being properly substantiated, and the Turkish Government had estimated the claims of foreign nationals at TL41 million, of which TL27 million were Greek claims." The total of TL41 million for foreign claims is also reported in TNA:PRO, Athens, No. RK16119/8, March 6, 1956, but it gives TL35 million as the claims of Greek nationals.

Table 23: Total damage to Greek property

	Theodôropoulos	*Chrêstidês*
Damages to 265 dwellings	TL3,036,980	TL3,036,980
Damages to businesses	23,122,639	23,122,639
Damages to graves/cemeteries	854,860	854,860
Damages to Greek-government property	90,000	
Totals	27,104,479	27,014,479
Total claimants	1,070	1,070[178]

The only complete text of a submission by a foreign government on behalf of citizens whose property had suffered damages was that of the British government sent to the Turkish foreign ministry on October 25, 1955[179] (see Appendix D). The claims submitted by the British embassy in Ankara represented forty-eight British citizens and totaled TL1,488,813.16.[180] The round figure in Warren's memorandum to Washington is thus in error. The completion of formal evaluations and payments of damages was to continue well into 1957, and it would seem that this list of forty-eight claimants stayed relatively constant as late as March 4, 1958, when some claims had not yet been vetted.

As for the claims submitted by the Greek minority and Orthodox Church, the figures vary, within the same general magnitude, probably due to various pressures that affected estimates over time. The most practical way to approach these assessments would be to examine the "statistics" of Theodôropoulos (who wrote his report in January 1956) and Chrêstidês (who wrote his long study in the latter part of 1957, considerably after the compensation law of February 28, 1956).

---

[178] Theodôropoulos, *Sêmeiôma*, p. 21; Chrêstidês, *Ekthesis*, p. 189. The same figures, save for an additional TL90,000 claimed by the Greek government for its consulate, are repeated elsewhere, as in Greek embassy, Athens, Dispatch No. 490T, November 10, 1955.

[179] The date does not agree with that given by US ambassador Warren's report, which dated the British submission of claims to November 15, 1955; see above.

[180] TNA:PRO, Ankara, Dispatch No. 1492/12, No. RK1481/3, March 4, 1958.

Table 24: Total damage to Greek and Greek Orthodox properties

Claimant	Theodôropoulos (in TL)	Chrêstidês (in TL)
Greek minority	c. 65,000,000	68,000,000
Greek Orthodox Church	35,000,000	19,933,450
		+
		19,121,155
		=
		39,054,605
		(finally reduced to 12,739,705)[181]

The preliminary estimate of damages to Greek and Armenian schools was TL450,000, with requests for immediate assistance coming to TL28,000[182] (out of total claims of TL69,578,744 by all Turkish nationals).[183] The aid committee report on its activities of November 30, 1955, revealed that it had collected TL8.5 million from forced levies, but had received claims for about TL70 million from Turkish nationals (as claims by foreign citizens went directly to the Turkish foreign ministry). These claims from Turkish citizens (mostly ethnic Greeks, Jews, and Armenians) did not include claims for churches, schools, or other religious establishments.[184]

The sources on applications give four categories of claimants from among Turkish nationals and provide information on foreigners as well, specifically:

- Foreign citizens
- Turkish citizens (Greeks, Armenians, Jews, Turks)
- The Greek Orthodox Church and other religious institutions
- Schools, etc.[185]

The aid committee was almost the sole source of funds for paying the claims of Turkish nationals. How did it manage to do so, given the enormous disparity between claims and ability to pay? What did the committee pay out and how much did it disperse?

---

[181] Theodôropoulos, *Sêmeiôma*, pp. 20-21; Chrêstidês, *Ekthesis*, pp. 190-192 (which, by the way, mistakenly comes up with the sum of TL40,054,605 when adding TL19,933,450 and TL19,121,155). Alexandris, *The Greek minority*, p. 259, gives slightly different figures.

[182] Chrêstidês, *Ekthesis*, p. 199.

[183] National Archives, Foreign Office Dispatch No. 666, American Embassy, Ankara, October 15, 1955; TNA:PRO, No. RG10344, January 25, 1956, reports TL69.5 million.

[184] National Archives, Foreign Office Dispatch No. 215, American Consul General, Istanbul, December 2, 1955.

[185] See footnotes 182-184 above.

As we saw, the committee's funds were applicable only to the claims of Turkish citizens. Since the records of the aid committee do not seem to have been published or made available as yet, our analysis is necessarily restricted to sources that emanated from interested parties, governments, and institutions. We have already seen that, following the announcement of its creation on September 20, the committee began to gather funds through "donations" from the private sector and soon amassed TL3,413,000 to begin its work. This levy continued for the next five weeks so that the committee raised the TL8.5 million already mentioned by November 30.[186] Theodôropoulos notes that by the end of December, this had grown to TL9.5 million, a figure that seems to have remained static in terms of any further contributions.[187] Accordingly, the ratio of available funds to damage claims was approximately 13.7 to 100. Further, as the chart below indicates, from September 30 to November 30, the Turkish lira lost most of its value in the underground currency markets.

Table 25: Devaluation of Turkish lira, September-November 1955

Currency market (official rate of exchange of $1 to TL2.80)

Date	$1 = TL
September	7.80
October 15	8.50
October 31	9.40
November 13	9.50
November 30	10.00

These data show that the actual compensations paid were even more insignificant—and profoundly skewed against the victims—since the damages were reckoned at the official exchange rate. According to Chrêstidês—and there is some logic to his presentation, which must rest on an unnamed contemporary source—the committee decided to give preference to claimants who had the greatest need. Thus, the TL28 million worth of claims of those who were in the worst financial condition were given preference out of the total of TL69,578,744.[188] This, of course, does not mean that the committee

[186] National Archives, Dispatch No. 883, November 30, 1955; in Dispatch No. 51867, sent by the foreign ministry to the Greek embassy in Washington, the minister informed the Greek ambassador that the Greek minority had, to date, been given only TL2.5 million of its TL63 million claims.

[187] Theodôropoulos, *Sêmeiôma*, p. 21; this is followed, as we saw, by Chrêstidês, *Ekthesis*, p. 197, as late as 1957.

[188] Chrêstidês, *Ekthesis*, pp. 196-201, is the most informative as to the division and outlay of the funds of the Istanbul aid committee, and much of his information is confirmed in other sources.

paid out the entire TL28 million. Even if it had desired to do so, the sums at hand were completely insufficient. Thus, most of these "preferred" claims were drastically cut. Given the absence or lack of the committee's records, however, one must attempt to make sense of figures reported by various sources and which are often inconsistent.

In analyzing the aid committee's procedures, we shall be concerned primarily only with Turkish citizens (Greek, Armenian, Jewish, and Muslim Turkish). The committee further divided this second category into four smaller subdivisions:

- Claims of TL1-5,000
- Claims of TL5,000-10,000
- Claims above TL10,000
- A special list of Orthodox indigents drawn up by the patriarch.[189]

The claimants in the first two categories numbered about 2,250 persons who had settled their claims by November 30, 1955, against a *total* disbursement of either TL2 million or TL2.5 million (the sources are not uniform on this matter).

The third category contained approximately 2,200 claimants whose applications were still being vetted at the time of the committee's November report. Theodôropoulos's next report (mid-January 1956) indicates that the aid committee had disbursed a total of TL4,380,000 by that time. Chrêstidês relates that, by the beginning of 1957, the committee's total disbursement was TL8,040,000.[190] As a result, very little of the original TL9.5 million still remained in the hands of the aid committee.

These figures help to give us a general idea of the amounts awarded to the third category, whose claims far surpassed those of the first two. It is difficult to give exact figures for there may be items included in these two large sums that were exclusive of the four subdivisions described above. Nevertheless, the differences among the awards noted by November 30, 1955, and the latter two amounts are considerable in terms of proportions and indicate a much greater award to those in the third subdivision, possibly over TL5.5 million. Chrêstidês gives some interesting proportions between claims and awards:

---

[189] National Archives, Foreign Office Dispatch No. 215, American Consul General, Istanbul, December 2, 1955; National Archives, Foreign Office Dispatch No. 883, American Embassy, Ankara, November 30, 1955; Theodôropoulos, *Sêmeiôma*, p. 22; Greek Embassy, Washington, No. 4850, Athens, on remuneration of Greek nationals, and the text, in translation, of the Turkish newspaper *Zafer*, dated November 24, on aid paid out by the Istanbul aid committee; documents sent by Athens on December 1, 1955.

[190] Chrêstidês, *Ekthesis*, p. 199; Theodôropoulos, *Sêmeiôma*, p. 22.

The Committee paid out damages to all those it deemed justified for compensation, varying sums that represented a portion of their…claims. This percentage reached, in the very rarest of cases as much as 50 to 60 percent of the claims. But in the majority of cases, the grants represented barely 10 to 20 percent of claims. Thus the Aid Committee on the sum total of the TL28,000,000 claims submitted to them [the claims of the neediest only] paid out, by the end of January 1957, a total of 8,040,000.[191]

Chrêstidês does not say anything about the judgments regarding the third category, which had the most substantial claims. They may, or may not, have been carried over to the compensation law of February 28, 1956.

What of the last group, the list of indigents presented to the aid committee by the patriarch? According to Warren's report of November 30, they numbered 2,736 Greeks who received TL60 each, for a total of TL164,160. Warren produced the following tabulation, which was not always consistent as to the numbers it reported:

2,250 Turkish nationals	TL2,000,000 paid
2,200 Turkish nationals being vetted	
2,736 indigent Greeks	164,160 paid
Total 7,186 claimants	**TL2,164,160 paid**[192]

These figures are close to those of Theodôropoulos and Chrêstidês in general, but there are inconsistencies. Regarding the 2,250 Turkish nationals, for example, the Greek sources mention TL2.5 million and usually attribute these payments to ethnic Greeks rather than to all Turkish nationals. This is possibly a wrong attribution as to payees, and the number may not be correct. Warren is also inconsistent when he adds the 2,250 Turkish nationals to the 2,200 persons being vetted, since he gives a total of 4,433 (as opposed to 4,450) in the introduction to his report. As he also gives no compensation figures for the 2,200 claims being vetted, we have to go to Theodôropoulos and Chrêstidês to reconstruct these data.[193] We know that the claims of the Greek minority amounted to TL63 million, and that this figure represented 90.5 percent of the total claims of all Turkish nationals (who claimed TL69,578,744). If we then apply this percentage to the total of 8,040,000 paid out by the aid committee to Turkish nationals by January 1, 1957, it

[191] Chrêstidês, *Ekthesis*, p. 199.
[192] National Archives, Foreign Office Dispatch No. 883, American Embassy, Ankara, November 30, 1955.
[193] Chrêstidês, *Ekthesis*, p. 199; Theodôropoulos, *Sêmeiôma*, p. 22.

yields a payout to ethnic Greeks of TL7,276,200 or 11.5 percent of their total claims. Again, however, this is highly speculative.

This clear disparity between claims and compensation brings us back again to the larger political and economic scene of Turkey and Greece. If, on January 1, 1957—sixteen months after the pogrom—the aid committee had disbursed only TL8,040,000 on claims of TL69,578,744 from 7,186 Turkish nationals, the historian must seek to explain this as a political and economic phenomenon. Clearly, the compensation process was dragged through a long and labyrinthine course that involved the Turkish government's political leadership, its foreign ministry, the tax system, and the respective bureaucracies. It is already evident that behind this disproportion between claims and awards, there lay a policy designed and followed by the government and its bureaucracy. Further, it is obvious that the ministers and their officials, who administered the final payments and the process of reducing claims, pursued their task slowly, at times very inefficiently, but always persistently, with the goal of avoiding any substantial assessment and compensation. The heads and administrators of the aid committee admitted openly that their policy was to give "immediate" but insignificant aid to claimants. The record confirms this strategy. Not only did the final compensation amount to no more than 11.5 percent of claims that amounted to almost TL70 million, but this latter sum itself was reduced very substantially by the Turkish policy of delay and refusal to acknowledge the pogrom's actual material consequences. Menderes created the aid committee as a convenience to allay the anxiety of the victims, and of the Greeks in particular, but also as a way of paying off the largest claimants, Turkey's own citizens, in nickels and dimes. The related legal measures, such as the quit claims declaring that the signer had received sums of money that he or she never did, were particularly intended to stop the claims from going any further. The payments themselves were in liras whose value had been drastically diminished by inflation and was thus unrepresentative of the true value of the businesses, goods, and houses for which compensation had supposedly been made. Lost days of business and work were simply ignored, and although legislation was meant to relieve businesspeople from the tax burden imposed by the destruction of their businesses, these laws were often so manipulated that many victims ended up losing their businesses and having to seek employment at a time when the economy did not need extra workers.

The longer that payments were delayed, and the longer many could not find employment, the more likely it was that their small businesses would close forever. This state of affairs, of course, imposed pressure not only on the Turkish authorities to pay, but also on the minorities (especially the Greeks), and on the Greek nationals to reach a solution that would expedite the compensation. The Greeks realized that if they did not repair their businesses immediately, they would have to close them. Soon, the Greek consul-general and the Greek minority were urging the Greeks to reestablish their businesses to the degree possible. And they began to exert pressure for a quick settlement even at a lower price, although not of course at the depths to which the aid committee had driven the compensations.

This policy of attrition against the claims and claimants was quite open and intrepid. In his report of October 3, 1955, as we saw above, Michael Stewart had recounted the virtual admission of the secretary-general of Istanbul's chamber of commerce that the principle was to cut down the damage claims so that the entire sum could be covered by the aid committee's available funds of TL9.5 million. He further concluded that the committee's fundraising activities would not meet the level of claims, and that there was "little likelihood that the compensation finally paid will account for more than a small proportion of the losses suffered," which meant that the "minority communities will clearly have to rely on their own energies and resources to restore their futures."[194]

The US consul-general in Istanbul described the aid committee's strategy as follows: "It is the policy of the Committee to reduce the claims as much as possible, to pay a certain percentage of the final figure. Before receiving any compensation each claimant is required to sign a paper stating that he has received full payment for damages sustained and that he has no further claims."[195] The US ambassador agreed, as is evident from his dispatch, already cited above, of December 1, 1955, by which time this policy had become more widely known: "The Committee agreed to pay in general only a percentage of each loss, depending on the degree of assistance each person must have in order to get re-established....[T]he chairman of the Istanbul Committee accented the Committee's purpose was to give 'aid,' not to pay compensation except for approved claims for less than TL10,000 which would be paid in full."[196] Once the aid committee's policies generally became known, the victims/claimants as well as the Greek government itself were in a state of despair; as they were also fully cognizant of the Turkish government's cynical role in the pogrom, they began to realize that Menderes's statements on rapid and substantial compensation were hollow.

---

[194] TNA:PRO, Ankara, Dispatch No. 202E, October 5, 1955.
[195] National Archives, Foreign Office Dispatch No. 127, American Consul General, Istanbul, September 23, 1955.
[196] National Archives, American Embassy, Ankara, Dispatch No. 228, December 1, 1955.

Table 26: Sources on damage claims

Source	Date	Funds raised by aid committee	Other funds contributed	Claimants		Claims (Turkish lira)		Payments (Turkish lira)	
				All Turkish citizens	Turkish citizens of Greek origin	All Turkish citizens	Turkish citizens of Greek origin	All Turkish citizens	Turkish citizens of Greek origin
Théodoropulos	12/31/55	9,500,000		3,110			65,000,000	4,380,000	
Chrèstidès	1/31/57	9,500,000					68,000,000	8,040,000[6]	674,000[7]
Greek embassy (Washington, DC)	12/1/55	4,000,000[1]							2,500,000[8]
	12/17/55			2,133	2,735		63,000,000		2,500,000[9]
National Archives (Washington, DC)	9/10/55		110,000[3]						
	10/18/55			4,443		69,578,744			
	10/27/55						79,000,000		
	11/30/55	8,500,000[2]	106,000[4]	2,250[5]	2,736			2,000,000	3,000,000[10]

[1] As of 11/29/55
[2] By that date
[3] Schools
[4] Schools
[5] 2,200 to be vetted
[6] Inclusive of payments to Greek minority equals 8,714,000
[7] 535,000, schools; 50,000, cemeteries; 89,000, medical clinics
[8] 11/29/55
[9] 11/24/55
[10] Total sum as per Warren: 164,160, destitute; 203,000, Greek patriarchate; 93,000, Şişli cemetery; 88,000, medical clinics in Pera

1. Dēmētrios Kaloumenos is honored by the academy of Athens on November 29, 1979, for his photographic documentation of the pogrom; sitting directly behind him is Kōnstantinos Tsatsos, president of the Greek republic (courtesy of Dēmētrios Kaloumenos).

2. Adnan Menderes (courtesy of Dêmêtrios Kaloumenos).

*3. Athênagoras I, ecumenical patriarch of the Orthodox Church
(courtesy of Dêmêtrios Kaloumenos).*

4. Alexandros Papagos (courtesy of Dêmêtrios Kaloumenos).

5. Kônstantinôs Karamanlês (left) with Adnan Menderes (right), as F. R. Zorlu looks on; Euangelos Averôf-Tositsa is half-hidden behind Karamanlês (courtesy of the Historical Archives Service of the Greek ministry of foreign affairs).

6. *Patriarch Athênagoras with Fahrettin Kerim Gökay (middle), vali of Istanbul, in 1954*
(© *Dêmêtrios Kaloumenos*).

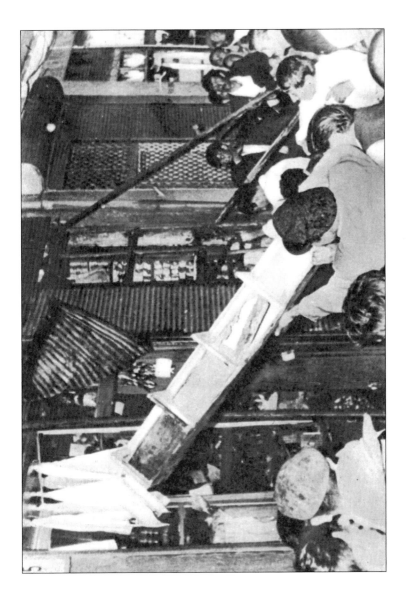

7. *Rioters batter in the front of a Greek shop* (The Illustrated London News *picture library*).

8. One of many youthful bands that led the rioting, driving through the streets, waving flags, and shouting slogans (The Illustrated London News picture library).

9. *A crowd of mainly young men demonstrates in an Istanbul street, shouting anti-Greek slogans (The Illustrated London News picture library).*

*10. A portrait of Kemal Atatürk is held above a speaker
(*The Illustrated London News *picture library).*

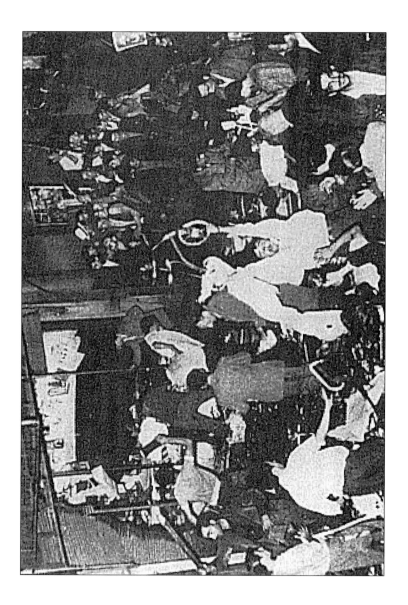

11. Destruction of a Greek store (The Illustrated London News picture library).

12. Troops stand by an overturned car after rioters have passed (The Illustrated London News picture library).

13. Tanks gather in Istanbul after the proclamation of martial law
*(*The Illustrated London News *picture library).*

*14. Wreckage is strewn in a Beyoğlu street
(The Illustrated London News picture library).*

15. The Illustrated London News *coverage of the pogrom;*
the subhead under the headline reports £100 million of damage.

16. *Pedestrians strolling over destroyed goods, with six ruined stores in background, İstiklal Caddesi, Beyoğlu* (© *Dêmêtrios Kaloumenos*).

17. *Three destroyed Greek shops (on the left), İstiklal Caddesi (© Démétrios Kaloumenos).*

18. *Destroyed shops, damaged goods, and pedestrians on Yüksek Kaldırım (© Dēmétrios Kaloumenos).*

19. *Two destroyed shops next to the Türkiye Garanti Bankası, which remained untouched, Galata, Karaköy* (© *Dēmētrios Kaloumenos*).

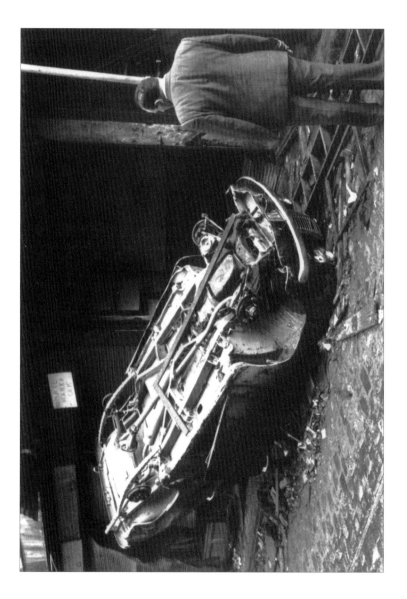

20. *Overturned and burned car, tires and wheels stripped, Galata, Karaköy (© Dêmêtrios Kaloumenos).*

21. A line of destroyed minority shops, with goods strewn on the street; the name of one sign, Meyer, suggests a Jewish owner, Karaköy (© Dêmêtrios Kaloumenos).

22. *Destroyed shops on the left, and Turkish sanitation workers sweeping up the debris in the street across from a subway station, Galata, Karaköy (© Dēmḗtrios Kaloumenos).*

*23. The Bon Marşesi and Motola stores completely looted, Karaköy
(© Dêmêtrios Kaloumenos).*

24. *Unidentified store, completely looted and gutted, Galata, Karaköy (© Dēmētrios Kaloumenos).*

25. *The typesetting area of the Istanbul Greek-community newspaper* Embros *after the pogromists' attack, Tünel, Beyoğlu (© Dēmētrios Kaloumenos).*

26. *The Lumiyer photography studio, with co-owner Matthaios Kaloumenos
(brother of Dêmêtrios), Tünel, Beyoğlu (© Dêmêtrios Kaloumenos).*

27. Another view of the Lumiyer studio (© Démétrios Kaloumenos).

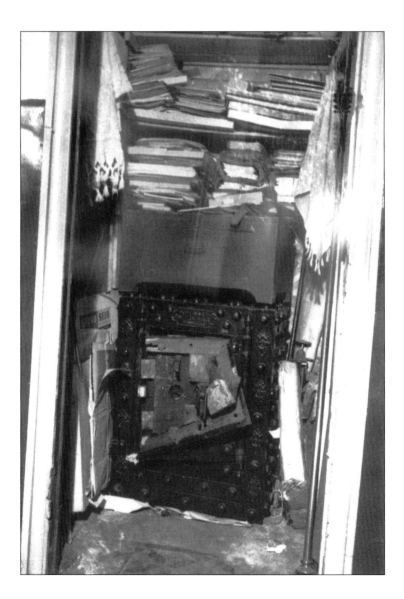

28. The Lumiyer's looted safe (© Dêmêtrios Kaloumenos).

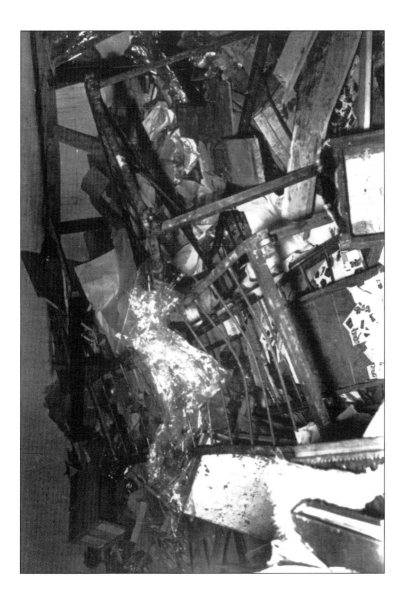

29. *Boyas Brothers furniture store, Tünel, Beyoğlu (© Démétrios Kaloumenos).*

30. *The owner overseeing the damage in the Roussos hat shop, Galata, Karaköy* (© *Dēmētrios Kaloumenos*).

31. Employees cleaning up after the attack in the Royal pastry and chocolate shop, Karaköy (© Démétrios Kaloumenos).

32. *Destruction of Meger furniture shop, Galata* (© *Dêmêtrios Kaloumenos*).

33. Looted house, Ortaköy (© Dêmêtrios Kaloumenos).

34. *Looted house, Edirnekapı (© Dēmētrios Kaloumenos).*

35. Looted "house-store" (residential building with a store on the ground floor), with a Turkish soldier, who took part in the looting, standing guard (see Chapter 3), Kumkapı (© Dēmētrios Kaloumenos).

36. Another view of the "house-store" (© Dêmêtrios Kaloumenos).

37. *Destroyed equipment, Holy Trinity outpatient clinic, Taksim (© Dèmètrios Kaloumenos).*

*38. Burned and destroyed lobby and ceremonial hall of the
Zappeion school for girls, Taksim (© Dêmêtrios Kaloumenos).*

39. Destroyed classroom of the Zappeion school (© Dêmêtrios Kaloumenos).

40. Another destroyed classroom of the Zappeion school (© Dēmētrios Kaloumenos).

41. Another view of the damage to the Zappeion school (© Dêmêtrios Kaloumenos).

42. *The World Council of Churches mission examines the destruction of the Church of the Zoodochos Pege, Balıklı (© Démétrios Kaloumenos).*

43. WCC representatives examine the burned ossuary, Church of the Metamorphosis, Şişli cemetery (© Dēmétrios Kaloumenos).

44. *Another view of the ossuary, Church of the Metamorphosis, Şişli cemetery (© Démétrios Kaloumenos).*

45. Desecrated tombs, Church of the Metamorphosis, Şişli cemetery
(© Dêmêtrios Kaloumenos).

46. *WCC representatives examine the desecrated tombs of the ecumenical patriarchs, Zoödochos Pēgē, Balıklı (© Dēmētrios Kaloumenos).*

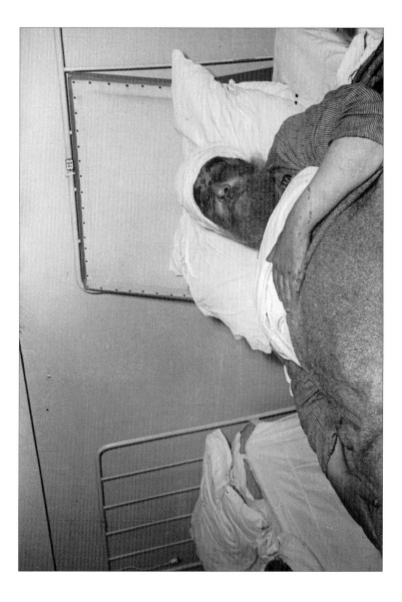

47. Bishop Gerasimos of Pamphilos, abbot of the Zoodochos Pege monastery, lies in a hospital of Balıklı after being beaten during the pogrom (© Dēmētrios Kaloumenos).

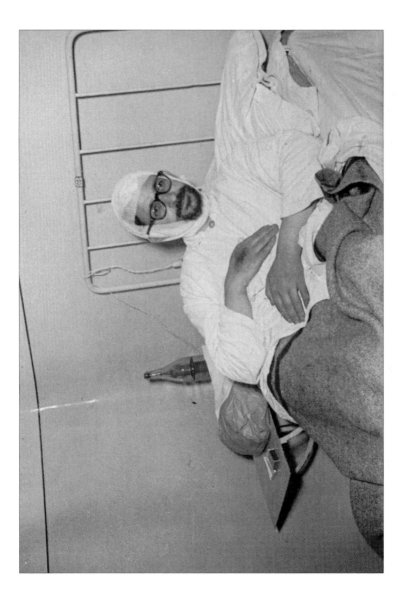

48. *The novice Euangelos Mastorakēs, of the Zoodochos Pege monastery, after being beaten* (© *Dēmētrios Kaloumenos*).

49. The WCC mission examines the ruins of Saints Constantine and Helen, Samatya (© Dêmêtrios Kaloumenos).

50. *The WCC mission examines the ruins of St. Menas, Samatya (© Dêmêtrios Kaloumenos).*

51. Head uncovered, Patriarch Athénagoras prays before the overturned altar table of the destroyed Panagia, Belgratkapι (© Démétrios Kaloumenos).

52. *Saints Constantine and Helen, Samatya, in ruins (© Démétrios Kaloumenos).*

53. Saints Theodoroi, Langa (© Démétrios Kaloumenos).

54. Saint Menas, Samatya, gutted and roofless (© Démétrios Kaloumenos).

55. *St. George Kyparissas, Samatya, burned and bell thrown from belfry*
(© Dêmêtrios Kaloumenos).

56. Entrance to Panagia Altı Mermer (© Dêmêtrios Kaloumenos).

57. Panagia Altı Mermer, bell thrown from belfry (© Dêmêtrios Kaloumenos).

58. *East and south walls of Panagia Altı Mermer; south wall is supported by iron rods to prevent collapse (© Dèmètrios Kaloumenos).*

59. After being cleaned, only shell of Panagia Altı Mermer remains (© Dēmētrios Kaloumenos).

60. St. John, metochion *of Mount Sinai, Masalla Caddesi, Fener
(© Dêmêtrios Kaloumenos).*

61. *Ruined icons, altar, analogion, chancel screen, and stasidia of Panagia Ouranon, Salmatobruk* (© Dēmētrios Kaloumenos).

62. Damages to icons, altar, and parts of nave of St. Paraskeue, Hasköy (© Dēmētrios Kaloumenos).

63. *Destroyed agiasma, Panagia Vlachernón, Ayvansaray* (© *Dēmétrios Kaloumenos*).

64. Damaged altar, chandelier, and icons, with evidence of arson, Zoodochos Pege, Balıklı (© Dēmētrios Kaloumenos).

65. *Icons hacked and vestments ruined, St. Nicholas, Galata, Karaköy (© Dēmḗtrios Kaloúmenos).*

66. Mural image of Moses defaced, St. Nicholas, Galata, Karaköy
(© Dêmêtrios Kaloumenos).

*67. Eyes on the icon of Christ gouged out and arms of Christ slashed on the
Crucifixion, Christos Soter, Galata (© Dêmêtrios Kaloumenos).*

*68. Icons removed from iconostasis and damaged. St. Nicholas, Τοπκαπι
(© Dêmêtrios Kaloumenos).*

69. *Small icons hacked into pieces, St. Phokas, Ortaköy (© Dēmētrios Kaloumenos).*

70. Burned altar, Holy Trinity, Taksim (© Dêmêtrios Kaloumenos).

*71. Only right forearm and hand remain on Crucifixion,
St. Nicholas, Galata, Karaköy (© Dêmêtrios Kaloumenos).*

72. Desecration of epitaphios, St. Nicholas, Galata, Karaköy (© Dēmētrios Kaloumenos).

73. *Another view of St. Nicholas, Galata, Karaköy (© Dēmḗtrios Kaloumenos).*

74. *Desecration of Crucifixion and figure of the Virgin, St. Kyriake, Kumkapı (© Dēmētrios Kaloumenos).*

75. Desecration of epitaphios, St. John of the Chians, Galata, Karaköy (© Démétrios Kaloumenos).

76. Desecration of the kouvoukli, St. Demetrios, Tahtakapı (© Dēmētrios Kaloumenos).

77. Euangelistria, Yenişehir (© Démétrios Kaloumenos).

78. *Smashed episcopal throne amid general destruction, St. Demetrios Kanavos, Tahtakapı* (© *Dēmētrios Kaloumenos*).

79. Damaged episcopal throne and iconostasis, St. Demetrios, Kuruçeşme
(© Dēmētrios Kaloumenos).

80. Destroyed vestments on floor of sanctuary, St. George,
metochion *of Jerusalem, Fener (© Dêmêtrios Kaloumenos).*

81. Some of the diplomats involved in the Greek dispute with Turkey following the pogrom, including (left to right): Menelaos Anagnostopoulos, Vyrōn Theodōropoulos, Theodōros Geōrgiadēs, and Iōannēs Kallergēs. Also in the photograph are (far right) Nikos Damtsas, translator for the patriarchate, and (next to him) the patriarchate's archivist, Tentes. (© Dēmētrios Kaloumenos).

82. Adnan Menderes is deposed at Yassıada (İrtibat Bürosu archive).

83. The heads of the Menderes government in the dock of the accused (right to left): Mahmud Celal Bayar, Adnan Menderes, Fatin Rüştü Zorlu, Mehmet Fuat Köprülü, and Fahrettin Kerim Gökay (İrtibat Bürosu archive).

84. Patriarch Athénagoras, flanked by his two Greek translators, testifies at Yassıada (İrtibat Bürosu archive).

85. Attorney Cemal Orhan Fersoy defends his client, Zorlu (İrtibat Bürosu archive).

86. *In the dock: (far right) Hasan Polatkan, minister of economics, and (next to him) Fevzi Lutfi Karaosmanoğlu, formerly a member of the Demokrat Parti and later founder of the Hürriyet Parti (İrtibat Bürosu archive).*

87. *Two soldiers lead Menderes to his final incarceration before his execution on the island of İmralı* (İrtibat Bürosu archive).

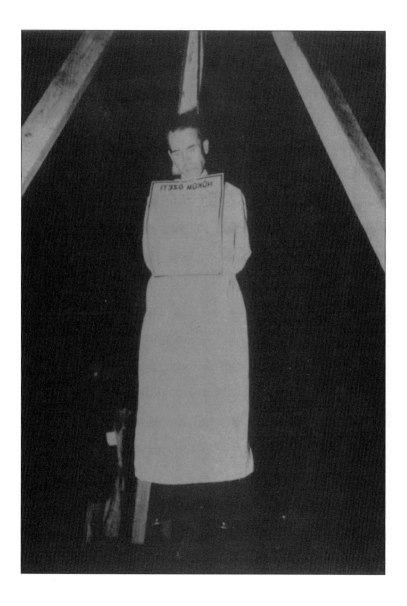

88. Hasan Polatkan on the gallows with the hüküm özeti *pinned to his collar*
*(*İrtibat Bürosu *archive).*

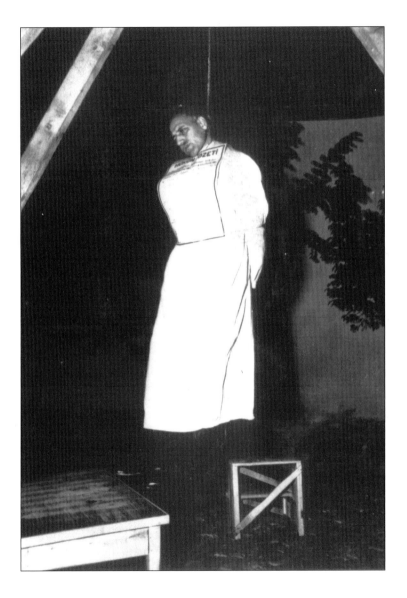

89. Fatin Rüştü Zorlu on the gallows with the hüküm özeti *pinned to his collar*
(İrtibat Bürosu *archive)*.

90. Adnan Menderes on the gallows with the hüküm özeti *pinned to his collar (*İrtibat Bürosu *archive).*

CHAPTER FOUR

FROM PAPAGOS TO KARAMANLÊS (THE ECONOMICS AND POLITICS OF COMPENSATION CONTINUED)

W hen the Turkish government finally agreed to "restore the honor" of the Greek flag with a special military ceremony in Izmir in the latter part of October, the Greek government began to have faint hopes that perhaps Menderes's promises might be real—but this weak note of faith and optimism vanished quickly in light of the aid committee's policies and activities. The Greek government then instructed its diplomats in Washington, at NATO headquarters in Paris, and at the UN to make strenuous efforts to enlist outside support, and corresponding pressure on the Turkish government to live up to its obligations. Without going into details here, these efforts were generally unsuccessful as American, British, and NATO interests lay elsewhere, specifically in Cyprus and in fighting the Cold War. Indeed, the situation regarding Cyprus continued to worsen from the point of view of Greek interests. In Turkey, Fatin Zorlu's rise to power, not only in the foreign ministry, where he had two active and capable diplomats as collaborators in Nuri Birgi and Mahmut Dikerdem, but also in Menderes's councils, led to extremely aggressive policies toward Greece and Cyprus. Zorlu's hostility to the Greek side was such that members of the Greek government hoped that he might be replaced. Zorlu was also behind the activation of a more general anti-Greek policy among the Western diplomats posted in Ankara and throughout Europe and the United States. It was obvious that the Cyprus issue had now become a national Turkish issue and that Zorlu was the driving force behind it. Even the most casual perusal of declassified Greek, US, and British diplomatic archives will impress the reader with the sharpness and hostility in the exchanges between Greek and Turkish diplomats meeting in Ankara. Such meetings are often documented in the conversations of Greek *chargé d'affaires* Theodôros Geôrgiadês and Birgi, and between the Greek ambassador and Zorlu. In effect, the pogrom had very considerable consequences on the foreign policies of both Greece and Turkey, as each side sought to rally foreign support in its confrontation with its opponent.

THE GREEK CAMPAIGN FOR COMPENSATION

Greek frustration over the slowness with which the claims were processed is strongly reflected in Greek policy and diplomacy. The first news of the "decimation" (literally, the "tenthing") of the damage claims of the Greek minority at the hands of the Turkish aid committee set off a number of protests to the Turkish government, as well as Greek diplomatic moves to have the US and NATO pressure Turkey to pay the appropriate compensation, and to do so in a timely manner. The Greek ambassador in Washington addressed an *aide-mémoire* to William O. Baxter at the State Department on the Turkish government's sluggishness in living up to its promises (symptomatically, the memo was dated October 14, 1955, the last day on which claims could be submitted to the aid committee):

> The Royal Greek Government is…well aware of and seriously concerned by the fact that five weeks after the occurrence of the riots, the Turkish Government has not yet taken any effective measures of compensations [*sic*] proportionate to the scope of the damage itself, and has rather had recourse to inadequate measures as public collections etc. As a result up to this day only few of the riot victims have received any compensation at all, and the amounts paid are of the nature of 500 to 1,500 T[urkish] liras [about 180 to 540 US dollars at the official rate of exchange.][1]

Throughout November and much of December, Greek diplomats continued their efforts to gain support on the matter of compensations at the same time that the Turkish foreign ministry was carrying out its own efforts to generate an effective counterattack in the same circles. The Greek government did not neglect the diplomatic front in Ankara and had hopes, momentarily, of persuading Turkey to improve the compensation situation— especially after the flag ceremony in Izmir, when relations seemed to improve, at least superficially. These hopes, as well as stiffening Turkish resistance to the Greek proposals, emerge from the two meetings in Ankara between Iôannês Kallergês and Menderes. In preparation for these meetings, the Greek foreign ministry had sent specific and careful instructions to its ambassador, who was to express the official thanks of the Greek government on the matter of the restoration of honor to the Greek flag and, in particular, for Menderes's goodwill and statements on preserving Greek-Turkish friendship. At the same time, in his conversations with Menderes, Zorlu, and other Turkish officials, Kallergês was to emphasize, carefully, that the Greek government attached special importance to the rapid and satisfactory solution of matters with

---

[1] Ypourgeion Exôterikôn, No. 4228/B/29, October 14, 1955.

Turkey, for only on such a solution could better relations be based. Against this general background, the Greek ambassador was to set forth the following views and requests of the Greek government.

First, the Greek government believed that it was to the mutual interest of the two countries to stabilize relations, and it was well-disposed to this provided that the Turkish government demonstrated an understanding of the Greek position and offered full satisfaction of Greece's just request. As such, although the Greek government was pleased with the moral satisfaction provided by the flag ceremony, there was still a need to carry out, appropriately, the material restitution of the vast damages suffered by the victims of the pogrom, especially as Greek public opinion was following the matter very closely. The ambassador was then to spell out the direct means by which this solution was to be reached, that is, the specific measures by which the Turkish government would compensate Greek citizens and assure their security. These measures would then become part of a binding exchange of letters or agreements between the two governments.

Second, the matter of the Greek minority and Greek Orthodox Church in Turkey was governed by the treaty of Lausanne, which gave (and, in fact, continues to give) the Greek government every right to intercede on behalf of, and to protect, both the Greek minority and the Church. In this spirit, the Greek government asked that all delays, especially intentional ones, be ended in the matter of compensation for the minority and the Church.

Third—and here we must add that the letter of instruction to Kallergês certainly overloaded him with additional burdens—the Greek ambassador was to renew efforts to get the Turkish government to use more restraint in dealing with Greek fishermen who fished in Turkish waters. Finally, and this was an especially onerous burden, Kallergês was to renew Greek efforts to get the Turkish side to meet on the matter of establishing the maritime boundaries dividing the two nations (this was not a new proposal, as the countries were already discussing this matter through duly appointed committees).[2]

In the ambassador's second meeting with Menderes on November 11, the latter refused to accept the former's written memorandum (as outlined above), arguing that he already knew what the position of the Greeks was and that he had already given money to the Greek schools and would resolve the outstanding damage claims. It seems that in their first meeting, Menderes had accepted the principle of some type of binding exchange of letters, but nullified that agreement in the second meeting. It was in this second meeting, as we have previously seen, that Menderes asserted that the Turkish government was not

---

[2] Ypourgeion Exôterikôn, No. 46321, October 24, 1955.

bound by any law to give compensation but that he, personally, chose to do so as a matter of honor. Perhaps of greater significance was the fact that Menderes repeatedly explained to Kallergês during their second meeting that he had to be very careful in his negotiations as he was expecting to be attacked, not only from the opposition but also from the nineteen members of his own DP who were splitting from the party, during the meeting of the Turkish parliament on November 28. Indeed this was prophetic inasmuch as the meeting of the DP deputies was to be a political disaster for Menderes and his party.[3]

In trying to explain to the foreign ministry why the exchange of binding letters was never again mentioned after the initial meeting, Kallergês argued that it was due to the fact that Menderes did not have full command of French and, as there was no translator at hand in their first meeting, he probably did not understand to what he had agreed. In the second meeting, however, Zorlu was present, and he did all the translating from Turkish into French and from French into Turkish. With this advantage as intermediary, Zorlu took the opportunity to draw Menderes into the most rigid of positions regarding Kallergês's proposals. Kallergês goes on at great length to describe the difficulties he encountered with Menderes at the second meeting, especially in regard to a specific timetable for resolving damage claims, which reflected the anxieties of both Greek and Turkish governments. On the one hand, the Turkish government did not have the financial wherewithal for rapid and full payment; on the other hand, the Greek government was faced with the mass destruction of the Greeks of Istanbul. Delay meant institutionalizing, to a disastrous degree, the material and psychological condition of the Greeks. After such exasperating insistence by the Greek ambassador on setting a specific date by which to resolve the issue, Menderes abandoned the ongoing Turkish tactical answer of "very soon" and set the deadline of March 30, 1956. As has already been pointed out, this date was far off the mark.[4]

Thus, the Greek effort to extract an exchange of letters embodying the agreed-upon terms for compensation, as well as an open acknowledgment of Greece's rights as guarantor of the Greek minority in accordance with the treaty of Lausanne, was neither attained nor even really discussed. This failure, and the accompanying collapse of Menderes's government on November 28, led to further deterioration of Greek-Turkish relations. Indeed, these seemingly hopeless conditions led to the realization, in Greek governmental quarters, that the situation was fast becoming chaotic. Thus, three months and a week after the pogrom, the new Greek prime minister, Kônstantinos Karamanlês,

---

[3] See below on the dissolution of Menderes's government.
[4] Ypourgeion Exôterikôn, No. 3476, November 12, 1955.

wrote a severe memorandum to the Greek foreign minister on what he considered to be, and termed, the continuous indisposition and lack of any element of goodwill on the part of the Turkish government in honoring its obligations and verbal promises to compensate the pogrom's victims. He noted that public opinion in Greece was at a boiling-point and had to be calmed by a fair Turkish response. In addition, members of the Greek parliament had made serious representations in their sessions, calling on the Greek government to account for the lack of financial and political satisfaction. Karamanlês stated in his memorandum that, "We can no longer tolerate the situation and we seek an immediate closing of this account [matter]."[5] The foreign minister was ordered, furthermore, to inform John Foster Dulles and Köprülü (who, after the political crisis at the end of November, had replaced Zorlu as foreign minister) of Greece's wishes on this score.

The aid committee's actions had played a crucial role in the deterioration of Greek-Turkish relations, as its conduct stood in stark contradiction to Menderes's rosy promises that all would turn out well and that equitable reparations would be made to the pogrom's victims. In addition, the Cyprus issue had begun to weigh heavily on relations. Moreover, it was not only the Greek parliament that was disturbed by the rocky road that Turkish compensation had taken. From the beginning, both the Turkish political opposition and, especially, Menderes's own party were equally distressed.

Hadi Husman, a member of the DP's parliamentary group (representing Istanbul), had submitted a series of eight questions on the pogrom to his group that he wanted to be discussed and answered on the morning of November 28, 1955, prior to the Turkish parliament's session. It seems that the parliamentary group's executive committee was able to avoid the matter, however, as it came at a time when Menderes was extremely vulnerable politically. Menderes, of course, had faced a similar problem with his parliamentary group on September 12. The fact that it would not subside indicates clearly that the party was being split along ideological and disciplinary lines. It confirms that Menderes wanted to deal with the compensation issue personally, not collegially or institutionally, which reflected his growing authoritarian and centralizing tendencies, both in regard to his own party and to the Turkish government in general. It was also part of his general policy of avoiding any subject that could betray his involvement in the pogrom. It is probably indicative of the fact that, although more and more was becoming known about the events and the reparations for them, the details were probably known only to a more limited circle,

[5] Ypourgeion Exôterikôn, No. 53601/T4 Ep., December 12, 1955.

which included Menderes, Zorlu, Köprülü, Bayar, and Polatkan at the higher levels, and the members of the aid committee at a considerably lower level. Husman may also have intended his questions to help expedite the matter of compensation for his own city of Istanbul.

Husman's very first question went to the heart of the compensation issue, namely, whether the value of damages suffered by "our compatriots" had been determined. He also wanted to know which government or private agency had carried out the assessments, and what had become of all the funds, whether in the form of assistance or raised through fundraising drives, intended for the partial compensation of victims? Of particular relevance was his request to be told the actual proportion of payments to the "firmly" established assessment of the sum total of damages? It is obvious, from the manner in which he stated his questions, that Husman had become aware of what was actually going on in the aid committee. He clearly knew that the committee was paying out only a portion of the real damages and that it was important to know whether or not the Menderes government was going to legislate (perhaps at the parliamentary session of November 28) a resolution of the matter. His fifth question asked: "Are these present-day compensations [of the aid committee] the compensations that the Government had promised the day after the events [the pogrom] or, is the Government intending to go further and to make payments specifically from its general budget?" Furthermore, Husman asked, if there was such intention to make further payments, could the government tell the DP parliamentary group whether such funds would come from the current or next year's budget, and what the form and amount of such aid would be? While these first six questions seemed to refer to damages suffered by Turkish citizens, the next one concerned itself, briefly, with the extent and assessment of damages suffered by foreign citizens, the government's intentions regarding compensation, and the total amount of compensation to be paid. (If the government had not already compensated foreigners, Husman wanted to know what it planned to do about the destruction of their property?) Finally, the eighth question queried the government on its plans regarding the damages suffered by the religious and educational institutions, which, Husman concluded, "must recover their former state."[6]

This policy of minimal (and minimizing) compensation that emerged

[6] Ypourgeion Exôterikôn, Ankara, Dispatch No. 3587, November 26, 1955. The Greek ambassador's dispatch contains a formal translation of Husman's petition to the executive committee of the DP deputies' group in which he asks that answers be given to the eight questions at the group's meeting on November 28. The Greek ambassador accompanies the text with a commentary on the eight questions: "It is questionable whether these questions will be discussed in the meeting of the Turkish General Assembly as I have been informed that there

from the government's budget and from the aid committee's actions was thus reflected in the reactions of both the Greek and Turkish parliaments. Both Menderes and Karamanlês were particularly sensitive to the respective opinions of their legislative bodies, as well as to those of the press and the public more generally in their respective constituencies. Karamanlês's new government was not yet firmly established and Menderes's government was tottering on the edge of political collapse. Meanwhile, the political maneuvering round and about the Cyprus issue intensified. Nonetheless, there were differences in the financial situation of the two governments. Greece's economy, although temporarily frozen by Papagos's illness and disability in his last few months, was still in better condition than that of Turkey. The Greek request for a $46-million loan from the United States in order to balance its budget was far lower than Turkey's comparable request of $300 million, which Menderes had hoped to get from the US just prior to the pogrom in order to meet the immediate necessities of his government. Now, with the widespread destruction in Istanbul, the Turkish treasury was faced with massive demands for compensation, the sudden unemployment of thousands, and shortages of certain necessities and commodities. Although Karamanlês was as yet untested, he had already had considerable experience as minister of public works after the large-scale destruction of the Second World War and Civil War. In preliminary conversations with American representatives, the prospects for the Greek loan were quite favorable, whereas the US had initially refused the larger loan to Turkey. As for international political advantage, there is no doubt that Turkey enjoyed priority over Greece. In the case of British relations with the two countries, it is quite clear, both from its diplomacy and from the telling commentaries of Foreign Office officials on the steady stream of reports from their representatives in Turkey, that Britain had taken the initiative in keeping Turkey in its camp in the dispute over Cyprus. The annual report for 1955 submitted by the British ambassador in Athens is characteristic in this regard:

> In this despatch which I have the honour to submit as my annual review of developments in Greece during 1955 I regret to record that the most notable feature of the past year has been the sharp decline in Anglo-Greek relations which are now at as low an ebb

is an effort within the Parliamentary Group to prevent the Assemblyman, Mr. Husman, from putting forth these questions, for the Government is not in a position to provide satisfactory answers to the questions." The matter of why it was not in such a position is undoubtedly complex, but it is not unlike the experience of Kallergês, who tried repeatedly to get answers to such questions but was largely unsuccessful, as both Menderes and Zorlu avoided specific commitments on the matter.

as they have been at any time since the First World War....There
were, indeed, other regrettable developments during the year. The
decline in Greece's friendliness to us was reflected in a worsening
of her relations with the United States and all her North Atlantic
Treaty Organization allies (amounting in the case of Turkey,
almost to a suspension of relations).[7]

The ambassador's annual report is a litany of complaints of Greek hostility,
irrationality, and inactivity. Although some of these complaints might have
been justified in terms of British policy on Cyprus, many were not. In fact,
the pogrom and the political interests pursued by the United States and
Britain in Cyprus turned out to be shortsighted and continue to plague
American policies in that part of the world. Thus, these actions were not to
"do good in the long run," to echo the remark cited in the previous chapter
by a commentator in the Foreign Office.

Behind Kallergês's inconclusive meetings with Menderes and Zorlu,
and the memo by Karamanlês that expressed Greek frustration with Turkey,
there lay the debris of what had been a virtual political war of some three
months' duration carried out by Greek and Turkish memoranda, attacks, and
defenses, all of which had been further aggravated by Dulles's "neutralist"
declaration. Much of this diplomatic "war" from September to December
1955 was waged over the Greek claims for justice and the Turkish effort
to defend the violence by shifting the blame for these acts from Turkey to
Greece, that is, to Greek policy over Cyprus, which, the Turkish argument
ran, had "provoked" the "national" violence that led to the destruction of
Istanbul's Greek community. In the beginning, the Turkish government did
not dare state its case so illogically and cynically. But with the passage of time,
and as the shock of the tumultuous events was absorbed into daily life on the
local scene, the controversy of Cyprus began to replace the pogrom, now over,
in Turkey's official stance and policy statements. For much of September and
well into October, in fact, the matters, first, of fixing responsibility for the
pogrom and, then, of assessing damages for compensation were to dominate
the political and diplomatic relations of Greece and Turkey. Further, the
censorship of the Turkish press by General Aknoz, and the subsequent civil
restrictions of the martial-law command, played a role in Turkish public
opinion. Toward the end of October and the beginning of November, a
marked change by the Turkish government from a more passive stand to an
extremely aggressive one was to be seen both on the issue of compensations

---

[7] TNA:PRO, Ankara, Dispatch No. 5, January 16, 1956; TNA:PRO, Athens, Dispatch No.
58, March 23, 1956.

and of the Cyprus question.

In this first phase of the diplomatic war, the Greek government undertook a fairly well-organized campaign to marshal support. Its activities centered on the United States primarily, but also on NATO, the United Nations, the World Council of Churches, and, of course, the Turkish government itself. In addition, Greek diplomacy involved, in particular, the Greek American community and its Church, which was under direct administration of the ecumenical patriarchate. Internally, the death of Premier Papagos, preceded by his rather long illness, as well as the initial instability of the new Karamanlês government, were not fortuitous events for Greece. The country's parliament repeatedly criticized both the old and new governments for what it considered (wrongly) to be their pusillanimity in the face of the pogrom. Official Greek documents refer to this diplomatic "handicap" repeatedly, and while it can be said that the Greek government often used this argument to justify its hard positions in dealing with Turkey, there was some truth in the matter. By and large, Greeks were so aroused by the pogrom's willful violence that no special effort was required to incite their political anger.

As such, the Greek government's response and method were not unintelligent, but relatively well-organized, and in the end achieved some success, although, of course, not all the success to which the government had aspired. The diplomatic campaign operated on several fronts, and the Turks had to organize their own efforts to withstand those of the Greeks. In the short term, the Greeks succeeded in forcing the Turkish government to proceed to some type of reparation to the victims of violence. In the long term, however, Turkish efforts ultimately succeeded (not only in Turkey but in Cyprus). In the end, Istanbul witnessed the definitive destruction of its Greek community and the effective elimination of the Orthodox Church as a viable Greek institution in Turkey. Compensation was reduced to levels far below what they should have been, the Greek government was forced to accept this, and much Greek property was alienated over the years. Politically, the pogrom's consequences and aftermath were to render void the terms of the Lausanne treaty insofar as its application to the Greek community of Istanbul was concerned, whereas Turkey successfully managed to retain its effective guardianship over the Turkish Muslim community in Greek Thrace. It should also be noted that the Greek effort in 1955 to define the maritime borders between the Greek islands and the Anatolian coast was rejected by the Turkish government that very year. Today, it has still not been settled, and the Turkish air force periodically and systematically continues to violate Greek airspace, as it has for decades.[8]

[8] Vryonis, "American Foreign Policy in the Ongoing Greco-Turkish Crisis as a Contributing

FEAR AND DISHARMONY IN THE GREEK COMMUNITY

In the aftermath of the pogrom, the Greek consulate-general in Istanbul operated in a much more socially turbulent and politically acid atmosphere. The Greek consul-general himself ultimately became responsible for what turned into a veritable flood of duties that threatened to drown him in terms of the political, economic, and social needs that overwhelmed the local Greeks. Agis Kapsambelês had to deal with the *vali* of Istanbul, General Aknoz's martial-law command, the security police, the city's *defterdar*, the aid committee, Istanbul's chamber of commerce, and many other organizations. His office also had to gather data on everything related to the destruction and pending reparations. The claims of Greek citizens had to be prepared through his office and then forwarded to the Turkish foreign ministry, after which the consul had to follow each one of over 1,070 cases. In addition, he also had to make policy suggestions to the Greek foreign ministry. Accordingly, his relations with the Greek community of Istanbul were complex and a major area of responsibility. Although the Turkish government chose to ignore it, the consul also had certain responsibilities toward the Greek minority as well, at least according to the Lausanne treaty. Finally, his relations with the patriarchate were intense and often difficult, as Patriarch Athênagoras had his own programs and policies, and yet often needed the support of the consul.

When confronted by all these duties, obligations, and concerns—many of them new and others greatly intensified—after September 6-7, the Greek consulate of Istanbul found itself desperately understaffed. It successfully requested temporary funds, both to increase staff and to give small grants to the neediest of the indigent who no longer had homes or food. The documents and reports coming out of the consulate are sufficient in themselves for a separate study. Although Kapsambelês signed nearly all of them, it is impossible that he could have written or dictated them all, as is clear from the valuable analysis of the pogrom composed and signed by former consul Vyrôn Theodôropoulos in January 1956, who also wrote many other reports signed by Kapsambelês. Generally speaking, the Greek consulate seems to have functioned well and on a practical basis. The reports reveal clear perceptions and a broad understanding of the entire complex of new and older problems that beset the local Greeks but also Greek-Turkish relations. Judgments and recommendations are always balanced and realistic, and the consul's personal passions, especially in the more frustrating matters, reveal only a zeal for duty, not any animus toward the persons or institutions involved.

Factor to Destabilization," UCLA *Journal of International Law and Foreign Affairs*, Vol. II, Number 1, 1997, pp. 69-89.

Farther afield from Istanbul, and given the obvious importance of the US, the Greek foreign ministry and its representatives in Washington, Chicago, New York, Boston, and elsewhere in the United States paid particular attention to American legislative bodies, the State Department, and the far-flung American mass media. UN headquarters in New York was yet another political bazaar in which the ministry had to negotiate. In Europe, as well as in Africa, the Middle East, and Latin America, Greek diplomacy was called upon to disseminate specific information on the pogrom, most crucially at NATO headquarters in Paris. The events of September 6-7 brought immediate problems to the functioning of NATO, supposedly a harmonious alliance of lesser and greater powers concerned with the fate of the Western world. As mentioned earlier, the Turkish attack on Greek religious institutions had provoked outcries from the Soviet-dominated patriarchs of Russia, Romania, and Bulgaria. The protests of the WCC, of which the ecumenical patriarchate of Constantinople was a member, were more effective, however. The appeal to the council by the Greek authorities elicited a quick and rapid response, much to the annoyance of the Foreign Office, which referred to the council's representatives, ironically, as "the good bishops."

There was disharmony between secular and ecclesiastical authorities on the Greek side, too, however. After Turkey's foreign ministry announced on September 14 that foreign citizens had to prepare their claims for compensation through their diplomatic representatives, the work of the Greek consulate in Istanbul intensified, as it had to oversee almost 1,100 applications of Greek citizens that, as we have seen, had to be submitted no later than the evening of October 14. It was at this time that serious differences with the patriarch began to arise. Although the patriarch had responded to the consul's advice that he should quickly turn to the aid of those Greeks who were left hungry and often homeless, he refused to heed the Greek diplomat on certain other matters. In his report of September 11 to Athens, Kapsambelês writes of the disarray and semi-paralysis of the patriarch and hierarchs of the holy synod. Since many of the latter had been harassed or even attacked during the pogrom, while others had witnessed the frightful scenes of that night, the violence had disoriented them. The patriarch himself, according to the report, was so shocked that he was unable to respond. The Greek consul indicated in his dispatch that he was sending Athens a copy of the patriarch's telegram to the Turkish prime minister on the following day, that is, September 12, two days after the first official Greek government protest and verbal note. Kapsambelês wrote: "Substantially, this is the first official act of the Most Holy Ecumenical Patriarch. I fear that the Ecumenical Patriarch was overpowered psychologically and was unprepared for the great tribulation."[9] He was of the opinion, further, that the patriarch, because of the dire necessity, should have quickly called a meeting of the *Endemousa* Synod (the patriarchate's permanent standing synod), in which the entire matter of the pogrom could have been discussed and appropriate measures taken. It would seem that the patriarch had agreed to this earlier on, but, on the eleventh, the patriarchal *syncellus* (secretary) and the metropolitan of Philadelphia informed Kapsambelês that the meeting that he had sought with the patriarch had been postponed. In the afternoon of the eleventh, the consul learned from conversations with the metropolitans of Imvros and Philadelphia that the patriarch's stance had not been approved even by the body of hierarchs. Furthermore, Alexandros Chatzopoulos, the Greek member of the Turkish parliament, and the leaders of the Greek community had also expressed their displeasure with the weakness of the patriarch's stance. It was only on the evening of September 10 that the patriarch dared to leave the walls of the patriarchate to visit the destroyed monastery at Balıklı. Kapsambelês asked once more for a meeting with His All Holiness on the twelfth, but this, too, was refused. Although the consul constantly asked the patriarch to call a meeting of the *Endemousa* Synod, the patriarch continually refused, fearing that the discussions and decisions taken therein would be leaked to the Turkish government.[10]

Generally, one can assume that the patriarch was indeed shocked by the events, but not overly so, as he had had very good relations with *Vali* Gökay. The latter had cautioned the patriarch two to three weeks before the pogrom that he should not leave the confines of the patriarchate as awful things were about to occur. He had also assured the patriarch of his safety, however, by informing him that he had greatly enhanced and reinforced the patriarchate's security by substantially increasing the armed guard around it. One must surmise, therefore, that the patriarch was not taken by surprise, and that he was prepared for what actually occurred. He had been visited soon after the outbreaks by Ahmet Salih Korur, undersecretary to the prime minister and Menderes's messenger, who had offered him TL1 million to settle all damages to the churches. The patriarch, intelligently, refused such a pittance.

Two weeks later, the patriarch had hardened his position toward the Greek consul. We learn that the latter had held consultations over a ten-day period with the metropolitans of Chalcedon, the Princes Islands, Helioupolis, Imvros, Ainos, Proikonesos, Pergamon, and Chalkê in regard to summoning the *Endemousa* Synod. He found them all cooperative, but they had serious

---

[9] Ypourgeion Exôterikôn, Istanbul, Dispatch No. 3916, September 11, 1955.
[10] *Ibid.*

doubts as to whether the patriarch would summon the synod. Kapsambelês had also spoken with the patriarchal representative, the metropolitan of Philadelphia, who had informed him that during the meeting of the regular synod on September 22 (during which the patriarch gave an account of the program to aid the needy), the patriarch announced that as soon as this work of assistance had been finished, he would convene the *Endemousa* Synod. Kapsambelês asked the metropolitan to convey to the patriarch his careful explanation of the need for such a meeting. This time, the patriarch replied that he was exasperated with the constant meetings of the consul with his hierarchs. In his long report on the matter to Athens, Kapsambelês maintained that the Greek community remained annoyed by the patriarch's conduct and that six of the metropolitans were ready to resign in protest over it. Kapsambelês told Athens that he had advised them against such behavior, as their resignation would have a negative effect.[11]

Kapsambelês also had to assist and accommodate the two WCC missions, whose purpose was to assess the damages to Orthodox religious establishments and to the Greek community at large, assure the patriarch of their support, and seek to supplement the aid to the poor.

In addition to its role as the principal source of critical information on the pogrom—and on its political, economic, and psychological effects on the Greeks of Istanbul—the consulate was also the conduit for informing the Greek government about the pessimism and defeatism among the Greeks and on how best to combat it. Specifically, it had to combat the tendency of the Greeks to flee, to Greece and elsewhere. The reports from the consulate during the month of September are marked by, among other things, continual reference to the Greeks flooding the consulate, not only for assistance but for passports to leave Turkey:

> ...[T]here is now to be seen, only two days after the Pogrom, a predisposition [for the Greeks] to abandon the city, which threatens to take on the nature of mass flight. I am making every effort to calm our compatriots in every way, though I do not deny them passports for Greece for if I do so, it is precisely then that we shall promote this predisposition to flee. However, I advise them not to be hasty and to wait a few days at least for the further evolution of affairs....Naturally, there are cases when it would be inhuman for me to insist that certain Greeks should remain, as in the case of young female students....[12]

[11] Ypourgeion Exôterikôn, Istanbul, No.1545/9/23, September 29, 1955.
[12] Greek Embassy, Washington, No. 38596/T4 Ep., Athens, September 15, 1955; in yet another document signed by Kapsambelês, 250 Greeks were issued passports to depart

On the psychological effects of the events of September 6-7, Theodôros Geôrgiadês informed Athens on September 15 that although the material damages were undoubtedly serious, the psychological damages were equally so:

> There is a danger that the Hellenic element of Constantinople will suffer a loss of morale and thus a flow of emigration abroad will be generated. Such a flow must, at all costs, be halted. First of all, we have the obligations to ask that the Consulate-General of Constantinople raise the spirits of the Greek minority, assuring them that the danger has passed, and urging the workers and the shopowners to return to their work.
>
> Parallel to this we must take care that the damages and destruction that have taken place should come to the attention of the international public, hoping that it might produce a general revulsion in such a manner that the Turkish Government, fearful of a new outcry against them, will take measures for future security.[13]

Istanbul for Greece. In Ypourgeion Exôterikôn, General Department of the Gendarmerie to the Ministry of Foreign Affairs, No. 29/691/5ia, September 25, 1955, the following figures on departures are given.

1. Greek citizens   69
2. Greek students   61
3. Greeks-Turkish nationals   51
Total individuals   181

[13] Greek Embassy, Washington, No. 39941/T.E., September 21, 1955, Geôrgiadês Memorandum from Ankara to Athens, Dispatch No. 2805, September 15, 1955; in Ypourgeion Exôterikôn, Istanbul to Athens, Dispatch No. 1454, September 14, 1955, Kapsambelês briefly outlined (in Memorandum No. 71) measures to be taken for keeping the Greeks in Istanbul:

> For this purpose efforts of both a negative and positive nature must be made.
> A. Negative Efforts:
> a) One must restrain and fight against defeatism and flight.
> b) The denial of permits for indefinite stay in Greece of whatever citizenship-applicant, and the request that all such should return after the termination of their period of stay.
> c) Obligation of students from Constantinople in Greece to return at the end of their studies.
> B. Positive Efforts:
> a) A consideration of a method by which the Turkish government will honor its promises and assurances as to the security and compensations of the damaged citizens.
> b) Extension, by the Turkish Government, of damages to Turkish citizens.
> c) The finding of a sum of money as aid so that the work of the small crafts and house repairs can begin again, as there is no hope that they will receive compensation [from the Turkish government].
> d) Securing a sum of money for the salaries of priests and deacons.

The question of repairing the destroyed or damaged dwellings, shops, churches, schools, newspapers, offices, and other institutions was very much in the economic forefront in the days, weeks, and months that passed after the pogrom, as was the issue of the political significance of repairing the damaged property. Given the small scale of assistance by the aid committee, and the time it took to gather and vet the applications for government aid—of which, in any case, only a tiny fraction were approved—the Greek authorities soon had to face the problem of an immediate need of funds on the part of many claimants.

The problem of how, if, and when the Greeks should repair and reactivate all their businesses and institutions came to a head very quickly, indeed, within the first five or six days after the pogrom. Quarterly taxes were also due by the end of September, and schools would soon begin the new year. The Menderes government called for all workers and storeowners to work intensively to repair their shops, and it sent the minister of education to inspect the needs of minority schools with a view to providing the absolutely minimal aid that would enable them to receive and teach their students in a timely fashion. Menderes was anxious to return a city that had ground to a screeching halt to some semblance of order and normality. The presence of the international congresses in Istanbul at the time of the pogrom had, as already noted, filled the city with journalists, conferees, professors, economists, and foreign police officials from all over the world, who were critical observers of the course of events and particularly of the destruction.

That this was not a pogrom that transpired far removed from public and international attention was of some assistance to the Greeks, as they had distinguished witnesses to their suffering, to the extent of the violence, and to the passive conduct of the Turkish government, police, and armed forces. The Turkish government's predictable tardiness in assigning blame and paying satisfactory compensation now placed the Greek side, at least momentarily, in the dilemma of choosing between two rather undesirable paths of action. It was to the Greeks' political advantage to exploit Turkish sluggishness and to leave the raw wounds of destruction unattended throughout the period of assessment and reparation and thus further expose the nature of the Turkish government's crime. On the other hand, such delay would have finalized the demise of the economic base of the Greek businessmen and Greek communities scattered throughout Istanbul. This would have led not only to the final collapse of many businesses, but would have been the fatal blow to the morale of the Greeks and pushed them to mass flight from the city. The Greek government and the Greek people were not yet ready psychologically to abandon Istanbul after 2,500 years of living there. The other consideration was that even if Turkey had been willing to pay compensation, it was already evident that economic conditions, as well as a prevalent social mentality among Turkish bureaucrats (which was further compounded by a racist attitude), made it highly unlikely that there would be full and just compensation for the Greeks, no matter how long they waited. That is why many did not even bother to apply for compensation. And when they did proceed to immediate repairs, they had to pay for most of them out of their own pockets, as had been predicted and indeed later witnessed by Michael Stewart, the British *chargé* in Istanbul.

In the event, both Greece's *chargé* in Ankara and its consul-general in Istanbul stressed the singular importance to their government of the Greeks of Istanbul remaining in the city that had been their traditional home. This need was also tied to their Church—represented by the ecumenical patriarch, *primus inter pares* in the entire Orthodox Christian world—which had existed for almost two millennia, from the time Byzantium had been renamed Constantinople and then on through the city's transformation into Istanbul. While the gross error of persuading the community to stay would not be long in manifesting itself, the Greek government and, especially, its foreign ministry heeded the advice of their knowledgeable diplomatic representatives in Turkey. The Greek foreign minister thus gave the appropriate directions to the Greek missions in Ankara and Istanbul on September 14, one day before the actual receipt of one of the reports:

> We consider correct the decision to put the [Greek] schools in operation as quickly as possible, both so that the educational program not be disturbed but also because at the beginning of the school term the Turkish Government shall be forced to pay the necessary amounts for repair of the buildings. As for the churches we regard that it is purposeful that they shall not function for the present so that for a while they shall remain as visible proof of Turkish arson and so that the available funds shall be used preferentially for the schools. As for the stores we think that this should not be delayed for reasons that are both psychological and practical. However it is necessary that the Greek minority should, for a long time, avoid expansion of commercial and industrial investment in awaiting the evolution and exact, actual intentions of the Turkish Government. Further it is to be hoped that, at least for the present, this restraint on large enterprises will deflect newer manifestations of envy and provocation from the side of the Turkish public and from the side of the competing Turkish businesses.[14]

---

[14] Ypourgeion Exôterikôn, Athens to Istanbul, No. 39172/Tourk 4. Epi., September 14, 1955.

THE POGROM AND THE US

The two verbal notes, the early pronouncements of Menderes, of the semi-official Turkish radio, and of the Anatolian News Agency were the basis of the Greek foreign ministry's diplomatic strategy, which required continual and rapid accumulation of reliable data on the damages inflicted by the violence. The ministry also gathered eyewitness accounts, information from other foreign missions in Turkey, and Turkish and foreign press coverage. Once it processed these data, the ministry disseminated them quickly to the strategic points of diplomatic pressure where they could be brought to bear in explaining and supporting the Greek case. Finally, the ministry composed an extensive and clearly structured memorandum that formed the foundation of a unified document that stated the Greek case in the same manner to all embassies, consulates, and diplomatic missions. By October 11, the ministry had circulated this memorandum to all its missions so that they could integrate and unify the Greek response in their battles with the Turkish diplomatic service, but also with British, and often US, diplomacy as well. Henceforth, this basic document would be merely updated and/or supplemented so that the task of pressing the Greek case would be relatively simple. It should be added here that the Greek military had its own representatives in Istanbul, Ankara, and Izmir; in fact, the first call for an illustrated "Black Book" on the pogrom came from the Greek military.[15]

The ministry of the presidency of the government—that is, the ministry that functioned as the prime minister's executive agency—had a special section, the directorate of the press, headed by Geôrgios Rallês (who was to be a future prime minister himself). Soon after the pogrom, Rallês issued a directive to all press offices abroad to follow and clip all reports in the foreign press related to the attacks. The material was then gathered, excerpted, and arranged according to the twenty-one countries from which it originated. Issued as a compact booklet, it became an important source of foreign views on the events from September to November 1955. Consisting of sixty-two pages, it contained *précis* (often long and detailed ones), with extensive quotes, of 149 newspaper and magazine articles that contained very important information. This document, known as the *Ektakton Deltion #1* (*Special Bulletin 1*) circulated throughout all the press offices in the Greek diplomatic network. Although Rallês's office informed the foreign ministry that a second *deltion* was in development and that it would subject the Turkish press to

---

[15] Ypourgeion Proedrias Kyvernêseôs, *Ektakton Deltion #1*, November 1955; it is contained in Ypourgeion Exôterikôn, No. 33361/A, *Septemvriana 1955*, and was sent to the Greek press offices in Washington, London, Paris, Rome, Bonn, Bern, Belgrade, Istanbul, Cairo, Ottawa, Buenos Aires, and Pretoria, as well as to the press service in Berlin, Brussels, and Jerusalem.

the same scrutiny, it has not been possible to ascertain whether it was ever completed and circulated, although there is indirect evidence in a number of reports that refer to the Turkish press, and even quote or translate from this bulletin, that it was completed in some form.[16]

Greek policymakers understood *ab initio* the strategic role that their diplomatic representatives had to play in the United States as Greece had been a primary political, military, and economic "beneficiary" of American power and policy between 1946 and 1955. They also realized that the British government was committed to a hard line on Cyprus and that it would fight any Greek attempt to set the agenda at the United Nations on the Cyprus issue. This was clear, among other things, from the Anglo-Turkish alignment in opposition to Greece. Although Greek diplomats were active in Britain, the political climate was such that no support could be expected from this quarter in the matter of the pogrom. In the beginning, the British government itself was hesitant to protest formally and submit damage claims for the destruction of the property of British citizens in Turkey. Although Dulles generally supported the British over Cyprus, the US had its own interests, so that this stance allowed some room for Greek diplomatic efforts in Washington, at least initially. After all, British power and influence had suffered a general decline after the Second World War, particularly in Greece and Turkey, where the US presence replaced that of the British. US funds soon became the basis for economic planning in both Greece and Turkey, and US military experts, along with those funds, rebuilt the military forces of the two countries, with effects on the developing police and intelligence agencies in both of them.[17]

Against such a background, Greek policymakers could not ignore the obvious need for US support. What they did not understand initially, however, was that the American public and nation had just undergone, and had hardly begun to recover from, the McCarthy era, during which the junior senator from Wisconsin had branded many politicians, civil servants, educators, and journalists as communists and traitors, and had transformed American public opinion with his anticommunism. The media were particularly affected by the country's mood. Although the fact that major parts of the globe had been converted into political and potential military theaters of Soviet-US conflict was a reality aside and apart from the domestic political landscape, the US

---

[16] Ypourgeion Exôterikôn, No. 43871, and W4266, sent to Washington *et al*, October 17, 1955.

[17] TNA:PRO, No. RK1201/1, London, January 18, 1955, was a ninety-seven-page analysis of the Turkish armed forces. It described the dominant role played in their training by US officers and technical experts as well as the enormous US financial aid to develop these forces.

government, the State Department, and American public opinion chose to see all these grim political realities against the background and hateful atmosphere of McCarthyism.

This new political reality was to have a long-term effect on America's relations with both Greece and Turkey. Greece had only recently emerged from the devastation of the Second World War and its own civil war. Indeed, because the Greek Civil War had demonstrated the strength of the indigenous communist party, the country was labeled as "unstable." Turkey was seen in a different and much more favorable light: it was considered politically "stable," a young country rapidly becoming a democracy, and a nation of warriors faithful to the goals of the West. Although much of this was and is debatable, Turkey's strategic location on the borders of the Soviet Union and of the oil-rich Middle East was never debatable. In their totality, these perceptions were, and remain, institutionalized in the departments of state and defense, in American business, in the White House, and in the American media and public opinion. Unfortunately, in most, albeit not all, of the aforementioned domains of American life, substantial knowledge of the respective geographies, histories, and politics of Greece and Turkey—to say nothing of the rest of the world—was, simply, lacking.

While the Greek government and Greek public opinion were better informed on much of this world, they knew considerably less about the US government, the American public, and the American mass media, or about the latter's crucial role in (mis)shaping American public opinion. As was to become evident in crucial matters, the Turkish government understood the United States—and so molded its relations with it—in a much more realistic, and therefore effective, fashion. The Greek lack of understanding of the nature of American society and politics was to produce a very rude awakening when Greeks encountered both during the controversies over Cyprus and compensation for the pogrom.

The initial disappointment of the Greek government's representative in Washington, Phaidôn Anninos-Kavallieratos, was expressed in his telegram to Athens of September 9. He was reacting to what he considered to be an indifferent response to the violence of September 6-7 on the radio broadcast of station RCS on the evening of September 8, which was attributed to the State Department: "The State Department expressed its relief at the manner by which the Turkish Government had handled the anti-Greek demonstrations. The State Department advised Greece and Turkey to deal cautiously with the Cyprus issue."[18] Kavallieratos lodged an official complaint with the

---

[18] Ypourgeion Exôterikôn, unnumbered, Washington to Athens, September 9, 1955.

appropriate State Department officer, Jeffrey C. Kitchen, objecting primarily to the fact that, after this horrendous assault on the persons and property of the Greeks of Istanbul, the only statement the State Department had made to the American public was that the department had been pleased at how the Turkish government had "handled" what in effect had been a pogrom of great magnitude. Kitchen denied that this had been a formal statement by the department and promised to investigate the matter. (If he did so, there is no evidence of it in subsequent documentation to which I had access.)

In response the next day to a telegram from the Greek foreign minister on September 12, Geôrgios V. Melas, the Greek ambassador in Washington, stated that he had just returned from New York, where he had been in contact with the *New York Times*. He added that all efforts to contact American officials were being made, that the Greek American community was active concerning the pogrom, and that letters were being sent to the press and interviews conducted: "However, the policy of the press, undoubtedly inspired by governmental circles, aims at suppressing news on the events that occurred so that the Turkish factor not be offended. For they [the us government] attribute special significance to it [Turkey] and it is not desirable that the situation be further exacerbated."[19] Three days later, the Greek ambassador to the United Nations, Chrêstos Palamas, echoed those remarks:

> For some days I have expressed, to my journalist friends of the American press here at the United Nations, my surprise and also the pain of Greek public opinion at the fact that the American press felt no necessity to condemn the Turkish medieval barbarities. From their vague answers and inability to answer I had the impression that the policy of the United States Government was not a stranger to the [journalists'] position. Today I confirmed, from an absolutely reliable source, that the State Department has proposed to the editors of the major American newspapers (the New York Times, the Herald Tribune and others) that they should strive to avoid commentaries on the events in Turkey or, as he told me, "to play down the whole affair."[20]

On September 18, following Dulles's memorandum to Greece and Turkey, the Greek ambassador lodged a strong protest concerning it.[21] On

---

[19] Greek Embassy, Washington, No. 3755/8/29, September 13, 1955.
[20] Greek Embassy, Washington, Dispatch No. 2104, September 16, 1955. This statement is basically correct, but the *New York Times* was occasionally criticized by the State Department for publishing "confidential reports" and information; C. L. Sulzberger successfully refuted this charge.
[21] Greek Embassy, Washington, No. 3841/B/29, September 18, 1955.

the same day, the *Washington Post* and *Herald Tribune* announced that the Turkish government had hired the former governor of New York, and 1948 Republican presidential candidate, Thomas Dewey as its legal adviser, with a $150,000 annual retainer.[22]

A comparable abstention by the Chicago press from detailed reporting of and commentary on the events of September 6-7 soon became obvious. As a result, a group of Greek Americans and the local Greek bishop (Ezekiel) called on the offices of the local press, where they protested what they considered to be the State Department's "silence" on the destruction of the many Greek churches in Istanbul: "Of these newspapers only the Chicago American published [short] articles herein attached....The representatives of the other newspapers, the Chicago Tribune, the Sun Times and the Daily News informed the committee that they would request information from the State Department."[23] This consular report reflects, once more, both the uninformed nature of the American press and its close relations to the State Department in matters of foreign policy. The same document reported that Archbishop Michaêl, head of the Greek Orthodox Church in North and South America, had formally sanctioned an organized effort to combat the general indifference of the American media to the violence and destruction to which Orthodox churches and parishes had been subjected on the night of September 6-7. In this campaign to inform public opinion in the Chicago area, some 22,000 telegram forms were prepared. Of these, 7,500 were handed out by the presidents of the eleven Greek parishes in the area to their parishioners. They were sent, in succession, to President Eisenhower, Dulles, the chairmen of the relevant congressional committees, and the parishioners' representatives in the House and Senate. Another 7,500 telegram forms were sent to the Greek Orthodox parishes and organizations in Detroit and Cleveland, while the remaining forms went to church communities in the broader region.[24]

The mindset of American public opinion and of the State Department against which Greece struggled during this time became, if anything, more firmly institutionalized throughout the last half of the twentieth century. Greece was to become newsworthy only when and if it occasionally became

---

[22] Ypourgeion Exôterikôn, No. 1348/127/6, September 23, 1955.

[23] Ypourgeion Exôterikôn, No. 3582/D/2, Chicago to Washington, October 5, 1955.

[24] Ypourgeion Exôterikôn, No. 3581/D/2, October 5, 1955; Ypourgeion Exôterikôn, No. 3671/F/2, Chicago to Washington, October 12, 1955: "Greek organizations of Chicago are becoming increasingly active....Bishop Ezekiel...visited Mayor Daley and the Mayor proclaimed October 23, a day of prayer 'of the victims of Turkish rabble rousing.'" The *Chicago Daily News* published the public proclamation.

a "problem"—as with Cyprus, for example. In truth, the dispute among Greece, Turkey, Great Britain, and the United States over the pogrom, and the assessment and payment of damages, was dominated and permeated by the sharpening Cyprus conflict. Greece attempted to separate these two issues and to treat each in isolation, but Turkey insisted from the outset in treating the pogrom and its aftermath as a mere and insignificant aftermath of the Cyprus issue. The British government concentrated primarily on the future of Cyprus and openly devalued the pogrom as a largely irrelevant matter, subordinating it to Britain's immediate imperial interests. Dulles and the State Department were somewhat more amenable to positions that were far less set than they were to become after Dulles's departure. US interests were less regional than global, and concerned with NATO, the Balkan Pact (a US-sponsored "treaty of friendship and cooperation" among Greece, Turkey, and Yugoslavia signed in 1953), and the Cold War. The dichotomy in American policy on the issues of compensations and Cyprus manifested itself early. On October 19, Karamanlês, newly installed as prime minister (his government had won its vote of confidence on October 12), received the US ambassador and explained to him the Greek government's *sine qua non* for reestablishing good relations with Turkey. First was a special ceremony that would swiftly render moral satisfaction to the Greek officers serving in NATO's Izmir command. Second was the rapid and just realization of formal Turkish promises to restore the physical infrastructure of Istanbul's Greek community (Karamanlês added that the US government would have to display an active interest in this matter). Third was the demand that the Greek churches be rebuilt quickly to bolster Greek morale. Finally, Karamanlês asked that the Turkish ambassador in Athens, who had played an active role in the pogrom's aftermath, be replaced. The involvement of the ambassador's subordinate consuls in Thessalonikê in the incident of the explosive device had not endeared him to Greek authorities. The only one of the earlier Greek demands that did not appear in Karamanlês's list was the stipulation that those responsible for the pogrom be identified and brought to justice. Although Karamanlês did not present this important demand to the US envoy, however, it was never abandoned by the Greek government.[25]

The responses of the US government and media to the pogrom shocked Greek public opinion. They also raised the issue, for the first but not last time, of US respect for the security and honor of a NATO ally. Did the American

[25] Ypourgeion Exôterikôn, No. 45208/T.4 Ep., October 19, 1955. US help in pressing the Turkish government on compensations was requested by the Greek foreign minister during the visit of William Oliver Baxter, head of the Greece-Turkey-Iran Desk in the State Department, Ypourgeion Exôterikôn, Memorandum of November 30, 1955.

government completely ignore the Greek request to press Turkey to fulfill its promises of just compensation? Actually, the archival evidence indicates that US foreign policy was not rigidly "anti-Greek" in all its manifestations. The following is taken from a confidential report from the Foreign Office sent on September 10, 1955, to its missions in Athens, Ankara, and Istanbul:

> ...2. The U.S. Government welcomed the offer of compensation for riot damage made by the Turkish Government but at the same time they wished the Turkish Government to know that the United States Government were shocked over these events and especially over the apparent lack of police intervention in riots which appear to have been the result of co-ordinated planning. They were also concerned over the effect that these developments would have on NATO and the Balkan Alliance....
>
> 3. The Ambassador was then instructed to say in regard to Cyprus that the United States Government considered that the interests of the three Governments primarily concerned—as indeed of the free world at large—would be best served if they maintained flexible positions and showed willingness to consider all proposals put forward in good faith. In the United States view the British proposals were in accordance with the principles of the United Nations Charter. The proposed Tripartite Committee to discuss possible forms of self-government for Cyprus seemed to them a reasonable and fruitful suggestion....
>
> 4....The United States Government could not but feel that the developments of the last few days would help the Greeks command widespread sympathy at the United Nations. World opinion was focussed [*sic*] on Turkey and early moderate and responsible action by the Turkish Government would seem timely.
>
> 5. The United States Embassy have also reported that the United States Ambassador in Greece has been instructed to convey to the Greek Government the gratification of the United States Government both on the "exemplary calmness" of the Greek people following the recent riots in Turkey and on the steps taken by the Greek Government to ensure the safety of Turks in Greece....[26]

The State Department's instructions to the US ambassador in Athens indicate a much wider political vista than that of the British. It recommends openness in discussions on Cyprus and its potential self-government so as to avoid a showdown in the United Nations; it is openly critical of the violence on September 6-7; it indirectly blames the Turkish government for its failure

---

[26] TNA:PRO, No. 5828, September 10, 1955.

to stop the pogrom; and, in the end, makes a friendly gesture to the Greek government for protecting the Turks who live in Greece. These instructions were openly offensive to Turkey on practically all grounds. Ambassador Warren found that Menderes was tied up on September 11 with last-minute preparations for the extraordinary parliamentary session the next day, so he met with Zorlu and delivered to him, orally, the first paragraph of the State Department's message, and handed him the written text of an *aide-mémoire* that also included the second paragraph. Whereas Zorlu reserved official reply until he had more time to examine the document more closely, he took the opportunity to express his opinion to the ambassador (the text retains its telegraphic form):

> Zorlu's reaction, after reading, was strong and unfavorable. Turkey could not, he said, be asked always to make sacrifices. However deplorable the Istanbul and Izmir incidents, Turkey had already been prepared to [suffer], and this should not and could not be used as a lever to force the Turks to make substantial concessions contrary to their interests [and] of stability in [the] Eastern Mediterranean. The Prime Minister and Birgi and he himself repeatedly told the Ambassador and [Foy] Kohler [that the] United States should avoid interfering in the Cyprus question and complicating an issue which is not our affair and which we [United States] apparently do not understand. United States pressure on [the] British has been responsible in considerable measure in obliging British to bring the three parties face to face with the undesirable results we now witness.

Zorlu's retort to the *aide-mémoire*, Warren, and the United States was clearly aggressive and somewhat irascible, alleging that because of its interference, the US had been responsible for the disintegration of Greek-Turkish relations. He concluded with a warning: "Here too, much depended on United States actions, and again he [Zorlu] hoped we would not interfere in a way disruptive of [the] status quo—upon which Greek-Turkish relations [are] founded."[27] The British reply to the State Department's message to

---

[27] National Archives, Ankara to Washington, Dispatch No. 381, September 12, 1955. By September 15, the situation in Athens was so desperate that Ray Thurston sent Senator Homer Capehart's personal message to Dulles. The senator informed Dulles that he had not been able to send this telegram to him because of the Turkish censorship:

> Strongly urge that both you and the President make statement for international press, as well as United States, showing United States sympathy and friendship for Greek peoples everywhere as result Ist.-T. [Istanbul-Turkish] riots which from first-hand observations and knowledge were absolutely unwarranted, unjustified,

Turkey had been far more analytical and rational than that of the agitated Zorlu, but it, too, had been characterized by half-suppressed alarm and anxiety. The Foreign Office had expressed its satisfaction that the United States was supporting the British proposals regarding Cyprus, but it had done so with urgent reservations. Before proceeding to an examination of these reservations, however, we need to glance momentarily at Zorlu's heated reference to Foy Kohler, the counselor posted to the us embassy in Ankara.

Zorlu told Warren that he had repeatedly "warned" Kohler against interfering in Turkish affairs. It is relevant to a discussion of us behavior toward Greek demands for swift and just compensation of the pogrom's victims that Kohler continued to "interfere" in this matter; indeed, he was quite persistent long after Zorlu vigorously expressed his displeasure in the matter. Three weeks later, on October 7, the American counselor sent a memorandum of his conversation with Zorlu's close colleague, Nuri Birgi; it was entitled, "Religious Desecrations during the Istanbul and Izmir riots." Kohler therein describes his earlier discussions with Birgi's predecessor as secretary-general of the Turkish foreign ministry, Melih Esenbel, on September 24.[28] Birgi inaugurated his side of the discussion with the customary Turkish protocol of repeating the regrets over the recent violence, and he finished his introduction by saying that the Turkish government was still studying the matter and that he much appreciated the concern of the Americans:

> He [Birgi] felt that this was a somewhat delicate problem which could not be handled too heavy-handedly or too obviously…but [he] was thinking along the lines of…an appropriate counter-propaganda campaign.

> barbarous, with millions of dollars worth physical damage and unpardonable scene [*sic*] desolated many churches, cemeteries, and unbelievable acts which I do not believe we, the world leaders, can permit to go unchallenged.
> I would not worry about Turkish reaction, but say something to hold Greece's friendship. From talks with many Greek government officials and others here [Athens], I observed that they cannot possibly understand no statement from any high us official and lack [of] initiative on the part of the us press on Istanbul riots while we have heretofore made so much to do, as they put it, about one priest being put in jail."

The latter was a reference to the Hungarian archbishop, Joseph Cardinal Mindszenty. National Archives, Dispatch No. 674, September 15, 1955.

[28] Ambassador Warren had sent a telegram to the State Department referring to the talks with Esenbel and giving the contents of the latter's remarks, which were general and vague, as were those of Birgi. At the end of his telegram, Warren remarks: "While we have heard many private expressions [of] profound regret [on] this particular aspect, there have in fact been no specific references thereto as official public statements." National Archives, Dispatch No. 487, September 24, 1955.

To emphasize my presentation, I took along with me and showed Mr. Birgi the issue of Time Magazine, dated October 10 enclosing a double-page spread of horror pictures from the Istanbul riots, including two specifically on religious subjects. When Mr. Birgi remarked about the inaccuracies in this Time coverage, I told him I thought this was relatively restrained and accurate as compared with some of the treatment the Turks still had to look forward to. I said that Time was much better researched and much more carefully presented than many other publications which would be interested in dealing with the subject. Mr. Birgi agreed with this.[29]

Birgi's responses to the persistent American counselor betray a certain lack of deeper understanding. When his interlocutor stated that the Turkish government needed to pay attention to the international revulsion over religious desecrations, his answer that the government would mount a propaganda campaign to obviate this reaction pointed to a fundamental failure, both to understand Kohler and to grasp the moral basis for the horror expressed internationally. The two men met again, possibly in early November, at which time Kohler deplored the uselessness of the ongoing exchange of bitter Greek and Turkish notes and curtly "urged the Turkish Government to try and get the claims question settled."[30] In light of these three telling episodes, one can surmise that the State Department did make efforts to pressure the Turkish government to hasten the necessary compensation for the events of September 6-7.

With Cyprus, too, the State Department made certain statements, at least in the beginning of this period, that the Foreign Office anxiously considered to be potentially unfavorable to British interests in Cyprus and, by the same token, potentially favorable to the Greeks. This was to result in a frantic effort by the British government to rally Dulles to its side in the approaching showdown in the United Nations. Ray L. Thurston, *chargé* at the American embassy in Athens, had relayed a telegram to Dulles on September 15 by Senator Homer Capehart, which had urged the US government to condemn the "unbelievable acts" against the Greek community in Turkey; two days later, he sent his own letter to Dulles in which he criticized Birgi's remarks that the Greek government should be left to "collapse":

Views expressed by [the] Secretary General of the Turkish Ministry of Foreign Affairs...show complete lack of understanding [of the]

[29] National Archives, Foreign Office Dispatch No. 145, Ankara to Washington, October 24, 1955. On the effect of the three *Time* magazine articles in Turkey, National Archives, Foreign Office Dispatch No. 190, Ankara, November 10, 1955; a translation into English of the editorial of A. E. Yalman in *Vatan* that appeared on November 5, 1955, is included in this dispatch.

[30] TNA:PRO, Ankara to London, No. RG10344/116, November 22, 1955.

Greek internal political situation. As [an] indication [in] our recent telegram, [the] Rally Government [the party in power in Greece at the time was called the "Greek Rally"] is trying desperately to maintain [a] moderate position and any change would be in the direction of more emotional and intransigent Greek line and [would worsen] the Greco-Turkish relation....We are concerned that it is clearly in the United States interest to support [the] present government, at least for the time being, and to help maintain its moderate stand.[31]

THE POGROM AND NATO

Of great concern to Dulles and the US were the consequences of the pogrom's political aftermath for NATO and the Balkan Pact. NATO had planned joint military exercises on its southeast wing in which both Greek and Turkish military units were to participate and in which Greek waters, airspace, and airports were to be used. But beyond these practical matters, Dulles was concerned with the first major rift in the system of alliances that the US and western Europe had created to fight the Cold War. In addition, this breach in Greek-Turkish relations had shown, in a flagrant manner, that regional interests and disagreements were sufficient to weaken NATO at a crucial time.

Early on the morning of September 7, Kanellopoulos revealed to the Turkish ambassador in Athens that he had asked NATO's secretary-general to call a special meeting of the alliance's council of deputies; Kanellopoulos had also ordered the families of the Greek officers posted to the NATO command in Izmir to return to Greece by special airplane.[32] On the ninth of the month, Kanellopoulos cabled US general Alfred B. Gruenther, Supreme Allied Commander Europe, that Greece would not be participating in that month's joint military exercises and he then went on to announce the decision to the Greek parliament. Kanellopoulos justified the swiftness of the measure, as he had not first informed NATO, on the grounds of pressing internal political necessity: "The attacks on the Greek officers and their families, and the pillaging of their dwellings in Smyrna bear witness, completely, to the guilt of the police and military authorities in that city. For, they could have intervened and halted this...."[33] He went on to explain that the gross violation of national dignity necessitated a swift reaction, as, otherwise, the fragile government would have fallen victim to the incensed public opinion

[31] National Archives, Foreign Office Dispatch No. 706, Athens, September 17, 1955.

[32] Greek Embassy, Washington, Dispatch No. 37965, September 9, 1952.

[33] Greek Embassy, Washington, Dispatch No. 3797/B/29, September 15, 1955, contains a copy of the Kanellopoulos telegram to General Gruenther.

of the entire Greek nation. Kanellopoulos appealed to General Gruenther, for whom he expressed great respect, to try and understand the Greek predicament and either to call off the military exercises or else hold them without Greek participation.[34]

On September 8, NATO's secretary-general, Lord Ismay, called a special meeting of the NATO council to discuss the pogrom. Ismay set the general theme around which the meeting carried out its discussions, commenting that this was "the greatest blow which [had] been inflicted so far on the prestige and ideals of NATO." His decision to call the meeting was in part based on the specific information of an attack on the Greek officers and Greek consul in Izmir passed on to him through General Gruenther from US admiral William Morrow Fechteler, commander-in-chief of NATO forces in southern Europe. Turkey's representative to NATO at the time, Mehmet Ali Tiney, essentially repeated the line of his government that it (the government) was surprised by the events of September 6-7, for which the communists were responsible, and that Turkish public opinion had become agitated over the Cyprus issue, "for which Turkey must reject all responsibility." Geôrgios Exêntarês, the Greek representative to NATO, countered that he could not, unfortunately, accept his Turkish colleague's version of events. He pointed to the weakness of the Turkish government's effort to shift the blame onto the communists and stated that the circumstances of the disorders pointed to the involvement of the government itself, seeing that Turkish soldiers had participated in the rioting.

Ismay then suggested that a gesture was needed to show the world that NATO was united. The American representative, however, Edwin M. Martin, thought that Ismay was exaggerating the ill effects of events on the Atlantic alliance, while the British representative, Cheetham, considered it "undesirable" for NATO to investigate the pogrom.[35] Consequently, this first meeting of the NATO council failed and Ismay called a second meeting for September 14. This subsequent gathering was not dissimilar to the first. Tiney brought a message from the Turkish government guaranteeing the security of the Greek participants to the planned exercises,[36] while Exêntarês replied that Greek public opinion would not allow participation. Moreover, he added, this abstention would allow time for Greek public opinion to let off steam, which was the best and only way for Greece to remain faithful to NATO.

[34] TNA:PRO, Paris, Dispatch No. 186, No. RG10344/17, September 10, 1955.

[35] TNA:PRO, Paris, Dispatch No. 182, September 8, 1955; for the full report of the permanent Greek representative to NATO, Exêntarês, Greek Embassy, Washington, Dispatch No. 3885, September 20, 1955.

[36] For all of the above, see Cheetham's report, TNA:PRO, Paris to London, Dispatch No. 589, September 14, 1955.

The French, Belgians, and Norwegians urged the Greeks "to let bygones be bygones" and the US ambassador, George W. Perkins, asserted that the Greek government had acted without thinking and without giving the Turkish side the opportunity for friendlier acts. Then, having rather prematurely concluded that, "The Turkish Government had now, in fact, done everything that could be expected of it," he asked, "Would not the Greeks reconsider their haste?"[37]

The allies' comments in this second meeting, as in the first one, were consistent and uniform: the disturbances of September 6-7 were not of major importance. Furthermore, the principal agent in these disturbances, the Turkish government, was rewarded with the council's statement that the government had done everything that one could have possibly expected from it. Exêntarês nevertheless insisted that Greek public opinion would not allow his government to participate. Ismay finally accepted Greece's resolution and asked if it could then participate in the following month's exercises. Exêntarês replied that this would depend entirely on the conduct of the Turkish government.

The mounting pressure on the Greeks, especially from the Americans, to return to NATO's military exercises could not have escaped Exêntarês's attention. In fact, this was noticed by Melas, the Greek ambassador in Washington, who communicated the matter to Athens on September 16, in response to two cables from Stefanopoulos sent to him on the previous day. In the first cable, Stefanopoulos had requested that Exêntarês inform the US representative to NATO that unfortunately the Greek government could not rescind its decision to refrain from participating in the alliance's exercises, but that this was for the good of NATO lest some untoward incident occur between the Greek and Turkish militaries. Stefanopoulos went on to say that, because of the Turkish stance and so long as it existed, Greece would have to put off participating in NATO exercises even beyond September, but that positive suggestions from NATO to the Turkish side regarding the situation would undoubtedly help.[38]

The second telegram had been addressed to the embassy in Washington itself and began by presenting Exêntarês's conclusions of the NATO meeting on September 14:

> Mr. Exêntarês finally drew the following conclusions:
> The spirit which generally prevailed in the Council was one of exerting pressure on the Greek Government to participate in the exercises. At the end Ismay proposed the compromise solution by

---

[37] *Ibid.*
[38] Greek Embassy, Dispatch No. 3789, September 15, 1955.

which we absent [ourselves] from the exercises of September but
participate in those of October.

I [Exêntarês] was struck by the fact that the Turkish crudeness
was considered as a very minor matter and the Turkish side was
rewarded by the Americans. There prevails a spirit of covering up
the disturbances with superficial solutions.

At the bottom of this document, Stefanopoulos says to Melas: "I ask that you
inform me of your understanding of this matter."[39]

Melas sent his reply to these documents to the minister on September
16. He had already informed Stefanopoulos on the fifteenth, in reply to the
first document, that the American pressure on himself and Kavallieratos for
Greek participation in NATO's exercises had begun to weigh heavily on both
of them. "…[A]side from the danger of diplomatic isolation, our abstention
from the exercises exasperates especially those here [American officials], and
should this abstention continue indefinitely it would worsen our position.
The Americans are especially sensitive on this issue…but I think that our
return to the exercises must be accelerated."[40] Melas added that it should be
suggested to the Greek press that any talk of political neutrality was a danger
to be avoided.[41]

Although the Greek representatives in Paris and Washington were
"receptive" to US and NATO pressure, and were particularly moved by the
threat of diplomatic isolation, the Greek government was so unstable,
especially following the death of Papagos and the events of September 6-7,
that it could not afford to back down from its stand. It therefore informed
NATO that until Turkey lived up to its promises on compensation, Greek
military forces would not participate in the exercises to be held in October.

By September 20, Admiral Fechteler had spoken with Kanellopoulos
and with the Greek chief of staff, General Kônstantinos Dovas, at which
time Kanellopoulos told the admiral that, in regard to the "insults to Greek
national honor during the September 6, Izmir events," the Greeks demanded
satisfaction on the violation of the Greek flag and on the attack on Greece's
NATO officers and their families, and that these demands were separate from
the demand for just compensation for the far greater damages in Istanbul.[42]
Accordingly, while the Turkish "amends" for the Izmir events and Turkish
reparations for the much greater destruction wreaked on the Greeks of
Istanbul were part of the same, larger issue for the Greek government, they

[39] Greek Embassy, Dispatch No. 3806, September 16, 1955.
[40] Ibid.
[41] Ibid.
[42] National Archives, Dispatch No. 764, September 21, 1955.

were treated differently and separately. On September 28, the foreign ministry in Athens sent a copy of Kanellopoulos's undated memorandum to Fechteler to the Greek embassy in Washington. In it, the Greek minister expressed his regret for the decision not to participate in the exercises, and offered complete use of Greek airspace and airports, save for the Turkish contingents.[43]

Fechteler reported to the US ambassador to Athens, Cavendish W. Cannon, that, after these conversations, his review of the available information showed that the Turks felt that they had made a sufficient effort to apologize to the Greeks and so the latter's demands were, according to the Turks, something new. Nonetheless, Fechteler added, he would bring the matter up with Menderes and "suggest [that] Turks take initiative in arranging [an] appropriate ceremonial expression [of] regret along lines demanded by [the] Greeks." According to the admiral, the Turks insisted that this last apology lead "to immediate resumption of Greek participation in NATO [and Balkan Pact] exercises." Indeed, when Fechteler put the matter before Menderes, the latter agreed to such a ceremony, asking what the Greek government wanted exactly.[44] Consequently, General Dovas outlined a flag ceremony that would satisfy five requests[45] and which seems to have been successfully realized without incident on October 24.[46] After Turkey's communications minister, representing his country (it was standard practice for the communications ministry to be responsible for ceremonial functions), addressed the matter of proper apology and friendship, the Greek ambassador also spoke briefly:

> Thank you for your friendly welcome. The honor paid to the Greek flag and the sincere expression of regret by the Turkish Government for the sorrowful events of September 6 constitute a formal manifestation of the Turkish Government's desire to restore the injured honor of the Greek nation. Today's official ceremony, which is duly appreciated by the Greek Government, is a fortunate beginning for smoothing the relations between the two nations which have been seriously shaken after the tragic events of September 6. The Greek Government feels that the same

[43] Greek Embassy, Washington, Dispatch No. 2706, September 28, 1955.

[44] National Archives, Foreign Office Dispatch No. 497, Athens, September 26-27, 1955.

[45] National Archives, Foreign Office Dispatch Nos. 698 and 1047, Ankara, October 22, 1955. These five requests included: inviting all Greek officers in Izmir; the presence of the two Turkish generals serving in the NATO command at Izmir, with a group of their officers; the presence of Generals Read and Richard A. Grussendorf (commander, Sixth Allied Tactical Air Force), and some of their officers; the presence of Izmir's *vali*, district commandant, and mayor; and Greek and Turkish military units and a Turkish band.

[46] National Archives, Foreign Office Dispatch No. 708, Ankara, October 24, 1955, and Dispatch No. 705, October 24, 1955.

spirit of understanding will prevail with regard to our request for a
quick and complete material restoration of damages suffered.[47]

The next day, the Greek ambassador returned to Ankara, his spirits raised
by hopes that this good beginning might continue into the next phase of
the troubled relations, which concerned the compensations. His return was
also a partial relief for the Turkish foreign ministry, which had feared that
his absence might be followed by a rupture of diplomatic relations. In fact,
the ambassador was pleased and recommended to his government that the
families of the Greek officers in Izmir return to the city. The US ambassador
informed Washington that his Greek colleague had requested an audience
with Menderes to express his government's thanks for the Izmir ceremony
and then "to request expeditious settlement [of] claims for material damages."
More significant, Warren was told by the Greek envoy that, "Claims [are] now
(repeat now) scaled down from early exaggerated [sic] estimates [ranging to 3
billion liras] to 'reasonable' figures of 30 million liras for churches, 30 million
liras losses [for] Greek subjects and 79 million for Greek-origin Turks."[48] It
should be repeated here that the policy of scaling down claims had more to
do with Turkey's general economic incapacity and Greece's fear of prolonged
compensation negotiations than with exaggerations, although there were
elements of the latter as well.

On November 9, the US ambassador in Athens reported to Dulles on the
instructions that the Greek foreign ministry had given to its ambassador in
Ankara as to what was to be presented to the Turkish government concerning
the rapid settlement of claims, which was to be based on an exchange of
binding agreements. Further, on the basis of the treaty of Lausanne, the
Greek ambassador was to take an active role in furthering the matter of
the damages suffered by the ethnic Greek minority (that is, Turkish citizens
of ethnic Greek origin). Finally, he instructed the ambassador to settle all
maritime and fishing disputes.

After the Greek foreign minister had discussed these measures with
Ambassador Cannon, their discussion moved on to NATO:

> In [the] ensuing discussion it became clear that Greeks consider
> cooperation with NATO [as] still dependent on [the] progress
> on claims settlement....I restated NATO expectations after [the]
> Izmir flag ceremony and urged earnest reconsideration [of the]
> present Greek attitude mentioning as [an] example a certain
> denial of Greek airfields to Turkish planes on NATO mission even

[47] *Ibid.*
[48] National Archives, Ankara, Dispatch No. 724, October 27, 1955.

for emergency landings. He said they wanted to move forward by degrees and gave [the] substance [of the] instructions to Exindaris at Paris to explain [the] Greek position to Ismay. I said this didn't sound good enough for Admiral Fechteler's purpose and suggested [that] he ask [the] Prime Minister to authorize instructions for speedier resumption [of] NATO activities.[49]

Cannon's observations, however, seem to be contradicted by what we know of the Greek foreign minister's discussions in Paris during the NATO ministers' meeting. He met with both Dulles and Perkins, the US ambassador to NATO, as well as with Macmillan and French foreign minister Antoine Pinay. The meeting with Perkins concerned the Greek request for a loan, to which Perkins was receptive; in fact, he complimented the Greek government for having finally righted the Greek economy. The meeting with Dulles (which occurred just before the flag ceremony in Izmir) centered on Greek-Turkish relations. The new Greek foreign minister, Spyros Theotokês (who had replaced Stefanopoulos after Karamanlês became prime minister on October 6), reiterated his government's position regarding the prompt and just payment of damage claims, which, he said, was a difficult and painful situation that had to proceed slowly as the only basis on which bilateral relations could be restored. Dulles seemed to agree and informed the Greek minister that it was highly unlikely that Turkey would receive the large loan it had asked for, at least in the immediate future. As for the Cyprus issue, Dulles said he would be glad to try and promote understanding but that he could make no definite promises. In the event, the minister's conversations with Macmillan on the subject were frank but friendly.[50]

Late in December, Melas sent a report to Athens on his most recent conversation with Assistant Secretary of State for Near Eastern Affairs George V. Allen about the compensation issue. Melas had indicated to him that they were dragging along very slowly, whereupon Allen abruptly "drew my attention to our absence from the meeting of the [NATO] Ministers and to the weakening of the Balkan Alliance [Pact]." Melas then continued:

> He [Allen] added that the Congress would soon be called upon to decide on foreign aid which the President will propose. At this time the Congress will certainly take into account the contribution of each [country]. His declaration contained a clear warning on

---

[49] National Archives, Foreign Office Dispatch No. 1214, Athens, November 9, 1955.
[50] For this interesting memorandum by Theotokês, Ypourgeion Exôterikôn, Athens, to Karamanlês, No. 47004/I. T., October 29, 1955; Greek Embassy, Paris, October 24, 1955, to Greek Embassy, Washington, No. 4359; Ypourgeion Exôterikôn, Paris, to Karamanlês, NATO, Dispatch No. 229.

the necessity for us to improve our relations with Turkey. I replied to him, is it not paradoxical that we who create allies should now be condemned for the consequences of Turkish aggressive actions? The Assistant Secretary also expressed the malaise of the State Department on the indictment of the Turkish consuls of Thessalonikê lest this condemnation result in a breach of relations between Greece and Turkey.[51]

Melas then told Theotokês that, although Greece had the right to indict the Turkish consuls, it was his opinion that the court case definitely had to be avoided and that "we" simply had to be satisfied with the return of their passports, following which, if the Turkish government did not remove them, they could be expelled as *personae non gratae*.

The pressure now came directly from the State Department, and it is obvious that US-Greek relations had entered a period in which the issues of compensation and Cyprus would weigh more heavily on Greece. At the same time, the impending court case against Turkey's consular personnel in Thessalonikê had become an issue for both British and American diplomats, as well as for the relations between the Greek foreign ministry and the State Department. Both the British and Americans feared that this prosecution would again bring Greek-Turkish relations to the breaking-point. This position once more reflected the desperation of the Turkish foreign ministry, which had every reason to fear a trial. Before turning to the diplomatic exchanges in Ankara itself, however, we need to look at one more aspect of the Greek campaign to influence opinion in the United States. This had to do with the extensive and well-established Greek American communities and the Greek Orthodox archdiocese in the United States, which was under the administrative jurisdiction of the ecumenical patriarchate.

THE POGROM AND GREEK AMERICA

We have already looked briefly at the roles of the Greek American community and its Church following the events, particularly in regard to the relative silence of the American media in Chicago. At that time, as is the case today, Greek immigrants and their American-born children were well-organized in more than 400 communities, each incorporated through state charters and with annually elected administrative boards and general assemblies of its members. The community's religious and a good deal of its social life revolved around its religious ceremonies, religious and ethnic holidays, and afternoon Greek school. The priest in a sense "belonged" to the community,

---

[51] Greek Embassy, Washington, No. 5129/B/29, December 21, 1955.

but his spiritual allegiance resided in the regional bishop and ultimately in the archdiocesan archbishop in New York. The majority of Greek Americans were well on their way to Americanization. Yet they still felt their Greek cultural roots—as well as their attachment to their villages, towns, and cities of origin—very strongly. They came to understand American politics and political patronage very early on and so were sufficiently politicized in that sense. The Greek-Turkish crisis over Cyprus and the devastation, of Greek churches in particular, in Istanbul had begun to sensitize them once again to their role in American politics.

The Greek embassy in Washington saw in this community a ready, willing, and natural ally. There were few families and villages in Greece that did not have relatives scattered throughout the United States. The embassy sought to alert the Greek American community to the events in Istanbul since the media were relatively silent, which is why most Greek Americans did not initially understand what had happened in Istanbul or why. The Cyprus issue had already begun to penetrate their communities, but, to the Greek Americans who evinced an interest (which was far from universal), it seemed that a small Turkish minority in Cyprus was blocking the will of the Greek Cypriot majority.

These Greek American communities, sprawled out and many of them distant from each other, possessed three elements of unity or identity. First, despite their different regions, there was a community of faith, and most acknowledged the spiritual leadership of the Greek Orthodox ecumenical patriarchate in Istanbul. Second, while the communities also had a strong secular identity that was essentially regional, there was one secular organization, the AHEPA (American Hellenic Educational Progressive Association), which had a national headquarters in Washington with chapters in most communities. It was tightly connected to the business and professional world as well as to the government in Washington. Finally, the third element of unity was the result of a peculiar mixture and union of Greek society and culture with semi-Americanization. Greek Americans' religious sensitivities were incensed by the facts of the pogrom, which soon became known in the various communities. There was particular outrage over the mass attack on, and burning and profanation of, so many Orthodox churches, as well as the attacks on the clergy. Secular Greek American "patriotism" was shocked by the unrestrained attacks on the Greeks, and on their homes and businesses. Accordingly, the leaders of the Greek churches, AHEPA, and the communities were ready instruments of action in the domains of the media, Congress (through their local representatives), and the White House. There was, however, one principal obstacle to this mobilization: the fact that the Greek Orthodox archdiocese of North and South America was spiritually and canonically under the administrative jurisdiction of the ecumenical patriarchate, which gave the Turkish foreign ministry a weapon in its diplomatic battles with Greece. (Turkey has utilized this fact of Greek Orthodox ecclesiology with considerable success over the decades. It has often applied the same tactic in its relations with the Armenian and Jewish communities abroad and in these communities' relations with their coreligionists in Istanbul.)

The mechanics and *modus operandi* of the Greek embassy in Washington, the Greek American communities, and the Greek foreign ministry were developed in the period between September 10 and October 3, 1955, and these would annoy the Turkish government for some time. On September 7, Kavallieratos, obviously responding to an inquiry from his ministry in Athens, replied: "The Archbishop of America, with whom I have communicated, is prepared to have the World Council of Churches protest against the religious desecration in Constantinople and Smyrna. But before he does so he desires instructions from the Patriarch and the approval of the Greek Government. I ask therefore…that if you approve [to] ask for instructions from the Patriarch for the Archbishop."[52] This indicates that the Greek government sought to inform the archbishop as well as the Greek American community of what had occurred on September 6-7, and to seek their help in disseminating this knowledge appropriately throughout the United States.

On September 8, Kanellopoulos replied to the embassy that in case the archbishop could not proceed with what had been suggested, the ambassador should do so, which was to say, to activate a response to the pogrom by Greek Americans and all Greek organizations in the United States, as "manifestations of protest are needed immediately."[53] On the same day, the embassy informed the ministry that, while the archbishop could not in fact, for obvious reasons, assume the leadership of such protests, he could inform his clergy to support this effort quietly. He was also willing to intercede with the World Council of Churches. On the other hand, the ambassador continued, having spoken with the general secretary of AHEPA, the latter undertook to use all of the organization's chapters in the United States to send letters of protest to Dulles, to local representatives in the House and Senate, and to the local press, to support the patriarch and the Orthodox Christians of Turkey, and, especially, to deplore the destruction of Istanbul's churches.[54] The ambassador had received a draft copy of the circular that AHEPA would send to its numerous

[52] Greek Embassy, Washington, No. 3687/B/29, September 7, 1955.
[53] Greek Embassy, Athens to Washington, Dispatch No. 3716, September 8, 1955.
[54] Greek Embassy, Washington to Athens, No. 3716/B/29, September 8, 1955.

chapters, and included it in his cable to Athens. Although coming from a secular organization, the AHEPA draft focused exclusively on the acts of violence and attacks on the patriarch and the Orthodox faithful, and protested "against the unprecedented acts of religious intolerance which caused centuries-old and venerated shrines of Orthodoxy to be outrageously desecrated and brutally destroyed."[55] It ended by asking the United States government to protect the Orthodox minority and ensure that such outbreaks did not recur.

The Greek foreign ministry sent its mission in Washington whatever information it had managed to gather regarding the destruction and acts of violence so that the embassy could update the archbishop, AHEPA, and the public more widely.[56] In his instructions to the ambassador on September 18, Stefanopoulos asked that, in agreement with Archbishop Michaêl, a meeting be held among the ambassador, the archbishop, Eugene Carson Blake, president of the National Council of Churches, and Bishop Merrill of the Episcopal Church in order to prepare a protest of the destruction of the churches through the National Council. Stefanopoulos told the ambassador that the patriarch was not opposed to this, as it was an ecclesiastical matter. Nevertheless, Archbishop Michaêl's participation did not need to be publicized. At the same time, Stefanopoulos indicated, the archbishop should arrange with the other churches of the WCC for prayers and services to be held on the three following Sundays on behalf of the Orthodox Christians of Istanbul, since the latter could not "carry out their religious obligations by reason of the destruction of their churches and their cemeteries...."[57] Stefanopoulos also reported in his telegram that, out of eighty Orthodox churches in Istanbul, only ten had been saved. Meanwhile, the Greek Americans of Chicago had convinced Mayor Richard Daley to designate a Sunday of prayer on behalf of Istanbul's Orthodox Christians.

Finally, on September 19, Kavallieratos reported that Archbishop Michaêl had sent an encyclical to all the Greek Orthodox communities of the United States urging them to send telegrams to the US government protesting the recent harsh persecution of Orthodox Christians in Turkey. Kavallieratos sent the foreign minister a copy of the encyclical, which read:

> Dear Communicants,
> I ask that you send, immediately, to the State Department and to your representatives in the Congress, telegrams of protest against the desecration by the Turkish mob of Churches, Monasteries,

[55] *Ibid.*
[56] Greek Embassy, Athens to Washington, No. 38683, September 10, 1955.
[57] Greek Embassy, Athens to Washington, No. 39812, September 18, 1955, and No. 39813, September 18, 1955; there is no further information on Bishop Merrill in these dispatches.

Schools and Cemeteries.
Please, also urge that [the other] pious Christians send as
many telegrams as possible.[58]

Michaêl also added a note that the State Department and representatives of
Congress be urged to recognize officially the Greek Orthodox Church in the
armed services.

The Greek American community's involvement in the issue of the pogrom
brought additional headaches both to the State Department and, especially,
the Turkish government, whose response was not long in coming. On
September 27, Palamas, Greece's representative to the United Nations, had
a rather sharp exchange with his colleague and Turkey's representative, Selim
Sarper. The latter informed Palamas that his government sought information
on the activities organized under the leadership of Archbishop Michaêl to
inform US official and public opinion about the anti-Greek violence in Turkey
and the need to defend the patriarchate. He asked Palamas if this was correct,
and then, according to the Greek official:

> ...he asked me if the Greek Government thinks that these efforts and
> manifestations will serve any useful end save to increase the agitation
> instead of the calming of passions. If, however, he said, Greece is
> looking forward to the dissolution of the Greek community and a
> shattering of the Patriarchate's position by the further incitement of
> nationalist tempers in Turkey, then the above manifestations could
> be justified. It is fated that Turkish public opinion shall consider the
> Greek minority [in Turkey] and the Patriarchate responsible—even
> though and in fact they are not responsible—for anti-Turkish
> efforts abroad. In politics, he said, the innocent pay for the mistakes
> of those who are really responsible.[59]

Although Palamas's reply to his colleague was brusque, he told the ministry
that it was a serious matter. Kanellopoulos then replied to both Palamas and to
the Greek ambassador in Washington that initially the government's general
line on Greek-Turkish relations was that the archbishop should not appear
to be involved in anti-Turkish mobilizations. Thus, he asked the embassy to
indicate the exact form of the archbishop's involvement. Both Kavallieratos
and Palamas responded, respectively, that the archbishop had not had a
role in any attempts to mobilize American public opinion on Cyprus.[60]

[58] Greek Embassy, Washington, No. 3875/B/29, September 21, 1955, which also contains
the text of the archbishop's encyclical.
[59] Greek Embassy, Washington, No. 2334, September 27, 1955; on Turkish threats to the
Greeks of Istanbul, see also Ypourgeion Exôterikôn, No. 4020, October 1, 1955.
[60] Greek Embassy, Athens to Washington, No. 41606, September 28, 1955.

Furthermore, the archbishop had taken action "only after having received detailed descriptions of the orgies [*sic*] in Constantinople against the Church, at which time he organized with other hierarchs, with Greek Americans and with AHEPA and GAPA [the Greek American Progressive Association, the Greek-language competitor to the English-language AHEPA at the time], a movement [in regard to the churches]."[61] As letters and telegrams began to deluge the American government, they were joined by letters from members of Congress, including Senators John Kennedy and Lyndon Johnson. The speeches of Senator Capehart and of the well-known Washington journalist Drew Pearson also drew considerable national attention to the pogrom and to the diplomatic struggle that ensued from it.[62]

Greek diplomacy in the United States was, therefore, very active and had some success in stirring the State Department to put a certain amount of pressure on Turkey regarding compensation and the error of the pogrom. But Greece failed to halt Dulles's recruitment of the Latin American countries in the crucial vote over self-determination for Cyprus. The mobilization of the Greek Americans can also be regarded a success in the struggle to inform American public opinion about September 6-7. By and large, however, Turkey's status in the halls of the State Department and NATO was, ultimately, little affected. Perhaps the most important consequence was on Menderes's government, which found itself confronted by a difficult political, diplomatic, and economic challenge. In effect, this increased the weakness of the Turkish foreign ministry, as well as of the government as a whole.

A FECKLESS ALLY

Of all the diplomatic fronts, the scene of the most intense struggle was played out in Ankara, where Turkish and Greek diplomats confronted each other in the context of Turkey's attempt to dig out from under the asphyxiating political debris of the pogrom's aftermath. The deleterious effects of the violence weighed heavily on international opinion, as both the UK and US governments believed. According to the British, the US had committed

---

[61] Greek Embassy, New York to Athens, No. 2360, October 1, 1955, and Greek Embassy, Athens to New York, No. 42147, September 29, 1955.

[62] On the addresses of Capehart and Pearson, see Ypourgeion Exôterikôn, Chicago to Athens, No. 4225-D/2.T, November 21, 1955, announcing that the senator's talk would take place on November 27 in Chicago. Previously, Capehart had also held a press conference, Ypourgeion Exôterikôn, No. 4273. Melas sent a lengthy letter on the significance of Pearson's national television broadcast at 2:30 PM, October 30, 1955, on the subject of the pogrom. The report to Athens contained the six-page text of the entire speech, Greek Embassy, Washington to Athens, Ypourgeion Exôterikôn, No. 4433, October 30, 1955.

impressive sums of money and technical manpower to their common ally: "America's continued contribution and expansion of the Turkish armed forces and Turkey's military budget, and the presence in Turkey of thousands of Americans in administering it, kept America foremost among foreign countries in Turkish minds."[63]

The US evaluation of the Turkish government's performance was increasingly negative, however. Perhaps the most penetrating analysis of Turkey's situation, and particularly of US presuppositions for its heavy financial investment, was that of the US consul-general in Istanbul, Arthur Richards. Indeed, his analysis was not only highly relevant to Turkey's situation in 1955 but was almost prophetic regarding more recent times. His three-page report to the State Department three weeks after the pogrom was entitled, "Implications of the Istanbul Disturbances of September 6, 1955," and dispensed with the many details of the pogrom and its immediate aftermath and instead focused on "certain implications of the disturbances [that] should receive [the] careful attention of those concerned with our relations with Turkey and with the capabilities of Turkey as an ally and as a partner in NATO." Richards summarized these implications broadly, logically, and with telling force.

> 1. Anti-Greek and, by extension anti-minority feeling, had been on the increase for some months before the events of September 6. Those events, though staged over the Cyprus issue and set off by the reported attack on Ataturk's birthplace, fundamentally were an anti-Christian and anti-minority outbreak of the type frequently recorded in Turkish history.
>
> (Implications)
>
> (a) We believe that social instability has been demonstrated by the disorders and has serious implications as regards the implementation of U.S. policies toward Turkey.
>
> (b) We believe that there are indications that there is a slackening of the secularization movement and the reform institutions by Ataturk which is having an adverse effect on cooperation between the people of Turkey and Western people.
>
> 2. Several incidents involving violence against the Greeks occurred in Istanbul during the week prior to September 6. Turkish Government officials knew that anti-Greek demonstrations were being planned....Furthermore there was elaborate advance planning for widespread destruction of the property of the indigenous Greek community, which plans involved many people

---

[63] TNA:PRO, Ankara, Dispatch No. 5, January 16, 1956.

and careful preparations.

(Implications)

(a) We have believed that the Turkish security police are effective. If that were true, they should have been aware of this advance planning which was known to many people (Ref. ConGen telegram No. 159).

(b) On the other hand, if the Turkish Government were aware of these plans and failed to take effective preventive actions, this would indicate that the Government was indifferent or inefficient, or both.

3. Demonstrations started at approximately 1900 hours on September 6; they got out of hand by 2000. Meanwhile police and military forces, though on hand, were perplexed and completely inefficient. After mid-night [*sic*] martial law was declared. Only after this were control measures started. Isolated incidents continued to be observed as late as 17:30 on September 7.[64]

(Implications)

(a) It appears the ineffectiveness of the security forces was based either (1) on lack of leadership, (2) on general ineptness, (3) on the fact that the Police and the Military forces were in sympathy with the attackers, or (4) on circumstances that security forces had orders not to intervene. Furthermore it is now apparent that adequate procedures do not exist for alerting and placing security forces in effective operation in potentially dangerous situations.

(b) Regardless of which of the foregoing reasons apply, we believe this would suggest the need for a reappraisal of our evaluation of the mechanics of the Turkish security forces and the effect of such mechanics on the capabilities of those forces.

4. In recent years fundamental economic trends and changes have been set in motion which are altering the basis of Turkish life, e.g., the trend toward industrialization which in turn brings greater numbers of country people into the cities, makes them dependent on salary jobs, and increases their vulnerability to economic fluctuations. The discontented among these, together with the depressed elements of the city, provided a favorable atmosphere for violence. There were thus great numbers of people

---

[64] "Military forces available in and around the city of Istanbul on September 6, were: 16-20,000 infantry from the 66th and 8th Divisions; 50 M-47 tanks of the 3rd armored brigade, and a tank battalion of 25 M-36 tanks. Senior us Military Advisors state that the infantry units were, at most, one hour from the center of town, and tanks could have been in place at any location in the city within 30-45 minutes." See National Archives, Foreign Office Dispatch No. 138, Istanbul, September 29, 1955.

who were ripe for widespread looting and vengeful vandalism.

(Implications)

(a) The economic distress which is apparent in and around Istanbul has been felt by lower classes principally because of the Government's inability to set up and maintain a system effectively controlling prices and distribution of goods. Thus the distress apparent in and around Istanbul might have been alleviated by adequate planning in this field and a constructive economic policy on the part of the central government.

(b) We believe that the lack of planning continues to reflect a fundamental weakness in Turkey's management of its economy.

5. Estimates of damages to property range up to one billion liras. Short term economic consequences of this destruction include: (1) Expenditure of sums to repair buildings and restock shops from materials available locally will increase considerably already dangerous inflationary pressures; (2) Depleted exchange reserves will be further burdened by the pressure to replace imported stocks; and (3) Tax collections in Istanbul (normally made before October 1) will be substantially reduced this year.

Long term consequences include: (1) Diversion to repairs and replacement of funds which might have been destined for investment in development projects; (2) Decreased tax collections in 1956 and 1957 by reason of deductions allowable to victims on damages and to those who make contributions to the aid campaign; and (3) Continuing attempts by minorities to transfer capital and to emigrate to other countries.

(Implications)

(a) The disorders and the evidences [*sic*] of governmental pressures on private firms to contribute toward reparation only thirteen years after the capital levy of 1942 [*varlık vergisi*], would seem to us to indicate that there is not yet reasonable security of private investments in Turkey.

(b) We believe that the implications of these economic consequences affect both the economic stability of the country and its present and future ability to support an effective military establishment.

Richards understood the problems facing Turkey directly, and those affecting its ally, the United States, indirectly. Having made an almost irrefutable case against the policies of both Turkey and the United States that had led Turkey down the path of social, economic, and political instability, he put himself and his analysis on the horns of a very difficult dilemma. Although his last implication was that Turkey could not, then or in the future, financially support "an effective military establishment"—which was a position that seemed contrary to Dulles's global policies—he ended up generally supporting precisely those US and Turkish policies that had led Turkey into seemingly inextricable difficulties: "We wish to make it clear that the conclusions set forth in this despatch do not imply changes in our policies *vis-à-vis* Turkey. We are suggesting only that certain aspects of their implementation should be reappraised."[65]

Richards's analysis of the pogrom's implications are, in a sense, repeated in the US ambassador's "Briefing paper submitted to the Department of State on October 18, 1955." The report characterizes the events of September 6-7 as "a grave embarrassment for the Turkish Government, and on the domestic front they have raised questions regarding the Government's responsibility and the patent inadequacy of the measures taken to prevent or suppress mob violence." The report adds that the government's internal stability was undermined, with especially disastrous economic effects, and that "the reputation and prestige of Turkey as a responsible member of the Western community of nations ha[d] been tarnished." Finally, the ambassador concluded, the strained relations with Greece were at breaking-point and the consequences for NATO were also very serious.[66]

Another report, this one the British ambassador's annual analysis of Turkey for 1955, must have been chilling not only to those in the Turkish government who got wind of it, but also to the American government, especially in regard to the ambassador's comments on Turkey's poor economic condition:

> As Turkey's economic difficulties grew, she tended to exploit her position as the Eastern bastion of NATO in support of her claims for further help. Her persistent dunning of the Americans throughout the year, combined, as it was, with a rigid refusal to accept American advice on the measures which she should take to put her economic house in order, lost her a good deal of the abundant good will she had hitherto enjoyed in America. Matters were not improved by Monsieur Zorlu's visit to Washington in early June, nor by the Turkish Government's successive attempts to gain the direct support of the Republican Party for their claims by by-passing [*sic*] the American Administration.

The report pointed to inflation, the failure to halt economic decline, and the default in payment of foreign debts:

> In short, the Turkish Government continued throughout the year

---

[65] *Ibid.*
[66] National Archives, Foreign Office Dispatch No. 153, Ankara, October 18, 1955.

their policy of living beyond their means. They spent more than their revenue, they imported more than they could pay for, they invested more than was prudent, they used the Central Bank to finance deficits of the Budget, the State Enterprises and the Soil Products Office and they tried to curb inflation by decree without adopting the measures of retrenchment needed to stabilize the economy. The result was an expanding note circulation, a steady rise in prices, increasing difficulty in selling Turkish export produce, the dwindling of most imports other than capital goods, growing internal shortages, the stoppage of many factories dependent on imported supplies and an increase in foreign indebtedness in spite of the operation of many agreements, for the liquidation of arrears. Against this background, the hopes placed in the possibility of drilling for oil (due to start in 1956) seemed exaggerated.[67]

Greece confronts Turkey

It is against this background that one should examine the diplomatic encounters of the Greek and Turkish foreign ministries in Ankara. Turkey's difficult position, as well as Greece's anxiety over Turkey's ability to pay just compensation, emerge very distinctly during the period from mid-September to early November. The war of nerves in Ankara was set off with the first Greek verbal note to Turkey on September 10, which accused the Turkish government of being responsible for the violence on September 6-7. Zorlu refused to accept the note because of its accusatory nature and returned it to Geôrgiadês, of whom he asked whether the Greeks wanted to improve or embitter relations. When the latter replied "improve," Zorlu suggested eliminating the accusations against the Turkish government and resubmitting the note.[68] After some small changes, the note was resubmitted, but Zorlu still found it unacceptable and informed Geôrgiadês that he would reply to it later.[69] Nuri Birgi, in discussing the Greek-Turkish crisis with the US ambassador, was similarly condescending in answering the ambassador's

[67] TNA:PRO, Ankara, No. RK1011/1, July 16, 1956.
[68] National Archives, Ankara, Dispatch No. 8437, September 16, 1955. In his report to Young in the Foreign Office, TNA:PRO, No. RG10344/35, Stewart analyzes his conversations with Birgi: "The subject of the Istanbul and Izmir riots came up only once and passed. I saw nothing from Birgi's manner which suggested that he was either particularly ashamed of what had happened or was at all worried about the consequences which these riots would have on the Turkish Government's position abroad."
[69] Ibid.

question as to his opinion on the "fall" of the Greek government and the ill effect of such an event should it occur. Birgi said that perhaps it would be better if the Greek government did fall.[70]

At a meeting on October 8, 1955, Birgi handed Geôrgiadês a memorandum in which he lodged a number of complaints about the Greek government's conduct. These complaints were to become a regular part of Turkish tactics in the ensuing diplomatic confrontation. The memorandum, which was an informal note, began with an objection to the inquest concerning the Turkish consular staff in Thessalonikê and the affair of the explosion on consular grounds.[71] Birgi asserted that the Greek charges of Turkish consular responsibility for the explosion could not be true. He then referred to what he called injurious publications in the Greek press concerning the incidents in Istanbul and Izmir on September 6-7. In particular, the memorandum dwelled on and criticized Greek diplomats abroad who had given themselves over to allegedly anti-Turkish propaganda, citing the Greek embassies in Washington, Madrid, Ottawa, and Damascus as examples. He also complained that a private organization had been charged by the Greek government to prepare the publication of a "Black Book" on the pogrom, illustrated with photographs. Birgi's memorandum exemplified the anxieties of the Turkish government over its international image at a moment of political and economic vulnerability. Turkey's foreign service had been active in information-gathering itself, as a reaction to what it feared might happen internationally. Looming on its horizon now were the trials of its diplomats in Thessalonikê, Greece's energetic efforts to focus the attention of international public opinion on the pogrom's horrors, and, finally, the "memorialization" of the pogrom in a *Black Book*— which frightened the Turkish government in particular.

The possibility that the entire consular staff of Thessalonikê would be publicly interrogated was also frightening, indeed a nightmare, not only for the Turkish foreign ministry but for the very security of the Menderes government. Menderes and others had—foolishly in hindsight—proclaimed in public that whoever had planned the explosion in Thessalonikê had also planned the pogrom. In his memorandum, Birgi argued that according to international practice, consuls were interrogated in their homes and not in public. He suggested that he would have no objections to such an interrogation. Of course, the real question, which neither Birgi nor British diplomats who also addressed this specific case addressed, was whether such consular privilege was invalidated when a crime was committed.

---

[70] National Archives, Dispatch No. 407, Ankara, September 15, 1955.
[71] Ypourgeion Exôterikòn, Ankara, Dispatch No. 3051, October 9, 1955.

In this connection, it should be noted that the foreign ministry was fearful that details on the pogrom would be leaked despite the censorship imposed under martial law. As for the Greek *Black Book*, it did become a subject of considerable diplomatic notice and apprehension. The archival materials give a good deal of information on this elusive document, which does not seem to have ever circulated. Birgi informed Geôrgiadês that his memorandum had no official character but was presented in order to "facilitate" Geôrgiadês's reports to the Greek government. The pretext, in other words, was that the memorandum was a communication between two friends that drew "attention to the events which could harm the existing friendship." In the event, the three "non-complaints" about court trials, the *Black Book*, and Greek diplomatic activity were to appear in practically all the communications between the two countries during October and early November.

On October 14, five days after receiving the memorandum, Geôrgiadês presented his government's reply to Birgi. The response, which was undoubtedly composed by Geôrgiadês after consultation with his superiors, was quite terse but vigorous, and spared neither the secretary-general nor his government. It attacked what it considered to be the superficiality of the Turkish government in thinking that a few shallow expressions of regret sufficed to erase what Turkey called "simple incidents which can be easily forgotten." It said that Turkish authorities erred if they believed that the attacks on Istanbul's Greek community would not have grave consequences, for public opinion against Turkey in Greece was at its height. The secretary-general had complained about the Greek press, but, the Greek statement insisted, the Greek press was justifiably critical of a Turkish government that had permitted the violation of the Greeks of Istanbul and of their churches. The Greek press, the Greek reply continued, was free to express the indignation of the Greek people, as "[t]he violent reaction of Greek public opinion is due to the offense given to its national dignity." It was thus the obligation of the Greek press to describe the tragic catastrophe and "expose faithfully the saddened sentiments and indignation of the Greek people. The Greek Government cannot…limit the freedom of the Press." This last retort was the answer to Birgi's accusation that the Greek government had not suppressed the Greek press. Indeed, in a counterattack, the Greek statement accused the Turkish government of allowing the Turkish press to fanaticize Turkish public opinion by printing false rumors against and demonizing the patriarch and the Greek community of Istanbul.

As for Greek diplomats, the reply stated that it was their duty to inform world opinion about the truth of the destruction suffered by the Greek community, especially in light of Turkish diplomatic activity, which had begun to circulate documents transferring the blame for the pogrom from the Turkish government to the Greeks. Regarding the "Black Book," however, the Greek government asserted that it would not interfere since the publication was a private initiative. At the end of all of this, Birgi exclaimed rhetorically that "the Greek reaction might cause one to believe that there exists between Greece and Turkey a hostility containing an international problem." Geôrgiadês replied that this was not an exaggeration but a fact, as the situation created by the Turkish government had added yet another, new international problem to those that already existed. Finally, Geôrgiadês concluded by stating that the Greek government could not interfere with the judicial authorities in Thessalonikê, which meant that, in effect, Turkey's consular staff would not be given any special treatment.

Birgi understood, of course, that the Greek reply was a direct onslaught against the Turkish government and its foreign ministry; as such, he objected both to the spirit and content of the "unofficial" Greek reply, and he refused to accept it. His brief answer adhered generally to the unchanging Turkish line: "We [the Turkish government] have expressed the opinions that it is not to the utility of the two countries to exaggerate the gravity of the event of September 6 and thus to present it as constituting an international problem."

The exchanges between Geôrgiadês and Birgi are far more interesting than the cut-and-dried unofficial notes, as their personalities emerge along with the views of their respective ministries (in contrast to their respective governments). Geôrgiadês ultimately cut off the arguments as they became, particularly on Birgi's side, less substantive and more repetitive. British consul Michael Stewart characterized Birgi as talkative and expansive. Geôrgiadês seems to have been more reserved; he finally halted their last discussion when he saw that the conversations could not proceed profitably:

> I fear, Mr. Ambassador, that our conversation continues, without result; let us try to give a resume. If your request has as its object to ascertain what in particular the Greek Government expects, at this moment, from the Turkish Government, which it would consider as satisfaction I can request this of my Minister and I shall communicate to you the results.
>
> Mr. Birgi [answer]: I have posed no question and I ask that you transmit nothing on this subject to Athens, for perhaps we would find ourselves before new and unforeseen demands.[72]

[72] Ypourgeion Exôterikôn, Athens, No. 53082, December 12, 1955; this contains both the four-page text of the conversation and a longer section on the exchanges between Greek and Turkish officials. The text in Ypourgeion Exôterikôn, Ankara, No. 3086, October 15, 1955, has only the text but a slightly longer Greek analysis.

It is obvious that the Greek government's diplomacy had begun to have an effect outside Turkey with consequences for the Turkish government itself. Birgi had pointed to the tight censorship of the Turkish press, in contrast to the relatively uncensored Greek press, but it would have made little difference in changing Turkish public opinion, which, if anything, had already become violently anti-Greek thanks both to the influence of the Turkish press for many months before the pogrom and the censorship imposed by martial law. Further, according to contemporary reports, the pogrom whetted the appetites of many Turks in Istanbul and adjacent regions for further opportunities to attack their Greek neighbors (there are consular reports to this effect). Aside from the matter of damage evaluations and payments to the Greeks and minorities, there were now the added Turkish demands regarding the Thessalonikê trials, the *Black Book*, and Greek diplomatic activity. In the light of circumstance, however, the Greeks were not ready to abandon any of these points without substantial concessions on the part of Ankara on compensation. On the diplomatic front, the Greek line had become hard and fixed, unbending before Turkish threats, NATO requests, or "silent" US pressure.

On October 23, the Greek embassy in Ankara telegraphed Athens that its *chargé* (the Greek ambassador was still absent) had been received by Menderes and, separately, by Zorlu, who had prepared a response to the initial Greek verbal note of September 10. As his reply was harsh, however, Zorlu had decided to withhold it in the light of some improvement in relations.

> The Minister [Zorlu] then touched upon the propagandistic undertakings of the Greek diplomats abroad. I stated that the activity of the representatives has as its purpose to shed light [on the disturbances] because of the hostile announcements of the Turkish Embassies. Then Zorlu announced that it would be necessary for the Greek Government to send out an encyclical to the Greek diplomats to halt the relevant propaganda and especially to desist from provoking international public opinion with the events of September. He added that he himself would send such a circular to the Turkish representatives [abroad]. He then asked me if it is certain that we would send out a similar Greek circular. I answered that we would communicate his desire to my government but that I could not know beforehand what would be its decision.
>
> On this matter, the Minister told me that in regard to this he is offering a "truce," that is, he will send out an encyclical today that they [Turkey's representatives] desist from further propaganda in the hope that the Greek Government will send a

similar encyclical to its representatives.[73]

On first sight, it is a little surprising that the hardliner Zorlu took the initiative to halt this diplomatic imbroglio unilaterally, or at least to offer a "truce" (which obviously implied a resumption of the conflict at another time). His hurry to call a halt to the matter was consonant, however, with the Turkish government's apprehension in the face of the almost inescapable consequences and aftermath of the pogrom. Although the specific date of the meeting is not mentioned in the telegram, the fact that it was received in the Greek foreign ministry at 5:16 AM on the twenty-third makes it almost certain that the meeting had transpired on the twenty-second, which was only two days before the agreed-upon flag ceremony in Izmir. The fact that Zorlu referred to his government's present policy on Greek-Turkish relations and to the "favorable statement of the Prime Minister" (probably Menderes's agreement to the ceremony) undoubtedly expressed the hope that this agreement somehow or other augured a favorable turn in Greek-Turkish relations, in his eyes at least.[74]

It is significant, then, that a coincidence of events flowed out of the small, temporary thaw of the flag ceremony. On the day Zorlu made his "unilateral" offer, Geôrgios Rallês received an urgent telegram from the Greek foreign ministry:

> By way of confirming today's telephone conversation and in reference to the relevant correspondence with you I have the honor to ask, by virtue of newer developments, and also by way of the order of the President of the Government [Karamanlês] that you proceed immediately to the necessary action to halt, indefinitely, the publication and circulation of the Black Book concerning the atrocities of September 6.[75]

Following Admiral Fechteler's initiative (and, with Menderes's approval, his conversations with Kanellopoulos and General Dovas) for a formal ceremony in Izmir, the Greek government had evidently decided to stop the already advanced work in Washington on the *Black Book* as a sign of its willingness to contribute to the flag ceremony's success. On the same day, making a virtue of necessity, Zorlu ordered Turkish diplomats abroad to suspend further propaganda.

Inasmuch as the *Black Book* and the Greek-Turkish diplomatic encounter

[73] Ypourgeion Exôterikôn, Ankara, No. 3158, October 23, 1955.
[74] *Ibid.*
[75] Greek Embassy, Washington, No. 4412/B/99, October 28, 1955. However, the original, withdrawing the *Maurê Vivlos* from publication and/or circulation, had already been sent by Rallês on October 22, Ypourgeion Exôterikôn, Athens, No.45433/T4. Ep.

reveal the nature and scope of the Greek campaign, a quick glance at the third element of the presentation of Greek arguments and actions against the Turkish government is of no little interest. Their crystallization is embodied in two documents. The first, out of which the second emerged, was the long and detailed memorandum that was circulated to all major and many lesser missions of the Greek government around the world. The second document was the *Black Book* itself, which—such are the mysteries of diplomacy— achieved its goals without being circulated. The memorandum or *ekthesis* consisted of three parts: the *ekthesis* proper on the causes of and conditions for the pogrom; an appendix containing data on the events and their aftermath; and a photographic appendix documenting the areas of destruction. Its primary intention and function was to serve as a credible guide through the disarray of, and often confusing data on, the violence. Most of its contents could be freely and publicly used as needed, with the exception of three classified paragraphs.[76]

---

[76] Greek Embassy, Washington, No. 43871/T.4. Ep., Dispatch No. 4266, sent from Athens, October 11, 1955; the Greek text has been published in Tsoukatou, *Septemvriana*, pp. 219-254, as Kavounidês's *Ekthesis*.

The foreign ministry's memorandum was divided into nine sections: 1) introduction; 2) causes and conditions; 3) "the new excuse"; 4) staging the cause; 5) proof of conspiracy; 6) blaming the communists; 7) the Turkish government's responsibility; 8) extent of damages; and 9) general thoughts and conclusions. After orienting the reader as to the memorandum's general purposes, the introduction proceeded to survey the destruction of homes, stores, schools, and churches. It also described the physical violence (beatings, forced circumcisions, rape, and murder) perpetrated against Istanbul's Greeks, as well as the desecration of their religious institutions. The document charged that the Turkish press had attempted to downplay the destruction, and protect the Turkish government, with its assertions that the disorders had resulted from the "spontaneous" exasperation of the Turkish people following the incident at the Turkish consulate in Thessalonikê, or—taking another tack—that the pogrom had been the product of a communist conspiracy.

In the second and third sections, the memorandum addressed previous Turkish policy on the Muslim minority in Western Thrace and then moved on, in the fourth section, to discuss the Thessalonikê consular affair. As this episode was critical to the case, and had a direct bearing on the events in Istanbul and Izmir, the next section pointed, convincingly, to the government conspiracy behind the violence. Section Six then dispatched the attempt to scapegoat the communists—a patently absurd scenario that was easily refuted. Section Seven, again, dealt with the Turkish government's responsibility for the pogrom—which was clear, for example, from the refusal of police or soldiers to intervene in the destruction—while Section Eight reviewed the wide extent of the devastation. Finally, the general conclusions in the last section led to a provocative question: What were the effective solutions going to be for the many serious problems caused by the pogrom of September 6-7?

The memorandum was supplemented by an appendix of nineteen pages with accounts from contemporary eyewitnesses (largely non-Greek). It also contained a series of photographs of ruined churches, businesses, and other Greek establishments.

The memorandum makes clear that there was nothing spontaneous about the pogrom, that, indeed, it had been planned ahead of time, that communists played no significant role in it in any way, and that the Turkish government was fully informed that such an outbreak would occur and did nothing to prevent it or halt the general destruction of the Greek community after it had begun. This general introduction set the tone for the entire document. Section Four dealt with the facts of the explosion in Thessalonikê, its perpetration by the Turkish government, and its function within the overall context of the pogrom. Following upon this section, the next one endeavored to prove that the pogrom was the result of a government conspiracy and that the disturbances were, in fact, aimed at destroying the property and community of Istanbul's Greeks. The evidence was both detailed and compelling.

This very brief *précis* of the memorandum illustrates the crucial points around which Greek diplomats argued henceforth in their relevant functions (and which have been discussed and developed throughout this study). The document constituted the institutionalization of a uniform paper that was meant to give greater consistency and integration to the Greek case, along with some very convincing arguments. The letter of instructions that accompanied its transmission read:

> To:
> All royal embassies
> The Permanent Representative in NATO, Paris
> The Permanent Representative in the United Nations, New York
> General Consulates: San Francisco, Alexandria, Jerusalem,
>   Cairo, Nicosia, Marseilles, New York, Chicago, Skopje
> Royal Consulates: Antwerp, Hamburg, Boston, Port Said,
>   Trieste, Tunis
> Sub-Consulates: Casablanca, Mansoura [Egypt], Minia [Egypt],
>   Toronto, Tanta [Egypt]

Its careful organization and detailed nature made the document one of the most important tools in the arsenal of Greek diplomacy. The repeated Turkish objections to Greek diplomatic activity were such that one understands that the latter was so effective that Turkey sought some respite from the consistent hammering from its neighbor. In short, Greek persistence was having a decided effect on the Turkish government; to a lesser but definite degree, it was also having an effect on the State Department, which quietly began to pressure Turkey on the compensation issue.

At a second level, the Greek foreign ministry envisioned a publication that would circulate more broadly, and in a more simplified and readable form, among the general public. This was why the ministry quickly began to prepare the *Black Book*. Both its development and vigorous Turkish opposition to it are evident in a substantial number of documents. It was to stimulate anxiety in both the Greek parliament, which chaffed at the delays in its publication, and the Turkish foreign ministry, which was afraid that it might appear at all. One should note here that the *Black Book* flowed, in many ways, from the same vision that had led to the prior memorandum. The vast work of assembly, editing, and analysis of consular and ambassadorial reports had been finished as of late September. Rallês's project in collecting the reports of the foreign and Turkish media had proceeded well, as had the collection of photographs. By late September to early October, all the material had been edited and integrated into the general memorandum. Early on in this first phase, the idea of a second booklet for broader circulation was conceived.

On September 14, the Greek general staff addressed a brief query to the foreign ministry about a possible "booklet on vandalisms in Turkey": "We have the honor to ask you to inform us in the Greek Staff of National Defense if it is true, as has been reported in the press, that one is going to publish a booklet concerning the vandalisms in Turkey. For the Ministry of Defense and the General Staff are able to contribute to its composition by furnishing data."[77] The foreign ministry's reply four days later confirmed the newspaper report.[78] By October 3, the foreign ministry's directorate of churches was asking Rallês's office to submit the *Black Book* for examination and approval, adding that, "despite the fact that the production of the aforesaid Album is already in danger of losing its timeliness, we consider its continuation useful."[79]

The physical inability to publish the *Black Book* in time, along with the Greek defeat in the United Nations on placing Cyprus on the General Assembly agenda, forced the foreign ministry to abandon any hope of employing it to immediate effect in the international arena and to settle for using it for some advantage in the long-term run of Greek-Turkish relations.

On October 17, Rallês's office announced to the Greek embassy's press office in Washington that the document was finally ready: "...[W]e approve of the publication of the Album...by AHEPA, at our own expense. The text consists of about 35 typed pages, and accompanied by 17 photographs, it shall be sent to you so soon as its contents are approved by the Ministry of Foreign Affairs....Please inform as to how many copies will be needed for America and the Anglophone lands. Please submit expense budget."[80] On the

[77] Ypourgeion Ethnikês Amynês, General Staff of National Defense, to the ministry of foreign affairs, No. 0041/61, September 14, 1955.
[78] Ypourgeion Exôterikôn, Athens, No. 39477/Tourk. 4, September 17, 1955.
[79] Ypourgeion Exôterikôn, Athens, No. 4238/EB/39, October 3, 1955.
[80] Ypourgeion Proedrias Kyvernêseôs, Athens to Washington, No. 1636/A/0211, October 17, 1955.

same day, Rallês submitted to the foreign ministry, as requested, an account of the publication's production, and he informed the ministry that his office had approved Kavallieratos's proposal for AHEPA to appear as the book's formal publisher. "We now await your return of the text, approved, so that we can send it to Washington for the further procedures," he concluded.[81]

Three days later, a member of parliament, Gerasimos Vasilatos, raised the issue of the *Black Book* in the chamber, asserting that the government had not yet sent the documents on to Washington: "It is as if the grievous fact were not enough....We have not seen, up to this day, the *Black Book* with the photographs, the statistics and the gathered data so that world public opinion might be informed of Turkish violence....[and] the President of the Government and the Minister of Foreign Affairs are asked why they have neglected the execution of their National duties."[82] This intense political pressure from certain deputies was to continue until the end of December, with the government in the difficult position of having to negotiate with Turkey while informing parliament of the details.

On October 18, the ministry returned the text of the *Black Book* to Rallês with a few alterations and suggested that Rallês include Senator Capehart's recent letter to the State Department, which referred to the extensive damages arising from the pogrom as well as to the Turkish government's responsibility for it. The communication concluded, "As the printing and circulation of the *Book* have been delayed and it is in danger of losing its timeliness, we ask that every effort be made to hasten the relevant procedures."[83] The next day, Rallês informed the ministry that his office had made the necessary changes and had sent everything to Washington.[84] Three days later, Kavallieratos indicated the number of copies to be printed and where they were to be sent. As to the requested budget, Kavallieratos informed Rallês that without the actual copy and photographs (which had not yet arrived), it would be very difficult to

---

[81] Ypourgeion Proedrias Kyvernêseôs to the ministry of foreign affairs, No. 1589/A/9915, October 17, 1955; Rallês informed the foreign ministry that his office had approved the *Black Book*'s publication and sponsorship by AHEPA, and he asked for the manuscript's return from the ministry. It seems that its author, A. A. Pallês, had already finished the text before October 4. Pallês, by the way—son of the famous Greek linguist and translator, Alexandros Pallês—had had an excellent English education and distinguished diplomatic career, and was the author of several noteworthy books.

[82] Ypourgeion Exôterikôn, Athens, No. 4667, October 26, 1955, which had received the document, by way of the ministry of the presidency of the government, from the Greek parliament.

[83] Ypourgeion Exôterikôn, No. 45102/T.4, Ep., October 18, 1955, to the ministry of the presidency of the government.

[84] Ypourgeion Proedrias Kyvernêseôs to the ministry of foreign affairs, No. 1651/A/10277, October 19, 1955.

give a budget, but he would make an estimate based on the number of copies to be printed and the size of the typescript. Kavallieratos asked for a total of 80,000 copies, 50,000 of which were to be distributed in the United States and 15,000 in Britain.[85]

This documentation, while not complete, gives a clear picture of how the *Black Book* was prepared and the activities of the Greek embassy and press office in Washington. Birgi had been correct when he charged that the *Black Book* was essentially a Greek-government operation, for it was the only entity at the time that could finance its publication and, more important, had the confidential information and government reports that made up the volume. He was also correct in fearing the political and international consequences of the *Black Book* for Turkey. What he was unwilling to admit, however, was that the Turkish government itself was not an innocent, surprised bystander to the pogrom. It had authored and executed the idea. In the end, he also did not realize that the continual delays in publication would eventually lead to the book's marginalization. Being oblivious to that reality, he and his colleagues unwittingly transformed the *Black Book* into a weapon for continued pressure on their government, despite the endless delays. In effect, the *Black Book* ended up having a greater impact on Turkish anxieties and diplomacy than it would have had if it had been published and then forgotten. As things turned out, and as we have seen, one day after the Greek ambassador in Washington requested 80,000 copies of the *Black Book*, the foreign ministry urgently telegraphed Rallês, copying the ambassador, ordering a halt to any further work on the volume in the light of the new turn in government policy toward Turkey.[86]

It is clear that following the flag ceremony in Izmir, both sides hoped that the vicious atmosphere in their relations would abate. This was most evident on the Greek side by the hopes expressed in a message by Theotokês to Karamanlês: "I have the honor to inform you that subsequent to the rendering of moral satisfaction [in Izmir], I think that we can dispatch instructions to our authorities abroad that they suspend all open propagandistic manifestations against Turkey."[87] On the very same day, however, Geôrgios Exêntarês sent Karamanlês a copy of a second telegram by Theotokês to Karamanlês. It had a

---

[85] Greek Embassy, Washington, No. 4341, October 21, 1955; the *Black Book* was printed but never circulated. See Sarrês, *Ê allê pleura*, II A, p. 129, who saw the title page only, on which Chrêstidês wrote, "it was pulped." I wish to thank Wing Commander Panagiôtês Skoutelês, who was kind enough to give me a photocopy of the entire booklet, on the basis of which my analysis has been made.

[86] Ypourgeion Exôterikôn to the ministry of the presidency of the government, No. 45433/T.4, Ep., October 22, 1955.

[87] Ypourgeion Exôterikôn, Paris, No. 2294, October 24, 1955.

completely different spirit from the previous one: "With especial satisfaction I received your telegram…announcing the attainment of the first objective goal in the series of efforts which you have planned in the foreign policy of the Government. This very good beginning provides additional strength to us for the continuation of the labors protecting our country's interests and the success of our national aspirations."[88]

The foreign minister's two telegrams to Karamanlês were in effect contradictory, as the first spoke of a general relaxation of "open… manifestations against Turkey" whereas the second one referred to a "truce" as the first success in a campaign to force Turkey to come to terms on compensation. It could not have been otherwise, however; as Karamanlês was to point out to Turkey (and as his predecessor, Papagos, and others had done), a ceremony had merely symbolic value. A tiny parade, Greece's flag raised and its national anthem played, and a fine banquet at which the Turkish minister of communications and the Greek ambassador to Turkey made brief but pointed speeches, did not address the crux of the matter, which was Turkey's failure to come to realistic terms with the substantive financial requirements for compensating the pogrom's victims.

Again, on the same day, October 24, Karamanlês gave very specific instructions to the Greek ambassador soon to go to Ankara that revealed a forceful policy for future negotiations on the difficult issue of compensation. Karamanlês had already indicated his policy in an earlier exchange with Menderes. On the eve of the flag ceremony at Izmir, and two days before his government won its vote of confidence, Karamanlês had spoken in parliament on the issue of Greek-Turkish relations. The next day, he had called a press conference on the subject. It is obvious that he had to take a firm stand on the matter given the dynamics of Greek politics. Menderes found the views expressed by the new prime minister both in his speech and press conference to be offensive and addressed them in a memorandum or "letter" to Karamanlês, which naturally forced the latter to reply, and to do so in a manner that would not compromise him politically in Greece.

Menderes wrote sharply to Karamanlês that Turks found the events of September 6-7 "regrettable" and that his government had formally apologized and promised compensation. He then continued:

> As deplorable as they are, the events in Istanbul and Izmir, whose damages have been repaired accordingly by the efforts of the Turkish Government there, these efforts should remain henceforth within normal limits. Consequently the Turkish Government has

[88] Ypourgeion Exôterikôn, Paris, No. 2295, October 29, 1955.

deemed it necessary to take care that the effects of these events
should not remain. However it is impossible for the Turkish
Government to succeed herein all by itself...and the Greek
Government should add to this its own efforts....Accordingly the
events in question shall not, and cannot be characterized in any
way except as having been accidental and of a passing nature....

It is for this reason that the communiqué which the Greek
Government made to the press [October 11] has been viewed by
the Turkish Government as disquieting....

Karamanlês thanked Menderes for his frank discussion of the problems
between their two nations, and in particular for his references to the letter
that the late Papagos had sent him and for the Turkish premier's hopes for the
future of bilateral relations. He pointed out, however, that there seemed to be
a vast gulf separating the two governments as to the extent and nature of the
events of September 6-7.

As it appears that the Turkish Government considers the events as
being of a passing nature, and it has the apparent conviction that
after the giving of promises for moral and material compensations
that a forgetting and pardon will automatically follow...the Greek
Government wishes to emphasize the fact that in order for the
present crisis to pass, one must create the necessary preconditions
and the Turkish Government must carry out its declarations
concerning moral and material compensation by actual deeds.

Karamanlês went on to state that this included, specifically, satisfaction for
the events in Izmir. Karamanlês further reminded Menderes that Kanellopoulos
in his note of September 19 had indicated to the Turkish prime minister that
the Greek government was going to monitor the matter of compensations
closely and that, in this respect, it had not introduced any new demands but
had simply reiterated ones that had been made from the outset, which, as
far as the compensations were concerned, had to be resolved quickly. It was
certainly clear, Karamanlês remarked pointedly, that the Turkish government
had an insufficient understanding of the degree of exasperation and anger
that the events of September 6-7 had provoked in Greece. The continuing
demonstration of this popular displeasure in the Greek press simply reflected
the Greek people's feelings. Consequently, it was only when the Turkish
government carried out its promises of material and moral compensation that
the Greek government would be in a position to move positively to restore
bilateral relations. Karamanlês closed by assuring Menderes that, "The Greek
Government in no way desires the weakening of the bonds of alliance as it is

always dedicated to the doctrine of collective security."[89]

Thus, although the government had changed in Greece, there had been no basic change in Greece's formal demands for restoring good relations with Turkey. US ambassador Cannon—as well as Menderes, Zorlu, and Birgi—had hoped in vain that Papagos's replacement might be more pliant, and that the flag ceremony in Izmir would satisfy him. It should be added here that although it was a mere ceremony, the choice of Izmir was particularly sensitive to Turkish national sentiments and İnönü eventually exploited this event in his attack on Menderes's handling of the Greek-Turkish crisis.

As mentioned above, on the very same day the flag ceremony was concluded, Karamanlês sent his personal instructions to the Greek embassy in Ankara, which have already been described. To repeat briefly, he told Kallergês (not yet returned to Ankara) to express the thanks of the Greek government for this first step in the difficult effort to reestablish good relations as well as for Menderes's good offices in the undertaking. The ambassador was to explain to the prime minister that the Greek ambassador had spoken rather soberly at the ceremony in Izmir because Greek public opinion would have been further agitated by any sign of warmth. He was also to explain to Menderes, to the foreign minister, and to other ministers that the Greek government considered it especially important that all outstanding bilateral issues be rapidly and satisfactorily resolved, as that was the only way Greek public opinion could be mollified. Specifically, the Greek government wanted to know the specific measures for reparations to Greek citizens, to the Orthodox Church in Turkey, to the Church's institutions, and to the communal institutions, businesses, and private property of the ethnic Greek minority, for whose protection, Karamanlês insisted, Greece retained "every right of action...by the Treaty of Lausanne." Additionally, he wanted these measures to be drawn up within fifteen days. Finally, Karamanlês also wanted a solution to fishing rights between the two countries and a renewed effort to delineate their maritime borders.[90]

Thus instructed, Kallergês had the two critical meetings with Menderes—on October 30, without the presence of Zorlu, and on November 11, with Zorlu present—that were discussed earlier in this chapter. In the first meeting, Kallergês put forward Karamanlês's points. Menderes agreed to compensate Greek citizens following his approval of the claims process. At that time, an exchange of binding letters between the two governments would take place. (It is noteworthy that Menderes actually told Kallergês to ask Zorlu for a

---

[89] Greek Embassy, Washington, No. 4566/T.4, Ep., October 22, 1955.
[90] Ypourgeion Exôterikôn, Athens, No. 46321/T.4, Ep., October 24, 1955.

reply within fifteen days of the time the Turkish minister received the Greek communication.) The prime minister assured Kallergês that this would occur quickly. Menderes also undertook to restore the Greek minority's churches and schools to the *status quo ante*. However, Menderes added, since this matter involved Turkish citizens, foreign intervention would only hinder the process. Menderes also agreed to proceed with measures to deal with fishing and maritime borders. Finally, he said that trials would ascertain the guilt for the pogrom, as well as the suitable punishment.[91]

Among the Greek ambassador's more urgent demands had been that Turkey pay TL27,014,479 to Greek citizens who had suffered damages; that the assessment of claims be carried out by a five-man committee consisting of two Turks, two Greeks, and an individual acceptable to both governments; that the last payments be made by the end of March 1956; that the government facilitate both the import of goods and currency exchange; and, finally, that Turkey enact the necessary legislation for all these measures by the end of 1955.[92]

As we have seen, however, the second meeting on November 11 was much less harmonious. Kallergês thought that this might have been due to the fact that Menderes did not have a complete command of French and the energetic Zorlu effectively intervened as translator throughout the meeting. Zorlu's interventions, at least according to Kallergês, were accompanied by extensive discussions with Menderes, who was moved, little by little, into hard and unbending positions by his acting foreign minister. First, and most important, Menderes abandoned his earlier agreement to a binding exchange of letters on compensation. As mentioned previously, it was at this meeting that Menderes insisted that the Turkish government was not legally bound to pay damages to anyone—a proposition that Kallergês had already heard from the British embassy—and that it was only because of his "personal honor" that Menderes had agreed to do so, although there could not be any outside interference on this matter as it would be interpreted as foreign intervention in Turkey's internal affairs. When on occasion Zorlu had spoken to him in a coarse and harsh manner, Kallergês asserted that he had answered in kind. In his report, Kallergês stated that he was impressed by Menderes's sincerity, who seemed to be genuinely interested in dealing with the problem. Without going into any further detail, perhaps the most important point was Menderes's statement that he hoped to bring a draft bill before parliament within twenty days to regulate compensations and provide a specific budget

---

[91] Ypourgeion Exôterikôn, Ankara, No. 3212, October 30, 1955.
[92] Ypourgeion Exôterikôn, Athens, protocol number illegible, November 10, 1955.

for them. Following Karamanlês's instructions, Kallergês pressed Menderes incessantly for a date by which reparations would be paid; after much evasion, he was promised that it would happen "by the end of March 1956."

A second issue emerged repeatedly, however, in Menderes's efforts to justify his delays in legislating the necessary financial measures, which Kallergês found to be of particular, and political, interest.

> Throughout the duration of our conversations it seems that it is internal difficulties which bother Menderes the most, as he told me repeatedly. This was so despite the Martial Law, as he had to take into account Turkish public opinion as well as the hostile criticisms of the [Republican] People's Party and of the recent splintering off of twenty [nineteen, actually] of the Assemblymen of his own party. It is probable that the latter will emerge in a vigorous manner in the Grand National Assembly when it returns to its legislative duties on November 16.[93]

Certain items presented by Kallergês to Menderes were not rejected until December (the mixed committee for damage claims, fishing rights, and maritime borders). Menderes had also danced around the stance of the Greek government as protector of the rights of the Greek minority given that the treaty of Lausanne guaranteed this right along with the Turkish government's rights to protect the Turkish minority in Greek Thrace. The Greek diplomatic efforts did succeed, however, in one very important goal: Menderes promised legislation to deal with the bulk of the damage claims. He thus eventually introduced the subject to his cabinet and finance minister. What does not emerge from these two meetings is the fact that Zorlu's aggressive policies in the foreign ministry had finally gotten the upper hand and, increasingly, the Cyprus issue began to compete successfully with the matter of the pogrom and the daunting problem of compensation.

On November 8, Kallergês sent a coded dispatch to Athens informing his ministry that the Turkish foreign ministry had handed out an *aide-mémoire* in French that day to the embassies in Ankara (although not to the Greek embassy) in which the Greek government had been attacked, the destruction in Istanbul and Izmir on September 6-7 had been justified, and the blame for the pogrom had been shifted from Turkey to Greece. The document also attempted to justify the Menderes government's new position on Cyprus. It was most probably Zorlu's inspiration, but it was composed by his subordinate Birgi, who, in his conversations with the foreign diplomatic community in Turkey, sought to justify the document as a truthful analysis.

---

[93] Ypourgeion Exôterikôn, Ankara, No. 3476, November 12, 1955.

It was a hasty compilation of data, positions, and accusations. Certainly, the composition, contents, and arguments pointed to Birgi as the author, as it was very similar to the contents of his previous memoranda and notes to Geôrgiadês.[94] Although it began with the admission that the events of September 6-7 were "deplorable" and regrettable, it rapidly and completely led to the proposition that the Turkish state and people were not responsible for the violent attacks on the Greeks and other minorities. The very second paragraph, the longest one in the document, claimed that the real cause of all that the Greeks had suffered that night was none other than the Greek government. The "deplorable events," according to the *aide-mémoire*, were preceded by a number of other events that implied the moral responsibility of the Greek government. In an effort to explain the apparent paradox of the Greek government seeking to destroy the Greek minority and Greek nationals resident in Istanbul, the document alleged that this had occurred because the Greek government had, over the years, manufactured a Cyprus issue, which, in turn, had produced powerful emotions and indignation among Turks. The intense activity of the Greek press further provoked the Turkish press to a similarly heated agenda of news coverage on Cyprus. This all fed the indignation of the Turkish people over the way the Greek government allegedly treated the Turkish minority in Greek Thrace. Finally, the document asserted that the pogrom's violence was justified by the explosion within the Turkish consular complex in Thessalonikê, as well as by the "warning" that the Turkish Cypriots were to be massacred by the Greek Cypriots on August 28, 1955. "It is now in these circumstances, and as a result of incessantly accumulating emotion, that the event of September 6-7 was provoked," the document insisted, adding that, "However, the Greek Government, passing over these antecedents in silence…attempts, even today, to show that these events constitute a case in isolation and without antecedents, due exclusively, if not to the initiative, at least to the encouragement of the Turkish authorities."[95]

The *aide-mémoire* goes on to attack Greece for ignoring and belittling Turkish efforts at sympathy for and understanding of the events' victims, and, above all, for successfully bringing the pogrom to the attention of world opinion and, in so doing, turning it into an international affair, "thus preventing by this means these events from being forgotten by public opinion

---

[94] For the French text and Greek translation, Ypourgeion Exôterikôn, Ankara to Athens, No. 3382, November 8, 1955; Ypourgeion Exôterikôn, Ankara, No. 3434, November 9, 1955, contains not only the French text in question, but also the French text of the calendar of events, which Birgi composed, covering the period of September 7 to October 30. See also Ypourgeion Exôterikôn, Washington, No. 6208, November 26, 1955, conveying Melas's comments.

[95] Ypourgeion Exôterikôn, Ankara, No. 3434, November 9, 1955.

and therefore being kept within their proper proportions."[96] Furthermore, the document continues, the Greek government was waging the battle over compensations in order to gain advantage on the issue of Cyprus's future: "It is certain that these events would have never taken place if the Cyprus Question...had not been led to where it is by the Greek government." Consequently, "Whatever the deeply regrettable character of these events and destruction, one cannot in any way consider them as anything else but accidental—in which the responsibilities do not fall exclusively on Turkey, which was as badly damaged as any other country."[97]

The meetings between Birgi and Geôrgiadês had been anything but amicable. The upcoming matter of compensation had been sufficient, in and of itself, to render Greek-Turkish relations difficult at best and disastrous at worst. For the Greek government, bringing those responsible for the pogrom to justice, and swiftly and justly remunerating the victims, was the *sine qua non* for improving relations between Greece and Turkey. In contrast, the Turkish side chose to consider the pogrom as a done deed to be forgotten, with oral and written apologies, and the *promise* of indemnities, sufficient as a response. The *aide-mémoire* had said nothing that had not been previously stated by the Turkish government in its frantic effort to disclaim events that it had so carefully planned and efficiently executed. The Turkish government was not only ambivalent about assigning blame, but now stated that it had all been the Greek government's fault. Turkey's claim that it had already paid for the damages was specious on two counts: the amount of the actual pittances doled out by the aid committee; and, even more so, the fact that there had been no substantive financial action taken by the government to that point.[98]

THE INTERNAL PRESSURE ON MENDERES

However, the two months that had passed was sufficient time for the pogrom to become "domesticated"—that is, to become a part of Turkey's daily life and for the shock it had initially provoked, both inside and outside the country, to begin to wane. Meanwhile, the Greek government's systematic efforts had begun to have an effect in international circles and public opinion. Politically, the Turkish *aide-mémoire* was a kind of "wake-up call," a sign that the Turkish government thought that it was losing the diplomatic battle and that its new

---

[96] *Ibid.*

[97] *Ibid.*

[98] Every event presented by the *aide-mémoire* as having been caused by others—that is, the Greek government—was in effect planned and executed by Menderes's government (see Chapters 1 and 2).

position on and claims in Cyprus, which had been vigorously stated at the tripartite conference in early September, were now threatened. Theotokês remarked:

> From the circulation of this *mémoire* it is clear that the Turkish Government, as a result of the events of September and of the energetic Greek reaction that resulted in an international projection of the events, found itself in a diminished position and in the position to take action by way of counterattack. Certainly the naive and unacceptable accusations of the responsibility of Greece for the events will not influence those who know well their creation and course. On the other hand it is apparent that the preparation of the *mémoire* was necessitated by the uneasiness that Turkey would be excluded from further agreements on the future of Cyprus.[99]

This change in Turkish diplomacy was also noticed by Palamas:

> From the day after the anti-Greek events, the Turkish Mission [to the United Nations] followed cautiously a policy of silence obviously because of its diminished international position, of which it had become aware. But I have observed, now for some days, that this tactic of "live by escaping notice" is coming to an end. The Turkish Mission has begun to take initiatives, behind the scenes, to inform [in consonance with the known Turkish positions] as a result of the recent developments in Cyprus. There are other indications that the Turkish Government believes that enough time has passed so that the events of September 6 have been forgotten and that they can now return to a policy of counterattacks on the basis of their unbending views on Cyprus.[100]

The American consul in Izmir also remarked on the changes in tone of Turkish foreign policy in his bimonthly report, listing this fact as an important new development.

> Such shame as the Turks may have felt about the events of September 6-7, is fast dissipating. The Turks maintain a firm stand on Cyprus....

---

[99] Ypourgeion Exôterikôn, Athens, unnumbered, November 10, 1955. On November 17, 1955, Theotokês sent his own memorandum (Ypourgeion Exôterikôn, No. 4963/T.4, Ep.) to the Greek ambassador in Washington as well as to Cannon in Athens, and he asked the ambassador to forward a copy to the appropriate officer in the State Department; he characterized the Turkish memorandum as "a new manifestation of the impertinent and arrogant anti-Greek policy of today's Turkey. It expects, at the least, a partial resurrection of shaken Turkish pride with the aim of the renewal of Turkish rigidity on the Cyprus question."

[100] Ypourgeion Exôterikôn, New York, No. 3005, November 29, 1955.

The wave of self-criticism which followed the September riots seems about spent. For a time, the Turks were abject in their shame not only for specific acts of pillage, arson and sadism, but for the basic lack of self-control revealed by the events of that terrible night. Recently the tone has changed. Now once again, Turks are lifting their heads in defiant pride and saying that the rampage against the Greeks was a completely natural outburst provoked by the atrocious conduct of the Greeks themselves, who got only what was coming to them.[101]

In two of Michael Stewart's reports to London (November 8 and 15), he states that a much friendlier tone had recently entered into Greek-Turkish relations, so that the Turkish *aide-mémoire* "astonished" the foreign diplomatic community in Ankara. Stewart criticized the Turkish foreign ministry for the note and characterized it as "obviously a blunder [that] apart from its effects on Turco-Greek relations has done the Turks no good with the foreign Missions here." The British diplomat had not yet investigated the timing of the delivery, but he writes that the note must have taken some weeks to prepare given the vast material that had to be processed in order to provide it with the appropriate and supporting appendixes: "none the less [*sic*] I think it probable that paragraph 9 of the Aide Memoire gives the real essence; the Turkish Government probably fear that their silence during the last two months on the question of Cyprus, coupled with the loss of ground in their international position as a result of the riots of the sixth of September, might have led the Greeks and others to believe that a change of strategy on the Turkish attitude on Cyprus is possible...."[102] Johnston of the home office had taken note of the basic changes in these policies, having been informed of them by the British embassy in Athens; he now foresaw a new Greek-Turkish crisis over the compensations.[103]

As it had been the first to experience Turkey's policy changes in detail, Greece took the decision it felt would best fit its immediate policies vis-à-vis the unexpected *aide-mémoire*. Having long ago separated the Cyprus question from the issue of compensation, it decided to ignore the Turkish note for the present and not make an open issue of it, as this would have further complicated the already complex negotiations over compensation. Furthermore, both Kallergês and Stewart noted that the document had not only been disregarded by the foreign missions in Ankara but that it had

[101] National Archives, Foreign Office Dispatch No. 8, Izmir, April 4, 1956.

[102] TNA:PRO, Ankara, No. RG10344/106, November 8, 1955; also TNA:PRO, Ankara, No. 1491/209/15, November 15, 1955.

[103] TNA:PRO, London, No. RG10344/112, November 16, 1955.

actually damaged Turkey's standing. There were much broader implications behind the Turkish allegations, however, which did not pass unnoticed. Theotokês remarked on them in a letter to various foreign embassies. The *aide-mémoire* stated openly that Turkey's primary concern was Cyprus, and that compensations were to be relegated to a secondary or tertiary position:

> The Greek Government sees that the submission of this *mémoire* proves that the Turkish Government has no real repentance and no awareness of the most important and sole responsibility of the tragic events. Simultaneously, this action demonstrates that there exists no genuine disposition from the Turkish side for the normalization of its relations with Greece, despite our good will. In charging Greece with this responsibility and by virtue of this new worsening of our mutual relations, Ankara is seeking, obviously, to evade the execution of its obligations to compensate material damages. The Greek Government considers it advantageous, at least for the present, to ignore the Turkish *mémoire* and avoid further public confrontations, and to turn its attention to obtaining, in the degree possible, a full satisfaction of our outstanding demands.
>
> In the case that, because of Turkish bad faith, no satisfactory solution for our just demands results, we shall find ourselves obliged to re-consider the entire nature of our relations with Turkey.[104]

His two meetings with Kallergês came at a time when Menderes was struggling on all fronts to save his government as well as himself. The Greek campaign to exert pressure on Turkey thus encountered a weakened Turkish government, which was to bring results of sorts. All indications point to Turkey's prime minister being eager to settle with the Greek government and, thus, freeing himself from a situation that had put Turkey in an increasingly unfavorable light on the international scene.

Five days later after his second meeting with Kallergês, Menderes raised the matter of compensation to his cabinet and asked it to cooperate on a rapid introduction of the necessary measures.[105] He stated that the claims for damages from the Greek side had reached TL104 million but that, in effect, the real damages were much lower. The cabinet discussed the matter at great length and, taking their cue from Menderes's assertion of much lower real damages, decided, first, to ask parliament for TL50 million as an initial appropriation and, second, to assign the matter to the finance ministry, which was actually going to submit the bill on the issue to parliament. Menderes

---

[104] Ypourgeion Exôterikôn, Athens, unnumbered, November 10, 1955.
[105] Ypourgeion Exôterikôn, Ankara, Dispatch No. 3500, November 18, 1955.

also added an important item: the ministry was to announce the bill in order to calm public opinion.

As soon as the cabinet's decision became known, however, the proposed measure provoked opposition from the nineteen deputies who had bolted from the DP. Kapsambelês reported to Athens from Istanbul that "the 'Group of Nineteen' has declared…that it will vote against the compensations law so long as the Government, which it considers to be responsible for the events, refuses to name, to the National Assembly, those responsible for the events."[106] The internal opposition from within his own party had, in fact, become one of the most troublesome features on Menderes's domestic political horizon, about which he had repeatedly expressed himself in his meetings with Kallergês.

Hasan Polatkan, the finance minister, announced the measure in the semi-official newspaper *Zafer* on November 24:

> The Government immediately, on the day after the grievous events of September 6, had declared, with certainty, that all those who suffered damages would be compensated. To this end, the newly formed Aid Committee had urgently begun its labors and began to assist those in immediate need by means of the funds it had raised from the Mayor's office, the Chambers of Commerce, the banks and the Red Crescent. Thus there were compensated [*sic*, this passage utilizes "assistance" and "compensation" interchangeably] 2,735 individuals and three institutions.
>
> In addition, there commenced the compensation of those who had submitted claims for damages, on the invitations to do so through the radio and the press. Up until today, 2,133 of them were fully compensated.
>
> Parallel to the activity of the Aid Committee the Government also began to take measures for dealing with those damages which it has not been possible to compensate by the [original public] fundraising.…
>
> Because many of those who suffered damages are now subject to taxation, they have been invited to submit, within a set period of time, the appropriate papers on the basis of which the relevant damages can be ascertained. Thus, some have submitted their claims to the Tax District to which they belong, and others who are foreign citizens have sent their claims to their embassies. A group of fifty Tax Inspectors has been established that will examine the claims submitted and will estimate the actual percentage of their claims that constitute the true damages.

[106] Ypourgeion Exôterikôn, Istanbul, Dispatch No. 1981, November 22, 1955.

As I have mentioned above, the Government will prepare the appropriate draft bill, to be submitted to the National Assembly, for all those damages which it has not been possible to cover through the fundraising among our people and institutions.[107]

Menderes acted promptly following the meetings with Kallergês since, in addition to consistent Greek pressure, the upheavals within his own party had caused him great concern. In his efforts to establish rigid control of the DP, however, Menderes had imposed a strict discipline that was anything but democratic. Conditions within the party were such that any criticism of the government was characterized as an attack and, as such, was actionable by the DP's disciplinary and central committees. This situation had come to a head with the pogrom and threatened the party's very existence. The resignation of nineteen members because of their arbitrary condemnation by the two committees in question led to a new political party that now threatened to attract even more DP members. The Group of Nineteen now demanded legislation or a judicial ruling that gave DP members the right to defend themselves against charges raised by party disciplinary and control mechanisms, or, as they called it, "the right of proof" (*ispat hakkı*). Furthermore, toward the end of October, Menderes had persuaded his party, without any significant debate, to introduce a bill in parliament that would have ensured Menderes's absolute control, both of his party's members and of their presence in parliament. According to this measure, all deputies who were either removed or retired from a party were automatically expelled from the national assembly. Thus, the internal affairs of the governing party and the state would become identical.

Once out of the *Demokrat Parti*, the Group of Nineteen founded the Freedom Party. The discontent within the DP finally boiled over in the party caucus of November 29, which Menderes had tried to head off several days earlier. Kallergês, who had followed the course of the party crisis closely, reported that, three days before the scheduled meeting, procedures had been initiated to remove Mükerrem Sarol from the party. His removal was crucial as he was one of Menderes's closest colleagues and advisors. According to the newspaper *Vatan*, he was accused of factionalism and—this is significant—opposed to "the right of proof." Specifically, he was charged with persuading Menderes to embrace his opinion, which led the central committee to oppose it also. This, the charge went on to state, resulted in the removal of the Group of Nineteen. Finally, Sarol was accused of debasing the name of the

---

[107] Greek Embassy, Washington, No. 5067/B/29, December 17, 1955, which contains a copy of Polatkan's announcement, sent by the Greek Embassy, dispatch No. 3585.

party by having introduced the law on the expulsion of deputies. Kallergês commented that, "It is clear that the removal of Mr. Sarol was intended to calm the Group of Nineteen Assemblymen who had split off, and...formed the Freedom Party....But even more so, the intent...was to halt the massive transfer of *Demokrat Parti* Assemblymen to the new party. This danger which threatens the *Demokrat Parti* is a reality."[108]

Menderes's government was thus forced to resign as a result of the party caucus's stormy session. Both the majority's discontent and its vehemence completely disarmed Menderes, as the attacks against certain key ministries were rapid and intense. It is true that the corruption in three ministries in particular had become scandalous and widely known: those of Sıtkı Yırcalı (commerce minister), Polatkan (finance minister), and Zorlu (acting foreign minister), who also sat on the critical exchange (currency) committee and so controlled all applications for currency exchange and import permits.

The corruption in granting import permits was especially flagrant, as was manifested in the importation of trucks and tires from East Germany. Despite the shortage of foreign exchange, applications for these imports were approved for a number of large companies, which derived massive profits from the enterprise. The imported tires were practically useless, so the operation was essentially a swindle of the Turkish public. Among the many bids for import licenses to purchase the tires, the only one granted was to a certain Mr. Soyungenç, who turned out to be related by marriage to Polatkan. Most of the political fallout at the party caucus fell on Zorlu's head, however, as he was involved in many scandals, with the East German truck-and-tire episode being only one. His colleagues charged that he had taken huge bribes from the French company that had been contracted to build the Gediş dam—5 percent for himself and 5 percent for the DP—and that he had sent his mistress on expensive shopping junkets to Paris where she frequented the

---

[108] Greek Embassy, Washington, Dispatch No. 3653, sent from Ankara on December 3, 1955; for the characterization of the domestic politics of the issue, Karakuş, *40 yıllık*, p. 289: "In October 1955, the Demokrat Parti suffered a great split. This had been long awaited. They had given their heart to the Demokrat Parti but they could not now find even a part of it. Having been named the 'Founders,' Bayar, Menderes, Köprülü, and Koraltan during the years of opportunity, they now renounced the promises they had given to create a society with democratic rights and freedoms. But, from the time that they acceded to power each day they approved measures to limit these rights and freedoms and soon they opened the road to great troubles within the party." Much remains to be studied and written on the *Demokrat Parti* and Menderes, but the following are helpful: Emrullah Nutku, *Demokrat Parti neden çöktü ve politika'da yitirdiğim yıllar 1946-1958 siyasi anılarım*, Istanbul, 1979; Ahmed Hamdi Başar, *Demokrasi Buhranları*, Istanbul, 1956; Metin Toker, *Demokrasimizin İsmet Paşalı Yılları 1944-1973. DP Yokuşu aşağı 1954-1957*, Ankara, 1991; and Rıfkı S. Burçak, *On yılın anıları (1950-1960)*, 1998.

establishments of the French *grands couturiers*.[109]

The caucus finally demanded the resignation of the entire government, which is what occurred. For the moment, the party had asserted itself against its leader and the leaders of the government, and Menderes's position was immeasurably weakened. Yet the prospect of İnönü waiting in the wings, and the possibility that the DP would lose its power and authority, forced it to reconfirm Menderes as leader and to allow him to form a new government without, to the degree possible, the other ministers who had also resigned. (An interesting note to Zorlu's political collapse as acting foreign minister was the charge that his corruption was so shameless that he had managed to arouse the mistrust of the US government. A reason that Ankara had failed to receive the $300-million loan it had sought from Washington, critics alleged, was Zorlu's widespread reputation for corruption.)

The fall of Menderes's government aroused Greek political sensitivities regarding the ability and willingness of any Turkish government to pay swift and just compensations for the destruction of September 6-7. There were few Greek politicians who were not glad to see the removal of the man who had treated them so arrogantly. At the same time, however, they understood that this would have no effect on the Cyprus issue, for example, and that it was all only a matter of domestic Turkish politics.

Menderes now had to form a new government, with new ministers and new and more liberal governance. British ambassador Bowker, in his annual report to London, was skeptical of this new and "reformed" government, however.

> The new Government's programme expressed the intention of introducing certain more liberal political measures, and bills were soon prepared to restore the right of proof in the case of slander, to repeal illiberal amendments in the Electoral Law which were introduced in 1954, and to increase the pensionable period for Government officials to 30 years, thus giving judges, in particular, more security of tenure. There were also references to the possibility of setting up a Committee to study Constitutional reform. These developments were hailed by some sections of the press and public as marking a return to a more democratic form of

---

[109] For the evidence and charges in the party caucus, Greek Embassy, Washington, Ankara, No. 3644, December 12, 1955, which is included in Athens to Washington, No. 53060/T/2, December 10, 1955; Greek Embassy, Washington, Ankara to Athens, No. 3653, December 3, 1955, which includes Athens to Washington, No. 53086/T/2, December 10, 1955; Greek Embassy, Washington, Athens to Washington, No. 33050/T/2, which includes Istanbul to Athens, No. 2072, December 3, 1955; Ypourgeion Exôterikôn, Istanbul to Athens, No. 2032, November 30, 1955; and Ypourgeion Exôterikôn, Ankara to Athens, No. 1323, December 12, 1955.

government, but doubts remained in many quarters about the real extent of the Prime Minister's change of heart. And indeed by the end of the year it could not be said that he had given convincing evidence of such a change.[110]

Thus with no prospect of real change, Menderes prepared for the parliament's vote of confidence. As he feared, it was to be as stormy as his own party's caucus, but the issues were to be more sharply drawn and set against a much broader perspective. Although the favorable vote was a foregone conclusion because of the DP's huge majority, it is nevertheless of interest and germane to our subject. İnönü, as leader of the opposition, made the first speech, a detailed and long address that attacked every major aspect of Menderes's premiership. Attributing the fall of the government to the badly damaged economy, he also attacked the increasing abuses of government and violation of democratic rights. Referring to Menderes's foreign policy toward Cyprus, Greece, the Balkans, and the Baghdad Pact, he pointed out the immeasurable harm it had caused Turkey's national interests. He warned parliament not to fall into the hands and control of bodies extraneous to it—a clear reference to the machinery of the *Demokrat Parti*—and devoted considerable attention to the pogrom of September 6-7, observing that there had still been no precise explanation of the events and that, although three months had passed, nothing had yet been resolved. Blaming Greece in part for the Cyprus imbroglio, he did not spare Menderes either:

> There was thus created the tense situation toward which the Prime Minister's speech of August 24 contributed. In the London meetings neither side avoided exaggerations. Nevertheless Greece, whose prestige was shaken by the myth circulating that [the Turks would be] massacred in Cyprus on August 28, took all necessary measures to protect against [similar] episodes. In contrast our Government remained under the burden of the events of September 6-7.

Then turning to Menderes's "fickle foreign policy," İnönü compared Menderes's August 24 remarks, in which he had attacked Greece as though the two countries were at war, to the Turkish prime minister's remarks on September 21, when he had said he would cut off the tongue of anyone who spoke against Greece. He also accused Menderes of imposing martial law for such a long period in order, primarily, to stifle dissent. He then made a stinging attack: "Mr. Menderes and Mr. Köprülü had acknowledged, from the podium [on September 12] that they had been informed ahead of time

---

[110] TNA:PRO, Ankara, No. 5, January 16, 1956.

as to the events that were about to unfold. Thus Mr. Adnan Menderes bears most serious responsibility for the events of September 6-7. Consequently, it is necessary that he be removed from the Government and from the office of Prime Minister."[111]

Four days later, Kallergês reported a particularly painful defeat for Menderes in parliament (December 20) that concerned Zorlu, Polatkan, and Yırcalı, whose fates had not been settled at the long parliamentary session of December 16:

> During yesterday's stormy session, the National Assembly decided, by an overwhelming majority, to send the former ministers of Foreign Affairs, Economics, and Commerce to the Assembly's Investigating Committee [and to indict them]. They did this despite the wishes of the Turkish Prime Minister, who had asked that they be sent to the Disciplinary Committee of the Demokrat Parti.
>
> Mr. Menderes, disturbed once more by the serious blow of disobedience from among the members of the Demokrat Parti, and upset also by the irritation of Turkish public opinion on the trial of the Turkish consul of Thessalonikê, summoned the Greek member of the Turkish General Assembly, Mr. Chatzopoulos. He asked him to go to Greece immediately and thus to set before you [Karamanlês] verbally, the difficulties that the Turkish Government is encountering. And, he asked that you, in understanding these difficult circumstances, make every effort to lower the tension in Greek-Turkish relations....
>
> Mr. Chatzopoulos tonight departed for Istanbul and thence will proceed by plane to Athens.[112]

Menderes's desperation over his own political future is quite evident. On the other hand, Karamanlês had by now despaired of Turkish compensation to the pogrom's victims, and had already given instructions (on December 12) to Greece's representative to NATO to inform Köprülü (who had been reappointed foreign minister after Zorlu's removal at the end of November) that relations between Greece and Turkey were on the verge of degenerating into a more dangerous confrontation:

---

[111] Ypourgeion Exôterikôn, Athens to KYP, No. 55405/7.4, Ep., January 2, 1956, to which is attached the Greek ambassador's report on the discussions of the National Assembly, document No. 3780, January 17, 1956, during the long session on the vote of confidence in the new Menderes government.

[112] Ypourgeion Exôterikôn, Ankara to Athens, Dispatch No. 3799, December 21, 1955; another six members of the *Demokrat Parti* were to bolt and join the Freedom Party.

Having ascertained the continuing reluctance and the lack of even the most elemental good will from the side of the Turkish Government in regard to honoring their obligations and to carrying out their oral promises for the compensation of the victims [of September 6-7], we must take all possible measures. We think it would be well...that you speak with Mr. Köprülü and ask him to find a manner of rapid and effective solution of the matter. We ask that you emphasize, to him, that we consider as unacceptable the stance of the Turkish Government, which even after three months have passed since the tragic events, and despite the promises of Mr. Menderes, has taken not a single governmental measure nor has it dispersed even the smallest sum from the Public Treasury....The Greek Government...is obliged to inform the Turkish Government as to the serious consequences following upon the unjustified stance of Ankara. The Greek Government has been exposed to Greek public opinion which, justifiably, is troubled and is unable to understand the unacceptable delay.

Because of this, we can no longer tolerate such a situation and we demand an immediate settlement...so as to avoid any further unfavorable developments in our relations with Turkey.[113]

Alexandros Chatzopoulos's "informal" and "unofficial" visit to Athens had actually been initiated by Turkey's ambassador to Greece, who found his position in Athens increasingly difficult and ineffective. He advised Ankara to use Chatzopoulos as an intermediary for lessening the mounting pressures on Greek-Turkish relations and to alleviate the political crisis.[114] Charles Peake, the British ambassador, spoke with Theotokês on the twenty-ninth of the month and asked about the foreign minister's conversations with Chatzopoulos on the previous day. Theotokês replied that Chatzopoulos described the new Turkish government as shaky, and that the latter thought it quite unlikely that the bill on compensation would pass unless Greece quashed the judicial proceeding against the Turkish consuls in Thessalonikê. Theotokês added that the Greek government could not do this until the compensation bill had actually passed. Peake replied that:

...[T]his seemed to me frankly childish. Surely the Turkish Government could be told confidentially that proceedings against the consul-general would be quashed and they could go ahead with their legislation. He [Theotokês] said that he was seeing Mr. Hadjopoulos [*sic*] again in company with the [Greek] Prime

---

[113] Ypourgeion Exôterikôn, Athens to Paris, No. 53601/T.4, Ep., December 12, 1955.
[114] Ypourgeion Exôterikôn, Istanbul, Dispatch No. 1981, November 21, 1955.

Minister and would try to persuade Mr. Karamanlis to give
him [Chatzopoulos] a suitable message which he could take back
with him.[115]

The explosive device on the grounds of the Turkish consular complex in
Thessalonikê had been contrived and utilized to manufacture the excuse and
signal for the simultaneous outbreak of the organized destruction of Greek
property in both Istanbul and Izmir. Immediately after the explosion, technical
experts from the Greek armed forces had been called in to investigate the
incident. After a forensic examination, the investigators concluded that the
dynamite used could not have been thrown into the 3.5-meter-high walled
complex but must have been set on the ground by someone inside it. Further,
the two police officers on guard outside the walls had been in a position to see
if anyone had entered the complex, but had not observed anyone doing so.
Furthermore, the photograph that had appeared, crudely altered and falsified,
in the special edition of the Istanbul *Ekspres* on the afternoon of September
6 could not have reached Istanbul, been developed, and published in such a
short period of time, as there were no flights from Thessalonikê to the Turkish
city, and the drive by bus or automobile would never have made it in time
for the special edition. The Greek photographer who had been commissioned
to take the photograph, and others as well, was identified, and still had the
negative of the photograph used by the Turkish newspaper: he had been
commissioned to take the picture by the Turkish consul's wife some days
before as a "souvenir" of the couple's stay in Thessalonikê. The Greek military
investigators indicated that the explosion had been ignited by the lighting
of a slow-burning fuse placed on the ground. Hurling such an explosive at
a minimum height of 3.5 meters from outside would have constituted a
lethal danger to the man attempting to do so. Clearly, the evidence from this
series of observations and deductions was compelling (in fact, it was used
at Yassıada, when the Menderes government was found guilty of planning
the pogrom). It is curious that Menderes and other Turkish officials (and
particularly the *vali* of Ankara) had, early on, alleged that the "terrorists" who
had organized the pogrom in Istanbul and Izmir were the same ones who
had perpetrated the incident in Thessalonikê. In the light of all this (of which
both Menderes and the Turkish foreign ministry were, of course, aware)
the trial in Thessalonikê was of major concern to the Turkish government.
Turkey's intense efforts to have the case dismissed, and all the defendants
released, assumed much broader political significance, therefore, especially
because the Turkish government's connivance in this matter—a probability

---

[115] TNA:PRO, Athens, Dispatch No. 769, December 29, 1955.

broached in the confidential handwritten comments on documents of the Foreign Office—would have become apparent to one and all. Birgi's complaints to Geôrgiadês always included the "trumped-up" charges against the Turkish consuls in Thessalonikê as a major source of irritation.[116] What is less comprehensible is Peake's insistence that the Greeks had trumped up these charges in order to put more pressure on Turkey. The Southern office in London understood the situation far better than its representatives in Athens and Thessalonikê.

As soon as censorship was ended on December 19, the Anatolian News Agency announced the arrests of the Turkish doorman of the Thessalonikê consulate as well as of the student Engin, in connection with the explosion. Two days before, the Turkish consul-general and his assistant had also been charged and summoned to appear before a Greek court. As the consul-general refused to accept the summons to appear, it was attached to the door of the consulate. The Anatolian News Agency charged the Greek government, in turn, with manufacturing the case for political purposes.[117] On December 21, the agency announced that Turkey had warned Greece that should it persist in its present behavior and take any serious action against the consuls, Turkey would respond with its own drastic measures.[118]

It would thus seem that Chatzopoulos's "unofficial" visit to Athens had come at an opportune moment since, despite the fact that the positions of

---

[116] For the report of the military technical committee that examined the site of the explosion, Greek Embassy, Washington, No. 39435/Tourk. 4, Ep., September 17, 1955; for Birgi's complaints and charges, Ypourgeion Exôterikôn, Ankara, Dispatch No. 3061, October 10, 1955; Greek Embassy in Washington, No. 53082/T/4, Ep., December 10, 1955; and TNA: PRO, Athens, No. RG10344/6, January 4, 1956. The British ambassador in Athens followed the advice and "information" of the British consul in Thessalonikê in dismissing the charges against the Turkish consuls. But he seems to have done so under the persuasive influence of the Turkish ambassador in Athens, Settar İksel: "The formal charge against the Turkish Consul General can, as Mr. Wall points out, be dismissed almost without comment. On the face of it the indictment is absurd and my Turkish colleague [Ambassador İksel] informed me that it rested entirely on the deposition of one man, who was serving a prison sentence of four years for fraud and who apparently came into contact with the kavass...in prison." On June 20, 1956, the British embassy in Athens sent the results of a part of the trial to London, Dispatch No. 1031/35/56, No. RG 10344/4: "The Appellate court of Salonika has now issued its decision on the supplementary enquiry by the investigating magistrate. The Consul-General Monsieur Mehmed Ali Belin and the Consul Monsieur Deni Kalp [*sic*], are acquitted as the enquiry did not produce sufficient evidence to justify their indictment. The Cavass, Mehmed Hassin, has been indicted on a charge of having perpetrated the explosion and of having explosives in his possession and the student, Oktay Engin, is also indicted on the charge of having instigated the Cavass."

[117] TNA:PRO, Ankara, No. RG10344/133, December 30, 1955.

[118] TNA:PRO, Ankara, No. RG1902/2, December 22, 1955.

Menderes and Karamanlês were, diplomatically, as distant as they could be, both men desperately wanted a solution. The Greek government decided to find an acceptable means of quashing the court proceedings in Thessalonikê (which it was to do after considerable delay), and Menderes submitted his bill on compensations on December 27, pushing it through committee until parliament finally enacted the legislation on February 29, 1956. The exchanges over the matter of Turkish governmental responsibility and compensation had taken about six months to resolve. In the eyes of the pogrom's victims, this had been an inordinately long time because of the dire circumstances into which they had been forced; for the Turkish justice system and the state administration, it was simply one more problem—in this case involving "troublesome" minorities—with which they had to deal. The long delays in passing some kind of legislation, however, were to be far outstripped by the malfunctioning of the compensation mechanism, which was to leave long-term injustice in its wake. It is one of the many unkind ironies of this entire history that these delays also heightened the animosity and suspicion between Turks, on the one hand, and the Greek, Armenian, and Jewish minorities as a whole, on the other.

On the morning of January 1, 1956, the Turkish ambassador in Athens called on British ambassador Peake, who conveyed the contents of their conversation to London:

> On the subject of Greco-Turkish relations he expressed himself as being encouraged at the way things now appeared to be moving. In the first place the Greek Minister of Foreign Affairs, appeared to be more flexible then he had been hitherto. He had told my Turkish colleague that the Government would not insist on the Turkish Government considering more than the passage of [the] bill about compensation for the victims of [the] riot as a condition for improvement of relations. At the same time the [Greek] Prime Minister had decided to quash proceedings against the Turkish consular officials in Salonica.[119]

THE LAW ON COMPENSATIONS

The Turkish ambassador had every reason to be pleased with the momentary lessening of bilateral political tensions, as Turkey was now freed of the specter of an open trial in which the matter of Turkish governmental responsibility in both the consular affair and the pogrom would have been at the center of worldwide attention. Henceforth, all attention focused

[119] TNA:PRO, Athens, Dispatch No. 774, January 1, 1956.

on the compensation law itself, which was so terse that it did not account for the specific processes, institutions, and committees by which it would function. It is obvious that at the time of its approval, hardly anyone knew how it would be implemented. This led to confusion and delay in both the finance and foreign ministries, which resulted in administrative paralysis. The law consisted of a very brief statement and contents that articulated its basic principles.

> Official Gazette #9247—January 3, 1956
> Law regarding compensation to be paid to persons who suffered loss during the disturbances in Istanbul and Izmir on September 6/7, 1955.
> Law No. #6684
> Article 1. The Government is authorized to pay compensation to persons with actual and judicial status who suffered loss during the disturbances in Istanbul and Izmir on September 6/7, 1955, in accordance with the principles accepted by the Council of Ministers. The total amount will not however exceed 60 million Turkish Lira.
> Article 2. Payments under the above Article will be made by Treasury Bonds, free of interest and payable within one year, to be issued by the Ministry of Finance.
> Article 3. Bonds which are not presented for payment after one year from the validity date of the Bond will be subject to prescription in favor of the Treasury.
> Article 4. This Law will come into force from the date of its publication.
> Article 5. The provisions of this Law will be executed by the Council of Ministers.
> February 29, 1956[120]

The typed comments attached to the copy of the English translation of the law are of some interest. The commentator notes that compensation will not be paid for losses due to theft or for losses of precious objects. Although the commentator tends to present the Turkish plans for payment as substantial, he ends his comment by stating that, "…we know that Turkish [i.e., Turkish citizens' and therefore primarily minority] claims were being scaled down…." The paralysis of action and administrative confusion were reported by the British embassy to London on April 25, 1956:

---

[120] TNA:PRO, Ankara, Dispatch No. 1491/13/56, No. RK10110.8, March 6, 1956; on the same day, the parliament passed a bill that referred to Paragraph 2 of Law No. 6684, namely, that funds paid out by the Istanbul aid committee were freed from inheritance and transfer taxes.

We learned from Istanbul in March that no compensation had
been paid to British or other foreign nationals; that the Istanbul
Relief [Aid] Committee were awaiting instructions from the
Ministry of Finance to deal with the smaller claims; and that the
Ministry of Finance Inspectors (paragraph 6 of our letter under
reference) were equally awaiting instructions to deal with the
larger claims.

The Ambassador therefore left an Aide Memoire with the
Secretary General of the Ministry of Foreign Affairs on March
29, asking if the necessary instructions would be issued shortly,
and the Counsellor followed this up with the Acting Head of
2nd Department at the Ministry of Foreign Affairs, Mahmut
Dikerdem, on April 25.

Dikerdem said that our lists, in common with those
submitted by other Missions, had been sent to the Ministry of
Finance where they were being examined.

The counsellor expressed the hope that an early reply would be
forthcoming and Dikerdem gave the conventional assurances.[121]

Some administrative order was brought to the chaotic situation with a
decree in the first half of July. The text was lengthy (six pages, single-spaced),
but so bureaucratic that it was often unclear, although it did describe the
processes and stages, as well as the various bodies that would be involved in the
statement, assessment, and final judgment on compensation to be paid in any
given case. The decree consisted of twenty-one articles, which were gathered
under four separate sections: the first delineated the general provisions of
the compensation procedures; the second was concerned with the process of
assessing losses; the third defined the authority(ies) responsible for assessment
of damages; and the fourth and final section was entitled, simply, "Payment."
The structure set up within the ministry of finance was now established,
although the work of assessment and payment was to drag on very slowly over
the next two years and, in some cases, into the early 1960s.[122]

---

[121] TNA:PRO, Ankara, Dispatch No. 1491/18/56, No. GK10110/9, April 25, 1956.

[122] TNA:PRO, Ankara, Dispatch No. 1491/27/56, No. RK10110/13, July 24, 1956; these
claim files, crucial for the entire course of compensation, have not yet made their appearance
although similar documentation has appeared in regard to the damages and repairs of the
churches. Also, we have the entire list of British claims, but only some of the corresponding
payments.
The ruling's protocol code was,
"Decree No. 4/7474
O. G. No. 9345-10th July 1956,"
and began:
"On the strength of the letter dated May 6, 1956, No. 114415/24-7000 from the Ministry

of Finance, the Council of Ministers decided on June 19, 1956, in accordance with Article 1 of Law No. 6684, to put into effect the following Regulations regarding the principles determining the losses suffered by actual and legal persons during the incidents that occurred in Istanbul and Izmir on September 6-7, 1955."

The decree's first section defined the entities that qualified for compensation, whether actual or legal persons, as "those having suffered damages on September 6-7, 1956"; it also determined the type of items for which compensation was allowed. Article 4 of this section was detailed and described how decisions were to be reached on "the amount of loss to be paid":

The applicant had to prove that a formal application had been submitted to any of the following offices: *vilayet, kaymakamate, defterdarlık,* fiscal department of the compensation committee, or the Council of State (with proof provided from the respective office); and the loss was not to have been already paid by the compensation committee [!].

Foreign citizens' applications were to be on record in the ministry of foreign affairs, etc.

• If legal bodies, trusts (*vakıflar*), churches, hospitals, and schools had not already applied, they had to do so at the office of the *defterdar* within one month. (Thus, there is already an implication that these institutions were not to be paid directly, but that the department of the Istanbul *vakıflar* would undertake the cost of repairing and rebuilding them.)

Article 5 of this section then traces the routing of applications, which was evidently a complex and not often uniform procedure. The applications made to the various offices were to be "examined by the Inspectors of the Ministry of Finance and/or by the Accounts Experts…[and] forwarded to the Commissions through the *defterdarlık*…together with the investigation reports within thirty days…." The procedures were similar for foreign citizens, except that their records were distributed through the foreign ministry to the commissions, which are later defined (Section Three, Article 13) as the three-person bodies estimating the damages and deciding on the amounts to be paid. Finally, the first section stipulated that "a number is given and a file made out for each application sent to the Commissions."

The second section set the principles that determined the extent of losses. While the "standard" procedure here (Article 6) is neither exact nor completely clear, it seems to have involved a first stage of examination in the case of applicants with the "required books and documents," in which the inspectors of the finance ministry and/or the "accounts experts" examined the declarations of loss and all other relevant materials, and then—if necessary—further examination by an estimates commission. It then appeared, although the text is ambiguous, that this commission returned the case file to one of two initiating offices for "the period for the examination and delivery of the report [to] be decided." If the combination of processes above could not determine loss and payment, then Article 8 (below) would apply.

Article 7 listed the procedures to be applied when the applicant was able to furnish books and documents for:

• loss ensuing from the destruction of or theft from a safe;
• goods that were totally damaged;
• goods that were partially damaged;
• amortization for total damage;
• amortization for partial damage.

In the case of damage to church property, the *vakıflar* allowed an *ilave* (inflationary adjustment) each year. In Article 8, the decree went on to enumerate ten measures to assist assessors in resolving those cases in which preliminary examinations and estimates had been inconclusive.

Section Three defined the authority of certain offices to estimate and determine compensation. More important, it created the estimates commissions:

Article 13 stated that within fifteen days from the date on which the regulations came

From the archival evidence, it is difficult to detect any logic as to how a particular case was chosen or vetted. It is obvious, therefore, that no given group of applications, whether of Greeks or other nationals, was reflected in any special or predetermined manner in the vetting and payments processes. That is to say, the few statistics that have been available to this study indicate that individual claims from all groups were handled at random and over a long period. Britain attempted to monitor the procedures at regular and reasonable intervals. At the end of September 1956, the British embassy in Ankara still had no information on any sums being paid out to British claimants. Thus, over a year after the events, some six months after the enactment of legislation, and two and a half months after the cabinet's decree authorizing payment, there was no evidence that British claimants had received anything.[123]

On October 13, 1956, the British consulate in Istanbul reported on a conversation with the *defterdar* (on October 5) as to the status of British

into force, estimates commissions of three persons—each composed of a ministry of finance inspector, an accounts expert, and a treasury lawyer—would be constituted by the ministry of finance. These commissions would have the authority to examine, determine, and estimate the losses suffered during these incidents and to decide on the amounts to be paid according to Law No. 6684 [of February 28, 1956]. The inspector of the ministry of finance would preside over the commission[s].

The finance minister had complete jurisdiction over the estimates commissions, which had wide powers to request all papers and data, and call in other experts. Nonetheless, the commissions were not bound by any of this: "It [they] may reach a decision on the basis of the principle of a total estimate and by majority vote."

Article 16 listed eight items that the commissions were obliged to furnish when they delivered a final decision, of which the most important were: "The subject and quantity of the damage for which indemnification is based; the reason and points on which the determination and estimate are based; the amount of loss to be paid." On completing a particular case, the commission was required to sign its decision and return it with the file to the local *defterdarlık*.

The fourth and final section was entitled, simply, "Payment." Article 18 ruled that the *defterdarlık* must, within thirty days of receipt of the documents and decision of the commission, inform the person concerned, after which the latter needed to apply to the same office. If the case had been decided favorably, the applicant was then paid in cash or treasury bonds (and could also request a copy of the decision). Article 19 differentiated between "ordinary" damage claims and those of certain institutions "such as churches, schools, and hospitals," whose compensation might be "undertaken by the General Directorate of the *Vakıflar*…through the local *Defterdarlıklar*." This seems to indicate that, while the repairs on churches and other institutions were immediately handled by the department of the Istanbul *vakıflar*, the actual evaluations and payments went through the commissions, and probably from the amounts voted by the Turkish parliament on February 28, which would have meant a further reduction of the original damage claims. The sums indicated for rebuilding and repairing the churches were, in any case, quite limited given the extent of the damages (see Chapter 5).

[123] TNA:PRO, Ankara, Dispatch No. 1492/12/56, No. RK10110/16, September 26, 1956.

claims. The report is of some interest in that it begins to give a picture of the procedures (which is incomplete but nevertheless indicative of the process):

> When I saw the Defterdar on October 5, I asked him what progress was being made with the settlement of claims for compensation. He told me that six committees were at work in Istanbul, each one under an Inspector of Finances. They were vetting each claim and in many cases were interviewing the claimant in order to establish more correctly the value of stock in his shop on the night of the riot, and so on. Comparisons were also being made between the figure given for stock destroyed and the figure of the shopkeeper's annual turnover given in his tax-returns last year. Many such comparisons were proving to be very interesting. I asked when this vetting of claims should be finished and I was told in six weeks or in a maximum of two months.
>
> As far as the Defterdar knew, there had not so far been any trouble with claims submitted by British Subjects. There was not a special committee dealing with foreign claims and it was a matter of luck how the claims came up for scrutiny....His general line was to assure me that no difficulties would be made over British claims since he was sure that no exaggerated British claims would have been submitted.
>
> I have not yet heard of any BS [British subject] who has been summoned to appear before a Committee. I should add that it seemed pretty clear from the way the Defterdar spoke that no payment would be made until all the claims had been vetted.[124]

The few bits of information indicate that only six committees (the so-called commissions of three tax specialists mentioned in the cabinet decree in July) were present to face the literal deluge of foreign and local claims. Thus, these six bodies of a total of only eighteen men had to deal with many thousands of claims. The report's conclusion, that all claims would be paid at the same time, is not borne out by the evidence. The *defterdar*'s obliging reply, of only six weeks to two months, to the question of how long the vetting would take was clearly another variant of the standard and presumably reassuring answer that was always so useful in all bureaucratic parlance.

Almost three months later, on December 28, 1956, the British embassy updated the Foreign Office on the situation:

> We have continued to remind the Ministry of Foreign Affairs about the outstanding questions in our Aide-Memoire but so far without results.

[124] TNA:PRO, Istanbul, Dispatch No. 091/20/56, No. RK 10110/17, October 13, 1956.

Meanwhile we understand from Istanbul that the investigation commissions are still working; that they have so far vetted only 50% of the claims submitted; and that it will probably be about two months before this vetting process is completed for all claims. No money will be paid until the work of the commissions is finished. There has still, so far as we know, been no trouble over claims submitted by British subjects.[125]

It is clear, then, that by December 28, sixteen months after the pogrom, ten months after the compensation legislation, and six months after the cabinet decree on the evaluation commissions, there were still no payments forthcoming to British victims. The *defterdar* was again reassuring, claiming that it would all be done within two months and that some 50 percent of all claims had been vetted. According to the cabinet decree, however, once the vetting was over, the documents were to be returned to the *defterdar* and the claimant informed within thirty days where to apply for payment. None of this seems to have occurred as of the end of 1956, at least so far as British subjects were concerned.

The malfunctioning of the vetting-and-payment process is apparent in the length of time that it took to accomplish its purposes. (Since the archives that contain the extensive documentation issuing out of the entire process of investigation, assessment, and compensation have yet to see the light of day, one must extrapolate the nature and reality from the available evidence.) The most obvious purpose of this particular administrative apparatus was to deal with the claims for damages. But there were within this purpose, two additional political motivations. First, to satisfy the insistent Greek government and thus ease the pressure on the relations between the two countries; in the same line of thought was Menderes's desire to improve his government's image both domestically and internationally. The unspoken goal, however, was once more to institutionalize a major scale-down of damage claims in the final stage of a series of such scale-downs that had been initiated by the aid committee. The more these procedures were drawn out, the less actual value was restored to the victims, if for no other reason than the unceasing inflation of the Turkish lira. There is no other obvious reason for not having created more than six commissions to process the thousands of claims. In the end, the estimates equaled only a portion of these claims, and the actual amounts disbursed as final payments were only a portion of the "corrected" claims (an analysis that is borne out by the evidence, incomplete though it may be). In short, the final payments were so small that they

---

[125] TNA:PRO, Dispatch No. 1492/18/56, No. RK10110/18, December 28, 1956.

constituted the finale of the material destruction that occurred on the night of September 6-7, 1955.

On March 4, 1958, the British embassy in Ankara once more admitted that it was not sure of the status of claims two years after the legislation on compensations and some thirty months after the events. Although the report began by asserting that "it is more than likely that the…compensation by the Istanbul authorities is virtually completed," it then informed London that the embassy will ascertain from the local authorities if "the payment exercize [*sic*] has been completed." In effect, the *Annex* to the report (see Appendix E), listing the names of the forty-seven British subjects who applied for damages in Istanbul, indicated that only twenty-three of the forty-seven claims had been paid in full or partially. Thus, as almost half of the British claims had still not been paid at this late date, the report raised an important question for the first time: "Subsequently we must decide in the light of the information obtained, what action, if any, should be taken vis-à-vis the Turkish Government in regard to the claims which have only been partially settled."[126] The realities of Turkish intent were apparent once more, despite all the rhetoric about full, just, or rapid compensation. Notwithstanding the soothing replies of Dikerdem or the *defterdar* that there was no foreseeable difficulty with the British claims; that British claimants had not indulged in exaggerating or bloating their applications; and, as Köprülü had assured Kallergês, that the amount of TL50 million would be sufficient for the claims (and supplementary funds would be appropriated if it wasn't), the commissions were to prove relentless in slashing claims.

From this *Annex*, updated to March 4, 1958, we see that, of the TL1,681,250 in claims submitted by forty-seven British citizens in the Istanbul area, the finance ministry and its evaluation commissions completed procedures and payments for twenty-three. Of these, far and away the largest claimant was Caraco & Co, with damages of TL942,500, for which it received only TL172,712, or 18.3 percent of the claim. Was the payment diminished some 81.7 percent because it was so high? Let us look at how, *grosso modo*, the other twenty-three smaller claims fared. They equaled a total of TL379,055, but received only TL92,986, or 24.5 percent, a percentage only slightly higher than that for Caraco & Co. This again amounts to a reduction of some 75.5 percent. When the claims of these two groups are combined, they amount to TL1,321,555, on which the finance ministry paid only TL265,698, or about 20 percent. Again, that is a reduction of some 80 percent for twenty-three claims.

There is a salient element missing from the British report, however. The

[126] TNA:PRO, Ankara, Dispatch No. 1492/12, March 4, 1958.

evaluation commissions were supposed to inspect the applications files to see if the estimates were correct, but the British document reveals only the final amount of compensation. Was it the same as the "true" assessments of the commissions? Or were there actually two different figures? The question is obviously relevant to the analysis of the entire process. What was the real point to the exercise, and what were the politics and economics behind it? Finally, how did the victims see the procedure?

Not a great deal can be gleaned from the sources presently available. Nevertheless, there are certain indications that one must examine closely. From the rather small number of interviews that have been published, the following cases are relevant as partial evidence of the nature of "compensation." The first is the testimony of H. H. on Balat cited extensively in Chapter 3. He mentioned the area's four communities: Jews (four synagogues), Armenians (one church), Muslims (three mosques), and Greeks (three churches). He states that forty Greek shops were looted and destroyed, giving the names of the owners, businesses, and locations. He was even a member of the DP (and attended the third trial at Yassıada in 1960). In short, he is extremely well-informed and precise, and he obviously experienced the violence personally. It was he who made the accusations against the local Turkish leader and organizer of the destruction in Balat, a certain Talat Bey, which led to his arrest. His terse comment on compensations is striking: "The Turkish State compensated us for almost 10 percent of the damages that were suffered."[127] The second testimony is that of Dêmosthenês Th., who not only refused to reveal his name and address, but also the area in Istanbul in which he lived. Having closed his shop, he and his wife went home early, having been warned about what was about to happen. His store was looted and then caught fire. He ran back to his shop because the safe had a large amount of money in it (as it was the beginning of the month). On arrival, he found the safe opened, thrown into the street, and the money gone. He managed to save only the deeds that had recorded the shop's sale to him. Looters even chased him as he ran back to his home:

> I was completely destroyed. The damages amounted to about 16,000 Turkish liras. Even though all these data were recorded in writing, I was not paid compensation. After some months, they summoned me with other Greeks, Armenians and Jews, and they paid me damages of only 1,000 Turkish liras, telling me that indeed this was very little. I could, if I wished, take it, or not. I accepted the money so that I could begin, again, from the

[127] Tsoukatou, *Septemvriana*, pp. 127-131.

beginning. I signed a piece of paper which they would not allow me to read.[128]

The rate of compensation (or, rather, "aid") was 1/16 or 6.25 percent. Safes being opened by acetylene torch was a common crime during the pogrom, and as the events transpired at the beginning of the month, the pogromists often found plenty of cash in the safes that were robbed. This was one of the more difficult aspects of proving actual loss of cash; the cabinet decree went into considerable detail on the calculation of such losses, but it was done, more or less, at the partial or complete expense of the businessperson.

These first two reports dealt with damages to businesses. The two that follow deal with damages to dwellings, and were initially cited, more extensively, in Chapter 2. The first one comes from Petros Sarantês, who lived in Bakırköy:

> ...[T]he vandals, under the leadership of a young newspaper-seller, then went off to the Greek dwellings. They looted and wrecked about ten of them. I think that our house was the first....It was an old wooden, two-storey house with a very large garden. They smashed the door, wrecked and then looted it.
>
> My parents and I exited from the back door into the garden and passed the night up in the trees....
>
> Some days later the *muhtar* visited us...to express his sorrow. A month later, he gave me a remuneration that was merely symbolic. I think it was just enough to repair one broken window....[129]

The second account is that of Gedikoulianê Iôannidou-Môysidou; here again is part of her testimony from Chapter 2: "When we went to see our store...a great catastrophe! They had said they would reimburse us for the damages down to the last dime. Unfortunately, none of this happened. And even if a few received compensation for damages, this was not enough to buy a candle for the church."[130]

The case of the Greek storeowner, Athênodôros Tsoukatos, was also briefly examined in Chapter 2. Owner of the Eifel store in Galata and also part-owner of the clothing store Great Ekselsiyor in the Tünel district, his story is illustrative. Both stores suffered general destruction and thorough looting, so that all their ledgers disappeared, along with their goods. In the Great Ekselsiyor, the damages were estimated at TL300,000. But since Tsoukatos

---

[128] *Ibid.*, p. 159; this probably refers to the period during which the aid committee was active.

[129] *Ibid.*, pp. 161-162, again a reference to the aid given by the few organizations that were activated by the government immediately after the violence.

[130] *Ibid.*, p. 100.

was unable to present his books, he received no compensation whatever. Strangely, however, the commission found enough "evidence" to level an additional TL100,000 fine on his profits! Consequently, as Tsoukatos relates, he had to sell the building of his Eifel store to pay this new, added debt, but as this, too, was not enough to cover the new taxes levied against him by the commission, his furniture and even his bed at home were confiscated.

The insufficiency of the reparations came as no surprise to the Greeks. There were Greek businessmen who refused even to apply, since they knew that, even in the best of circumstances, the effort would not be worth the reward.[131] In some cases, the Greek owners themselves undertook the restoration and restocking of their stores. Further, as happened with Tsoukatos, the commission could rule against a claimant and simply impose additional taxes on the ailing business. By mid-September 1955, the Greek government had sent officials to investigate the issue of compensations. In no case did they find any payment larger than 20 percent of a claim.[132] Although no complete catalogue of all these processes of claims, assessments, and payments has yet come to light, we have not only the list of British citizens, but a partial list reproduced by Chrêstidês of Greek *établis* claimants who received payments (Table 27A).

Chrêstidês's data give us a comprehensive picture of the mechanics for vetting and scaling down the original claims of the pogrom victims. After the submission of the Greek claims to the courts, the latter pared them down by TL1,359,011.97 from the sum of the original forty-two claims of TL3,433,444, which amounted to a 40-percent reduction. Despite the legal standing of the awarded sums, a second and even more drastic reduction followed, however. The commissions cut another TL1,560,181.03 from the already lowered total sum of TL2,074,432.03. Thus, the final sum paid out to the victims was TL514,249, which represents a total reduction of 85 percent from the original claims. Moreover, most of these savagely reduced claims were to be paid in treasury bonds redeemable one year later, without interest. Upon return of the files to the *defterdar*, the latter was to notify each claimant within thirty days, after which the claimant had to apply again to the *defterdar* for the issuance of the treasury bond.

The archives of the Greek foreign ministry confirm and enrich Chrêstidês's list of compensated Greek nationals. One catalogue (reproduced in Appendix F) enumerates 220 such cases. Arranged in alphabetical order

[131] TNA:PRO, Ankara, Dispatch No. 202E (1491/123/55); No. RG 10344/70, October 5, 1955.
[132] See above, in the text, for reference to the "war" on compensations.

Table 27A: Greek *établis* claimants who received compensation

Name	Type of business	Amount of claim (TL)	Estimate of court specialist (TL)	Final estimate of commission (TL)	Court estimate as % of original claim	Final payment as % of court estimate	Final payment as % of claim estimate
Anastasiadês Iôannês	electrical goods	105,477.00	29,980.00	29,980.00	28.0	28.0	
Vasilakos Vasileios	watchmaker	49,500.00	10,000.00	10,000.00	20.0	20.0	
Veletsos Kleovoulos	cobbler	50,000.00	26,500.00	12,000.00	53.0	45.0	24.0
Veltras Epameinôndas	cloth	26,312.00	11,000.00	3,361.50	42.0	31.0	13.0
Volakês Alexandros	grocer	23,935.00	5,000.00	5,000.00	21.0	21.0	
Gasparakês Dêmêtrios	perfumery	50,000.00	25,000.00	13,000.00	50.0	52.0	26.0
Gizês Kôn/tinos	leather goods	51,300.00	38,000.00	15,000.00	74.0	39.0	29.0
Delapollas Petros	metallurgist	145,000.00	68,000.00	20,000.00	47.0	29.0	14.0
Dismanês Dêmêtrios	grocer	24,060.00	2,350.00	2,350.00	9.8	9.8	
Exarchos Anastasios	butcher	60,000.00	12,500.00	8,000.00	21.0	64.0	13.0
Theocharês Anastasios	grocer	38,830.00	25,000.00	10,000.00	64.0	40.0	26.0
Istorios Grégorios	fashion	35,000.00	29,800.00	10,500.00	85.0	35.0	30.0
Kalogeras Michaêl	building materials	37,400.00	22,000.00	14,000.00	59.0	64.0	37.0
Karapiperês Kôn/tinos	cloth	66,000.00	27,000.00	11,000.00	41.0	41.0	17.0
Katsanos Nikolas	businessman	241,025.00	418,761.00	45,000.00	87.0	11.0	9.0
Katsanos Stelios	businessman	241,025.00					
Kozakês Athanasios	blacksmith	366,100.00	29,964.00	5,000.00	8.0	17.0	2.0
Kourtelês Geôrgios	corsets	281,098.00	281,098.00	60,000.00	21.0	21.0	
Kritsês Lênas	pastry shop	198,026.00		34,279.00	17.0		
Kônstantinidês Ermin	watches, glasses	116,108.00	86,700.00	18,000.00	75.0	21.0	16.0

Name	Business						
Kōnstantinidēs Kōn/tinos	cloth	126,512.00	115,000.00	42,500.00	91.0	37.0	34.0
Kōnstantinou Iōannēs	grocer	53,000.00	22,800.00	2,000.00	43.0	9.0	4.0
Lambropoulos Paikos	men's clothing	30,561.00	26,167.53	7,871.01	86.0	30.0	26.0
Liazē Argyrios	furniture	53,725.00	31,850.00	7,500.00	59.0	24.0	14.0
Liazē Siderēs	furniture	27,725.00	16,870.00	6,000.00	61.0	36.0	22.0
Magoulas Nikolaos	cloth	28,850.00	28,850.00	3,500.00	12.0	12.0	
Manikas Dēmētrios	electrical goods	259,643.00	239,463.00	30,000.00	92.0	13.0	12.0
Mauros Stylianos	shoemaker	55,545.00	34,740.00	2,000.00	63.0	63.0	4.0
Melas Nikolaos	tailor	44,492.00	42,000.00	12,752.20	94.0	30.0	29.0
Bayias brothers	furniture	88,635.00		10,000.00	11.0		
Bellas Pantelēs	grocer	20,850.00	17,860.00	4,500.00	86.0	25.0	22.0
Noios Nikolaos	buttonmaker	22,508.00	22,500.00	4,000.00	18.0		
Papavramidēs Agath.	grocer	16,620.00	12,335.00	2,000.00	74.0	16.0	12.0
Papathanasiou Kōn/tinos	jeweler	125,756.00	103,000.00	14,155.29	82.0	14.0	11.0
Parisēs Iōannēs	shoemaker	13,541.00	13,601.00	1,500.00	11.0		
Patounas Dēmētrios		60,000.00	54,698.00	4,000.00	91.0	7.0	7.0
Siōtēs Kōn/tinos	barbershop	12,308.00	8,400.00	1,500.00	68.0	18.0	12.0
Skarpelēs Achilleus	furnituremaker	83,257.00	33,701.50	5,000.00	40.0	15.0	6.0
Strakarēs Geōrgios	restaurant	50,472.00	48,694.00	10,000.00	96.0	21.0	20.0
Tsikos Apostolos	furnituremaker	24,249.00	24,249.00	8,000.00	33.0	33.0	
Chatzēs Athanasios	photography store	7,000.00	7,000.00	2,000.00	29.0	29.0	
Chrēstakēs Geōrgios		22,000.00	22,000.00	7,000.00	32.0	32.0	
Total		**3,433,445.00**	**2,074,432.03**	**514,249.00**	**61.0%**	**25.0%**	**15.0%**

(according to the Greek alphabet), it also records case numbers, original sum of damages, and final sums approved and paid, although it does not include the intermediate step of evaluation of damages by the courts and their real-estate specialists. A second register of claimants reproduced in Appendix F lists fifty-one cases of Greek nationals not included in the first list of 220. This catalogue records original claims, final payments, and final evaluations, but also includes figures and percentages of reduction of the original claims by the courts and their specialists. We thus get a statistical glimpse of the process of double reduction of the initial claims.

It is apparent from this second catalogue—and, as such, noteworthy—that the court proceedings and decisions of the court-appointed specialists were, with few exceptions, far more accepting of the original claims than the three-man tax committees. Clearly, these committees not only violated the courts' decisions, but had the power to do so, since, as in so many other areas of Turkish life, the courts did not have *de facto* authority to back up their decisions. It is also obvious that the role of the tax committees was not to render a just settlement; rather, it was to effect a systematic and radical reduction of the original claims. Decree 4/7474 of July 10, 1956, gave the commissions the final authority to determine evaluations and compensation—which is to say that it gave them the right to reduce the claims so drastically as to vitiate any sense of genuine compensation. Indeed, the commissions even violated the decree's specific provision of prompt payment once the final vetting was over. These delays entailed the further injustice of holding on to treasury bonds for one year without the accrual of interest. Furthermore, there was no specific provision for inflation in the decree and, as we shall see in the case of the damage claims for church parishes, whatever interest accrued to the amounts given by the state for church repairs was reimbursed to the state.[133]

Of the 271 cases of Greek nationals under examination in the two lists mentioned above, the claims came to TL9,876,332 for the first list and TL3,959,443.90 for the second, for a total of TL13,835,775.90. The payments, however, come to TL1,843,104.32 for the first list and TL738,845.65 for the second, for a total of TL2,581,949.97, or only 18.7 percent of the original claims.

These claims, and the evaluation and reduction processes to which they were subjected, present the analyst with important data for examining the Turkish government's policies on compensation, especially because they

---

[133] Chrêstidês, *Ekthesis*, pp. 210-211. The texts of the 220 and fifty-one cases, respectively, derive from loose, unnumbered, and largely undated documents sent to the Greek foreign ministry, undoubtedly by the Greek consulate in Istanbul. It is significant, however, that each of these 271 cases provides an official case number assigned by the Turkish department of taxation.

represent just over a quarter of the total number of claimants of Greek nationality. The claims presented by Britain, and the final payments for them, are also significant. Although small in number and without figures regarding intermediate court procedures, they nevertheless reveal that the Turkish government finally agreed to pay only 20 percent (or a total of TL266,053) of the original claims made by British subjects (which amounted to TL1,321,555).

Accordingly, the Turkish policy on compensations was actually, and no doubt intentionally, an apparatus meant to oversee the liquidation of what had become the Turkish government's debt. Did the victims have any recourse? The answer was forthcoming in the case of the Istanbul silver and crystal merchants Isaac and Raphael Caraco, who were Jews but also British citizens. As we have already seen, their firm had applied for damages through the British consulate and embassy. In their application, they had asked for compensation of TL754,742 (the figure of TL942,500 is also given in the sources), but the evaluation commission lowered it to TL172,712.[134] The Caraco firm decided to seek redress and so had the British consulate send their file, with an accompanying letter stating their case, to the Foreign Office in London. The letter asked the Foreign Office "kindly to oppose the decision of the Turkish Valuation Commission which wrongs our Company" and to "safeguard the interest of our Company by taking up our claim."[135] The letter pointed out both contradictions and illegalities in the compensation process. For example, the compensation award, dated April 17, 1957, was announced to them only on January 24, 1958, over nine months later, despite the clear instructions in the cabinet decree of July 1956 that claimants were to be notified of their awards within thirty days after the file had been returned to the *defterdar*. Isaac and Raphael Caraco also stated that their firm's account book and official papers were in order and had been presented in the due course of the procedures. According to their letter of appeal, however, the two government offices that dealt with their claim, the court-appointed specialist-expert and the commission, arrived at thoroughly contradictory conclusions.

> Whereas the Damage Valuation Commission's...report found that the records and accounts, which had not been damaged...were in order, and in spite of recording at end of page two of the report established by Court appointed experts and based on books...that

[134] TNA:PRO, Ankara, Dispatch No. 1492/23, No. RK1481/6, April 3, 1958. As the appellants note, there is a discrepancy between the two figures as to the amount of the original claim of the Caraco firm, which the commission's decision attempts to explain as, "[being] due to the fact that the first application included the loss of profit and moral damages."
[135] *Ibid.*

as per books records [*sic*], the stock held by our firm amounted to 663,754 Liras, it is stated at the conclusion [*sic*] part of the report without any material reason or supporting evidence being shown, that the stock in hand was worth TL150,000 only, which is in contradiction with the points they had themselves sanctioned in the same report....

The Valuation Commission in its report puts forward the fact that it does not appear from the report that the warehouse was visited by the surveyors appointed by the court to ascertain the stocks held as against the stocks shown in the legalized account books as per Art. 1 above, to justify the reduction in the amount shown in the books down to 150,000 T. Liras.

There is no reasonable and logical ground to assume—unless there is a definite proof to the contrary—that either the judges or the experts appointed by the court to ascertain and value damages suffered by us as a result of the case have not gone through and examined every place in our premises; in fact they have done so.

It is argued in the report that it would have been impossible for the whole of the goods kept in the warehouse to be destroyed in such a short time. This conclusion seems to have been reached by the Valuation Commission on the assumption that the only entrance to the warehouse would be through the shop. In point of fact this assumption is not in accordance with the actual state of things in view of the fact that the street door entrance at the back of İstiklal Caddesi was opened and that the contents of the warehouse were partly destroyed and partly lifted, so that this resulted in the total loss of the merchandise held in the warehouse. This was duly noted by Mr. Coppola of the British Commercial Attache's Office, who had been sent on the spot by the British Consulate General on 7th September 1955 in the morning to see things for himself.

The Caraco firm's letter was accompanied by an English translation of the commission's decision on the case. The claim was originally submitted on October 5, 1955, finally passed on to the commission on March 8, 1957, and finally decided on April 17, 1957, and the Caraco firm was finally notified only on January 24, 1958, some nine months after the commission's decision. In short, the firm was finally notified twenty-seven months from the date of its original submission, while its claims were cut by 78 percent.[136]

Aside from this inside view of the workings of the commissions that the Caraco case offers, it also raises the important issue of appealing the

[136] See footnote 134.

commissions' decisions. Actually, the British chancery in Istanbul had raised the issue with London, and then brought the question to the attention of the relevant officer in the Turkish foreign ministry, who confirmed that there had been many appeals of foreign citizens through their respective missions in Turkey and that they had all been forwarded to the finance ministry:

> But the answer of that ministry was that the law under which the Commissions to assess compensation were set up made no provisions for any appeal against the Commissions' Awards. Hence he could personally hold out no great hopes that anything could be done for the British claimant who wished to appeal....
>
> He agreed that if there was no provision for appeal it was difficult to see what was the purpose of allowing claimants to demand copies of the Commission's findings [such as that forwarded to the Caraco brothers]. In answer to a question he said that all the money voted for compensations arising out of the riots had not been exhausted; so the payment of further increased compensation is not ruled out purely by exhaustion of the funds.[137]

With a certain relief, the British Foreign Office accepted the opinion that the compensations law provided no avenue for appeal. Indeed, it did not provide any such possibility and all matters of final evaluation and payment were controlled by an administrative apparatus whose primary function was to reduce claims. The commissions were so parsimonious that, as late as April 1958, two years and seven months after the pogrom and over two years after the relevant legislation had been enacted, the slowly grinding bureaucracy had neither spent all the compensation funds nor vetted all the claims.

The analysis of the actual vetting, reevaluation, and payment of compensations has brought us to the end of a long and twisting road. From the first days of damage lists and estimates immediately following the events of September 6-7, 1955, to the beginning of the actual payments, close to three years elapsed. If one judges from the records of the department of the Istanbul *vakıflar* and the Greek Committee for Repair (*6-7 Eylül Hey'et*), the compensation was still in process even after the overthrow of the Menderes

---

[137] TNA:PRO, Ankara, Dispatch No. 1492/25, No. RK1481/6, April 30, 1958; the home office addressed a letter of instruction to the chancery of the British mission in Turkey: "Although you have been concerned in the collection and presentation of the claims of British subjects to the Turkish authorities, we assume that this was done mainly for reasons of administrative convenience and efficiency and that you have to date played no part in prosecuting the claims. Prosecution we understand has been left to the British subjects themselves....Therefore we consider that Caraco should press their own case and...exhaust the available Municipal remedies."

government. Every step of this long and detailed analysis has been difficult because of the inaccessibility of much relevant documentation. Nevertheless, the general outline of events, trends, and policies is clear. This holds true for the continually changing estimates and financial aspects of the damages, assessments, and payments, as well as for the policies of both the Greek and Turkish governments, which remained consistent and tempered only by daily conditions and reconsiderations of lesser and greater events and details. The extent and cost of damages began slowly to increase as more knowledge, and the specific consequences, of the destruction became known. Conversely, and more dramatically, the assessments of this damage began a downward spiral as the Turkish government became more conscious of the sheer cost of restoring what had been destroyed. Because little has come to light on this issue that is of an official nature, the analysis here has been shaped necessarily by the available evidence. In the end, the number of damaged and looted businesses must have been between 4,000 and 4,500, whereas about 1,000 dwellings were damaged and about 2,500 looted. The cemeteries, monasteries, schools, and other communal institutions that were damaged, looted, or completely destroyed were far smaller in number, while there were at least ninety-two churches and *agiasmata* that were damaged and/or destroyed (this issue will be treated in the next chapter).

The first estimates of damage were very large, ranging from several million to one or two billion Turkish liras. (Even under the black-market rate of nine Turkish liras to one US dollar—which was slightly over three times the legal, if completely unrealistic, exchange rate—TL2 billion amounted to roughly $220 million.) These were the estimates of the Turkish tax department and foreign banks in Istanbul. The Istanbul aid committee established on September 20, 1955, however, was obliged to raise funds (in effect, forced levies) from the private sector and, on instructions from Menderes, to pay damages primarily to Turkish citizens (including minorities). This indicated, from the beginning, that Menderes intended to dispense with the obligation of paying damages through the use of public funds. He insisted that there was no binding legal obligation on the Turkish government to compensate the victims of violence. Consequently, the aid committee's director began to enforce a grim policy of paying "aid" rather than compensation, which was quickly accompanied by the policy of systematically reducing the assessments of most of the initial claims.

The formal figures themselves illustrate the general and massive reductions of the initially anticipated compensations. It is obvious that private-sector levies could hardly meet the demands of the 7,186 Turkish nationals who submitted claims, to say nothing of the damages claimed by the churches and religious institutions. In the event, the aid committee's director explained that the group's payments were not intended as compensation, even at the vastly lowered total claims, but only as a small, partial, and temporary aid program to assist the victims in riding out the destructive aftermath of the events. Thus, by the end of July 1957, the committee had paid out only TL8,040,000 on TL28 million of total claims, and these only to the neediest Turkish nationals, that is, to those whose small claims fell into the two categories of TL1,000-TL5,000 or TL5,000-TL10,000 (and there is no evidence as yet that the total budget of the aid committee ever surpassed TL9.5 million). These smaller claims amounted to 40.2 percent of total claims of Turkish nationals, but their payment represented 84.7 percent of the entire aid-committee budget. The question arises, naturally, as to the disposition of the applications of the remaining Turkish nationals, whose claims exceeded TL10,000 and added up to a total of TL41,578,744. One assumes that most of these were dumped into the general compensation process and the appropriations provided by the law of February 29, 1956, and the cabinet decree of the same summer, which amounted to no more than TL60 million, which also had to cover the cost of repairs of churches, and the claims of other institutions and foreign citizens.

In this second period of reassessments and partial payments, the sum total of submitted claims must have run close to the following figures (in Turkish liras):

Table 27B: Total claims

	Claims (TL)	Budget (TL)	Sources of funds
7,186 Turkish nationals	69,578,744	9,500,000	private levies
1,296 Foreign citizens	34,035,479		
Religious institutions	?	10,000,000	Turkish government
92 Greek Orthodox			
religious institutions	39,045,065		
Secular property		50,000,000	Turkish government
Totals	142,659,288	69,500,000	

We see from the authorized budgets and (massively reduced) claims that the entire financial magnitude had shrunk greatly even before the individual claims (almost 8,500) were reevaluated and cut further. Before these reductions, the budgeted funds were approximately TL73 million under the estimated claims. Consequently, while the claims of British subjects were cut by 80 percent and those of Greek nationals by 81.3 percent, the claims of the 7,186 Turkish nationals were reduced by 86.35 percent. Without going into details here, the Turkish government allotted only TL10 million for the damages to all religious structures and institutions—or close to a 75-percent reduction. The details that emerge from the evaluation process, therefore, point to the system's ferocity, as well as to its obvious intent.

Clearly, therefore, although the Greeks won the diplomatic battle to force the Turkish government to proceed with compensation, the Turkish government won the war on assessments and final payments. Turkey rejected the Greek proposal of a mixed, five-member committee to carry out the evaluations. The law of February 29, 1956, and the decree of the same year intentionally avoided any mention of the right of appeal against the decisions of the evaluation commissions. Thus all attempts at appeal, particularly those of foreign missions, were rejected out of hand. Moreover, in almost every case, the commissions rejected the reduced estimates of the court-appointed specialists, and made even further and more drastic reductions in evaluations and final payments. The Greek government, however, saw the issue in a much broader context. It insisted on compensation for moral as well as for material damages, and, consequently, called for the exemplary punishment of those guilty of organizing and executing the pogrom. The moral damages, in other words, were as destructive as the material costs, but little attention has been paid to this aspect of the violence. It remains to consider the Greek demands for punishment of those responsible for the events of September 6-7, 1955.

TURKISH JUSTICE

Among the most frequent instructions flowing out of the Greek foreign ministry were the orders to the Greek ambassador in Ankara to update Athens on the progress of the court proceedings on this matter and to remind both the Turkish prime minister and foreign ministry that the just resolution of these proceedings was a precondition for reestablishing better relations between the two countries. Fundamental to any analysis of the judicial proceedings immediately following the pogrom are the extensive files, first, of the courts-martial established after the imposition of martial law and, second, of the civil courts that inherited the task of the military courts after martial law was lifted. Both sets of files are, unfortunately, currently unavailable. The more crucial files are undoubtedly those from the courts-martial, whose procedural rules prohibited public coverage of the proceedings since the cases were tried *in camera*. The verdicts of proceedings were announced tersely from time to time, through communiqués issued only to the press (this changed when the civil courts took over). It is hoped that future researchers will have access to the military- and civil-court files; in the present circumstance, reference will be made to the military communiqués and to Hulusi Dosdoğru's account of his own trial in 1956 in a civil court.

As the martial-law command began to wind down its operations (its authority was to expire in early February 1956), the military courts had to prepare to turn over their unfinished proceedings to civil courts. According to a US embassy dispatch, the acting minister of defense, Şemi Ergin, was summoned to parliament on January 20, 1956, to brief it on the work to date of the courts-martial. There, he presented some general statistical data:

Table 28: Cases related to participation in the pogrom

Arrested for suspected role in pogrom

In Istanbul	3,813
In Izmir	424
In Ankara	171
Total	4,408
Released	3,933
In Istanbul	3,525
Sentenced by military courts	228
Acquitted by military courts	61
Accused held for trial	288
Total	577

Cases turned over to civil courts

In Istanbul	394
In Izmir	134
In Ankara	162
Total	690 [138]

These figures are not internally consistent but give some idea of the scope of the numbers. The types of crimes for which some were convicted and others were still awaiting trial included destruction and looting of property, hostile action against foreign governments, murder, sabotage, seduction (rape), and communist propaganda. The author of this US report commented that, "Ergin's statement is of particular interest as it appears to confirm rumors that some incidents involving murder and rape did occur during the riots despite earlier statements to the contrary by other Government spokesmen." Among those arrested were sixty-seven persons suspected of being, or previously identified as, communists. Of these, twenty-six were found to have participated in the disturbances.

On February 11, 1956, the martial-law authorities sent a document

---

[138] National Archives, Foreign Office, Dispatch No. 332, Ankara, January 25, 1956.

summarizing their work to the civil courts investigating the pogrom. The military asked that twenty-four individuals (seventeen from Istanbul and seven from Izmir) be indicted for their responsibility for the events. The first part of this military report gave a short review of the Cyprus crisis and its beginnings. The second part attempted to make a case for Soviet sponsorship of *enôsis* in Cyprus. Part Three was an attack on the Cyprus is Turkish Association and its supposedly dominant role in the events of September 6-7. Part Four gave a chronological framework for the events, while Part Five referred to those points of the criminal code that were considered relevant. The charges and the names of the accused followed at the end of these twenty-one pages (see Appendix G).

This report was well-summarized by British ambassador Bowker in a dispatch he sent to London on February 21, 1956:

> You will see...that the blame for the riots has been laid on the "Cyprus is Turkish Association"; and that the Secretary-General of the "Cyprus is Turkish Association," Kamil Onal, is accused of being the ringleader even to the partial exclusion of the President [*sic*] of the Association, Hikmet Bil. The original version that the Communists were to blame has been dropped, presumably through lack of any corroboration, although the report makes the most it can out of Communist participation in the riots and their interference in the Cyprus problem generally, and underlines the communist contacts of Kamil Onal himself.[139]

What is striking is the complete silence on any intimation or even question of the role of the government or some element of the state, given the close relations among Menderes's government, Hikmet Bil, and the KTC. The well-organized nature of the pogrom is also passed over in silence. But as a highly placed military official remarked to a member of the American diplomatic staff in Istanbul, as reported by the US consul: "Perhaps indicative of the reasons for present public apathy is the informal personal comment volunteered by the Chief of Staff of the Martial Law Command to a senior member of the Consulate General staff. The Chief of Staff characterized the indictment and the proceedings as an outrage (*kepazelik*) and an attempt by the Prime Minister to relieve himself of the guilt which many believe he feels because of the disorders."[140]

By this time, Menderes's attempts to hide his own culpability and that of his government had become a matter of public discussion, particularly after

---

[139] TNA:PRO, Ankara, Dispatch No. 34, No. RR10110/5, February 21, 1956.
[140] National Archives, Istanbul, Dispatch No. 306, February 20, 1956.

the appearance of the article of the noted Turkish journalist Hüseyin Cahit Yalçın in the newspaper *Ulus*, which supported İnönü and the RPP. The article appeared rather soon after censorship was lifted and after İnönü's attack on Menderes in the debate preceding the vote of confidence of December 16. Yalçın, adhering closely to the unduly strict laws governing the media, launched his attack on Menderes by referring to the latter's own statements, as well as to those of Köprülü, both of whom had publicly stated that the government had known ahead of time of the planned demonstrations. Yalçın continued by remarking that there were sufficient numbers of police and gendarmerie in the city so that it should not have been necessary to call in the army hours later. Indeed, by twelve noon of September 6, the authorities had been notified of the explosion in Thessalonikê. Not only were security measures not taken, but the sizable forces on hand had refused to respond, both at the beginning and, in fact, throughout the disturbances. Both Istanbul's governor and the interior minister were well-informed but did nothing; and, although the attacks had begun before Menderes had even left the city for Ankara, he, too, did nothing. Thus, Yalçın asked, since Menderes had done nothing in the face of all this, should he not have been held responsible? Moreover, while martial law could punish looters, it could not bring legal action against the government: "The Commander of the Martial Law cannot issue a communiqué saying, 'I have arrested the Prime Minister.' We wonder if it is not for this reason that the Martial Law's investigations have been marking time for the past four months?"[141] Yalçın concluded:

> Is the Prime Minister's arrest necessary or not? Nothing can be said in this respect for the present, namely until the facts are exposed as the result of parliamentary investigations. But it is necessary to clarify the position and role of the Prime Minister, who was present from the very beginning of the incidents and who failed to show his existence before relieving the three commanders in Istanbul from their duties, expelling the district Governors, and conducting investigations concerning the Governors.
>
> How could Adnan Menderes be brought to Premiership, after his whole cabinet had changed and when he is suspected of being primarily responsible for the September 6/7 events? How can investigations be conducted concerning him as long as he remains Prime Minister?[142]

Yalçın had put his finger into the wound. That is to say, he exposed the

---

[141] National Archives, Ankara, Dispatch No. 309, January 13, 1956.
[142] *Ibid.*

complete dependence of judicial decisions, military and civil, on the whims of a prime minister who had created a dictatorial premiership and—although formally governing through parliament—had in reality enforced his will, and laws, through the *Demokrat Parti*. It was precisely for this enormous constitutional crime that he and his two ministers were executed in 1960-1961. Indeed the twenty-four indictments sought by the martial-law command were part of a larger cover-up through which Menderes sought to escape his own crimes.

The comments of the Foreign Office upon receiving Ambassador Bowker's observations on the martial-law command's report were very perceptive: "The Turkish Government will be hard put to place before the Grand National Assembly a convincing account of these trials, which are conveniently being held in camera, and the reasons for the absence of communists from the list of accused....This report will not please the Greeks and we can expect them to accuse the Turks of endeavoring to wriggle out of an uncomfortable situation at the expense of a few nationalists who were put up as a front for the misdeeds of those in positions of responsibility." A second commentator on Bowker's report made a similar, if more acerbic, evaluation of the entirety of the Turkish legal process: "This report is a miserable effort and will convince no one. It can be picked to pieces by any determined critic."[143] Adnan Menderes's ten-year rule as prime minister was a decade during which he accumulated oppressive dictatorial powers that in the end brought destruction not only to him and his associates, but also to what should have been the more normal democratic development of Turkish society. When one examines it closely, his arbitrary conduct was shocking, and ranked him with other such examples in the latter half of the twentieth century.

Understandably, the authoritarian tendencies of such a prime minister also manifested themselves in the everyday functioning of the judicial system. Of considerable interest is the analysis of the Turkish legal system submitted to the British embassy by J. W. Perkins on April 12, 1955. The report was sent to London by Bowker, who described Perkins as the honorary adviser to the embassy on Turkey's judicial system. Bowker wrote:

> Mr. Perkins is shortly retiring from the practice of law and this memorandum is in the nature of a swan song. It is as interesting as it is depressing....
>
> Mr. Perkins' memorandum is mainly concerned with civil proceedings and on this I have very little to add....
>
> There is one...aspect of Turkish justice which concerns

[143] TNA:PRO, Ankara, Dispatch No. 34, February 21, 1956.

this Embassy but is naturally not treated by Mr. Perkins in his memorandum. That is the readiness of the Government to use the processes of law for political ends.

The laws of any state may be expected to provide for its own security and when national issues are involved the main fault of Turkish justice in Western eyes is that it is a secret justice. Political trials of political offenders such as Communists are normally held in camera and there is no way of judging whether they are convicted on the kind of evidence that would convince a court in the United Kingdom or indeed on any evidence at all....Those who have been behind the Iron Curtain are struck by the similarity.

More open and more reprehensible is the Government's use of its influence in matters affecting relations between the political parties. For example, the recent crop of prosecution of journalists, though they were covered by the law were instituted by Ministers for political purposes....

Political interference with justice is naturally one of the main grievances of the opposition People's Republican Party since last summer when the Government passed a new law permitting the compulsory retirement of judges without reason given, after twenty-five years' service....The judges have no constitutional protection, and it appears that they now begin to receive political directives on how to deal with cases in their courts which they dare not resist. And the draft bill now before the National Assembly... which will increase the powers of the judges, already wide, to order arrests without trials is likely, in practice to extend the influence of the Government still further....

All these observations on governmental interference in justice are borne out by a whole host of testimony regarding the pogrom. Perkins observed that:

[A]lthough people are always dissatisfied with the courts they are faced with the fact that criticism of the administration of justice is as taboo as criticism of the army. There is in fact not a breath of public criticism, of complaint in the press, in legal journals, in the Grand National Assembly or elsewhere....

The Ministry of Justice makes no effort to improve the administration of Justice. The Government has other matters to attend to and is even averse to fostering real independence of the Judiciary.[144]

Having followed this skimpy outline of the court proceedings, their

[144] TNA:PRO, Ankara, Dispatch No. 75, April 12, 1955.

outcome in 1957 surprised no one, given the presuppositions described above. The announcement in the Turkish press of the final verdicts in the civil trial was unsensational and passed without editorial comment. The Criminal Court of the First Instance acquitted all twenty-four individuals who had been accused of responsibility for the pogrom. The court adjudged the evidence as inconclusive and argued that the charges of premeditated criminal acts were unsubstantiated. The prosecution "dropped all charges and requested acquittal of all accused on the grounds that the island of Cyprus is Turkish, forming part of the motherland. The Turkish people could hardly remain indifferent to the continuous provocation in Cyprus and Greece. Thus the September disturbances were in substance the resulting product of such provocations."[145] On January 24, 1957, therefore, Turkish justice ruled that no Turk was responsible for the pogrom. Kônstantinos Karamanlês rightly saw all this as confirmation that the matter was fundamentally over as far as Turkey was concerned. The reaction of the US ambassador to Turkey, Avra Warren, verged on the incomprehensible, however. Contrary to the Greek prime minister's belief that there was nothing more to expect from Turkish justice, Warren found the acquittals to be proof of a substantive and strong judicial system in Turkey. Indeed, Warren insisted that "there are no indications that the Government of Turkey will not (repeat) not continue to search for the riot perpetrators."[146]

It is, of course, difficult to comprehend the good ambassador's faith, as it betrayed either singular gullibility or a less-than-hidden political agenda. His own consuls' analyses should have raised doubts in Warren's mind about Menderes's innocence. In the event, the military coup of May 1960, and the subsequent trial that found the Turkish premier and his colleagues criminally responsible for the pogrom, was to prove how far-fetched the US envoy's sanguine assessment in 1957 truly was.

---

[145] National Archives, Foreign Office Dispatch No. 633, Istanbul, January 25, 1957.
[146] National Archives, No. 1787, Ankara, January 31, 1957.

CHAPTER FIVE

THE ATTACK ON THE
GREEK ORTHODOX CHURCH

O f all the ruin and hatred unleashed by the pogrom against the Greeks, the destruction of the Greek churches, monasteries, and cemeteries was the most conspicuous. The flames consuming the Holy Trinity in Taksim, the Euangelistria and Saint Athanasios in Kurtuluş, the Metamorphosis in the Greek cemetery of Şişli, and St. Constantine on Kalyoncu Kulluk lighted up the Istanbul sky and were visible as far west as Bakırköy and Yeşilköy. The fires consuming the churches of the Taxiarchs and St. Paraskeue, along with the episcopal residence in Tarabya, were visible to the regions east of the Bosphorus and often the thunder and roar of the demonstrators could also be heard across the body of water separating the two continents. In Kadıköy itself, the burning edifice of the local Church of the Holy Trinity lit up the streets of the area. In old Istanbul, many churches scattered along the old Byzantine land walls were burned; when a Swiss journalist visited the region the next day, he reported that, "In the old city between the...Patriarchate and Yedikule one saw only the blackened walls of the churches as though they had been bombarded." The churches of the Panagia at Belgratkapı, Zoodochos Pege at Balıklı, and Panagia Altı Mermer had been torched. From Yedikule to Yenikapı and Kumkapı, arson demolished the churches of St. George Kyparissas, Saints Constantine and Helen, and St. Menas.[1] There are disparate accounts testifying to the use of gasoline and dynamite in these acts of destruction. The fire most often led to explosions as it built up pressure within a church and eventually destroyed the roof and whatever remained inside the structure. Wooden pews, holy icons, and other sacred objects perished. In some cases, the paint on icons melted (and transmogrified the holy images). Where fire did not entail complete destruction, the demonstrators themselves finished the job with the tools with which they had been uniformly supplied for their task. The air of Istanbul and its environs was filled with the light of a massive conflagration and the shouts of those responsible for it. This noisy drone of relentless

---

[1] Ypourgeion Proedrias Kyvernêseôs, *Ektakton Deltion #1*, November 1955, *passim*.

destruction was periodically interrupted by the sudden outburst of flames, falling church roofs, and dynamite, and coexisted with another sensation: the acrid odor resulting from the combined smells of burning wood, plaster, clothing, foodstuffs, shoes, and chemicals.[2]

RELIGIOUS FANATICISM IN KEMALIST TURKEY

The all-out attack on Greek religious institutions involved over 90 percent of the Greek churches, but it also included, on a much smaller scale, Armenian and Catholic churches, as well as one synagogue. In his initial report, Istanbul's chief of police had indicated that while a small percentage of Turkish business establishments had also been looted, not a single mosque or other Muslim religious establishment had been touched. It is certainly significant that the Turkish government took care beforehand to protect only one Greek religious complex, that of the patriarchate. It made no similar effort to protect any other Greek churches, monasteries, or cemeteries,[3] despite the official Kemalist ideology—not only of the government, but of the relatively autonomous armed forces—of defending Turkey's secular state, which supposedly ensured both religious freedom and constitutional equality to all its citizens. Despite this official secularism, however, there can be little doubt that the violence of the attacks on the Greek religious establishments was due not only to the chauvinism (nationalist sentiment) or need and want (class sentiment) of many of the demonstrators, but also to religious fanaticism, which was deeply rooted in many Muslims living in Istanbul. Both Muslim and non-Muslim communities had substantial numbers of impoverished members, so that economic envy and difference were not unique to either group. Moreover, many non-Turkish but Muslim minorities were not interested in Cyprus or other international disputes. Rather, it was confessional identity that largely differentiated all the component groups of Istanbul's society. Occasionally, official Turkish, British, and US analyses attempted to minimize the role of religious differences as a motive for the pogrom's violence and fanaticism; invariably, however, both US and British analysts kept returning to the terrible combination of ignorance and religious fanaticism.

Nevertheless, in speaking of religious passions, one should be careful to make certain distinctions. There is, no doubt, for example that, by 1955, secularism had become one of the seven so-called pillars of the Turkish state created by Atatürk. The degree to which this policy had succeeded could be

---

[2] Ypourgeion Exôterikôn, Istanbul to Athens, No. 1086, September 16, 1955.
[3] The same is true of the invasion of northern Cyprus by the Turkish army in July 1974, as well as of the subsequent fate of Greek religious institutions there.

seen in Turkey's major cities, whereas it was much more marginal elsewhere. Thus, the governing class and certain urban groups were its basic supporters. The older Ottoman social and religious legacies were, however, deeply rooted, and the majority of the Turkish and Kurdish populations still constituted two rural societies that remained loyal to these traditions. Even Turkish urban centers were partially "ruralized" as villagers began to move into them for a "better" life and brought their religious values with them. Thus, alongside increasing poverty, the ongoing immigration brought its rural piety to Istanbul. The minorities in particular were sensitive to the growing "provincialization" and "Islamization" of the neighborhoods in which they lived and worked.[4]

The religious fanaticism at the core of the pogrom's fury is thus clearly apparent; from the point of view of Islam's role in Turkish society, it is also important. Menderes's ten-year premiership coincided with the state's gradual political and fiscal opening to Islam, which, indeed, had never gone away and was deeply rooted in the identity of modern Turks and in their national sentiments.[5] The US mission in Turkey paid particular attention to the new developments in the country's religious life and to their social and political significance. Early on, Menderes had understood that the somewhat subdued loyalty of the average Turk to Islam had nevertheless to be taken into account politically. Its presence in the pogrom was unmistakable. Somewhat later, US diplomatic reports began to pay attention to and comment on a variety of forms in which Islam was emerging from its political circumscription. The American consul-general in Istanbul reported to the State Department in June 1957 on the "Political Developments in Istanbul," focusing primarily on domestic and international aspects of Turkish policies. At the end of what was a matter-of-fact analysis, he added: "This year the festival of Ramadan

---

[4] See the striking poem, "The Saga of Istanbul," in Talat Halman, *Contemporary Turkish Literature: Fiction and Poetry*, Rutherford, 1982, p. 302, and Nüzhet Erman's poem, "The Turkish Alphabet," in the same anthology, pp. 296-297, on the social background as some Turkish poets saw the state of this rural element, both in Anatolia and in the sprawling city of Istanbul. See also Tsoukatou, *Septemvriana*, pp. 99 and 102.

[5] For the older views, Lewis, *The Emergence of Modern Turkey*, pp. 411-418. The study by Niyazi Berkes, *The Development of Secularism in Turkey*, New York, 1988, remains fundamental for the onset of secularism and its early relations to Turkish Islam. Feroz Ahmad's introduction is of particular interest. The recent Turkish literature has developed entire, and new, political, historical, and sociological sections on the political resurgence of Islam in Turkey during the 1990s: Mustafa Özel, *Refahlı Türkiyet*, Istanbul, 1997; Orhan Gökdemir, *Devletin din operasyonu öteki İslam*, Istanbul, 1998, second printing; Uğur Mumcu, *Tarikat, Siyaset, Ticaret*, Ankara, 1999, twenty-fifth printing. For a masterful and rich analysis of the rise of Islam as the new, and crucial, element in Turkish indentity, M. Hakan Yavuz, *Islamic Political Identity in Turkey*, Oxford, 2003.

was more widely and more conspicuously celebrated than in previous years. The mosques were jammed to capacity. Many Moslems, even among the sophisticated classes, attempted to observe the month-long fast."[6] Later in the year, the US consul in Ankara informed Washington of the specific efforts to win Kurdish votes, and the subsequent political gains, by the DP in extending its political patronage to the Nurcu brotherhood, a dervish order:

> According to unconfirmed reports from Izmit contacts who have friends and relatives living in Eskishehir, the Kurd mystic Said Nursi secretly is being used as a propagandist by the Democratic Party in its electoral campaign in the Kurdish provinces. Nursi is believed to be one of the most influential Kurdish religious leaders. For many years he has been living in quasi-exile in Eskishehir as a result of his part in the 1925 Kurdish uprising under Sheikh Sait.
>
> In the 1950 electoral campaign, Nursi was credited with swinging a large number of Kurd votes to the then opposition Democratic Party when he publicly revealed a dream in which he claimed to have been told that a D.P. victory would greatly benefit the Kurds.[7]

By 1958, Menderes's support of and relations with highly conservative religious groups had begun to attract the attention of the Turkish press and to provoke the criticism of secularist circles. Members of one group (loyal to Sheikh Nursi mentioned above) were arrested for "reactionary activities" in Nazilli (a town near Izmir). A second group, which consisted of the followers of the Ticani dervish order, was arrested for the same reasons in the town of Mihalicik, in the district of Eskişehir. A us embassy dispatch attributed to both groups a program of "forcible overthrow of the existing order." Although both the dispatch and the Turkish authorities referred to these groups as insignificant, the report also indicated that the manifestations of the Nursi order "assumed quite sizeable proportions and that [it]...operated with remarkable lack of restraint," attacking the secular regime in a violent manner and proclaiming the religious message that the sheikh was a divinely ordained prophet whose mission was to return Turkey to a godly regime. The dervish order attacked the person of Atatürk in particular, and urged people to shed

---

[6] National Archives, American Consul General, Istanbul, to Washington, No. 385, June 13, 1957.

[7] National Archives, Ankara to Washington, No. 67, October 17, 1957. Sheikh Sait (or Said) led a major Kurdish national and religious uprising in eastern Anatolia in 1925. This rebellion was part of the political evolution of the Turkish Kurds' desire for a national state; in the event, it was brutally crushed by Atatürk. See Andrew Mango, *Ataturk: The Biography of the Founder of Modern Turkey*, Woodstock, 2000, pp. 421-426.

their blood for Nursi's cause, as "the day of victory was imminent." The embassy report also remarked that the Ticanis had attacked and mutilated monuments and statues honoring Atatürk upon Menderes's electoral victory in 1950. It concludes: "Istanbul circles do not tend to attribute special importance to the reported instances of regressive acts. However, the openness and boldness with which these leanings have been manifesting themselves occasionally is a source of some concern. Concensus [*sic*] in the matter is that this has to be attributed to the laxness with which the present administration has been enforcing secular principles and, in particular, to the concessions made to the conservative and reactionary elements for the purpose of securing their political support."[8]

The American *attaché* in Istanbul filed a second "Report of New Reactionary Activity" in early December 1958. The Istanbul press had reported a new encounter between Menderes and Nursi, which raised the hackles of the city's secularists. When Menderes had visited the town of Emirdağ (in the province of Afyon Karahisar), Sheikh Nursi had raised the green flag of Islam with the insignia of the sultanate above the central mosque, in a salute to the prime minister, and then bestowed his religious blessing on Menderes. The latter was then addressed as the "Restorer of the Faith" and had over fifty sheep sacrificed in his honor. In the October 20, 1958, issue of *Dünya*, H. Alpar exclaimed: "The fact no longer admits denial that the ruling party is making one concession after another to the elements of reaction. Whither are we going?!" In the October 22 issue of *Vatan*, S. Tancu entitled his piece, "Our Muslim Premier," and proceeded to castigate Menderes: "When a few men one day started reciting the Qu'ran in the GNA [the Grand National Assembly]...when a few attempted to preach reaction at the mosque in Bursa...we dismissed them as freaks...and we did not attach too much importance when the head of the Department of Religious Affairs proclaimed that the Qu'ran could not be read in the Turkish script....What shall we now think?...How interpret the fact that the Prime Minister seemed to feel no concern upon seeing the displayed green flag carrying the emblem of the Sultanate...?" The American consular report, which quoted the article above, correctly interpreted the Turkish government's silence in the face of

[8] National Archives, Istanbul to Washington, No. 50, April 17, 1958. The report then adds the following remarks from the April 9, 1958, edition of *Hürriyet*: "In the present instance [of the Ticanis] close to thirty persons were taken into custody, the majority being women. Report has it that one of the women arrested was in an advanced state of pregnancy although her husband had been away for over a year. On being asked how she could reconcile this with her religious fervor, it appears that she retorted by claiming that there was no reason for astonishment over her condition since this was a simple case of immaculate conception."

such criticism as evidence of its "determined unwillingness to engage in any outspoken move liable to alienate the support which it receives from the conservative segment of the population."[9] Peyami Safa, who commented on this matter in *Milliyet* on October 24, drew some reasonable conclusions: "If those who hung the green flag of the Caliphate from the minarets have nothing to do with the 'Disciples of Light' [Nurcu] movement, then the incident must be regarded as the deed of a few unbalanced individuals. But if this is not the case and the so-called 'Disciples of Light' are working as a network of political reaction, deceiving also a part of our Youth…then this movement is more serious than thought and one must ascribe to it the features of a regular conspiracy."

It is surely important to note that the religious groups were operating actively and forcefully in the western Anatolian region that included Afyon Karahisar, Eskişehir, Izmir, and Bursa, that is, in important areas closely connected to Istanbul. The US report, however, did not make any systematic effort to tie these groups and episodes to one another or, more important, to the heartland and eastern areas of the country. Today, with the advantage of hindsight, and with two religious parties heading Turkish governments in the past decade, we can understand somewhat better these earlier manifestations of religious conservatism as the beginning of a vigorous return of Islam to the society and politics of modern Turkey. Despite their inability to see what lay ahead, these early diplomatic reports understood that these episodes involving mystical religious groups were important, and that their importance was confirmed by the fact that the Turkish government kept relatively silent on the matter and did not allow much public coverage of and attention to the subsequent trials involving the groups. By 1959, in fact, the US diplomatic reports no longer present these events as isolated, disjointed occurrences unrelated to each other, but as part of a broad religious phenomenon looming on the horizon of modern Turkish society.

The very difference in the reports' titles reflects this change. In the two basic reports of 1959 (January 26 and December 30), the titles are, respectively, the "Status of Islam in Turkey…" and "Islam in Turkey…." The 1958 report had contained the key phrase, "reactionary activities." Thus, the new titles were more "neutral" and comprehensive, and implied that the earlier titles were no longer sufficient to describe a much broader phenomenon. US diplomats began to perceive that such "exotics" as Nurcus and Ticanis were part of the wider phenomenon, broadly speaking, of a reemergent and conspicuous Islam. Nevertheless, the newer and more comprehensive reporting of the US mission

[9] National Archives, Istanbul to Washington, No. 35, December 4, 1958.

in Turkey remained timid regarding the future significance of these Islamic manifestations, and attempted to explain the clash of secular and religious as essentially the product of two extremes (secularist and fundamentalist) in which the common sense of the Turkish people and government would bring a calm and evolutional solution to the problem.

The first of these two US reports, "Status of Islam in Turkey—End of 1958," was a fairly complete, if not systematic, analysis of what the US mission had observed during the year. The report saw the Islamic experience of the Turkish people in modern times as being divided into three phases over the last 150 years, during which the "struggle between rational and theological forces" had been restricted in the first phase to a "whittling away of the prevailing obscurantism of medieval Islam." In the second phase, Atatürk and İnönü had made a frontal attack on Islam's formal practices and attempted to replace them with modern nationalism. The third phase was seen as the first eight years of Menderes's premiership, in which the DP had begun to utilize and support that part of Islam in Turkey that still had deep roots: "...The eight years of the Menderes regime has increasingly tended to tolerate, if not to encourage, religious expression in Islamic tradition." This period of toleration and support of Muslim practice and sentiment had naturally resulted in removing many of the older constraints that had inhibited their open expression. The report saw this largely in the growing crowds at the mosques, the increase in women wearing the *çarşaf* (the large, kerchief-like veil that hides most of the nose, chin, and parts of cheeks), and the growing numbers saying the daily prayers. Further, the report took this increase in ritual observance as an indicator also of a change in mentality. The transliteration of the Qu'ran, or its Turkish translation, no longer aroused the criticism it once did. The Nurcus and their green flags had dropped out of the Istanbul press, while wearing the *çarşaf* no longer provoked stiff opposition and was increasingly associated with poverty. Talismans, meanwhile, had become ubiquitous and men had substituted the beret for the fez.

Perhaps the most important indication of change, however, was the DP's use of religious sentiment "to persuad[e] the people of their [the DP's] devotion to the preservation of Islam." The report went on to state that the DP had begun to attack the Republican People's Party in religious terms and that one DP deputy had gone so far as to condemn the RPP as Zionists and freemasons and to praise himself as having consulted Beduizzaman Said-i Nursi: "He [said] that if Menderes withdraws as Prime Minister, Turkey will collapse...[and] the Imams and Muezzins toured all the villages [of the district of Erzerum] during the election time and worked for our Party." According to the US report, Atatürk's efforts to block the Ottoman heritage by inventing the Turkish historical and solar linguistic theses had foundered after his death as they were obviously artificial creations, without any basis in historical and linguistic reality.[10] The study of Ottoman history and culture eventually replaced the historical fictions of Atatürk, with Köprülü's students laying the brilliant scholarly foundations for the research in and understanding of Ottoman history and culture. The study of this once powerful Islamic empire, the report concludes, "has led to a renewed feeling that Islam is a normal patriotic and respectable part of Turkey's heritage....Mr. Menderes seems to have been stating nothing but the truth when he said that 'the Turkish nation was born Moslem, and it will live as a Moslem nation.'"[11]

The US mission's second report sent to Washington largely corroborated the first one. However, the analysis was disappointingly shallow in light of what we know now:

> The religious group prefers to promote those aspects of Turkish Islam which it best understands—the superstitions—and traditions of dress and conduct of the past which usually do not have their origin in Islam at all, but which symbolize ignorance and intolerance of the pre-republican past. At the other extreme are [sic] a group of republic-trained secularists who are in their own way as truly reactionary as their enemies, and who long for the days of Ataturk when any manifestation of religious feeling was frowned upon and religious activity frequently punished....
>
> Everyone, however, is aware that change is taking place and that the present Administration is more tolerant of religious and pseudo-religious activity than its predecessor. That the Government intends to use its power and its funds to establish itself as a defender of the Faith has for several years been accepted as fact by everyone. Most moderate intellectuals have accustomed themselves to this and worry less than they did a few years ago at the sight of new mosques, of increased budgets for the Presidency of Religious Affairs, and of other official homage to the concept of Islam.

Significantly, the report commented on the gradual fear creeping over moderate secularists, causing them to refrain from expressing secular ideas or statements that might provoke the "religionists" to violence at some future date. This was certainly a change in mentality, which confirmed religion's

---

[10] In the United States, the Turkish government succeeded in suborning much of the field of Ottoman studies to its political interests and causes; see Vryonis, *The Turkish State*, 1991, pp. 89-131.

[11] On all the above, National Archives, Ankara to Washington, No. 2, January 26, 1959.

strong return to Turkish society by the middle and late 1950s.[12]

RELIGOUS FANATICISM AND THE POGROM

The resurgence of Islam in Turkey, its perennial role as a basic element in Turkish national identity, its long history of military and religious conquest (and legal disenfranchisement) of the Christian peoples, and the pitiful decline of this once powerful empire in the face of Christian Europe and the Balkan peoples, constitute the historical background for the analysis of the religious factor in the pogrom of September 6-7, 1955. The Islamic revival in Turkey during the 1950s, and the increasing and open politicization that arose from its own religious dynamic—as well as from the determination of Menderes's government to exploit this dynamic—helps us better to understand the pogrom's violence. The rise of Islamic sentiment fused with the economic deprivation of the poorer residents of Istanbul, who were also indoctrinated with the chauvinism of the new state administration and its policies toward the minorities. This chauvinism had had an ugly history in any case, from the very onset of Kemalism in the 1920s and 1930s—and particularly during the earlier part of the Second World War (until the defeat of Nazi Germany at Stalingrad), when the Turkish government had expected the Nazis to emerge victorious from the war. The diplomatic reports of the British, US, and Greek missions were unanimous in ascribing a major role in the violence inflicted on the Greeks (and on other minorities and some non-Greek foreigners) to religious fanaticism. A sampling of these diplomatic dispatches, as well as of other documentation, bears out the religious character and even religious justification of such acts. On occasion, the Turks even asserted that the Greeks "got what they deserved."

One should begin with Ambassador Warren's extensive report sent to Washington in early December 1955. Warren acknowledged that the pogrom

---

[12] National Archives, Istanbul to Washington, No. 2, July 23, 2002. For a report on the activities of the Naqshibandi order in northwestern Anatolia, TNA:PRO, Izmir to London, No. 502, February 2, 1959:

> A meeting of 102 women did in fact take place in a private house at Bergama on January 26....When the police entered they found 102 women performing what was thought to be a religious ceremony of the Nakshibandi order under the leadership of the owner of the house...Shaziye Pashaoglu, known as the "Sheikh."... All the women, most of whom were between the ages of 40 and 55, pleaded their innocence and said that they were merely engaged in reading a "mevlut," i.e. prayers for the dead, and that they had done nothing against the law. However, as certain books and pamphlets found in the house suggested that the Nakshibandi ritual was being performed they were all committed for trial....Some of the women who were present are believed to belong to well known families of Bergama.

was primarily anti-Greek, aimed at both Greek nationals and Turkish citizens
of Greek origin, "because of a belief that these Greeks and the clergy of the
Greek Orthodox Church secretly supported the efforts of Greece to annex
Cyprus." Echoing the conclusions of Istanbul's police chief, however, he stated
that "riots...stirred against the Greeks...seemed to change into a riot of the
economically depressed section of the population against all signs of wealth
and prosperity." This statement flew in the face of the evidence, including
that provided by the chief of police that the preponderant majority of attacks
were carried out against the businesses and homes of the Christian and Jewish
minorities and not on those of Turkish Muslims, prosperous or otherwise.
Warren's report was further distorted by his refusal to accept any possibility
that the Turkish government was somehow implicated in the pogrom, either
by acts of commission or a predetermined stance of studied "neutrality." As
we saw in Chapter 2, he explained away the government's responsibility by
claiming that the Turkish police and army were not trained or equipped to
suppress the pogrom, thus ignoring the reality that: (a) police and soldiers
had openly *supported* the demonstrators during the course of events; (b) after
the imposition of martial law, both police and soldiers had proved quite
effective in suppressing further vandalism; (c) the Turkish government had
decided, *before* the pogrom, to protect both the ecumenical patriarchate and
the Greek consulate, and did so very easily; and (d) in certain isolated cases,
lone or a few individual police officers were able to disperse mobs and prevent
destruction.

Warren spent an entire page in his report on the subject of "Anti-Foreign,
Anti-Christian Implications," stating that, "As a carry over from the period
of the 'capitulations,' a mild [*sic*] atmosphere of mutual distrust and dislike
exists between Moslem Turk circles and most minority groups."[13] The use
of the adjective, "mild," to characterize the "distrust and dislike...between
Moslem Turk circles and most minority groups" was hardly appropriate
and actually falsified the hatred and fear that characterized these relations.
Furthermore, Warren's attempts to persuade the State Department that the
pogrom was neither anti-foreign nor anti-Christian were both unconvincing
and bizarre: "The attacks on the 81 Christian churches have caused a great
deal of comment. But by excluding all Greek Orthodox Churches, it is seen
that only 7 of the approximately 95 Christian and Jewish houses of worship in
Istanbul were molested." It is difficult to respond to this kind of "reasoning."

---

[13] The so-called regime of capitulations, in effect in later Ottoman times, entailed the forced
granting of special legal rights to various great powers that made them immune to the laws of
the Ottoman state or to the wishes of its governments. See Nasim Sousa, *The Capitulary Regime
of Turkey: History, Origin and Nature*, Baltimore, 1933.

Clearly, Warren's only purpose in devising such a line of "argument" was to disguise the implications of, and reasons for, the pogrom.

This exercise in manifest disorientation was also behind Warren's disingenuous attempt to explain away the livid nature of the attacks on Greek institutions. On the one hand, the US ambassador claimed, the riots were a consequence of the Cyprus issue and of the fact that the hierarch Makarios was the Greek Cypriots' leader, which, for Warren, implied that all non-Cypriot hierarchs and clergy of the Greek Orthodox church were active supporters of the Cypriot archbishop. (The fact was that the ecumenical patriarch and his clergy were anything but supporters of a Church that was, after all, completely autonomous and independent of the patriarchate.) On the other hand, Warren asserted—without any self-consciousness, it must be added, about the obscene justification he was providing for the violence—that, "The attacks on the Greek Orthodox Cemeteries can be explained only on the supposition that perhaps some of the organizers of the riots expected to find caches of arms and ammunition there"! While one demonstrator was said to have accused the abbot of the monastery at Balıklı of hiding weapons in its storehouse, no such accusation was ever recorded about the church, charnel house, or large number of graves in the cemetery. Further, Warren's incredible assertion (these "caches of arms" that the pogromists were desecrating cemeteries to find were presumably meant for some uprising or other, or for support of the Greek Cypriots) does not explain why hundreds of marble crosses on graves were smashed, why corpses and bones were exhumed, burned, knifed, and strewn on the ground, or why some pogromists took the time to defecate on a large number of graves. The fact is that even Warren had to admit, in other parts of his lengthy memorandum, that "75 Greek Orthodox Churches were attacked and *desecrated* [stress added]," and that these churches were "desecrated in a manner most offensive to Christians, that is the holy sacraments were destroyed." (On this, see the relevant section in Chapter 2).

This thirty-page report signed by Warren betrays multiple authorship, in fact, and the lack of an analytically unifying editorial hand. One part of the memorandum contends that the acts of violence carried out against the Greek Orthodox religion were motivated by secular animus based on political (if mistaken) reasoning, whereas other parts point to religious desecration and, therefore, religious fanaticism. Aside from these internal contradictions, there is a failure to understand the basic fusion of two contradictory forces in Turkish society: religious fanaticism and secular chauvinism. In its own contradictory and confused manner, however, this long memorandum clearly testifies to the violent convergence of both these forces during the pogrom.[14] Interestingly, the earlier reports from the US consulate in Istanbul, which was obviously much closer to events, set the element of Islamic fanaticism in its proper place alongside poverty and chauvinism as a basic motive force of the violence. The US consul-general's conclusion on this matter was probably the best statement of the role of religious intolerance on the night of September 6-7: "Anti-Greek and by extension anti-minority feeling, had been on the rise for some months before the events of September 6. These events, though staged over the Cyprus issue and set off by the reported attacks on Ataturk's birthplace, fundamentally were an anti-Christian and anti-minority outbreak of the types frequently recorded in Turkish history."[15] The US consular reports were composed at the time of the pogrom, or soon thereafter, and so their authors were eyewitnesses, both from the consulate as well as in other parts of the city. For them, the element of religious extremism was omnipresent; by contrast, Warren, at his desk in Ankara, was geographically and visually distant from the hourly grinding-on of the violence.

On October 12, 1955, the British consulate in Istanbul reported on damages to the property of British nationals and in so doing drew a specific picture of incidents affecting three such nationals. In the first, a Mrs. Binns was stabbed and a few days later a group of Turks attempted to burn her house. In the second, the house of a Mr. Turbini was attacked by a group of Turks with whom he had had differences. As Turbini was engaged in procuring Turkish-government contracts, he had to compete in a sector in

[14] National Archives, Ankara to Washington, No. 228, December 1, 1955. Warren's reports are, on occasion, confused and confusing, and the British official, Michael Stewart, often thinks of him as gullible. Warren's gullibility stands in sharp contrast to his own consul and officials, including Richards, Carp, Kohler, and Wendelin, who are perceptive and convincing. An earlier report by Wendelin (National Archives, Ankara to Washington, No. 153, October 18, 1955) is somewhat broader than that of the ambassador, and includes the skeleton of the later thirty-page memo. Wendelin makes a much more specific reference to religious fanaticism as a factor in the pogrom:

> This intrusion of the religious issue into the situation undoubtedly contributed to the unprecedented scope of the mob attack against the Greek Orthodox churches and cemeteries. However it would be unwise to assume that it was a purely religious fanaticism that moved the crowd in this instance.

Accordingly, Wendelin gives a much more balanced picture of the factors that incited the pogromists.

[15] National Archives, Istanbul to Washington, September 29, 1955. Of the urban depressed and the poor peasantry who settled in Istanbul, Richards stated: "The discontented among these, together with the depressed elements of the city, provided a favorable atmosphere for violence. There were thus great numbers who were ripe for widespread looting and vengeful vandalism." Richards was of the opinion that sober economic policies could have neutralized the socioeconomic factors of the pogrom.

which graft and racketeering were common, so it is assumed that this was the source or cause of the attack on his house. The third case concerned a Mr. Hammond, who was married to a Turkish lawyer, about whom the report relates: "It is quite possible that the attacks were directed against her, perhaps by disgruntled clients or else by fanatical Muslims who objected to a Muslim woman marrying a Christian and a foreigner." This particular consular document concluded that these three incidents were indeed isolated, and one could add that their causes may have been the result of personal differences or aggravations. Nonetheless, it went on to state the conditions in Istanbul that gave rise to these conflicts and to many other attacks:

> It is unfortunately true that recent riots have stirred up the latent religious fanaticism and xenophobia of the Turkish masses, and that, in such an atmosphere, any real or imaginary grievance is more likely to issue in a resort to violence than would normally be the case....
>
> We have heard several reports of foreigners living in outlying areas having to put up with rudeness and unpleasantness from shopkeepers and the like, and Mr. Turbini has told us that his Turkish servants have been warned that they would be well-advised not to go on working for infidels. So long as this atmosphere persists, there is always the possibility of incidents....

The handwritten comment of Johnston at the home office on this report, which is attached to it, is in agreement with the consulate in Istanbul:

> The explanations for the various attacks seem reasonable enough.
>
> Paragraphs 6 and 7 probably outline very concisely the present position in which the minorities find themselves today in Turkey, and particularly those of Christian faith. It is probably also against this background that numbers of foreigners [resident in Turkey] were reported to have enquired during the latter half of September at our Visa Offices in Turkey about details of immigration to Commonwealth countries.
>
> Once the mob, and in particular the Muslim element has been roused to the pitch that was reached on September 6/7 it will take a long time for the germ of xenophobia and religious fanaticism to die in the blood of the masses.
>
> It has been reported in Lambeth Palace [offices of the archbishop of Canterbury] that a Greek correspondent has written "next time it will be a massacre." This is very likely the case.[16]

---

[16] TNA:PRO, Istanbul to London, No. 1490/10/55, October 12, 1955.

This view was pithily seconded in the newspaper report of Noel Barber in the *Daily Mail*, who said that the attacks were carried out "with the terrible twin weapons of violence [and] bitter fanatical hatred allied to cold, precise instructions."[17]

As the Greeks were the pogrom's main victims, their perception of the role of religious extremism in the broader spectrum of Turkish violence was vivid and accurate as to detail, particularly in the attacks on churches, monasteries, cemeteries, and the clergy. Perhaps the most lucid analysis was that of Christoforos Chrêstidês in his *Ekthesis*. As a practicing lawyer in both Greece and Istanbul who was also fluent in Turkish and visited Istanbul frequently to consult with his clients (which included at least one Muslim Turk who was a member of parliament), Chrêstidês was certainly a Greek who was well-informed on greater and lesser developments on the Turkish scene. He believed that the key to understanding the pogrom's dynamics and violence lay both in Menderes's failed economic and political policies and in the fact that the majority of the Turkish population had remained bigoted and reactionary religious extremists. When his economic and domestic policies had faltered and begun to fail, Menderes turned to the Cyprus issue and to conservative religious policies that would appeal to the religious majority, Chrêstidês wrote. He saw, as did the American diplomats, that, as the harsh secularist policies of Atatürk and İnönü had failed to penetrate the majority of the Turkish population in any significant way, Menderes had exploited this basic political reality. Chrêstidês also realized that this religious intolerance was paralleled by a general xenophobia that had always been latent in this large sector of the population. Accordingly, Chrêstidês saw the Cyprus problem combining with latent religious fanaticism (and chauvinism) to disorient the general attention and concerns of many people away from Menderes's unsuccessful policies (and, above all, from his dictatorial measures and tendencies).[18]

Greek diplomats and politicians, and the Greeks of Istanbul as a whole, were sorely taxed to evaluate Turkish attitudes at the time, or to assess the proper measures to take to face the gloomy future of Greek-Turkish relations. Five weeks after the pogrom, I. Ivrakês, the Greek cultural attaché in Turkey, submitted a detailed memorandum to the Greek ambassador in which he analyzed Greek-Turkish relations. The events of September 6-7 had forced Ivrakês to reconsider the past and future of these relations. In so doing, he was

[17] *Daily Mail*, September 14, 1955; also, TNA:PRO, London, No. 371/117712, 198335, September 21, 1955.

[18] Chrêstidês, *Ekthesis*, pp. 177-180, although his generalizations regarding religious fanaticism need qualification.

clearly conscious of the effects that politics and, especially, abrupt political events had on all cultural relations. His first observation was significant, namely, that Greek-Turkish friendship had been based on a negative foundation, defined by the current Western alliance against the "communist threat." He reasoned that this was a fragile basis for the friendship inasmuch as any event that called this political assumption into question would also provoke the immediate collapse of the relationship. It was also "negative" because there were really no organic elements in the relationship that gave it elasticity, a broad spectrum of common interests, common culture, or other necessary ingredients. Ivrakês reminded the Greek ambassador that he had written all this to him prior to the pogrom: "Unfortunately, the most recent dramatic events were fated to demonstrate the truth of this [earlier] statement and to shatter, to its very roots, the relations of the two countries. The question now posed is to what degree is it possible to rebuild Greek-Turkish friendship, and more generally the cultural relations of the two countries?" If Turks did desire a rapprochement, they did so only because of the momentary need to restore relations, according to Ivrakês, who also believed, as did many others, that the older religious traditions and intolerance had not only survived the Kemalist purges, but had been supported, manipulated, and exploited by Menderes, most recently and spectacularly in the pogrom. He concluded by asserting, pessimistically, that cultural relations could only be restored through a very limited reference to a small circle of intellectuals and Westernizers.[19]

Finally, while the proposition that religious fanaticism contributed to the pogrom was not commonly held by many Turkish observers, many of them did favorably compare the Ottoman era (as a period presumably characterized by freedom of religious worship and an absence of cruelties at the expense of the Christian sects) with the intolerance of the pogrom. Indeed, leftist authors such as Aziz Nesin and Hulusi Dosdoğru, as well as the political activist Hasan Dinamo (all three of them arrested as communists as part of the cover-up of the pogrom), condemned Menderes and the *Demokrat Parti* as "hoodlums" who had destroyed, raped, killed, and burned. For, as we shall see at the end of this study, there were Turkish Istanbulis who braved the pogromists and came to the defense of their fellow citizens who were Greek. The three men mentioned above in particular condemned Menderes's deceit and abuse of power. Yet perhaps the clearest condemnation of the pogrom came from the Turkish journalist, Falih Rıfkı Atay, in the newspaper *Dünya* just five days after the violence:

[19] Ypourgeion Exôterikôn, Istanbul to Athens, No. 437, October 14, 1955.

During the past one hundred years systematic efforts have been made to turn our country into a European state. Laws based on the principles of European jurisprudence have been enacted, and the granting of political and social liberties has contributed to Turkey no longer being looked upon as a kind of medieval dungeon. Unfortunately, certain internal events, which have received great publicity throughout the world, create the impression that there exists in our country something that has not changed. Ignorance and fanaticism from time to time raise their heads, and the way they manifest themselves makes one suspect that the progress we have achieved and of which we are so proud has no deep roots but is purely superficial and provisional....

Since the Turkish Constitution was proclaimed, repeated revolutions and disorders have occurred, and on each occasion attempts have been made to fasten responsibility on some individual. The only ones really responsible and who are exploited by those behind these disorders are: Ignorance and Fanaticism. Whenever our politicians find themselves in a tight corner, they make use of these two elements without considering the harm they do to the country....

We must undertake a fresh campaign, a campaign to civilize and educate our people. Our political parties, whose leaders are educated men, must make up their minds to cease in future to exploit the fanaticism and ignorance of the people in their political quarrels.[20]

As we have seen, Ecumenical Patriarch Athênagoras stated in his formal memorandum to Menderes of November 22, 1955, that he saw "[t]hese terrible events...[as] a persecution of the Church and of its Christians and...a deep wound in the history of the life of the Patriarch, a wound which, because of the Ecumenical position of the Patriarchate and because of the nature of the events had world-wide reverberation."[21] The archbishop of Canterbury had characterized the events as "a night of terror...inflicted upon the great Church of Constantinople and upon the life of the Orthodox Christians."[22]

---

[20] Journalists' Union, *The anti-Greek riots*, p. 63; Ypourgeion Exôterikôn, Istanbul to Athens, No. 433, September 11, 1955, includes a Greek translation of this text. The article originally appeared in *Dünya* on September 11, 1955.

[21] Ypourgeion Exôterikôn, Istanbul to Athens, No. 1986, November 22, 1955, sent on November 27. Archbishop Michaêl of the Greek Orthodox Church in North and South America had similarly condemned the pogrom as an act of persecution of the Church, Greek Embassy, Washington to Athens, No. 3875, September 21, 1955.

[22] PRO No. F0371/117712, 198335, October 12, 1955. Some Turkish authors such as Nesin and Dosdoğru dubbed the pogrom as another St. Bartholomew's Day massacre; for a

The change that Menderes had brought to Turkish foreign policy on Cyprus in 1954 gave free reign to the Turkish media and extremist groups to proceed with an intense and successful campaign to direct public opinion against the Greek community and churches of Istanbul. This resulted in the widespread use of unfounded rumor and propaganda. As the political atmosphere of Istanbul became more oppressive for the local Greeks, the press and other elements began to hurl accusations against the patriarch, calling him variously to account for the patriarchate's finances, for allegedly having become enmeshed in the policies of the Greek government on Cyprus, for open support of Greece against Turkey, and for allegedly raising funds for EOKA.

This frenzy of attacks on the patriarch and the patriarchate was, of course, based on false rumors. As emerged from his battle with the Greek consul, Kapsambelês; from his circumspect conduct and relations with the Church of England and the World Council of Churches (to which he continually stressed his loyalty—as a Turkish citizen—to Turkey); and from his wish to avoid all demonstrations on the Christian churches' part (since he believed that, by and large, he would receive the necessary reconstruction funds from the Turkish government), the patriarch was indeed faithful to his obligations to the Turkish state. He refused to become involved in political issues and expressed his irritation at Kapsambelês regarding what he considered to be the latter's over-involvement with the holy synod. It was precisely this neutrality that earned him the disrespect of many victims of the pogrom, who looked upon him as their spiritual leader. Until the very end of his life, Athênagoras observed an official policy of friendship with the Turkish state and Turkey more generally. Nonetheless, despite his manifestly non-political stance, both he and the patriarchate were dragged into the vortex of Greek-Turkish relations—and enmity—and, in the final analysis, were exploited by Turkey to pressure Greece over unrelated political and territorial issues. Turkey realized that the more it pressured and threatened the patriarchate, the more Greek politicians would be intimidated. As Turkey's permanent representative to the UN remarked to his Greek counterpart, Palamas, "It is fated that Turkish public opinion shall consider the Greek minority and the Patriarchate responsible—even though and in fact they are not responsible— for anti-Turkish efforts abroad. In politics…the innocent pay for the mistakes of those who are really responsible."[23]

By the time the pogrom occurred, the patriarch had not only been subjected to the incessant condemnation of the Turkish press and extremist

brief account of the Turkish press attacks on the patriarch, see Chapter 1.

[23] Greek Embassy, Washington to Athens, No. 2334, September 27, 1955.

groups, but some Orthodox churches and Greek stores had also actually been attacked. Had not Kerim Gökay, Istanbul's *vali*, increased the number of soldiers and police guarding it, there is no doubt that Turkish rioters would have inflicted heavy damage on the patriarchate as well, as they did with over 90 percent of the other Greek religious institutions in the region. While the mob did, in fact, attack the patriarchal grounds on the night of September 6, managing to break a few windows, it was easily driven away by the soldiers and police guarding the premises.

Despite the martial law imposed after the violence, which remained in effect until early 1956, religious passions continued to rage; if anything, as US consul Katherine Bracken had noted in her report on anti-minority sentiment, events had actually accentuated resentment toward the non-Muslim elements of the population. By the end of 1955, before martial law was lifted, the patriarch was subject to additional pressures as a result of two new false rumors, the most serious of which was that Cyprus's Turkish mufti, Dana Efendi, had been murdered by Greek Cypriots. Although it was untrue, this rumor proved to be so disturbing—and dangerous for the Greeks—that, on December 9-10, General Aknoz took drastic measures, deploying tanks and soldiers at all of Istanbul's strategic points, which had not seen this kind of operation since September 7. On the morning of December 10, Aknoz also called a formal meeting of the press in which he condemned the events of September 6-7, which, he said, had been exploited by Turkey's enemies. He then called attention to the rumor about Dana Efendi, which, as with the pogrom, he blamed on communists. He categorically denied the rumor and informed the press that he had assured Kapsambelês, who had visited him on the previous day, that the Greek community would be in no danger. He was also visited by Alexandros Chatzopoulos, who, too, was assured that the Greeks of Istanbul were safe. That same morning, Aknoz posted Turkish soldiers in every Greek school and church,[24] thus helping to alleviate the fear of the Greek and other minorities.[25]

At the same time that the rumor about the mufti was circulating, a member of parliament introduced yet another series of rumors in that body. According to the December 24, 1955, edition of *Vatan*, deputy Şeyhan Sinan Tekelioğlu addressed the following question to Menderes: "Is the Government aware that there is, in the Archives of the Patriarchate in Fener, a document, signed by the entire Holy Synod, which asks for Russian

---

[24] Ypourgeion Exôterikôn, Istanbul to Athens, No. 2100, December 12, 1955; see also Ypourgeion Exôterikôn, Istanbul to Athens, No. 2172, December 17, 1955, for the text of the Turkish newspaper *Journal d'Orient*, December 17, 1955.

[25] Ypourgeion Proedrias Kyvernêseôs, No. 1964/A 12736, December 30, 1955.

assistance in establishing a Patriarchal State. If he [Menderes] knows this, what does he think of it?"[26] (That day's edition of *Vatan* had also carried an attack by the newspaper's owner and editor, Ahmet Amin Yalman, against the Greek judicial system in connection with the trials of the two Turkish consuls in Thessalonikê.) The Greek government addressed this accusation on December 27, 1955, through a Radio Athens commentator who responded on the program regularly broadcast to Greek-speakers in Turkey. He ridiculed the charge of conspiring to create a "Patriarchal State," since there never had been one in history (in contrast to a papal state), and the very institution was completely foreign to the ecclesiology and theology of the Orthodox churches. He then asked, "Is [this charge]…just gross folly or is it a new signal for new uprisings and vandalism?"[27]

These two episodes, the first more serious than the second, were symptomatic of the rumor mill that, according to many Turkish, Greek, and foreign observers, had created the climate for the pogrom—which continued long thereafter, with more or less intensity depending on the situation in Cyprus. By mid-December 1955, the Turkish columnist, Peyami Safa, writing in *Milliyet*, titled a piece, "All Lies":

> For some days now, rumors have been raging and put into motion all the networks of intrigue and incitement that had created the atmosphere of September 6. Someone approaches and says to you:
> "Have you heard the news? In Cyprus they murdered Dana Efendi."
> A lie! We are journalists and we have at our disposal all kinds of means to get the news.…We inquire, we research, and we utilize the network of our reporters.…There is no such thing, it is a lie.
> And another says to you:
> "Have you heard the news? This time it is true: The entire house of Atatürk in Salonika was completely blown up."
> A lie. This time there was no bomb, not even a rock the size of a hazelnut thrown at the house of Atatürk.

[26] Ypourgeion Exôterikôn, Ankara to Athens, No. 1368, December 27, 1955. The text was taken from the Istanbul Greek newspaper, *Apogeumatinê*; see also Ypourgeion Exôterikôn, Athens to Istanbul, No. 55386 EK/3a, December 30, 1955.

[27] TNA:PRO, London, No. RK 10110/1, January 6, 1956. Tekelioğlu's charges were historically and politically senseless to such a degree that they did not arouse the Turkish government's interest. The latter was much more concerned with the pending questions of compensation legislation and the cessation of the Thessalonikê trials against their consuls. But to the unknowing masses, this was yet one more tasty political morsel. The publication of *The Inside Story of the Patriarchate* by Ali Karakurt in 1955 was to be a particular irritant for Patriarch Athênagoras (see TNA:PRO, London, No. 30, April 2, 1958), and he actually began legal proceedings for libel, but then dropped the matter.

"Have you heard the news? The massacre of the Turks in
Cyprus has begun."
A lie!
"Have you heard the news? England granted Cyprus to
Greece and the latter granted bases to the English."
All lies.
All the sources, whether governmental or informal, to which
we turn tell us that nothing has happened in Cyprus which is of
concern to Turkey....All are lies.
I assure all the innocent children of the fatherland that all
these rumors are pure lies.
And, I also assure that these concoctions of lies will not be
able to create a new September 6.[28]

By 1958, suspicion and hatred of the patriarchate had become deeply
rooted in a significant portion of Turkish public opinion and had added yet
another layer to latent religious fanaticism and virulent chauvinism. For the
Turkish government, it was a readymade tool that was extensively used to
exert pressure on the Greek government and to get Western governments
to recognize this religious force. To a certain degree, but increasingly, the
Turkish government itself was affected by this hostility to the patriarchate.
This, too, was a legacy of the pogrom. Without going into any great detail,
the documentation of the three years following the pogrom sufficiently
illustrates a kind of institutionalization of this hostility.

As the struggle over Cyprus intensified, Turkish enmity toward the
patriarchate became an increasingly integral element of Turkish religious
feelings. In late April 1957, the situation of the patriarchate occasioned a
new evaluation of its status by the US embassy in Ankara: "Public clamor for
punitive action against the Patriarchate has been at a particularly high pitch
in the past few days, especially in the Istanbul Press. Consul General [Robert
Graham] Miner [in Istanbul] believes that the Government of Turkey is
certainly tolerating, if not encouraging the press campaign since it could
be terminated by invoking any one of several articles of the press law and
probably by mere word of advice to the editors."[29] Although Miner believed
that Menderes's actual stance toward Patriarch Athênagoras was personally
friendly, he also thought that Menderes had encouraged the attack on the
patriarchate on the grounds that the UK's release of Makarios from his exile,
and the latter's invitation to New York by then-Governor Averill Harriman,

[28] The text appeared, in Greek translation, in the Istanbul *Apogeumatinê*, December 18, 1955,
at a time when the local political atmosphere was charged with wild anti-Greek rumors.
[29] National Archives, Ankara to Washington, No. 2427, April 21, 1957.

put an entirely new complexion on the matter. The US embassy report quoted Miner's observation that "the Patriarchate is less secure than at any time since 1925." The report also stated that while the Turkish government had deemed it "folly to interfere with the Patriarchate" in the past, it now considered pressure on the patriarchate as very useful in pressuring Greece, as well as western Europe and the US. The report also saw this new stance as "dovetail[ing] nicely with Islamic psychology, re the 'infidel' and Kemalist ideas on 'the oil and water' character of religion and politics."[30] It concluded, finally, that the embassy would continue to monitor the situation.

This state of affairs was emphasized by Miner himself in his monthly survey of political developments in Istanbul filed the same month. The public concern with Cyprus was characterized as an "intense preoccupation":

> Istanbul was angry this month. Reactions to the various discouraging...developments of the month for the most part varied only in the degree of hatred and bitterness displayed toward Greece, the Greek minority here, the Patriarchate, Great Britain and, in some instances, the U.S....
>
> The prime local target of the rising tide of feeling was the Patriarchate. A widespread and persistent campaign demanded its removal to Greece. The city won popular approval when it suggested that all or part of the Patriarchal buildings might be condemned in the course of [the] Istanbul urban improvement plan."[31]

Such were the passions that three Istanbul newspapers (*Milliyet, Tercüman,* and *Tan*) urged the government to reconsider its alliance with the West and seek more advantageous relations with the Soviet Union.

In yet another evaluation, a State Department report to Dulles about a year later indicated that the Turkish government had continued to treat the patriarchate in a very rough manner despite the general public relations between Menderes and Athênagoras. According to Warren, "public animosity against the institution...could easily burst into flame at any moment....Thus it seems likely that the Patriarchate will continue to be blamed for any actions taken on Cyprus under the leadership of the Cypriote clergy."[32] The US view of the patriarchate's gloomy situation seemed to be confirmed by the British. The British ambassador reported on May 1, 1957, that, upon inquiry in the Turkish foreign ministry, he had been informed that the matter of expelling the patriarchate from Istanbul, as well as of limiting Greek work permits,

---

[30] *Ibid.*
[31] National Archives, American Consul General, Istanbul to Washington, No. 333, May 6, 1957.
[32] National Archives, Ankara to Washington, unnumbered, April 10. 1955.

had been under discussion for some time, but that these measures would not be implemented unless the Greek government proceeded to actions that would justify them.[33] Further British reports confirmed this worsening of the patriarchate's position.[34]

This hostility seems to have infected a part of the Turkish political and journalistic elite. A vitriolic, racist, and antisemitic expression of this intolerance appeared in the pages of *Hürriyet*, not unexpectedly. Written by its night editor, Selçuk Candarlı, and entitled, "Nourish a Viper," it appeared on February 11, 1958, and was a general anti-minority attack:

> The time has come to speak openly. There is a minority hostile to anything Turkish, yet we want to consider this group as brothers. The greatest part of this minority, despite our attitude, awaits the occasion to attack us when our backs are turned....
>
> How can the national economy be strengthened while we have these sycophants with us ? What is it to Apostol, Mişon, and Onnik whether Turkey regains her economic strength? If black-market conditions prevail and continue to ravage the country, this only facilitates their business. They don't care whether the cost-of-living figures go up or down. If their rackets are uncovered, Apostol will flee to Greece, Mişon to the Promised Land, and Onnik to America [as there was, presumably, no independent Armenia at the time], where he can vilify Turkey where for so long he has obtained his daily bread.
>
> We are running out of patience and can no longer tolerate such a hostile minority. Our country is open to those who call it their fatherland and who share our troubles. The rest can all leave as soon as possible. We don't want to nourish vipers in our bosom.[35]

Menderes apparently wrote the stiff reply (published in the DP newspaper, *Havadis*, on February 15, 1958) that attacked *Hürriyet* (which had promised

[33] TNA:PRO, Ankara to London, No. 1783/47, May 9, 1957.

[34] On the worsening condition of the patriarchate, see TNA:PRO, Ankara to London, No. 1783/50, May 31, 1957, and TNA:PRO, WCC to FO, No. RK1781/20, December 20, 1957. TNA:PRO, Ankara to London, No. 1783/50, April 2, 1968, files a report on court action begun by the patriarchate against Ali Karakurt for his book and the Turkish prosecutor's office's rejection of the patriarch's petition. The British chancery in Ankara described the book as "pretty poor, sensational stuff full of weird stories of conspiracy by the Greek Orthodox Clerics...against the Turkish State."

[35] National Archives, Ankara to Washington, No. 67, February 19, 1958.

[36] For an analysis of the reasons that kept minorities on the DP's side, see the interesting paper by Betty Carp, assistant attaché to the US consul-general in Istanbul, entitled "Attitude of the Istanbul Minorities in Recent Elections," National Archives, Ankara, No. 17, November 21, 1957.

to support Menderes in the 1957 elections, but had failed to do so).[36] Miner reported that Turkish newspaper attacks on the Greeks and the patriarchate were silenced for an entire week. Clearly, the Turkish government had the power, if it so chose, to put an end to the attacks on the patriarchate. It may have been that this intervention had been due to political reasons, a matter of internal politics. Not only had *Hürriyet* not supported Menderes, but the vote of the Istanbul minorities had been very important, as they had continued to support the DP. In the final analysis, the choice between the RPP and DP left the minorities no real alternative. *Hürriyet's* racist assault called to mind the harsh days of the İnönü regime and its quasi-fascist racism. Obviously, the pogrom had been no less horrific for the minorities. In 1957, however, much in need of their votes, which were estimated at 90,000, the DP successfully wooed them, even the Greeks (who were the last to come over). Menderes had bowed to the political necessity of the domestic situation without, however, radically changing his Cyprus policy or his government's behavior regarding the patriarchate and the Greek minority. Indeed, wooing the Greek minority in view of the elections, and intervening with the press, were both temporary measures that, once effective, were then suspended as the established order of politics was back on course.

A last, illuminating incident is of particular interest for the light it sheds on the Turkish elite's views on the pogrom and the patriarchate. Canon H. M. Waddams, general secretary of the Church of England Council on Foreign Affairs, requested and was given a meeting with the Turkish ambassador in London (and future prime minister), Ali Suat Hayri Ürgüplü, to discuss the canon's anxieties about the ecumenical patriarchate. On January 4, 1957, after the meeting, which lasted fifty minutes, Waddams sent a summary to the Foreign Office, accompanied by a short letter in which he asked a certain Young of the ministry for his comments.[37] Waddams had apparently been displeased by the blunt aggressiveness of Ürgüplü, who presented a side of Turkish diplomacy that, if accurate, was anything but subtle or refined. In summarizing his main impressions of the conversation, Waddams found the ambassador to be almost completely negative (with one exception). At the beginning of their meeting, the canon had expressed his interest in obtaining information from the ambassador on three points: the events of September

---

[37] TNA:PRO, Church of England to FO No. RK1041/1, January 4, 1957:

> I must confess that I am somewhat alarmed and am inclined to feel that a policy of saying nothing may very well play into the hands of the extreme elements.
> I should very much value your comments on the matter if it is not pressing too much on your time.

6-7; a bill introduced in the Turkish parliament for the expulsion of the patriarchate from Istanbul; and the arrest of important members of the Greek community (probably a reference to the arrest of *Ellênikê Enôsis* members and the closing of the organization). However, "the Ambassador began by emphasizing the extremely low standard, both morally and educationally, of the Greek Orthodox clergy and stressed that their influence…was anti-Turkish." Ürgüplü then returned to his interlocutor's original questions:

> In regard to the riots…they were notable for the fact that there was no loss of life, and the Turkish Government could easily put right the material damages, but, if provocation by the Greeks continued in Cyprus and elsewhere, it was more than likely that there would be another riot, only this time it would be a massacre and the police and the troops would probably be on the side of the rioters. He added that life was cheap in the Mediterranean, that fighting was the Turkish national sport, and that Turks outnumbered Greeks by three or four to one.
>
> He then went on to say that the Radcliffe proposals for Cyprus…would be accepted by the Turks as a basis for further development. If, however, the Greeks refused this the Turks would ask for Partition of the Island, and, if that were refused the Turks would insist on the revision of the Treaty of Lausanne, which would end the matter once for all by exchanging the whole of the Greek population of Turkey-in-Europe for the Turks in Thrace and elsewhere.
>
> I said twice very emphatically that any such solution would be a calamity….
>
> My own comment on this is that I very much fear it may be true (Waddams).

Waddams's further comments bear rereading as he realized that Ürgüplü's violent reactions indicated what many other Turks thought about the Greek minority. Their security can only be ensured, Waddams stated, "if the British and American Governments, particularly the latter, are prepared to make it clear to the Turkish Government that they will in no circumstances countenance any such developments as that suggested by the Ambassador and that they require guarantees of some sort that the Turkish Government is civilised enough to secure the safety and well-being of the minorities within the boundaries of its State."[38]

[38] TNA:PRO, London, No. FO371/130194 XC198479, January 3, 1957. Viscount (Cyril John) Radcliffe's proposals in the latter part of 1956 to secure an agreement on a system of self-government for Cyprus collapsed after the fall of Antony Eden, and his replacement as prime minister by Harold Macmillan, and under the pressure of the Turkish government. See

The MP Francis Noel-Baker was not the only Briton to react to the revelations of Canon Waddams and to Ürgüplü's mention of a possible massacre in which police and army would participate—and, by implication, the Turkish government would be involved. The memorandum also startled officials in the Foreign Office, which had been so discreet and even timid in raising the question of compensations for British citizens who had suffered damages in the pogrom. The first reaction in the Foreign Office was one of consternation that the Turkish ambassador would have made such a belligerent statement. The Foreign Office realized that the Turkish government had been telling Britain's ambassadors and consuls one thing, while Ürgüplü had thundered out something completely antithetical. In the past, the Foreign Office had tended to play down several aspects of the pogrom, and had defended the Turkish government's remorse and desire for full compensation. Both assertions turned out to be false. Ürgüplü, after all, was not a lone and idiosyncratic official; he represented the mindset of other Turkish officials in regard to the patriarchate and the minorities. Noel-Baker had understood this and expressed it succinctly to the British secretary of state: "Waddam's account is the latest of a series of indications which have come to my notice that the Turks have been talking in this strong and, in my view, highly undesirable way for some time....In these circumstances, it would seem to me to be of the highest importance to bring it to the attention of the Turkish Government that both the British Government and public opinion in this country would react in the strongest way to any suggestion of renewed violence against the Greeks in Turkey or to any interference with the Oecumenical Patriarchate."[39]

But the relevant department of the Foreign Office was less concerned over Ürgüplü's blunt threat than over the contradiction between his statement and the Turkish government's official policy. Indeed, the Foreign Office's concerns were quite different from those of the Anglican canon and British MP. On January 7, 1957, C. T. Brant of the Foreign Office's Southern Department entered his analysis of the Waddams-Ürgüplü conversation into the official files. This document deserves close attention:

It is incredible that the Turkish Ambassador, his country's

Brandon O'Malley and Ian Craig, *The Cyprus Conspiracy: America, Espionage and the Turkish Invasion*, London, 1999, pp. 37, 47, and 55-56.

[39] TNA:PRO, London, No. FO371/130194 XC198479, January 3, 1957; in his memorandum, Waddams had commented of the conversation with the Turkish ambassador: "It seems remarkable to me that such things could be uttered in cold blood in London, for surely it must show that he is quite convinced that the British Government would permit the Turks to carry out these threats without any serious results to them."

representative in London should have uttered such serious threats about his Government's attitude towards the Greek minority in Istanbul, and to the Church of England Council on Foreign Relations above all people. Anything better calculated to alienate the Council completely, and to confirm its fears that the Turks and not the Greeks are the disturbers of the peace in the Eastern Mediterranean, could hardly be imagined. One can only presume that the Turks are contemplating resorting to threats if they fail to achieve their objectives over the Cyprus question by negotiation. One is, too, quite convinced that the threat is no empty one, and that although the Istanbul Riots of September, 1955, were such a sorry performance on the Turks' part, there would be little hesitation on the part of the Turks in provoking some further incidents to lead to a renewal of the trouble.

...In particular, the Turkish Ambassador's utterances cut the ground completely from under our feet in the matter of the Oecumenical Patriarchate. In both Mr. Young's letter to Canon Waddams at RK 1781/8 and my letter to Colonel Barron at -/10, we have taken the line, based on evidence given us by Ankara and Istanbul, that the Turks are not deliberately provoking the Greek minority, and that they are in fact anxious to avoid any further strain on their relations with Greece. In view of this clear divergence, we should, I suggest, admit frankly to the Council that the Ambassador's statements are completely out of line with what we have previously understood from the Embassy at Ankara. We should in view of this seek some enlightenment from the Turkish Government via the embassy at Ankara, and so we should inform Canon Waddams....[40]

Brant had begun to understand that Ürgüplü's threats constituted a reality in Turkish policy, and so needed an explanation as to why they conflicted with Turkey's official line. He was concerned with the fact that, "In particular, the Turkish Ambassador's utterances cut the ground completely from under our feet in the matter of the Oecumenical Patriarchate," and confessed that the Foreign Office had accepted Ankara's claims about establishing good relations with Greece and ensuring the safety of the Greek minority and the patriarchate.

A second analysis attached to the text of the Waddams-Ürgüplü conversation is that of John Edgar Galsworthy. It is shorter but agrees, in part, with Brant:

This was a remarkable piece of stupidity on the part of the

[40] TNA:PRO, London, No. RK1071/1, July 1, 1957.

Ambassador. Perhaps knowing that he was on the verge of leaving he felt free to vent his spleen against the extremely philhellene Church of England. It seems clear to me that he was deliberately trying to make Canon Waddams' flesh creep. I would be inclined to invite the Canon to call and to tell him quite frankly that we are baffled by this outburst; that we have no evidence that it conforms to Turkish Government policy; but that we have asked for advice from Sir J. Bowker [the UK's ambassador in Ankara] and will let him know its import....[41]

Like his colleague, Galsworthy was concerned primarily with the incompatibility between what Turkey claimed was its official policy toward Greece, the Greek minority, and the patriarchate, and Ürgüplü's statements to Waddams. Neither British official considered the possibility that there may have been a "sanitized" policy fabricated by the Turkish government for American and European consumption and a real policy, known only to the upper echelons of government. In the end, Nuri Birgi's response to the British ambassador to Ankara confirmed the truth: he refused to apologize for Ürgüplü's remarks.[42]

As we have already seen, the US diplomatic mission in Turkey was ordered to investigate the massive desecration of Greek Orthodox churches, monasteries, and cemeteries. Indeed visitors to the scenes after the desecrations, as well as eyewitness accounts, were so numerous that this aspect of the general violence is undeniable. The US embassy sent at least four reports to the State Department (at the latter's request) on this specific issue. On the evening of September 23, Warren had already had a lengthy discussion with Melih Esenbel, acting secretary-general of the Turkish foreign ministry, who "recognized that these [desecrations] had not received publicity abroad in any way commensurate" with their gravity. Warren added that, "While we have heard many private expressions [of] profound regret on this particular aspect, there have in fact been no specific references thereto in official public statements."[43]

[41] TNA:PRO, London, No. RK1781, January 9, 1957.

[42] There is more British documentation on the course of this episode in Ankara and on Birgi's "explanation" to Ambassador Bowker, as well as on the former's refusal to issue an apology for his ambassador in London: TNA:PRO, London to Waddams, No. RK1071/1, January 11, 1957, and No. FO371/130194 XC198479, London to Ankara, April 11, 1957; TNA: PRO, London to Noel-Baker, No. RK1071/1(a), July 14, 1957; TNA:PRO, No. RK1781/7, with documents dated February 7, 12, and 14, 1957. Finally, for the episode's "resolution," see Bowker's letter to London, No. 1783/32, March 15, 1957, outlining Birgi's hard line and refusal to apologize.

[43] National Archives, Ankara to Washington, No. 487, September 24, 1955.

Since no formal acknowledgment by the Turkish government was forthcoming on this matter, the US embassy returned to the issue after Birgi had replaced Esenbel as secretary-general. In a meeting called specifically to discuss religious desecrations, US counselor Foy Kohler informed the State Department that he had tried to impress on Birgi the serious concern of the US regarding them and the "possible consequences thereof." Birgi, however, much as his predecessor had done, tried to avoid the issue by first asserting that Turkey had taken no final decision on the matter. As has already been noted, Birgi did not consider this to be a serious, let alone a moral, issue, but merely a spinoff of the larger Cyprus problem. After all, according to him, incidents of desecration were nothing new. He saw the matter "practically," not as an issue to be faced morally in which the facts of the case were painfully obvious. Rather, he proposed that Turkey organize "an appropriate counter-propaganda campaign"—in effect, a reflection of the real attitude of much of the Menderes government to the ethical violations of the pogrom and of Turkey's guilt in this matter.[44]

In October 1955, *Time* magazine published three articles and photographs on the pogrom and Turkey, all of which were quite critical of the country, albeit mildly so. Although the issue containing the first article was not allowed to circulate in Turkey (as it included details of the violence), the second issue did circulate, "and it served to bring home to the Turks the very real concern of outsiders with respect to the religious desecration that took place during the riots."[45] Despite the censorship and Menderes's strict press laws, which tended to bridle the press, *Vatan's* publisher called his readers' attention to the serious nature of the charges concerning the religious vandalism and other matters, and warned them that other foreign media had become much more hostile to Turkey than *Time* had been with its three articles.

The Greek foreign-ministry summary of events that was sent to all Greek diplomatic missions on October 11, 1955, dwelt on this issue in two sections:

> All the historical churches of the Queen of Cities [*Vasileuousa*, a common Greek description of Istanbul/Constantinople] were destroyed, the sacred vestments and vessels were desecrated most shamefully as the mob polluted in a beastly manner the holy altars as well; the priests were mocked publicly and tortured. The Bishop of Pamphilos was hurled into the flames, a nonagenarian monk

---

[44] National Archives, American Embassy, Ankara to Washington, No. 245, October 24, 1955.
[45] *Ibid.*

was burned alive, the graves of the dead were looted, their bones scattered, the skulls of the deceased Patriarchs and the sacred chalices and patens were used as urinals, while buried bodies were knifed; and statues and works of art in the Greek cemeteries were destroyed.[46]

In closing, the memorandum clarified that all the churches that were attacked were also, in fact, desecrated.

THE DESECRATION OF GREEK ORTHODOX CHURCHES

That the religious fanaticism that violated the Greek community of Istanbul is a fact—and not a figment of Greek, Christian, or Western prejudice—emerges from the examination of the very attacks on the community's religious life and institutions. The evidence of planned desecration is so overwhelming as to point to clear organization and strategy. It is also clear that, because of the specific definitions of such matters in Orthodox canon law, the assault on the institutional and liturgical core of their faith struck every Greek as, indeed, systematic desecration.

In Orthodoxy, desecration (*vevêlôsis*) is essentially a religious term that refers to the violation of any and all things sacred (*ta iera*), which are constituted of all that is dedicated to God and sacralized by His presence. In this sense, a church building is not a sacred building until the religious ceremony is held that consecrates it to God. The same holds true for all objects in it. The Greek canons draw a further distinction between the sacred and the holy. The holy refers to God but the object in question has not been consecrated to Him, and can thus be possessed by an ordinary individual. That is the case, for example, of a chalice (for communion wine), paten (metal tray for communion bread), icon, or metal or wooden cross, while it is being crafted and before its placement in the church. As such, it can be bought and sold, or gifted, freely, according to secular law, or melted down or reshaped to some other use. Once it is consecrated to God, however, and filled by His presence, it becomes sacred and, one might say, "in His sole possession." It can no longer be bought or sold, melted down, or recrafted. Consecration changes the object's status—indeed, its essence—completely, and any violation of this sacredness is a violation of the inviolable, and therefore subject to severe punishment.

Defilement or pollution (*miansis*) is a specific act of "soiling" the

---

[46] Greek Embassy, Athens to Diplomatic Missions Abroad, No. 43871/T.4.Ep., October 11, 1955; see also National Archives, American Embassy, Ankara to Washington, No. 228, December 1, 1955.

consecrated object and constitutes an element of desecration. It consequently denotes the specificity of desecration and is usually marked by the *physical* soiling of the consecrated object, most often in the case of the pogrom involving the urination or defecation upon these objects, or in places and parts of a church or cemetery. Another form of desecration to be seen during the pogrom was that of lampooning and ridiculing sacral liturgical acts and funereal practices (condemned by Orthodox canon law as *empaigmos*).[47]

Everything in an Orthodox church, monastery, or cemetery, including the buildings themselves, is thus sacred and is the domain and "possession" of God. Any act, and in some cases even statements, that disturb this state constitute a religious violation. Included in this sacred domain are, as said above, the physical structure, altar, *antimension*, *aeras* (tetragonal cloth covering the chalice and paten), chalice and paten, *exapteriga* (small metal plates carried as banners), icons and *iconostasis*, episcopal throne, pulpit, lectern, books and manuscripts (as well as the case holding them) used for the liturgy, candle-holders and candelabra, the standing-pews for the communicants, sacerdotal vestments, crosses, graves, and, of course, the bodies of the dead in the case of cemeteries. Any form of attack on any of these constitutes an attack on God, for their consecration (*kathierôsis*) is to Him, and so all are sacred. Even the crime of stealing is differentiated by whether the theft involves a secular or consecrated object. In Greek, theft is *klopê*, whereas the legal term for stealing sacred objects, both in the secular legal system of the Greeks and in the canon law of the Orthodox, is *ierosylia* (or sacrilege), which is a crime against God and religion. Finally, in matters of desecration and pollution, the canons draw attention to the intent of the act. The ethical nature of any violation of the sacred is determined by the intention of the individual or group committing it. Thus, if the act is accidental (and therefore unintentional), there is no desecration—although it does demand expiatory punishment of some sort (prayers, abstentions, etc.); if, however, the desecration is intentional, it brings heavy religious (and often secular) punishment in its wake.

Brief descriptions of these countless acts of vandalism and desecration were presented in Chapter 2. Here, the only point that bears repetition is the particular moral violence of many of these acts, such as the fact that defiled graves were marked by extensive defecation on the smashed gravestones, a practice that was also noted in the case of church altars (as with the Church

---

[47] On these acts and on their canonical definition, consult G. A. Rallês and M. Potlês, *Syntagma tôn theiôn kai ierôn kanôn*, Athens, 1992, reprint: Volume I, p. 80; Volume II, p. 682; Volume IV, pp. 150, 427, 450, 463, and 695; Volume V, pp. 413 and 414; and Volume VI, pp. 80 and 262.

of the Metamorphosis at Şişli described by Noel Barber). The religious rage of the demonstrators, more generally, seems to have been focused on the Greek Orthodox dead. It was as if these attacks were a compensatory violence for the prohibition against killing living Greeks, signs not only of religious hatred and a desire to desecrate and pollute a "competing" confession, but physical attacks on the actual bones, heads, and bodies of the deceased, who, in a sense, were symbolic victims, substituting for their living descendants, who had been safeguarded—with notable exceptions—by the pogrom's organizers. The eyewitness identified only as T. I. P. S., who was mentioned in Chapter 2, was of the opinion that this religious fanaticism, in active collaboration with the chauvinism of groups such as the Turkish National Union of Students, played an important role in "the manner by which the application and execution [of the pogrom] was inculcated into the demonstrators by the religious leaders in the mosques. Their sermons were full of hatred and passion."[48]

We also return once more to the correspondence of Despoina Portokallis, whose intrepid investigation of the pogrom's aftermath was cited in Chapter 3. We have already quoted from her reports on the destruction of Greek shops and dwellings, and on the harsh economic conditions imposed on the Greek minority and Greek nationals after the pogrom. Her attempts to investigate what had actually happened to many of the churches are no less remarkable and furnish us with extensive detail as to the specific vandalism. In her first letter (September 7-8, 1955), she observes that, "No church survived untouched. After looting them, they set all on fire." A friend from another part of the city tells her that the "churches of St. Constantine [and Helen], of Holy Trinity [in Taksim], of Christos [Soter, in Galata], St. Nicholas and St. Therapon are destroyed."[49] By her second letter, written fourteen days after the pogrom, Portokallis had managed to move extensively around the city and ascertain the extent and intensity of the violence:

> When I wrote...the first letter I had not yet gone out. But afterward when I did venture out...! It is one thing for people to tell you about it but it is entirely different when you see it with your own eyes. The newspapers reported that the bombing of London was not its equal....
>
> The churches were "virania" [desolations]. They say that once you go inside [them] you do not know on what you are treading.

---

[48] Tsoukatou, *Septemvriana*, p. 179; it is very difficult to determine the accuracy of this statement. Palaiologos, *Diagramma*, p. 2, makes a similar statement: "It was completely organized and completely secret. Those who had been initiated into the movement had been summoned to the mosques and swore on the Qu'ran to keep the plan a secret."

[49] Despoina Portokallis to Tatiana, September 7-8, 1955.

Is it ash? Dirt? Did they burn it? Did they remove the marble [floors]? No one knows. For one is treading upon scorched earth. The cemeteries have all become [mere] earth.

All those things that were above the earth have been buried, and all that was interred has been exhumed and placed above the earth. The cemetery is now guarded by soldiers with bayonets affixed to their rifles....Everyone must see the cemeteries of Şişli and Balıklı, even small children, so that they can recount this to their own grandchildren later. The Church of the Metamorphosis [at Şişli], its offices, and the ossuaries are all burned....They [the demonstrators] gathered all the white bones and poured gasoline on them...and burned them all. On the feast of the Holy Cross, they allowed everyone into the cemetery where the Patriarch delivered the *Trisagion* prayers [on behalf of the departed] atop the ashes of the bones from the ossuary....On the other side of the city, from Kontoskali [Kumkapı] to San Stefano (Yeşilköy), is now a great wasteland.[50]

In her third letter (October 6), Portokallis refers to the raids after the pogrom, during which police searched Turkish houses whose inhabitants were suspected of having participated in the attack and having looted churches:

Many Turks are cheeky and declare that the Greeks did all this, that they conceal bombs in their homes, and that it was the Greeks who had burned the churches. The police [now search the homes of pogromists and] take away what has been stolen, as well as silver icons. When the police arrest the thieves, the latter ask: "Is it not you who put us up to these things? Why are you arresting us now? You even told us that you would give us twenty liras!" The relatives of those now imprisoned are boiling mad: "What are they doing to us on behalf of the Infidels?"

Portokallis then proceeds to elaborate on the desecration of the cemetery of Şişli, criticizing Noel Barber's report for having skipped over the details. She writes that the dead were all exhumed and scattered about, the church burned (only its blackened walls remaining), and all of its marble facing smashed:

All the bones of the two ossuaries were thrown out and burned. You see the heads, arms, and the joints from the legs....No matter how hard I try I cannot really describe this to you. For you cannot understand it if you do no see it....They stripped off the gold and silver from the icon on my godmother's stone grave, and smashed

---

[50] Despoina Portokallis to Tatiana, September 20, 1955. In another district, the priests' vestments were thrown into the streets and used to decorate the local donkeys.

the glass covers of all the photographs and then tore them up....They took out the skulls [from graves] and stuck them on wooden sticks and paraded them in the streets.

Portokallis concludes mournfully: "All the churches were burned, a few of which still have the *iconostasis* and pulpit, as in the case of St. Nicholas in Galata....For [the rioters] would gather the [smashed] pews, lecterns, icons, *epitaphioi*, and whatever else was combustible and place it all in the center... [and] pour gasoline on it and burn...everything." (Portokallis does, however, give specific examples—albeit few in number—of local authorities, often alone and pistol in hand, dispersing mobs that were intent on destroying a particular church.)[51]

In her fourth letter (October 17), Portokallis writes that "people here are terrified as we walk about and gaze upon the churches." She describes visiting the churches of Christos Soter (Christ the Savior) in Galata and Saints Constantine and Helen in Pera: the *kantiles* (glass oil-lamps hanging in front of the *iconostasis*) and chandeliers no longer existed; the icons had all been smashed; and the *pankaria*, pulpits, and thrones had also all been shattered. She is almost elegiacal in her summation:

> They say that throughout the city there are churches where only the front wall has remained standing...and even the skeleton [of the church] has collapsed, and where the standing wall has only uncovered holes for windows and door. They say also that in the district of Vefa they took out [from the church the large] crucifix and, as they were parading it about, from behind they were beating it and throwing stones at it. They did this as they sang songs and mocked it. That is to say that, after 2,000 years, they have regressed to the state of civilization of that time.

She closes her letter with an item from the Istanbul daily, *Cumhuriyet*, reporting that the rioters had smashed the mausolea of the Greek patriarchs in the cemetery of Balıklı and had thrown their remains out on the streets.[52]

Perhaps the patriarchal committee's reports on damages shall one day surface. As this matter now stands, one must rely on portions of the *vakıflar* documents dealing with the costs, contracts, and materials for repairing and rebuilding a large number of, but not all, the damaged churches, cemeteries, and monasteries. Dêmêtrios Kaloumenos's photographic archives are an excellent, and specific, visual source as well. Nevertheless, Portokallis's

---

[51] Despoina Portokallis to Tatiana, October 6, 1955; she includes a description of how the interior of the *Megalê tou Genous Scholê* was burned.

[52] Despoina Portokallis to Tatiana, October 17, 1955.

testimony is extremely important, not only for the specific data it adds to our knowledge, but also because of her broader understanding of the events. She combined her very considerable analytical ability with her perception of the details surrounding the pogrom.

In the eyewitness accounts of the violence and vandalism, such as Bishop Gregory's memorandum and Despoina Portokallis's correspondence, one finds data on specific acts of desecration. The bishop's data are reliable, one assumes, inasmuch as they were prepared for the patriarch, who was responsible for submitting damage claims to Menderes on behalf of the churches. Specifically, Gregory reported on the attacks sustained by the churches of Christos Soter, St. Nicholas, St. John of the Chians (all three located in Galata), the Koimesis of the Theotokos (in Palio Banio), and St. Phokas (in Ortaköy). Although the report is quite good, it gives rather general descriptions of damage for the first church, while satisfying itself by repeating that, since the attacks were similar in each case for the others, there was no point in going into the same details for all five churches. Is the report reliable? All doubts may be satisfied by consulting Kaloumenos's evidence, which begins from the morning after the pogrom. A tabulation of this body of photographic evidence, which documents the damages in thirty-nine churches, monasteries, and cemeteries, is necessary as it is far more detailed than any written or oral testimony. Consequently, I list below the damaged items from the churches in the bishop's report, and, parallel to that, record Kaloumenos's photographic documentation of destroyed or desecrated objects.[53]

[53] The name of Dêmêtrios Kaloumenos has appeared repeatedly in this study, and indeed he has performed an invaluable service to a better historical understanding of the pogrom. Having photographed the ruins and destruction under very dangerous and difficult circumstances, he managed to preserve his photographic archive. Since then, it has enriched our knowledge of these events in a most remarkable way. Selecting a relatively smaller number of photographs from his archive, Kaloumenos published an album of 279 of them that he had taken of the destroyed or damaged churches, monasteries, cemeteries, *agiasmata*, businesses, and dwellings of the Istanbul Greek community. The first edition, *Ê staurôsis tou Christianismou* (Athens, 1966), featured a commentary in Greek and English and was accompanied by two introductions. All 279 photographs were numbered and each was accompanied by an identification index in the narrative itself. A second edition was printed in 1978, with the same photographs. The third edition, which appeared in 1991, was printed on paper far superior to that of the first two printings, and the photographs are therefore far clearer and sharper. Unfortunately, however, this edition's editor introduced confusion into the identification legends of many photographs, often misattributing them to the wrong church or, in a few cases, attributing the same structure to different churches. This regrettable error arose from a much more serious, indeed tragic, accident: Dêmêtrios Kaloumenos lost his eyesight as the result of being struck by an automobile, and so can no longer help us to clarify these inexplicable changes in the third edition. Perhaps those familiar with the churches photographed can help to clarify the issue in the future although most of the photographs are identifiable with certainty. Finally,

Table 29: Damage to Christos Soter

Bishop Gregory's report	Kaloumenos photographs
vestments	vestments
chalices, patens	altar
Gospels	sacred books
icons	icons
iconostasis	*iconostasis*
chandeliers	chandeliers
pews	pews
manoualia	pulpit
lecterns	episcopal throne
pulpit	crucifix
episcopal throne	baptismal font
all sacred objects	*kouvoukli*
only columns left[54]	*epitaphios*[55]

The photographs confirm the destruction of most of the sacred items reported by the bishop; in addition, they also document the desecration of the crucifix on the altar, the baptismal font, the *kouvoukli* (or funeral bier, the elaborate wooden cage-screen in which the *epitaphios* resides), and the *epitaphios* itself (the embroidered brocade depicting the dead Christ). Kaloumenos's photographs also document the various "styles" of desecrating icons and *iconostasia*: split or "blinded" (that is, the eyes punched out); smashed and burned; and stripped of the silver adornments to various parts of the body of the painted subject. The pictures also record the damages to meeting and reception rooms, and the church generally. The photograph of a chair hanging from a lavish, if damaged, chandelier is a testament to the fury of the unknown pogromist who hurled the chair.

one should note, in the third edition, the new essay by Professor Neoklês Sarrês, which is an excellent analysis of the social, economic, and political evolution of Turkish Istanbul, as well as Turkish society in general.

[54] Greek Embassy, Athens to Washington, No. 4274, EK/39, October 14, 1955.

[55] Kaloumenos, photographs, roll 4a, nos. 3A, 4A, 6A, 7A, 9A, 17A, 20A, 21A, 22A, and 42A-44A; roll 5, nos. 2, 4, 5, 11, 39, 41, 44A, 5, 6A, 7A, 11A, 12A, and 18.

Table 30: Damage to St. Nicholas of Galata

Bishop Gregory's report	Kaloumenos photographs
icons	icons
doors	pulpit
everything desecrated	*pankari*
and destroyed[56]	*iconostasis*
	pews
	altar
	iron rails
	sacred vestments
	offices
	crucifix
	liturgical objects
	kouvoukli
	gynaeconitis
	epitaphios
	priest's library
	candelabra
	chandeliers[57]

The photographs present a variety of desecrations: smashing, cutting and hacking, "blinding," "mutilation" (of body extremities, or *akrôteriasmos* in Greek) and defacement of murals.

Table 31: Damage to St. John of the Chians

Bishop Gregory's report	Kaloumenos photographs
same level of	*iconostasis*, altar
destruction and burning	icons, *pankari*
icons of narthex	chalices, pews
chalices	sanctuary, lobby
vestments	candlesticks, chandelier
patens[58]	candlelabra[59]

---

[56] As in footnote no. 54.
[57] Kaloumenos, photographs, roll 2a, nos. 1A-6A and 16A-44A; also rolls 2b, 3, 4, and 6.
[58] As in footnote no. 54.
[59] Kaloumenos, photographs, roll 9, nos. 3A-36A.

Table 32: Damage to Koimesis of the Theotokou

Bishop Gregory's report	Kaloumenos photographs
mass destruction	destruction of left side
manoualia	altar, sanctuary
icons	icons
chalices	chalices
sacred books	altar table
patens	candlestick
pankari	candlelabra
cell of deacon[60]	pews
	smashed objects lying about[61]

Table 33: Damage to St. Phokas

Bishop Gregory's report	Kaloumenos photographs
suffered same fate as	icons
above churches[62]	baptismal font
	cabinets
	liturgical objects
	offices
	icon frames
	kouvoukli
	tables
	sacred books
	reception
	windows[63]

On the basis of this rough comparison of the written episcopal report and the photographic evidence, one quickly notes that they are basically in agreement and that the photographs flesh out in considerable, if not complete, detail the furious activity of the pogromists.

The same conclusion emerges from a similar examination of the letters of Despoina Portokallis. Kaloumenos's photographs testify to the total destruction of a number of churches, including the Panagia (Belgratkapı),[64]

---

[60] As in footnote no. 54.

[61] Kaloumenos, photographs, roll 34, nos. 9-32.

[62] Kalounenos, photographs, as in footnote no. 54.

[63] Kaloumenos, photographs, roll 6, 11A, 14, 17A, and 22; roll 21, nos. 1-7; roll 22, nos. 2-11 and 26-44.

[64] Kaloumenos, photographs, roll 1, nos. 10-15.

Saints Theodoroi (Langa),[65] St. Menas (Samatya),[66] St. George Kyparissas (Samatya),[67] Panagia (Altı Mermer),[68] and the Church of the Metamorphosis at the cemetery at Şişli.[69] The totality of damages photographed by Kaloumenos can be broken down into the number of each type of desecration or destruction perpetrated. Although neither his photographs nor the many written testimonies give us a quantitatively exact picture of the damage (Kaloumenos did not photograph everything, and much of the destruction was absorbed into the nondescript debris that could not be identified but that literally covered the floors of most churches), the quantitative categorization of each particular type or act of desecration is nonetheless of some interest. Keeping in mind that Kaloumenos was active in only thirty-nine institutions, the resulting data are significant.

Table 34: Desecration to churches

Desecrated objects photographed	Number of churches in which the particular desecration occurred
1. altars	38
2. liturgical objects (chalices, patens, etc.)	32
3. icons	32
4. *iconostasia*	29
5. pews	28
6. candlelabra	26
7. building structures	24
8. church furniture	21
9. chandeliers	20
10. crucifixion	19
11. candlesticks	18
12. *kouvouklia-epitaphioi*	18
13. sacred vestments	17

[65] Kaloumenos, photographs, roll 7b, nos. 19 and 20; roll 9, no. 45.

[66] Kaloumenos, photographs, roll 16a, nos. 6A, 3A and 9A.

[67] Kaloumenos, photographs, roll 16a, nos. 11A-15A and 23A.

[68] Kaloumenos, photographs, roll 16a, nos. 24A-26A and 30; roll 16b, nos. 11, 12, and 16. These two rolls show the destruction of this large church, which covers the entire floor with a thick layer of debris and burned beams, and then, later, after the entire floor had been cleaned and the debris removed.

[69] Kaloumenos, photographs, roll 36, nos. 16A and 17A.

14. pulpits	16
15. *pankaria*	15
16. windows	14 or 15
17. episcopal thrones	14
18. sacred books and manuscripts	13
19. lecterns	13
20. iron railing of *solea*	10
21. doors	9
22. bells	9
23. crosses	9
24. staircases	6
25. frescoes	2+
26. *agiasmata*	very many
27. tombs	7?

Although Kaloumenos photographed the destruction selectively, in order to illustrate the nature of the attacks and because many of the sacred objects had been reduced to rubble, his work is even more valuable. As he photographed almost 45 percent of the structures and their contents, his images are representative, not only of the various forms of desecration but of the desecratory "preferences" of the enraged rioters. Altars, icons, *iconostasia*, pews, candelabra, the buildings themselves, chandeliers, crucifixes, and the *kouvouklia-epitaphioi* in particular engaged their attention. Not far behind was the desecration of cemeteries, and of the corpses buried therein and the bones in the ossuaries. Along with the abuse of corpses, defecation was particularly marked in the cemeteries, although altars also seem to have been systematically polluted with urine and feces. The Kaloumenos photographs bear horrible testimony to this sadder aspect of human behavior and confirm the depth and fury of the rioters' religious fanaticism.

THE NUMBER OF VIOLATED ECCLESIASTICAL INSTITUTIONS

Having dealt with the religious climate in Turkey that fed into the pogrom, it is time now to attempt to determine the number of religious institutions actually damaged and/or destroyed, and then to proceed to the enormous problem of compensations. While the various Greek communities ultimately had to undertake all the negotiations on damage claims with the department of the Istanbul *vakıflar*, which was to monitor the matter, the Committee for Repair and Compensation of Damages Suffered by the Churches and Charitable Institutions Because of the Incidents of September 6-7 (*6-7 Eylül hadiseler dolayısıyla Kilise ve Müessesatı Hayriyede vukua gelen hasarları tamir ve telafisi için teşkil edilmiş Hey'et,* hereinafter referred to as the Committee for Repair or *6-7 Eylül Hey'et*) was critical to the initial submission of claims. It was through this large and complex Greek committee that the vast majority of the Greeks' ecclesiastical claims passed before reaching the *vakıflar* for final approval and determination of compensation. According to the legislation of February 29, 1956, and the enabling act of the following July, the Greek communities would not directly receive the sums of money claimed as compensation. Whereas each community was to submit its claims through the Committee for Repair to the department of the *vakıflar*, the actual repair and rebuilding were assigned to the contractor who had bid successfully for the particular project. Once work began, contractors submitted invoices for work done to the Committee for Repair, and eventually the *vakıflar* would examine the invoices and decide on the appropriate payment. In other words, moneys never passed directly into the hands of the Greek community (unless the community itself had bid successfully as the contractor). This constant system of inspection and approval generated an entire body of documents intended to record the rebuilding process in all its details. Although the entirety of this extremely important body of materials was not accessible for the present study, the documentation concerning seventy-four Greek religious institutions was, in some cases, extensively so.

Very soon after the pogrom, the patriarch convened a meeting of the secular representatives of each Greek community. One such was Symeôn Vafeiadês, who lived in the district of Kuzguncuk, had his business in Gemiş, and seemed well-informed on this important matter; he described his participation: "A very few days after [the events], the Patriarch sent out an encyclical asking all the community governing boards to send one representative each to participate in the election of a representative council that would undertake the task of repairing the churches, Greek institutions, etc. The community of Kuzguncuk appointed me to represent it. Thus it was that I found myself, with another seventy representatives at this special session."[70] This committee, elected by the communities' representatives, took the lead in negotiating with the contractors, and above all with the *vakıflar*, in restoring both the buildings and their furnishings. It was only thanks to the information gathered and the damages catalogued by each community, especially regarding religious institutions, that the patriarchate was able to

---

[70] Tsoukatou, *Septemvriana*, p. 63.

distribute its first such official list, which can be found in the report sent by the US consulate in Istanbul to the State Department on September 27, 1955.[71] Following are the relevant parts of this report (original—and inconsistent—spelling of names has been maintained):

> A survey of the damage inflicted on public establishments of the Greek Community of Istanbul during the rioting on the night of September 6-7 shows that the destruction caused has been extremely widespread. In fact, only a very small percentage of community property appears to have escaped molestation. Although there are as yet no figures available assessing the damage sustained, the number of establishments attacked and the nature of the destruction caused in the course of the night under reference convey a clear picture of the scope of the devastation. In most cases the assault on these establishments involved a thorough wrecking of installations, furniture, equipment, desecration of holy shrines and relics, and looting. In certain instances serious damage was inflicted on the buildings themselves by fire.
>
> Information received from the Greek Orthodox Patriarchate shows that of the 95 houses of worship listed on the books of the Archbishopric of Istanbul 61 were either completely or partially damaged. Eight of them became the victims of flames. The religious edifices thus affected are identified as follows:
>
> 1. Aghia Triada, Taksim—Wrecked, pillaged and destroyed by fire
> 2. St. Constantin, Kalyoncu Kulluk—Wrecked, pillaged and destroyed by fire
> 3. Metamorphosis, Cemetery of Shishli—Wrecked, pillaged and destroyed by fire
> 4. Sotiros Christou, Galata—Wrecked and pillaged
> 5. Saint Nicolas, Galata—Wrecked and pillaged
> 6. Saint Jean, Galata—Wrecked and pillaged
> 7. Saint Dimitri, Kurtulush—Wrecked and pillaged
> 8. Saint Athanase, Kurtulush—Wrecked and pillaged
> 9. Saint Elethere, Kurtulush—Wrecked and pillaged
> 10. Evangelistria, Kurtulush—Wrecked and pillaged
> 11. Ghenethlion tis Theotocou, Beshiktash—Wrecked and pillaged
> 12. Saint Phocas, Ortakoy—Wrecked and pillaged

[71] I wish to thank the Greek journalist Alexis Papahelas, who gave me a copy of this critical document twelve years ago. Thereafter, it was conveyed to Helsinki Watch, which published it in their booklet, *The Greeks of Turkey*; I have published parts of it in Greek American journals and newspapers.

13. Saint Dimitri, Kurucheshme—Wrecked and pillaged

14. Ton Taxiarhon, together with residence of Bishop, Arnavutkoy—Wrecked and destroyed by fire

15. Saint Haralambos, Bebek—Wrecked and pillaged

16. Evanghelismos tis Theotokou, Boyacikoy—Wrecked and pillaged

17. Taxiarchon, Istinye—Wrecked and pillaged

18. Saint Nicolas, Yenikoy—Wrecked and pillaged

19. Saint Paraskevi, Tarabya and residence of Bishop—Wrecked and destroyed by fire

20. Saint Paraskevi, Buyukdere—Wrecked and pillaged

21. Saint Jean, Yeni Mahalle—Wrecked and pillaged

22. Saint Constantin, Pashabahche—Wrecked and pillaged

23. Genethlion tis Theotocou, Kandilli—Wrecked and pillaged

24. Saint George, Chengelkoy—Wrecked and pillaged

25. Prophet Ilia, Uskudar—Wrecked and pillaged

26. Agia Triada with residence of Bishop, Kadikoy—Wrecked, pillaged and destroyed by fire

27. Saint Georges, Kadikoy—Wrecked and pillaged

28. Saint Jean Chrysostome, Kadikoy—Wrecked and pillaged

29. Saint Ignace, Kadikoy—Wrecked and pillaged

30. Saint Dimitri, Buyukada—Wrecked and pillaged

31. Dormition of the Virgin, Buyukada—Wrecked and pillaged

32. Metamorphosis tou Christou, Buyukada—Wrecked and pillaged

33. Saint Georges, monastery, Heybeliada—Wrecked and pillaged

34. Saint Spiridon, monastery, Heybeliada—Wrecked and pillaged

35. Zoodochos Pighi, Balikli—Wrecked and destroyed by fire

36. Genethlion tis Theotocou, Beligradiou—Wrecked and pillaged

37. Saint Constantin, Samatya—Wrecked and pillaged

38. Saint Paraskevi, Samatya—Wrecked and pillaged

39. Saint Georges, Samatya—Wrecked and pillaged

40. Saint Minas, Samatya—Wrecked and pillaged

41. Dormition of the Virgin, Exi Marmara—Wrecked and pillaged

42. Saint Theodore [*sic*], Vlanga—Wrecked and pillaged

43. Saint Elpida, Kumkapi—Wrecked and pillaged

44. Saint Kiriaki, Kumkapi—Wrecked and pillaged
45. Saint Nicolas, Topkapu—Wrecked and pillaged
46. Saint Georges, Edirnekapu—Wrecked and pillaged
47. Dormition of the Virgin, Edirnekapu—Wrecked and pillaged
48. Another Dormition of the Virgin, Edirnekapu—Wrecked and pillaged
49. Taxiarchon, Balat, Egrikapu—Wrecked and pillaged
50. Panagia tis Soudas, Egrikapu—Wrecked and pillaged
51. Dormition of the Virgin, Blacherne, Ayvansaray—Wrecked and pillaged
52. Saint Dimitri, Xiloportis—Damaged
53. Dormition of the Virgin, Valinu—Damaged
54. Saint John Prodrome, Valinu, monastery—Wrecked
55. Saint George Potira—Wrecked
56. Vierge Mouchliotissa, Phanar—Wrecked and pillaged
57. Saint Nicolas, Cibali—Wrecked and pillaged
58. Saint Haralambos Chapel, Cibali—Wrecked and pillaged
59. Dormition of the Virgin, Vefa—Wrecked and pillaged
60. Saint Paraskevi, Haskoy—Wrecked and pillaged
61. Aghioi [*sic*] Therapon—Damaged.

In addition to the above religious establishments the following properties belonging to the Monastery of Mount Sinai, said to contain irreplaceable objects of art of Byzantine origin and religious relics of great value, apparently, also suffered serious destruction and pillage:

1. Monastery of St. Georges ti [*sic*] Kremnou, Heybeliada
2. Monastery of St. Georges, Fener
3. Monastery of St. Georges, Eynikoy [*sic*, Yeniköy]

Reports show that the dependencies of the religious edifices hit were also not spared and that very serious damage was inflicted on presbyteries and well-appointed community meeting headquarters, libraries, dispensaries attached to these establishments....

Reports on hand indicate that the rioting crowd hit with particular frenzy at the important Greek Orthodox community centers: the central cemetery at Shishli and the cemetery of the Patriarchs of Balikli. The former sustained particularly extensive destruction. Crosses and statues were knocked down, sepulchers and vaults opened and the remains of the dead removed and

dispersed. At Balikli, the sarcophaguses of the Greek Orthodox
Patriarchs were desecrated....[72]

Again, it bears repetition that the list above includes only about 65 percent of
the religious institutions of the Greek community of Istanbul.

The second list of attacked religious institutions, which one must again
assume was of patriarchal origin, was sent by A. I. Frydas, an official of the
Greek foreign ministry, to the Greek embassies in Washington, London,
Paris, and Beirut, and to the consulates in Jerusalem and Alexandria. Frydas
considered this to be an important document politically, and he accompanied
it with a brief letter in which he commented that:

> As to the significance of each of the destroyed churches, we note
> the following:
>   a) The church of St. George of Psamatheia [Samatya] and of
> the Panagia Mouchliotissa go back to the Byzantine era.
>   b) The *Agiasmata* of the Panagia Balıklı, Panagia Vefa, and
> Panagia of Vlaherna are of historical importance, as is the Sinaitic
> *metochion* [chapter] of St. George.
>   c) These churches are important either because of their size,
> or because they serve a well-populated district, or because they
> are wealthy and beautiful: Agia Trias in Staurodromion [Beyoğlu],
> St. Athanasios in Kurtuluş, St. Menas in Psamatheia, Saints
> Constantine and Helen in Psamatheia, St. Demetrios in Kurtuluş,
> Christos in Galata, St. Nicholas in Galata, St. John of the Chians
> in Galata, the Taxiarchs in Mega Reuma [Arnavutköy], Agia Trias
> in Chalcedon [Kadıköy], Prophet Elias in Skoutari [Üsküdar],
> St. Panteleimon in Kuzguncuk, and St. Demetrios in Prinkipo
> [Büyükada].[73]

Frydas essentially "rated" the most important Greek churches and
agiasmata according to historical pedigree, ecclesiastical significance, and
demographic/economic importance. His report is certainly important, but,
unfortunately, the copy available for this study was incomplete, as the second
page was missing. Included in this lost page was the remainder of a list of
vandalized institutions that were under the jurisdiction of the archbishop of
Constantinople (that is, the ecumenical patriarch), as well as the names of the
first of the thirteen ecclesiastical establishments under the administration of
the metropolitan of Chalcedon (Kadıköy). By reconstructing the contents of
the missing page, I have deduced the number of twenty-one missing churches

---

[72] National Archives, American Consul General, Istanbul to Washington, No. 132,
September 27, 1955.
[73] Greek Embassy, Athens to Washington, No. 42071 EK/3a, October 3, 1955.

from the archbishopric of Constantinople's truncated list and nine from that of the metropolitan of Chalcedon. Accordingly, Frydas's catalogue included the following numbers of vandalized religious institutions:

Archbishopric of Constantinople	51
(of which 21 were added by emendation)	
Metropolitanate of Chalcedon	23
Metropolitanate of Derkon	7
Metropolitanate of Princes Islands	4
Total	75

This list adds another ten damaged churches and *agiasmata* to the sixty-seven in the catalogue of the patriarch:

St. Demetrios, Sarmaşık

St. Nicholas, Heybeliada

St. George, Bakırköy

Panagia, Göksuyu (*agiasma*)

St. George, Fener (*metochion* of Jerusalem)

Panagia, Vlah Saray

Saints Constantine and Helen, Tarabya

St. Panteleimon, Kuzguncuk

St. Kyriake, Tarabya (*agiasma*)

Metropolitanate of Derkon[74]

The sixty Istanbul *vakıflar* files (which are far from complete) yielded ten more damaged institutions:

Prophet Elias, Arnavutköy

St. Nicholas, Samatya

St. John, Kumkapı

St. George, Ortaköy (cemetery church)

St. Kyriake, Paşabahçe

[74] *Ibid.* I have been able to reconstruct page two of this report with some high degree of probability on the basis of report no. 132 from Istanbul to the State Department in Washington, as well as other evidence. Even higher probability lies in the estimated numbers of damage and destruction in new Istanbul.

Panagia, Yeniköy, Boğaziçi

Saints Kyriake and Onoufrios (2 *agiasmata*)

St. Panteleimon, Çengelköy (*agiasma*)

St. Panteleimon, Hasköy (*agiasma*)

In his *Ekthesis*, Chrêstidês adds two more names to the list of damaged churches and *agiasmata*: St. Paraskeue of Arnavutköy and St. Paraskeue of Sirkeci (*agiasma*). Finally, Kaloumenos documents the damage at the Analepsis in Samatya. The total of desecrated institutions is therefore ninety.[75]

This is a partial testimony to the number of religious institutions in which a particular sacred object, or a building as a whole, was somehow desecrated.[76] With access to a much larger sampling of the documents of the *vakıflar* and of the Committee for Repair, these numbers will undoubtedly increase. Further access to the archives of the individual communities will also add to the number in this particular table.[77]

In the event, the documentation here is far from complete, as the sources on which it is based have many gaps. They do, however, help us to understand not only the fury and extent of the destruction but also much of its specificity. Even the number of religious institutions attacked may not be complete; nevertheless, the data include the vast majority of institutions that suffered damages. It is probable that the number of damaged *agiasmata* and similar gravesites is greatly deficient. That part of the available Istanbul *vakıflar* and Committee for Repair data is not only incomplete; the very basis on which it was drawn up was selective. On closer examination, for instance, it emerges that no provisions were made for restoring or replacing lost or damaged objects, which were not only numerous in the Christian institutions but often of considerable value. By way of example, there was no or very little provision for stolen or destroyed icons, sacred vestments, chalices, patens, *artophoria*, or other items. Thus, a detailed catalogue of such losses cannot be precisely reconstructed from this documentation.

---

[75] On the number of damaged religious institutions that emerges from my access to a part of the Istanbul *vakıflar* and Committee for Repair documentation, and for the detailed information that it provides, see the discussion below.

[76] According to the official report of the special mission of the World Council of Churches, which went to Istanbul to investigate the destruction to churches, the number was much larger: "Out of 80 Greek Orthodox churches, 29 were completely destroyed by fire." See TNA: PRO, London, FO371/11712, no. 198335, October 12, 1955.

[77] The documentation will be discussed in greater detail when the matter of compensation for damages to ecclesiastical institutions is analyzed further; see TNA:PRO, London, FO371/117712, no. 198335, October 12, 1955.

CHRISTIAN UNITY WITH THE GREEK ORTHODOX OF ISTANBUL

The patriarchate's situation on the morning of September 7, 1955, was desperate. The churches were shut down, and a great many of them were in no state to function. The clergy and hierarchs had been attacked physically as well as morally, and had been paraded and mocked publicly; the soup kitchens that had provided meals for the poor, aged, and schoolchildren had all been destroyed.

The violence and fanaticism had shocked the entire community, but especially the clergy (whose beards and attire had made them obvious and defenseless targets). A few days later, the seeming indifference of John Foster Dulles and his British allies had a concomitant effect on the Greeks of Istanbul. As we have seen, the psychological atmosphere that had prepared the way for the pogrom continued to intensify and to distress the patriarch in particular, who had become the center of Turkish anger and opprobrium. Fearful of appealing to the outside world (so as not to stoke anti-patriarchal hatred in Turkey), Athênagoras decided on a "pro-Turkish" policy and put his faith in Menderes—in short, he decided to continue the official line he had adopted from the time he first assumed the patriarchal throne. While it was the only realistic policy under the circumstances (he could not rely on foreign powers, as Turkey clearly enjoyed their favor, or on Greece, which was still suffering the devastating effects of German occupation and civil war), it did have certain consequences. First and foremost, although he understood that the Turkish government was implicated in the pogrom, Athênagoras refused to state any opinion on the matter, even years later at the Yassıada trials. Further, and more immediately, he incurred the bitter criticism of many Greek Orthodox hierarchs, clergy, and parishioners, as is evident from a variety of testimonies. This bitterness is still alive in many of the Greek refugees who sought asylum in Greece and other countries after the events. It was commented on by a number of foreign observers as well, a fact that will be discussed below.[78]

Athênagoras did not emerge from the militarily secured patriarchal compound until the afternoon of September 10, when he went out to examine the ruins of the church, *agiasma*, and patriarchal and other graves at the monastery of Zoodochos Pege in Balıklı.[79] Following Agis Kapsambelês's advice, Athênagoras had turned to the immediate care of his flock, many of whom were homeless and facing the grim prospects of hunger and surviving

---

[78] Remarks critical of the patriarch have already been encountered in Despoina Portokallis's correspondence, in various diplomatic reports, and in some of the oral testimony collected by Tsoukatou, *Septemvriana, passim.*

[79] Ypourgeion Exôterikôn, Istanbul to Athens, No. 3916, September 11, 1955.

the oncoming winter. Any appeal to a foreign power seemed futile and, at any rate, would have aroused the Turkish foreign ministry. What then did the patriarch decide to do? He informed the Greek consul-general that, taking as his basis Greek foreign minister Stefanos Stefanopoulos's statement that Greek-Turkish relations would continue, he was, "[c]onsequently...obliged to advance under the light of this policy as our central axis of struggle...."[80] He emphasized that a psychological campaign to combat defeatism was of the first order of importance. (Indeed, he pursued this line for the remainder of his life, until his death in 1971).[81] He proposed specific measures: to halt Greek flight from Turkey; to pressure the Turkish government to keep its promises for the security and compensation of both Greek nationals and Turkish citizens of Greek origin; to fund the reconstruction of dwellings and small businesses (since there was no hope for real compensation at this level); and to find immediate funds to allay the pressing needs and pay the salaries of priests, deacons, teachers, and others. Although it was decided to leave the damaged churches as they were (pending compensation for their

[80] Ypourgeion Exôterikôn, Istanbul to Athens, No. 1454, September 14, 1955.

[81] I observed this during a stay in Istanbul in the months of July-August 1959. On August 16, I attended a service in the church of St. Mary of the Mongols at which the patriarch was present. At the end of the service, a reception was held across the street in the community hall. During the reception, the patriarch addressed his flock on the significance of the Dormition of the Virgin and on the important history of this particular church. My diary records the following notes on the address:

> Then he spoke of the vicissitudes which had fallen on the Greek Community in Turkey, emphasizing first its great antiquity (Byzas) and its historical tradition (Byzantine Civilization and Orthodoxy) and he stressed a point which he continuously stressed throughout his address: Even though quantitatively the community had decreased since 1453 and especially after 1923, qualitatively the community was as strong as ever since the traditions remained among a smaller number of people. Then he moved on to the events of September 6/7, 1955. Without mentioning the brutality and cowardice of the disturbances, without mentioning the destructions, he reminded the congregation that Turkey was his own fatherland and the fatherland of the community; that they were all free to worship in their own churches, to have their schools, hospitals, organizations, etc. He continued, in the same spirit, that the Greeks should love the Turks and Turkey, that nothing can come of the principle, "I shall love you if you love me." For if love is not complete, not even if it is 99 percent, the fact that one percent is not present makes it as if there were no love at all....He then criticized those who left Istanbul after the troubles as having deserted their duties and the community. Then turning to the Greek visitors from the city of Thessaloniki he humorously stated that if ever the Greeks of Turkey should come to them, "they should turn all of us away without even offering us the customary glass of water."
>
> A few middle aged women were silently shedding tears and wiping their eyes as the Patriarch spoke....

rehabilitation), the patriarch ordered that services be held in three churches: the patriarchal church (St. George in Fener), the church of Feriköy (probably the Holy Apostles), and the Panagia in Beyoğlu. The liturgies were celebrated behind closed doors, and the patriarch officiated without his official vestments, as a sign of mourning for the destroyed churches.[82]

The Greek government moved quickly to draw the attention of the Christian world to the plight and desecration of the Greek Orthodox churches in Istanbul. The Orthodox churches of Russia, Romania, and Bulgaria had meanwhile responded on their own and with the permission of their governments, of course. Because of the Cold War, however, the Greek government was wary of finding itself on the same side with the Soviet Union. The Church of Greece was less hesitant on that count and vigorously denounced both the pogrom and the British and American positions on Cyprus. Of particular interest were the letters sent by Greek Muslim communities in Greek Thrace that condemned the attacks on the Greek minority in Istanbul. The patriarch's formal and politically correct stance was to be responsive to the remonstrations against the pogrom by foreign Christian churches and institutions while eschewing any demonstrations of a political nature. Athênagoras could openly receive representatives of foreign religious bodies since the patriarchate was a member of the World Council of Churches and its suffragan archbishop in the United States (as indicated in the previous chapter, the Greek Orthodox archdiocese in the US is under the jurisdiction of the ecumenical patriarchate, not the Church of Greece) belonged to the National Council of Churches. But Athênagoras was always correct in these relations, carefully stressing two basic facts: Turkey was his fatherland, of which he was a loyal citizen; and he rejected any demonstrations, or acts of a political nature, undertaken on behalf of the patriarchate. The Turkish foreign ministry tried to maintain a formal and correct attitude to the patriarchate, but hid its real hostility behind the veil of formal diplomacy and threats to Greece's diplomatic representatives, as well as behind the voice of "public opinion" and the controlled Turkish press.

Given the patriarchate's situation, the Greek government hastened to mobilize the foreign religious institutions to which the patriarchate had formal connections. As mentioned in Chapter 4, Athens had been briefed by its embassy in Washington on September 7, and simultaneously sent formal instructions to its permanent representative to the WCC in Geneva, about actions to assist the Greek Orthodox Church in Istanbul. This constituted

---

[82] Ypourgeion Exôterikôn, Istanbul to Athens, No. 1448, September 14, 1955; the dating is possibly inaccurate as it would not fall on a Sunday.

the opening of a religious front in support, and an effort to break the political isolation, of the patriarchate. The Greek ambassador in Washington reported that Archbishop Michaêl was willing to lodge a protest with the WCC against the desecration and looting of the Greek churches in Istanbul. But before doing so, he wanted the approval both of the patriarch and of the Greek government.[83] The ambassador requested that the foreign ministry discuss this request with the patriarch. Simultaneously, Kanellopoulos instructed Greece's representative in Geneva to intervene urgently with the council:

> We ask that you draw the attention of the World Council of Churches to the unprovoked and barbaric actions of the mob which took place under the toleration of the Turkish authorities in Constantinople and Smyrna.
> The fact that this madness of the mob against the Orthodox Christians continues and that the churches are publicly undergoing attacks has created a most serious alarm over the safety of the Ecumenical Patriarchate and of His All Holiness the Patriarch.
> We instruct you to ask, immediately, of the appropriate authorities of the World Council of Churches that they proclaim their serious concern to the Turkish Government, by telegram, and that they condemn all the deeds of the Turkish mob, which has violated every sacred concept and human right.[84]

Athens also asked that the council contact churches that did not belong to it.

Among the most ardent and important supporters of the patriarchate, and of Istanbul's Orthodox Christians, was the Church of England. Such was the tenacity of the Anglican clergy in this matter that Britain's foreign secretary and foreign ministry both became annoyed with the Church's involvement in the country's foreign policy, which was inextricably bound up with the US (without whose support Britain could do very little), as well as with the UN and Turkey, which were critical to British interests in Cyprus. Such were these political interests that the Foreign Office had to contend with the Church of England's criticism of Britain's ally, Turkey. Hence, the ministry's Southern Department began to monitor the Church's activities and, especially, its declarations on Turkey, the pogrom, and relations with the patriarchate. But the extent of the September violence had been such that, having determined the facts, the archbishop of Canterbury asked the Southern Department for specific information on damages to Greek churches and attacks on Christians. The archbishop told the department that while he had been assured that there

---

[83] Greek Embassy, Washington to Athens, No. 3687/B/29, September 7, 1955.
[84] Ypourgeion Exôterikôn, Athens to Geneva, No. 37963/dis, September 7, 1955.

had been no damages or attacks on Anglican clergy, he wished to be informed of the extent of the destruction of the Greek Orthodox churches. He added that "news had reached Lambeth Palace that the monastery on the island of Halki had been attacked and that the abbot had been injured. It had also been heard that two Metropolitans and other Greek Orthodox clergy had been injured in and around Istanbul during the riots, and there was some doubt whether the Phanar had been damaged or not."[85]

Three days after his request to the Southern Department, the archbishop of Canterbury made his first public statement on the pogrom, which was released to the British press on September 15:

> The Archbishop of Canterbury has sent a telegram to His All Holiness the Oecumenical Patriarch of Constantinople expressing his profound grief and horror at the destruction of Orthodox Churches in Istanbul. Riots were specially directed against the Orthodox Churches, many of which are reported to have suffered destruction, as well as against the shops and houses of the Greek population.
>
> The Archbishop trusts that all Christian people in Great Britain will support with their earnest prayer their Orthodox brethren in Istanbul and the whole of the Orthodox Church in bearing this evil which has been inflicted upon them; and hopes that they will take any opportunities which may be offered through the Inter-Church Aid of the British Council of Churches, or by other means, for giving practical help to them.[86]

The Church of England was to maintain this stance of solidarity with the patriarchate and its flock, in sharp contrast to the stance of the Foreign Office.

As the days passed and became weeks, the details of the pogrom gradually replaced the vague and sparse information that had followed in the immediate aftermath of the events. On September 22, the British consul-general responded to the Foreign Office's request for information to be relayed to John R. Satterthwaite, chief of the Archbishop of Canterbury's office of information. Although it did not begin to approach a full catalogue of vandalized churches, the report was nevertheless specific in its details and gave the first estimates of Greek religious institutions attacked and damaged. The report's second paragraph is of interest:

> You [Satterthwaite] are correct in concluding that the Church of England clergy and property in Turkey have not suffered in

---

[85] TNA:PRO, London to Istanbul, No. FO371/117710 XC198373, September 12, 1955.
[86] TNA:PRO, London, No. FO371/117711/198335, September 15, 1955.

the riots. Demonstrators who made their way on two or three occasions to the Crimean War Memorial Church, were kept out of the grounds owing to the prompt action of the caretaker who kept the iron gates closed and telephoned the Consulate-General for protection which the Turkish authorities speedily provided in this case.[87]

The consul's memorandum explained that the specific data contained therein had been provided by the British embassy's chaplain, Rev. C. W. Piper, the patriarchate, and the Greek consulate-general. It reported that while the patriarchal church and complex had suffered no damages due to its protection by the Turkish police, seventy-two out of the eighty-three [sic] Greek churches had been damaged, eight to ten had been completely destroyed, and that massive damage had been effected on the great Greek cemetery at Şişli. Further, thirty-two Greek and eight Armenian schools had been damaged, and the tombs of the Greek patriarchs in the cemetery at Balıklı had been smashed and the bodies cast out. A copy of the dispatch was passed on to Rev. Satterthwaite so that the archbishop of Canterbury now had a formal statement by the British government on the extent of the Turkish attacks on the Greek Orthodox community of Istanbul. The archbishop was also in contact with the Greek embassy in London. Soon after September 15, the Greek embassy had forwarded to the archbishop a copy, in English, of Kapsambelês's memorandum on the attacks on Istanbul's Greek churches. Upon receipt of this list, the archbishop asked for a full and detailed accounting of the damages wreaked on the Greek Orthodox community, requesting that it be sent to him as quickly as possible.[88]

The earlier list of damages requested by the Foreign Office on the archbishop's behalf had been sent to the ministry on September 22, but the latter did not forward it to the archbishop until October 13, a delay of three weeks.[89] Consequent to this three-week delay, the archbishop had been forced to brief himself from other sources, as he had to prepare his address to the Convocation of Canterbury on October 12. The address to the convocation of clergy was well-prepared, carefully structured, and both a direct and nuanced analysis of the pogrom. Inasmuch as the Church of England is the officially

---

[87] TNA:PRO No. G10344/48, September 22, 1955.

[88] Ypourgeion Exôterikôn, London to Athens, No. 3505/b/13, September 27, 1955.

[89] TNA:PRO, London, No. RG10344/48, October 13, 1955. Among the handwritten comments attached to this document was the following note on the two churches: "The Panaghia, a major eyesore, would have been small loss, but I am grieved about S. Mary of the Mongols, which is a building of great historic value and interest." It is interesting to see that there were people of such "esthetic" sensitivity in the Foreign Office.

recognized confession of the British state, the archbishop of Canterbury is as much a political as a religious figure. As such, his address on "the suffering of the Greek Orthodox Church" had official and respected standing. As the archbishop's intent was to inform his clergy directly of the official view of the pogrom as seen by the Church of England—and not the Foreign Office—one can understand the concern of Eden, Macmillan, and the Foreign Office itself, all of whom had formally presented the violence as an unfortunate incident that had somehow gotten out of hand and for which the Turkish government was truly repentant but not responsible. According to the UK government, since Turkey had expressed its regrets and had promised to pursue the culprits, one had to get on with the business of running the world. *Sub rosa*, there was considerable resentment in the halls of the Foreign Office at the "worthy clerics" for interfering in affairs that were presumably none of their business. The UK's foreign ministry repeatedly expressed its displeasure at what it considered to be the seduction of the Anglican church by Greek propaganda (*sub rosa* also, of course, many in the ministry realized or strongly suspected that the Turkish government was implicated in the events).

Under the circumstances, the archbishop of Canterbury's remarks at Church House, Westminster, were to have a marked effect in shaping British public opinion on the pogrom, Cyprus, and the Foreign Office's attachment to its Turkish alliance. Following are parts of the address (which was entitled, "The Primate's Speech on the Sufferings of the Greek Orthodox Church").

> Right Reverend, Very Reverend, Venerable and Reverend Brethren, I wish to draw your attention again to the fearful calamity which just over four weeks ago befell a Church with which the Church of England has had for many years the closest and most brotherly relations. I refer to the destruction which was wrought on the night of Tuesday September 6th on the Greek Orthodox churches and other institutions in Constantinople at the hands of the Turkish mob. The fact of it is known here; but partly due to difficulties in getting reliable information, partly due to the fact that the events of one day are quickly submerged by those that follow, the British public has not...been made aware of the appalling nature of the catastrophe which occurred.
>
> Much information has reached me from various sources and of a reliable kind. Because it is little known, I think I should give you a short summary of it, that you may realize what a night of terror was inflicted upon the great Church of Constantinople and upon the life of the Orthodox Church, tragic in itself and in its abiding effects.
>
> Let me begin by saying that to the best of our belief the

Turkish Government had no previous knowledge of the riots and was as surprised and horrified by them as were the International Police experts assembled in Constantinople as its guests....

There is, however, clear evidence that the whole operation had been carefully planned beforehand by some powerful and efficient body of persons. Thus the riots broke out widely in separated places simultaneously at what must have been a prearranged time....

There was a deliberation and controlled efficiency about the riot which makes it almost more devilish....

The Phanar itself, the residence of the Oecumenical Patriarch, was itself saved...as it happened there was a guard of soldiers, stationed there....Elsewhere the police for some hours of the rioting for the most part looked on. But it is significant that according to our information when they tried to restrain the crowds, they had no difficulty in doing so—an indication perhaps that the whole thing was engineered and never really uncontrollable....[90]

Having perceptively described in detail the nature and character of the "riots," the archbishop implied that they had been organized from higher up; rather than attributing the destruction to the sudden impulses of a frenzied crowd, therefore, he informed his clergy that it had been carefully planned, and its specific purpose was to attack the Greek community in all its elements. He went on to speak of the numbers of churches and schools struck, the furious onslaught that desecrated the two large Greek cemeteries, and the need for Christians to respond to the devastation of the Greek community not only with prayers but with material aid.

The convocation address added to the discomfort of the specialists in the Southern Department, while the Greek foreign ministry saw its efforts finally meeting with some success in British quarters. Most of all, the archbishop's comments encouraged the patriarchate, which finally felt that it was not alone and had not been forgotten in a world long hardened by the struggles of the Cold War. With this opening act in the ongoing drama, the archbishop of Canterbury became a central player and so his requests to the Foreign Office for information on the events of September 6 were attended to very carefully. Criticism was, generally, reserved for his colleagues; none of the

---

[90] TNA:PRO, London, No. 70371/17712 198335, October 12, 1955; see also TNA:PRO, London, No. RF10344/79, October 18, 1955, in which Satterthwaite thanks Johnston for having sent him the Istanbul consul's report on damages, adding: "It would appear that the psychological damage caused during the rioting is even more serious than the material damage. A correspondent has written recently that there is a complete breakdown of confidence and even the most responsible Greeks are now saying 'it will be a massacre next!'"

Foreign Office documents examined manifests even the slightest expression of disrespect for the primate of the Church of England, unless, of course, he, too, was meant to be included in the sarcastic phrase, "worthy clerics." Other bishops and canons were not treated so gingerly, however, especially because they became familiar callers and visitors to the Southern Department.

In this vein, Canon Waddams wrote to Johnston in the Foreign Office about "allegations from Turkey that the Turkish Government was implicated in the riots which took place on September 6," seeking "confidentially...any evidence that this was the case."[91] The archbishop of Canterbury had hinted at this by stating that while, on the one hand, "to the best of our knowledge," the Turkish government had not been involved, on the other hand, the entire affair was perhaps "engineered and never really uncontrollable." Further, during the special session of the Turkish parliament on September 12, Köprülü had, of course, confessed openly that the Turkish government had known well ahead of time of the demonstration. Hence, the question now raised by Canon Waddams on November 2, two months later, should not have come as an unwanted revelation to Johnston (especially because the running, hand-written comments scrawled on their reports indicate clearly that the Southern Department's staff understood that the Turkish government must have been implicated in the pogrom). As Waddams's question had been conveyed on behalf of the archbishop of Canterbury, Johnston prepared a written answer that, however, he had no intention of sending but would only use in his attempt to answer the canon. This non-circulating document, stamped "Personal-Confidential," was essentially evasive, avoiding any direct answer to Waddams's question:

> We have received a number of varying reports about these riots, including some to the effect that certain Turkish authorities had foreknowledge that the riots were going to take place and failed to forestall them. But it is very difficult to get to the bottom of the story and it is still not at all clear where the responsibility lay for the extensive organization of the riots, or what purpose it was hoped they could achieve. The Turkish Government, as you know, have blamed the Communists.
>
> Whatever the truth on all this may be it is, I think, fairly evident that the extent of the damage done during the riots came as a genuine, and severe shock to the Turkish Government, and that, after some apparent initial delays, the Turkish authorities took firm and effective measures to restore law and order.
>
> Needless to say, the foregoing, inconclusive as it is, is

[91] TNA:PRO, London, No. RG10344/98, November 2, 1955.

forwarded to you in strictest confidence. But I hope that it will give you the sort of guidance that you require.[92]

On November 15, Johnston wrote up the minutes of his meeting and conversations with Waddams. He asserts that Waddams was "satisfied" with the Foreign Office's official explanation on the "vague" nature of the responsibility for the events of September 6-7. Waddams told him that in a day or two he would be meeting with the bishop of Malmesbury, who, as a member of the World Council of Churches mission to Istanbul, was just now returning from Turkey. Waddams then explained that the archbishop of Canterbury was concerned with the precarious condition of the patriarchate; the Anglican primate was also afraid that, as many in the Istanbul Greek community were dissatisfied with the patriarch's policy toward the Turkish government, they might decide to emigrate to Greece. Should this occur, the importance of the patriarchate would be lessened and would thus affect the future relations of the Church of England with the Russian Orthodox church. Attached to these notes was a brief memorandum written by Johnston on November 11:

> I do not think that we can divulge in any way that the Turks were implicated; were we to say that the Turkish Government was involved in responsibility we would undoubtedly be subjected to unbounded public criticism, and Turco-British relations would become strained. In any case this point is material to our consideration of an official protest, and until we have considered with the Legal Adviser the evidence now in our possession we cannot pronounce on either a protest or a claim for compensation, and, therefore cannot really make a statement attributing blame....[93]

Once more, the document speaks for itself. Ironically, the Foreign Office's legal adviser did indeed ultimately assign responsibility to the Turkish government for the destruction of the property of British nationals during the pogrom. In any case, the ministry's policy was clearly to avoid all formal or public mention of Turkish governmental responsibility in the pogrom, in sharp contrast to the approach of the Church of England. Indeed, the activities of the archbishop of Canterbury and his clergy demonstrate a course of action that was fully independent of the Foreign Office. Although the Church had asked the ministry for data on the damages inflicted on the Greek community,

---

[92] TNA:PRO, London, No. RG10344/98, not dated but attached in the files to Waddams's letter of November 2, 1955, in which he asks for an appointment so that Johnston could "give him a line" on the responsibility, or not, of the Turkish government.

[93] TNA:PRO, London, No. RG10344/98, November 5, 1955.

it relied on its own information in the end, which was gathered by the Church of England Council of Foreign Affairs. Furthermore, as opposed to the British government, the Church freely and openly discussed the evidence in question, which was far more accessible than the Foreign Office thought. Although its relations with it were friendly and proper, the Church avoided both the misinformation and example of the Foreign Office.

The Church of England, like the National Council of Churches in the United States, was a member of the World Council of Churches and participated actively in its activities and policy formulation. Together, the three entities played a crucial role in bringing the pogrom to the attention of their respective networks and nations. The WCC mission to Istanbul, for example, which left for the city on November 7, had been preceded by the earlier WCC envoy, Rev. Maxwell, who had gone to Turkey only a few days after the riots. The council's general secretary, Willem A. Visser't Hooft, had entrusted him with a personal message to the patriarch, which was published in the press and was translated into Greek by Greece's UN mission. It was brief but very reassuring: "The World Council of Churches, which is concerned for the good condition of all its member-Churches, wishes to express its profound sympathy to Your Holiness in the face of the present circumstances. It also wishes to provide every assistance which is needed and therefore summons its member-Churches to offer prayers that we might live in peace and so that prudence might prevail."[94] On returning to Geneva, Maxwell submitted a detailed, confidential report whose main points, however, were circulated by the general secretary to the leaders of twenty churches in various countries, and included the following actions:

a) Assurances to the Patriarch of [our] sorrow and our solidarity with him;
b) Demands for full reparations on the damages;
c) Demands for assurances from the Turkish Government that such violent behaviour shall not be repeated.[95]

One such letter, sent to Archbishop Spyridôn of Athens, was a composite of quotes from the Maxwell report and the message of Visser't Hooft. Part of the latter's message read as follows:

[94] The text is preserved, in Greek translation, in Palamas's report, Ypourgeion Exôterikôn, New York to Athens, No. 2374, September 30, 1955. Maxwell's mission and Visser't Hooft's press release are undated therein. The Palamas dispatch not only refers to the activities of the WCC representative in Athens, but gives some information on Nolde's activities as well. The date of Maxwell's mission to Istanbul is set by National Archives, No. 782.00/9-2955, September 28, 1955, as having taken place five days later than the pogrom.

[95] See the previous footnote.

What has happened to the Orthodox Church in Constantinople is
even worse than we were led to believe in the first reports. It is one
of the greatest destructions wrought upon the Christian Church
in our times. And it adds one more tragic chapter in the history of
sorrows in the Eastern Mediterranean Church. It is hard to believe
that it was possible for such crimes to be committed in this era of
the Doctrine of Human Rights....

Every Church participating in the World Council of
Churches must feel that the burden which the stricken Church is
obliged to bear is also its own burden.[96]

During this earlier period, the WCC had appointed an official, O.
Frederick Nolde, to act on its behalf in the United States and to effect contacts
and conversations with the UN secretary-general, Dulles, Greek and Turkish
representatives, and Archbishop Michaêl. Nolde's efforts were singularly
unsuccessful. It is clear that his diplomatic actions were diametrically opposed
to those of the council. Rather than striving to foster a wider dissemination of
information on the pogrom and the perilous condition of the Greek Orthodox
community in Istanbul, he in effect tried to short-circuit this effort. It is clear
that he was not in agreement with the council's goals, as we shall see.

Nolde's activities were reported in detail by the British mission to the
United Nations on October 28, 1955, in a dispatch to London. This report
began with the statement that the mission had denied Nolde's request for an
audience with its highest official: "Since Mr. Nolde's request for an interview
[with the British minister of state] was clearly of an embarrassing nature, it was
decided that it would be preferable that Mr. Nolde should be received by the
Permanent Representative rather than by the Minister of State." At his meeting
(October 17) with Pierson Dixon, the UK's permanent representative, Nolde
stated that the WCC had initially wished to express its views on the pogrom in
Istanbul through a letter to the UN secretary-general and then to circulate the
letter to all members of that body. However, he continued, he had proposed an
alternative approach to the council that had been accepted. A letter would still
be addressed to the secretary-general, but it would not circulate. Furthermore,
this alternative letter would be purely for the secretary-general's information
and would state that Nolde had discussed the question with the UN's Turkish,
Greek, US, and UK representatives. When Nolde put the crucial question to
Dixon as to whether the latter would lend his approval and name to this letter,
the British diplomat instantly refused:

Sir Pierson had it very much in mind that the Greek Government

---

[96] TNA:PRO, London, No. RG10344/64, October 4, 1955.

were behind this move on the part of the World Council of Churches and that they might make some use of the move in the future....

Sir Pierson then explained to Mr. Nolde that this really was a matter between Turkey and Greece, and we did not think it right that we should be brought into it....Mr. Nolde then said that he thought that for his purpose it would be sufficient if he were to omit any reference to the United Kingdom in his letter and merely let his authorities in London and Geneva know that he had had a talk with us as well as other delegations. This seemed to be the best course, and Sir Pierson agreed with it.

We have since heard from Mr. Nolde that, on reflection, he has decided that it would be preferable if, in his letter to the Secretary-General, he merely stated that he had conferred individually with the representatives of a limited number of governments; he would not mention governments by name, thereby avoiding both the dangers of specific enumeration and the implications of omission.[97]

Nolde readily and successively abandoned practically all his demands of Dixon and seems to have done so easily. All he seems to have insisted on was the freedom to tell his superiors that he had consulted with the British representative. Nothing was to be mentioned in the letter.

Two weeks earlier, Nolde had trotted through the same futile exercise in his effort to meet with Dulles. This was denied, but he was briefly seen in New York on September 28 by Dulles's special assistant, Roderic L. O'Connor. In his report, O'Connor mentioned, among other things, that Nolde had complained to him

that he had been under heavy pressure from the Orthodox Greeks in the World Council of Churches to take some strong action of protest in this situation. He said that he realized that any precipitous action would be inflammatory and that he was merely asking to see me to present his point of view and one or two suggestions as to how the situation might be remedied.

He specifically asked me if he could state to his Greek colleagues that he had brought this matter "directly to the Secretary's [Dulles's] attention." I said that I felt he could say that so long as he did not state that he had brought it "personally" to the Secretary's attention.

O'Conner offered to submit Nolde's outline of what was to have been

---

[97] TNA:PRO, New York to London, No. RG10344/97, October 28, 1955.

discussed with Dulles to the State Department: "I said I might be able to give him some reaction but couldn't promise it and he did not press the point."[98] Little came of this meeting except that William Baxter of the State Department replied to O'Connor that he hoped the latter would send Nolde to him since Baxter had had frequent contact in the past with the WCC emissary, who had been "very understanding and constructive in his ideas." Nolde had always consulted him before his trips to Cyprus and this was now an opportunity for Baxter "to tell him some of the measures which Turkey has already taken to redress the wrongs and to let him know of efforts we are continuing to make to improve Greek-Turkish relations."

While one can sympathize with the difficulties of Nolde's position, and the pressures he encountered from all sides (including the Greek insistence that the issue of the pogrom be introduced in these important quarters and the refusal of Dulles and the British minister of state to see him or even formally consider his proposals), one cannot help but reproach the expediency of his ethical and professional standards. He seemed to make a special effort to avoid antagonizing the powerful, while, at the same time, keeping his position within the council secure. It did not take the Greek foreign ministry long to determine his real *modus operandi*, and Greek representatives in the United States were ordered to exclude him from any committees, planning, or visits that concerned the Greek Orthodox community of Istanbul. Nolde was certainly correct in referring to Greek anxiety and pressure on the World Council of Churches, but even he had to admit in his outline-memorandum, which he had prepared for Dulles, that "the tragic destruction of the Turkish riots has been established beyond question."[99]

Indeed, following the events, the WCC sent a special mission to Istanbul to survey the situation and renew contacts with Greek Orthodox communities, Turkish officials, and certain Turkish institutions. When Rev. Maxwell

[98] TNA:PRO, New York to Washington, No. 782.00/9 2858, September 28,1955.

[99] *Ibid*; for Baxter's desire to cultivate Nolde, see Baxter's letter to O'Connor, National Archives, Washington, No. 5787, October 5, 1955:

> It seems apparent from the informal memorandum left with you by Mr. Nolde that he is not insistant [*sic*] on any public departmental action at this time and was satisfied in having brought the views of the World Council of Churches to the attention of the Secretary....
>
> If you have no objection, I would like to get in touch directly with Mr. Nolde....Mr. Nolde has called on me several times in the past, before visiting Cyprus and after, and I have found him very understanding and constructive in his ideas. I should like to be able to tell him some of the measures which Turkey has already taken to redress the wrongs and to let him know of efforts we are continuing to make to improve Greek-Turkish relations.

returned to Geneva from his factfinding trip to Istanbul immediately after the pogrom, he proposed a special council mission to follow up on his visit. The archbishop of Canterbury had referred to this new mission in his convocation address, and announced that it would consist of the Bishop of Malmesbury (UK), Rev. Edward Hardy (US), Rev. Robert Tobias (US), Rev. Charles Westphal (France), Rev. Maxwell himself (Geneva), and possibly a representative from Sweden.[100] Finally, the five clergymen (the Swedish representative did not participate in the end) departed for Istanbul on November 6, and after their return filed their report, dated November 15.[101]

The mission's official memorandum was succinct, substantive, and precise; it indicated that its members not only understood what had transpired during the pogrom but also appreciated its effects on the victims. By way of introduction, the report stated that the council undertook its mission "to express personally the feelings of the Christian world and the Desire of Christian bodies represented in the World Council to 'bear one another's burdens' [as] a practical means of demonstrating that concern." Furthermore, as "[t]he Mission went in the name of the 162 Churches cooperating in the World Council...," it ultimately reported directly to these churches.

First and foremost, the mission described the desolation presented by Istanbul's Greek community:

> The Mission saw everywhere the remains of the appalling destruction of September 6th. Out of 80 Greek Orthodox churches, 29 were completely destroyed by fire, 34 badly damaged and 8 less seriously—only 9 remained intact; 4,000 shops were destroyed, their contents thrown into the streets, and 2,000 homes utterly ruined....Several feeding centers have been set up especially for the aged and poor children to give them at least one hot meal a day. Not only were churches, shops and homes the target of the demonstrators, but also the cemeteries. The great cemetery of Shishli was the scene of ravage and desecration—monuments were smashed and overturned, graves were opened, bones thrown out or burned and the chapel utterly gutted....The scene [at Balıklı cemetery] is impossible to describe. Here the tombs of the Patriarchs had been opened and bones left exposed; the church and monastery completely destroyed by fire....Many of the 2,000 homes are still without windows or doors and are bare of furniture and utensils. Shopkeepers lost their stocks, professional men their equipment and the poor what little they had.

---

[100] TNA:PRO, London, No. 70371/17712 198335, October 12, 1955.
[101] National Archives, Istanbul to Washington, No. 210, November 25, 1955.

As for the immediate prospects of saving the Greek Orthodox community and restoring its confidence in its future in Turkey, the memorandum pointed strongly to the role of the Turkish government and indeed to its obligation to right the wrong, to compensate and restore, to preside over a reconciliation of Greeks and Turks, and, finally, "to reassure the minorities concerning their future security."

The most practical part of the report dealt with interchurch aid. During its stay in Istanbul, the mission had ample opportunity to see the wretched living conditions of many Greek families after the events. Partial relief had been furnished by the WCC's division of international aid and its refugee service, as well as by the Turkish Red Crescent. The patriarch had also successfully recruited the assistance of those Greeks who were better off financially in "adopting" and assisting the destitute families. Still, the mission saw ample room for assistance. In fact, having refused any major aid for fear of being accused by the Turkish government and masses of "betraying" Turkey to foreigners, the patriarch asked for a scanty amount of money to relieve those now suffering. The mission proposed the following:

> We therefore recommend that an appeal be made to the member Churches for 75,000 dollars (25,000 sterling) to be sent to the Patriarch for the relief of his people. This would go far towards helping our brethren in their need and it would give practical expression to the reality of the fellowship in the World Council of Churches. This need is urgent and immediate. Over 1,000 homes are without doors and without glass in their windows, no blankets for their beds, and winter rapidly approaches. Many people have no clothes other than those they stand up in, and though the food centres enable them to have one hot meal a day, it is important that as soon as possible they be enabled to live in their own homes protected from the weather and able to have the utensils necessary to cook their own food. They look to their Christian brethren for help, shall they look in vain?[102]

The text speaks for itself. It undoubtedly played an important role in eliciting the concern of a wide spectrum of Christian churches and thus of widening the circle, above and beyond diplomatic efforts, of those now aware of the facts. This detailed report of the widespread suffering of the Greek Orthodox of Istanbul would certainly have affected a large part of world public opinion, which, until that time, had been given a distorted picture of September 6-7 (linked to efforts to blame the Greek community for the violence), as well as

[102] *Ibid.*

of the rights and wrongs of Greek, Turkish, British and US arguments over Cyprus. It is only because of Dêmêtrios Kaloumenos's photography that we even have visual documentation of the mission's visits to the ruined Christian institutions of Istanbul's Greek community.[103]

The Foreign Office followed the mission with considerable curiosity and asked for a full report from the British consulate in Istanbul, which sent it out on November 15; it thus reached London before a meeting had been arranged in the Southern Department with the Bishop of Malmesbury. The report was a succinct summary of what was to become the mission's memorandum. Johnston noted especially the comments of the consulate on the difficulties that Athênagoras was having with his own flock over his pro-Turkish policy and refusal to travel to the United States to gain the support of American public opinion. The report notes that had the patriarch done so, it would have further disadvantaged the local Greek Orthodox community. Further, it reports on the bishop's comments on the visit to the *vali* of Istanbul. What particularly caught Johnston's eye was the bishop's exchange with Gökay, the latter stating to the former "that he had done everything in his power to prevent the agitation whipped up over the Cyprus issue from resulting in a recourse to violence....On September 6, he had forbidden the students' demonstration which formed the curtain-raiser to the riots, but had been overruled by higher authority. His attempts to secure prompt military intervention to restore order had also been frustrated."[104]

Johnston's first reaction to the consular report was immediate interest in the data it revealed, of which, astonishingly, he had not been aware. He criticized the bishop's expectations for the mission's visit and memorandum, but nevertheless found the latter "interesting." He also found the information on the patriarch's difficulties with members of his own flock confirmed by his previous conversations with Canon Waddams. It was indeed curious that the ministry, or at least a critical member of the Southern Department, had not been aware of this situation; it is even more curious that the ministry had to be alerted to and informed of it by two clerics of the Church of England. Even more astonishing was Johnston's reaction to the bishop's report of his conversation with the *vali*, who had been a critical figure in the pogrom. In his commentary, Johnston remarked that, "The report of the visit to the Governor of Istanbul is revealing, in that it is the first [?] occasion on which we have heard that the responsibility for delaying measures to deal with the demonstrations lies at the door of Turkish ministers."[105] Johnston

---

[103] Some of these photographs have been included in this volume.
[104] TNA:PRO, Istanbul to London, No. RG10344/10, November 16, 1955.
[105] *Ibid.*

claims that this was the first time that the Southern Department had heard of Turkish governmental responsibility for September 6-7. Yet, by November 15, this was Turkey's worst-kept secret, as it had been widely discussed and assumed in many quarters, including İnönü's RPP and the DP's own meetings on September 12. Gökay's own continuing tenure as *vali* of Istanbul was threatened over the matter, and his temporary replacement as the official in charge of Istanbul on that September night, Interior Minister Namık Gedik, had been forced to resign before the special session of the Turkish parliament in a desperate effort by Menderes to blame the pogrom on expendable officials. All this was certainly known to British diplomats, and Michael Stewart's reports to London almost spelled it out. In any case, if we are to believe Johnston, then here, too, the Foreign Office had gotten rather crucial information from a member of the Anglican clergy.[106] Johnston's closing comments on the bishop's discussions with the British consulate in Istanbul did not speak well of the reputation for efficiency that the Foreign Office enjoyed in many circles: "In view of the amount of information which the Bishop of Malmesbury appears to have obtained during his short visit to Istanbul, I have written asking that he should let me know when he next comes to London, in order that I might have the opportunity of meeting him and hearing at first hand an account of his visit."

The Church of England, World Council of Churches, and National Council of Churches succeeded in a kind of united action on behalf of the pogrom's Greek Orthodox victims. While they attracted the attention of the US, British, and Turkish governments, however, they had very little effect on the State Department or Foreign Office. The Turkish government tried to ignore them entirely, while the Greek government, of course, had taken the initiative to alert and press them to denounce the pogrom and call for compensation to the victims. Although these prominent religious bodies

---

[106] A correspondence ensued between the bishop and the Foreign Office official, and a meeting was arranged for December 12. I have not yet seen the record of this conversation, although there is a short, handwritten note from one of Johnston's colleagues, who testifies to having read a report by the bishop of Malmesbury that was at least sixteen pages in length: He comments: "A very long winded report which is full of repetitions, I get the impression that the worthy clerics have been somewhat misled by their reception in thinking that they may have achieved more than they in fact have done (cf. especially the visit to the Governor of Istanbul and the result in Government circles)" [TNA:PRO, London, No. RK10110/16, December 22, 1955]. The signature at the end of this acidic response is not legible, but it is clearly not that of Johnston. One thing that the bishop did do was to enlighten Johnston on the patriarch's difficulties and the definite implication of the Turkish government in the disturbances of September 6-7. Thus, the anonymous commentator denied results "in Government [Turkish] circles"; by Johnston's own admission, however, the results of the bishop's observation on Turkish governmental responsibility had some result in another government's circles.

ultimately did not have the political power to sway the governments of the United States, Britain, and Turkey, they did succeed in two ways. First, and perhaps most important, they gave their constituents (162 churches) a more precise and accurate knowledge of the pogrom's violence; as such, they were instrumental in raising global awareness of the events and, thus, played a crucial role in forming international public opinion. At the same time, they introduced a certain apprehension in the governmental circles of the US, UK, and Turkey. There is also no doubt that their labors added to the considerable discomfort that characterized Turkish diplomacy in the pogrom's aftermath, not just in the United States and western Europe, but as far afield as Australia, South Africa, and Canada. Finally, in this period of tragedy and suffering, the World Council of Churches fellowship mission encouraged the Greek Orthodox of Istanbul to rebuild and carry on (if only temporarily).

As we have seen, the autonomous Church of Greece was also a member of the WCC, and so it and its archbishop, Spyridôn, also received copies of the reports and news of the council. Obviously, the Church and clergy of Greece were particularly outraged by the savage attacks on the Orthodox Church and clergy of Istanbul, as well as by the destruction of Greek dwellings, schools, and businesses. Many of the clergy in Greece had relatives in Istanbul, while others had gone to the theological school at Chalkê. Generally, the Orthodox population of Greece needed very little "sensitizing" to the events in the city. The Greek press was full to overflowing with coverage; indeed, to the large body of foreign correspondents who were already in the city to cover the five international conferences were now added a considerable number of Greek journalists. The testimonies of fleeing refugees filled the pages of Greek newspapers, as did, soon after, Kaloumenos's photographs. Finally, the names and numbers of attacked religious sites, businesses, and dwellings began to appear in Greece, often in entire lists that had been specially composed. All told, the Greek public was well aware and knowledgeable of the details of the frightful event. Even today, fifty years later, Greeks still lament what has come to be called the "black night of Hellenism."

On September 21, 1955, which was designated a day of national protest and mourning by the Church of Greece, Archbishop Spyridôn delivered a message to the Greek people over Radio Athens. It was to be a fiery oration. Although originally scheduled for 11:00 AM, it did not begin until 11:25, purportedly because the Greek government had tried to delete some passages that were construed as insulting to the country's allies. Spyridôn, however, not only read his entire message as he had written it, but left no doubt in his national audience that it was indeed "extreme," and that it reflected the outrage of the majority of the country (Spyridôn was not only archbishop of all Greece, but also president of the Panhellenic Enôsis Committee).[107] Some of his most explicit statements did in effect reflect Greek anger and the political atmosphere at the time:

> ...Greece is mourning today....We are mourning for the acts of violence and the ruins. We are mourning for the burned Churches and the outrage. We are mourning for the miserable attitude of the Christian world. Before these abominable acts, the Powerful keep silent, our friends assume a hypocritical attitude, and the authors of the cruelties jeer us, just because they are tolerated by those whose guilt is certain and proved....
>
> The alleged defenders of civilization and Freedom have not yet realized to what extent they have ill-treated the ideals by supporting the acts of violence, and what arms they have offered to those considered their enemies. And yet, at the time when the powerful Russian Empire protected the Orthodox of the East, the barbarians never dared to commit such sacrileges....[108]

The archbishop's diatribe was effectively ignored by the State Department and Foreign Office. The US embassy in Athens criticized the address as an attack, primarily, on the US and Britain, which it was to a real extent. The US embassy was offended by the charges of American hypocrisy; it failed to understand, however, that the issue of Cyprus, followed by the pogrom's violence, was to mark a major turning-point in Greek opinion—not only of the public but of politicians, diplomats, academics, and clergy as well—toward both Britain and the United States. One need only recall the annual report for 1955 of the British ambassador to Athens in which he remarked regretfully that the year had marked a turn in the course of Greek-British relations that had been worse than any since the end of the First World War. The US embassy had to admit, however, that "the Archbishop's message found a responsive audience."[109]

Whereas the reaction of the Protestant churches to the pogrom and to the plight of the Greeks in Istanbul had a lively and developed history, the same was not true of the reaction of the Orthodox churches of eastern Europe. The ecclesiological and cultural ties between the patriarchate of Constantinople and the other autonomous Orthodox churches of the Balkans and eastern

---

[107] National Archives, Athens to Washington, No. 333, October 10, 1955.

[108] *Ibid.* Elting's comment is brief but meaty: "More than a protest against incidents in Turkey, the Archbishop's address is an invective against the attitude of the big powers [i.e., the US and Britain], alleged to be motivated by 'self-interest, hypocrisy and deceit.' Noteworthy is...the remark that 'when the powerful Russian Empire protected the Orthodox of the East, the barbarians never dared to commit such sacrileges.'"

[109] The text of the prelate's speech had been published in *Kathimerini*, September 21, 1955.

Europe had traditionally been very strong. After the Byzantine empire was destroyed by the Ottoman sultans, the principal patrons of the ecumenical patriarchate had been the Russian tsars and the Romanian princes and *boyars*. Despite occasional differences, the patriarchate and Mount Athos were generously patronized by Russians and Romanians. With the decline of the Ottoman empire and the military and territorial expansion of the Russian state to the northern shores of the Black Sea, Russia's rulers became, in effect, the "protectors" of the Orthodox Christians in the Ottoman Balkans. Consequently, the tradition of Russophilia was deeply rooted in the national psyches of Greeks, Bulgarians, and Serbs. This was the case, furthermore, not only because of the common ties of strong Byzantine and Byzantine-Slavic cultures and religion, but also because Russians, Serbs, Bulgarians, and Greeks had a concurrent, and strong, political interest in common in the nineteenth and early twentieth centuries: the removal of Turkish rule in the Balkans. It was to this shared religion and political interests that Archbishop Spyridôn had referred in his angry address.

The Bolshevik Revolution had brought an abrupt hiatus to this tradition, however, as the Soviet government supported the new Turkish state during the long and bitter Anatolian war between Greece in Turkey that broke out in 1919 and lasted for three years. Although the Soviet Union did not destroy the Orthodox Church (or Islam) within its domains, it badly crippled it and subjected it to ruthless control. The conflict over Cyprus in the 1950s, and particularly the dramatic events of the pogrom, gave the Soviets an opportunity at the height of the Cold War to loosen the bonds between Greece and the Western camp. In this matter, the common cultural traditions and religious bonds of the Bulgarian, Romanian, and Russian churches could once again be put to practical, political use. On September 20, the Russian Orthodox patriarch, Alexii, and his holy synod, in a release to *Pravda*, issued a declaration on the violence in Istanbul:

> From newspaper reports we have learned of the grievous events which occurred in Istanbul on September 6, when a number of Orthodox Churches were plundered and destroyed, violence was committed to and wounds inflicted on very reverend hierarchs of the Oecumenical Church, and the editorial offices of Greek newspapers were destroyed.
>
> The Russian Orthodox Church, through us, expresses deep sympathy with the Oecumenical Church of Constantinople and the Greek people which had to experience this grievous suffering.
>
> The Russian Church has always felt profound, heartfelt love, forever ineradicable, for the Church of Constantinople, which was

for centuries its Mother Church. Therefore the deep sorrow felt by us because of the events which have occurred is understandable.

We rely on the grace of God—He is our refuge and strength (*Psalms* 45:2)—that he will stretch forth His mighty hand and restrain those who cause woe from further manifestations of violence, and will, in the future also, help our fraternal Church to lead the Orthodox Greek people along the path of safeguarding the Holy Faith and Its Sacred Objects.[110]

On the same day and in the same newspaper, a Soviet committee published the corresponding political message:

The situation has been aggravated on the one hand through the violation of the Cypriot people's right to self-determination, and on the other because of the persecution of the Greek Minority in Turkey.

The committee considers it its duty to state that devotion to the great ideal of peace in no way means toleration of the coercion being applied to the population of Cyprus or the Greek minority in Turkey.

The committee states that the standpoint of the Government of the USA and other member countries of NATO shows that this bloc of states serves the interests of the strong to the detriment of the weak. The strengthening of peace on the basis of justice... demands not different blocs of states, but sincere cooperation of all countries, cooperation capable of guaranteeing collective security and respect of the rights of each country.

The committee addresses to the UN General Assembly the demand that the question of the Cypriot people's right to self-determination be examined.[111]

Six days later, the Romanian patriarch, Justinian, and his synod unsurprisingly joined the Russian Church in condemning the Turkish attacks. Their statement generally followed the structure and content of the Russian synod's earlier one, condemning the destruction of the Greek churches and homes and referring to the attacks on the clergy and the faithful. It also included a reference to the role of Romanians in the life of the Orthodox Christians during the period of Ottoman rule: "The ancient relations between our Church and the Oecumenical Patriarchy [*sic*] in Constantinople, the fact that among the devastated and destroyed churches some had been endowed and founded through the faith of our ancestors, increases our sorrow even more."[112]

---

[110] TNA:PRO, London to Satterthwaite and Slack, No. RG10344/57, September 22, 1955.
[111] *Ibid.*
[112] TNA:PRO, London, No. FO371 117711 198335, contains an English translation of

The Bulgarian Church followed suit. The actions and statements of the Eastern Orthodox churches were no doubt facilitated by the Cold War, with the respective states finding the role of their national churches convenient in their face-off with the Western powers. The seeming political isolation of Greece from its Western allies over the Cyprus issue and the pogrom seemed an opportune moment for the Soviets to woo Greece away from its alliance. The US and Britain—as well as the Greek government itself, of course—were not going to let that happen. The series of Greek governments that had come to power in postwar Greece had fought a drawn-out and bitter civil war with the forces of the Greek communist party. Consequently, the country was torn asunder into two highly polarized camps, and it was impossible for the victors to accept any accommodation with the Soviet system. It was politically impossible, therefore, for the Soviet effort of using the Orthodox churches to bring Greece out of the West's embrace to succeed in any meaningful way.[113]

THE MUSLIMS OF WESTERN THRACE

A final note on religious diplomacy has to do not with Christians, but with the Muslim communities of Greek Thrace. According to the treaty of Lausanne, the Greek minority was not only to remain in Istanbul and the Muslim minority in Greek Thrace, but both ethnic minorities were accorded full civil and political rights, and were allowed the intervention of their respective motherlands to defend their rights. The issue had already arisen when the Greek government insisted on speaking on behalf of the Greek

the statement of the Russian patriarch and holy synod on September 20, 1955, as well as the declaration of the Romanian patriarch and holy synod, dated September 28, 1955. For the similar pronouncement of the Bulgarian clergy and synod, see TNA:PRO, London, No. RG10344/66, September 30, 1955.

[113] On the Greek government's negative reaction to any Soviet proposal, see Kavallieratos's report, Greek Embassy, Washington to Athens, No. 3896, September 23:

> I communicated supplementary details to the [US] authorities, as these were transmitted to me in your message No. 40463, in regard to the message of the Patriarch of Moscow. I once more emphasized the political aims of such a message. And to the question [of the US authorities] as to what were, in my opinion, the purposes, I answered that obviously this is a matter of Soviet interference in Greek affairs. And, the proof of it lies in the United Press news according to which a representative of the Soviet Embassy in Athens announced that Russia is willing to cooperate with Greece on all matters if the Greek Government should agree. My [US] interlocutor expressed his belief that the political sense of the Greek Government and of the people would not allow us to fall victims to such purposes. I replied that I am certain that the American Government will find a means of supplying us with the necessary assistance.

minority in Turkey. Nonetheless, Menderes basically refused to discuss such intervention, while the Turkish foreign ministry always denied this right on the grounds that the Greek minority was made up of Turkish citizens who were completely, and inalienably, under the jurisdiction of the Turkish state. Meanwhile, in the 1950s, Menderes's government had begun to cultivate the Kemalist secularist and nationalist ideology in Greek Thrace through the Turkish consulate there, in order to wean the Turkish minority, as well as other non-Turkish Muslims, to a Turkish nationalist identity. Accordingly, the Turkish consuls in Western Thrace became missionaries of Turkish nationalism, inculcating their ideology in the teachers of the local Turkish-language schools, who were brought to Istanbul for courses and seminars. Thus, ethnic Turkish communities gradually began to be penetrated by and divided into those with a modern nationalist outlook and those of the old school, who looked upon Islam as the basic element in their identity. During this time, Turkey's consuls not only exercised a kind of censorship over the region's Turkish-language newspapers, but also tried to create a Turkish national consciousness among non-Turkish Muslim minorities such as the Pomaks, Roma, and Circassians.[114]

Within hours of the outbreak of the pogrom, the Greek government ordered stringent security measures for the entire Muslim minority of Greece to ensure that no harm befell it. Indeed, in his speech in the Turkish parliament, İnönü had accused Menderes of being responsible for the pogrom and then compared his inaction in protecting the Greek minority with the Greek government's speed in securing the lives, property, mosques, schools, and businesses of the ethnic Turks in Greek Thrace. (Panagiôtês Kanellopoulos was the minister who specifically signed the order of protection.) Certainly, the position of the Muslim minority in Greek Thrace and the Dodecanese islands must have been extremely difficult in the immediate aftermath of the events. The shocking details began to flood the Greek press, first in Athens and Thessalonikê, then the provincial press, and finally the local, Turkish-language newspapers, *Milliyet* and *Trakya*, which gave relatively good and detailed coverage of the pogrom to their readers. In addition, Thrace received four daily Turkish newspapers from Istanbul—*Cumhuriyet*, *Milliyet*, *Vatan*, and *Hürriyet*—which continued to come to Xanthê regularly after the pogrom although delivery to Komotênê was halted after September 7. In the general mustering of Greek public opinion, the government solicited—or various organizations, cities, and villages spontaneously sent in—letters denouncing the pogrom. And so it was that Muslim villages, as well as

[114] See Chapter 1 of this study.

mixed and Greek villages in Greek Thrace, began to condemn the violence. Generally, the letters of protest from Greek Thrace came from local village assemblies or governing boards; some letters were quite detailed, indicating that the local Turkish-language press or a Greek newspaper had been read by the locals, while others were brief and general. Given the outrage that prevailed among their Christian neighbors, it would have been difficult for Muslim communities to refuse to sign such letters, or at least to approve them in a village's general assembly.[115]

A detailed report by Major Geôrgios Koklamanês, director of the rural gendarmerie in Rodopê, dated September 12, 1955, gives a vivid picture of the real difficulties in preserving order between Christians and Muslims in the region, which was now caught up in the uproar that followed the violence in Istanbul. The translation of the full police report, divided into five short sections, follows.

> I have the honor to report the following regarding order and security and on the situation that prevails in Komotênê following the events that took place and afflicted the Greeks of Constantinople and Smyrna.
>
> 1. The Greek population of Komotênê continues in a state of exasperation and volatility against the [local] Turks because of the frightful crimes which they [the Turks of Istanbul] carried out against our compatriots. All the [local] Greeks, regardless of their age and political persuasion, manifest their hatred and irritation toward the entire [local] Turkish element. The Greeks believe that despite the fact that they [the Turks] have lived amid civilized people for so many centuries, they have not managed, nor is it likely that they will ever manage, to dispel their primitive instincts and the habits of the jungle from which they are descended.
>
> The [Greek] youth of Komotênê has considered that the only thing that primitive people perceive, and through which their criminal instincts can be tamed, is power or force, and so they have come together from the very first day [of the pogrom]. They assembled in secret meetings under the leadership of the former head of the "Chi Organization," Theodôros Karadiamantês and made the decision to proceed to reprisals against the local Turks.
>
> But they were hindered from this by all those who took notice of this discussion and they [the youth of the Chi organization]

---

[115] Such letters were received by the Greek foreign ministry from the following villages in Western Thrace: Arisvê, Kalchan, Pandrosos, Arianoi, Filyrê, Krovylê, and Aratos; there were undoubtedly others as well. See Ypourgeion Exôterikôn, September 18, 1955, protocol number is effaced from the document.

have been persuaded that such activities are in opposition to Greek culture and to the national interests of Greece. Thus, they abstained from lawlessness and restricted themselves only to the mere expression of their exasperation against the crimes of Constantinople and against the local compatriots [of the pogromists].

Despite all this, the more hotheaded of the Greeks continue to threaten the [local] Turks and to seek the opportunity to express this exasperation. It is hoped, however, that with the passing of the first impact [of the pogrom] and because of the strict measures [of security] that have been taken, there will be no public demonstration whatever nor will order be disturbed in any manner.

2. The local Turkish population feared reprisals on the first and second day [after the pogrom] and so restricted its movements in and around the city.

Certain leaders [of the Turkish community], as well as their members in the Greek Parliament and others who have entered Greek political life, and the leader of their youth, constituted an exception. Especially such was the Turkish Deputy Consul, and those who accompany him, who circulated boastfully and even at night, which forced my officials to put him under surveillance.

3. After the passing of the first days [after the pogrom], the Turks took courage and began to circulate and to carry out their daily chores as before. Indeed, some of them, mostly their youth and above all those who belong to the "Young Turks" [that is, Kemalist nationalists and modernizers], in their private discussions expressed themselves in an improper manner at our expense, attributing our tolerance to weakness, and from time to time threatening us or the Greeks of Constantinople.

Specifically, one such young Turk, İsmail Ahmet, in a public discussion with other Turks, stated that the Turks have the best army and have no need of alliances. Another Turkish youth, by name Ali Mola Ahmet, in a conversation with the tailor Nicholas, stated that they should have massacred some [Greeks in Istanbul] so that [the rest of the Greeks] would come to their senses. A third Turk, in answering a [local] Greek who had threatened him with reprisals, replied, "the Greeks do not dare touch us."

This information was brought to the attention of the Nomarchês [Prefect] formally by the director of the ATE [Agricultural Bank of Greece]. In addition, the director denounced all the Turks, as they had all completely ceased paying their monthly loans, and he asked my opinion on whether it was conducive to Greek national interests to proceed with legal measures for collecting what was owed the bank.

4. According to information, which is as yet unconfirmed, the local Turkish Deputy Consul notified the Turkish inhabitants of Komotênê to abandon Greek soil. According to this same information, from the time of the "events" [pogrom] and thereafter, the Turkish Deputy Consul has intensified the secret immigration of local Turks from Greece and especially in the rural areas.

5. These contacts of the Turkish Deputy Consul, his irregular movements, and the very "servile" behavior of certain Turks who are obviously working under the command of the Deputy Consul, have raised suspicions in our service and among many Greeks of this town that perhaps a portion of the Turks, or the Turkish Government, desire to create episodes similar to the one in Constantinople and Smyrna attributable to the Greeks. This would then lessen unfavorable [to Turkey] public opinion worldwide.[116]

Excluding the theorizing on national psychologies—and the manifest racism—this report nonetheless conveys a clear picture of the situation faced by the Greek police. Koklamanês quickly isolated the critical factors in the drama: the heightened tension in the two communities over the pogrom had suddenly reversed the situation between the Greek and Turkish communities in Istanbul. It was now the Muslims of Greek Thrace that feared the rage of their local Greek neighbors. Koklamanês saw that there were divisions in each community, and he quickly seized upon these to neutralize the smaller, more violent element among the Greeks. In this, he obviously echoed the will of the majority of the Greek community to force those in the *Chi* organization to desist from violence. The Muslim community was also divided between their own more extremist youth and the older generation. The former were already converted apostles to the cause of the Turkish consulate whereas many in the older generation were fearful for their lives and possessions. The other

---

[116] For the Greek text, High Administration of the Rural Greek Gendarmerie of the District of Rodopê, Office of National Security, No. 132/1/135, sent from Komotênê to Athens, September 12, 1955, with a copy to the foreign ministry on September 20, 1955. *Chi* ("X" in the Latin alphabet) was an organization of the extreme right founded toward the end of the German occupation of Greece and associated with (then) Lieutenant-Colonel Geôrgios Grivas. It had close relations with the German authorities and, during the period of civil strife that enveloped Greece at the end of the Second World War, managed to incorporate many of the collaborationist elements of the Greek quisling regime; it also seems to have enjoyed the favor of pro-British circles in Athens in the immediate postwar era. Grivas, who was a native-born Cypriot, went on to found EOKA in the Fifties. See Giôrgos Margaritês, *Istoria tou ellênikou emfiliou polemou, 1946-1949*, Athens, 2001, pp. 516-517, and David Close, editor, *The Greek Civil War, 1943-1950: Studies in polarization*, London, 1993.

external factor, as mentioned, were the officials of the Turkish state. The constant reference in this short report to their activities is an unmistakable sign of their vigorous efforts to "nationalize" the entire Muslim minority and make it a willing instrument of Turkish foreign policy. The telling proof lies in the complaint of the director of the Agricultural Bank of Greece that all the Muslims who had taken out agricultural loans concurrently went into default on their payments. This had to have been orchestrated by the Turkish consulate, as no other entity could have guaranteed to replace the collateral on their loans that all these farmers were threatened with losing.

As time passed, however, the atmosphere of fear began to dissolve, with the Turks returning to their daily affairs and the threat of the Greek extremists being suppressed by the larger majority of Greeks who did not desire violence. Comparing September 6-7 in Istanbul and September 6-7 in Komotênê and throughout the areas in which the Muslim minority lived, the picture is clear. Still, the pressures and political requirements of the Turkish government increased, if anything. Ankara was continually looking to provoke episodes and false rumors that would give it an advantage over the Greek side on the Cyprus issue.

For example, in contrast to the offices of the eight Greek newspapers of Istanbul that were all destroyed and burned, the offices of the two Turkish newspapers in Xanthê, *Milliyet* (owned by Hamdi Hüseyin Fahmi) and *Trakya* (owned by N. Nuri), were not touched. And although they were on occasion subjected to pressure from the office of the minister of Northern Greece, they were not closed or under legal sanction during this critical period. The Turkish-language press of Western Thrace continued to publish regularly, in fact, and in the first week or so continued to write on the pogrom. *Trakya* in particular strongly criticized the outrages of September 6-7, and both newspapers continued to provide information on events in both Turkey and Greece. On September 16, *Milliyet* published a variety of articles that included a commentary on the political campaign of the *Synagermos* (Rally) Party and its preparations in light of the upcoming election. The paper announced that it would not be supporting this party and accused it of never keeping its promises to the Turkish minority. A second article reported on the return of Turkish teachers to Greek Thrace from special summer seminars in Istanbul. Of the fifty local teachers that had been sent to these seminars in Turkey, which were created especially for them, fifteen were *mollas* (that is, *mullahs*), who, the newspaper added, would "again cover their heads with the fez and turban as before" now that they had returned. This was a direct reference to the split in the Turkish community between the traditionalists and Kemalists.

The most relevant article, however, was entitled, "Sad Episodes in Istanbul and Izmir," and was, in effect, a very limited and selective annotation of the material regarding the pogrom in the Turkish press. The reportage began with the incident at the Turkish consular compound in Thessalonikê (from which "no damages were effected save for the breaking of some windows [of Atatürk's house]"). Still, the paper continued, as soon as the news spread:

> ...it produced a most violent reaction among the people and very numerous bands moved to Taksim and demonstrated....It has been concluded that evil minds exploited this situation and influenced the obvious emotions of the people and became the cause for the outbreak of incidents in the streets and in the various neighborhoods of Istanbul. The mob entered very many stores and dwellings of the Greeks and threw out into the streets furniture, utensils, commercial goods, and caused very great damage.
>
> Similar and sorrowful scenes also took place in Izmir where the Greek pavilion [in the Izmir international fair] and the Greek Consulate were burned.

In this short and selective recapitulation of events, *Milliyet* quickly noted the "true sorrow" expressed verbally by Turkish president Bayar, the political parties, and Turkey's National Association of Students, and then came to the most important concern of the Turkish minority in Greek Thrace:

> The Greek Government, having in mind what had taken place in Turkey, things worthy of the most severe condemnation, and realizing that these affairs could also arouse the people [of Greece], wished to head off such unnecessary behavior. It took all those measures necessary, in simultaneous action everywhere, and above all in Western Thrace, to preserve order. Accordingly, not even the slightest episode took place. During all this, the events in Istanbul and Izmir had provoked the most profound emotions among all classes of the Turkish and Greek populations.

The newspaper, in other words, confirmed that the Greek government had taken all the measures necessary to preserve the security of the Turkish and Muslim minorities in Western Thrace.

The newspaper was also extremely sensitive to, and issued a vigorous denial of, the reports that Turkish "refugees" from Western Thrace had taken part in the pogrom:

> A newspaper of Istanbul, after the abovementioned underhanded brashness in Turkey, published the most slanderous news that participating in these events were also Turkish refugees from

Western Thrace who had settled in Istanbul. Thus an effort was made to sully the name and honor of our fellow citizens [the Turkish minority of Western Thrace]. This journalist, who managed to pass over into the columns of such a distinguished newspaper, the name of which we do not wish to reveal, should have reckoned with the great evil that he could have caused with this slander, and he should feel some shame and troubled conscience....

We, as the conveyors and representatives of the opinion of the Turks of Western Thrace, deem it our ethical responsibility to declare to World Public Opinion that we reject this [accusation] and detest it.[117]

Clearly, the newspaper had adopted the official view of the Turkish state that the pogrom had been the deed of unknown conspirators who were enemies of Turkey. Furthermore, although the commentary's author mentioned damages to Greek shops and dwellings, he was completely silent on the destruction and desecration of Greek churches and religious institutions. Nor was a word written about the physical violence visited on the Greeks or on the destruction of the eight Greek newspapers in Istanbul. Still, despite all the partial reporting, *Milliyet* did at least apprise its readers of the great injustice done to the Greek Christians of Istanbul, and commented very favorably on the timely intervention of the Greek authorities to protect the Turkish Muslim minority.

Three days later, *Trakya* published a report on the aftermath of the pogrom that began with a statement that was in consonance with *Milliyet* on the question of responsibility: "All Turks, from the smallest [*sic*] to the highest, have condemned and cursed the incidents that took place on...September 6-7. All, from the [Turkish] Government and the National Assembly to the very villages in the most distant Anatolian reaches, agree that these incidents were not a Turkish deed but one of an organized conspiracy and plotting against the Turkish Government and Nation." *Trakya*, however, also reported the martial-law measures, the mass arrests, the large amount of looted property amassed in houses and elsewhere, the creation of the Istanbul aid committee, the fund drives, and the destruction of Greek schools and businesses. Still, as with *Milliyet*, there was no mention of the destruction of Greek churches and other religious institutions, although there was the same, albeit indirect, focus

---

[117] Office of the Press of the Ministry of Northern Greece to the Ypourgeion Proedrias Kyvernêseôs General Press Office, Athens, unnumbered; Greek translations of relevant sections from the September 16, 1955, edition of *Milliyet* of Xanthê as the Turkish text was unavailable.

on the Turkish community of Western Thrace and on the quick reaction of the Greek government to protect it.

> Turkish radio frequently reports on the ninth announcement of the Martial-Law Government of Istanbul. According to this announcement, certain people are circulating rumors that supposedly the Turks of Western Thrace are being oppressed. The Martial-Law Administration denies this, and orders all those who circulate this rumor to be reported and denounced. And indeed we here are astonished by these false rumors. It would seem that all this derives from the same source, as this suspicious and underhanded propaganda is attempting to keep the people of both countries in a high state of political agitation.[118]

According to the treaty of Lausanne, the Turkish minority of Greece and the Greek community of Istanbul were to be treated equally. The violence against the Greek community of Istanbul—with the apparent participation of Turks from Western Thrace—showed, however, that the two communities could be bound together in a crueler way: as hostages to each other. The Greek extremist right-wing organization *Chi* now called for reprisals against the Turkish minority in Western Thrace, as we saw from Koklamanês's report. Both *Milliyet* and *Trakya* agree on one point, however: the measures immediately taken by the Greek government were decisive in safeguarding the Turkish minority during the dangerous days following the pogrom. Indeed, in stark contrast to the Turkish police, which, on order of its superiors, had stood by as the Greek community in Istanbul was attacked, the Greek police forces protected the Turkish communities in those areas of the country where they might have been in danger from extremist vigilantes.

Meanwhile, in the midst of all the tension and apprehension affecting Greek Thrace, the Turkish consular authorities of Komotênê began to make their presence felt. On September 9, the secretary of the Turkish consulate in the town, Recip Mehmetoğlu, telephoned the Turkish-minority member of the Greek parliament and complained (in a conversation tapped by the rural gendarmerie) that the Greeks "have placed police detachments around the Turkish Consulate, around the Turkish community, and around the [Turkish] social foundations, and this is, according to them, freedom?" The Turkish deputy replied, however, that, "You must be thankful and you must express your gratitude to the Greek Government for the measures they have taken,

---

[118] Office of the Press of the Ministry of Northern Greece to the Ypourgeion Proedrias Kyvernêseôs General Press Office, Athens, unnumbered; Greek translations of relevant sections from the September 19, 1955, issue of *Trakya* as the Turkish text was unavailable.

in contrast to those [taken] by our people in Turkey [in regard to the Greek minority]."[119] This sentiment seems, on the face of it, to have been consonant with that of the Turkish minority, which undoubtedly did appreciate the security measures taken on its behalf. At the same time, of course, the deputy may also have been guarding himself against the unthinking Turkish consular secretary, given the probability that he understood that the Turkish consulate's telephones were under electronic surveillance.

In a dispatch to the foreign ministry, the minister of Northern Greece pointed out that both *Milliyet* and *Trakya*—and especially the latter newspaper, which had previously engaged in rather fierce criticism—had begun to lower the tone of their criticism of the pogrom. He refers specifically to the effort of both newspapers to protect the Turkish government against any charges or hints of responsibility for the events:

> This is due, according to our information, to the activities of the Turkish Consul-General in Komotênê, who has become extremely active in squelching the protests and manifestations of the Turkish communities over the incident of September 6, as well as to his agreement with the editors and owners of these newspapers….This is also apparent from the columns of these two newspapers, which ceased and desisted from their violent personal politics, which used to occupy most of the newspapers' space.[120]

The active intervention of the Turkish consulate had succeeded in restraining the local Turkish-language press and in largely halting the letters of protest from the Turkish and Muslim communities despite that fact that the measures of the Greek government had effectively removed the danger of reprisals by Greek extremists.

However, as the *Milliyet* article had implied, the Turkish—or, depending on one's point of view at the time, Muslim—community was not unified. Fifteen of the fifty Turkish teachers sent to the summer program of seminars set up specifically for them opposed Kemalism and, as *Milliyet* wrote, put on their turbans as soon as they returned. Furthermore, not all Muslims in the region were Turks, and inter-Muslim rivalries existed. This emerges from the letter, dated September 15, 1955, of one Hafuz (*sic*) Ali Reşad, in which the latter is presented as "President of the Organization of Islamic Union of all Muslims in Greece" and "Vice-President of Circassians in Greece." Addressed to the governor of Rodopê, the letter attacks Turks and alleges "that there is

---

[119] High Administration of the Rural Gendarmerie of Thrace, No. 125.4.52a, September 19, 1955, and received in Athens on September 17, 1955, Ypourgeion Exôterikôn, No. 271(?).

[120] Ministry of Northern Greece, Thessalonikê to Athens, No. 1486/T, October 3, 1955.

a great similarity between the white bear of the north [the Soviets] and the wolves of Anatolia [the Kemalist Turks]. These Young Turks assert that they are the descendants of the ancient Hittites and so have an ancient civilization, thus shamefully ignoring the truth of four to five thousand years of history and considering themselves Europeans whereas in effect they have become even more barbarous than before." If, Reşad continues, it was necessary to avenge the bomb in Thessalonikê supposedly thrown by the Greeks, would it not have been sufficient to do this with the Greek consulates of Istanbul and Izmir?

> Did not the Turks understand that, with all these acts of violence, they were destroying fellow citizens? Their ancestors never committed acts of violence against religious institutions and functions....They demonstrated through their vandalism that neither freedom nor human rights are respected in Turkey. Anyway, a nation that betrays its own religion cannot respect the religions of others. It is well-known that the Turks denied Muhammad's religion and took on the dogmas of Atatürk.
>
> Can the Turkish politicians and journalists who daily assert that the Turks of Western Thrace are being persecuted point out even one Greek violation of sacred institutions of the Turks, or of their personal freedom, or of the inviolability of their families?
>
> We in Western Thrace live, as a Muslim minority, in complete freedom and peace and not like those who live in Turkey deprived of every freedom.[121]

In reality, any discussion of the Muslim minorities of Greece at this point requires a broader context. The treaty of Lausanne provided for the protection and full rights for the Greek minority of the Istanbul area and for the Muslim minority of Greek Thrace. A comparison of these two minority communities and of the measures taken by their respective national—that is "host"—governments to protect them and ensure the treaty's implementation is by now unnecessary and needs only a brief comment. While the Turkish government had systematically organized the attack on and destruction of the Greeks of Istanbul, the Greek government implemented tight and effective security measures to protect the Muslim (both Turkish and non-

---

[121] The person, the "Organization of Islamic Union of all Muslims in Greece," and the "Circassians in Greece," are all unclear as to precise identity, but what is clear is that this letter indicates, along with other evidence, that the non-Turkish Muslims of northern Greece had not been absorbed into the ethnic Turkish community of Western Thrace at that time. The letter is dated September 15, 1955, and was forwarded by the governor of Rodopê to the foreign ministry in Athens.

Turkish) minority of Greek Thrace, as well as its property, religious and educational institutions, and press. Indeed, today, half a century later, Greek Istanbulis have, for all intents and purposes, disappeared whereas the Turkish communities of Greek Thrace have grown and prospered, especially in the quarter-century since Greece entered the European Union. In this respect, the Turkish government succeeded in turning the treaty of Lausanne into a unilateral instrument: while all provisions protecting the Greeks of Istanbul were systematically abrogated over the years, the accord was used ostensibly to "defend" and promote the Muslim minorities of Greek Thrace, which, in reality, meant allowing Turkey's consular authorities in the region to propagandize among and "chauvinize" the Muslim population, including those segments of it that were not ethnically Turkish.

THE POLITICS OF ECCLESIASTICAL COMPENSATIONS

Having briefly examined the process of reducing claims for compensation in Chapters 3 and 4, we also noted that compensation for destruction of ecclesiastical properties was not made directly to the respective Greek communities, but rather to the contractors who took on the job of repairs and rebuilding. Inasmuch as Christoforos Chrêstidês's *Ekthesis* remains the best available source on compensation for the damaged or destroyed churches, it is appropriate to return to it. Chrêstidês also had a rather remarkable collection of confidential documents at his disposal, including official documents that dealt with the damage claims of the churches and other religious institutions. In his report, he states that this material is to be found at the end as an appendix.[122] Unfortunately, it is missing from the manuscript and is not to be found in the Chrêstidês archive of the Center for Asia Minor Studies in Athens. Nevertheless, Chrêstidês stated that, of the TL60 million appropriated by the Turkish government for all compensation claims, TL10 million was dedicated to the Istanbul *vakıflar* to cover the rehabilitation of churches. Again, Chrêstidês gave the total of damage claims as being approximately TL40,054,605. Two things are worthy of note in this figure. The first is that, as mentioned, Chrêstidês had access to the patriarchate's official list of damages and claims to be submitted to the *vakıflar*. In it, the patriarchate had differentiated between damages to buildings (TL19,933,450) and damages to moveable property and objects (TL19,121,155).[123]

Chrêstidês then explains the consequent reduction of these claims in light of the Turkish legislation on the issue and Turkish economic "practicality":

---

[122] Chrêstidês, *Ekthesis*, p. 192.
[123] *Ibid*, p. 191; either Chrêstidês's arithmetic is in error or the two entries are.

...[I]t now became apparent that the damage [claims] had to be cut, in every way possible, to an insignificant amount. This would facilitate a rapid granting of the relevant governmental down payment that would permit the repair and rebuilding to commence. Because of all this, there were constant reexaminations of the tables of damages. The original hope for replacing all the destroyed church property was now abandoned and attention was now limited to ascertaining how much money would be needed for the churches to function once more with everything that was absolutely essential, but with no hope, any longer, of restoring them to that state that they had formerly enjoyed.[124]

By the latter part of 1957, over two years after the pogrom, the Church was forced to reduce its claims to TL12,739,705, which was still over the total of TL10 million allowed by law.[125] Even this minimal award, however, was further vitiated by the slowness of the procedures of assessment and payment, which fed into the incessant inflationary devaluation of the compensation.

Of the ninety identified churches, monasteries, cemeteries, and *agiasmata* that suffered damages, seventy-four appear in the archival materials of the Istanbul *vakıflar* and Committee for Repair, although these files are incomplete. It is to be hoped that future researchers on this issue will have access to the full archival sources, not only of the two institutions above but of the patriarchate, the various Greek communities, the Istanbul aid committee, and all other relevant organizations. It is noteworthy that the majority of claims negotiations was handled by the secular representatives of the larger Greek community. It should also be noted, again, that the documentation of damaged religious properties was the responsibility of the Greek communities and the Committee for Repair, and that the latter undertook the critical responsibility of dealing with the Istanbul *vakıflar*, or contracting out the work for repairs and reconstruction, and, finally, of allocating the funds provided by the *vakıflar* to the contractors.

As indicated previously, the patriarch summoned an assembly of the representatives from each of the many Greek communities early on to advise on the assessment and identification of damages, compensation, and related issues. In addition, the patriarch heeded the advice of Alexandros Chatzopoulos to accept the Turkish proposal of a three-man mixed (Turkish/ Greek) committee to monitor the process. This small committee was undoubtedly the architectural committee that appears later in the assessment process and was under the administrative authority of the Committee for

[124] *Ibid.*, pp. 191-192.
[125] *Ibid.*

Repair. The three-man mixed committee of architects seems also to have constituted the approval committee (*Kabul Hey'et*). A primary function of this committee was to be the liaison to the governing board of each Greek community as well as to the Committee for Repair. Their immediate contact in the *vakıflar* was the bureau of monuments and construction (*Abide ve Yapı İşleri Dairesi Reisliği*).

These then were the basic groups and institutions involved in evaluating, examining, approving, and paying for the damages to ecclesiastical institutions. The Committee for Repair and the architects' committee had to carry out a detailed survey of damages, while the bidding contractors had to list the damages systematically, estimate the quantity of materials and labor needed for repair, and, finally, itemize the cost. These cost estimates were based on the price and rate list promulgated annually by the ministry of public works (the *Nafia*). Once all the documentation was prepared, the architectural committee had to verify every item and declare it satisfactory or appropriate. This part of the process must have been carried out in conjunction with the community boards, although their names do not always appear in the documentation. When the three-man committee's documentation was in order, it was forwarded to the bureau of monuments and construction of the *vakıflar*, where it was examined and, if approved, forwarded to the *vakıflar* directory for final approval.

There is no suggestion in the accessible documentation that the evaluations had to be examined by the commissions established for that purpose in regard to secular property (see Chapter 4). In fact, it is possible that all such evaluations were ultimately examined by the *vakıflar*. In any case, legislation had already reduced Greek ecclesiastical claims by 75 percent and, as there is some evidence of rejection of specific assessments thereafter by the *vakıflar*, the final cuts were even more severe. It is thus apparent that a further reduction of compensations was inherent in the very process.

It was the duty of the Committee for Repair to put out each job to bidding. Those who bid successfully (including Muslim Turks, local Greeks, Armenians, and Jews) underbid the actual estimated pricing of the job, with the percentage of underbidding varying from case to case. While the awards to the successful bidders were made by the committee, they had to be approved by the *vakıflar*, which did not pay the contractors directly, as all these (and other) functions were carried out by the committee. The *vakıflar* simply deposited, periodically, sums of money into the Committee for Repair's account for the payment of contractors.

There was some allowance for additional work and materials that were not or could not have been foreseen, but such cases are limited in number in the available sources. The *vakıflar* could also allow for an extension of completion deadlines. This seems to have been frequent. All these contracts were subject to two processes: the first, which has already been mentioned, was the *eksiltme tenzilatı* (lowest bid), and the second was the allowance for inflation (*ilave*). A detailed study would have to examine whether the *ilave* was equal to the actual rate of inflation. This is a difficult and technical subject that need not concern us here, but it is doubtful whether the allowance for inflation was realistic, for the formal value of the Turkish lira had become greatly disproportionate to its real value. Finally, another matter that is marked by some uncertainty is the issue of the documents that identified, quantified, and priced materials, labor, and evaluations. These documents generally do not originate from the *vakıflar*, as their address and signatures are absent. They are usually signed by the three-man committee, which scrutinized them in detail.

The process of repairs was drawn out over a long time, to as late as 1966 (if not later), and it bears repeating that the available documentation for these seventy-four institutions does not indicate provision being made for repairing or replacing a significant number of items that were completely destroyed or stolen. The procedure for any case, but especially for those of churches and other institutions that suffered heavily, necessitated a very considerable documentation, as the items had to be listed in an identifiable and specific manner, and had to be measured both as to dimensions and, in cases such as cement or plaster, weight. In pricing, only those prices set by the ministry of public works were allowed, and each price had to be identified by its corresponding item number in the ministry's annual registry. The preparation of documentation was reduced to an almost meaningless task by virtue of the Turkish government's rejection *ab initio* of 75 percent of the value of the damage. The documents are nonetheless of interest for establishing the level of costs, the extent and degree of damages, and the actual amounts the Turkish government intended *not* to compensate. The extreme reduction of 75 percent of claims is possibly reflected very early in the patriarchate's order to the communities to reduce all their claims regarding religious property to 10/35, or 28.5 percent, of the initial damage assessments determined jointly by the Committee for Repair and the patriarchate before the claims were submitted. The source for this information and the calculation of the numbers will be discussed below.

Each case began with three documents, which were prepared by the successful bidder and submitted to the Committee for Repair. These three documents were:

1. The *Technical Specifications* (*Fenni Şartname*) were a rough, general, and concise document that consisted of two parts: a) a long list of numbers,

which referred to the items or materials requested by the repairwork that corresponded to the price list of the ministry of public works; b) a far longer, numbered list of both materials needed and in what place in the specific church they were to be used (this list is therefore a good general guide, by inference, to the damages in different parts of the given building). The *Technical Specifications* were usually signed by the architectural committee. As chief of the project (*İnşaat Şefi*), the head of the bureau in the *vakıflar* stamped the document, often also stamping the term, "Appropriate" (*Uygundur*), on the *List of Valuations*. He then sent the three documents of the successful bidder to the *vakıflar* directorate for final approval. If the latter approved, it stamped the *List of Valuations* "Approved" (*Onandı*) and dated it. If the document was deficient and thus not approved by the *vakıflar*, it was returned for correction, resubmitted, and the same procedure above was repeated.

2. The second document, which was accompanied by the *Technical Specifications*, was the *Register of Measurements* (*Metraj Cedveli*). It was always composed on finely lined paper with subtitles of materials under which were listed all materials required for the job. It was an extremely detailed list and provided the complete specifications of each material or item, as well as the numbers or volumes required. The measurements were either in area, volume, or weight, according to the material. It was signed by all three members of the architectural committee and forwarded along with the previous and succeeding documents. If approved, it was stamped by the bureau as *Onandı* and dated and sent on to the *vakıflar* directorate.

3. The successful bidder's third document was the so-called *List of Valuations* (*Keşif Özeti*). It was usually similar to the catalogue of materials and labor in the *Register of Measurements*, differing basically in that it actually applied the price/cost of each as set by the ministry of public works (and as identified by number in the *Technical Specifications*). This document set out the official price of each item and ended with a total of expenses for the work. It, too, was signed by the architectural committee, accompanied by the preceding two documents, and sent to the *vakıflar*, where it was stamped, approved, and dated.

When, and if, these documents were approved by the *vakıflar*, the Committee for Repair awarded the contract to the lowest bidder. Meanwhile, from the submission of the first three documents and the awarding of the contract until the completion of the job and final payment to the contractor, a host of other documents intervened. Without going into detail, it is sufficient for our purposes to mention only the more important three documents and procedures, whose purpose was to control the process once it had begun and possibly allow for certain variations or additions to the original contract.

1. The first of this second group of documents was issued by the Committee for Repair and constituted the *Installment Payments* (*Hakediş Raporu*). The committee periodically had to report and estimate the contractor's efficiency in satisfactorily and expeditiously finishing the work. The report always included the number of that specific installment payment. It also recorded the date of the contract, the period within which the work had to be concluded, the sum total of the original cost estimate, and the percentage by which the bid undercut the original estimate. If the architects' committee approved the speed and quality of the work, it signed the document of approval for the particular payment to proceed. The contractor also signed the document, which included the number of installments already paid, as well as the amounts and payments remaining. The document also recorded the *ilave*, that is, the additional sums added to the cost of the job because of inflation. Upon approval by the *vakıflar*, the committee paid the contractor.

2. The second document in this latter group was *Approval of Work Finished* (*Geçici Kabul Raporu*), and, while similar to the previous document, it was simply a way of monitoring the work's progress. It, too, was signed by the three architects and the contractor.

3. The third document of this second group was the *Final Certification* (*Kesin Kabul Raporu*), which acknowledged final completion of the work to the satisfaction of the three architects and contractor, all of whom signed it. It, too, included a list of payments; after approval, the Committee for Repair paid the contractor.

The contractors entered the preceding procedure when the "bids committee" (which was drawn from the Committee for Repair and organized and presided over the bidding process) advertised for tenders. By way of illustration, following are sixteen cases of specific bids.

An examination of a representative sample from this body of documents will perhaps demonstrate better than anything else the process of repairs (and compensation) and illustrate what was damaged, destroyed, or stolen. Following is a detailed analysis of two churches in particular, Holy Trinity in Taksim and the Taxiarchs in Balat. Although the files are not complete, the first consists of 110 pages and the second of 55 pages, which are sufficient in both cases to give us a clear idea of what happened.

The first file is entitled "Taksim: Holy Trinity and its Complex of Buildings"[126] and is certainly incomplete as the notes and correspondence of

---

[126] Istanbul *vakıflar*, file a, *Taksim: Aya Triada ve müştemilatı binaları*, contract date 4/11/57, contractors Gürleyig and Tanla.

Table 35: The bidding process for church reconstruction (in TL)

I. 05/19/56	A	B	C	D	E	F
	St. Kyriake, Kumkapı	Euangelistria, Yenişehir	Panagia, Eğrikapı	Saints Taxiarchs, Balat	St. Paraskeue, Büyükdere	
Keşif bedeli (assessed value)	11,069.90	7,640.43	13,423.38	13,908.00	6,388.57	
Teminat (guarantee)	830.24	573.03	1,006.75	1,043.10	479.00	
Belge tutarı (liability)	10,000.00					

Awards:
A. St. Kyriake: Haluk Önen and Aristo Yoanidis, *eksiltme* (reduction) of 22.5%
B. Euangelistria: Mehmet Atalay, *eksiltme* of 1%
C & D. No bids

II. 04/26/57	A	B	C	D	E	F
	Metamorphosis, Şişli	St. Nicholas, Topkapı	Saints Taxiarchs, Balat	Panagia, Eğrikapı	St. Paraskeue, Büyükdere	
Keşif bedeli	17,946.53	15,351.89	8,862.33	13,181.65	6,388.57	
Teminat	1,346.00	1,151.40	664.70	988.60	479.00	

Awards:
A. Metamorphosis: Zafiri Canoğlu, *eksiltme* of 6.5%
B. St. Nicholas: Zafiri Canoğlu, *eksiltme* of 11%
C. Saints Taxiarchs: Mènas Konstantinidès, *eksiltme* of 2.5% rejected
D. Panagia: Giuseppe Lemma, *eksiltme* of 2.51%
E. Parasekeue: Mènas Konstantinidès, rejected

III. 06/27/57	A	B	C	D	E	F
	St. John, Yeni Mahalle	St. Demetrios, Kuruçeşme	Euangelistria, Yenişehir			
Keşif bedeli	11,917.93	19,213.52	13,664.09			
Teminat	893.85	1,442.36	1,024.81			

Awards:
A. St. John: Zafiri Canoğlu, *eksiltme* of 3%
B. St. Demetrios: Zafiri Canoğlu, *eksiltme* of 12%
C. Euangelistria: Mènas Konstantinidès, *eksiltme* of 12.5%

IV. 08/12/57

	St. Athanasios, Kurtuluş	Panagia, Göksuyü	Saints Taxiarchs, Arnavutköy	Prophet Elias, Arnavutköy	Panagia, Tekfur Sarayı
Keşif bedeli	70,939.95	24,354.21	18,752.47	17,496.54	15,331.66
Teminat	5,320.50	1,826.57	1,046.44	1,312.24	illegible
Belge tutarı	80,000.00	30,000.00	20,000.00	20,000.00	20,000.00

Awards:
A. St. Athanasios: Rebi Gürleyig and İbrahim Tanla, *eksiltme* of 1%
B. Panagia: Zafri Canoğlu, *eksiltme* of 1%
C. Saints Taxiarchs: Ménas Konstantinidès, *eksiltme* of 1%
D. Prophet Elias: Ménas Konstantinidès, *eksiltme* of 1%
E. Panagia-Zafri Canoğlu, *eksiltme* of 0.7%

V. 08/17/58

	Paraskeue, Hasköy	Panagia, Salmatobruk	Agia Vlacherna, Ayvansaray	St. George, Edirnekapı	Panagia, Vefa-Zeyrek
Keşif bedeli	43,510.42	39,758.15	39,350.70	39,241.91	17,716.96
Teminat	3,263.28	2,981.85	2,951.85	2,493.14	1,328.77
Belge tutarı	55,000.00	35,000.00	35,000.00	30,000.00	15,000.00

Awards:
A. Paraskeue: Mehmet Atalay, *eksiltme* of 3%
B. Panagia: Kemal Mutlu, *eksiltme* of 8%
C. Agia Vlacherna: no bid
D. St. George: Kemal Mutlu, *eksiltme* of 14%
E. Panagia: Hasan Kasapoğlu, *eksiltme* of 1%

VI. 10/5/59

	Panagia Elpis, Kumkapı	St. George, Samatya	Prophet Elias, Arnavutköy	St. Demetrios, Sarmaşık	Panagia, Eğrikapı	Agia Vlacherna, Ayvansaray
Keşif bedeli	83,982.51	11,487.56	14,615.81	10,908.15	5,945.50	5,137.00
Teminat	5,449.13	861.57	1,096.19	818.11	445.91	398.77
Belge tutarı	50,000.00	10,000.00	7,000.00	5,000.00	3,000.00	3,000.00

Awards:
A. Panagia: Mehmet Atalar, *eksiltme* of 5%
B. St. George: Mehmet Atalar, *eksiltme* of 7%
C. Prophet Elias: Xenofôn Leóntopoulos, *eksiltme* of 5%
D. St. Demetrios: Mehmet Atalar, *eksiltme* of 7%
E. Panagia: Muzzafer Gürcihan, *eksiltme* of 36%
F. Agia Vlacherna: Muzzafer Gürcihan, *eksiltme* illegible

VII. 3/31/60

	Zoodochos Pege, Balıklı	Panagia, Altı Mermer	Panagia, Belgratkapı	St. George, Edirnekapı	St. Phokas, Ortaköy	St. John, Yeni Mahalle
Keşif bedeli	307,943.70	344,484.58	276,876.86	28,407.03	17,626.75	21,995.28
Teminat	16,067.75	17,529.38	14,825.07	2,130.53	1,322.01	1,649.65
Belge tutarı	200,000.00	250,000.00	200,000.00	20,000.00	15,000.00	15,000.00

Awards:

A. Zoodochos Pege (Meryem Ana): Ali Nahat Birgen, *eksiltme* of 15.1%
B. Panagia: İzzi Büyükyusal, *eksiltme* of 23.99%
C. Panagia: İzzi Büyükyusal, *eksiltme* of 23.99%
D. St. George: Osman Ada, *eksiltme* of 16.9%
E. St. Phokas: Osman Ada, *eksiltme* of 16.8%
F. St. John: Osman Ada, *eksiltme* of 16.7%

VIII. 11/22/60

	St. Constantine, Samatya	St. Menas, Samatya	St. George, Samatya	St. George, Heybeliada
Keşif bedeli	595,028.23	358,745.33	249,050.29	12,192.85
Teminat	27,551.13	18,099.81	13,702.51	914.46
Belge tutarı	400,000.00	200,000.00	175,000.00	8,000.00

Awards:

A. St. Constantine: Muammer Bakır, *eksiltme* of 28.95%
B. St. Menas: Ali Topaloğlu, *eksiltme* of 27.3%
C. St. George Kyparissas: Muammer Bakır, *eksiltme* of 28.95%
D. St. George: Kemal Mutlu, *eksiltme* of 1%

Table 36: Undated list of offers (bids) before the actual awards

Bidders' names	Amount of bid (TL)	Addition for inflation (%)
1. Şişli Metamorphosis		
(keşif bedeli: 214,295.30)		
Stratês Iôsêfidês	273,227.44	27.5
Necmi Ateş	316,949.77	47.9
2. Fener Aya Yorgi (Potiras)		
(keşif bedeli: 62,783.35)		
Stratês Iôsêfidês	83,180.82	32.5
Kemal Mutlu	89,277.78	42.2
Mehmet Atalar	83,999.88	33.8
İbrahim Tanla	83,385.35	36.0
3. Balat Aya Yani (Tur Sina)		
(keşif bedeli: 52,413.10)		
Mehmet Atalar	71,819.74	37.0
İbrahim Tanlar	73,330.09	38.0
4. Balat Panagia (Balino)		
(keşif bedeli: 71,419.75)		
Mehmet Atalar	91,224.90	27.7
İbrahim Tanlar	92,191.47	29.0
5. Ayvansaray Aya Vlaherna		
(keşif bedeli: 49,265.41)		
Hasan Hasapoğlu	58,142.34	18.0
Mehmet Atalar	67,641.28	37.3
İbrahim Tanlar	68,478.92	39.0
6. Sarmaşık Aya Dimitri		
(keşif bedeli: 7,320.63)		
Giannês Frangineas	12,705.73	73.6
Kemal Mutlu	10,720.00	46.4
7. Arnavutköy Profiti Ilia		
(keşif bedeli: 9,164.46)		
Hasan Hasapoğlu	10,600.60	17.8
Mênas Kônstantinidês	15,650.00	70.8
Giannês Frangineas	12,970.72	41.5
Kemal Mutlu	12,558.00	37.0
8. Arnavutköy Taksiarhis		
(keşif bedeli: 1,549.77)		
Mênas Kônstantinidês	2,700.00	74.3
Giannês Frangineas	2,050.56	34.2[127]

[127] Data on the bidding in tables 36 and 37 come from the rich files of the Committee for Repair, whose bid committee (*eksiltme komisyonu*) organized and carried out the bidding process: XXIV, XXV, XIV, XX, XVI, IV, XVI, XVII, XXX. The bid committee usually recommended the

the *vakıflar* are missing, as is much of the material from the Committee for Repair. Some of the installment-payment documents are also missing, but their contents are preserved, all of them in later documentation. Fortunately, the *Technical Specifications, Registers of Measurements,* and *Lists of Valuations* are accessible, and the final payment can be found in the *Final Certification,* which is still in the file.

The *Technical Specifications* consist of six full pages. They list the materials to be used in repairing the church; the parts of the church to be repaired; the reference numbers of each material or item in the 1956 registry of prices of the ministry of public works; and a detailed but partial listing and numbering of goods and items needed for the job with the price of each. Although reference is made to eighty-four such items, only forty-six are actually listed in the *Specifications.* They are, however, all listed in the *Register of Measurements* and *List of Valuations.* The *Specifications* also refer to some items needed for repairing the church's other three buildings or quarters—the reception hall, the hall in which its governing board met and its archives were kept, and the priests' and deacons' quarters—with the related materials and costs also laid out fully in the other two documents. The *Installment Payments* and *Final Certification* further inform as to the contractors, date of contracts, periods during which work was executed, original estimate of costs, bids, allowances for inflation, etc.

The *Technical Specifications* include the identification numbers for sixty-three items called for in the repairs, with reference to the official 1956 price registry. Forty-six items are enumerated in detail.

Table 37: Holy Trinity, Taksim, *Technical Specifications*	TL
1. Removal of broken glass, cleaning of putty; labor per sq. meter	1.5
5. Marble, limestone molding of iron door, all to be replaced	4,000
6. Repair of marble covering of door	200
8. First floor, left side, repair marble grill of windows, polish	400
9. Left side, replace damaged limestone door posts	1,000
10. Replace marble balustrade and staircase posts, *gynaeconitis*	4,000

lowest bidder, and the Committee for Repair then proposed the choice to the Istanbul *vakıflar,* which made the final decision.

Since, in the matter of assessments and payments, the documents of the Committee for Repair and *vakıflar* almost never had protocol numbers, identification depends mostly on dates, files of specific churches, and names of contractors. Accordingly, references in this book have followed, where possible, church name, contractor name, contract dates, and sums. All *vakıflar* documents are identified either by Arabic numerals or small Latin letters (i.e., 55 or a); all files from the Committee for Repair are indicated by capital Roman numerals (IV, XXV, etc.).

11. Replace parts of wooden balustrade	each 50
12. Limestone decorative frames of windows in church, bell-tower	each 2,000
13. As in #12 above 1 window	100
14. Replace all polished wooden stalls in *gynaeconitis* [which had been burned]	each 80
15. Hardwood benches in *gynaeconitis* to be repaired	each 35
19. Repair of 2 white sandstone columns in *gynaeconitis*	each 400
20. Repair of 2 white sandstone capitals	each 400
21. Repair 6 "profile" columns in *gynaeconitis*	each 100
24. Repair bishop's throne (marble; described in great detail)	9,000
29. Repair 2 marble basins in altar	each 150
32. Stationary resinous pine case in altar	260
33. Repair 1 resinous pine case in altar	50
34. Repair 1 resinous pine door in altar	50
35. Repair 2 polished carved wooden doors	each 175
36. Decoration of these 2 doors with silverleaf, etc.	each 1,000
39. Make ornamented plaster/putty molding for icon of Saints Constantine and Helen	1,000
40. Repair putty moldings for 9 icons	each 75
41. Repair of column and capital in narthex	1,550
42. Make new column of white marble for narthex	2 each 3,700
43. Repair of huge marble door and its base in narthex	1,600
44. Repair of marble cover of main door of narthex	300
45. Repair of iron of window	50
46. Clean and polish 8 columns in narthex, 8 inside church	each 75
47. Remove and replace damaged rock in walls of *gynaeconitis* and bell-tower [obviously damaged from fire]	1,000
56. Replace hardwood, ornamentation of two windows to right and left of entrance from narthex to church	each 150
57. Make 6 marble crosses, 3 on church doors, 3 over street doors	each 50
58. Repair edges of outside walls	each 50
59. Make new crosses destroyed on iron doors, 3 on outside doors and one on inside door	each 50
62. Repair framework of metal wire on 3 windows	each 280
[the document indicates two prices]	each 240

64. Galvanized metal thread [the document indicates two prices]	each 80
	each 50
65. Repair iron railings of stairs to *gynaeconitis*	each 30
67. Make a new marble altar table	3,000
69. Repair iron door leading from sanctuary to garden	75
70. All of outside of church, bell-tower to be scraped cleaned	the price originally given is TL15,000, but is penned out and replaced by TL7
71. Rubble to be cleaned and taken away	500
72. Broken marble to be removed	each 2.50
73. All broken marble and white sandstone to be removed	300
82. Make a pulpit balustrade of hardwood	750
83. Make two wooden angel statues	800
84. Make two holy altar tables of marble	each 500

Thereafter, the *Technical Specifications* provide a number but not all the items needed for repairing the church's other three units. This document indicates the prices called for by the ministry of public works, and in so doing gives us an idea of what such labors and materials cost. In addition, there are indications for specific damaged items: windows, frames, doors, roofs, columns, a pulpit, lecterns, icon frames, frames for doors and windows, the structure of the *iconostasis*, altars, a *gynaeconitis*, pews and seats, marble crosses, altar tables, railings, plaster, glass cases, bishop's throne, etc. Following is an incomplete and temporary sampling of materials needed, taken from the *Metraj Cedveli* of *Register of Measurements*:

Table 38: Holy Trinity, Taksim, *Register of Measurements*

Glass	22.43 sq. meters
Marble	91.86 sq. meters
Marble	148.55 meters [?]
Cement	425 kilos
Hardwood	142.55 sq. meters
Iron/Steel	60 kilos/28 sq. meters
Parquet	9.66 sq. meters
Paint	1,182.73 sq. meters
Whitewash	1,274.55 sq. meters

Lead, remelted	273 kilos
new	424 kilos
Faience	3.6 sq. meters
Plywood	5.17 sq. meters
White sandstone	20.32 sq. meters
Scaffolding	36.62 sq. meters
Pinewood	41.24 sq. meters
Wooden borders	20.32 sq. meters

Obviously, this list from the *Register of Measurements* is not complete, primarily because many items are listed per unit only.

The *Register of Measurements* and *List of Valuations* for this particular church are far more detailed and thus outline all the materials needed, their cost, and the totality of the work. The two documents are signed by the three-man architectural committee (although there are four sets of initials, not three, in this particular case), were approved by the bureau, and passed on to the *vakıflar*. The approval is dated September 28, 1957, and the outside page of the *List of Valuations* summarizes the total cost estimate at TL128,268.30 for the church and TL10,717.30 for the other three units for a total of TL138,985.60.

There follow seven *Installment Payments* and the *Final Certification*, which record the finances and payments over a period of time to the contractor. Of the *Installment Payments*, the file has the fifth report dated November 1, 1958, and its salient details are of some relevance. The contractors are named as Rebi Gürleyig and İbrahim Tanla and the essence of the contract and progress of the work is summarized as follows:

Table 39: Installment Payment

Report No. 5

1st cost estimate: TL138,985.60

Date of contract: 11/4/1957

Reduction (bid): 10.1% (TL14,037.55)

Period of work: 180 days

Cost of contract: TL124,948.05

Day to be finished: 5/2/58

Estimated increase: NA

Extension of time: 91 days

Percentage of increase: NA
New day to finish: 6/2/58
Increase of contract cost: NA
Guaranteed period: 6 months

The architects approved the work described in this fifth report and calculated a fifth payment of TL18,451.38. In the fourth report and installment, the contractors had been paid a total of TL94,885.01, which was most of the original cost of the contract. Inflation, however, had forced the architectural committee and the *vakıflar* to reevaluate the entire contract on December 30, 1958. By that time, inflation had gone up 26.33 percent and so the original basis of the contract (TL124,948.05) was increased by TL36,595.98.

The *Final Certification* for the completed work was drawn up on December 29, 1959. Although the date the original contract was put into effect was November 4, 1957, and the contract called for finishing the work in 180 days, it had taken the contractors almost thirty-two months to do so. The extension of the dates of completion had also brought the *ilave* into the accounting. The work was formally approved by the architectural committee (five signatures) and chief of the project, and stamped, as having been examined, and dated January 14, 1960. The bureau in the *vakıflar* stamped it as approved on January 15[?], 1960. By this time, the *Final Certification* included a special page listing the dates and amounts of each payment (in Turkish lira):

Table 40: Payments report from *Final Certification*

The reports	& Total	Deductions (fines)	Amount paid out
I. 4/5/58	18,492.21		16,624.50
II. 5/26/58	44,524.91		23,403.39
III. 7/25/58	79,264.70		31,231.08
IV. 9/25/58	105,545.06	4,500.00	19,126.04
V. 11/1/58	129,486.42	3,000.00	18,451.36
VI. 1/5/59	162,005.19		29,306.30
VII. 5/14/59	175,581.58		12,205.17
TOTALS		7,500.00	150,347.84
			+ 7,500.00
Subtotal	**175,581.58**		**157,847.84**

	less *eksiltme* (10.1%) - 17,733.74	
Total	157,847.84	157,847.84

The fines indicated above were occasioned by the failure at certain stages to perform as warranted, but the warrants were made good and the fines were deducted from the amount paid to the contractors. On such occasions, the architectural committee would issue a *Kusur Listesi*, that is, a list of deficiencies occasioned by the failure to finish contracted work. Such was issued to the *vakıflar* on July 11 (the year is not clear) for seventeen items and stamped by the bureau as *Onandı*.[128] The community itself applied to do a small part of the repairs, submitted the papers, finished the work, and presented a bill for TL6,077.75. It undoubtedly received a reduced payment.

There is some merit in examining the details of the damages and repairs of the Church of the Taxiarchs at Balat. This church did not undergo the enormous vandalism of other churches and so the documentation of repairs is less extensive and much more easily manageable as far as its essential details are concerned. We shall have to deal with the larger churches and their more extensive damages in the form of a general table. In order to understand the general applications, valuations, financial reductions, and payments, it is necessary to consider two basic contracts. In this specific case, these processes, labor, and payments went on during the better part of 1957, 1958, and 1959.

The first contract was awarded to Giuseppe Lemma on May 6, 1957, and the work contracted was finished on September 17 of the same year. According to the original contract, the work should have been finished on June 19, but as this period did not suffice, the contractor asked for and received an extension of three months (until September 19). The original assessment of the work to be done was TL8,862.33, but the reduction of value that accompanied the award of the contract, which amounted to 2.56 percent, lowered it to TL8,640.77. Because of the time that had passed between initial agreement and payment, Lemma was given a supplement, probably because of inflation, that raised the contract's value to TL10,149.28.

The work of the contractor, the materials, and prices are set out in the *Technical Specifications* and the two accompanying documents. The list of materials accompanying the first contract stipulate thirty-one items in the church and thirteen in its adjacent multipurpose building. This first contract

<hr>

[128] *Ibid.*

aims basically at repairing or replacing all structural and building elements of the church itself, and, although some religious items are included here, this category of damages (that is, religious objects) is reserved for the second contract and contractor. Thus, the recipient of the first contract is to repair or replace 20 categories of items.

Table 41: Materials list, 2nd *List of Valuations, Final Certification*

Types of objects	Item #	Size (m²)	Unit price (TL)	Cost (TL)
1. Windows	2	17.69	65.54	1,159.40
	3	1.63	21.31	34.73
	7	17.81	16.38	291.73
	8	71.53	6.96	497.85
	9	12.57	5.95	74.79
	19	1.54	68.59	105.63
	21	1 piece	25.00	25.00
	25	4.26	19.65	83.71
	26	1.79	12.07	21.60
2. Doors	4	100.00		
	5	15.14	12.72	192.58
	9	22.76	6.43	146.35
	10	21.19	4.47	94.72
	16	6.78	10.09	68.41
	22	1 piece	20.00	20.00
3. Stairs	23	1 piece	20.00	20.00
	29	6.00	63.33	379.98
	31	5 pieces	5.00	25.00
4. Floors	27	4.48	1.02	4.57
	28	4.48	21.31	95.47
5. Walls	9	24.07	5.90	142.01
	24	6.31	10.00	63.10
6. Balustrades	30	4.00	30.03	156.12
	32	4.00	25.00	100.00
7. Roof	9	84.66	5.66	479.17
8. Latticework	13	1 piece	750.00	750.00
9. Episcopal throne	12	1 piece	800.00	800.00
10. Pulpit	11	1 piece	200.00	200.00

	18	1 piece	300.00	300.00
11. Gospel lectern	15	1 piece	300.00	300.00
12. Cross	17	1 piece	10.00	10.00
13. Gorgona	20	1 piece	120.00	120.00
Total				7,748.00

There were, however, another TL2,401.70 added to the bill because of inflation, which brought it to a total of TL10,401.70. The *Final Certification* sets out the course of financing until final payment was made:

Table 42: Payment

1st cost estimate: TL8,862.33

Date of contract: 5/6/1957

Reduction: 2.5% (TL221.56)

Day to be finished: 6/19/1957

Cost of contract: TL8,640.37

New day to finish: 9/19/1957

Inflation award: TL1,286.95

Date finished: NA

2nd cost estimate: TL10,149.28

Final amount finally paid to Lemma: TL9,895.55

The second contract is, for the most part, about an entirely different category of repair; it deals, almost completely, with religious objects as opposed to building structure. The contractor is also a different individual, Mênas Kônstantinidês.

Although the itemized *Register of Measurements* and *List of Valuations* are much shorter (only sixteen to seventeen items), the cost of this work is double that of the structural repairs. There are two sets of *Technical Specifications, Registers of Measurements,* and *Lists of Valuations,* and there is a short letter to the *vakıflar* communicating the successful bid and asking for approval of the contract. There follow an *Installment Payments, Approval of Work Finished,* and *Final Certification* with attached table of payments. The two *Technical Specifications* are virtually the same save for the addition of a sixteenth item (incorrectly numbered 17 in the second) and a substantial increase in the *ilave*. The *Nafia* registry applied to the first specifications document was for 1956, whereas the second was the 1959 list. Thus, a total inflationary rate of three years and TL1,792.23 were added to costs, not only in the second series of specifications, but also in the second *List of Valuations* and other documents.

It is useful to examine these as they are relatively short and yet at the same time highly representative of what religious items and objects were covered and payable by the *vakıflar*. Simultaneously, they are indicative of a large number of items and objects that either were not damaged or were not replaced or repaired. From the documentation of all the churches that were completely destroyed, there is a large list of this latter category, which the *vakıflar* simply decided to exclude from compensation. We must therefore conclude with certainty that the following list of religious objects is highly "exclusive" in this respect—that is to say, a large number of damaged, destroyed, or stolen religious objects were excluded from consideration for compensation. For as we saw, the second contract is far more valuable, and costly, than the first. The fifteen or sixteen entries of the *Technical Specifications* (fifteen in the first and sixteen in the second) are identified in exactly the same manner, word for word, in both documents, and both are signed by the architectural committee.

The first set of documents is stamped March 13, 1958, by the *vakıflar*. The final date of approval of the second set is May 30, 1959.

Table 43: Materials list

	Cost (TL)	
Items	*3/13/58*	*5/30/59*
Repair and reconstruction of the templon (*iconostasis*)	2,000	3,000
New hardwood leaves (doors) for the *prothesis*	60	100
Repair and reconstruction of the two entry-doors to sanctuary	600	1,000
Repair and reconstruction of the main (hardwood) door of sanctuary	800	1,200
Repair and reconstruction of icon frame, left side, near sanctuary	400	600
New icon frame for left side of church	600	800
New hardwood cabinet with glass pane to house icon of the Resurrection	250	400
Repair and reconstruction of holy icon frame of Three Hierarchs	600	800
Repair and reconstruction of holy icon frame of St. George	700	1,000
Repair of the *Epitaphios*	350	500
Book stand in the lecterns	300 each	400 each (2)

Repair pews	35 each	50 each (51)
Make new pews	80 each	125 each (53)
Repair wood-and-glass cabinet for the candles	100	125
Iron doors in *gynaeconitis*	75 each	125 each (2)
Repair and reconstruction of door on right side of *templon* (*dimothira*)		100

A preparatory document to the final settlement had added items numbered 18 (26 pews) for TL6,500; 19 (an additional icon frame for TL450); and 20 (painting of an iron object for TL71.06), thus bringing the assessment for the work (after the omission of Item 14 above) to a total of TL20,464.89.

The repairs to the *templon* (*iconostasis*) is of interest in regard to the issue of compensation that was allowed, or disallowed, by the *vakıflar*. Items numbered 5, 6, 8, and 9 refer to "mukaddes tasvir çerçevesi," that is, to the "frame of the sacred icon [picture]." And, indeed, this phrase occurs repeatedly in the *Technical Specifications*, *Registers of Measurements*, and *Lists of Valuations*. But, with two very slight exceptions for retouching slightly damaged icons, there is no mention whatever of the repair or replacement of destroyed, damaged, or stolen icons in the totality of the documentation for the seventy-four vandalized churches that have been examined for this study. It is obvious that the *vakıflar* did not allow such compensation, repair, or replacement in its customary lists of damages. We shall see interesting examples that demonstrate this point for all the icons in the *iconostasis*, *proskenetaria*, and indeed throughout an Orthodox church. Thus, the documentation concerning repairs and replacement of icons is silent, whereas the photographic evidence gives eloquent testimony to the defacing, smashing, or hacking into pieces of numerous icons. And in churches where everything was destroyed and burned, the *vakıflar* documents make little mention whatever of the icons themselves. Accordingly, the exclusion of this one item alone is an indication of the mass exclusion not only of icons, but of many other cult objects and items, especially as most of these churches were literally drowning in sacred images, as is shown by a brief survey of photographs of their destruction.

In this light, the brief description of the restoration of and replacements in the front side of the *templon* (Item 1 of the *Technical Specifications*) should be examined closely. The Turkish word used to denote icon (as in the icons of the two unnamed saints in Items 5 and 6, as well as of the Three Hierarchs and St. George in Items 8 and 9) is *tasvir*, which means picture or design. The full phrase, *mukaddes tasviri*, in this context signifies a sacred picture, in reality, an icon. An icon is for the most part, in this circumstance, a two-dimensional painting usually, but not always, on wood. *Mukaddes tasviri* thus describes an icon. The word, *çerçeve*, refers to the wooden frame placed around the icon. In these four mentions of icons, it is only the icon frames that are being replaced or repaired. There is no repair or replacement of a single icon *itself.*

Returning to the contents of Item 1 in the *Technical Specifications* on "The repair and completion of destroyed parts therein," the word *tasvir* is used again, this time in conjunction with depictions of the True Vineyard (*Alethine Ampelos*), the angels, rooster, and crucifixion, and, more generally, of various religious motifs. Does it then refer to two-dimensional icons? In fact, the word *tasvir* has a more generic meaning as well, and is used here to refer to small, three-dimensional statues or objects carved out of wood and painted.

The very opening sentence of the descriptive paragraph of the *Technical Specifications* speaks of "the repair and reconstruction of damages to the carved wooden art on the front side of the twelve-by-six-meter *templon.*" These then are not painted, two-dimensional icons from the front side of the *templon.* They are wooden carvings or small sculptures of the *Alethine Ampelos*, the rooster, the angels, and the crucifix, as well as other subjects. But what were these objects? One reference to the *iconostasis* of the Church of St. Euphemia in Kadıköy answers the question. In this church, one sees that the top of the *iconostasis* is decorated with small, wooden, painted statues or representations of all the above objects. The *Alethine Ampelos* is represented by a small grapevine with three grape clusters and four leaves attached to a shortened but thick trunk. The rooster is also there, facing the crucifix atop the *templon*, crowing in his full feathery glory, signifying Peter's denial of Christ, and to be seen just to the left of the *Oraia Pyle* (central door of entry into and out of the sanctuary). All are atop the *templon.* In addition, a number of other smaller symbols, sculpted in the round and of wood, are also visible: the sacred chalice and spoon, cross, and serpent. So what has been replaced are these small objects sculpted in wood with their obvious references to the Gospels and the mysteries of the faith. It is clear, however, that Item 1 does not refer to icons at all.

The *Final Certification* for the completed work in the second contract was prepared on November 16, 1959, signed by the architects, confirmed on November 9, 1959, by the bureau (*vakıflar*), and then finally approved (*Onandı*) by the *vakıflar* directorate on December 31, 1959. The amount paid to Kônstantinidês amounted to TL19,134.67 after subtracting the reduction (bid) of TL1,330.22.[129]

---

[129] Istanbul *vakıflar*, file 5, *Haliç-Balat: Taksiarhis kilisesinin sabit müteferrik işler onarımı*, listed in the *Technical Specifications*, contract date 6/5/57, contractor Lemma; Istanbul *vakıflar*, file 55, contractor Kônstantinidês.

Having now examined the general process, the institutions involved, and some details as to how compensation and repair proceeded, it is time to evaluate the general import of the repair and compensation files that are partially available. The most practical approach is to take the cases of four large churches that suffered massive destruction. For this purpose, the churches of Saints Theodoroi of Langa, Saints Constantine and Helen of Samatya, Panagia Altı Mermer, and Panagia of Belgratkapı have been selected. Their destruction has already been touched upon, and one may consult earlier chapters for the narrative detail and relevant sources. After the rebuilding and repair of the four churches have been identified and analyzed, a summary of the salient details will be presented in two comparative tables: one that deals with the history of structural damages and rebuilding, and a second that summarizes the destruction and reconstruction of items and objects of Christian worship.

For the Church of Saints Theodoroi, the data of two fundamental contracts are accessible, at least in their essentials, and there is also a third and much smaller contract that is of peripheral interest only. The first of the two contracts was awarded to Stratês Iôsêfidês for carrying out the fundamental rebuilding and repairing of the church structure. The eighth *Installment Payment* provides the following information:

Table 44: Payment

Report No. 8

1st cost estimate: TL601,612.90

Date of contract: 12/14/1959

Reduction (bid): 23% (TL138,370.97)

(New) Period of work: 9 months

Cost of contract: TL463,241.93

(New) Day to be finished: 4/12/61

Extension of time: 4 months + 3 months

Since we do not have the *Final Certification*, we cannot ascertain the exact amount that the *vakıflar* paid out to the contractor but it may have been the final contract cost of TL463,241.93. However, there are certain irregularities that cannot be explained because of the incomplete nature of the documentation. That it may have been less might be extrapolated from the fact that this particular document gives a "value of work finished" on April 4, 1961—when this document was formulated—that is lower than the "first cost estimate." The new calculation of the amount owed the contractor was as follows:

Table 45: Payment

Value of work finished: 561,092.97
23% reduction: -129,051.38
Net value of work finished: 432,041.59
Amount paid until February 17,1961: 358,646.24
Amount remaining: 73,395.35

Thus according to this eighth installment report, TL432,041.59 is likely to be closer to the amount paid for overall repairs to the structure of the church, but it may be a little less.

A quick glance at the itemized expenditures of this considerable sum, approaching a half million liras, shows decisively that the contractor undertook to dig foundations, grade the land, and remove most of the damaged stone, cement, and plaster. When this was cleared away and the land leveled, he began the substantial labor of rebuilding. Out of a total of 134 itemized expenditures, twenty-one account for almost three-fourths of the expenses:

Table 46: Materials list, 7th *Installment Payment*

Item	Amount	Price/unit (TL)	Total price (TL)
13. 200 dz. cement	63.335 m³	102.71	6,493.84
14. 250 dz. cement	13.642 m³	112.08	1,528.99
15. 300 dz. cement	334.666 m³	125.34	41,947.04
16. B. A. casting mold	1,901.31 m²	15.50	29,470.30
18. Scaffolding	1,166.24 m²	1.55	1,807.67
19. Brick wall	59.63 m³	131.69	7,852.67
21. Interior plaster	1,635.72 m²	5.85	9,568.96
23. Ceiling plaster	933.21 m²	5.59	5,216.64
27. Mosaic flooring	303.54 m²	24.41	7,385.00
29. Marble flooring	485.00 m²	160.87	78,021.95
32. Plaster on arched surfaces	450.23 m²	14.02	6,312.22
33. Wooden seat covers	817.20 m²	43.30	35,384.76
34. Marseilles roof tiles	872.02 m²	14.25	12,426.28
38. Copper pipes	88.95 [*sic*]	70.81	6,298.55
44. Wooden flooring	204.68 m²	40.25	8,238.37
46. Interior glass doors	25.17 m²	92.87	2,337.54
60. Iron doors, shutters	5,866.50 kgs	6.77	39,716.20

66. B. A. of iron	16,416.756 kgs	2.93	48,101.09
67. B. A. of iron	9,609.501 kgs	3.06	29,405.07
50. Telarolu [*sic*] windows	125.46 m²	62.81	7,880.14
72. Stone wall	96.434 m³	48.07	4,635.58
Total			**390,028.86**

Thus, these twenty-one more expensive items in the first contract account for roughly 84 percent of the reduced payments of TL463,241.99. And this is all for the basic task of rebuilding the structure and the accompanying smaller building. This church building suffered massive damage, far worse than that of the Holy Trinity in Taksim.[130]

The second contract, unlike the first, preserves for us, in its larger file, a *Technical Specifications*, a *Register of Measurements*, and a *List of Valuations* that contains twenty-one items. Virtually all of these are liturgical:

Table 47: *List of Valuations, Approval of Work Finished* *(TL)*

1. A new *templon*	51,856.00
2. Pulpit	6,000.00
3. Episcopal throne	6,000.00
4. Lectern (*analogion*) 2 pieces	3,000.00
5. *Parathronion* (3 pieces)	2,400.00
6. *Pankari*	3,500.00
7. *Gorgona*	4,000.00
8. *Proskenetarion*	2,200.00
9. *Epitaphios*	6,500.00
10. *Exapteriga* closet	700.00
11. Closet for vestments	700.00
12. *Diskeli*	750.00
13. Glass-encased *epitaphios*	500.00
14. Wooden pews (54)	6,750.00
15. Funeral bier	750.00
16. Pews (46)	17,250.00
19. Icon frames (3 pieces)	4,500.00
20. *Anastasis* table	3,000.00
21. Wood flooring under pews	692.54
Total	**121,048.64**

[130] Istanbul *vakıflar*, file f, *Langa [Vlanga]: Aya Todori Kilisesi*, contract date c. 12/10/62,

The contract had been awarded to Mardiros Mançılıklıoğlu on October 8, 1965, for TL124,146.23 after a 5-percent reduction (bid). The exact amount paid to him at completion is missing, but must have been a little lower than the TL121,048.64 mentioned in the table above.

There is a third and much smaller contract, as evidenced by a *Register of Measurements* and *List of Valuations*, for whitewashing the building, which was assessed at TL2,101.32. But there are no details as to the actual amount paid. The two documents are dated October 5, 1962, and so were presented after the first contractor, Iôsêfidês, had finished his work on the church structure.[131]

In a short letter from the *vakıflar* (dated April 20, 1961, and numbered, by hand, 1638) to the Committee for Repair, the director of the bureau reported that, in its original application, the committee had applied for reimbursement of a total of TL774,407.33 for work materials. If one adds the original valuation of the three contracts discussed above, one comes to the following sum:

1st contract valuation	601,612.09
2nd contract valuation	130,684.24
3rd contract estimate	2,101.32
	734,397.65

This is a difference of only 10,009.68, and is accountable by the fact that the available documents in this file are incomplete. But, in round numbers, the letter corresponds to the papers in the files for the total assessments of the applications coming from the community of Saints Theodoroi; indeed, there is a difference of only 1.25 percent. Perhaps the total payments amounted to about TL551,000 (a careful estimate based on all the above), and therefore about 75 percent of the original valuations of the first contract, but, as payments lagged and inflation rose, the real value must have been less.

However, the second point of interest in this second letter seems to be the fact that the Committee for Repair had presented a second application to the *vakıflar* for an additional TL200,904.72, to which the bureau replied that this would be sent to the *vakıflar* directorate, with the detailed seven-page valuations, to see whether or not it would be included within the original application for TL774,407.33 worth of repairs. As it seems that the *vakıflar* was seeking to disqualify the second application, we must assume that the original application of the community of Saints Theodoroi was in effect larger than originally stated by the relevant file, and consisted of two applications:

contractor Iôsêfidês.
[131] *Ibid.* The penned-in protocol number of the letter is 1638, contract date c. 5/10/62, contractor Mançılıklıoğlu.

one for TL774,407.33 and one for TL200,904.72, for a total of TL975,312.05. Thus, the cuts in the applications loom even larger.[132]

Having analyzed the rebuilding costs of, and by implication the damages to, the Church of Saints Theodoroi in some detail, we see that the same general procedures, records, and figures emerge from the files of the churches of Saints Constantine and Helen of Samatya, Panagia Altı Mermer, and Panagia Belgratkapı. We shall content ourselves with the bare data as to the essential dates, statutes of limitations, reductions, and final payments for each community, for all the details, and even many of the figures, are often similar to those of Saints Theodoroi. In any case, the detailed data of the four churches will be summarized in the table that follows immediately after these few remarks concerning the other three churches.

The contract to rebuild the structure of Saints Constantine and Helen was awarded to Muammer Bakır on December 15, 1960, and the *Final Certification* was dated July 7, 1965, a period of four and a half years. The church had suffered violent destruction and thus the second contract—to restore it completely and refurnish it with many, if not all, of its liturgical effects and objects—was awarded on April 4, 1964, by which time most of the physical structure had been rebuilt and rehabilitated. The Kaloumenos photographs depict scenes of ruin that recall images of destruction from aerial bombardment. Indeed, Despoina Portokallis had made precisely that comparison on viewing these churches. Nothing survived of the church's interior, as the roof had disappeared and many of the walls had to be partially restored. Accordingly, it took a long time for the contractor to accomplish his task. Inasmuch as the detailed data will appear, for the most part, in the table that follows, the present examination will be limited to a brief survey of some of the vital statistics offered by the files.

Table 48: Payment

1st cost estimate: TL595,028.23

Date of contract: 12/15/1960

Reduction (bid): 28.95% (TL14,037.55)

Day to be finished: 10/14/1961

Cost of contract: TL422,767.56

New day to finish: 9/26/1962

2nd cost estimate: TL594,100.13

Actual completion date: 7/26/1962

[132] Istanbul *vakıflar*, file f, *Langa [Vlanga]: Aya Todori Kilisesi*, contract date c. 5/10/62, no contractor indicated.

The *Final Certification* was drawn up on July 25, 1965, and the total paid to the contractor was TL423,108.14

The second contract, awarded to Kônstantinos Sporidês, was intended to provide the church with some necessary religious furnishings and was finally paid out by the *vakıflar* at or after December 14, 1964:

Table 49: Payment

1st cost estimate: TL133,974.00

Date of contract: 10/18/1963

Reduction (bid): 1% (TL1,339.74)

Day to be finished: 4/17/1964

Cost of contract: TL132,634.26

Actual completion date: 4/17/1964

Guarantee period: 3 months

2nd cost estimate: TL119,804.00

The amount paid out to Sporidês, after completion of work, was TL118,605.96. It is obvious that some items were not allowed in the application for the second contract and so certain religious furnishings were not figured in.[133] One should also keep in mind that the *vakıflar* had probably already disallowed a substantial amount when the application was first submitted, as was the case in the early applications for the Church of Saints Theodoroi.

The two contracts that the Committee for Repair proposed to and were approved by the *vakıflar* for the Church of Panagia Altı Mermer (Ex Marmarôn) follow the basic lines of the other churches. The first contract was awarded on September 7, 1960, to Ali Birgen for structural work on the building. Its broad description was as follows:

Table 50: Payment, *Final Certification*

1st cost estimate: TL344,484.50

Date of contract: 9/7/1960

Reduction (bid): 23.29% (TL82,641.85)

Day to be finished: 5/6/1961

Cost of contract: TL261,842.73

Extension: 12/6/1961

2nd cost estimate: TL343,726.72

---

[133] Istanbul *vakıflar*, file 49, *Samatya: Aya Konstantin kilisesi*, contract date 12/15/60, contractor Bakır; same file 49, contract date 10/18/63, contractor Sporidês.

Actual completion date: 6/21/1963

Amount finally paid to contractor: TL261,266.68

The second contract, given to Giannês Frangineas on November 13, 1963, was again intended to provide new liturgical items and objects, but was temporarily interrupted by circumstances that issued directly from the Greek-Turkish crisis.

Table 51: Installment Payment

1st cost estimate: TL117,802.93

Date of contract: 11/13/1963

Reduction (bid): 1.5% (TL1,764.04)

Day to be finished: 5/12/1964

Cost of contract: TL116,035.89

Period of work: 6 months

Frangineas finished items numbered 1, 3, 6, 8, 14, and 16 (see table below) and submitted his claims for them to the *vakıflar* through the architects' committee and their Greek superiors:

	TL76,700.00
Subject to a 1.5-percent reduction:	- 1,151.00
	75,549.00
Paid for earlier work:	-34,175.50
	41,370.00 (*sic*)
Withheld for 10-percent guarantee:	- 4,137.00
Amount left to be paid:	TL37,233.00 (*sic*)

Soon after April 4, 1964, the date the invoice above was drawn up, the police and the tax office issued a formal declaration that forbade him to work any further and ordered him to settle his debts. The reason given was that Frangineas was a Greek citizen and that, following the Greek-Turkish crisis over the pogrom, the Turkish government had decided to take these measures against this Greek national. The contract was then transferred to Mardiros Mançılıklıoğlu, who was obviously of Armenian origin and undertook the contract on September 19, 1964, with a first assessment of TL23,680.43, a reduction of 1.5 percent, and a final sum of TL23,325.72, to be paid three months later on December 9, 1964, for remaining work. There were also two very small contracts for electrical work, estimated at TL8,124.20 (the sum paid out is not in the available documents), and for whitewashing the building, paid out at TL1,645.48.[134]

Kaloumenos's photographs once more present us with a site of complete desolation, piles of burned rubble and fallen stones, scarred and damaged walls, an image of utter destruction so thorough that the church is even devoid of any semblance of a roof. The piles of rubble within the church walls are penetrated by long beams placed after the destruction to keep the walls from falling in. There is twisted iron everywhere, and all the former contents of this large church have been reduced to broken bits indistinguishable from the entire bed of rubble. No altars or wall partitions remain. In a second set of photographs, Kaloumenos presents the spectacle of the bare, fire-eaten walls, uncovered by a roof, and the naked floor—a massive skeleton of what once was, like some part of a city abandoned after centuries of habitation. The massive costs of cement, plaster, marble, iron, and stone that are catalogued in the *vakıflar* files are mutely implied by these photographs, which directly document the complete devastation of everything inside the church. The beautiful *iconostasis*, with its gilded woodwork and elaborate half-doors, the major icons and countless smaller ones, the silver patens and trays, the colorful and sumptuous vestments and brocades, the massive chandeliers and candelabra, the mosaic floors, all vanished, destroyed in one brief night.

The fourth and last of this group of four churches is Panagia Belgratkapı (Panagia Veligradiou), near the Byzantine land walls and Belgrade Gate (so named after the Serbian settlers that were brought there by the Ottomans). The Committee for Repair and the *vakıflar* awarded the first contract to Ali Birgen on September 7, 1961. It is noteworthy that work on the church did not begin until exactly six years after its destruction on the night of September 6-7, 1955 (although a very small, insignificant effort was made in late 1958 but without any substantial effect). Much of the documentation is absent from the file that was accessible, but one can reconstruct the salient details from the fourth and last *Installment Payments* documents, one of which is dated April 12, 1962. The fourth installment included a list of 108 items for work on the church's structure, an additional forty-six items for rebuilding its additional building, and twelve items for electrical installations. It lists the following costs for the work on all three:

Work on church structure	TL213,218.03
Work on second building	11,945.47

---

[134] Istanbul *vakıflar*, file 36b, *Altı Mermer Kilisesi*, contract date 9/7/60, contractor Birgen; same file 36b, contract and renewal 11/13/63 and 9/10/64, contractors *ad seriatem* Frangineas and Mançılıklıoğlu; in the same file 36b, contracts appear for electrical work, etc., on 3/15/57 and 4/16/60, but without contractors' names.

Electrical installations ___9,901.00___
Total TL235,064.50

The conditions of the contract were as follows:

Table 52: Installment Payment

1st cost estimate: TL276,876.76

Date of contract: 9/7/1961

Reduction: 23.29%

Day to be finished: 4/6/1962

Cost of contract: TL210.454.03

Period of work: 7 months

New day to finish: 7/26/1962

Extension: 3 months

The amount to be paid out was, perhaps (it is not clear), approximately TL235,064.00.

The next contract went to the local community's governing board for repairs of the small adjacent building. The community's estimate was TL6,414.39, but the head of the *vakıflar*'s bureau (a certain Aşkan) cut it by 5.5 percent (TL356.23) to TL6,058.16. This seemingly insignificant detail reveals that the bureau head could—and so always did—impose the reduction of the original estimate proposed by the mixed committee of architects. Of further interest is that this short and simple application for a very small expenditure was presented to the *vakıflar* on or about April 12, 1958, but that the three-line reply was not given until October 28, 1958, six and a half months later.

The third contract went to Ömer Aydın Koksal for that part of the repairs that involved new furnishings for the church's liturgical life. It was approved by the *vakıflar* on October 8, 1965, with a 5-percent reduction. The first assessment of TL94,723 was thus lowered to TL86,949.70. The *Technical Specifications*, *Register of Measurements*, and *List of Valuations* closely followed the set menu of twenty to twenty-four standard items, always of hardwood. It is interesting to see that Items 17 and 18 from this menu were disallowed by the *vakıflar*, not only for the repairs of Panagia Belgratkapı but also for the three other churches. The actual payment of TL86,949.70 thus represented 92 percent of the original estimate. The one difference in expenditure in these standard items had to do with the first one, making a new *templon*. In this case, the final cost was set at TL36,491, which was considerably less than the costs of the *templa* of the other three churches. The variation in costs of this one set price (for the *templa*) was in part due to the varying sizes of the four churches. Finally, there was a very small contract for whitewashing the church building, originally estimated at TL1,172.13, but no indication was found in the file on the actual amount paid.

The sums of money expended on Panagia Belgratkapı were considerably less than those spent on the churches of Saints Theodoroi and Saints Constantine and Helen. The repairs of Panagia Belgratkapı represented less than half the expenses paid out on either of the other two churches and were more in the range of expenditures for Panagia Altı Mermer, with the funds spent on Panagia Belgratkapı being equal to 81.6 percent of the funds for repairing Panagia Altı Mermer. This was undoubtedly due to the smaller size of the church although the destruction was no less thorough.[135]

The next step in examining the archival documentation is to compare the costs and materials of rebuilding the four churches. Again, as previously indicated, the arrangements for the work and payment centered on two types of contracts: building infrastructure and religious effects essential to Christian cult practice. In the case of the first type, the following table represents twenty-one items of the much larger catalogue of materials and work that always included more than 100 items. The effort was made to restrict this list of twenty-one items to costs of about TL2,000 or more. In so doing, it became clear that these items represented the great majority of expenditures for work on the four churches. It seemed pointless for the purposes of this study to proceed to an analysis of the eighty or more remaining items since they were quantitatively marginal and without purpose to this analysis, in which estimates of church damage is only one important subject among many others. The percentage of total expenditures on these four churches' structures that these twenty-one items represent are: Saints Theodoroi, 90.28 percent; Saints Constantine and Helen, 87.21 percent; Panagia Altı Mermer, 74.17 percent; and Panagia Belgratkapı, 64.48 percent.

Although the seventy-four examined files (see Appendix H) documenting the procedures for reconstruction, repair, and payment represent three-fourths of the religious institutions that suffered damage, they are, for the most part, incomplete. Nevertheless, a brief table of essential contents is necessary and will identify, to the degree possible, churches, estimates, contractors, imposed reductions/bids, date of beginning of work, payments, and date of the work's completion. The more detailed analyses of these and many other items in the contracts/rebuilding of a number of heavily damaged churches inform us

---

[135] Istanbul *vakıflar*, file b, *Belgratkapı Panagia kilisesi*, contract date 9/7/61; same file b, contract date 4/14/58, contractor Mütevelli Heyet of Agia Triada; same file b, contract date 10/8/65, contractor Koksal.

about the many particulars so that there is no need to repeat them for each subsequent church individually. The simplified table of all these churches and institutions that appear in the available archival materials not only gives us a somewhat broader picture of the rebuilding and damages, but also helps us to understand better the economics and politics of compensation on the part of both the Turkish government and the Istanbul Greek community. In this respect, it serves to supplement the prior examination of the official Turkish policy of partial—indeed, fragmentary—compensation for the damages to Greek businesses, dwellings, and schools (which latter case has only been mentioned perfunctorily).

In the 196 extant contracts examined, the beginning and termination dates do not appear in all. The chronological spread of the dates on which contracts were finally completed, where recorded, are present in ninety-two, with the number of contracts executed annually over eleven years as follows:

Table 53: Chronology of completed contracts

1956	4
1957	36
1958	13
1959	6
1960	20
1961	2
1962	3
1963	1
1964	4
1965	2
1966	1
Total	92

During the first three years of efforts to repair the churches through government funds (as opposed to the communities' expenditures from their own resources), finished contracts constituted 57.6 percent of the ninety-two dated and/or finished ones. The accessible files, fundamentally incomplete in regard to final payments to contractors, indicate payments in 108 contracts for a total of TL3,430,185.48. There are, however, preserved in the available archives an additional seventy-one contracts whose assessments have survived, although there is no indication of final payments or many reduction percentages. These seventy-one assessments amount to about TL1,054,035.82.

Table 54: Materials to repair damages to four churches

Item	Saints Theodoroi Langa		Saints Constantine and Helen Samatya		Panagia Altı Mermer		Panagia Belgratkapı	
	Quantity	Value (TL)	Quantity	Value (TL)	Quantity	Value (TL)	Quantity	Value (TL)
200 dz. cement	63.255 m³	6,493.84	86.30 m³	8,863.87	43.496 m³	4,464.47	28.618 m³	2,939.35
250 dz. cement	13.642 m³	1,528.99						
300 dz. cement	334.666 m³	41,947.04	339.726 m³	42,581.26	125.00 m³	16,168.75	113.38 m³	14,277.65
B. A. kalibi	1,901.31 m³	29,470.30	1,890.63 m³	29,304.76	600.00 m³	9,300.00	767.96 m²	11,903.38
Scaffolding	1,166.24 m³	1,807.67	1,339.50 m²	2,076.22				
Brick wall	59.63 m²	7,852.67	79.28 m²	1,463.51	24.98 m³	3,289.35		
Plaster inside	1,635.72 m²	9,568.96	1,711.25 m²	10,001.81	1,020.00 m²	5,967.00	264.27 m²	2,579.27
Ceiling plaster	933.21 m²	5,216.64	920.35 m²	5,144.76	400.00 m²	2,236.00		
Mosaic floor	302.54 m²	7,385.00	257.57 m²	6,287.53	200.99 m²	4,882.00		
Marble floor	485.00 m²	78,021.95	727.59 m²	117,047.40	370.00 m²	59,521.90	267.47 m²	43,027.00
Plaster, curved surface	450.23 m²	6,312.22	560.60 m²	7,859.61	260.00 m²	3,645.20	428.99 m²	5,280.87
Wooden covers	817.20 m²	35,384.76	1,160.11 m²	50,232.76	530.00 m²	22,949.00	295.81 m²	12,808.57
Marseilles tiles	872.02 m²	12,426.28	1,183.70 m²	16,867.72	580.00 m²	8,265.00	329.28 m²	4,692.24
Copper pipes	88.95	6,298.55			78.35 (of zinc)	3,553.96	44.50	2,018.52
Wooden floor	204.68 m²	8,238.37	178.76 m²	7,195.09				
Inside glass doors	25.17 m²	2,337.54	46.83 m²	4,426.51				
Iron doors, shutters	5,866.50 kgs	39,916.20	2,090.00 kgs	14,149.30	949.00 kgs	6,424.00	2,200.00 kgs	14,894.00
B. A., of iron	16,416.76 kgs	48,101.09			5,000.00 kgs	15,300.00	2,971.71 kgs	9,093.42
B. A., of iron	9,609.50 kgs	29,405.00	10,626.92 kgs	32,518.36	9,488.01 kgs	27,803.00	4,100.05 kgs	12,013.15
Telarolu windows	125.46 m²	7,880.14	148.70 m²	9,339.85			31.11 m²	1,954.02
Stone walls	96.43 m³	4,635.58	75.46 m³	3,627.17				
Total cost of items		390,028.70		368,987.49		193,769.63		137,482.34
% of total estimates		90.28%		87.21%		74.17%		64.48%
Total paid out on claims		432,041.59		423,108.41		261,266.68		213,218.03

Table 55: Itemized damages to four churches

Works of Hardwood	Saints Theodoroi		Saints Constantine and Helen		Panagia Altı Mermer		Panagia Belgratkapı	
	Quantities	Value (TL)	Quantities	Value (TL)	Quantities	Value (TL)	Quantities	Value (TL)
Templon	74.08 m²	51,856.00	77.22 m²	50,554.00		45,122.00		36,491.00
Pulpit		6,000.00		6,000.00		6,000.00		5,000.00
Throne		6,000.00		6,000.00		6,000.00		5,000.00
Lectern	2 pieces	3,000.00	2 pieces	3,000.00	2 pieces	3,000.00	2 pieces	3,000.00
Parathronion	3 pieces	2,400.00	3 pieces	2,400.00	3 pieces	2,400.00	3 pieces	2,400.00
Pankari		3,500.00		3,500.00		3,500.00		3,500.00
Gorgona		4,000.00		4,000.00		4,000.00		3,500.00
Proskenetarion		2,200.00		2,200.00		2,200.00		2,200.00
Epitaphios table		6,500.00		6,500.00		6,500.00		6,500.00
Exapteriga		700.00		700.00		700.00		700.00
Vestment closet		700.00		700.00		700.00		700.00
Diskeli		750.00		750.00		750.00		750.00
Epitaphios cabinet		500.00		500.00		500.00		500.00
Stasidion	54 pieces	6,750.00	12	15,000.00	74	9,250.00	60	7,500.00
Funeral table		750.00		750.00		750.00		750.00
Benches	(46)	17,250.00	26	3,750.00	26	9,750.00	20	6,250.00
Icon frame	3 pieces	4,500.00	3	4,500.00	3	4,500.00	3	4,500.00
Anastasis table		3,000.00		3,000.00		3,000.00		3,000.00
Wood floor		692.64				1,571.58		
Wooden doors						433.93		
Window panes						175.87		
Door windows								
Metal parts						250.00		
Valuation		121,048.64		113,804.00		111,053.38		92,246.00
Payout		114,996.21		118,605.96		98,775.00		86,949.70

Further, the award of three contracts was set at a total of TL67.810.11, and the award of three *ilaves* in thirteen contracts came to TL106,636.97. The approximate total of paid and committed funds is thus:

TL3,430,185.48
1,054,035.82
106,636.97
67,810.11
TL4,658,668.38 in 196 cases.

Of the 196 contracts analyzed above, the table includes only seventy-four churches or religious institutions. The table depicting damages that was examined earlier included ninety churches. The list in the first table was itself, so far as one can tell, incomplete as to the churches attacked. But eighteen churches that were included in the first table are missing from the 196 contracts in the second one, and even the list of ninety is incomplete, as it is estimated that perhaps as many as 105 Greek religious institutions were attacked, to which must be added the smaller number of Armenian and Greek Catholic churches that were damaged.[136]

An additional observation needs to be made here. The Committee for Repair had itself become a miniature bureaucracy and, as a result, had regular, monthly expenses for staff, overhead, and other functions such as advertising, storage, and transport. It also had to submit monthly withholdings from employees' salaries and for the official government stamps attached to its statements. The tax-withholding document lists five architects, two secretaries, one accountant, one guard, one storage employee, one typist, and one janitor. The monthly salary for staff in 1958 was TL12,904, or TL154,848 per year. In five years (the processing of claims, contracts, and compensations went on for at least five years from 1955 to 1960), this would have amounted to TL774,240, thus adding another burden to the TL10 million allocated for reconstruction of all damaged Christian buildings of all ethnic groups.[137]

What these incomplete archives do not reveal is the work done by the Greeks with their own community funds. One would have to consult

---

[136] These eighteen churches are: Agia Analepsis, St. Demetrios (Büyükada), Agia Eleutheria (Kurtuluş), St. George (Fener), St. George (*metochion* of Jerusalem), St. George (Tarabya), St. Charalamos (Cibalı), St. Ignatios (Kadıköy), St. John (Kumkapı), Saints Constantine and Helen (Tarabya), St. Kyriake (Tarabya), Metamorphosis (Kandilli), Derkon metropolitanate (Tarabya), Panagia (Vlah Saray), St. Paraskeue (Arnavutköy), St. Paraskeue (Kaila Sirkeci), St. Paraskeue (Samatya), and St. Spyridon (Heybeliada).

[137] See *6-7 Eylül Hey'et* (Committee for Repair), file V, the two payrolls dated August and November, respectively, for the year 1960. It may be that salaries for earlier years were lower, but certainly after 1960 and until 1966, they were much higher.

the community ledgers for this important material. It is generally alleged by Istanbul's Greeks that the Turkish government's appropriation of TL10 million was quite insufficient for the repairs needed, and so the communities undertook to do this work, just as Greek businessmen had restored their own enterprises. In a detailed study of the Greek community of Cibalı, the author frequently refers to the local community archives. Indeed, the study closely examines the financial records of the community's governing board and states that: "In the following year [1956], the damages [to the Church of St. Nicholas] were gradually being repaired and on December 12, 1956, it was recorded in the financial register [of the community] that the expenses that arose [for 1956] from the destruction of September 6, 1955, had reached TL18,730." On glancing at the incomplete *vakıflar* file for St. Nicholas, one sees that there were some small repairs initiated and finished in 1957, for payments of TL1,226.97, TL2,115.64, and TL2,381.55, respectively. It is obvious, however, that the sum reported in the Cibalı community ledgers for 1956 has nothing to do with this archival file for Cibalı or with the funds paid out by the *vakıflar*. The sums are entirely different, and the dates of beginning and termination of work fall, respectively, into two different years, 1956 and 1957. Thus, the approximately TL5,700 paid out by the *vakıflar* would have entered the ledgers of the Committee for Repair whereas the TL18,730 were recorded in the ledgers of the community of Cibalı.[138] As expenses would have appeared in the ledgers of a community only in those cases in which it was the contractor—and, of 196 contracts studied, some eighty were contracted out to Greek community boards—it is possible then that this sum was contracted out in part to the Cibalı board.[139]

---

[138] Kesisoglou-Karystinou, *Tzimbali*, p. 115.

[139] Very soon after the pogrom, the patriarchate created its own reconstruction committee and gathered formally prepared lists of damage assessments from all the Greek communities in regard to their religious institutions. Traces of these detailed lists have emerged in the parts of the *6-7 Eylül Hey'et* archives available to the author. Copies must also exist in the patriarchal and Greek community archives. Three letters about damage assessments, sent by the *mütevelli hey'et* to the patriarchate, are particularly relevant. (One has seemingly contradictory dates, which complicates matters as the date is of some importance in the evolution of questions of assessments, submissions, and payments.) The president and general secretary of the community of Galata and of the Church of St. Nicholas wrote to the patriarchate's office of the great protosyncellus on November 7, 1956 (?):

In response to the encyclical of the Reconstruction Committee of the 23rd of October, we have the honor of bringing the following to your attention, in consonance with the catalogues of damages to the Sacred churches of our community that have been submitted to you: The damages to both our churches amount to TL170,304 and TL232,959, to the Church of St. Nicholas and to the Church of Christos Soter,

In the end, one can conclude that the economics and politics of compensation (read: rebuilding and repairs) of Greek religious institutions were, in their broad outlines, identical to those of the Greek (as well as Armenian, Jewish, and foreign) businesses, shops, and dwellings. The politics operated under the same conditions and policies set by the Turkish government—with one major exception: the victims suffered all the consequences of the aroused religious fanaticism of their Muslim neighbors. This is perhaps the one differentiating factor between the spirit of the attacks on Greek persons, shops, dwellings, and schools, on the one hand, and churches, cemeteries, and other religious institutions, on the other.

The unifying factor in economic policies lay in the driving animus within government circles to reduce the compensations to insignificance in both cases. The Turkish government's first step was to make a drastic reduction of Greek ecclesiastical claims from about TL40 million. As we saw, this consisted of two almost equal segments: for structural damages; and for damages to movable property and objects related to the practice of the religious cult. Menderes, however, then abruptly cut all Greek claims, ecclesiastical and secular, by specifically calling for a cap of TL60 million to cover all remaining claimants who had not been granted relief from the very restricted funds of the Istanbul aid committee. Further, of the funds appropriated on February 29, 1956, only TL10 million were to be allowed for damages to religious institutions (which must have also included the damage to a limited number of Armenian and Greek Catholic churches, as Israel undertook to repair the one synagogue that had been attacked). As a consequence, the Greek Church had to reduce its claims by 75 percent, and simply abandoned hope

respectively. But, in consonance with the predetermined percentage to be paid, the sums are:
for St. Nicholas church - 107,304 x 10/35 = TL48,665
for Christos Soter - 232,959 x 10/35 = TL66,560.

This letter was also sent to the central Greek ephorate of Galata and to the *mütevelli hey'et*. In the former case, the text seems to date the action to October 26, 1955, or 1956 (although probably the latter). The letter informs the office of the protosyncellus of the original lists of damage assessments that had initially been submitted to it. Further, the letter reveals that, at some point, a decision had been made that only a uniform percentage of the original claims for all churches would be paid, and that this percentage was 10/35, or 28.57 percent. Accordingly, the community could only apply for a sum that did not surpass this amount.

Finally, the president of the *mütevelli hey'et* of the Church of St. John in Galata wrote to the Committee for Repair on November 6, 1955, that the community had already submitted its catalogue of damages to the patriarchate in October and subsequent to specialist assessments of TL76,567.40. He was responding to the committee's request of October 23, 1955. All these letters indicate a centralizing effort on the part of the patriarchate to reduce claims, in a uniform and sweeping manner, by 71.53 percent.

of restoring the churches to the condition they had once enjoyed. Half of the claims for TL40 million were intended precisely for non-structural repairs, and it was in this area that most of the reductions took place in payments.

Still, things got worse. After this initial arbitrary reduction of three-quarters of the claims' value, the applications of various community boards were further and severely cut at a next stage, before the Istanbul *vakıflar* would even accept them for formal vetting. This emerges from the case of the Church of Saints Theodoroi in Langa. There is no regular application at this first stage, but only a short letter from the bureau of the *vakıflar* that states that it has received two applications for TL774,407.33 and TL200,904.72. It questions the former claim, however, and sends it back to the Committee for Repair, forcing it to reduce both amounts. When, finally, the necessary papers for the applications are drawn up, the two general assessments are for TL601,612.09 and TL130,684.32, respectively, a reduction of 22.3 and 35.2 percent for the corresponding claims. The bureau of the *vakıflar* then imposed further reductions of 23 and 5 percent, respectively, while the final payments fell to TL358,646.24 and TL119,996.21, respectively, for corresponding cuts of 53.7 and 48.6 percent. Thus, in the end, the original total of TL975,312.05 had been slashed to TL478,642.45, or a total reduction of TL496,669.60.

The view of Turkish policy was that the Greek communities should swallow the vast majority of the uncompensated damages to religious property. Perhaps the most striking exclusion that one notices in the *Registers of Measurements* and *Lists of Valuations* that the Greeks submitted to the *vakıflar* was the nearly complete absence of icons. The sacred icon was the central and omnipresent sign of Orthodox religiosity; intense civil wars had been waged in Byzantium to defend its sanctity and preserve its liturgical function. Thus, in the *vakıflar* documents issuing from the communities, one reads repeatedly of requests for new icon frames and new glass panes to cover them, as countless icons were lost in the destruction. Many churches, in fact, were completely burned, as were all their icons. We read continually of defacing of icons, and of their smashing and being used as fuel to kindle the huge fires that destroyed the churches. In one contract submitted to the *vakıflar*, fifty-eight icons are mentioned and described as to their painted saints. Still, there is no request in the application for their replacement. Indeed, with only two slight exceptions, in the 132 contracts of these applications, there are only two minor requests that an icon be touched up with a brush. Hundreds of icons were destroyed, but not one was replaced at the expense of the *vakıflar*. They were all replaced by the funds of the Greek communities.

Finally, along with the sacred icons, largely absent also from the *Registers of Measurements* and *Lists of Valuations* were the sacred silver patens and trays, the sacred vestments and embroidered coverlets, the sacred books and manuscripts. These rarely appear in the applications or in formal documents dealing with compensations; the same is true of damaged murals. In the end, the policy of the Turkish state was clearly to add on to the already heavy burden of the Greeks of Istanbul the major expenses of rebuilding their churches, repairing the damages to their cemeteries, and refurnishing their houses of worship with the necessary liturgical and sacred objects of their faith.

Table 56: Itemized damages of the Greek churches

	Agia Analepsis (Holy Ascension), Samarya[140]	St. Athanasios and *agiasma*, Kurtuluş[141]	Christos Soter, Galata[142]	St. Demetrios, Büyükada[143]	St. Demetrios, Edirnekapı-Sarmaşık[144]	St. Demetrios, Kurtuluş[145]	St. Demetrios, Kuruçeşme[146]	St. Demetrios Kanavos, school and Agia Vlacherna *agiasma*, Xyloporta-Tahtakapı[147]	St. Eleutheria, Kurtuluş[148]	Prophet Elias, Arnavutköy[149]	Prophet Elias, Üsküdar[150]	Euangelistria (Euangelismos-Annunication), Boyacıköy[151]	Euangelistria (Euangelismos), Yenişehir-Kurtuluş[152]	St. George, Bakırköy[153]	St. George, Boğaziçi, Yeniköy[154]	St. George and St. Panteleimon *agiasma*, Boğaziçi, Çengelköy[155]	St. George, Edirnekapı[156]	St. George, patriarchal church, Fener[157]	St. George, Antiphonetes Potiras, Fener[158]
bells, towers	■			■		■													
crosses	■			■		■									■				
baptismal font	■				■		■												■
crucifix	■			■	■	■								■					
proskenetarion	■	■		■		■					■	■		■		■			
vestments	■	■		■	■														
kouvouklli, epitaphios	■	■		■					■	■		■		■	■	■			■
murals	■	■				■													
icon frames	■	■		■			■				■			■		■			■
panikaria, gorgones	■	■		■	■	■	■	■	■	■	■			■	■	■			■
small templa				■															
doors	■	■		■		■	■			■	■					■			■
stairs	■	■		■															
chanters area																			
stasidia (pews)	■	■		■	■	■	■							■	■				
throne (episcopal)	■	■		■	■		■			■	■			■			■		
pulpit	■	■		■	■	■	■				■			■	■				
lectern	■	■		■	■	■			■		■			■					
chandeliers	■					■		■											
candlesticks	■			■	■		■				■					■			
candelabra	■	■			■	■	■	■			■								
railing	■					■													
cases	■			■		■													
books, manuscripts	■	■		■		■									■				
exapteriga	■	■													■				
manoualia	■	■													■				
aeras	■	■																	
antimension																			
paten	■	■		■		■	■	■			■								
chalice	■	■			■	■	■	■			■								
altar, sanctuary, prothesis	■	■	■	■	■	■	■	■		■	■			■		■			
reliefs	■	■		■											■				
icons, iconostasis	■	■		■	■	■	■	■			■			■	■	■	■		
narthex						■					■				■				
nave											■			■	■				
apse															■				
windows	■			■	■	■				■	■	■		■	■		■		
roof	■														■				
walls														■	■				
polluted, defiled		■												■					
desecrated	■	■	■	■	■	■	■	■	■	■	■	■	■	■	■	■	■		■
burned			■	■														■	■
damaged/looted	■	■	■	■	■	■	■	■	■	■	■	■	■	■	■	■		■	■
destroyed	■	■																■	■

Key to columns:

1. St. George, metochion of patriarchate of Jerusalem, Fener[159]
2. St. George Kremnos, Heybeliada[160]
3. St. George (cemetery church), Ortaköy[161]
4. St. George Kyparissas, Samatya[162]
5. St. George, Tarabya[163]
6. St. George, Kadıköy, Yeldeğirmeni[164]
7. St. Charalambos, Bebek[165]
8. St. Charalambos, chapel, Cibali[166]
9. St. Ignatios, Boğaziçi-Asya-Kadıköy[167]
10. St. John Prodromos, Balino, monastic metochion of Sinai[168]
11. St. John, Boğaziçi-Asya-Kalamış[169]
12. St. John of the Chians, Galata, Karaköy[170]
13. St. John, Kumkapı[171]
14. St. John, Kuruçeşme[172]
15. St. John, Boğaziçi, Yeni Mahalle[173]
16. Saints Constantine and Helen, Beyoğlu-Kalyoncu Kulluk[174]
17. Saints Constantine and Helen, Boğaziçi, Paşabahçe[175]
18. Saints Constantine and Helen, Samatya[176]
19. Saints Constantine and Helen, Tarabya[177]
20. St. Kyriake and St. Onouphrios aghiasmata, Arnavutköy[178]

Feature	1	2	3	4	5	6	7	8	9	10	11	12	13	14	15	16	17	18	19	20
bells, towers			■									■								
crosses			■									■					■			
baptismal font	■		■																	
crucifix			■	■								■				■			■	
proskenetarion			■									■						■		
vestments	■		■						■					■				■		
kouvouklin, epitaphios			■	■	■		■		■			■						■		
murals			■																	
icon frames			■															■		■
panhagia, gorgones	■		■	■	■				■									■		
small templa			■						■											
doors	■	■	■	■	■				■							■	■			■
stairs	■		■																	
chanters area			■																	
stasidia (pews)		■	■	■	■				■									■		
throne (episcopal)		■	■					■								■		■		■
pulpit	■	■	■											■	■			■		
lectern	■		■						■									■		
chandeliers	■		■						■					■						
candlesticks	■		■					■	■					■						
candelabra			■	■				■						■	■					
railing			■																	
cases			■	■				■						■						
books, manuscripts			■				■													
exapteriga			■						■									■		
manoualia			■						■											
aeras			■																	
antimension			■																	
paten	■		■						■											
chalice	■		■																	
altar, sanctuary, prothesis	■		■					■						■						
reliefs			■											■						
icons, iconostasis	■		■					■				■	■	■			■			
narthex			■																	
nave			■																	
apse			■																	
windows	■		■	■		■	■				■	■		■		■				
roof	■		■	■						■										
walls			■		■			■	■	■	■	■	■				■		■	
polluted, defiled					■															
desecrated	■	■	■	■	■	■	■	■	■	■	■	■	■	■	■	■	■	■	■	■
burned			■																■	
damaged/looted	■	■	■	■	■	■	■	■	■	■	■	■	■	■	■	■	■	■	■	■
destroyed			■																	

	St. Kyriake, Kumkapı[179]	St. Kyriake, Boğaziçi, Paşabahçe[180]	St. Kyriake *agiasma*, Tarabya[181]	Metamorphosis tou Christou, Büyükada[182]	Metamorphosis (Transfiguration), Boğaziçi, Kandilli[183]	Metamorphosis, cemetery church, Şişli[184]	Metropolitanate of Derkon, Tarabya[185]	Greek Orthodox metropolitanate, Kadıköy[186]	St. Menas, Samatya[187]	St. Nicholas, Cibali[188]	St. Nicholas, Galata, Karaköy[189]	St. Nicholas, Heybeliada[190]	St. Nicholas, Samatya[191]	St. Nicholas, Topkapı[192]	St. Nicholas, Boğaziçi, Yeniköy[193]	Panagia, Altı Mermer[194]	Panagia Balino, Balat[195]	Genethlia Panagias, Belgratkapı[196]	Panagia, Büyükada[197]	Panagia tes Soudas, Eğrikapı[198]	Panagia Mouchliotissa, Fener[199]	Panagia, Boğaziçi, Göksuyu[200]
bells, towers				■	■			■	■			■		■		■						
crosses				■	■			■	■			■		■		■						■
baptismal font	■			■	■			■				■		■								
crucifix				■	■			■	■			■		■								
proskenetarion				■	■			■	■			■		■								
vestments				■	■			■	■			■		■								■
kouvoukli, epitaphios				■				■	■	■		■		■		■						
murals				■				■	■			■		■								
icon frames				■				■			■	■		■		■						
panhiria, gorgones	■			■				■	■	■	■	■		■		■				■		■
small *templa*				■				■				■		■	■	■						
doors				■	■	■		■	■	■		■		■		■						
stairs				■	■		■	■		■		■		■		■						
chanters area				■				■				■	■	■								
stasidia (pews)	■			■		■		■				■		■	■	■		■	■	■		
throne (episcopal)				■				■			■	■	■	■	■			■	■	■		
pulpit	■			■				■	■	■		■		■		■						
lectern				■	■			■				■		■	■	■		■	■	■		
chandeliers				■	■			■			■	■	■	■				■				
candlesticks				■	■			■				■	■	■				■				
candelabra				■	■			■				■	■	■				■				
railing				■				■			■	■	■	■		■						
cases				■	■			■	■			■		■								
books, manuscripts				■	■			■		■		■		■								
exapteryga				■				■				■		■								
manoualia				■				■	■			■		■								
aeras				■				■				■		■								
antimension				■				■				■		■								
paten				■	■			■				■		■								
chalice				■	■			■				■		■								
altar, sanctuary, *prothesis*	■			■	■	■		■		■		■		■	■	■						
reliefs				■	■			■			■	■		■								
icons, *iconostasis*	■			■		■		■	■			■		■	■	■	■			■	■	■
narthex				■	■			■				■		■								
nave				■				■				■		■								
apse				■	■			■			■	■		■								
windows				■	■	■		■	■	■		■	■	■		■		■	■			
roof				■	■			■	■	■		■		■		■	■					■
walls				■	■			■	■			■		■		■	■	■				
polluted, defiled				■				■		■		■		■								
desecrated	■	■	■	■		■		■	■	■	■	■	■	■	■	■	■	■	■	■	■	■
burned	■					■		■				■		■		■						
damaged/looted	■	■	■	■	■	■	■	■	■	■	■	■	■	■	■	■	■	■	■	■	■	■
destroyed				■	■			■				■		■								

	Panagia Elpis, Kumkapı[201]	Panagia ton Ouranon, Salmatobruk, Edirnekapı[202]	Panagia Chantzirgiotissa, Tekfur Sarayı[203]	Panagia Vefa Zeyrek[204]	Panagia, Vlah Saray[205]	Panagia, Boğaziçi, Yeniköy[206]	Saint Paraskeue, Arnavutköy[207]	St. Paraskeue, Beykoz[208]	St. Paraskeue, Büyükdere[209]	St. Paraskeue, Hasköy (Pikridion)[210]	St. Paraskeue, Kazlıçeşme[211]	St. Paraskeue, Kaila, Sirkeci[212]	St. Paraskeue, Samatya[213]	St. Paraskeue, Tarabya[214]	St. Panteleimon agiasma, Boğaziçi-Asya-Çengelköy[215]	St. Panteleimon agiasma, Hasköy (Pikridion)[216]	St. Panteleimon, Kuzguncuk[217]	St. Phokas, Ortaköy[218]	St. Spyridon, monastery, Heybeliada[219]	Saints Taxiarchs, Arnavutköy[220]	Saints Taxiarchs, Balat[221]
bells, towers	■		■	■																	■
crosses	■								■												■
baptismal font	■																				■
crucifix	■	■							■												■
proskenetarion	■																	■		■	■
vestments	■																				■
kouvoukli, epitaphios	■		■	■														■		■	■
murals	■								■												■
icon frames	■	■										■						■		■	■
pankaria, gorgones	■		■	■					■									■		■	■
small templa	■																				■
doors	■		■	■													■	■	■		■ ■
stairs	■		■										■								■
chanters' area	■	■																			■
stasidia (pews)	■		■	■				■	■									■		■	■
throne (episcopal)	■	■							■												■
pulpit	■		■	■				■	■									■			■
lectern	■		■																	■	■
chandeliers	■								■												■
candlesticks	■																				■
candelabra	■								■												■
railing	■		■	■																	■
cases	■																	■		■	■
books, manuscripts	■																				■
exapteriga	■																				■
manoualia	■																				■
aeras	■																				■
antimension	■																				■
paten	■																	■	■		
chalice	■																	■	■		
altar, sanctuary, prothesis	■		■	■				■	■									■		■	■
reliefs	■						■													■	■
icons, iconostasis	■		■	■				■	■	■								■		■	■
narthex	■		■							■	■										■
nave	■																				■
apse	■																				■
windows	■		■	■				■	■							■					■
roof	■		■	■	■																■
walls	■		■		■						■			■	■	■	■				■
polluted, defiled	■			■		■												■		■	
desecrated	■		■	■	■	■		■	■	■	■	■	■		■	■	■	■	■	■	■
burned	■				■																■
damaged/looted	■		■	■	■	■	■	■	■	■	■	■		■		■	■	■	■	■	■
destroyed	■			■								■								■	■

	bells, towers	crosses	baptismal font	crucifix	proskenetarion	vestments	kouvoukli, epitaphios	murals	icon frames	panhagia, gorgones	small templa	doors	stairs	chanters area	stasidia (pews)	throne (episcopal)	pulpit	lectern	chandeliers	candlesticks	candelabra	railing	cases	books, manuscripts	exapteriga	manoualia	aeras	antimension	paten	chalice	altar, sanctuary, prothesis	reliefs	icons, iconostasis	narthex	nave	apse	windows	roof	walls	polluted, defiled	desecrated	burned	damaged/looted	destroyed
Saints Taxiarchs, Boğaziçi, İstinye[222]																																					■				■		■	
Saints Theodoroi, Langa (Vlanga)[223]																															■						■		■		■		■	■
Koimesis Theotokou (mistakenly Genethlia Theotokou), Beşiktaş, Palio Banio[224]																																					■		■		■		■	
St. Therapon, Sirkeci[225]																																					■				■		■	
Holy Trinity, Kadıköy[226]				■																	■												■				■			■	■		■	
Holy Trinity, Taksim[227]							■			■											■		■								■	■					■			■	■		■	
Koimesis Theotokou, Ayvansaray (Vlacherna)[228]							■		■	■																					■									■	■		■	
Zoodochos Pege, (Meryam Ana Monastery), Balıklı[229]	■	■	■	■	■	■	■	■	■	■	■	■	■	■	■	■	■	■	■	■	■	■	■	■	■	■	■	■	■	■	■	■	■	■		■	■	■	■	■	■	■	■	■
Totals	19	19	17	23	23	20	36	14	25	41	14	39	21	12	40	32	33	30	20	23	27	16	20	17	14	14	11	11	20	19	20	20	44	16	11	12	45	23	32	18	88	20	89	17

[140] Kaloumenos, photographs, roll 7b, nos. 23A, 24A, and 25A.

[141] National Archives, Istanbul to Washington, No. 132, 9/27/55, Carp Report; Greek Embassy, Athens to Washington, No. 42071, EK/3a, 10/3/55, Frydas Report; Istanbul *vakıflar*, St. Athanasios, Kurtuluş, *Hakediş Raporu*, 9/5/58.

[142] National Archives, Istanbul to Washington, No. 132, 9/27/55, Carp Report; Greek Embassy, Athens to Washington, No. 42071, EK/3a, 10/3/55, Frydas Report. This part of the missing text has been reconstructed on the basis of other evidence. Istanbul *vakıflar*, Christos Soter, Galata, *şartname, and keşif özeti* 10/21/57. Kaloumenos, photographs, roll 4a, nos. 3A, 4A, 6A, 7A, 9A, 20A-22A, and 42A-44A; roll 5, nos. 2, 4, 5, 11, 38/39, 41, and 44A.

[143] National Archives, Istanbul to Washington, No. 132, 9/27/55, Carp Report; Greek Embassy, Athens to Washington, No. 42071, EK/3a, 10/3/55, Frydas Report; Chrêstidês, *Ekthesis*, p. 87.

[144] Greek Embassy, Athens to Washington, No. 42071, EK/3a, 10/3/55; Kaloumenos, photographs, attributes roll 27, nos. 27, 36A, and 40A; roll 28, no. 8A/9. The attribution is seemingly confused inasmuch as a different view of the *iconostasis* is attributed both to St. Demetrios and to another church. Bids 11/7/58 and 1/4/60.

[145] National Archives, Athens to Washington, No. 132, 9/27/55, Carp Report; Greek Embassy, Athens to Washington, No. 42071, EK/3a, 10/3/55, Frydas Report; Kaloumenos, photographs, roll 15, nos. 23A-37A; roll 16A; roll 16a, nos. 1-6; Chrêstidês, *Ekthesis*, p. 59; Istanbul *vakıflar*, St. Dêmêtrios Kurtuluş, the two *şartnames*, 8/27/57.

[146] National Archives, Istanbul to Washington, No. 132, 9/27/55, Carp Report; in the emended text of Greek Embassy, Athens to Washington, No. 42071, EK/3a, 10/3/55, Frydas Report; Kaloumenos, photographs, rolls 25 and 26; Chrêstidês, *Ekthesis*, p. 95.

[147] National Archives, Istanbul to Washington, No. 132, 9/27/55, Carp Report; Greek Embassy, Athens to Washington, No. 42071, EK/3a, 10/3/55, Frydas Report; Chrêstidês, *Ekthesis*, p. 78; Kaloumenos, photographs, rolls 24, 25, and 30, nos. 24 and 26; roll 12, nos. 19A-21A.

[148] National Archives, Athens to Washington, No. 132, 9/27/55, Carp Report.

[149] Emended list of Greek Embassy, Athens to Washington, No. 42071, EK/3a, 10/3/55, Carp Report; Megas Reumiotês, *Syrriknosê*, pp. 47-50; Tsoukatou, *Septemvriana*, p. 76; Istanbul *vakıflar*, Prophet Elias, *şartname*, 8/24/59, and *Hakediş Raporu*, 3/5/60.

[150] National Archives, Istanbul to Washington, No. 132, 9/27/55, Carp Report; emended text of Greek Embassy, Athens to Washington, No. 42071, EK/3a, 10/3/55, Frydas Report; Chrêstidês, *Ekthesis*, p. 90; Istanbul *vakıflar*, Prophet Elias, Üsküdar, *şartname* and *keşif özeti*.

[151] National Archives, Istanbul to Washington, No. 132, 9/27/55, Carp Report; emended text in Greek Embassy, Athens to Washington, No. 42071, EK/3a, 103/55; Chrêstidês, *Ekthesis*, p. 94, seems to place it in nearby Bebek.

[152] National Archives, Istanbul to Washington, No. 132, 9/27/55, Carp Report; Istanbul *vakıflar*, Euangelistria, *şartname*, 3/1/57.

[153] Greek Embassy, Athens to Washington, No. 42071, EK/3a, 10/3/55; Istanbul *vakıflar*, 10/3/57.

[154] Emended text of Greek Embassy, Athens to Washington, No. 42071, EK/3a, 10/3/55, Frydas Report; Istanbul *vakıflar*; St. George, Yeniköy, *şartname* and *keşif özeti*.

[155] National Archives, Istanbul to Washington, No. 132, 9/27/55, Carp Report; emended text of Greek Embassy Athens to Washington, No. 42071, EK/3a, 10/3/55, Frydas Report; Istanbul *vakıflar*, *şartnames* undated, 10/21/57, and *keşif özeti*; Chrêstidês, *Ekthesis*, p. 90.

[156] National Archives, Istanbul to Washington, No. 132, 9/27/55, Carp Report; Greek Embassy, Athens to Washington, No. 42071, EK/3a, 10/3/55; Kaloumenos, photographs, roll 8, nos. 7-25; Chrêstidês, *Ekthesis*, p. 79.

[157] While the substantial police and military forces were able to defend the patriarchal compound when the church was attacked, some windows were broken; for photos of the soldiers, broken windows, and rocks and bricks that broke them, Kaloumenos, roll 1, nos. 2-6, 30, 33A, and 39.

[158] National Archives, Istanbul to Washington, No. 132, 9/27/55, Carp Report; Chrêstidês, *Ekthesis*, p. 78.

[159] Kaloumenos, photographs, roll 18a, nos. 1A-21A and 42; roll 18b, nos. 34 and 35; roll 19a, nos. 3A, 7A, 13A, and 20A; see also Kaloumenos, *Staurôsis*, 1978, Nos. 74-77.

[160] National Archives, Istanbul to Washington, No. 132, 9/27/55, Carp Report; Chrêstidês, *Ekthesis*, p. 86.

[161] Istanbul *vakıflar*, St. George cemetery church, Ortaköy, *keşif özeti*, documents dated to 1957-1958.

[162] National Archives, Istanbul to Washington, No. 132, 9/27/55, Carp Report; Greek Embassy, Athens to Washington, No. 42071, EK/3a, 10/3/55, Frydas Report; Kaloumenos, photographs, roll 16a, nos. 11A-18A and 23A; Chrêstidês, *Ekthesis*, p. 78.

[163] Although the Frydas Report notes this church as unharmed, the archival documents—

Istanbul *vakıflar*, St. George of Tarabya, and its two *şartnames* and *keşif özetis*—indicate that it was attacked and sustained certain damages. The principal *şartname* is dated March 1, 1957.

[164] National Archives, Istanbul to Washington, No. 132, 9/26/55, Carp Report; emended text of Greek Embassy, Athens to Washington, No. 42071, EK/3a, 10/3/55, Frydas Report; Istanbul *vakıflar*, St. George, Yeldeğirmeni, two *şartnames*, dated 5/5/57 and 10/24/57, and *keşif özeti*.

[165] National Archives, Istanbul to Washington, No. 132, 9/26/55, Carp Report; emended text of Greek Embassy, Athens to Washington, No. 42071, EK/3a, 10/3/55, Frydas Report; Istanbul *vakıflar*, St. Charalambos, Bebek, has three *şartnames*, one of which is dated 3/9/57.

[166] Kesisoglou-Karystinou, *Tzimbali*, pp. 115, 122, and 157.

[167] National Archives, Istanbul to Washington, No. 132, 9/27/55, Carp Report.

[168] National Archives, Istanbul to Washington, No. 132, 9/27/55, Carp Report; Greek Embassy, Athens to Washington, No. 42071, EK/3a, 10/3/55, Frydas Report; Kaloumenos, photographs, roll 19b, nos. 1-11; Chrêstidês, *Ekthesis*, p. 78; Tsoukatou, *Septemvriana*, pp. 127-130.

[169] National Archives, Istanbul to Washington, No. 132, 9/27/55, Carp Report. This catalogue of damaged churches places the Church of St. John in Kadıköy, but Kalamış must be near it and it is undoubtedly one and the same church. In Greek Embassy, Athens to Washington, No. 42071, EK/3a, 10/3/55, Frydas Report, it is mentioned as having survived untouched. Nevertheless, Istanbul *vakıflar*, St. John of Kalamış, *keşif özeti*, indicates basic repairs of massive window damage, structural repairs with cement, and new electrical installations.

[170] National Archives, Istanbul to Washington, No. 132, 9/27/55, Carp Report; Greek Embassy, Athens to Washington, No. 43071, EK/3a, 10/3/55, Frydas Report; Kaloumenos, photographs, roll 9, nos. 3-13, 35, and 26; Istanbul *vakıflar*, St. John of the Chians, a *keşif özeti* dated 12/27/56; the file is obviously missing a considerable number of other documents.

[171] There was a small building with an *agiasma* dedicated to St. John Prodromos in Kumkapı; Atzemoglou, *T'agiasmata*, p. 57.

[172] Kaloumenos, rolls 24 and 25; Istanbul *vakıflar*, St. John Kuruçeşme, *keşif özeti* dated 12/29/76; emended text of Greek Embassy, Athens to Washington, no. 42071, EK/3a, 10/3/55, Frydas Report.

[173] National Archives, Istanbul to Washington, No. 132, 9/27/55, Carp Report; Kaloumenos, photographs, roll 20, nos. 11A-34A; Chrêstidês, *Ekthesis*, p. 93.

[174] National Archives, Istanbul to Washington, No. 132, 9/27/55, Carp Report; Greek Embassy, Athens to Washington, No. 42071, EK/3a, 10/3/55, Frydas Report; Kaloumenos, photographs, roll 14b, Nos. 27A-35A; Istanbul *vakıflar*, Saints Constantine and Helen of Beyoğlu, a *şartname* dated 4/11/57 and *keşif özeti*.

[175] National Archives, Istanbul to Washington, No. 132, 9/27/55, Carp Report; Greek Embassy, Athens to Washington, No. 42071, EK/3a, 10/3/55, Frydas Report; Istanbul *vakıflar*, Saints Constantine and Helen, Paşabahçe, *keşif özeti*.

[176] National Archives, Istanbul to Washington, No. 132, 9/27/55, Carp Report; Greek Embassy, Athens to Washington, No. 42071, EK/3a, 10/3/55, Frydas Report; Istanbul *vakıflar*, Saints Constantine and Helen of Samatya, a very long *şartname* dated 11/17/62. The photographs in Kaloumenos (roll 16a) are wrongly attributed, at least in part, to Saints Constantine and Helen of Samatya; they seem to belong to the church of St. Menas, as per their attribution in Kaloumenos, *Staurôsis*, 1978, Nos. 112 and 113; also Chrêstidês, *Ekthesis*, p. 78.

[177] Greek Embassy, Athens to Washington, No. 42071, EK/ 3a, 10/3/55, Frydas Report; Chrêstidês, *Ekthesis*, p. 93.

[178] Istanbul *vakıflar*, St. Kyriake and St. Onoufrios of Arnavutköy were both *agiasmata* and

there is a *şartname* listing repairs to the former subsequent to the pogrom, dated 4/19/57; Atzemoglou, *T'agiasmata*, pp. 106-110.

[179] National Archives, Istanbul to Washington, No. 132, 9/27/55, Carp Report; emended text of Greek Embassy, Athens to Washington, No. 42071, EK/3a, 10/3/55, Frydas Report. Kaloumenos's photograph roll 29a (nos. 9A, 33A, and 40A) is erroneously attributed to Panagia of Eğrikapı. It is in reality St. Kyriake of Kumkapı, as properly identified in Kaloumenos, *Staurôsis*, 1978, nos. 212 and 213. Istanbul, *vakıflar*, St. Kyriake of Kumkapı has two *şartnames*, both undated, but the *keşif özeti* is dated 10/18/55.

[180] Istanbul *vakıflar*, St. Kyriake (an *agiasma*), a *şartname* dated 1/7/57; see Atzemoglou, *T'agiasmata*, pp. 129-130. It was a very small affair, as many such *agiasmata* were.

[181] Greek Embassy, Athens to Washington, No. 42071, EK/3a, 10/3/55, Frydas Report; Chrêstidês, *Ekthesis*, p. 93.

[182] National Archives, Istanbul to Washington, No. 132, 9/27/55, Carp Report.

[183] Istanbul *vakıflar*, Metamorphosis, Kandilli, 1/21/57.

[184] National Archives, Istanbul to Washington, No. 132, 9/27/55, Carp Report; Kaloumenos, photographs, rolls 36a, 36b, 36d, 36e, and 36f; Istanbul *vakıflar*, huge files of reports, *şartnames*, and *Hakediş Raporu* on damages, repairs, and costs. The documentation dates from 1957 to 1962, beyond the fall and execution of Menderes.

[185] Greek Embassy, Athens to Washington, No. 42071, EK/3a, 10/3/55, Frydas Report; Chrêstidês, *Ekthesis*, p. 93.

[186] Greek Embassy, Athens to Washington, No. 47021, 10/3/55, Frydas Report; Istanbul, *vakıflar*, Greek metropolitanate, Kadıköy, very little, including a *keşif özeti* dated 1/7/57.

[187] National Archives, Istanbul to Washington, No. 132, 9/27/55, Carp Report; Greek Embassy, Athens to Washington, No. 47021, EK/3a, 10/3/55, Frydas Report; Kaloumenos, photographs, roll 16a, nos. 6A-10A, which had formerly been erroneously attributed to Saints Constantine and Helen of Samatya; Chrêstidês, *Ekthesis*, p. 78.

[188] National Archives, Istanbul to Washington, No. 132, 9/27/55, Carp Report; Greek Embassy, Athens to Washington, No. 47021, EK/3a, 10/3/55, Frydas Report; Kaloumenos, photographs, roll 29b, nos. 6, 7, and 10; Kesisoglou-Karystinou, *Tzimbali*, pp. 115, 122, and 157; Istanbul *vakıflar*, St. Nicholas of Cibali. I have seen only a small portion of this latter file, dating to early July 1957, which does not even contain a *şartname* in it.

[189] National Archives, Istanbul to Washington, No. 132, 9/27/55, Carp Report; Greek Embassy, Athens to Washington, No. 47021, EK/3a, 10/3/55, Frydas Report; Kaloumenos, photographs, rolls 2b, 3, and 4; Istanbul *vakıflar*, St. Nicholas of Galata, two *şartnames*, one dated 10/21/57. The data of damaged and destroyed materials matches very well with Kaloumenos's photographic record. The report on the destruction wrought on the church at Galata had been submitted by the local ecclesiastical administrator and has been preserved in a dispatch sent by the Greek foreign ministry to its embassy in Washington; see footnote no. 85 in Chapter 2 above, as well as the extensive translation of it into English in Chapter 2.

[190] Greek Embassy, Athens to Washington, No. 47021, EK/3a, 10/3/55, Frydas Report.

[191] Chrêstidês stated that St. Nicholas of Samatya had not been damaged, but there is some evidence to the contrary, although perhaps the damage was not so severe; Kaloumenos, photographs, roll 7b; Istanbul *vakıflar*, St. Nicholas of Samatya, a *şartname* dated 12/29/56, as well as other documents.

[192] National Archives, Istanbul to Washington, No. 132, 9/27/55, Carp Report; Greek Embassy, No. 47021, EK/3a, 10/3/55, Frydas Report; Kaloumenos, photographs, roll 14a, nos. 14A-30A; roll 14b, nos. 17 and 18; Istanbul *vakıflar*, St. Nicholas, Topkapı, *şartname* dated 10/10/57 and plentiful documentation on damages and replacements.

[193] National Archives, Istanbul to Washington, No. 132, 9/27/55, Carp Report; there is very

little other than a short *şartname*, as I have seen it, in the file of Istanbul *vakıflar*, St. Nicholas of Yeniköy; *Makedonia*, 9/6/55; see Chapter 2 above.

[194] National Archives, Istanbul to Washington, No. 132, 9/27/55, Carp Report; Greek Embassy, Athens to Washington, No. 47021, EK/3a, 10/3/55, Frydas Report; Kaloumenos, photographs, roll 7a, No. 10A; roll 16a, Nos. 16A-21A and 30A; roll 16b, Nos. 2-4, 5A, and 6A; Istanbul *vakıflar*, Panagia, Altı Mermer, two *şartnames*, one dated 11/9/62, extensive damage and repair documentation

[195] National Archives, Istanbul to Washington, No. 132, 9/27/55, Carp Report; Greek Embassy, Athens to Washington, No. 47021, EK/3a, 10/3/55, Frydas Report; Kaloumenos, photographs. Here, roll 31 has recently been attributed to Panagia Balino in Fener, but some part of it appears to be of St. Demetrios Kanavos in Tahtakapı; it is rich material, but the material needs to be clarified.

[196] National Archives, Istanbul to Washington, No. 132, 9/27/55, Carp Report; Greek Embassy, Athens to Washington, No. 43071, EK/3a, 10/3/55, Frydas Report; Kaloumenos, photographs, rolls 4, 10-15; Istanbul, *vakıflar*, Panagia, Belgratkapı, three *şartnames* with many documents dating from 1957 to 1962.

[197] National Archives, Istanbul to Washington, No. 132, 9/27/55, Carp Report; Greek Embassy, Athens to Washington, No. 47021, EK/3a, 10/3/55, Frydas Report, states that the church was undamaged, but Istanbul *vakıflar*, Panagia of Büyükada, records extensive desecration and damages in three *şartnames*, all of which were filed on 3/23/57.

[198] National Archives, Istanbul to Washington, No. 132, 9/27/55, Carp Report; Greek Embassy, Athens to Washington, No. 47021, EK/3a, 10/3/55, Frydas Report; Kaloumenos, photographs, roll 29a, nos. 1-11A, 31A, and 33A-43A, formerly mistakenly identified as belonging to the church of Panagia Ouranon of Edirnekapı. Of these, 9A, 33A, and 40A are positively identified as Panagia Soudas of Eğrikapı by Kaloumenos in *Staurôsis*, 1978. Istanbul *vakıflar*, Panagia Soudas of Eğrikapı, has a considerable body of interesting documents from 1957 through 1960 that includes a *şartname* and extensively detailed documents as well.

[199] National Archives, Istanbul to Washington, No. 132, 9/27/55, Carp Report; Greek Embassy, Athens to Washington, No. 47021, EK/3a, 10/3/55, Frydas Report; Kaloumenos, photographs, roll 12, no. 12. See Kaloumenos, *Staurôsis*, 1976, nos. 50-53, and *Staurôsis*, 1991, where three photos are attributed to this church.

[200] Greek Embassy, Athens to Washington, No. 47021, EK/3a, 10/3/55, Frydas Report; Istanbul *vakıflar*, Panagia, Göksuyu, an extensive *şartname*, papers for 1957-1958.

[201] National Archives, Istanbul to Washington, No. 132, 9/27/55, Carp Report; Chrêstidês, *Ekthesis*, p. 79; Istanbul *vakıflar*, Panagia Elpis, Kumkapı, a small series of *keşif özetis* and a thick *metraj cedveli* indicate considerable desecration of and damage to the church.

[202] National Archives, Istanbul to Washington, No. 132, 9/27/55, Carp Report; Greek Embassy, Athens to Washington, No. 42071, EK/3a, 10/3/55, Frydas Report; Kaloumenos, photographs, roll 29a, nos. 1-11A, 31A, and 33A-43A; Kaloumenos, *Staurôsis*, 1978, has confirmed this identification for some photographs.

[203] The Panagia Chantzirgiotissa of Tekfur Sarayı must be the "second" church of the Virgin mentioned in the American document, National Archives, Istanbul to Washington, No. 132, 9/27/55, Carp Report; Greek Embassy, Athens to Washington, No. 42071, EK/3a, 3/10/55, Frydas Report; Kaloumenos, photographs, roll 1, nos. 7A and 9A-11A.

[204] National Archives, Istanbul to Washington, No. 132, 9/27/55, Carp Report; National Archives, Greek Embassy, Athens to Washington, No. 42071, EK/3a, 3/10/55, Frydas Report.

[205] Greek Embassy, Athens to Washington, No. 42071, EK/3a, 3/10/55, Frydas Report.

[206] *Ibid.*

[207] Chrêstidês, *Ekthesis*, p. 94.

[208] Greek Embassy, Athens to Washington, No. 47021/EK/3a, 10/3/55, Frydas Report; Istanbul *vakıflar*, St. Paraskeue, Beykoz, one *şartname* dated 1/3/57 with little material.

[209] National Archives, Istanbul to Washington, No. 132, 9/27/55, Carp Report; Kaloumenos, photographs, originally roll 35, nos. 1-35, now on diskette; Istanbul *vakıflar*, St. Paraskeue, Büyükdere, has no *şartname*, but has *metraj cedveli* and *keşif özeti*, etc.

[210] National Archives, Istanbul to Washington, No. 132, 9/26/55, Carp Report; Greek Embassy, Athens to Washington, No. 47021, EK/3a, 10/3/55, Frydas Report; Kaloumenos, photographs, roll 29b, nos. 11-14 and 19-23A; roll no. 30, nos. 3A-22A.

[211] Istanbul *vakıflar*, St. Paraskeue, Kazlıçeşme (outside land walls of Yedikule), all dated from 1956 to 1958; the *şartname* is dated 12/23/56.

[212] Chrêstidês, *Ekthesis*, p. 79.

[213] National Archives, Istanbul to Washington, No. 132, 9/26/55, Carp Report.

[214] National Archives, Istanbul to Washington, No. 132, 9/27/55, Carp Report; Istanbul *vakıflar*, St. Paraskeue, Tarabya, one *şartname* is dated 3/1/57 at the beginning of the repairs and the matter had not yet closed in 1962, five years later.

[215] This was an *agiasma* and therefore small by nature; Istanbul *vakıflar*, St. Panteleimon, Çengelköy, with little material that centers about January 1957; Atzemoglou, *T'agiasmata*, pp. 134-135.

[216] This is another of the smaller *agiasmata*; Istanbul *vakıflar*, St. Pantelemon, Hasköy, a few papers dated September 1957; Atzemoglou, *T'agiasmata*, pp. 89-90.

[217] Istanbul *vakıflar*, St. Panteleimon, Kuzguncuk, one *şartname* dated 1/15/57 and accompanying papers on materials and costs.

[218] National Archives, Istanbul to Washington, No. 132, 9/27/55, Carp Report; Kaloumenos, photographs, roll 6, nos. 11A, 14, 17A, 17, 18, and 22; roll 10b is mostly damaged dwellings of Greeks in Ortaköy; roll 21, nos. 1-7, and roll 22, nos. 2-11 and 26-44, are rich in details as to desecration of all types of sacred objects. Istanbul *vakıflar*, St. Phokas, Ortaköy, has two *şartnames* dated 3/15/57 and 10/21/60, respectively.

[219] National Archives, Istanbul to Washington, No. 132, 9/27/55, Carp Report; Greek Embassy, No. 47021, EK/3a, 10/3/55, Frydas Report.

[220] National Archives, Istanbul to Washington, No. 132, 9/27/55, Carp Report; Kaloumenos, photographs, roll 34, nos. 3A and 5A and *varia*, now on diskette.

[221] National Archives, Istanbul to Washington, No. 132, 9/27/55, Carp Report; Istanbul *vakıflar*, Saints Taxiarchs, Balat, one *şartname* of 3/13/57 went into 1958 and shows significant desecration.

[222] National Archives, Istanbul to Washington, No. 132, 9/27/55, Carp Report; Istanbul *vakıflar*, Saints Taxiarchs, İstinye, few documents, possibly few claims.

[223] National Archives, Istanbul to Washington, No. 132, 9/27/55, Carp Report; Kaloumenos, photographs, roll 7b, nos. 19 and 20; roll 9, nos. 4 and 5, now on diskettes; Istanbul *vakıflar*, Saints Theodoroi of Langa, has a *şartname* dated 1960 with the documents ending in 1966. The church had been destroyed and burned.

[224] National Archives, Istanbul to Washington, No. 132, 9/27/55, Carp Report, erroneously attributes this to the "Genethlia tes Theotokou" [Nativity of the Virgin]. It is one and the same church but the name is erroneous. Istanbul *vakıflar*, Koimesis tes Theotokou, Beşiktaş, a short *şartname*, 8/27/57.

[225] National Archives, Istanbul to Washington, No. 132, 9/27/55, Carp Report; Istanbul *vakıflar*, St. Therapon, Sirkeci, one *şartname* on structural damages, 1/3/57.

[226] National Archives, Istanbul to Washington, No. 132, 9/27/55; Carp Report; Greek Embassy, Istanbul to Washington, No. 47021, EK/3a, 10/3/55, Frydas Report; Istanbul

vakıflar, Agia Trias, Kadıköy, one *şartname* and one *keşif özeti*, both dated 3/2/57.

[227] National Archives, Istanbul to Washington, No. 132, 9/27/55, Carp Report; Greek Embassy, Athens to Washington, No. 47021, ER/3a, 10/3/55, Frydas Report; Kaloumenos, photographs, roll 14a, nos. 14A-30A; roll 4b, nos. 16A-26A; on references to and quotes from the sources on desecration and damages inflicted on the Holy Trinity of Taksim, see above Chapter 2. Istanbul *vakıflar*, Agia Trias, Taksim, is a detailed *şartname* and documentation of desecration, destruction, and rebuilding, running from 1957-1959.

[228] National Archives, Istanbul to Washington, No. 132, 9/27/55, Carp Report; Greek Embassy, Athens to Washington, No. 47021, EK/3a, 10/3/55, Frydas Report; Kaloumenos, photographs, roll 32a, nos. 21A-43A; see also Kaloumenos, *Staurôsis*, 1978, nos. 34-47.

[229] National Archives, Istanbul to Washington, No. 132, 9/27/55, Carp Report; Kaloumenos, photographs, rolls 16, nos. 37a, 37b, and 37c; Istanbul *vakıflar*, Panagia Balıklı has much documentation, and the process seems to have gone on from 1959 to 1964, although it may be that there are missing documents of differing dates.

CHAPTER SIX

CRIME AND PUNISHMENT, AND THE TRIAL OF THE MENDERES GOVERNMENT

G reece's efforts to obtain compensation and moral satisfaction for all the Greek victims of the violence resulted in a lengthy political and diplomatic struggle between it and Turkey. The final settlement of the compensation issue was protracted, and the actual rebuilding, repair, and payment to contractors went on as late as 1966, well after the military coup that overthrew Menderes's government, and resulted in the mass arrest of the leaders and representatives of the *Demokrat Parti*, and their trial and punishment. From the very beginning of the controversy over compensation, the Greek government had vigorously insisted on full and rapid payment (neither of which occurred). It had also insisted on justice, that is, on assigning responsibility for the pogrom's planning, organization, and execution. This was, however, by the pogrom's very nature, impossible since Menderes would have had to condemn himself, his ministers, and the chiefs of the security forces. Menderes and Köprülü had openly declared that both the Thessalonikê consular explosion and the pogrom itself were planned, that is, had resulted from a conspiracy. Nonetheless, it came as no surprise that the courts-martial and trials administered by General Aknoz, as well as the continuation of these trials by the civil courts during the first half of 1956, never raised the issue of governmental responsibility. By and large, these courts "reasoned" that because of the national furor over Cyprus, the demonstrations had been excusable and normal. Obviously, Menderes's government would never seek to fix responsibility for a vast crime of which it was, indeed, the parent.

Eventually, Greece's original demand for severe punishment of the pogrom's perpetrators fell on the scrap heap of unsuccessful diplomatic endeavors. Even the matter of compensation would be unsatisfactorily

---

[1] See the earlier chapters of this study; the compensations were generally rudimentary and parsimonious; National Archives, Ankara to Washington, No. 132, September 27, 1955, lists thirty-six of the Greek schools damaged.

concluded.[1] So it was that Greece, in despair, finally abandoned its efforts
to bring to justice those responsible for the crimes. This demand, however,
was to be satisfied, indeed completely fulfilled, in a most unexpected manner
almost five years after the fact. The military coup of May 27, 1960, brought
a massive purge and removal of the entire *Demokrat Parti* and its leadership
from Turkey's governing structure, and even from its political life. All of
the party's leaders, including the government ministers and parliamentary
deputies, were arrested, and its more than 50,000 urban and village *ocaks*
(district chapters) and *bucaks* (district subchapters) were extirpated forever.

From 1954 onward, Menderes had increasingly perverted Turkey's
constitution and gradually imposed an authoritarian hold on the Turkish
parliament. In the cities and provinces, all bureaucrats and elected officials
had to submit to local DP boards and heads. In a similar fashion, Menderes
assumed control of the security and local police, as well as of the labor unions.
State radio had become the political monopoly of the governing party, while
new legislation was used to bridle much of the Turkish press. With his large
majority in parliament (a product of his electoral law), Menderes battered
İnönü's party. At the same time, the corruption of Menderes's government
had become a commonplace. All these factors were highlighted in the
immediate fallout from the pogrom, and continued to escalate until the
crescendo of May 27, 1960, when Menderes was arrested. In many ways,
the pogrom itself, as well as the struggle over compensation, was played out
against this background of the material and moral corruption of Turkey's
leaders. In that (remarkable) sense, the internal rebellions within the DP
over Menderes's growing dictatorial powers and, especially, his cabinet's
corruption, threatened his political career in 1955-1956, and actually led
to his government's fall at the end of November 1955. İnönü's determined
reaction to these authoritarian measures is also remarkable and became such a
burden that Menderes and his party were later accused of an attempt to have
İnönü assassinated at the gate of Topkapı.

All these measures created, in effect, a dictator who enforced his desires
and protected himself by legislation in a parliament dominated by his party,
which could, furthermore, recruit thousands of loyalist thugs to attack not
only opposition leaders, but also newspapers that dared to criticize him. In
effect, as the supreme executive authority, Menderes ruled through the vast
DP organization that coexisted with the official organs of government.

By the end of 1954, Menderes's economic policies had failed; by the
end of his premiership, the value of the Turkish lira had fallen to less than
a third of what it had been at the start, decreasing from 2.8 to 9 to the
American dollar. Meanwhile, İnönü and his Republican People's Party

began to attack Menderes and the DP very aggressively despite the restrictive measures. Although Menderes's popularity among Turkey's rural population was a good electoral guarantee, the real political power was centered in the cities and the army. His authoritarian measures and corruption alienated university professors and students, and began to disturb many heads of the armed forces. All these factors, including the government-sponsored pogrom, reached a head in mid-1960. During the crisis in late 1959 and early 1960 that immediately preceded the coup, Menderes sought to ensure his political position in the face of an ever-widening chasm, but it became difficult even to maintain discipline within the DP's local branches, which had regional rather than national interests, and so he grew increasingly reluctant to call meetings of his own political party. Thus it was that he gained the support of General Rüştü Erdelhun, chief of staff of the Turkish armed forces, who personally guaranteed his security against any military coup. Among Menderes's many concerns and perceptions, his reliance on the army was perhaps the most critical, and the one in which he was most in error.[2]

The political degeneration of the crisis was marked by two events that transpired in parliament. In February 1960, the RPP introduced a number of measures calling for a corruption investigation of Menderes's cabinet. This was followed by an accusation that the national elections of 1957 had been rigged. So heated did the debates become that many deputies resorted to physical violence. It was obvious that Menderes's efforts to attack and destroy the opposition party had reached a very dangerous point. Two months later, on April 18, the DP's deputies established a parliamentary committee to investigate the activities of the RPP, although, apparently, they did so without even seeking formal approval of the parliament as a whole. It was then that İnönü issued his prophetic warning: "If you continue on this road, even I will not be able to save you."[3] As the assembly was controlled by a large DP majority, the party armed the new committee with vast powers aimed, ultimately, at destroying İnönü and his party. In effect, the committee took on unconstitutional powers, which would enable it to undermine the legitimate opposition and its right to criticize the government. Henceforth,

---

[2] For the crisis, Feroz Ahmad, *The Turkish Experience in Democracy, 1950-1975*, Boulder, 1977, pp. 52-99; also H. Bayram Kaçmazoğlu, *Demokrat Parti Dönemi toplumsal tartışmaları*, Istanbul, 1988, pp. 197-226, for an economic analysis of the *Demokrat Parti*'s policies and errors in the Turkish economy; and, finally Erik J. Zürcher, *Turkey: A Modern History*, third edition, London, 2004, pp. 221-240.

[3] Quoted by Walter F. Weiker, *The Turkish Revolution 1960-1961*, Washington, 1963, p. 15; Weiker's work is an excellent guide to the events that led to the military coup of May 27, 1960, and a concentrated presentation of the nineteen trials at Yassıada. For more detailed works on these subjects, see the footnotes below.

all criticism of the government was forbidden, including any criticism by the press of the committee, which replaced civil, administrative, and criminal law. The committee was also empowered with the right to imprison for periods of up to three years and to confiscate property and documents when and where it wished. In the end, the creation of the committee was the capstone in the growing structure of Menderes's authoritarianism. The "icing on the cake" for Menderes was İnönü's removal from parliament for one year.[4]

This series of events had been preceded by the illegal efforts to prevent İnönü from entering the city of Kayseri, where he had been scheduled to speak, on April 2. Through his officials in Kayseri, Menderes had blocked the train tracks and then ordered İnönü to return to Ankara. The latter refused and disbanded the blockade simply by appearing before the soldiers, who kissed his hand and allowed him to pass. By the end of April, the university students of Ankara and Istanbul began to demonstrate over the ongoing situation and professors began to attack the undemocratic measures. This led to clashes with the police and the violation of university asylum. Thereafter, clashes became a nightly affair. On April 21, over a thousand military cadets marched to the presidential mansion to demonstrate their opposition to the security measures. By this time, the officer corps was equally disturbed by and alienated from Menderes; behind General Erdelhun's back, thirty-eight generals and officers formed a junta and joined a conspiracy to seize power.

This they did, bloodlessly and almost effortlessly, in four hours, on May 27. Menderes's policies had provoked the first major military coup to remove a Turkish government and replace it with a military junta, although this one asserted that it would—and actually did—return the reigns of power to a properly elected government. Nevertheless, it had set a successful precedent for future coups and the open entry of the military into the civic and political life of the nation. Who could have foreseen, on October 15, 1961, when the military National Unity Committee (NUC) gave way to free elections, that the Turkish military was, in fact, in politics to stay and would exploit its new position in two other successful coups in the future, thus gradually consolidating its not-so-quiet intervention in all national matters? Indeed, one should recall the analysis of the pogrom by the then-US consul-general in Istanbul: "We believe that the complications of these economic consequences [of the pogrom] affect both the economic stability of the country and its present and future ability to support an effective military establishment."[5] As an institutionalized and dominant factor in Turkish political life, the military

---

[4] *Ibid.*
[5] National Archives, Dispatch No. 138, Istanbul, September 29, 1955.

would also eventually seek an economic expansion of its interests at the costly expense of the Turkish treasury and economy. As such, the US policy of arming Turkey and making military technology accessible to its armed forces remains, to this day, a basic factor in the militarization of Turkish domestic politics and of the Turkish economy.

After the complete and easy victory of the coup, the generals faced a difficult problem: What should they do with the large number of arrested ministers, deputies, and other members of the DP establishment? It was, without a doubt, the most complex of all the problems they had before them. Very quickly, and with some prodding from legal authorities and academics, General Cemal Gürsel, the head of the army who was the junta's leader, and his associates realized that, having removed a government by force, they were faced with the legal problem of justifying the removal. Menderes and his colleagues could not simply be released. The military first appointed the NUC, to run the government and draft a new constitution until a new government could be properly elected the following year; then, a seventeen-member cabinet was announced that reported to the NUC on a variety of civil matters. Of particular concern was the large number of political prisoners and what to do with them. It was decided to try them by a thirty-one-member High Investigating Committee that was appointed to prepare the trials for the 592 arrested defendants.[6]

---

[6] The literature on the trials is massive and for the most part of great interest. The new military authorities were anxious to make the proceedings known throughout the country as they wished to justify their coup to the public. Menderes was particularly popular in the countryside, where farmers had looked upon his measures favorably, and the more credulous of this rural society began to believe that he possessed some kind of semi-immortality (as he had survived an airplane crash).

The trials stretched out for the better part of a year. The best and most concise account is that of Weiker, *The Turkish Revolution*, pp. 25-47. Much has been written by Turkish authors who were either directly involved in the trials (as defendants or defense lawyers), or who were journalists attending them. In many ways, the most interesting and important book was by Hulusi M. Dosdoğru, *6/7 Eylül Olayları*, in which the author chronicled his own experiences during the pogrom, as well as his imprisonment and trial, and quoted extensively from the legal documents and from the minutes of the third trial (on the pogrom), pp. 95-308 and 309-367. His work is particularly important for the light it sheds on the vigorous role played by the local *Demokrat Parti* chapters and their leaders and boards.

The very detailed and well-integrated work of Neoklês Sarrês, *Ê allê pleura*, vol. II, A, pp. 186-273, is certainly the best treatment of Trial 3. Sarrês follows the major sections of the official court *gerekçe* (legal opinion) in establishing the pogrom's conspiratorial nature, the primary responsibility of Menderes, Bayar, Zorlu, and Hadımlı, and the guilt of others. He pays particular attention to the role of the local *Demokrat Parti* chapters in implementing the violence. Throughout his treatment of the trial, Sarrês brings to bear his thorough knowledge of all the Turkish literature that had been published on the subject at the time he wrote his book.

So vast were the dossiers that had to be compiled that it took the High Investigating Committee four months to prepare the indictments and the list of more than a thousand witnesses who would be called to testify. Inasmuch as the junta wished to justify its coup in the eyes both of Turkish citizens and the international community, it organized the systematic dissemination of news and information. Over 150,000 spectators were brought to witness some part of the trials over eleven months. Turkish radio was allotted a section in the courtroom to record every phase of the trials, and then dedicated one hour in the evenings, called the "Yassıada Hour," to the day's proceedings. Meanwhile, the Military Film Center (*Ordu Film Merkezi*) shot newsreels of the trials and showed them frequently to public audiences. In the end, the trials did manage to focus the interest not only of the Turkish but also of the world press to the extent that over four million lines were dedicated to them in the international press (with three Greek journalists among the correspondents covering them). Turkish reporters consumed more than 6,900 hours on telephones sending their stories, while the ministry of communications, which had been charged with preparing and operating the process, compiled an official photographic album of the tribunals from the very arrival of the principals until the execution of the verdicts. The album included 247 photographs depicting every phase of the lives and tribulations of the accused. Thus, just as the pogrom had been extremely well-covered by journalists and photographers, so also were the everyday dramas of the nineteen trials at Yassıada.

The 592 accused individuals fell within the purview of nineteen discrete trials, with the result that some were tried more than once. Menderes, for example, was tried in six different cases, and Zorlu and Bayar in three.

The Turkish authors and works on the pogrom and the trials include, among others: Salim Burçak, *Yassıada ve öncesi*, Ankara, 1976; Emrullah Nutku, *Demokrat Parti neden çöktü ve politikada yitirdiğim yıllar 1946-1958*, Istanbul, 1979; Mahmut Dikerdem, *Ortadoğuda devrin yılları: Bir büyük elçisinin anıları*, Ankara, 1977; Ahmet Hamdi Başar, *Yaşadığımız devrin iç yüzü*, Istanbul, 1971; Ahmet Emin Yalman, *Yakın tarihte gördüklerim ve geçirdiklerim 1945-1970*, Istanbul, 1972; Şevket Süreyya Aydemir, *Menderes Dramı?*, Istanbul, 1969; Fahir H. Armaoğlu, *Kıbrıs meselesi 1954-1959*, Ankara, 1963. Of special importance are the two books by Zorlu's lawyer, Orhan Cemal Fersoy, *Devlet ve hizmet adam Fatin Rüştü Zorlu*, Istanbul, 1979, and *Bir devre adını veren başbakan Adnan Menderes*, Istanbul, 1971.

For some details on the courts-martial held by General Aknoz in 1956: Emin Karakuş, *40 yıllık bu gazeteci gözü ile işte Ankara*, Istanbul, 1977. For other works on the Yassıada trials that have detailed information: Hulusi Turgut, *Menderes/Zorlu/Polatkan'dan yaptırılmayan savunlar: Yassıada Belgeler*, Istanbul, 1982; the massive work of Tekin Erer, *Yassıada ve sonrası*, Istanbul, 1965, is one of the most extensive, with all kinds of information, which is often slightly different from the official accounts; Rasih Nuri İleri, *27 Mayıs Menderes'in Dramı*, Istanbul, 1986, is extremely detailed.

Furthermore, as we have seen, the materials on which the prosecution based its charges were enormous. The burden on the defense lawyers was literally crushing. It was impossible for them to consult all the documentation on which the indictments had been based or to have more than a fleeting consultation with their clients. Fersoy, one of Zorlu's lawyers, justifiably complained that he was hopelessly constrained to prepare his defense by the very short time limits severely enforced on him by the court:

> For this case, up to the time of the defense, there were fifteen court sessions on different days. The carrying-out of the last investigations [by the court] and the reading of the indictments took fifty hours and twenty minutes. In addition, there was the hearing of ninety-seven witnesses. The first investigation was based on twenty-eight cartons of documents and then in addition twenty-nine cartons were added for the final investigation. These cartons contained thousands of pages of reports, journals, newspapers, vouchers, and other documents. Then there were the written proceedings of the session [more than 2,000 pages] and permission was not granted to consult them. So I made use of the notes I had written down during the sessions as well as of printed materials from the press.[7]

Further, the judges were free to attack the accused on political grounds. Despite the serious shortcomings of the proceedings as a whole—and here one recalls the Perkins memorandum on Turkish justice—and the fact that courts, judges, and justice in Turkey were compliant to the political demands of the government, the mountains of evidence, and the actions of Menderes's government, were so flagrant and violent that the latter's guilt of many of the accusations stood out even in these truncated proceedings.

Seventeen of the trials were incorporated into the more general crime of violation of the constitution (*Anayasayı İhlal*). The trial regarding the pogrom of September 6-7, 1955, was also one of the most important of the nineteen trials, second, indeed, only to the case of violating the constitution. In the event, some of the files of those in the pogrom case were merged with those in the case of violating the constitution. Thus, it is incorrect to state that those found guilty of the pogrom received only moderate jail sentences and small fines. They were also accused, on the very *basis* of responsibility for the pogrom, of violating the Turkish constitution.[8]

The relentless wheels of Turkish justice turned rapidly, and on September 13, 1961, the NUC announced that the tribunal's verdicts would be formally

---

[7] Fersoy, *Zorlu*, p. 230.
[8] On this eradication of the vast DP machine, Erer, *Yassıada ve sonrası*, pp. 454-460.

Table 57: Corruption cases

Case	Trial dates	Accusations	Sentences
The dog	10/24/60	Bayar forces İzmir zoo to purchase an Afghan hound.	Ökmen given 5 years and barred from public office; Bayar given 4 years, 2 months, and barred from office.
Pogrom of September 6-7, 1955	10/20/60-1/5/61	Conspiracy to destroy Greek property in Istanbul and Izmir; case merged with that of violating the constitution.	Menderes and Zorlu given 6 years; Hadımlı, 4 months, 15 days; Köprülü, Belin, Tekinalp, Uçar, and Engin acquitted. The civil rights of Gökay and Eriş deprived. Fines of TL375 and TL250, respectively, to Menderes and each of the others.
The infanticide	10/31-11/22/60	Menderes and a Dr. Atabey charged with aborting former's child.	Both acquitted.
Vinylex	11/4-11/26/60	Polatkan receives bribe to secure favorable terms for loans for N. Dolay and H. Altan.	Case merged with that of violating the constitution.
Fraud	11/11-12/3/60	H. Erkmen and B. Mandalinci for financial fraud.	Mandalinci acquitted; Erkmen given 6 months, and case merged with that of violating the constitution.
Sale of lots to government	11/8-11/26/60	N. Ökmen sells wife's lot to agricultural ministry at exorbitant price.	Ökmen given 5 years and barred from public office.
İpar, transport ships	11/15/60-1/19/61	Zorlu, Menderes, 3 ministers, and İpar violate currency laws.	İpar fined TL26,790,285 and sentenced to 2 years; Zorlu, Menderes, and Berk sentenced to 1 year each; Polatkan, Erkmen, and Ataman sentenced to 3 months each; cases merged with that of violating the constitution.
The mill	11/18/60-12/3/60	Minister Yırcalı sells government mill to businessman Ş. Demirkan.	Case merged with that of violating the constitution; statute of limitations expired.
Nurse Barbara	11/21-12/20/60	Exchange fraud of Koraltan and Polatkan.	Koraltan given 5 months, 25 days; Polatkan, 6 months. Both cases merged with that of violating the constitution.
Abuse of discretionary funds	11/25/60-2/2/61	Menderes and Korur.	Menderes given 14 years, 2 months; Korur, 8 years, 9 months.

Political monopoly of state radio	11/29–12/26/60	Menderes, Zorlu, Sarol, Kalafat, Yardımcı, Yırcalı, Aker, Shaman, and Kılıç.	Kılıç acquitted; all other cases merged with that of violating the constitution.
Topkapı events	12/2/60–4/17/61	60 accused of planned violence against İnönü.	16 acquitted; 9 given 3 years, 9 months, each; 9 given 7 years, 9 months. Cases of Menderes, Bayar, Yetkiner, and Aygün merged with that of violating the constitution.
Çanakkale/Geyikli events	12/27/60–3/10/61	Menderes and officials hinder movement of RPP politicians.	Cases of Menderes and 2 officials merged with that of violating the constitution; Sezgin given 10 years, Sezen, 7 years.
Kayseri events	1/9–4/20/61	Bayar, Menderes, DP deputies, Kayseri *vali*, and security official hinder campaign of İnönü.	Cases of Menderes and Bayar merged with that of violating the constitution; *vali* and security official get 4 years, 2 months; Kayseri DP deputies acquitted.
Demokrat İzmir newspaper	1/12–5/5/61	İzmir DP leaders recruit members and destroy anti-Menderes newspaper, *Demokrat İzmir*.	16 condemned, 14 acquitted; cases of Menderes, Hadımlı, and Tunca merged with that of violating the constitution.
Ankara-Istanbul events	2/2–7/27/61	Menderes, Bayar, and 117 (police, general, government officials) accused of firing on students and demonstrators, and violating university asylum.	Condemned but cases merged with that of violating the constitution; Bayar, A. Menderes, E. Menderes, Berk, Akçal, Yardımcı, Zorlu, Polatkan, Benderlioğlu, İleri, Erkmen, Husman, Ökmen, Ergin, Şaman, Ataman, Aker, and 51 others given prison terms; 41 acquitted.
Expropriation of property	4/17–6/3/61	Improper expropriation of property for construction.	Menderes and 1 other convicted; 7 acquitted; case of Menderes merged with that of violating the constitution.
National Front	4/27–6/21/61	Promoting anti-democratic goals of the *Vatan Cephesi*.	Menderes, Berk, Benderlioğlu, İleri, Koraltan cases, and 14 others are merged with that of violating the constitution; 3 others acquitted.

| Violating the constitution | 5/11-9/15/61 | 1. Confiscating property of People's Republican Party. 2. Demoting Kırşehir to status of *ilçe*, for political reasons. 3. Violating security of judges and independence of courts. 4. Anti-democratic alteration of electoral law. 5. Altering parliament's rules of order and regulation, and creating investigating commission. 6. Legislating Law 6761 on gatherings and demonstrations. 7. Decisions taken by the investigating commission before passing Law 7468. 8. Creating investigating commission with Law 7468 without authority of parliament. 9. Seventeen [eventually sixteen] of nineteen cases merged with this case. | Of the 395 present at the trial, 47 were acquitted and 348 received sentences that ranged from 4 years, 2 months, in prison to death.[9] |

[9] The sources utilized are basically in agreement as to the details in this table: Weiker, *The Turkish Revolution*, pp. 30-31; the journal *Hayat*'s insert, "Kararları," pp. 1-16; Turgut, *Yassıada ve sonrası*, pp. 44-99; and Erer, *Yassıada ve sonrası*, pp. 565-566. There were originally nineteen cases at Yassıada, but seventeen were subsumed into the overarching case of contravention of the constitution. The case of the sale of the state mill, however, was eventually dropped because the statute of limitations on it had expired, which left a total of eighteen cases, with sixteen included in that of constitutional violation.

presented to the accused on September 15. On that day, the communications ministry announced the decisions to the public, stating further that sixteen cases (including that of the pogrom) would be merged with the case of violating the constitution. On the same day, the NUC forbade any office or individual to give information on the trials except for the ministry of communications.

The trials had lasted for eleven months and one day, from October 14, 1960, to September 15, 1961. There had been 287 sessions over 203 days, lasting for 1,033 hours, in addition to the 1,068 hours for hearing the army of witnesses. Although the prosecution had asked for 228 death penalties, the court handed down death penalties in only fifteen cases. Thirty defendants were sentenced to life imprisonment, 402 were given shorter prison terms, 133 were acquitted, and five cases were dropped. The fifteen death sentences had to be approved by the National Unity Committee, which commuted twelve to imprisonment.[10]

Late in the evening of September 15, the vast majority of prisoners were shipped off to their prisons. The two to be hanged (Bayar had been spared as he was over sixty-five)—Zorlu (aged fifty-one) and Polatkan (aged forty-six)—were dispatched by military boat to the island of İmralı, whereas Menderes (aged sixty-two) was ill and the doctors did not approve his removal until the following day. Zorlu and Polatkan were hanged in the early hours of September 16 (3:05 AM). On September 17, Menderes was transported to İmralı and remained in his tiny cell long enough for the chief prosecutor of the court to read the sentence to him inasmuch as Menderes had been absent from the court proceedings following his illness. The former prime minister remained in his cell another ten minutes or so smoking a Yenice cigarette while two imams recited the Islamic funeral rites. He was then led to the gallows, upon which he was raised. His executioner placed the noose about his neck; Menderes recited his last prayers, and was hanged.[11]

The communications ministry photographed the three hanging bodies, draped in white robes upon which the *hücum özeti* (summary of charges) had been attached. On the day of execution, the same *hücum özeti* was affixed

[10] Erer, *Yassıada ve sonrası*, p. 566; his figure for the number of sessions, 272, is in error and should read 287. Weiker, *The Turkish Revolution*, p. 28, lists only 202, but the number is erroneous. The decisions were read out to the 574 accused in twenty-four sessions of twenty-four accused each during the course of the morning and afternoon. Only the decisions were read out. The printed *gerekçes* were given to the lawyers of the defendants. There were more than 130 lawyers present on September 15 when the decisions were delivered.

[11] For details of the hanging, Erer, *Yassıada ve sonrası*, pp. 626-642; for the photographs, see the photographic insert in this book. It is noteworthy that of the six executioners brought to İmralı, only two were ethnic Turks; the other four were Roma.

to the front door of each condemned man's home in Ankara. The verdicts were intended to operate on two levels. At the higher level, the tribunal condemned three of the four principal conspirators for violating the Turkish constitution. At a lower level, the entire organizational structure of the *Demokrat Parti* was extirpated. Thus, the party was destroyed at the lowest level while it was also decapitated at its summit. Still, the *vali* of Izmir, Kemal Hadımlı, was given one of the lightest sentences. And the two Turkish consuls of Thessalonikê, Mehmet Ali Belin and Mehmet Ali Tekinalp, as well as the consular doorman, Hasan Uçar, and the student Oktay Engin and certain others, were acquitted. This left the question unanswered, however, as to who had been responsible for the Thessalonikê episode. Clearly, the tribunal and the NUC were now solely interested in doing away with the highest leadership of the Menderes regime. It was enough to condemn Menderes, Zorlu, and Hadımlı, although the latter's sentence was a token one. A strong sign of this political strategy was that the indictments concerning the pogrom avoided charges of murder and rape, of which there had been evidence even in the civil trials of 1956. The *iddianame* specified that the pogrom had been a crime against Greek property and not against persons, although the civil cases of 1956 had referred to both rape and murder. These accusations were not carried over into the indictments of Menderes's government, obviously because the implications would have been tantamount to charges of a partial genocide.[12]

The military junta, with its professors of law, saw to it that the destruction of Menderes's government and its party cadres was based on a substantial legal underpinning. Of particular importance in this respect was the *gerekçe* inasmuch as it placed responsibility for the actual physical destruction of Greek property (and of the property of the Jewish and Armenian minorities) not only on the government but also on the presidents, boards, and numerous thugs of the local DP organizations. This combination of direction and organization of formidable acts of violence against various segments of Turkish society (religious and ethnic groups, political institutions, and the press) was not unique to the pogrom, however. It was, in fact, the base for charges against Menderes and his government in several other cases, all of which involved local officials, boards, members, and affiliates of the countless DP chapters.

***

Before proceeding to the general conclusions of this study, it is necessary

---

[12] Much of this has been discussed throughout the earlier parts of this book.

to address one final issue. This narrative of the pogrom, which had such a destructive effect on the Greeks of Turkey, has concentrated on an analysis and reconstruction of the decision to effect the violence, the actual execution of it, the extent of the damage, the diplomatic wars that raged around all these issues, as well as on the nature of their final "resolution." In so doing, this study has, of necessity, dealt with the grisly aspects of a particular Turkish government as well as with the criminality of its organs, which were charged with actually executing the pogrom.

There is, however, another side to the matter, and to Turkish society more generally, albeit very limited in extent: those Muslims and secularists (and Turkish communists) who came to the assistance of individual Greeks in those hours of cruelty and horror. The circumstances behind this assistance and support is evident from the fifty Greek eyewitness accounts preserved in Pênelopê Tsoukatou's book. Of these reports, at least ten refer specifically and clearly to critical assistance, warnings, and personal intervention to save Greek businesses, dwellings, and two churches, and even to stop rapes. In all these cases, those who intervened were Muslims and included Kurds, Turko-Cretans, Albanians, and Turks.

Symeôn Vafeiadês, who lived in Kuzguncuk (and later emigrated to Australia with his family), was in the produce business in Gemiş. On the morning of September 7, he set out to inspect his store and the damage it had suffered. As he passed through the commercial quarter, he relates that the destruction was so great that it appeared that a typhoon had passed over all the shops. Everything had been looted, or destroyed, and thrown into the streets. Because of the rains, the earth had turned to mud, which had mixed in with the olive oil, potatoes, and other matter that had been thrown on the ground. Such was the quagmire that it took many days to clean up. On finally arriving at his business, however, Vafeiadês was relieved to see that it had only suffered minor damage. It had been saved, he says,

> because a Turkish neighbor, a bookkeeper, who, immediately upon learning what was happening, contacted a *hamal* [porter], Hasan, and told him to run and save our business. He, with another Kurd, stood in front of the store and did not allow the demonstrators to destroy it. Thus, it survived with minor damage.
>
> We asked Hasan who had wished to destroy the store. He replied, "Do not ask me for you are acquainted with most of them, but I cannot tell you their names."[13]

---

[13] Tsoukatou, *Septemvriana*, p. 61; Vafeiadês gives a brief aside about Hasan: "Everyone believed that Hasan was a Kurd. In reality, he was of Armenian descent. In 1916, during the massacres, he was then a little boy and he had been taken in by a Turkish family. The fate of his

What is interesting in this incident is that the man responsible for saving the Vafeiadês business was a Turkish bookkeeper who obviously knew the owners personally, doubtlessly through business contacts, while the two men who actually saved the shop were a crypto-Armenian and a Kurd.

Another witness observed the beginning of the attacks in her neighborhood, on Sıraselviler Caddesi just to the east of İstiklal Caddesi. Soon after they began on the night of September 6, her husband returned from their shop, having quickly shut it to protect his wife, who was in her last month of pregnancy. The husband, not wishing to distress her, merely said to his wife that "the Turks have been aroused and are shouting." But she had seen the destruction in their own neighborhood and was already distressed. The testimony is of more general interest for it also draws a picture of how one person reacted to the pogrom and to the threat of violence. In the event, there was one aspect that the husband could not hide from his wife. She relates: "We had cases of beer at home. Half of the bottles were still full, but the others were empty. I saw that my husband was emptying all those bottles that were full into the sink, and then filling them with gas. He told me that in case the mob entered the apartment building and attempted to come up the stairs, he would set fire to the bottles and hurl them down on the mob since we were on the fourth floor." Indeed, soon after, the mob began to throw rocks and broke the window in their living room.

> At that moment our doorman, Sadık, came and asked us if we had a Turkish flag. Inasmuch as we are [sic] Greek citizens, we did not have one.
>
> Meanwhile, they [the rioters] smashed the outside door. Sadık, however, placed his body in front of the door and, while holding on to both doorjambs, shouted that everyone was absent and that only his family was present and that presently he would be displaying a Turkish flag. The demonstrators stated that they would return. And so they departed…in a hurry so that they could smash, destroy, rape, and plunder as many Greeks as possible. Sadık went out, he detached a Turkish flag, that is, stole it from another apartment building, and hung it outside our apartment building, and thus we were saved.
>
> Of course, our doorman was a Kurd and the next day the owner of the building rewarded him.[14]

parents remained unknown. When he grew up, he managed to locate relatives in France and he corresponded with them."

[14] *Ibid.*, pp. 107-108; the subject of the Greeks' reaction to their tormentors has been touched upon elsewhere and will recur in the documentation that follows.

The Kurdish doorman was fearless in facing the mob and, possibly, also felt an obligation to his employers.

Another witness relates what happened at Paşabahçe on the Asian shore of the Bosphorus. The large number of pogromists brought to the area on the ferryboat Üsküdar #72 simply overpowered the local police *komiser* (chief), but he nevertheless managed to keep them from destroying the apartment of Aristos Zekopoulos, who lived above his coffeeshop (which was destroyed). In addition, he halted the attack on the Church of Saints Constantine and Helen, although the soldiers sent to guard the church the next day broke its windows: "They also say that that the police *komiser* informed the police of the nearby suburb Beykoz, and the police chief of the latter refused to allow the ferryboat Üsküdar to dock, and...let the demonstrators disembark."[15] Such actions, rare in the police annals of September 6-7, managed to minimize the damages inflicted in these areas.

Yet another witness, who lived in Cihangir near Sıraselviler Caddesi, recounted how the doorman of the Nennan Apartments, Tahir Efendi, dissuaded the mob from looting the apartment of the well-known metropolitan of Ikonion, Iakôvos.[16] Maria Andreou Kanakês, a resident of Çengelköy, related the destruction of her family house at the hands of the rioters and of the cadets of the nearby military academy of Kuleli. In contrast, the family factory in Galata survived the savage destruction of most Greek businesses in the area: "My husband departed for Istanbul to see if his factory...which was in Galata...had been destroyed. On arrival, he saw a policeman, for whom he had done a favor the previous week, standing, watching, and guarding the front door."[17]

On most occasions, the Muslim fellow citizens of the Greeks were in no position to hinder or divert the mob, but nevertheless even when the property of Greeks was being destroyed, there were Muslims who attempted to console the victims and in some cases to give them sound advice. In Chapter 2, I cited Lilika Kônstantinidês's account of the destruction of her business. She and her husband had just returned home from the store when a Turkish employee came to inform them that it had been attacked. So the husband returned and took whatever measures to protect his property (including removing the cash from the register), and, finally, took a safe position from which he could monitor what was happening.

In a little while, a group of fifteen to twenty people...entered

---

[15] *Ibid.*, pp. 89-90.
[16] *Ibid.*, p. 85.
[17] In this case, a policeman broke ranks to repay a favor and managed to do so successfully.

[and] began to smash everything in the store....My husband
was watching from across the street as twenty years of labor was
reduced to ruins....A Turkish neighbor tapped him on the back
and said to him: "Leave. You cannot do anything, you will simply
become sick."[18]

The Turkish employee and Turkish neighbor were neither police nor soldiers
nor politicians and so could not alter the fate of the couple's store, but one
perceives in the concerns of the two Turks their regard and compassion both
for the store and for the well-being of the Kônstantinidêses.

Despoina Isaakidou's account is much more complicated and dramatic.
The family's house was near the Church of St. George in Edirnekapı and
her father owned a small snack-bar nearby. On the afternoon of September
6, a Turkish friend warned Mr. Isaakidês to close his shop and hasten home
to protect his family as something terrible was about to happen. Finally, his
house was attacked and the family was forced to flee (the attacker was the
Sergeant Kırmızı mentioned earlier in the book): "During the course of the
looting, a Turko-Cretan family came from across the street and gathered us in
their house to protect us.... " The next day, her mother and she decided to
revisit their vandalized home in order to get clothing for an infant sibling. On
arrival, they found the house "guarded" by three Turkish soldiers, but finally
got permission to enter. At that point, two of the soldiers seemed ready to
attack the mother and Despoina, while the third one stood guard outside:
"Then, like a *deus ex machina*, [a] Turkish friend of my father, who had tried
the previous evening to return to our house but found the roads blocked,
appeared. He ran into the yard and shouted at the soldiers: 'What else do you
want? You've burned down their livelihood [the shop], you've blackened their
souls. Leave their honor alone....' He was so furious that he grabbed both of
them and threw them out of the house."[19] This family had been violated in the
most fundamental way. Nevertheless, not only were there neighbors that took
them in and protected them, but a Turkish friend did not abandon his efforts
to find their house despite the curfew and the difficulties of the moment.

Kônstantinos Katsaros's family lived in Cihangir but had been summering
on Heybeliada; when they returned to their house in Cihangir the next day,
they learned that it "had been saved because our doorman, Ömer, probably of
Kurdish descent, prevented the barbarians from entering."[20] Peter Tsoukatos
was nine years old at the time and staying with his aunt; when he returned

[18] Tsoukatou, *Septemvriana*, pp. 101-102.
[19] *Ibid.*, pp. 147-148.
[20] *Ibid.*, p. 151.

to his family's house, "I learned that our apartment building had been saved because our doorman—a Kurd from Van—Mehmet...a *pallêkari* [a brave and stalwart youth], stood before our apartment building keeping guard and would not allow the mob to destroy it." Mehmet insisted that no Greeks lived in the building and had taken care to hang a Turkish flag in front of it.[21] Again, one notes the actions of a Kurdish doorman who took his duties seriously, as opposed to the looting and vandalism in which so many other doormen took part on that night.

Mênas Mauromatês, an inhabitant of Çengelköy, recounted that when the demonstrators attempted to enter his building, "Our Turkish cohabitants descended to the entrance and refused to allow the demonstrators to enter, saying that there were no Greeks in the building."[22] In her letter of September 20, 1955, to Tatiana, Despoina Portokallis comments on a few more good *komiseres*:

> In Paşabahçe on the Bosphorus, the good police *komiseris* who saved the church and people from pillaging and burning appeared; a *komiseris* with only a pistol in his hand saved the church of Feriköy. A third saved the island of Antigonê [Burgazada]. Imagine what would have happened if the entire police force had acted thus....In the *Pasaj* Agnavor [a shopping area in new Istanbul], the Turkish guard and his wife struggled with the mob....And they did not let them enter. Thus were these stores saved. The shopowners raised 8,000 liras as a reward to the guard and his wife for saving them. The other *pasajes* were given over to the flames."[23]

Certainly the most touching example of kindness and assistance at a very humble level is that of Hulusi M. Dosdoğru's care of an old Greek woman, her daughter, and a mentally handicapped dependent after the three were thrown out on the street of Ortaköy by the pogromists. Since Dosdoğru, a physician and writer, was arrested as a communist, he wrote his book to chronicle the event, as well as his arrest, imprisonment, and prosecution.

His account of what he witnessed and experienced in Ortaköy during the night of September 6-7 is not only well-structured, but is particularly detailed on the destruction of Greek shops and dwellings, as his balcony looked out on the central marketplace. When a wave of pogromists attempted to enter the apartment building, for example, they were blocked by a resident who

---

[21] *Ibid.*, pp. 157-158.
[22] *Ibid.*, p. 163; for yet another example of Turkish assistance, see p. 139, in which a Greek doctor's clinic was protected successfully by the Turkish doorman of the entire building.
[23] Despoina Portokallis to Tatiana, September 20, 1955.

happened to be the colonel in charge of provisioning the Turkish army. Having donned his military uniform, he and his son refused to allow the demonstrators entry. The latter insisted that there were Greeks in the building. The colonel maintained that they had moved out. Interestingly enough, the demonstrators then replied that this was the building where the communist doctor (Dosdoğru) lived and they insisted that they be allowed to go to his apartment and settle accounts. The colonel was adamant in his refusal and the matter ended there. It is clear that the demonstrators' leadership was extremely well-informed, not only on the Greeks but on Dosdoğru as well, an obvious indication of the involvement of the security police.

In the morning, Dosdoğru went out to purchase provisions from his Greek grocer only to find the marketplace a ruin. He managed to buy a newspaper and was able to read the accounts of the previous night. He then went to see the destroyed apartments, houses, and shops of his neighborhood and was shocked at what he saw. His description of Ortaköy's destroyed marketplace and Greek dwellings is an important primary source for the events in the area. Dosdoğru then became concerned with a very elderly Greek widow who lived in Ortaköy known as *Yiayia* (Greek for grandmother), who was in the poultry business with her husband. Well-known throughout Ortaköy for her generosity and kindness to the poor, whether Greek or Turkish, Dosdoğru finally arrived before what was left of her house.

> When I came to *Yiayia*'s house I could not believe what I saw. Refrigerators, pantries, mirrors, were smashed and piled up before the building. Beds and quilts had been cut up, their cotton stuffing, as though thrown out, was scattered throughout the neighborhood; shirts, shoes, blankets, carpets, *kilims*, were shredded. Pots and pans, glasses and plates, were smashed into bits. The iron of the beds was smashed to bits, chandeliers, shopwindows, tables, chairs, armchairs, couches, were smashed into small pieces with sledgehammers.
>
> Firewood, coal, gas, salt, sugar, butter and eggs lay poured out into the streets. Heaters and their pipes had been smashed into small pieces, and trunks with all kinds of goods were chopped up bit by bit.
>
> A little higher up from *Yiayia*'s house in a corner of the garden of her building, it was as though a bomb had exploded inside. The building had been transformed into a pile of rubble.
>
> Short, rotund, and though advanced in age, the red of her plump cheeks had not paled…she shed tears…as she contemplated the ruins. At her side was her daughter, Athêna…who now tore her hair and head: "I don't have anything, no passport [she lived in

Greece], no identity card, for they tore them to pieces. Now how can I return to my house," and she continued to weep.

Yiayia's hunting dog, Rex, had been savagely beaten with a club by the demonstrators. The poor animal's glance was turned toward *Yiayia* as though thanking her for saving its life from the hands of the mob.

The half-demented child, Osanna, lamented on her knees. Their heads crowded together, a voice came out from them but it was incomprehensible as to who said what. It was difficult to separate them but finally I was able to touch...*Yiayia's* shoulder. For awhile, she stared at my face and then she came to and cried out: "Look at what has befallen us...," and she fell at my feet.

I took her by the shoulder, raised her, and said to her, "Come now, let's get a grip on ourselves. There's no sense in our remaining here." And taking all three, I brought them to my house. They washed their faces and I gave them sedatives, and then forced them to eat a bowl of soup. They lay down for a while until *Yiayia's* oldest son came and took them.[24]

This account is important evidence that not all Turks approved of, let alone believed in, the cruel oppression of Greek Christians. As a leftist, Dosdoğru had been jailed on previous occasions by the government. On the night of September 7, the security police abruptly entered his apartment, began to abuse him and his wife, and arrested him as a communist who had supposedly taken part in the demonstrations. He was then taken to the military prison of Harbiye and left there to await his trial and fate. Knowing full well what was awaiting him even before his arrest, he was nevertheless moved by the unjust tragedy that had overtaken the three women who were left desolate with their badly beaten dog on the streets of Ortaköy. He aroused them from their shock, calmed them down, cleaned them, treated them medically, fed them, and then gave them rest and shelter. He was a veritable Turkish leftist Good Samaritan who carried out his medical oath as well as the oath and laws of humanity.

There is a later section in Dosdoğru's book that includes some of the experiences of his fellow detainees. Of special interest is the brief narrative of Oflu Hasan. Dosdoğru writes:

Hasan was in Galata taking his coffee on a street, when the riots began and a group of Greek owners of large ship-supply stores approached him. Hasan told them: "If you give me TL10,000, I'll take two or three men from the streets and defend your

[24] Dosdoğru, *6/7 Eylül Olayları*, pp. 29-30.

stores until the riots end." The storeowners paid him the money willingly. Accordingly, Hasan was able to save their stores on this street from the attackers.

The court-martial sought tax on this money. Now Hasan was in his cell, which was covered with rugs and prayer rugs and silk coverings. He had on his silk *robe de chambre* and was enjoying a smoke and drinking mouthfuls of thick black coffee…when he was brought an arrest warrant from the court-martial and the demand that he sign it.

Hasan said, "I shall read no farther. I do not understand the law. Leave the document and I shall show it to my lawyer. If he tells me to sign it, I shall do so."…

As the noncommissioned officer departed, Hasan said to me: "Look, doctor, at these men. When the police stood idly by as spectators, it was I who saved the stores of those men from destruction. That is to say, I persisted in those duties that the police abandoned, and they gave me money and did so willingly. And now they want me to give them money? Is this not impossible?"

And Hasan tore up the arrest warrant that he had been given to sign. "Look, doctor, after awhile, they will forget this [document] they gave me. I shall put my lawyer in motion. I shall ask for the arrest warrant, but they will not be able to find it in my file. The lawyer, at the first hearing, will ask: 'Where is my client's arrest warrant? Since there is no arrest warrant, how is it that you hold him under arrest? According to the law, I am demanding his discharge.'"[25]

And so it came to pass that Oflu was discharged from prison. As he departed with his rugs, prayer rugs, silk coverlets, and *robe de chambre*, with his coffee and brewing utensils, and supplies of cigarettes, he reminded Dosdoğru, "I told you that this is how it would end. Now good luck to you." He returned to his beloved street haunts awaiting other capital enterprises that the state did not provide the citizen.

This narrative clearly reflects some interesting aspects of the "facts of life" on the streets and in the prisons of Istanbul. It reflects, first, a street world that lived off society because of the crime and corruption of the government and police. There was a natural body of toughs, but toughs who were highly intelligent, and whose native intelligence and perception of the shortcomings of governmental and security services allowed them to provide those services to those of their fellow citizens who were able to pay for them. In other words,

[25] Dosdoğru, *Ibid.*, pp. 49-51.

they sold, illegally, their services to the public. Hasan was certainly extremely intelligent, and he feared neither the government nor the police, as he was familiar with lawyers and the rules of legal procedure, and had an excellent lawyer whom he paid to defend him. His personal standards of esthetics and comfort were not sacrificed even in the harsh circumstances of Harbiye prison; under his careful planning, jail was something that would be borne for a short period and under maximum comfort and ease. At worst, it was a matter of free rent. On the street, Hasan was fearless; certainly, the Greek shopowners knew who he was and decided that he was the man to solve their problems. No doubt he had performed earlier services for them or for those whom they knew. These smart street toughs in effect performed badly needed, if illicit, services for citizens who lived in a lawless state in which such things as security of property and human rights were not only neglected but were often violated by the state itself.

I have made the effort in this book to analyze the Turkish pogrom of September 6-7, 1955, which caused massive material and moral damage to the Greek minority and *établis* of the greater Istanbul region. In the half century that has elapsed since the attack, a considerable body of important materials that deal with it has emerged. A careful analysis of these sources enables one now to place the event within its historical context, and particularly within a political, economic, and social framework. This event constitutes an important chapter, not only for the fate of minorities in modern Turkey, but for the evolution and formation of the modern Turkish state and society. At the end of the ten-year rule of Adnan Menderes and the *Demokrat Parti*, many of Turkey's problems reached a stage of such disorder and seeming intractability that they ushered in five decades of political domination by the military. The latter's anti-minority and anti-religious policies, and its ambitions (occasionally successful, unfortunately) for territorial aggrandizement, were not only salient features of its political supremacy in Turkey, but were ingrained, until very recently, in the country's political establishment. This underdevelopment of democratic institutions and violation of human rights were blatantly manifested in the pogrom, in its consequences, and in post-pogrom Turkey.

Naturally, any treatment of the pogrom immediately becomes ensnared in the historical, political, and diplomatic literature, and depends on the points of view of the authors, politicians, and diplomats who have concerned themselves with the events. The DP government in Turkey was particularly vexed by this problem—specifically, by the question of responsibility for conceiving, organizing, and executing the violence. The Menderes government followed a policy of suppressing, and indeed destroying, evidence, and it resorted to martial law, kangaroo courts (both military and civilian), and suspension of free speech in an effort to redirect blame from itself onto others. Governmental control of Turkey's judicial system involved the bondage and corruption of the latter, as well as the tradition of the "gizli devlet," that is, the "hidden state" (or, as it's been called more recently, the "derin devlet," or "deep state").

Indeed, the treatment of Turkey's minorities during the Young Turk regime of the rapidly declining Ottoman empire established a ruthless tradition that became ingrained in Kemalist nationalism. Discriminatory legislation against minorities, particularly aimed at removing Greek *établis* from many professions and economic specializations, appeared in the 1930s. The most vicious of these efforts occurred during the Second World War, when the Saracoğlu government believed that Hitler and the Nazis' racist policies and theories would prevail, and Greece was occupied by the Germans (and thus unable to come to the assistance of the Greek minority in Turkey). The Turkish government enforced mass conscription of all Greek, Jewish, and Armenian males of the so-called "twenty generations" (ages 19-38) into labor battalions and then marched them off into Asia Minor to hard labor. This act was followed by legislation that imposed the so-called *varlık vergisi* (a confiscatory tax on property and estates), which provided that, within fifteen days of assessment on an individual or company, the assessed had to pay the full amount, with severe consequences for failure to do so. The Greeks, Jews, Armenians, and even Dönmes were taxed at ten times the taxes levied on Muslim Turks. Those unable to pay, including members of one's extended family, were sent off to Aşkale, Turkey's Siberia, and there consigned to harsh labor and to the rigors of the climate. Many died from the experience, and the measure destroyed the economic basis of these minority communities at one fell swoop. Accordingly, the late Ottoman tradition of hostility toward minorities stayed alive, and indeed thrived, to the end of the Second World War. The pogrom of September 6-7, 1955, was to prove to be a particularly violent continuation of this reality, surpassed only in the last twenty years of the twentieth century by the brutal suppression of the Kurdish minority in eastern Anatolia.

The immediate background to the pogrom was Turkish political life during the first five years of the DP's exercise of state authority and control of government. On the international stage, the decolonization of the British empire was to be dramatically played out in Cyprus and at the Suez Canal, both strategic sites in the waterways linking much of Europe, the Middle East, and India. The Eden government was, at the time, determined to retain control of Cyprus and, at the very least, maintain its strategic military base there. The Greek Cypriots' desire, which went back to the 1930s, to be united with Greece could not be stifled, however, and the issue was hotly contested with the Papagos government, whose attempt to defend the principle of Cypriot self-determination at the United Nations was particularly threatening to the UK. In the face of this effort, the British government turned to US secretary of state John Foster Dulles, who successfully recruited the votes in the UN to defeat the Greek challenge. At the same time, British foreign secretary Harold Macmillan prevailed upon Turkey to alter its policy on Cyprus and make vigorous representations as to its claims and rights on the island.

Previously, Turkey's foreign minister, Mehmet Fuat Köprülü, had formally announced that Cyprus was a British and not a Turkish concern, a statement for which he was to be severely criticized by a number of prominent Turks. Meanwhile, a Foreign Office official would comment in a confidential memorandum that "a few riots" in Turkey would serve Britain "nicely." Other factors no doubt played a role in Menderes's decision to take on the Cyprus issue and thus begin to give an ear and support to those who favored such a change in Turkish policy. By mid-1954, Menderes's economic policies had caused a shortage of foreign exchange (from overspending on imports), inflation, and increasing distress for most economic strata. It had become more and more obvious that the government lacked any sound, systematic economic program. Further, Menderes and his immediate circle progressively abandoned the original DP principle of wider participation in government for policies that crippled the opposition and violated democratic values. Cyprus would divert attention from this generally gloomy environment, and redirect passions and fanaticism toward the Greek minority and *établis* of Istanbul. In the remaining five and a half years of Menderes's premiership, these tendencies would so distort Turkey's political life and institutions that the system would collapse with the intervention of the Turkish military and the violent extinction of the *Demokrat Parti,* some of its leaders, and parliamentary deputies.

Menderes's new Cyprus policy was eventually accompanied by Fatin Rüştü Zorlu's appointment as acting foreign minister. Zorlu's replacement of Köprülü signaled an openly aggressive policy on Cyprus and promoted a small group in the foreign ministry that inaugurated a very hostile approach toward Greeks in general, whether of Cyprus, Greece, or, above all, Istanbul. This group around Zorlu composed Turkey's official position paper on Cyprus, and a few formed the core of his mission to the London conference. As for Zorlu himself, he not only became acting foreign minister, but Turkey's ambassador to NATO and president of the (foreign) exchange commission—in short, the second most important official in the Turkish government. His role in the pogrom seems to have been pivotal, and he was accused of having masterminded it in the third Yassıada trial.

A number of institutions used by Menderes after mid-1954 were, formally, organizations independent of the government, including the National Federation of Students, National Union of Students, Committee for the Defense of Turkish Rights in Cyprus, Organization for the Welfare of the Refugees from Western Thrace, and the Cyprus is Turkish Association. Far more important than these groups were the labor unions, for they provided a massive source of manpower obedient to the government's will. The most important, by far, of all these "independent" bodies, however, was the extremely well-organized *Demokrat Parti*, with its approximately 50,000 local chapters, particularly those in Istanbul, western Anatolia, and Turkish Thrace. In effect, the real political power and authority of a given area most often lay in the hands of the local DP president and board. Menderes utilized these branches to enforce his own (read: DP) decisions and plans. Consequently, local mayors and *valis* were, in all crucial matters, subservient to the local DP chapters, which, at this lower level, functioned as an instrument of illegal coercion, and illegal execution, of Menderes's policies. Whereas it was the student and other organizations that helped stoke the flames of public opinion over Cyprus and redirect chauvinist hatred from Cyprus and Greece to the Greeks of Istanbul, it was the local DP chapters that carried out the acts of destruction, arson, murder, rape, and religious desecration on the streets of Istanbul and its environs.

The Turkish press played an equally violent role in a campaign of hatred calculated to prepare the political atmosphere in Istanbul, and in the Turkish nation more generally, for the savage attacks on the Greeks. Most of the journalism was raw propaganda and highly inflammatory, and it placed the forty-five Greek communities, the ecumenical patriarchate, and the Greeks' churches, dwellings, businesses, and schools in the position of sacrificial victims, although the Greeks and the patriarchate were in no way responsible for the Greek government's policies on Cyprus.

On August 24, 1955, Menderes formally announced Turkey's radical policy change on Cyprus at a banquet honoring Zorlu and his diplomats as they prepared to leave for the London conference. He had cast the die. On the evening of August 29, some DP chapters attacked a small number of Greek Orthodox churches in the Istanbul region and inflicted substantial damage on them. The police made no effort to restrain the attackers. On the same evening, Zorlu sent a cipher telegram from London to Menderes asking for demonstrations in Turkey because of the weakness of the country's position at the tripartite conference. Although Zorlu was to deny at Yassıada that he had called for a pogrom, the tribunal found him guilty of having requested the violence that ensued.

The explosion of dynamite in the courtyard of the Turkish consulate in Thessalonikê was meant to be the signal for the pogrom. Although the Turkish government, and Menderes specifically, was to deny that it had conspired through its two consuls to set off the device, all the evidence points clearly to an "inside job." The evidence also indicates that, contrary to its contention that the pogrom had been a "spontaneous" reaction by the Turkish nation in the face of the explosion—and of the Cyprus issue more generally—the

Turkish government had made the decision for violence prior to its mission's departure for the London conference on August 24. Patriarch Athênagoras, forced to testify at Yassıada in 1960, under persistent questioning by the prosecutor, testified that the *vali* of Istanbul had placed security forces around the patriarchate to protect it two weeks *before* the pogrom, on August 24. Eight days earlier, on August 16, Hikmet Bil, a leader of the Cyprus is Turkish Association, had issued a secret directive to its members that they were henceforth free to determine themselves when action was demanded. On September 2, leaders of the DP and the government went to Eskişehir, where they recruited some 400 to 500 factory workers through the local DP chapter and shipped them to Istanbul on the state railways under their own *değnekçis* and security officers. After the events, many of these laborers were arrested and their loot confiscated, while the local security officers were transferred from Eskişehir to distant posts in eastern Anatolia. Finally, after the pogrom began on September 6, Menderes, Mahmud Celal Bayar, and other top government officials drove through the streets of Istanbul, and so were present when the violence began. After crossing the Bosphorus at Kabataş, they were in Haydarpaşa station until 8:20 PM and were updated by Interior Minister Namık Gedik about what was occurring in the streets. Before boarding the train, Menderes spoke to Zorlu in London and ordered him to return immediately to Ankara as the pogrom was well underway. Alaettin Eriş testified at Yassıada that Menderes could have halted the rampage had he wanted to.

In the five-year period leading to the Yassıada tribunals, the Menderes government circulated several differing and unconvincing explanations of the pogrom. At first, it attempted to blame the forty-five to fifty-five communists and leftists it arrested on September 7, but soon the martial-law tribunals realized that there was no evidence whatever for these detentions. Then Menderes shifted to a "psychological" explanation: namely, the spontaneous outbreak of Turkish fury over Cyprus resulting from national "psychosis." Then it was claimed that the violence had been perpetrated by some extremely well-organized but apparently mysterious and unidentifiable "enemies of Turkey." As the martial-law tribunals could not pinpoint any relevant persons or organizations, however, they sent a group on to the civil courts in February 1956 that was distinguished by the presence of the leaders of the Cyprus is Turkish Association. Nevertheless, here, too, the courts decided that no one was guilty, as the reaction of the demonstrators had been justified ostensibly by the "threat" to Turkish interests in Cyprus. Therefore, no one was responsible, not even those accused of murder and rape. Indeed, the foreign ministry, and its diplomats and acting minister, eventually charged the Greek government with responsibility for the pogrom!

In Chapter 2, the narrative was based on substantial eyewitness and other contemporary accounts of the destruction in order to present as detailed an account as possible of the attacks. This has not been attempted since Christoforos Chrêstidês composed his report sometime toward the end of 1956. Clearly, the violence was organized carefully, broadly, and covertly, according to a highly centralized and overarching plan. There was a massive marshaling of forces (the estimate by security police of some 100,000 people was conservative compared to other figures, including those of Menderes), a careful coordination of both public and private transport, and a carefully planned provision of the tools of destruction at the many strategic spots over a vast area of about forty square kilometers. Among the leadership of the larger (up to 5,000) and smaller (fifteen to fifty) groups were security officers, local DP officials, commissioned and noncommissioned officers, and even a bank president. Both large and small groups followed the orders of their leaders and showed remarkable cohesion and efficiency.

Not only were the preparations carried out effectively, the strategy of attacking in waves (usually three) was systematic. The first wave quickly broke down doors, smashed vitrines, metal shutters, and windows, and rapidly moved on to the next store, dwelling, or church. The second wave then fell upon the contents of a particular building and often threw out into the street furniture, foodstuffs, clothing, equipment, and store ledgers, and broke open any safe. The third wave finished the work of destruction both inside and outside a building, but not before it had thoroughly looted the property. The destruction of food and perishable goods was so great as to be asphyxiating. The major street surfaces were raised over half a meter by goods, oils, and textiles after cars and trams had run over and compacted them into a thick, greasy, and slippery layer atop the asphalt.

The larger groups usually marched to the accompaniment of slogans and patriotic songs, all liberally interspersed with nationalist or religious imprecations. Typically, a large group would march into an area or neighborhood along a main boulevard and then, upon a signal, would break up into smaller groups of fifteen to fifty, each with its own leaders and lists of buildings to be attacked. Once finished, they would await orders to rejoin the larger group and proceed elsewhere. Frequently, dwellings and businesses had been marked beforehand, indicating that those present were non-Muslims, whereas Turkish Muslims had been forewarned to fly a Turkish flag and turn on their lights. Practically all observers and reporters remarked that the police and soldiers not only tolerated the pogromists, but encouraged and often assisted them. The vast majority of police and soldiers refused to respond to the desperate pleas of Greeks, Jews, and Armenians for protection, often replying that, on that night, they were not officers of order or security but patriotic Turks. Important assistance to the pogromists was also rendered by the night watchmen in various neighborhoods who, along with some police, took part in the looting. The most glaring and intentional neglect of duty was that of Namık Gedik, the interior minister who had temporarily replaced *Vali* Gökay as head of Istanbul's security and refused to meet the requests of military and police to send reinforcements to stop the attacks. Indeed, his reply was an admonition to junior officers to desist from intervening in what he referred to as a national and beneficent act.

In the last fifty years, Britain and the us have declassified documents contemporaneous with the pogrom, as well as relevant ambassadorial and consular reports. Although the same is not true of the Greek and Turkish state archives, the records of both the Greek foreign ministry and of its embassy in Washington were made available for this study. Of the crucially important Turkish archives, the *gerekçes* and *kararnameler* of the Yassıada trials, as well as major portions of the Istanbul *vakıflar* documentation on the rebuilding of Orthodox churches and other religious institutions, have been largely, albeit not completely, accessible to the author.

As for the quality of the us and British memoranda, the final report sent by us ambassador Avra Warren to Washington on December 1, 1955, fell far below those of the us consuls in Istanbul and betrayed a general failure to understand the pogrom's origins or the Menderes government's responsibilities. It thus tended to reflect more what the State Department wanted to believe than the realities. By contrast, the reports of the British—and particularly Michael Stewart, the *chargé* in Istanbul—were generally superior to those of their American colleagues. Stewart quickly discerned both the government's responsibility for the pogrom and, especially, the role of the local DP chapters in Istanbul and adjacent areas in executing it. Equally noteworthy is the fact that some officials of the Foreign Office's Southern Department clearly perceived the pogrom's general structure and tended to the conclusion that Turkey's government was responsible both for placing the dynamite at its consulate in Thessaloníkê and for the Istanbul rioting more generally. Nevertheless, the matter of compensation to British subjects whose properties had been attacked was treated as quietly as possible so as not to arouse Turkish displeasure and thus affect the Anglo-Turkish alignment over Cyprus.

Despite prevailing censorship, the Turkish press, particularly *Milliyet*, managed to provide detailed coverage, and ample photographic documentation, of events. Greek reporting was also comprehensive, as Greece's major newspapers had their own correspondents in Istanbul. The memoranda of the two Greek consuls in the city (Vyrôn Theodôropoulos and Agis Kapsambelês) were both highly perceptive and reflected their extensive investigation of what had happened. The Frydas report (which was very detailed on damages to churches) and the Greek foreign ministry's final analysis of events are absolutely essential to understanding the entire issue.

Following the description of the attacks, this study proceeded to a specific analysis of the moral and material damages resulting from them, and of the economics and politics of Turkish compensation. Morally (and therefore legally), the pogrom was an illicit attempt by the Turkish government to destroy the Greek minority (which was legally but not practically guaranteed full Turkish citizenship) and *établis*, although both groups abided by Turkish law, paid their taxes, tried their lawsuits before Turkish courts, and, in the case of the Greek minority's men, performed their military service (often more than once) in Turkey's armed forces. Thus, the Turkish government's effort to destroy the Greek minority was a brutal violation of Turkey's constitution. In the case of the *établis*, furthermore, Turkey grossly violated its international treaty obligations. The abuse of its ethnic Greek citizens' human rights, in fact, also encompassed its Armenian and Jewish citizens, as well as foreigners living and working in the country. Suppression of minorities was an old phenomenon in Turkey: it had been employed in the past not only to cripple and eradicate minorities, but, as was the case in 1955, to distract popular sentiment and domestic critics from a government's economic policies or its slide into authoritarianism.

Although it is clear that the government forbade the demonstrators' local leaders from engaging in murder or massacre, and did not issue firearms, the rioters directed their violence not only against Greek property but also against the persons of the Greeks themselves. Accordingly, the events on the night of September 6-7 bore all the salient features of a pogrom. As with every pogrom in modern European history, this one was organized by the state and abetted by official state organs (and implemented on this occasion by the ruling party) with the intention of destroying a specific ethno-religious group that lived within the boundaries of the state and, in this case, was constitutionally guaranteed all the rights of citizenship. The pogrom was therefore, in the first instance, a crime of the state (as adjudged by the *gerekçe* of the third trial at Yassıada); consequently, every discrete crime perpetrated against the Greeks (property, institutions, and persons)—and there were many thousands of these—was also a crime of the state by the principle of overarching culpability for an agent's acts.

Thus, while it is true that instructions to the pogromists specifically precluded bodily harm, it did occur—despite the insistence of American and British diplomats that only one person perished during the attacks. A preliminary survey of the evidence now accessible points to anywhere from fifteen to thirty-seven Greek deaths. Hundreds of Greeks were physically assaulted and many of them beaten mercilessly, but many more such physical attacks remained unreported, out of the victims' fear. These assaults included rapes of women of all ages and even reports of the rape of young Greek males.

Sexual crimes, however, went largely unreported because of the shame culture of the Greeks. The sources are clear that there was a general reluctance of Greek victims and their families to report rape out of the reasonable fear that it would affect existing marriages or younger women's opportunities for marriage. Often, Greek girls were kidnapped and then raped (and in some cases murdered afterward); some older women and young girls were raped publicly. In rare cases, the victims are identified by name. Reports of physicians and hospitals were specific as to the recourse of rape victims to medical care. One Greek woman stated that rape was widespread and often extremely violent, as the perpetrators often scarred victims, either by cutting their faces with knives or viciously biting their breasts. All these crimes added to the general fear of Greek women, many of whom sought to flee Turkey. Patriarch Athênagoras made special reference to this crime, and to the horror it aroused in the Greek community, in his letter to Menderes: "Our children are poised for flight from [Turkey]. Especially the girls, for they are overcome by the fear of being raped." Conservative estimates placed the number of rapes at 200.

Turkish authors such as Aziz Nesin and Hulusi Dosdoğru refer to the sexual violation of both females and young males, whereas the imprisoned leftist Dinamo related that DP thugs had bragged openly about committing large-scale rapes in the very Greek homes that they had destroyed and looted. Finally, cases of forced circumcision of Greek and Armenian clergy are also cited in the documentation of the violence, and both Nesin and Dosdoğru refer to this as a crime that was not limited to two or three isolated incidents.

The crimes against property were better attested than those against the person. In the event, damaged or destroyed structures could not be hidden or made to melt away in the crowd, but remained long after the deed (in some cases until 1966). Consequently, Istanbul's gaping wounds became a regular feature of the city's landscape, which both inhabitants and visitors could neither escape nor ignore. The evidence was omnipresent.

The attack on the Greek institutions of the forty-five Greek communities was aimed primarily at eradicating these tenacious Greek settlements (which had managed to survive through the centuries of an often tumultuous existence) and secondarily at enriching the pogromists. This exterminationist strategy was predicated on ravaging the household base of the Greeks of

Istanbul so as to make their very presence untenable. This is readily apparent in the decision to attack a very large number of Greek dwellings, as well as by the fact that Greeks dwellings were largely identified beforehand. While we still have no reliable source as to the precise number of Greek homes attacked, the general estimate of the Greek foreign ministry's final analysis of October 11, 1955 (based on a number of reports identified in Chapter 3), seems to be the best (despite the round numbers): "There were destroyed, completely, 1,000 Greek dwellings, and those which were partially destroyed and pillaged amount to 2,500." So the general total of attacked Greek homes is about 3,500. This constituted a major socioeconomic disaster for the Greeks of Istanbul and led many to abandon their homes forever.

In addition to the loss of or serious damage to their households, the Greeks, of course, suffered financial disaster through the massive destruction of their businesses, while some 8,000 lost their jobs. Michael Stewart's dispatch on the economic consequences of the pogrom concluded: "The riots have left the Turkish authorities a considerable social problem with many poor people at least temporarily out of work and many of them homeless....So far it cannot be said that they [the Turkish Government] have been very active in discharging that responsibility." Four months after the riots, the victims were still desperately awaiting assistance from the Turkish government. In any case, the destruction wreaked on Greek businesses seems to have been even more widespread, and severe, than that caused to Greek dwellings. It destroyed not only the economic base of the Greek community but the economic basis of the community's entire institutional life.

When the noted journalist and author Metin Toker attempted to traverse the city of Istanbul during the later hours of the pogrom, he encountered a city still in the throes of destruction. The streets were impassible (for vehicles), as they were clogged and choked with debris, ash, and destroyed goods, and so he trudged, on foot, atop this semi-gelatinous stratification of devastation while "alongside of us, strange people with cudgels and resembling robbers were, on the one hand, smashing this and that and, on the other hand, waging a merciless war on wealth...." He recounted that every place was on fire and that the police and government had disappeared. The semi-official Turkish journal, *Ayın Tarihi* pithily summarized the economic situation:

> The waste of our wealth from the destruction is calculated in the neighborhood of one billion [Turkish lira]....
>
> A city of 1,500,000 cannot live without a market. Indeed, a large city means a marketplace. Today, Istanbul is a city without a market.

The setting of damages at TL1 billion is worthy of note. Chapter 3 concerned itself with the two fundamental issues—number of businesses damaged or destroyed and damage assessments—which became the focus of conflict between Greece and Turkey. The first attempts at an accounting of Greek (and other) businesses attacked centered on the reports of Istanbul's chief of police, the *Ellênikê Enôsis*, the Greek consulate in Istanbul, the ecumenical patriarchate, and Istanbul's chamber of commerce. From these estimates, one can extrapolate a range of 4,000-4,500 Greek businesses damaged. But the actual assessments of damage soon became a contested battlefield, particularly between Turkey and the victims, especially the Greeks, who had sustained far and away the greatest destruction. It is unlikely that the exact value of the total of Greek damages will ever be known; moreover, even the process of evaluating damages varied over time, not only because of the Turkish state's ever-shifting interests and abilities to pay, but also because of the changing interests of the Greek state. Compensation for entire categories of items was arbitrarily excluded, as was restitution for bodily injury (even murder). Further, Greece insisted on the trial and severe punishment of those responsible. The Turkish economy's decline and the increasing troubles in Cyprus were additional irritants in the matter of damage assessments and payments.

The initial estimate of damages to Greek property (of both Turkish and Greek citizens) was approximately TL1.05 billion. These early and very substantial estimates were soon ignored by Turkey, however; already in financial straits, the government quickly imposed a long-term policy of arbitrary claim reduction. The first such move, which disturbed both Greek Istanbulis and the Greek government, was Menderes's decision to pay compensation through private funds. He hoped thus to relieve the government of a particularly onerous economic weight that bore down heavily on the already over-burdened public debt. For this general purpose, Menderes created a private organization, the Istanbul aid committee, in September 1955, and he ordered it to begin raising funds from the private sector to pay off the claims that were to be submitted. The group was able to raise only about TL9.5 million, a sum woefully inadequate to deal with the situation. As a primary goal of the aid committee was to reduce the size of damage claims (primarily of Turkish citizens), and its president openly stated that its aim was not compensation but rather immediate "aid," the derisory amount it raised actually served its purposes. As Michael Stewart noted: "The minority communities will clearly have to rely on their own energies and resources to restore their futures."

On September 14, 1955, the Turkish foreign ministry announced that all foreign citizens who had suffered damages had to submit their claims through their respective diplomatic representatives. As the funds of the newly constituted aid committee were intended for Turkish citizens, however (and were in any case insufficient), there was no provision yet for compensation to foreigners. (Menderes had created the aid committee quickly—and in full knowledge of the inadequacy of funds—to help quell the domestic and international outcry over the pogrom, and to prove his government's good intentions.) More significantly, the committee's very limited funds were meant to initiate the government's policy of reducing assessments to the point that they would ultimately become an inconsequential liability for the Turkish treasury. This latter agenda was in force until at least 1966, when compensations were still being processed. To the very end, Menderes continued to deny any responsibility on Turkey's part to pay compensations.

With the passage of time and Turkey's evident inability to pay equitable compensations, Greece took its own measures that were, in part, based precisely on the realization that Turkey was not in any condition to honor victims' claims. This entailed two decisions. The first was a diplomatic offensive to force the Menderes government to accept its financial responsibilities and, so, initiate formal legislation to furnish funds for compensation. The second was to pressure the victims themselves to settle for fractional compensation on practical grounds (Turkey's economic distress). Meanwhile, Greece continued to insist throughout the compensation dispute that Turkey fix responsibility for the violence and, having done so, proceed to the severe punishment of the perpetrators so as to secure the minorities against repetition of the same crimes in the future.

With the failure of the Istanbul aid committee to meet the victims' claims, the Greek government urged the Greek community of Istanbul to accept—as the Greek government did—the drastic reduction of the original damage assessments of approximately TL1.05 billion to a total of TL135,069,084. Even this sum, however, was far beyond the TL9.5 million available to the aid committee.

The Greeks realized that delay in compensation was to their great disadvantage and so the Greek government decided to pressure Menderes to agree to legislation that would remedy the situation to some degree. Menderes, however, found himself under increasingly difficult conditions domestically. Turkey's policy on compensations was already known publicly. In the light of these realities, Greece initiated a systematic diplomatic campaign, in Ankara and abroad (Europe, the Middle East, the US, the UK, Canada, and Australia), including the UN and NATO. Its efforts were particularly focused on the latter organization and on the United States. Both areas were vital in the looming crisis over compensations and were to have a substantive influence on it—although Greek diplomacy's greatest impact was on Menderes and his cabinet, particularly in the foreign ministry under Zorlu and his colleagues. As the Cyprus controversy increasingly agitated the relations of Greece, Turkey, Great Britain, the United States, and NATO, the pogrom had become a distinct liability for Menderes and for his domestic and foreign policies.

Greece's principal weapon in the compensations dispute was its systematic exposure of the details regarding the pogrom and of the Turkish government's responsibility for it. All this transpired at a time when the opposition was continually hammering Menderes, not only for the pogrom, but for his failed economic policies, his increasingly dictatorial governance, and governmental corruption of scandalous proportions. In addition, the Greek government's decision to place Turkey's two consuls in Thessalonikê on trial for the dynamite conspiracy put Menderes's government in danger. As a result, Greece gained a formidable advantage in the compensations dispute. The first sign of Menderes's willingness to negotiate came after NATO intervention, with the official Turkish ceremony of raising the Greek flag over NATO headquarters in Izmir. Zorlu and Birgi chose to interpret this ceremony as a full satisfaction of Greek demands, but that was definitely not the view of Greece, which informed Turkey that bilateral relations could only be restored by Turkish legislation on equitable compensation. Raising the Greek flag in Izmir, playing the national anthems of the two countries, and making brief after-dinner speeches were, for Greece, merely symbolic gestures and of little substance.

Reflecting, and an effective example of, this diplomatic struggle were two key Greek documents: the government's detailed analysis of the pogrom and the so-called *Black Book*. Turkish diplomats abroad had early taken note of the Greek memorandum (which had been distributed on October 11, 1955) as they were soon faced by a unified attack from various Greek missions. They also knew of the pending publication of the *Black Book* since Greek authorities had purposely made its preparation known. The rumor that it was to be accompanied by graphic photographs of the pogrom's crimes particularly exercised the Turkish foreign ministry. Under the pressure of this Greek diplomatic offensive, Turkey prepared its own formal view of the night of September 6-7 in a memorandum that it distributed to all the foreign embassies in Ankara except for that of Greece. The document attempted to shift the blame for the pogrom onto Greece—a ploy that obviously convinced no one and was more an indication of the difficult international position in which Turkey found itself.

Under specific instructions, and with a very aggressive agenda, from Prime Minister Kônstantinos Karamanlês, the Greek ambassador in Ankara sought and attained two meetings with Menderes in October and November 1955. Both Menderes and Zorlu had given signs of wavering in their resistance to Greek demands for legislation on compensations. Just prior to the flag ceremony in Izmir, Zorlu had unilaterally called off the Turkish diplomatic offensive against Greece and asked that Greece do the same, which led to Greece's decision to suspend publication of the *Black Book*. Menderes was now under increasing pressure, both from the opposition and within his own party. He complained to the Greek ambassador that his most difficult problem at this stage, in fact, was criticism arising in his own party, and he asked that the Greek side show some understanding of his troubles. It seems that by the second meeting, he had decided to lighten his political burdens by agreeing to the sought-after legislation as a means to ending the Greek-Turkish standoff. Although he and Zorlu had rejected Karamanlis's request for a mixed evaluations commission (which was to prove fatal to the expeditious and equitable remuneration of the victims), he nevertheless informed the Greek envoy that he would draft a bill to be submitted to parliament within twenty days. Menderes's cabinet agreed to an appropriation of TL50 million—yet another example of Turkey's formal policy of radically reducing compensation for claims that, even after their initial voluntary reduction, still added up to almost three times the appropriation requested from parliament. In any case, in return for the compensation legislation, the Greek government dropped the charges against the two consuls in Thessalonikê.

The diplomatic struggle over this legislation had taken the better part of six months and was finally "resolved" because both sides stood to gain from the resolution. A realistic examination of the law of February 29, and the enabling act (which spelled out the law's enforcement in great detail) of July 10, 1956, however, leads to certain conclusions. While the Greek side had, generally, won most of the diplomatic battles, it was the Turkish side in the end that won the overall war over compensation. The sum total of Greece's diplomatic effort consisted of the successful drive to bring Turkey to the point of legislation. In substance, however, Greece lost the war for equitable and rapid compensation. While it yielded to the pressure to enact legislation, Turkey rejected Karamanlês's demand of a mixed evaluations committee of Greeks and Turks. More important, Turkey arbitrarily reduced Greek claims from over TL135 million to less than TL60 million (which were to cover not only Greek claims but also those of Jews, Armenians, a small number of Turks, and foreigners). Worst of all, this radical reduction of claims was then followed by a further, and *systematic*, reduction resulting from the procedures of both the Istanbul aid committee and the tax commissions, against which no appeal was allowed. (As for expeditious payment, this, too, was merely a catchphrase intended to lull international complaints, as the compensation process dragged on at least until 1966—in other words, for eleven years, and five years after Menderes, Zorlu, and Polatkan were hanged.)

The attack on Greek Orthodoxy was comprehensive and included the systematic destruction of the majority of its churches and large numbers of *agiasmata*, monasteries, and cemeteries. Such was the fury of the attackers that many churches were burned and, in some cases, reduced to barren walls and ashes. On the morning of September 7, the Orthodox churches presented a mute testimony to the crowd's rage. This fundamentally anti-Christian violence involved some 90 percent of all Greek Orthodox churches, as well as some Armenian and Catholic churches, although a synagogue was also attacked. It is significant that the Turkish state took precautions to protect only one Greek church: that of the ecumenical patriarchate in Fener. Of course, not a single mosque was touched. This violence against Greek religious institutions was the consequence not only of a fervid chauvinism, or even of the economic resentment of many impoverished rioters, but of the profound religious fanaticism in many segments of Turkish society.

The Menderes decade (1950-1960) corresponded with the sociopolitical reawakening of Islam in Turkey, which the *Demokrat Parti* chose to exploit and encourage, not only electorally but also through support of religious schools and the building of mosques. The dervish orders reappeared, and many of their followers actively supported DP candidates in elections. There was also a noticeable increase at prayers in mosques, with the equally noticeable opposition of secularists. US diplomatic reports from Turkey describe the rising sociopolitical importance of Islam at the time. In fact, the reports of American, British, and Greek diplomats all agreed that the violence of September 6-7 was also indicative of religious fanaticism; even some Turkish commentators referred to the fact that the Menderes government had exploited this fanaticism in the course of the violence. Patriarch Athênagoras, in his sorrowful letter to Menderes, referred to the pogrom as "a persecution of the Church and of its Christians...."

The State Department was particularly disturbed by the extensive desecration suffered by Greek religious institutions and requested no less than four reports on these acts. In his dispatch to Washington, US ambassador Warren declared that "75 Greek Orthodox Churches were attacked and desecrated." The more detailed reports of Greek diplomats in Turkey describe the desecration of sacred vestments, vessels, icons, and *iconostasia*, and the shameful and "unmentionable" pollution (defecation and urination) of sacred altars; the public mockery, beating, and circumcision of clerics; the exhumation and knifing of the Greek dead in cemeteries; the burning of ossuaries; the public mockery of Greek religious ceremonies; the destruction of Gospels, liturgical books, and manuscripts; and the slicing and gouging of icons. The texts describing these desecrations are all confirmed by Dêmêtrios Kaloumenos's comprehensive photographs.

As with the Greek community's secular infrastructure, so also in the matter of its religious institutions, the Greek foreign ministry acted immediately to publicize the grim details. Concurrently, it alerted major Christian organizations in the United States, Great Britain, and western Europe, and moved to rally the National Council of Churches in the US, the Church of England, and the World Council of Churches in Europe in support of the beleaguered patriarchate and the Greek Christians of Turkey. In many ways, Greece's efforts to muster Western support for the pogrom's victims were much more successful with the Christian churches of the West than with Western governments, and particularly the governments of Greece's allies, Britain and the United States. All three Protestant bodies mentioned above quickly demonstrated active concern for the distress of the Greek Orthodox Church. In particular, the Anglican Church and the World Council of Churches expressed persistent interest in the plight of the Greek Orthodox and applied continual pressure on various governments. The archbishop of Canterbury, his bishops, and clergy adopted a very aggressive policy in support of Orthodox Christians that was often antithetical to Turkish interests and policies. Such were the Church's differences with the Foreign Office that the latter came to resent Anglican expressions of support for the Greek victims as dangerous to Britain's policies toward Turkey and as constituting unwarranted clerical interference in those policies.

Thus it was that the Christian pulpit brought substantial moral support to the Greek Orthodox Church in this historical moment of great tragedy. At the same time, Christian solidarity constituted an additional, disquieting factor for Turkey's foreign ministry. The Orthodox (primarily Russian, Bulgarian, and Romanian) churches of the Soviet bloc, as well as the Orthodox Church in Yugoslavia, all condemned the pogrom against their mother church, and the Soviets even briefly entertained the thought that events, and the attendant disgust of the Greek people and government with the indifferent political stance of both the US and Britain, provided an ideal opportunity to woo Greece away from NATO and the Western alliance. But these efforts were not (and indeed could not have been) fruitful, as Greece had just emerged from a destructive civil war between right and left.

In passing, one must also note Greece's policy toward its own Muslim minority in Western Thrace (and elsewhere). After the pogrom, the minority was in immediate danger from Greek extremists who were intent on wreaking revenge. The measures that were immediately taken by Defense Minister Panagiôtês Kanellopoulos were aimed at, and succeeded in, securing the life, property, schools, and mosques of Greece's Muslim citizens. This fact is corroborated by examining the two Turkish-language newspapers in Greek Thrace at the time. The Greek government also had to contend with the attempts of Turkey's consular authorities in the region to provoke local reactions that might have compromised Greece and, so, provided some "justification" for Turkish conduct toward the Greeks of Istanbul. The local Turkish-language press also condemned the pogrom and the oppression of Istanbul's Greek minority. A comparison of Greek and Turkish policies toward their respective minorities is indeed revealing and puts the latter in a very harsh light. İsmet İnönü, the leader of the opposition in Turkey's parliament in 1955, made this particular comparison and used it to attack Menderes's policies and to denounce the pogrom.

Once the pogrom had wreaked its devastation, Turkey's radical policy of forcing the victims to swallow over 80 percent of their losses succeeded in the pauperization of the Greek communities, which set the stage for their final expulsion and flight from Turkey. Ironically, although Greece's efforts to obtain equitable and expeditious compensation collapsed, its demands for affixing responsibility—and severely punishing those who were guilty—for the events was, some six years later, achieved in a most unexpected manner. The military coup of May 27, 1960, brought 592 members and collaborators of the *Demokrat Parti* to trial, and condemned and punished the vast majority. The third tribunal found the Menderes government guilty of conspiracy to destroy the property of the Greek community of greater Istanbul. This crime of conspiracy was subsumed into the larger crime of violating the Turkish constitution, a charge that carried the death penalty. For this latter crime, Adnan Menderes, Fatin Rüştü Zorlu, and Hasan Polatkan were hanged on September 16 and 17, 1961. While the three men were hanged for their crimes, however, their policies of eradicating Turkey's minorities were continued by successive governments, as the most recent, albeit decades-long, violent repression of the Kurds bears out.

***

And what of this post-pogrom or, rather, post-Menderes era, and of the fate of the Greek minority and *établis* in greater Istanbul? What changes did the militarization of political life bring to the Greeks of Turkey? This question goes far beyond the ever-shrinking Greek-minority and *établis* communities, since this shrinkage occurred within the broader spectrum of ethnic politics and religious developments in Turkey. In other words, this process included and involved all those ethnic and religious elements within Turkey that did not fit into the Kemalist chauvinist program. The military intervention in the country's political life forcefully tightened Kemalism's grip, not only on the Greeks but also on the Kurds, Alawis, Assyrian Christians, Armenians, Jews, Dönmes, and Islamic "fundamentalists." The domestic intensification of Kemalism was concurrent with two powerful political forces external to Turkey: the increasing role of the European Union in the country's politics and economy, and the gradual rise of Islamic fundamentalism in neighboring lands of the Middle East. These factors led to contradictory forces and tendencies within Turkey in the last decade of the twentieth century. On the one hand, the former increasingly imposed uniform policies regarding human and civil rights and freedoms as societal values of fundamental importance. On the other hand, the latter began to impel Islam toward a return to its own fundamentals as a creed and, therefore, to varying forms of political action.

In the last half of the twentieth century, however, Turkey's professional military class became the preeminent political factor in the life of the Turkish citizen, as the generals pursued a kind of neo-Ottoman imperialism and diverted a significant part of the nation's economic wealth to the creation of a massive and extremely well-armed military force, equally well-developed on land, sea, and air. One purpose of this huge Turkish military machine was its political imposition on its neighbors—which was done, of course, with the tacit approval of the political and military arms of the US government.

Having asserted this control over Turkey's government, the military not only diverted massive funds to advanced equipment. It also intensified its suppression of the rights and freedoms of ethnic and religious minorities, as well as of the country's citizens as a whole. In this, the military proved itself to be a worthy successor to the oppressive regime of the Young Turks. The demographic decline of both the Greek and Jewish communities in Turkey during the latter half of the twentieth century was a direct result of the Menderes and post-Menderes policies and persecution of minorities, as well as of the restriction of the rights and liberties of Turkish citizens more generally. This restriction was manifest in the legislation that empowered the state to deprive citizens—and, above all, minorities—of their legal, cultural, and property rights, and in the police brutality that enforced these laws with the systematic use of arbitrary incarceration and torture. The tax laws, in particular, were manipulated through the decades to impoverish minorities. And the growing power of the military was later utilized to crush the efforts of Turkish Kurds for independence, or at least autonomy and the right to inhabit their native villages and homes.

Indeed, the entire history of the last fifty years of Turkish society is tied to the imperialism of the Turkish general staff, which has successfully utilized its forces to impose its territorial aggression and conquest. In effect, the spirit of the pogrom of 1955, whose motive force was the final destruction and expulsion of the Greeks from Istanbul, was continued and finally consummated by successive governments and the activities of the Turkish general staff. While the "National Unity Committee" junta destroyed the Menderes regime and (through the Yassıada tribunals) found him and Zorlu guilty of planning and executing the pogrom, and had them hanged, along with Polatkan, for violating the Turkish constitution, General Cemal Gürsel proved to be a vigorous and willing heir to the pogrom's spirit. As it happened, successive Turkish governments continued Menderes's aggressive violations of the Greek community. Furthermore, after the invasion of Cyprus in 1974— following the aborted, Greek-inspired coup against Archbishop Makarios— these policies were reconceived to carry out the ethnic cleansing of the Greek Cypriot majority in the occupied north. This policy, intended to Turkify northern Cyprus, was attended by willful destruction that strongly resembled the acts perpetrated by the Menderes government against the Greeks of Istanbul. This ethnic cleansing was also applied later, with us weapons, in the destruction of the Kurdish villages of southeast Anatolia, which reduced the region to a semi-desolate landscape.

Of primary interest for the purposes of this book is a brief examination of the fate of the Greeks of Istanbul, the Princes Islands, and the larger islands of Imvros and Tenedos. Today, the number of Greeks left in the former imperial capital of the Ottomans (and the Byzantines) is somewhere between 1,000 and 2,500. The exact number is unknown. The formerly populous isles of Tenedos and Imvros were very heavily Greek prior to 1955; today, Greeks make up no more than a handful of inhabitants. Thus, only about 1 percent, or a bit more, of the original Greek community has survived in the greater Istanbul area. Turkey's military (and military-dominated) governments thus carried out a successful internal "cleansing" as far as the country's Greeks were concerned. The first phase of this purge was, of course, the pogrom, which occurred within the larger context of the Cyprus problem; in that sense, it was part of that problem and, thus, a factor in the larger thinking of the Turkish military establishment. Nevertheless, a second factor independent of the Cyprus problem motivated the pogrom: the opportunity to bring an end—through a final, violent removal—to the actual *presence* of the Greek community, and its significant role, in the life of Turkey's largest and most famous city.

In mid-November 1962, the Greek consul in Istanbul, Themistoklês

Chrysanthopoulos, sent an important, secret report to Athens entitled, "The Future of Hellenism in Istanbul," which detailed further repression of the local Greek communities, including two measures that are particularly noteworthy. The first was the military junta's decree, No. 5/1248 (June 21, 1961), entitled, "Review of Public Benefits Foundations." These legal foundations—churches, schools, etc.—were now deprived of their freely elected governing boards, which were transformed into simple executive organs charged with carrying out the orders of the general directorate of the Istanbul *vakıflar.* This decree openly violated Article 40 of the treaty of Lausanne, which regulated the internal life of the Greek communities in Istanbul and of the Turkish and Muslim communities in Greek Thrace.

Equally symptomatic of this anti-Greek minority policy was the partial abrogation of the compensation funds legislated by Menderes in February 1956 for rebuilding the churches and other religious establishments attacked in the pogrom:

> The government arbitrarily cut TL3 million from the TL10 million agreed upon for rebuilding the churches, schools, etc....As a result, the holy churches of Panagia Belgratkapı, Saints Constantine and Helen, and St. George Kyparissas of Samatya remain half-built; and the Metropolitanate palace of Derkon in Tarabya, as also the school of Üsküdar, cannot be rebuilt."[1]

These measures radically reduced the initiatives that the Greek communities could undertake to carry out their communal life, and made them literally the legal and financial hostages of the state through the Istanbul *vakıflar.* This new state of affairs not only paralyzed the community's self-

---

[1] Ypourgeion Exôterikôn, Istanbul to Athens, Dispatch No. EP 2782/M13, November 15, 1962. Of interest in the matter of the total spent on ecclesiastical rebuilding by the Istanbul *vakıflar* is the information in the lengthy memorandum, "Questions in Suspense Between Greece and Turkey (Top Secret)" of 1964, dated between May 25 and September 16, Greek embassy in Washington. It is sixty-three pages long, of which p. 11 refers to expenditures on "gutted churches"; p. 21 to the embargoed properties of the Greeks expelled from 1957 to 1960; and pp. 24-25 to the initial legislated sum of TL60 million to cover all losses, and to the losses suffered by Greek merchants.

On the connection of the Armenian deportations during the First World War, which led to their extermination, and the massive conscription of Greeks, Jews, and remaining Armenians later in the twentieth century, see, above all, Frank G. Weber, *The Evasive Neutral,* New York, 1979, pp. 101-116. Also, Jacob M. Landau, *Pan-Turkism: From Irredentism to Cooperation,* second edition, Bloomington, 1995, pp. 111-147; K. B. Bardakjian, *Hitler and the Armenian Genocide,* Cambridge, 1985, pp. 3-36; and Bruce R. Kuniholm, *The Origins of the Cold War in the Near East,* Princeton, 1994, pp. 28-29. I wish here to express my gratitude to Dr. Rouben Adalian and Mr. Aram Arkun for assistance in the references of some of the above and for having provided me with some of the English-language materials.

governance; at a higher level, the community's three larger governing bodies were in fact destroyed as functioning institutions. In other words, the very factor that had led to the final revitalization of the economic, cultural, and religious life of the Greek communities, the dissolution of the *tek mütevelli* system, was no longer operable. The communities soon fell under the complete control of the *vakıflar*, which, as an instrument of a hostile government, began to act accordingly. As for the arbitrary sum of TL7 million left to rebuild ecclesiastical institutions, it became even more ridiculous in light of the real cost of the destruction wreaked on the religious life of Greek Christians.

The second phase of the plan to rid Turkey of its Greeks centered about the Turkish government's decision in 1964 to expel the Greek *établis*—that is, the Greek nationals—once and for all from the country. Although the decision was technically directed toward the *établis* alone, it affected a large part of the Greek minority that, ostensibly at least, held Turkish citizenship. This move, like the pogrom itself, was closely tied to the Cyprus issue, and was set off by the constitutional breakdown of the Cypriot state, which had recently gained its independence. This collapse was accompanied by armed conflict between the Turkish minority and Greek majority in December 1963 and well into 1964. The aggravated situation on the island verged on open war. At the outset, Turkey exerted systematic pressure on the *établis*, both as political retaliation against Greece and in order to proceed apace with the extinction of the Greek community.

Pressure on the *établis* was already evident, however, with the contracts that were awarded for rebuilding the churches after the pogrom. In at least one case, after having won the bid, an *établis* contractor was removed from the work and ordered to put his affairs in order and depart from Turkey on the specific grounds of the Cyprus issue. The situation of the Greek element in the city had increasingly worsened after Menderes's overthrow on May 27, 1960. The community's harassment reached such a level that, by November 15, 1962, the Greek foreign ministry asked for, and received, the report mentioned above from consul Chrysanthopoulos.[2] He cited the aggressive attitude and behavior of the Turkish bureaucracy toward both Greek *établis* and Turkish nationals of Greek origin, particularly in matters concerning property. The widespread intermarriage between these two bodies of Istanbul Greeks had mixed their property and wealth so that often their estates were transferred from the registry of (and the legal protection theoretically given

---

[2] Ypourgeion Exôterikôn, Istanbul to Athens, Dispatch No. EP 2782/M13, November 15, 1962.

to) Turkish citizens (ethnic Greeks) to that of the Greek *établis*.

On August 5, 1963, the Istanbul police systematically and formally began to inform all Greek *établis* who owned businesses to transfer title to Turkish citizens. In each case, the person summoned presented him- or herself to the respective police precinct, was read the decree, and then forced to sign a statement that he or she had been duly informed of the law. As of December 6, 1963, twenty-nine such statements were signed.[3] It is obvious, as this process continued, that the Turkish government had larger plans to expropriate the businesses, property, and wealth of Greek nationals.

Thus, on March 13, 1964, the Turkish government "denounced" the convention signed by Greece and Turkey in 1930 concerning "establishment" (that is, the presence of Greek citizens in Istanbul), as well as commerce and navigation (both maritime and by air, as we shall soon see). The convention stipulated that it remained in effect until six months after it was repudiated by a signatory, which meant in this case that it would lapse on September 16, 1964, at which time Greek nationals would have their work permits repealed and, then, be expelled from Turkey. Most of these Greek nationals had been born in Turkey (as had their parents and, in many cases, their grandparents), but the decision to expel them was, as already mentioned, taken because of the heightening of the Cyprus conflict. The measures had been planned in detail: *établis* stores were to be closed; workers to depart; and all *établis* bank accounts to be blocked and severe taxes imposed on them. These men, women, and children were allowed to leave with only a one-way ticket, two suitcases (about forty kilos), and TL200 (that is, about $20-22). They lost everything else. Further Greek marriages were forbidden, so as not to complicate the ultimate seizure of property and assets, since the new spouse would, very probably, come from the Greek minority and therefore be a Turkish citizen.

These anti-minority measures, it should be noted, also had dire consequences for the Armenian and Jewish communities. As we saw earlier in this study, some 500 Jewish stores were destroyed in the 1955 pogrom according to the Istanbul police, and conditions for Istanbul's Jews had become oppressive. Between 1955 and 1964, the number of Jews in the city

---

[3] Ypourgeion Exôterikôn, Athens to Brussels, Dispatch No. D8716-53, December 6, 1963. For further details, see Ypourgeion Exôterikôn, Athens to Washington, Dispatch No. D8611-1, January 3, 1964, concerning the Greek minority in Imvros and Tenedos; Ypourgeion Exôterikôn, Athens to NATO and EU, Dispatch No. D860-129, August 26, 1974; Ypourgeion Exôterikôn, Athens to all embassies, No. D860-156, September 10, 1964; Ypourgeion Exôterikôn, Athens to Washington *et al.*, Dispatch No. DT860-144, September 4, 1964; Ypourgeion Exôterikôn, Athens to NATO and UNESCO, Dispatch No. DT860-225, October 17, 1964.

had declined by 62.4 percent as circumstances became difficult:

> Turkish xenophobia, especially toward the ethnic minorities living in Turkey for hundreds of years, was again illustrated with the situation of the Jewish minority in that country, which was reported on in the issue of April 5, 1964, of the large Israeli German-language daily, *Tages Nachrichten* (independent, Tel Aviv), and said, among other things, the following:
>
> "The general hatred against foreigners in Turkey has greatly affected the Jewish minority of that country. As a matter of fact, there were over 85,000 Jews [Turkish citizens for generations] some ten years ago there, while their total number at present is just 32,000. The Turkish authorities are interfering in all internal affairs of the Jewish community, and even the appointment of a Rabbi must be approved by the Turkish government."
>
> Previous reports published in the Israeli and Jewish world press described the terror under which the Turkish Jews were living. Among other things, the fact that they were forbidden to speak their mother tongue [Judeo-Spanish or Ladino] and compelled to speak Turkish only. The report also mentioned the existence of antisemitic Turkish newspapers.
>
> As is well known, extremely tragic were the conditions of the Jewish minority...during World War II, when—pressed by the Nazis—immense inhuman taxes were imposed on the Turkish Jews. Thousands of them could not pay these taxes, and they were deported to far-outlying mountain regions, where many of them died of hunger and epidemics.[4]

As this entire anti-Greek minority effort was conceived within a larger and aggressive anti-Greek policy, we must now turn to other events that occurred simultaneously. The Greek foreign minister, Stauros Kôstopoulos, prepared an official, eighteen-page memorandum for NATO's secretary general, Dirk U. Stikker, in which a very broad range of unilateral Turkish violations of agreements and arrangements was set forth.

In the first of the seven broad areas covered by this memorandum, Kôstopoulos informed Stikker that Turkey had denounced the Greek-Turkish convention on establishment, commerce, and navigation, and had rejected Greece's proposals to negotiate a new one. At the same time, the Greek foreign minister added, Turkey had undertaken a series of measures against Greek nationals established in Istanbul, including 156 deportations and the

---

[4] Ypourgeion Exôterikôn, Athens to Washington and London, Dispatch No. DSK412-77, April 11, 1964.

withdrawal of more than 400 work permits as the prelude to deportation. The deportations themselves were carried out on short notice, with the deportees allowed to take next to nothing. Before the *établis'* stores were closed, the premises and merchandise were seized, and the seizure orders were accompanied by a demand for immediate payment of the entire current year's taxes.

Kôstopoulos then noted that Turkey had suspended the 1955 agreement eliminating visas between itself and Greece, and that, furthermore, General Gürsel, president of the Turkish republic, had asserted that "Greco-Turkish friendship is dead. Nothing remains of this friendship…and it is not possible to foresee what the future holds in store."

The memorandum then enumerated a number of measures taken against the ecumenical patriarchate and Greek Orthodox Church, including: the stripping of Turkish citizenship from two metropolitans and their subsequent deportation; the summary trial and guilty verdict of an *établi* vicar for officiating in church—followed by deportation; the deportation of the chaplain of the Greek consulate at Izmir; and the closure of the patriarchate's printing facility. At the same time, Kôstopoulos added, a violent campaign against both the patriarchate and the Church was being waged in the Turkish press.

The Greek foreign minister then accused Turkey of stepping up, again, the attack on the Greek minority more generally. He cited an intensification of attacks and anti-minority manifestoes, flourishing anti-minority graffiti, and widespread window-breaking in both churches and schools—all of this intimidation accompanied by open boycotts of Greek businesses. In addition, the Greek orphanage (165 children) was closed on grounds that it was "unsafe," although it had repeatedly applied for permits to repair and rebuild, which were denied. Finally, morning prayers—as well as the production of ancient Greek drama—had been prohibited in the Greek-minority schools.

Next, the memorandum dealt with an issue that the Greeks had tried to settle with Turkey in a manner satisfactory to both sides even before the pogrom: territorial waters. Without going into detail here, Turkey had clearly, and unilaterally, challenged the international maritime regime by radically altering basic facts to its own advantage. Namely, it had extended its territorial waters from the edges of mouths of bays and established an additional twelve-mile zone of territoriality that forbade fishing to foreign fishermen. Both acts violated older practice as well as international law, all without any consultation with the affected neighbor, Greece.

The final particular in the memorandum touched upon a new phenomenon: the violation of Greek airspace. These violations by the Turkish air force (flying us aircraft) had begun on January 2, 1964, and had recurred nine times through May of that year. They included flights over Greek Thrace and the islands of Samos, Kastellorizo, Chios, and Lesvos, as well the Maritza airfield and over Greek military vessels. Although violating Greek airspace was a relatively new type of Turkish aggression, it was to become a permanent fixture (down to the writing of this book). Although US military aid—which made possible much of the hardware used by the Turkish air force—was legally bound to defensive use, the US government never attempted to restrain this misuse of its assistance, with the notable exception of the Carter administration. It is clear from Kôstopoulos's memorandum that Turkish expansionism had quickly spread from Cyprus to the Aegean Sea and the Greek islands, and that it was bound tightly to the measures taken against the Greek community of Istanbul.

What was the final effect of the Turkish denunciation of the convention of establishment on the Greek *établis* and ethnic minority of Istanbul? The figures vary but are absolute in regard to the Greek *établis*: they were all eventually expelled from Turkey. For reasons already mentioned, however, the law was so framed that it resulted in a much larger expulsion of those members of the ethnic Greek minority who were officially—and constitutionally and, therefore, legally—Turkish citizens. The Turkish students of the expulsion, Hulya Demir and Rıdvan Akar, place the number of Greek *établis* and ethnic minority expelled as a result of the secret decree of 1964 (No. 6/3801, prepared on September 16, 1964) at between 35,000 and 40,000. The Greek scholars Neoklês Sarrês and Aristarchos Eleutheriadês place it at 12,000 Greek *établis* and 36,000 Greek minority, for a total of 48,000. When Demir and Akar wrote their book in 1994, they estimated that only 3,500 Greeks had been left in Istanbul. Today, only between 1,000 and 2,500 are left. Needless to say, the property of the expellees was confiscated and sold. The decree stated: "Any act in connection with the transfer of ownership of immovables and of other real rights over immovables which are situated in Turkey and belong to persons of Greek nationality, as well as any other act which would have as a consequence the transfer of the above rights, is hereby suspended."

Meanwhile, the Turkish minority of Greece has retained its numbers— indeed grown—as well as its property, mosques, schools, and newspapers. One needs to be reminded of this as Turkey continually claims—against all reality— of "corresponding" damage to the Turkish minority in Greek Thrace. Turkey's expulsions were in a sense the last major blow to the Greeks of Istanbul. To this day, litigation over properties continues, but drags out as the Turkish state refuses to pay. From 1964 to the present, various efforts have been made to prevent the Greek victims from receiving proper compensation.[5]

The secret decree of 1964 became the basis for large-scale confiscation

[5] For the extensive text of Kôstopoulos's memorandum, composed on June 11, 1964, see

of Greek properties. In 1980, Turkish authorities *retroactively* invalidated all wills and testaments of the *établis* and thus denied them the right to designate heirs. As late as the meeting of the Greek and Turkish prime ministers at Davos on February 11, 1998, the right of Greek nationals to designate heirs was denied in Turkish courts. As a result, Alexandros Alavanos, a Greek MEP at the time (and now head of Greece's leftwing *Synaspismos* party), raised the matter in the European parliament in 1994, thirty years after Turkey had first enacted the secret decree that alienated the properties of Greek nationals.[6]

As for the islands of Imvros and Tenedos, they lost all rights to the local autonomy guaranteed them by the treaty of Lausanne, which was never enforced in their defense. Soon, the government decided to build a large school for training Turkish teachers, and it would eventually build a substantial Turkish military base on Imvros. Turkey placed a "deputy" director in every minority school who, in effect, turned the Greek directors into powerless and dysfunctional figureheads. Minority schools thus passed directly into the hands of Muslim Turkish officials—whose salaries, nonetheless, were paid by the respective communities.

By 1975, however, the Turkish military and local administration were frustrated by their failure to effect a full ethnic cleansing of the two islands. (The Çanakkale provincial authorities had begun to confiscate minority property soon after 1968).[7] Thus, the National Security Council (the real power behind Turkey's formal government) took measures to accelerate the process of de-Hellenization. In yet another secret decree (No. 206, January 28, 1975), the NSC (under the leadership of Turkish president, and former admiral, Fahri S. Korutürk) laid out a rigorous, detailed, and systematic plan to hasten and complete the ethnic erasure of the Greeks of Imvros and Tenedos. This decree also displayed both the military elite's marked continuity in exercising power over the Turkish government and its racist mentality regarding Turkey's minorities.

Ypourgeion Exôterikôn, Paris to Washington and United Nations, Dispatch No. 4260/140/14, June 18, 1964.

[6] The entire Turkish text and its English translation are published in Alexandros Alavanos, *The Greeks of Constantinople: People Without Rights of Succession*, Athens, 1994, pp. 14-15 and *passim*. The main reason the decree was not published in the official government gazette was because, according to law, its constitutionality could have been challenged for ninety days.

[7] The confiscations of July 16, 1968, were officially announced in the newspaper *Gökçeada*, which decreed the *istimlak* (confiscation) of 373 properties belonging to 344 persons and legal persons. A second such *ilan* (announcement) in *Gökçeada* of May 25, 1990, announcing the confiscations of the properties of eighty-four individuals, was also available to the author. Thus, the process was ongoing. For a very concise and reliable account of this process, see Aristide Caratzas, "The Turkification of Imbros and Tenedos: The Destruction of Two Greek Communities in Turkey," *The GreekAmerican*, July 8, 1994.

The decree begins with a bland statement of the ethnic constituency of Imvros over a ten-year period:

Turks (%)	Greeks (%)	Years
5.0	95.0	1960
22.5	77.6	1965
61.0	39.0	1970

There were already three stages of Turkification prior to 1964: 1934-1951: Unsuccessful period....Land given to 28 [Turkish families] was sold to the local Greeks and the [Turkish] émigrés deserted the island; 1951-1962: A period that functioned to the advantage of the Greeks....1962: A period in which many coordinated measures were taken. The general staff [of the Turkish armed forces] demands procedures for altering the [ethnic] situation on behalf of the Turks.

> The NSC decided on article 35, March 27, 1964....Immediate application of all these measures approved....Militarization of the island [and of Tenedos]; provision of the necessary economic support for government policy....This decision consists....of twenty-seven articles which can be summarized under five headings. The necessity of the Greeks to immigrate [from Imvros], as we destroy their economic power through the confiscation of their arable lands. There shall be enforced on them an educational system carried out in the Turkish language. We shall refurbish the older Turkish buildings and build newer ones to establish Turkish culture on the island. We should exercise care in selecting public officials who will carry this work out on the island.

These measures had a certain success in the beginning, but the increase of the Turkish population was not reliable...as 75% of them consisted of males.

The New Method [of Turkification] from 1975...

The landed [agricultural] estates of state production that have been established on the island shall be re-organized....A new Turkish population will be established on the island to work these estates....The open-air penitentiaries must be closed. The original reason for their founding was to force the local Greeks to emigrate. Now, however, it seems that they disturb our Turkish settlers....We must, at this point, find secondary jobs for the Turkish population so that the agricultural settlement will succeed....Even though the Greek element is abandoning the island in large numbers as a result of our policies of [land] confiscations, nevertheless, the commercial life of the island is still in their hands, especially in the transport sector.

If the commercial monopoly of the Greeks is not broken, they will not completely abandon the island....Accordingly, the government took the following decision No. 7/10381 in August 1975...:

> Immediate confiscation of land [of the Greeks] for the creation of public works in the most significant parts of the island; appointment of a strong and competent *mufti* [for Islamization of the island's life]; building of massive prisons on the model of the type on İmralı island...which will furnish prisoners to work in the fields; a fast boat to hinder smuggling; a school for the rural gendarmerie to be built on the island....
>
> Measures limiting the authority of the churches over the [Greek population]: prohibition of church involvement in educational and related activities; metropolitans [of the Church] to be given no special treatment; the Greek church to be required to participate in Turkish national celebrations; the Greeks on the island to be forbidden to participate in Greek national holidays; Greeks forbidden to re-purchase lands from the emigrants who shall decide to leave Imvros.[8]

This last phase of Turkification of the two islands was virtually complete in the 1990s. The Greeks had been crippled economically by the large-scale confiscation of their lands; threatened and abused by soldiers and convicts; and assaulted by the courts and the Çanakkale administration. They were forced in the end to seek refuge in Greece and elsewhere. Thus, Imvros's militarization was complete, as was the full Islamization and Turkification of both Imvros and Tenedos.

This same policy of conquest, occupation, militarization, and ethnic cleansing was applied by the Turkish army in Cyprus in 1974 and thereafter. There is no point here in any detailed analysis of this matter as very much

---

[8] The Greek translation of the text was published in the Athens daily, *Eleutherotypia*, April 28, 1988. For the general oppression of these two islands, Geôrgios Tenekidês, *Imvros kai Tenedos. Istoria/Nomiko kathestos*, Synchronê Pragmatikotêta, Thessalonikê, 1986. For crimes of rape and murder, *Violations of Rights of the Greek Minority of Imvros and Tenedos*, sent by the Panimbrian Society of Athens to H. van der Broek, chair of the EEC council of foreign ministers, Brussels, October 3, 1991. Also, the undated memorandum of the Greek foreign ministry entitled *Imvros and Tenedos*. In 1964, Imvriots owned c. 61,346,905 square meters of land. In 1990, only 164,095 square meters were left in their hands. The expropriations had alienated over 99.77 percent of their land. By 1991, only about 300 Imvriots, or some four percent of the original population, were still to be found on the island.

has already been written on it, not only by Greeks and Turks, but also by British and Americans. It is sufficient to refer here to the lengthy (198-page) and detailed report, complete with documentation and eyewitness accounts, issued in 1977 by the Commission on Human Rights of the Council of Europe.

The commission found the Turkish government and its army guilty of repeated violations of the European Convention on Human Rights. Moreover, it concluded that, "having found violations of a number of Articles of the Convention, the Commission notes that the acts violating the Convention were exclusively directed against members of one of the two communities in Cyprus, namely the Greek Cypriot."[9] Still, with some rare exceptions, the commission's clinical analysis of the evidence submitted by the Greek Cypriot government avoided many details from the documents and testimony. These details were furnished only to the nineteen member-states of the Council of Europe, but were so shocking that they were not publicized. The *Sunday Times* of London, however, managed to obtain a copy of the secret version of the findings:

> It amounts to a massive indictment of the Ankara government for the murder, rape and looting by its army in Cyprus during and after the Turkish invasion of summer 1974.
>
> Allegations made by the Cyprus government against Turkey covered systematic killings of civilians who were not involved in the 1974 fighting; repeated raping of women aged from 12 to 71, often brutally in public; the torture and savage and humiliating treatment of hundreds of Greek Cypriots, including children during their detention by the Turkish army; and charges of extensive looting and plunder which were supported by unpublished United Nations documents.[10]

In the event, occupied northern Cyprus was subjected to a massive and detailed ethnic cleansing. The majority of Greek Cypriots were expelled; their properties and businesses seized; and churches converted into mosques, destroyed, defaced, turned into stables or public latrines, or, along with Greek cemeteries, desecrated. The toponymy of northern Cyprus was completely

---

[9] Council of Europe, Commission on Human Rights, *Report in response to charges by the government of Cyprus concerning atrocities committed by Turkish troops in Cyprus*, Strasbourg, June 1977.

[10] *Sunday Times*, "What secret report tells about Turk atrocities," January 23, 1977. For Karpasia, John Fielding's report on his "unchaperoned" visit to that area is brief, but highly indicative of the violence unleashed on the local Greek communities, their villages, churches, and graveyards.

Turkified, and, among other things, the Turkish military continues to maintain some 40,000 troops on the island over thirty years after the invasion.

At the same time, the illegal settlement of Anatolian Turks has, fatefully, changed the demography of Turkish Cyprus, a large part of which has preferred to leave its homeland. The devastation of Greek cultural monuments, meanwhile, has reached tragic proportions and been accompanied by looting of archeological sites, churches, museums, and private collections—and, consequently, the flooding of the major auction-houses in Europe, Canada, and the United States.[11]

These general policies were all evident in the pogrom, in the expulsions of Greeks from Istanbul, and in the ethnic cleansing of Imvros and Tenedos. In the last two decades, the policy of Turkish military aggrandizement has shifted to the Aegean Sea and the Greek islands there. The build-up of land, air, and naval forces (including numerous landing craft) has been accompanied by

---

[11] On cultural and religious destruction by the Turkish side, see the catalogue and description of the Cypriot department of antiquities, *The destruction of the cultural heritage of the occupied part of Cyprus*, Nicosia, 1994, 23 pages, kindly furnished by Dr. Patroklos Stavrou. From the Turkish side, see especially the bitter reports of the Turkish Cypriot journalist Mehmet Yasin, entitled "Perishing Cyprus," which appeared in the Turkish Cypriot weekly *Olay* in four issues, April 6, May 3, 10, and 17, 1982. A typed, thirty-nine-page, English version of the text has circulated. Patroklos Stavrou, "The plundering of the cultural heritage and the falsification of the national identity of Cyprus by Turkey," lecture delivered at the National Gallery, Athens, May 11, 1984. For a detailed account of the theft and smuggling of the Kanakaria mosaics, Dan Hofstadter, *Goldberg's Angel*, New York, 1994, and, especially, the brief summary of the trial in federal court in Indiana in 1989 and 1990, *Kanakaria Mosaics: The Trial*, Nicosia, nd, which reprints the judgment of Chief Judge Bauer, Circuit Judge Cudahy, and Senior Circuit Judge Pell.

The Turkish government decided to rely for its demographic base not so much on Turkish Cypriots, but rather on heavy, and illegal, colonization by tens of thousands of Anatolian Turks, in addition to the large Turkish military force occupying the north, much of which would ultimately settle there. As a result of these settlement policies, many Turkish Cypriots eventually decided to leave Cyprus. This illegal settlement, whose intention was to alter the demographic reality of northern Cyprus and drive out the Greeks who had remained, was for a time denied by the Turkish government and, in particular, by the US State Department in the person of its special Cyprus negotiator, Nelson Ledsky. Needless to say, this demographic base could be a useful instrument should occasions present themselves for further aggrandizement in the south. Costas Yennaris, *From the East: Conflict and Partition in Cyprus*, London, 2003, page 268; *Turkish Colonization: A Threat for Cyprus and its People*, ministry of the interior, republic of Cyprus, Nicosia, nd, pp. 1-24. The numbers were monitored and commented on by the Turkish Cypriot press as well as that of mainland Turkey. The matter was brought before the US Congress by Lee Hamilton, chairman of the subcommittee on Europe and the Middle East in the hearing of Rozanne L. Ridgway, assistant secretary for European and Canadian affairs, State Department, June 19, 1986.

various claims on Greek islands, demands for their demilitarization, and unceasing violation of Greek airspace, including civil-aviation corridors. Simultaneously, Turkey continues to press its accusations of violations of the rights of the Turkish minority in Greek Thrace. A careful comparative investigation by Helsinki Watch (now Human Rights Watch), however, indicates very clearly that the violations of the rights of the Turkish minority pale in significance when compared to the violations endured by the ethnic Greek minorities in Istanbul, Imvros, Tenedos, and northern Cyprus.

Despite the radical turn, some years back, in Greek foreign policy that has led to the unquestioning support of Turkey's accession to the European Union, the Turkish military continues to pursue its provocative policy of violating Greek airspace. At the same time, the Turkish military finds it difficult to subscribe to the institutionalization of civil and human rights for all of Turkey's citizens.

Although the pogrom of September 6-7, 1955, occurred half a century ago, its legacy is caught up, even today, in a larger web of regional and international interests. This web is, indeed, the key to understanding important parts of this ongoing history. The "success" of the Turkish military behemoth during the last fifty years has, in fact, made the Turkish state a persistent violator, not only of the human and civil rights of its minorities, but also of those of its vast ethnic Turkish majority.

COMMUNITIES UNDER THE
ARCHDIOCESE OF CONSTANTINOPLE

In his detailed and invaluable study of the pogrom of September 6-7, 1955, Christoforos Chrêstidês gives the following vital and detailed statistics on the numbers of families, churches, and institutions that existed in the larger Greek community of Istanbul and its environs on the eve of its destruction (see *Ekthesis*, pp. 26-36).

Community	Statistics
I. Old City	
1. Cibalı (Tzimbali)	Families: no information
	Church of St. Nicholas
	Grammar school, 4 grades
	School food program
	Philoptochos Adelphotês
	Cultural club
2. Balat	Families: 24
	Church of the Taxiarchs
	Grammar school, 4 grades
	School food program
	Philoptochos Adelphotês
	League for Clothing the Poor
	Daycare center
3. Tahtakapı (Xyloporta)	Families: 45
	Churches: St. Demetrios; Panagia Vlachernon
	Grammar school, 3 grades
	Philoptochos Adelphotês
	Cultural club
4. Potiras	Families: 45
	St. George
	Philoptochos Adelphotês

5. Edirnekapı	Families: 102 St. George Grammar school, 4 grades *Philoptochos Adelphotês* Cultural club School food program Clinic
6. Balino	Families: no information Church of the Dormition of the Theotokos *Philoptochos Adelphotês*
7. Kumkapı (Kontoskalion)	Families: 405 Churches: Panagia Elpis, St. Kyriake Grammar school, 6 grades School food program *Philoptochos Adelphotês* Cultural club Clinic
8. Yenikapı (Vlanga)	Families: 205 Saints Theodoroi Grammar school, 6 grades School food program *Philoptochos Adelphotês* Cultural and art club
9. Samatya (Psamatheia)	Families: 304 Churches: St. George; St. Menas; Saints Constantine and Helen; The Assumption; St. Nicholas Grammar school, 6 grades 3 *Philoptochoi Adelphotêtes* Cultural club
10. Muhli (Mouchlion)	Families: 110 The Panagia *Philoptochos Adelphotês* Cultural club
11. Topkapı	Families: 62 St. Nicholas *Philoptochos Adelphotês*
12. Belgratkapı (Veligradion)	Families: 16 The Panagia *Philoptochos Adelphotês* Clinic

13. Altı Mermer (Ex Marmarôn, in a state of dissolution)	Families: 17 The Panagia *Philoptochos Adelphotês*
14. Tekfur Sarayı (Ayvansaray)	Families: 32 The Dormition of the Theotokos *Philoptochos Adelphotês*
15. Salmatobruk	Families: 23 The Dormition of the Theotokos *Philoptochos Adelphotês*
16. Eğrikapı	Families: 27 The Dormition of the Theotokos *Philoptochos Adelphotês*
17. Fener (Phanarion)	Families: 314 Seat of the ecumenical patriarchate Patriarchal church of St. George Schools: *Megalê tou Genous Scholê* (*Gymnasion*); Iôakeimeion School for Girls; Marasleios Grammar School School food program *Philoptochos Adelphotês* Cultural club

II. New City

1. Beyoğlu (Pera/Staurodromion)	Families: 7,700 Churches: The Panagia; Holy Trinity; Saints Constantine and Helen *Gymnasia*: Zographeion (boys); Zappeion (girls); Central School for Girls Grammar Schools: Zographeion; Zappeion; Central School for Girls; Holy Trinity; Saints Constantine and Helen; Nane; Ainalıçeşme, Tarses Vareidou (private) School food programs Various brotherhoods, associations, and clubs Athletic association Clinic

2. Kurtuluş (Tataula)	Families: 1,975 Churches: St. Athanasios; St. Demetrios; St. Eleutherios Grammar school, 6 grades School food program *Philoptochos Adelphotês* Cultural club 2 Athletic associations Clinic
3. Galata	Families: 1,250 Churches: Christ the Savior; St. Nicholas; St. John of the Chians Grammar school, 6 grades School food program *Philoptochoi Adelphotêtes* Cultural club Athletic association
4. Feriköy	Families: 1,289 The Holy Apostles Grammar school, 6 grades School food program *Philoptochos Adelphotês* Cultural club Clinic
5. Propodôn Kurtuluş (Euangelistria)	Families: 375 Euangelistria Grammar school, 5 grades School food program *Philoptochos Adelphotês* Cultural club Club of the Friends of Education Clinic
6. Hasköy	Families: 60 Church and *agiasma* of St. Paraskeue Grammar school, 3 grades *Philoptochos Adelphotês*

III: European shore of the Bosphorus	
1. Beşiktaş (Diplokionion)	Families: 122 Churches: The Panagia Palaiou Baniou (Paşa Mahalle); The Panagia Diplokioniou Grammar school, 5 grades *Philoptochoi Adelphotêtes* Cultural club
2. Ortaköy (Mesochôrion)	Families: 180 St. Phocas Grammar school, 5 grades School food program *Philoptochos Adelphotês* Cultural club
3. Kuruçeşme (Xerokrinê)	Families: 17 St. Demetrios *Philoptochos Adelphotês*
4. Arnavutköy (Mega Reuma)	Families: no information *Agiasmata*: St. Onouphrios; Prophet Elias Grammar school, 6 grades School food program *Philoptochos Adelphotês* Cultural club
5. Bebek (Şile)*	Families: 85 St. Charalambos Grammar school, 4 grades *Philoptochos Adelphotês*
6. Boyaciköy (Vafeochôrion)	Families: 96 Euangelistria Grammar school, 6 grades School food program *Philoptochos Adelphotês* Cultural club
7. İstinye (Sosthenion, Stenê)	Families: no information St. Nicholas; *agiasma* of St. Marina *Philoptochos Adelphotês*

* This is how Chrêstidês presents the data although Bebek is on the European shore and Şile is on the Asian shore of the Bosphorus, and the two areas are quite distant from each other. The two communities might have been joined administratively because of the latter's decline.

8. Yeniköy (Neochôrion)	Families: 220 Churches: The Panagia; St. George (cemetery); *agiasma* of Panagia Phatnes Grammar school, 6 grades School food program *Philoptochos Adelphotês* Cultural club

IV. Metropolitanate of Chalcedon on the Asian shore of the Bosphorus

1. Kadıköy (Chalcedon)	Families: no information Churches: Holy Trinity; St. Euphemia; St. Ignatios (cemetery); St. George in Yeldeğirmeni; St. John Grammar schools: 6 grades in Kadıköy; 3 grades in Kalamış; 3 grades in Yeldeğirmeni School food program *Philoptochos Adelphotês* Cultural club in Moda Clinic
2. Üsküdar (Skoutari or Chrysoupolis)	Families: no information Prophet Elias Grammar school, 6 grades *Philoptochos Adelphotês* Cultural club
3. Kuzguncuk (Chrysokeramon)	Families: no information Churches: St. Panteleimon; St. George Grammar school, 5 grades *Philoptochos Adelphotês* Cultural club
4. Çengelköy	Families: no information Church of St. George; *agiasma* of St. Panteleimon Grammar school, 5 grades *Philoptochos Adelphotês*
5. Kandilli	Families: no information The Transfiguration Grammar school *Philoptochos Adelphotês*

6. Paşabahçe	Families: no information
	Church of Saints Constantine and Helen;
	chapel of St. Kyriake; *agiasma* of the Panagia
	Philoptochos Adelphotês
7. Beykoz	Families: no information
	St. Paraskeue

V. Metropolitanate of Derkon (European shore of the upper Bosphorus)

1. Yeni Mahalle	Families: 77*
	St. John; *agiasma* of John Prodromos
	Philoptochos Adelphotês
2. Büyükdere (Vathyryax)	Families: 121
	St. Paraskeue
	Grammar school, 6 grades
	School food program
	Cultural club
3. Tarabya (Therapeia)	Families: 144
	Churches: St. Paraskeue;
	St. George; Saints Constantine and Helen
	(cemetery); *agiasma* of St. Kyriake
	Grammar school, 6 grades
	School food program
	Philoptochos Adelphotês
	Athletic association

* Chrêstidês gives a figure of 90 families on p. 91 of his *Ekthesis.*

VI. Metropolitanate of Derkon (European shore of the Sea of Marmara)

1. Bakırköy (Makrochôrion)	Families: 490 St. George *Philoptochos Adelphotês* Cultural club
2. Yeşilköy (Agios Stefanos)	Families: 119 St. Stephanos Grammar school *Philoptochos Adelphotês* Cultural club Club of the Friends of Education

VII. Metropolitanate of Prinkiponeson

1. Kınalıada (Prôtê)	Families: no information Churches: The Panagia; The Christ *Philoptochos Adelphotês*
2. Burgazada (Antigonê)	Families: no information Church of St. John Monasteries: The Christ; St. George Karypes Grammar school, 6 grades Cultural club
3. Heybeliada (Chalkê)	Families: no information Churches: St. Nicholas; St. George of Kremnou; Holy Trinity (Theological School); St. Spyridon Sketes Grammar school, 6 grades *Philoptochos Adelphotês* Cultural club
4. Büyükada (Prinkipo)	Families: no information Churches: St. Demetrios; The Panagia Monasteries: St. Nicholas; The Christ; St. George Koudounas 2 Grammar schools, 6 grades *Philoptochos Adelphotês* Cultural club

LISTS OF THE DEAD IN THE POGROM

As indicated in Chapter 3, the lists below are based on the Helsinki Watch (now Human Rights Watch) report, The Greeks of Turkey, published in 1992 as part of the organization's "Denying Human Rights and Ethnic Identity" series. As is immediately evident, the lists are problematic; nevertheless, they are the only source from which a reconstruction of the actual number of victims of the progrom can be attempted.

I. ATZEMOGLOU'S LIST

1. Father Chrysanthos Mantas, burned to death after being soaked with gasoline; body thrown into a well.
2. Bishop Gerasimos of Pamphilos, beaten viciously, died later.
3. Metropolitan Gennadios of Helioupolis, beaten at home in Yeniköy, died a few days later.
4. Unknown priest of Edirnekapı, completely disappeared.
5. Unknown priest of Chalkê, found dead in Chalkê.
6. George Erpapzoglu(?), sexton of church in Paşabahçe, murdered in dynamited church.
7. Unknown sexton of neighborhood of Anadolu Hisar, murdered on the altar.[1]
8. Avraam Anavas, killed in the Moton store.[2]
9. Olga Kimiadou, beaten to death, heart attack.[3]
10. Thanasês Misiroglou, murdered in his store.
11. Eve Yolma, dragged outside Working Girls' Hostel, raped, and murdered.
12. Unknown "disrespectful" Greek lynched in the area of Yeni Cami.[4]
13. Isaak Uludağ, educator of Beşiktaş, burned alive in his school.[5]
14. Theopoula Papadopoulou, Üsküdar, raped and murdered.
15. Giannês Balkês, found dead on a street of Makrochôri (Bakırköy).
16. Kônstantinos Chatzopoulos (father of MP Alexandros Chatzopoulos), beaten savagely in his house and died soon after.

[1] Reported in *Cumhuriyet*, 9/7/55.
[2] Reported in *Cumhuriyet*, 9/8/55.
[3] Reported in *Hürriyet*, 9/8/55.
[4] Reported in *Milliyet*, 9/8/55.
[5] Reported in *Cumhuriyet*, 9/8/55.

17. Avakoum İpekçi, died from fright.

II. KOUMAKÊS'S LIST

18. Zênovia Charitonidês, raped and died on the night of the pogrom.
19. Asêmenia Parantônopoulos, raped and died on the night of the pogrom.
20. Twenty-year-old-woman kidnapped from the Working Girls' Hostel, raped, and died.
21. George Korpovas.
22. Emmanuêl Tzanetês.
23. Nikolas Karamanoğlu.

III. *MAKEDONIA*'S LIST, 9.13.55

24. A youth who died from fright.
25. Unknown owner of a naval-supplies store in Pera committed suicide.
26. Unknown youth lynched.
27, 28, 29. Three unidentified bodies dug out of destroyed shops.
30, 31. Two unidentified bodies washed ashore in the Golden Horn, aged approximately sixty-five and twenty years of age.
32. A certain George (full name unknown), approximately sixty-five years old, died from fright, Paşabahçe.
33. Alexandros Chatzopoulos's mother.

IV. TSOUKATOS, *SEPTEMVRIANA 1955*

34. Alexandros Iatropoulos, teacher, succumbed to violent beatings in the Fener district

V. YELDA, *AZALIRKEN*

35, 36, 37. Three burned bodies found in a sack in Beşiktaş.*

---

* Atzemoglou, *Mnêmes*, pp. 61-63; Leônidas Koumakês, *The Miracle*, Athens, 1982, pp. 54-55, speaks of the death of over twenty people.

AREAS IN WHICH GREEK BUSINESSES WERE ATTACKED IN ISTANBUL ON SEPTEMBER 6-7, 1955

I. NEW CITY

Abanoz	Hamalbaşı	Perşembe Pazarı
Babuk Pazar	Kalyoncu Kulluk	Şişli
Balık Pazar	Karaköy	Sıraselviler
Bankalar Caddesi	Kumbaracı	Syrian Market
Beşiktaş	Kurtuluş	Taksim and
Beyoğlu	Maçka	İstiklal Caddesi
Cihangir	Meşrutiyet	Tarlabaşı
Dolapdere	Nişantaş	Tepebaşı
Feridiye	Osmanbey	Tünel
Fermeneciler	Pangaltı	Yüksek Kaldırım
Galata	Parmakkapı	
Galatasaray	Pasaj Kristaki	

II. OLD CITY

Ayasofya	Edirnekapı	Mahmut Paşa
Kapalı Çarşı	Eminönü	Mısır Çarşı
Aksaray	Fener	Samatya
Ankara Caddesi	Gedikpaşa	Sirkeci
Babıali Caddesi	Hassırlar	Tahmis
Bahçekapı	Kapalı Çarşı	Tahtakapı
Bakırköy	Koska	Vefa
Balat	Küçükkapı	Yedikule
Cağaloğlu Caddesi	Küçükpazar	Yenikapı/Langa
Çarşıkapı Caddesi	Kumkapı	Yeşilköy
Cibalı	Laleli	
Defterdar		

III. EUROPEAN SHORE OF THE BOSPHORUS

Arnavutköy	Ortaköy
Bebek	Sariyer
Boyacıköy	Tarabya
İstinye	Yeni Mahalle
Kireçburnu	Yeniköy
Kuruçeşme	

IV. ASIAN SHORE OF THE BOSPHORUS

Anadolu Hisar	Kandilli
Beykoz	Kuzguncuk
Çengelköy	Paşabahçe
Göksu	Üsküdar
Kadıköy	Yeldeğirmeni
Kalamış	

V. PRINCES' ISLANDS

The attacks on these islands took place primarily on Heybeliada and Büyükada.

Sources: For references and sources, see the relevant sections in Chapter 3.

CATALOGUE OF DAMAGES TO PROPERTY OF BRITISH SUBJECTS ON SEPTEMBER 6-7, 1955

The document is presented, with slight modifications in punctuation and usage, but with spelling kept intact. Unless otherwise indicated, all amounts are in Turkish liras.

ANNEX I: ISTANBUL—DAMAGE TO OR LOSS OF PROPERTY

1. Isaac and Raphael CARACO & CO.

303 Istiklal Caddesi, Beyoglu: China and silverware shop completely destroyed with contents.

Total (including TL187,813 for loss of profits)   TL942,500.00

2. Jacques CARACO

71, Financillar Istanbul: 36½ percent interest (TL38,168.64) in the firm Billuri, which owns a china and silverware shop and show rooms which were destroyed. Also loss of a fur mantle, valued at TL10,000, belonging to his wife, which was in the fur shop Stanovic, 413 Istiklal Caddesi, which was destroyed.

Business	*38,188.64*
Personal	*10,000.00*
Total Value	*48,188.64*

3. Messrs. J. W. WHITTAL & CO LTD

Retail shop at 252 Tarlabashi Caddesi, Beyoglu: Destroyed. Also merchandise lying on consignment in the shops of other retailers, lost when the shops were destroyed. Also a record player (value TL750) belonging to Mr. K. E. Whittal, which was destroyed in the firm's shop.

Business	*12,390.00*
Personal	*750.00*
Total	*13,140.00*

4. Theoharis L. LATOPOULOS

Grocery shop at 37 Faik Pasha Caddesi, Beyoglu: Smashed and contents destroyed or looted.

Value   *12,850.00*

5. Antonio CARUANA

Monumental masonry business at 39 Yenisehir Sirdar Yener Caddesi, Beyoglu: Heavily damaged with most of its contents.

Total estimate of damage   *65,120.00*

6. Mrs. Sophia NOCK

Cinar caddesi, Yel Ufurdum Sokak 2, Buyukada, Istanbul: Lost a large quantity of furniture and personal property stored in three different places at Haskoy, Istanbul, all of which were destroyed. The three addresses were:

Mrs. F. Tekmazoglu, Aynali Kavak Sokak 20;

Mr. D. Petridis, Cakirgoz Sokak 12;

Mr. D. Sokolaridis, Iskele Caddesi 6.

Total estimate of loss   *60,025.00*

7. Leon WILLIAMS

Imitation jewellry and perfume shops [*sic*] at 172/2 Istiklal Caddesi, Beyoglu: Completely destroyed.

Total value of shop and contents   *10,000.00*

8. Giovanni MIZZI

161/1 Tarlabashi Caddesi, Beyoglu: Heating and electrical goods shop badly damaged and many of the contents destroyed and looted.

Total estimate of damage and loss   *9,000.00*

9. Santo N. SPINOCCHIA

3 Okchumussa Caddesi, Galata: Electrical goods shop badly damaged; dining room and bedroom suite lost at the furniture shop of Messrs. Cirigotis, 116 Meshrutiyet Caddesi, Beyoglu.

Business   *11,000.00*
Personal   *14,750.00*
Total estimate of damage and loss   *25,750.00*

10. Messrs. Sidney NOWILL & CO.

P. O. Box 1154, Galata: A quantity of paper lost which was stored with the printing firm Yorgi Furtuna, 47 Gelipdede Caddesi, Beyoglu.

Total estimate of loss   *870.00*

11. Ulysses GRISETI

203-5, Tershane Caddesi, first floor, Galata: Office premises of the shop belonging to two firms with which he is associated were completely wrecked. Also damage to his house at Therapia and to his car.

Total estimate of loss and damage   *34,922.51*

12. George GENOVESE

2 Aynali Pasaji, Beyoglu: Shoemaker's shop completely destroyed.

Damage estimated at   *6,000.00*

13. Kornilyos GALYA

7 Saksi Sokak, Pangalti, Istanbul: Small repair shop destroyed.

Total value of shop and contents estimated at   *1,586.00*

14. Edward J. JAMIESON

69/2 Meshrutiyet Caddesi, Beyoglu: Nameplates of his shop smashed (TL110). Also clothes lost which were left with the Yildiz dry-cleaning establishment at 255 Meshrutiyet Caddesi (TL570).

Total damage and loss estimated at   *1,980.00*

15. Antonio MANGIUM

248 Kurtulush Caddesi, Sinemakoysavash Sokak, Cicek Apt., Kurtulush: Two shops—a small foundry and repair shop at 133/135 Yelkenciler, Kalafat Yeri, Galata, and a general store at 32 Sirdar Omar Caddesi, Beyoglu. Both damaged. Damage also to his house at the Kurtulush address.

Total loss and damage estimated at   *43,050.00*

16. N. ZERVOUDAKIS

28 Eski Gumruk Sokak, Galata: Ship's chandler's shop attacked and badly damaged.

Total estimate of damage after judicial survey   *4,205.50*

17. Arthur BENNET

Hacopoulo Ap., Istiklal Caddesi, Istanbul: Flat with all contents, including valuable antique furniture, porcelain and silverware completely destroyed.

Total estimate of damage   *129,790.00*

18. Amadeo GAUCI

Embassy Residence, Istanbul: House at Haskoy attacked, furniture destroyed and clothes stolen.

Total estimate of damage and loss   *3,000.00*

19. Leopold CALOCI

29 Yuksek Kaldirim, Galata: Printing shop wrecked and printing machine smashed.

Estimated loss   8,000.00

20. Antigoni PAVLOVICH

21 Turna Sokak, Elmadag, Beyoglu: Shop at Gelipdede Caddesi, 2 1/1, Beyoglu: Destroyed with all contents.

Total estimate of damage   27,950.00

21. The Commercial Bank of the Near East Limited

Premises attacked, windows broken and a certain amount of interior damage.

Total estimate of loss   4,425.00

22. Nicolas STELIANIDES

Veli Konagi Caddesi 59, Nishantash, Istanbul: Family vault at Shishli Orthodox Cemetery damaged, his wife's and other relatives' tombs destroyed and desecrated. Also the door of his house damaged when attacked.

Total estimate of damage   4,500.00

23. Mario BORG

5/1 Bekar Sokak, Beyoglu: Two suits lost at a dry-cleaning establishment which was destroyed.

Total estimate of loss   700.00

24. George PELLEGRINI

Mechanic at H. M. Consulate General, Istanbul: Blankets, sheets and pillows looted from his house.

Total estimate of loss   200.00

25. Charles SCHEMBRY

Market Officer at H. M. Consulate General, Istanbul: Two armchairs and a sofa destroyed at the shop of Joseph Pavlovich at Kumbaraco Yokushu, Beyoglu. Also 9 metres of furnishing fabric stolen. Also damage in the flat of Mr. Schembry's mother at 54/31 Piremici Sokak, Tepebashi, Beyoglu.

Total loss and damage estimated at   1,115.00

26. Miss Mary VRETENITICHITCH

10 Herman Sokak, Hamal Bashi [*sic*], Beyoglu: Damage to the gate of her country house in Buyukada.

Estimated at   60.00

27. Joseph BONNICI

3/1 Ak Apt.,Nokaloglu Sokak, Silahsor Caddesi, Bomonti, Istanbul: Two suits and three skirts lost from the shop of Nico Bicakcioglu at 347 Halaskar Gazi Caddesi, Shishli.

Total loss estimated at 650.00

28. C. BRANCALEONE

55 Feslegen Sokak, Hamalbashi, Beyoglu: One overcoat and one suit lost at the tailor's shop Ipocrat Kerameris, 29 Hacopoulo Pasaji, Beyoglu.

Total loss estimated at 450.00

29. E. H. JONES

50/9 Rumeli Caddesi, Osmanbey, Istanbul: One wrist watch lost in the shop of V. & A. Koracides Bros. of 60 Necatibey Caddesi, Galata.

Total estimate of loss 350.00

30. Spiro MAMA

18 Bogurtlen Sokak, Therapia, Istanbul: House next to the house of the Orthodox Metropolitan at Therapia damaged.

Total estimate of damage 1,500.00

31. Philip PAVLOVICH

147 Meshrutiyet Caddesi, Tepebashi, Beyoglu: Family vault at Orthodox Cemetery at Shishli destroyed and desecrated.

Damage estimated at 1,500.00

32. Nicholas AZZOPARDI

Caretaker at the Crimean Memorial Church at Istanbul: His mother's tomb at the Therapia Cemetery damaged.

Estimated cost of repair 500.00

33. Andrea GENOVESE

Night watchman at H. M. Consulate General, Istanbul: House damaged.

Estimated at 230.00

34. Mr. B. S. BASSOUS

P. O. Box 119, Alexandria, Egypt: Luggage destroyed at Greek Airlines office.

Total estimate of loss £300.00

35. Alexander WARRINGTON

Macka Palas, No. 3/12 Machka, Istanbul: Two fur capes and a fur mantle lost at the dealer's shop when it was wrecked.

Total estimate 19,000.00

36. Miss E. CUMING

Assistant Naval Attache's Office, H. M. Consulate General, Istanbul: Some pieces of domestic silver lost when the shop was destroyed in which they were waiting to be sold.

Total estimate of loss   *950.00*

37. Mr. G. P. MURRAY

Dogan Bey Caddesi, Buyukada: Panes of glass broken in his house.

Total damage estimated at   *26.00*

38. Michael Charles HOLMES

British Consulate General, Istanbul: Certain items of clothing lost at the cleaner's.

Total estimate of loss   *325.00*

39. Mrs. Adelaide MANGO

65 St. Charles Square, London: Her late husband's grave damaged and desecrated at the Greek Orthodox Cemetery.

Total estimate of damage   *500.00*

40. Mrs. Froso BORG

Gulmez Hasan Sokak, Buyukdere, Istanbul: Her husband's tomb destroyed at the Orthodox Cemetery.

Total estimate of damage   *450.00*

41. Mr. A. A. DAWSON

3 Sucu Bahche Sokak, Arnavutkoy: One suit and a pair of shoes lost.

Total estimate of loss   *260.00*

42. Miss Esther CUPPA

Now resident in Greece: Some furniture which was stored in a Greek school building was lost when the building was destroyed.

Total estimate of loss   *2,500.00*

43. Captain A. P. PATERSON, R. N.

c/o H. M. Consulate General, Istanbul: One suit, one pair of trousers and one uniform suit lost at a dry-cleaning shop and laundry which was destroyed.

Total estimate of loss (£37.00)   *290.00*

44. Lieut. Commander R. S. BRYDEN, R. N.

H. M. Consulate General, Istanbul: Clothes lost at a cleaner's shop which was destroyed.

Total estimate of loss   *110.00*

45. Mr. and Mrs. Victor BINNS

4 Fenerli Turbe Sokak, Rumeli Hisar: Their house attacked in broad daylight on September 15, set on fire and four rooms of the house burnt.

Estimate of damage   *(not yet available)*

46. Mr. T. HAMMOND—School master at Robert College

Attempts made to set on fire his house at 11/13 Ashiyen Yolu, Kayalar, Bebek, on September 7, and again on September 8. Also another attempt on September 12 to set on fire the house on the outskirts of Robert College to which Mr. Hammond had moved, and a large piece of stone thrown through one of the windows of his house on September 19.

Estimate of damage   *(not yet available)*

47. Mr. and Mrs. A. B. TUBINI

147 Koybashi Caddesi, Yenikoy: An armed attack on their house on September 13, presumably with the object of doing personal violence.

Estimate of damage   *(not yet available)*

48. Mr. Harry WHYTE

c/o Alfons Torres, 31 Pershembe Bazar, Caddesi, Galata: Typewriter destroyed.

Estimate of damage   *75.00*

Total   TL**1,488,813.00 [plus £551]**

Source: TNA:PRO, Ankara, Dispatch No. 360, October 26, 1955. Annex II of the same document lists injuries inflicted on three British citizens. One person was stabbed inside her house at Rumeli Hisar, a second "was arrested and roughly handled by the police," and the third was "threatened by rioters at the Londra Oteli, Beyoglu." Annex III lists small-scale damage to British shops in Izmir.

Catalogue of compensation to British subjects for damages incurred on September 6-7, 1955

Annex I: Istanbul—Damages to or Loss of Property
[attached to the British Embassy's report of March 4, 1958]

Serial number	Name	Amount claimed (TL)	Amount paid (TL)	% Paid
1.	Caraco & Co.	942,500	172,712	18.3
2.	Jacques Caraco	48,188		
3.	J. W. Whittal & Co.	13,140	11,921	90.7
4.	Latopoulos	12,850		
5.	Caruana	65,120	10,000	15.4
6.	Mrs. Nock	60,025	8,000	13.3
7.	Williams	10,000	5,000	50.0
8.	Mizzi	9,000		
9.	Spinocchia	25,750	3,000	11.7
10.	Nowill	870		
11.	Griseti	34,922		
12.	G. Genovese	6,000	2,000	33.0
13.	Galya	1,586		
14.	Jamieson	1,980		
15.	Mangium	43,050		
16.	Zervoudakis	4,205		
17.	Bennet	129,790	25,800	19.8
18.	Gauci	3,000	2,000	66.7
19.	Caloci	8,000	4,000	50.0
20.	Pavlovich	27,950	10,000	
21.	Near East Bank	4,425		

22.	Stelianides	4,500		
23.	M. Borg	700		
24.	G. Pellegrini	200	200	100.0
25.	Schembry	1,135	600	52.9
26.	Vretenitichitch	60		
27.	Bonnici	650		
28.	Brancaleone	450	450	100.0
29.	Jones	350		
30.	Mama	1,500		
31.	P. Pavlovich	1,500		
32.	Azzopardi	500	400	80.0
33.	A. Genovese	230		
34.	B. S. Bassous	£300	TL1,500	c. 71.0
35.	Warrington	19,000	4,000	21.1
36.	Cuming	950	950	100.0
37.	Murray	26		
38.	Holmes	325		
39.	Mango	500		
40.	F. Borg	450	450	100.0
41.	Dawson	260	260	100.0
42.	Cuppa	2,500	1,500	60.0
43.	Paterson	290	290	100.0
44.	Bryden	110		
48.	Whyte	675	650	96 .0
49.	Yamut	£60	TL420	100.0
50.	Edwards	1,200 (rejected)		
	Total	**c. 681,250**	**266,053**	**15.8**

Izmir			
Horstein	2,732	1,000	
HMG's Typewriter	200		
Polycarp Buttigag	215	215	
SS Livorno	£105.17	840	
SS Brescia	198	198	
SS Brescia	£22.10		13.3
Total	**c. 4,345**	**2,253?**	

Source: TNA:PRO, Ankara, Dispatch No. 1492/12, No. RK1481/3, March 4, 1958, Annex I.

CLAIMS FOR COMPENSATION BY GREEK NATIONALS AND FINAL PAYMENT BY THE TURKISH GOVERNMENT

Case Number	Claimant's Name	Original Claim	Final Sum Paid
209	Alexios, Geôrgios Iôannou	19,960.00	4,000.00
91	Alexiadou, Katina Dêmêtriou	17,100.00	2,500.00
412	Aetras, Nikolaos Dêmêtriou	32,126.00	2,000.00
808	Albertês, Nikolaos Michaêl	3,526.00	1,000.00
927	Anastasiadês, Zacharias Michaêl	537,600.00	124,397.73
367	Anastasiadês, Iôannês Kônstantinou *	105,477.00	29,980.98
293	Andreadou, Maria Panagiôtou	7,575.00	1,000.00
904	Andriôtês, Iakôvos Iôannou	420.00	90.00
1015	Anninos, Stylianos Alexandrou (share)	3,964.00	15,823.84
281	Antôniou, Kônstantinos Antôniou	102,000.00	17,500.00
1047	Apergê, Frangiskê, wife of Nikolaos	12,000.00	2,000.00
783	Armaos, Nikolaos Antôniou *	1,585.00	800.00
305	Asterês, Chrêstos Nikolaou *	43,672.00	8,000.00
190	Vavoulas, Geôrgios Nikolaou	72,350.00	18,500.00
420	Valsamakês, Antônios Dêmêtriou	2,014.00	1,800.00
628	Varlas, Dêmêtrios Panagiôtou	6,000.00	1,500.00
66	Varesês, Stefanos Spyrou	23,735.00	5,000.00
8	Vasalios, Geôrgios Dêmêtriou *	48,340.00	1,505.00
116	Vasilakos, Vasileios Geôrgiou *	49,500.00	10,000.00
252	Vatê, Ermionê Nikolaou	16,200.00	4,000.00
253	Vatê, Charikleia Nikolaou	36,000.00	2,000.00
12	Veletsos, Kleovoulos Geôrgiou *	50,000.00	12,000.00
134	Veltras, Epameinôndas Nikolaou	26,312.00	3,361.50
605	Vikopoulos, Stergios Kônstantinou	23,800.00	9,000.00

259	Vlavianos, Kônstantinos Michaêl	8,275.00	2,200.00
53	Volakês, Alexandros Iôannou	23,955.00	5,000.00
347	Vonortas, Dêmêtrios Iôannou	123,700.00	15,000.00
833	Vranê, Smarô	14,125.00	3,000.00
909	Gavala, Marika	25,000.00	1,000.00
428	Gadê, Maria	3,600.00	1,160.00
1040	Ganetidês, Nikolaos Charalambous	2,245.00	350.00
120	Garbês, Chrêstos Iôannou	37,910.00	7,500.00
965	Garyfallou, Frangoulês Kallinikou	221,320.00	25,944.47
340	Gasparakês, Dêmêtrios Geôrgiou *	50,000.00	13,000.00
990	Gerardos, Kyriakos Panagiôtou *	144,577.00	50,000.00
426	Giannakarelês, Dêmêtrios Iôannou	13,066.00	6,700.00
396	Giataganas, Chrêstos Spyrou	34,755.00	1,500.00
657	Ginas, Êlias Eustratiou	5,672.00	1,850.00
471	Gioulekas, Iôannês-Nikolaos Iôannou	12,000.00	3,000.00
207	Giôkas, Geôrgios Stefanou	8,500.00	1,000.00
365	Gizês, Kônstantinos Markou	51,300.00	15,000.00
625	Glytsos, Kônstantinos Emmanuêl	88,752.00	8,000.00
584	Glypsês, Alexandros Spyridônos	13,710.00	4,000.00
84	Daniolos, Michaêl	15,000.00	4,000.00
29	Dapollas, Geôrgios	34,963.00	7,000.00
109	Devliôtês, Athanasios	8,350.00	2,000.00
955	Legaitas, Anastasios	13,530.00	1,250.00
592	Delatolas, Antônios	59,160.00	1,500.00
800	Delatolas, Petros	145,510.00	20,000.00
388	Dermou, Alikê	15,000.00	2,000.00
93	Dêmêtriadês, Michaêl Geôrgiou	4,650.00	500.00
530	Dimantês, Dêmêtrios	24,060.00	2,350.00
673	Diamantopoulos, Dêmêtrios	8,950.00	500.00
859	Doukoglou, Antônios	16,589.00	4,000.00
101	Doupês, Êlias	25,350.00	1,500.00
195	Douratsos, Natalês	30,286.00	5,000.00
297	Droumpoulas, Theofilos	26,037.00	6,500.00
350	Dorizas, Menandros *	33,940.00	10,000.00
362	Droumpoulas, Kônstantinos	23,670.00	2,500.00
165	Exarchos, Anastasios	60,000.00	2,000.00
214	Exarchos, Stauros	36,695.00	5,000.00

973	Zampikou, Charikleia	37,500.00	12,500.00
893	Zarida, Angelikê	34,950.00	3,500.00
343	Zarokôstas, Panos	82,300.00	5,446.00
229	Zaharatos, Geôrgios	11,986.00	3,050.00
729	Zelê, Eleutheria	40,000.00	500.00
596	Theotokas, Iôannês	22,500.00	3,000.00
104	Theocharês, Anastasios	38,530.00	10,000.00
245	Iatropoulos, Menelaos	5,150.00	1,700.00
174	Itsios, Simos	35,000.00	10,500.00
58	Iôannou, Aristotelês	26,000.00	4,000.00
302	Kavalarês, Iôannês	33,870.00	3,500.00
894	Kangelarês, Apostolos	22,080.00	1,500.00
884	Kalligarês, Stauros	6,000.00	4,000.00
238	Kalogeras, Michaêl	37,460.00	14,000.00
50	Kapellos, Stefanos	20,000.00	4,500.00
600	Karakygiannês, Chrêstos	15,760.00	1,000.00
233	Karagiannopoulos, Nikolaos *	267,205.00	45,000.00
996	Karametsês, Chrêstos	1,945.00	860.00
107	Karapiperês, Kônstantinos *	66,000.00	11,000.00
22	Karvelês, Athanasios *	37,000.00	8,250.00
967	Katanos, Stergios	241,025.00	45,000.00
966	Katanos, Nikolaos	(241,025.00)	
2	Katsês, Athanasios	480,000.00	130,000.00
3	Katsês, Petros	64,000.00	5,000.00
895	Klôsteridês, Nikolaos *	3,350.00	750.00
555	Kongourês, Iôsêf	101,290.00	19,241.00
458	Kozakês, Athanasios	366,100.00	5,000.00
553	Kolaros Brothers	36,895.00	2,500.00
496	Kolisanês, Marinos	12,000.00	1,500.00
263	Kollios, Andreas	30,000.00	0.00
278	Kontorouchas, Chrêstos	35,500.00	9,000.00
872	Kotrôtsios, Kônstantinos	4,000.00	300.00
117	Kounadês, Dêmêtrios *	57,670.00	8,919.89
48	Kounadês, Fôtios *	83,980.00	14.100.88
14	Kounanidês, Fôtios	50,100.00	12,140.00
166	Kourtalês, Geôrgios	281,098.00	60,000.00
1042	Kountanas, Chrêstos	2,149.00	750.00

389	Kourtesês, Markos	35,780.00	1,500.00
180	Krithariôtês, Euangelos	1,000.00	900.00
465	Kyritzês, Lenas	198,025.00	34,279.00
680	Kônstantinidês, Ermenios *	116,108.00	18,000.00
617	Kônstantinidês, Êraklês	2,300.00	250.00
325	Kônstantinidês, Kônstantinos and Geôrgios *	125,512.00	42,500.00
475	Kônstantinidês, Kônstantinos and Miltiadês	46,278.00	22,000.00
402	Kônstantinidês, Sôkratês	26,420.00	50.00
910	Kônstantinou, Elenê	2,300.00	700.00
106	Kônstantinou, Iôannês	55,000.00	2,000.00
971	Lambropoulos, Paikos	30,561.00	7,271.01
45?	Leipsanos, Antônios	14,000.00	2,500.00
821?	Lembesopoulos, Euripidês	9,662.00	2,000.00
486	Liazê, Argyrios *	53,725.00	7,500.00
484	Liazê, Siderês	24,795.00	6,000.00
462	Lafas, Dêmêtrios	30,500.00	3,000.00
260	Langos, Chrêstos	13,995.00	1,500.00
326	Logothetês, Geôrgios	35,500.00	6,500.00
524	Lorandos, Kosmas *	5,000.00	2,000.00
92	Loukatos, Dêmêtrios	9,815.00	2,500.00
10	Loufakês, Iôannês *	42,175.00	5,000.00
90	Lykiardopoulos, Eustathios *	5,737.00	700.00
89	Magoulas, Nikolaos	28,850.00	3,300.00
949	Makkou, Marika	10,500.00	3,500.00
477	Makrês, Kônstantinos Nikolaou	10,180.00	2,000.00
769	Makrês, Savvas	28,700.00	5,000.00
9	Makrês, Fôtios	28,183.00	2,000.00
372	Manthios, Theodôros *	40,000.00	6,000.00
923 (872?)	Manikas, Dêmêtrios *	239,693.00	30,000.00
179	Mantzoukas, Stauros	13,295.00	6,000.00
488	Ma[r?]inos, Iôannês	7,200.00	1,000.00
1	Mastorakês, Antônios	91,565.00	10,000.00
1032	Markopoulos, Nikolaos	5,330.00	750.00
683	Mauromaras, Panagiôtês	8,900.00	2,500.00
685	Mauros, Stylianos *	55,545.00	2,000.00
146	Mauroudês, Theodôros	8,000.00	3,000.00

35	Mermêngas, Dêmêtrios	7,402.00	2,000.00
468	Mesolongitês, Têlemachos	14,400.00	750.00
827	Metretikas, Iôannês	92,600.00	1,500.00
563	Melas, Nikolaos *	44,492.00	12,752.50
132	Menopoulos, Dêmêtrios	10,000.00	2,500.00
817	Mytakidês, Vasileios	15,000.00	2,000.00
188	Michaêl, Nikolaos *	7,780.00	2,000.00
32	Bagias, Nikêtas *	88,635.00	10,000.00
86?	Belias, Iôannês	31,550.00	3,000.00
61	Belias, Pantelês	21,450.00	?
31	Bournakos (?), Iôannês	435.00	200.00
8?	Myrôdia, Sofia	15,000.00	2,100.00
150	Mytilênaios, Geôrgios	10,965.00	1,500.00
369	Morfitês, Emmanouêl	9,250.00	276.25
45	Nintês (?), Dêmêtrios	12,700.00	2,100.00
198	Nomidou, Thalia	47,322.00	4,000.00
301	Nomikos, Kônstantinou *	128,600.00	45,000.00
138	Noios, Nikolaos *	22,508.00	4,000.00
330	Nonnês, Êlias	16,765.00	2,500.00
261	Noutsios, Panagiôtês	17,500.00	2,000.00
310	Dêmos, Dêmêtrios * [out of order in the original]	14,000.00	3,000.00
44	Xenakês, Iôannês	5,997.00	3,000.00
78	Oikonomou, Dêmêtrios	30,010.00	3,500.00
41	Oikonomou, Iôannes Panagiôtou	10,520.00	3,500.00
640	Pagônês, Michaêl *	10,500.00	600.00
21	Panopoulos, Nikolaos *	43,000.00	8,000.00
266	Pantazopoulos, Leônidas	4,736.00	700.00
194	Papavramidês, Agathangelos Athanasiou	16,620.00	2,000.00
267	Papavramidês, Leandros Athanasiou	37,200.00	3,679.78
79	Papadês, Dêmêtrios	18,050.00	2,000.00
130	Papadês, Leônidas	5,000.00	1,000.00
164	Papadês, Iôannês	11,000.00	2,000.00
394	Papadopoulos, Vasileios *	54,000.00	10,948.00
549	Papadopoulos, Geôrgios	2,022.00	450.00
905	Papadopoulos, Leônidas	1,455.00	400.00
227	Papatheodôrou, Kônstantinos *	129,756.00	14,155.79

558	Papanastasiou, Iôannês	8,249.00	2,000.00
495	Parisês, Iôannês *	13,541.00	1,500.00
972	Pastellas, Euthymios	526,190.00	65,000.00
543	Patounas, Dêmêtrios	60,000.00	4,000.00
501	Patrianos, Agamemnôn	2,851.00	750.00
727	Paulidês, Nikolaos	986.00	986.00
200	Pachnês, Kônstantinos	3,472.00	500.00
254	Pekounês, Antônios *	98,500.00	11,000.00
400	Pouplidês, Alexandros	18,042.00	3,000.00
46	Prelorentzou, Charikleia	2,500.00	750.00
196	Razês, Antônios	5,815.00	1,000.00
735	Rafaletos, Kônstantinos *	99,000.00	43,000.00
341	Roussos, Angelos	30,015.00	21,700.00
44	Sgourdaios, Theodôros	7,475.00	2,000.00
681	Santamourês, Mirkos	1,000.00	500.00
142	Sarrês, Iôannês	3,397.00	2,000.00
16	Sygrinê, Dêmêtrios	47,000.00	3,000.00
847	Sigounês, Michaêl	1,000.00	100.00
70	Siôtês, Kônstantinos	12,308.00	1,500.00
613	Skarpelês, Achilleus *	83,257.00	5,000.00
991	Solômos, Êlias *	63,200.00	15,000.00
556	Souliôtês, Êlias	11,160.00	2,500.00
47	Spyratou, Anastasia	2,500.00	500.00
508	Spyrou, Spyros	5,010.00	932.50
28	Stamargas, Euangelos	16,150.00	4,662.15
236	Stamatiou, Michaêl	45,530.00	1,055.00
519	Stafylias, Dêmêtrios	25,000.00	5,000.00
234	Stefanidês, Iakôvos	3,360.00	500.00
54	Strakarês, Geôrgios *	50,472.00	10,000.00
71	Strantzalês, Kônstantinos	30,949.00	2,000.00
520	Stratos, Fôtios	15,925.00	5,000.00
219	Stylianou, Chrêstos *	21,420.00	4,000.00
802	Synodinos, Antônios	125.00	125.00
773	Schoinas, Nikolaos	11,926.00	4,000.00
213	Tzinetas, Chrysostomos	9,500.00	3,500.00
570	Tzakanika, Feurônia	21,560.00	3,500.00
201	Tsampos, Theodôros	14,543.00	2,500.00
500	Tsikos, Apostolos	24,249.00	8,050.00

632	Tsoukatos, Athênodôros Panagiôtou	288,650.00	65,245.00
235	Fourtounas, Geôrgios	18,800.00	2,000.00
395	Frangantônê, Aglaia	6,700.00	750.00
311	Chaskopoulos, Dêmêtrios	9,595.00	4,000.00
248	Chaskopoulos, Stauros	11,430.00	6,315.00
403	Chatzêgeôrgiou, Tarsê	22,437.00	6,500.00
96	Chatzês, Athanasios	7,000.00	2,000.00
810	Chatzêparas, Dêmêtrios	56,225.00	3,500.00
108	Chatzopoulos, Geôrgios	9,000.00	3,500.00
82	Chrêstakês, Geôrgios	22,000.00	7,000.00
417	Chasapidou, Euthalia (Eudoxia?) *	59,010.00	6,000.00
947	Psaltês (?), Kônstantinos	3,214.00	800.00

The asterisk (*) indicates a case that also appears separately with the intermediate court/specialist evaluation of the original claim.

The cases are arranged alphabetically according to the Greek alphabet. There is no mention of the intermediate court procedure during which the real-estate specialist reevaluated the claim and usually pared it down before passing it on to the three-man tax committee that made the final reduction and often imposed taxes on the claim.

Fifty-one additional cases in which the court procedure is included, from the Greek ministry of foreign affairs (not included in the preceding 220 cases).

Name	Case number	Original claim (TL)	Court evaluation (TL)	% of claim	Final award (TL)	% of claim	Tax (TL)
Dallas, Vasileios	987	47,316					
		47,316	9,000	19	3,750	7.9	8,500
Dedes, Vasileios	175	45,570	19,000[1]	41.7	7,500	16.5	0
Delêgiannês, Dêmêtrios	287	54,134	13,775	25.4	13,000	24	22,194
Drosinos, Gerasimos	509	69,000	50,000	72	0	0	
Emmanouêlidês, Sergios	346	87,625	NP		20,000	22.8	19,000
Gouverês, Nikolaos	382						
Chaitalês, Apostolos	184	42,210	NCE		2,000	4.7	0
Inglesês, Aristeidês	761	51,400	NP		5,000	9.7	
Kônstantinidês, Z. Karapiperês, S. Stauropoulos	323	126,512	115,000	90.9	42,500	33.6	18,000
Kaiktsakês, Nikolaos	156	118,875	NCE		21,000	17.7	55,000
Kallinikos, Anastasios	361	62,667	62,667	100	18,826	30	40,000
Kazelas Brothers	997	38,931	35,849	92	8,725	22.4	0
Kazelas, Geôrgios and Kônstantinos	862	45,000	NCE		5,000	11.1	0
Keramarês, Ippokratês	280	5,550	3,700	66.7	3,000	54.1	0
Kônstantinidês, K. and S.	351	84,930	82,580	97.2	22,000	25.9	0
Kontomerkos, Chrêstos	27	58,000	32,000	55.2	6,000	10.3	0
Koukoularês, Iôannês	75	56,250	NCE		1,000	1.8	0
Leivadas, Grêgorios	141	42,100	NP		6,000	14.3	0
Lennas, Charalambos	464	55,735	52,635	94.4	17,000	30.5	0
Leukaros, Frangiskos	575	75,705	62,000 (?)	(81.9)	8,250	10.9	0
Liagourês, Nikolaos	601	75,650	59,000	78	12,500	16.5	0
Loukrezês, Kônstantinos	982	41,855	36,300	86.7	9,000	21.5	0
Mazarakês, Dionysios	701	50,599	50,599	100	15,000	29.6	2
Moustakês, Gerasimos[3]	317	61,500	2,800	4.6	3,000	4.9	
Melas, Nikolaos	563	41,489	15,011.95	36.2	12,752	30.7	5,600
Moukas, Vasileios	129	52,000	NCE		6,000	11.5	
Barotsês, Alfonsos	313	88,000	85,964	97.7	27,000	30.7	

[1] Disallowed.
[2] In abeyance.
[3] Payment is only for furniture, or for merchandise completely looted, and could not be evaluated.

Benadon, Vitalês	310	68,000	NP		15,000	22.1	0
Nanopoulos, Charalambos	485	44,300		NCE	5,050	11.4	2,150
	1003	526,327	406,151	77.2	103,808	19.7	100,000
Palavidês, Dêmêtrios[4]	1003	406,151	406,151	100	89,433	22	94,122
Palavidês, Dêmêtrios and Giotos, Leônidas, 50% each		36,050	36,050	100	14,315	40	
Pantazês, Iôannês	616	71,625	36,950	51.6	20,000	28	0
Papageôrgiou, Geôrgios and Panagiôtês	961	187,932	176,516	94	107,000	57	60,555
Papadopoulos, Antônios[5]	514						
Paparfiou, Nikolaos[6]	169	46,227	46,227	100	9,000	19.5	0
Papas, Euangelos (50% share)	24	40,000		NCE		7,500	18.8	0
							0
Patounas, Têlemachos	192	105,390	80,000	75.9	50,000	47.4	
Pitikas, Symeôn (50%)[7]	183	73,750	64,964	88.1	21,000	28.5	7,000
Plytas, Giôrgos	4	14,500		NCE	3,500	24.1	0
Smyrnaios, Stamatios	125	11,500		NCE	3,330	29	0
Smyrnaios, Kônstantinos	249	4,750		NCE	1,500	31.6	0
Terzakopoulos, Nikolaos	479	15,282	11,441	74.9	2,908	19	3,138.42
Tranakas, Dêmêtrios	237	26,000		NCE	3,000	11.5	0
Triantafyllidês, Dêmêtrios	644	51,455	18,350	35.7	5,300	10.3	0
Tsariôtês, Nikolaos	958	82,695	82,695	100	18,490	22.4	19,000
Tsitourês, Dêmêtrios[8]	409	99,000				0.0	
Vasileiadês, Iôannês[9]	325	70,000	58,000	83	15,000	21.4	2,000
Vasos, Paulos	271	9,150		NCE	996	10.9	0
Venetês, or Papadopoulos, Gerasimos, Christoforos	25	46,940	41,874	89.2	6,000	12.8	0
Xanthou, Elenê	715	46,344	27,750	59.9	8,000	17.3	0
Zacharopoulos, Panagiôtês and Euthymios	1022	51,670	28,120	54.4	17,972	34.8	0
Zellê, Eleutheria	729	40,000		NCE	500	1.3	0

[4] There are two separate reports; it may be that the two reports represent their respective phases of the process.

[5] Left for Greece.

[6] There is a separate record with the same case number and identical figures for Paparrodou, Nikolaos; one of the two names is most likely a misspelling.

[7] A second entry gives slightly different figures.

[8] He left for Athens where he remains.

[9] He did not bring his papers

NP = No papers

NCE = No court evaluation

Two further cases in which the court procedure is included, from Chrêstedês's *Ekthesis*:

Name	Original claim (TL)	Court evaluation	% of claim	Final award (TL)	% of claim
Dismanês, Dêmêtrios	24,060	2,350	9.8	2,350	9.8
Chatzês, Athanasios	7,000	7,000	100	2,000	29

Fifty-three additional cases, most of which went through the courts were for claims of TL3,595,443, or 20.5 percent of all claims, with final payments of TL738,845.

Sources: Geôrgios Kavounidês, Ekthesis, Greek Embassy, Washington, No. 4266/B/29, October 17 (and 11), 1955, and also Christoforos Chrêstidês, Ekthesis; Kavounidês's report is now available in Pênelopê Tsoukatou, Septemvriana 1955. Ê nychta tôn krystallôn tou Ellênismou tês Polês, pp. 221-252.

Catalogue of accused
for crimes perpetrated
on September 6-7, 1955

Kamil Önal
Charged under Penal Code Articles 128, 296, 311, and 71
Section II, pgs. i and ii: Adana press statement; burning Greek papers in Taksim, Sept. 4; press statement, Sept. 6; demonstrations beginning in Taksim Square; destruction of correspondence.

Hikmet Bil
Charged under Penal Code Articles 128 and 80
Circular after receipt of Küçük letter; burning Greek papers, Sept. 4; drafting statement of Cyprus is Turkish Association, Sept. 6.

Hüsamettin Canöztürk
Charged under Penal Code Articles 128 and 80
Burning Greek paper, Sept. 4; drafting statement of Sept. 6.

Orhan Birgit
Charged under Penal Code Article 128
Drafting statement of Sept. 6.

Nedim Üskiden
Charged under Penal Code Article 128
Drafting statement of Sept. 6.

Aydın Konuralp
Charged under Penal Code Articles 128, 274, 311, and 71
Distribution of Cyprus is Turkish placards; removal and destruction of correspondence in student federation headquarters sealed as evidence.

Hurşit Şahsuvar
Charged under Penal Code Articles 128, 80, 296, 311, and 71
Burning Greek papers, Sept. 4; distribution of placards; removal and destruction of sealed correspondence.

Öztürk Türker
Charged under Penal Code Articles 274, 296, and 71
Removal and destruction of correspondence sealed as evidence.

İsmail Türker
Charged under Penal Code Article 296
Removal and destruction of correspondence sealed as evidence.

Gündüz Gölün
Charged under Penal Code Article 128
Burning of Greek papers, Sept. 4.

Vedat Pekgirgin
Charged under Penal Code Article 161
Propagation of exaggerated reports of Thessalonikê explosion in Turkish consulate.

Göksin Sipahioğlu
Charged under Penal Code Article 161
Propagation of exaggerated reports of Thessalonikê explosion in Turkish consulate.

Mürşit Yolgeçe
Charged under Penal Code Articles 128, 71, and 311
Inciting crowds during demonstration in Taksim-Cihangir section.

Serafim Sağlamel
Charged under Penal Code Articles 128 and 311
Inciting crowds during demonstration and disorders in Kadıköy.

Osman Tan
Charged under Penal Code Articles 128, 311, and 71
Active participation and incitement of crowds during disorders in Büyükdere-Sariyer (Bosphorus) area.

Mustafa Eroğlu
Charged under Penal Code Articles 128, 311, and 71
Active participation and incitement of crowds during disorders in Büyükdere-Sariyer (Bosphorus) area.

Erol Demircioğlu
Charged under Penal Code Articles 128, 311, and 71
Active participation and incitement of crowds during disorders in Büyükdere-Sariyer (Bosphorus) area.

Sources: National Archives, State Department, No. 306, Istanbul, February 20, 1956; TNA: PRO, Ankara, Dispatch No. 34, No. 1493/3/56, No. RR 10110/5, February 21, 1956, for the final report of the martial-law command on the trials held under its authority and the one remaining trial to be handed over to the civil courts.

APPENDIX H: DETAILS OF REPAIR WORK TO GREEK ORTHODOX CHURCHES

Church, Place, Contractor	File numbers: Istanbul vakıflar	Archival documentation: 6-7 Eylül Hey'et	Contract date	Date finished	1st keşif bedeli valuation	% of bid reduction	Job award	Installments payments	İlave	Final payment
Athanasios, Kurtuluş	#c	X(c)								
1. Gürleyig and Tanla			8/22/57	3/20/58	70,939.95	1.0	70,230.55		9.18%	76,677.69
2. Electrical work					2,760.10					
Christos Soter, Galata	#14	I, IX, XIII								
1. Leóntopoulos			11/5/57	1/13/58	11,825.00	9.45	10,707.00		20.0%	11,744.30
2. *Mütevelli Hey'et*				7/14/58					TL4,383.14	4,101.96
3. *Mütevelli Hey'et*					2,425.23					2,250.19
4. Zachariadés					3,800.00					
5. ?					6,172.60					
This and all other files are incomplete. Original evaluation of damages to Christos Soter was TL237,959 but was reduced by 71.43% to 66,500 (28.57% of original)										
St. Demetrios, Tahtakapı	#6									
1. *Mütevelli Hey'et*				2/18/57			3,620.16			
2. *Mütevelli Hey'et*				10/24/57						
3. ?			2/11-24/57						TL2,468.59	6,485.10
St. Demetrios, Kurtuluş	#d	VII								
1. *Mütevelli Hey'et*			7/5/57		11,810.69					11,810.69
2. ?			8/28/57				34,757.06		8.13%	
St. Demetrios, Kuruçeşme	#h	XIV(a)								
1. Canoğlu			7/30/57	11/30/57	19,213.32	12.0	16,923.74		28.86%	21,807.63
2. ?			4/19/57		7,097.71					
St. Demetrios, Sarmaşık, Edirnekapı	#39	II, III, VI, XXX								
1. Atalar and Katipoğlu			11/9/59	1/4/60	10,908.15	7.0	10,144.58			10,139.33
2. ?			7/23/57		969.24					965.24

	Ref		Date 1	Date 2	Amount	Factor	Amount	Cost / %	Final
3. *Mütevelli Hey'et*, makbuz			2/6/59		1,004.55				1,000.00
4. ?					3,816.98				
5. ?					685.50				
6. *Mütevelli Hey'et*, list of damages totals TL38,550.00									
Prophet Elias, Sts. Taxiarchs, Arnavutköy	#9, #37	IV(c), X(c)							
1. *Mütevelli Hey'et*		XXX, V, VII	7/19/57		3,506.49				3,250.46
2. Kónstantinidēs			8/16/57		17,496.54	1.0	17,321.58	19.34%	20,637.76
3. Leóntopoulos			11/4/59		14,615.81	4.0	13,885.02	11.70%	15,395.38
Prophet Elias, Üsküdar	#15	V, VII, XIX							
1. *Mütevelli Hey'et*			3/17/60		7,841.09				7,271.46
2. *Mütevelli Hey'et*			4/27/59		8,896.46			(cost) TL8,974.78	8,896.46
3. *Mütevelli Hey'et*					1,963.76			(cost) TL1,842.42	
Euangelistria, Boyacıköy	#46								
1. *Mütevelli Hey'et*			5/6/57					TL5,1024.00	
2. ?					515.18				
Euangelistria, Kurtuluş, Yenişehir	#48	IV, XIV(a), XXV, XXVI							
1. *Mütevelli Hey'et*			5/23/57		4,658.85	13.0			4,022.54
2. Kónstantinidēs			7/25/57	9/10/57	13,664.09	12.5		20.0%	12,286.68
3. Frangineas			9/2/57	12/1/58	7,640.43	2.5		TL7,448.69	7,448.69
4. *Mütevelli Hey'et*			c. 3/27/58		c. 1,600.00				1,520.00
5. *Mütevelli Hey'et*			6/15/59				8,285.74		8,283.74
6. *Mütevelli Hey'et*			1/7/60		520.00				520.00
7. *Mütevelli Hey'et*					26,241.84				26,241.84
8. *Mütevelli Hey'et*			7/15/63		4,637.00				4,637.00
There is an undated list of destroyed or damaged items with the stamp of the *Mütevelli* office for a total of TL135,454.									
St. George, Bakırköy	#23, #28								
1. *Mütevelli Hey'et*					2,557.79				

	#	Codes	Date 1	Date 2	Amount 1	%	Amount 2	Cost/TL	Final
St. George, Çengelköy	#30								
1. *Mütevelli Hey'et*			1/21/57		4,887.16				
2. *Mütevelli Hey'et*					3,583.38				
3. *Mütevelli Hey'et*			c. 11/19/58		1,212 64 (?)				
4. *Mütevelli Hey'et*			11/19/58		7,840.65			TL7,858.21	
5. *Mütevelli Hey'et*					3,404.00			5.883%	
6. *Mütevelli Hey'et*			2/14/60					TL11,607.59	
7. ?					2,400.00				
St. George, Edirnekapı		V, VII,							
1. Ada		XVI(b), XVII(e)	3/31/60		28,407.03	16.9	23,006.20		
2. Mutlu			3/17/55		39,241.91	14.0	33,748.04		
St. George Potiras, Fener Antiphonetes	#42	V,XXX, XXXV, XVII(b), VII							
1. *Mütevelli Hey'et*			c. 3/15/60		2,124.17			(cost) TL1,903.30	
2. *Mütevelli Hey'et*			c. 11/11/57		3,966.23			TL4,759.48	
3. Iosefidés, bid					62,784.35	(not yet awarded)		TL83,180.02	
St. George, Heybeliada		V,VII, XVII(b)							
1. Mutlu, bid			11/22/60		12,192.85	1.0			
2. Patriarchate, *makbuz*			2/8/60						3,179.10
St. George, Ortaköy	#3								
1. ?			12/8/56		3,098.03			TL3,598.31	
2. *Mütevelli Hey'et*			4/24/57					(cost) TL60.00	
St. George Kyparissas, Samatya		VIII, XVII(b), XVIII							
1. Bakır			12/5/60	3/12/65	249,050.29	28.95	176,950.23		153,716.36
2. Katipoğlu and Atalar			11/5/59	5/1/60	11,487.56	7.0	10,681.43		12,025.77
St. George, Yeldeğirmeni	#34	XXI							
1. *Mütevelli Hey'et*			c. 1/24/57		4,095.10			(cost) TL4,126.00	3,943.94
2. *Mütevelli Hey'et*			c. 4/16/58		1,444.50				1,281.80

			Date				
3. *Mütevelli Hey'et, makbuz*					TL950.00	(cost)	804.70
4. *Mütevelli Hey'et*					TL2,091.40	(cost)	2,091.40
5. *Mütevelli Hey'et*			c. 4/8/57	5,070.90			4,529.72
(There is an undated, unstamped list of 52 categories of damaged items for a total evaluation of TL201,735)							
St. George, Yeniköy, Boğaziçi, *metochion* of Jerusalem	#12	XIX, IX					
1. Patriarchate			12/29/56	2,389.38			
			1/21/59	1,945.06	32.80%		1,945.06
					TL1,977.16		
2. Patriarchate			12/3/58	3,540.10			3,540.00
3. Patriarchate, *makbuz*			5/10/57		TL1,083.80		924.69
St. Charalambos, Bebek	#40	VII					
1. *Mütevelli Hey'et*			3/9/57	2,735.75	20.0%		
					TL3,382.90		
2. *Mütevelli Hey'et*			c. 2/23/57	1,749.80	TL1,927.61		1,749.80
3. *Mütevelli Hey'et*			c. 8/13/58	4,639.84			
4. *Mütevelli Hey'et*			c. 1/12/61		TL5,193.38	(cost)	5,131.11
St. John, Balat, *metochion* of Sinai		XXX, VII					
1. Atalar, bid				52,413.81	TL83,180.82		
2. Ada, *makbuz*			c. 1/22/60		29,432.93		
St. John of the Chians, Galata	#1	I, VII(b)					
1. *Mütevelli Hey'et*			1/7/19/57	11,445.25			9,803.41
2. *Mütevelli Hey'et*			c. 12/27/58	715.00			
3. *Mütevelli Hey'et, makbuz*			c. 5/31/60				6,500.00
4. *Mütevelli Hey'et, makbuz*			c. 3/16/58				3,030.03
5. Zachariadès, bid			2/6/58	10,370.00			10,870.00
6. Zachariadès, bid			8/3/57		TL6,700.00	(cost)	

Immediately after the pogrom, the patriarch sent an architect and interior decorator to assess the damages. They found them to be about TL76,567.40, and this very detailed list was sent to the patriarchate in October. In a letter dated 11/5/55, the community added TL5,000 and TL9,500, for a total of TL91,067.40.

Item	#	Ref	Date 1	Date 2	Amount				Final
St. John, Kalamış	#19								
1. ?			c. 1/7/59		4,140.98			20%	TL4,969.19
St. John, Kuruçeşme	#4								
1. ?			c. 12/29/56		479.76				
St. John, Yeni Mahalle		V, VII, XIV, XVI							
1. Canoğlu			7/30/57	12/5/57	11,917.93	3.0	11,560.39		
2. *Mütevelli Heyet*					1,695.00				1,685.38
3. *Mütevelli Heyet*				9/1/61	3,275.00				
4. Ada			9/8/60?	12/9/60	21,995.28	16.7	18,322.07		18,094.68
Saints Constantine and Helen, Beyoğlu	#47								
1. Lemma			5/28/57	8/13/57	6,121.54	7.0	5,693.03	29.59%	7,377.71
2. *Mütevelli Heyet*			5/10/57		3,444.84			13.09%	
Saints Constantine and Helen, Paşabahçe	#32								
1. *Mütevelli Heyet*								(cost)	TL114,50
Saints Constantine and Helen, Samatya	#49	VIII(a), XVIII(b)							
1. Sporidēs			10/18/63	12/14/64	133,974.00	1.0	132,634.26		118,605.96
2. Bakır			12/15/60	9/6/62	595,100.17	28.9			422,108.14
St. Kyriake and St. Onouphrios, Arnavutköy	#55								
1. *Keşf özeti*				2/24/58 ?	1,472.82				
2. *Keşf özeti*				4/19/56	1,882.04 +50.00				
St. Kyriake, Kumkapı	#j	XXIV(a)							
1. *Mütevelli Heyet*					35,841.64				TL39,932.98
2. Önen & Íoannidēs, bid			5/19/56		11,069.90	22.5			

Item	Ref	Numerals	Date	Amount	Rate	Amount	Note	TL / %	Total
St. Kyriake *agiasma,* **Paşabahçe**	#17	XXXV							
1. ?			c. 1/7/57	807.68				20.0%	
Metamorphosis, Kandilli	#31								
1. Paschalidēs			3/11/57	1,885.69				TL2,240.00	2,203.56
Metamorphosis, Şişli	#25a, b, c	V, VII, XXVIIIA, XXX, XXXV							
1. Çelikoyar			4/24/60	305,782.22	5.75	288,294.74	10 payments	16.78%	310,452.32
2. Canoğlu			5/1/57	17,946.63	6.5	16,780.00		11.54%	18,717.24?
3. Electrical work									
4. *Belediye*; graves			3/24/58					TL4,805.00	89,125.00
5. Work on graves									
Metropolitanate, Kadıköy	#20								
1. Metropolitanate			2/28/57					TL680.00	
St. Menas, Samatya	#24a								
1. Gürsoy			4/20/57	2,137.21	1.0	2,115.84			1,567.71
2. *Mütevelli Heyet*			3/12/57	1,336.97			(cost)	TL1,446.00	
St. Nicholas, Cibalı	#24a, b								
1. *Mütevelli Heyet*			c. 3/14/57	1,336.97		1,336.97	(cost)	TL1,446.45	1,336.97
2. Gürsoy			4/20/57	2,137.21	1.0	2,115.84	1,567.71		
3. ?			5/27/57	2,381.55					
St. Nicholas, Galata	#21	I(a, b, c)							
1. Leóntopoulos, *makbuz*			11/5/57	12,830.66	9.82	11,570.06	3		12,991.28
2. *Mütevelli Heyet*			c. 12/24/60				(cost)	TL15,400.00	
3. *Mütevelli Heyet*			c. 2/23/57; 4/12/57	8,578.66			(cost)	TL10,143.37	8,578.66
4. *Mütevelli Heyet, makbuz*			11/24/58				(cost)	TL12,253.87	12,253.87
5. *Mütevelli Heyet*			12/29/59				(cost)	TL5,750.00	5,750.00
6. *Mütevelli Heyet, makbuz*				5,556.88?			(cost)	TL6,137.17	6,137.17

A letter from the Galata community president to the patriarch's protosyncellus, dated 11/7/56, detailed the damage valuations. The protosyncellus replied that only 10/35 of damages could be claimed from the *vakıflar*. Thus only 28.57% of original damage claims could be submitted, or:

	Original damage claims		Amount of damage claims to be submitted
St. Nicholas	TL170,304	(original claim x .2857)	TL48,655
Christos Soter	TL232,954	(original claim x .2857)	TL66,560

The protosyncellus informed the community that the ratio of claimed damages for all churches was to be 28.57% of total claims of each.

	Original damage claims	Date	Amount of damage claims to be submitted			
St. Nicholas, Samatya	#28					
1. *Mütevelli Hey'et*		12/29/57	1,307.49	(cost)		TL982.50
St. Nicholas, Topkapı	#26b					
1. Canoğlu	XX, XXII	5/6/57	15,351.89	11.0		13,401.66
2. *Mütevelli Hey'et, makbuz*	XXIII, XXIV	2/28/57	552.49	(cost)		TL535.36
3. Kalogeras		7/31/57	2,068.00	2.0	2,026.64	1,850.24
4. Konstantinidês		7/22/59	19,942.40	1.5	19,942.04	19,642.91
St. Nicholas, Yeniköy	#11					
1. *Mütevelli Hey'et*	XXIII(b)	3/31/58	99.95			
2. ?		4/9/57				TL4,405.61
3. *Mütevelli Hey'et, makbuz*		5/15/58			TL2,105.71	1,967.98
4. Gavrilês and Yagobian, *makbuz*		11/27/57				2,300.00
Panagia Altı Mermer	#36b					
1. Birgen	XVI(e)	9/7/60	344,484.50	23.29	261,842.73	261,266.68
2. (a) Frangineas		11/13/63	117,802.93	1.5	116,035.89 (3)	67,594.05
		4/17/64				(75,549.50?)
(b) Mançıklıoğlu (continues)		9/10/64	23,680.93	1.5	23,325.72	23,225.50
3. Whitewash		10/5/62	1,645.58			
4. Clean up		3/15/57	3,000.00			2,895.15
5. Electrical work		4/16/60	8,124.20			

Name	#	Ref	Date	Amount		*ilave* (+27.73%)				
Panagia Balino, Balat		XXX								
1. Atalar, bid				71,419.75		91,224.90 (no acceptance document)				
Panagia, Belgratkapı	#b									
1. Birgen			9/7/61, 7/21/62	276,876.76	23.29	210,454.03				c. 235,064.48
2. *Mütevelli Hey'et*			4/14/58, 10/28/58	6,414.39	5.5	6,058.16				6,058.15
3. Koksal			10/8/65	94,723.00	5.0	89,986.85				86,949.70
Panagia, Büyükada	#41									
1. *Mütevelli Hey'et*			c. 3/20/57	5,656.78		4,754.07				
Panagia, Eğrikapı Souda	#38	IV, VII(d), XX								
1. Gürcihan			11/3/59, 12/2/59	5,945.50	36.0	3,805.12			TL565.60	4,167.10
2. Lemma			5/6/57, 8/19/57	13,181.65	2.51	13,117.04			TL767.50	12,787.50
3. *Mütevelli Hey'et*			5/28/57						(cost)	
4. ?			2/25/61	19,078.55						
Panagia Elpis, Kumkapı	# i	V(a), VII(d), VIII(b)								
1. Katipoğlu and Atalar			11/7/59	108,350.42	4.20	102,754.17	3	28.79%	TL24,179.71	92,829.46
2. Katipoğlu and Atalar			10/20/60							
Panagia, Göksuyu	#e	X(c)								
1. Canoğlu			3/19/57	24,354.21	1.0	24,110.67	2	6.93%		24,784.35
Panagia Muhli, Fener, Haliç	#43									
1. ?			c. 11/8/58	3,3407.97	(possibly part of #1?)					
2. *Mütevelli Hey'et*			4/13/57						TL5,572.74	
Panagia ton Ouranon, Salmatobruk		XIV(b)								
1. Mutlu, bid			3/17/58	39,758.15	8.0	36,577.50				
Panagia, Tekfur Sarayı, Chantzirgiotissa		X(c), XI-XIII								
1. Canoğlu			8/19/57, 3/27/58	15,331.66	c. 7.0	15,224.34			TL4,301.17	19,396.10
2. *Mütevelli Hey'et*			9/19/59							3,033.00

	Ref		Date A	Date B	Amount		Amount 2		Final
3. *Mütevelli Hey'et, makbuz*				11/14/57	1,971.88				1,955.45
4. D and V. Ramadanoğlu			1/23/58	2/15/58	2,180.50	18.35	1,780.00	1,780.00	
5. Könstantinidês?					38,172.83?				
6. Parasoğlu			5/17/58?	6/15/58	14,335.47	0.5	14,265.79		14,256.74
7. ?, *makbuz*				3/7/65					13,086.55
Panagia, Vefa Zeyrek		V, XV(a), XVI(b)							
1. Kasapoğlu			3/20/57	10/27/58	17,716.96	1.0	17,599.79	TL20,444.25	20,324.25
2. Patriarchate, *makbuz*			3/12/58					TL4,347.63	4,326.49
3. Kasapoğlu, *makbuz*			5/20/65						120.00
Panagia, Yeniköy	#43	XXIII							
1. *Mütevelli Hey'et, makbuz*				12/26/56	1,253.90			TL1,233.90	1,233.90
St. Panteleimon, Çengelköy	#16	XXXV							
1. *Mütevelli Hey'et*				1/7/57	462.10			TL456.56	
2. ?				7/3/57	1,250.00				
St. Panteleimon, Hasköy	#7	XXXV, VII(d)							
1. *Mütevelli Hey'et*				9/19/57	3,101.95			TL3,195.00	
St. Panteleimon, Kuzguncuk	#27								
1. *Mütevelli Hey'et*			2/28/57		2,199.80				
2. ?								TL679.59	
St. Paraskeue, Beykoz	#18								
1. ?				1/3/57	428.52				428.92
2. *Mütevelli Hey'et*					568.50				472.92
St. Paraskeue, Büyükdere	#9	XX(e)							
1. Canoğlu			6/5/57	6/19/57	6,388.57	3.0	6,196.91	TL7,325.20	7,325.20
2. Kalogeras				8/1/57					1,820.84
St. Paraskeue, Hasköy	#19	VII(d), XVI(b)							
1. Atalay, bid			3/17/58	2/29/60	43,510.42	3.0	42,205.11	3,569.30 (last installment)	
St. Paraskeue, Kazlıçeşme	#8								
1. ?			12/19/56		527.64				

St. Paraskeue, Tarabya	#45	XXVIIIb								
1. *Mütevelli Heyet*			8/6/57		3,320.09		3,009.73			
2. *Mütevelli Heyet, makbuz*			2/15/63		1,307.45			(cost)	TL2,865.20	1,307.45
St. Phokas, Ortaköy	#26a, 29	XVI(e)								
1. *Mütevelli Heyet*				8/4/57	4,321.45			(cost)	TL4,562.56	
2. Electrical work					4,118.90					
3. *Mütevelli Heyet* ?			4/5/61		3,100.00					
4. Ada			9/8/60	12/31/60	17,626.75	16.8	14,665.66			14,041.46
Sts. Taxiarchs, Arnavutköy	#37	X(c), XXX								
1. *Mütevelli Heyet*			6/1/57		6,747.64			(cost)	TL7,979.80	6,747.64
2. Kônstantinidês			8/16/57	12/24/57	18,752.47	1.0			TL19,458.19	19,458.19
3. ?			c. 8/24/59		1,549.77				TL2,075.12	
Sts. Taxiarchs, Balat	#10	XX, XVII(a)								
1. Lemma			6/5/57	9/16/57	8,862.23	2.5	8,640.77		TL10,149.28	9,895.55
2. Kônstantinidês			7/22/59	10/21/57	20,104.57	6.5	18,797.77		TL19,134.67	19,134.67
Sts. Taxiarchs, İstinye	#10									
1. *Mütevelli Heyet*			1/3/57		850.13					
2. *Mütevelli Heyet*			5/15/57		144.00					
Sts. Theodoroi, Langa	#f	V(b), VII(d)								
1. Mançılıklıoğlu			10/5/65	2/28/66	130,680.24	5.0	124,146.23	2		c. 119,996.21
2. Whitewash			c. 5/10/62		2,101.32					
3. Iôséfidês			c.12/14/59		601,612.90	23.0	463,241.93	8		c. 463,241.43

Letter of Istanbul *vakıflar* to the 6/7 *Eylül Heyet* speaks of a *keşif* of TL200,904.72, and rejects a newer *keşif* of TL774,407.33, evidently of additional damages.

Theological School, Heybeliada		XXIII						8		
Koimesis Theotokou, Beşiktaş	#2	XXXV	9/13/59	3/8/60	6,526.33			(cost)	TL6,526.22	5,361.48
1. *Mütevelli Heyet*			12/28/56		1,295.00				TL1,034.35	
2. ?			8/27/57		1,535.33					

Name	Ref	Date	Amount	Rate	Amount	Misc	TL / Amount	Final
St. Therapon, Sirkeci	#23 IX(a)							
1. ?		1/3/57	3,285.25					
2. *Mütevelli Heyet*			5,000.00					
Holy Trinity, Kadıköy	#33 VII(d)							
1. *Mütevelli Heyet*		11/10/60			22.80			22.80
2. *Mütevelli Heyet*		4/22/57	5,050.90					4,529.57
Holy Trinity, Taksim, Beyoğlu	#a VII(a)							
1. Gürleyig and Tarla		4/11/57	138,985.60	10.10	124,948.05	8		157,847.84
2. *Mütevelli Heyet*							TL6,077.75	5,861.54
Vlacherna, Ayvansaray	VII, XVI(b), XXX							
1. Gürcihan, *makbuz*		7/13/60						3,621.89
2. Mutlu, *makbuz*		8/23/60						2,500.00
3. Mutlu, *makbuz* (43,357.00 collected by 9/15/60)						(no date)		
4. Cezairliyan, *makbuz*		8/1/6					TL65,453.39	27.40
Zoodochos Pege, Balıklı	#44a, b, c XVI(e)							
1. Birgen, äid			307,943.70	15.1	261,444.24 (no further documents available)			
2. Pepinyani		10/11/62	8,000.00	18.75	7,850.00			7,850.00
3. Turanlıgıl		4/29/57	2,600.00	13.33	2,600.00			2,600.00
4. Şahin and Sağlık		6/15/56	43,050.00	15.1	36,549.75		TL42,550.00	36,124.95
5. Kônstantinidês		9/13/63	59,165.82	5.75	55,763.79		67,874.83	63,672.03
6. *Mütevelli Heyet*		12/3/59	4,150.02				TL4,199.02	
7. *Mütevelli Heyet*		1/7/63	11,413.56			(cost)	TL14,382.49	11,413.26
8. Electrical work		4/16/59	904.00					

I. Governmental and institutional archives

A. GREAT BRITAIN
The National Archives, Public Record Office, Kew Gardens

1955
FO371/117710   198335
FO371/117711   198335
FO371/117712   198335
FO371/117713   198335
FO371/117714   198335
FO371/117717   198335
FO371/117718   198335
FO371/117721   198335
FO371/117742   198335
FO371/123844   198479
FO286/1262   198373
FO286/1263   198373
FO286/1271   198373
FO286/1279   198373

1956
FO371/117741   198479
FO371/123858   198479
FO371/123999   198479
FO371/124008   198479

1957
FO371/124003   198426
FO371/130194   198479
FO371/130225   198426

1958
FO371/136272   198426
FO371/136509   298426

1959
FO371/136519   198426
FO371/144527   198479
FO371/144798   198479

B. GREECE

Greek embassy, Washington, DC
File B29, *Tourkia*, September-December 1955
File B32, NATO, November-December 1955
Greek ministry of foreign affairs, Athens
Political Directory, Section on Turkey
Yp. Ex., *Tourkia, 4 Epeisodia genika*, #35,000-56,000, August-December 1955

C. TURKEY

Yüksek Adalet Divanı Kararları, Yassıada (1960-1961) consist of some 1,300 pages. They do not include the *tutanaklar*, or proceedings, of which at least one copy is in the library of Turkey's Grand National Assembly, thus allowing access to a limited number of Turkish authors. The legal opinions and decisions include the following:

Esas No: 1960/1   *Türk Milleti adına yargı hakkını kullanmaga yetkili ve numeralı geçici kanunun 6 ncı maddesi hükmünce kurulmuş Yüksek Adalet Divanı'nın Anayas'yı Ihlal Davası ve bu dava ile birleştirilen diger davalar hakkındaki Kararı*
Esas No: 1960/2   *Köpek davası kararı gerekçesi*
Esas No: 1960/3   *6/7 Eylül Olayları davası kararı gerekçesi*
Esas No: 1960/4   *İstanbul-Ankara Olayları davası kararı gerekçesi*
Esas No: 1960/6   *Arsa satışı yolsuzulugu*
Esas No: 1960/7   *Topkapı Olayları*
Esas No: 1960/8   *Bebek davası*
Esas No: 1960/10   *Zimmet ve irtikap davası gerekçesi*
Esas No: 1960/11   *Vinylex ortaklığı yolsuzulugu kararı gerekçesi*
Esas No: 1961/8   *Istimlak yolsuzlukları davası kararı gerekçesi*
Esas No: 1960/13   *İpar Transpar Şirketi döviz kaçakcılığı davası kararı gerekçesi*
Esas No: 1960/18   *Türk P. K. Ko. Kanununa aykırı hareket davası kararı gerekçesi*
Esas No: 1960/20   *Radyo davası kararı gerekçesi*
Esas No: 1960/21   *Örtülü ödenek davası kararı gerekçesi*
Esas No: 1960/30   *Çanakkale İskele ve Geyikli 31. inci kilomtre Olayları davası kararı gerekçesi*
Esas No: 1960/31   *Kayseri Olayları davası kararı gerekçesi*
Esas No: 1960/32   *İzmir'de yayınlanan "Demokrat İzmir" gazete ve matbaasın'ın tahribi davası gerekçesi*
Esas No: 1961/7   *Vatan Cephesi davası kararı gerekçesi*

Also, Part III, *Sanıkların mufassal hüviyet listesi*, gives the names and identification of each accused person, 592 all told.

D. UNITED STATES

National Archives, Washington, DC
Turkey, consular and ambassadorial reports from Turkey to the State Department

central files 782.00 (plus dates—i.e., 782.9.3.55—in the DCR or RMR central files). For specific dates and numbers, see the footnotes.

E. Greek Orthodox ecclesiastical institutions

A substantial part of the files of individual Greek Orthodox ecclesiastical institutions that were repaired or rebuilt through the funds allotted to the Istanbul *vakıflar* was accessible, although in many cases the individual files were incomplete. In any case, they follow no uniform protocol numbering. Rather, they are kept in separate files for each institution, which is how they are identified here. These files include, for the most part, documents generated by the various Greek committees recognized by the *vakıflar* as official organs of the evaluation process and all other processes involved in bidding out each job to contractors, checking the latter's performance, and final payments. For details on these committees, see Chapter 5. The files that were accessible included the following:

Name of church	*File #*
1. St. Athanasios and *agiasma*, Kurtuluş	c
2. Christos Soter, Galata	14
3. St. Demetrios, Kurtuluş	d
4. St. Demetrios, Sarmaşık	39
5. St. Demetrios, Kuruçeşme,	h
6. St. Demetrios Kanavos, *agiasma*, Vlacherna	6
7. Prophet Elias, Arnavutköy	9 and 37
8. Prophet Elias, Üsküdar	15
9. Euangelistria (Annunciation), Boyacıköy	46
10. Euangelismos (Annunciation), Yenişehir	48
11. St. George, Bakırköy	23 and 28
12. St. George, Çengelköy	30
13. St. George cemetery, Ortaköy	3
14. St. George, Yeldeğirmeni, Kadıköy	34
15. St. George, Yeniköy, Boğaziçi	12
16. St. George (Panagiou Tafou), Fener	42
17. St. Charalambos, Bebek	40
18. St. John, Kuruçeşme	4
19. St. John of the Chians, Galata	1
20. St. John, Kalamış	19
21. St. John, Kuruçeşme	4
22. Saints Constantine and Helen, Paşabahçe	32
23. Saints Constantine and Helen, Beyoğlu	47a and b
24. Saints Constantine and Helen, Samatya	49
25. St. Kyriake, *agiasma*, Paşabahçe	17
26. St. Kyriake, Kumkapı	j
27. Saints Kyriake and Onoufrios, *agiasma*, Arnavutköy	55

28. Metamorphosis, Kandilli	31
29. Metamorphosis, Şişli	25a-c
30. St. Menas, Samatya	24a
31. Metropolitanate, Kadıköy	20
32. St. Nicholas, Cibalı	24a and b
33. St. Nicholas, Galata	21a-c
34. St. Nicholas, Samatya	28
35. St. Nicholas, Topkapı	26b
36. St. Nicholas, Yeniköy	11
37. Panagia, Altı Mermer	36b
38. Panagia, Belgratkapı	b
39. Panagia, Büyükada	41
40. Panagia, agiasma, Göksuyu	e
41. Panagia Elpis, Kumkapı	I
42. Panagia Soudas, Eğrikapı	38
43. Panagia Muhli, Fener	43
44. Panagia, Yeniköy, Boğaziçi	13
45. St. Panteleimon, agiasma, Çengelköy	16
46. St. Panteleimon, agiasma, Hasköy	7
47. St Panteleimon, Kuzguncuk	27
48. St. Paraskeue, Beykoz	18
49. St. Paraskeue, Büyükdere	9
50. St. Paraskeue, Kazlıçeşme	8
51. St. Paraskeue, Tarabya	45
52. St. Phokas, Ortaköy	26a and 29
53. Saints Taxiarchs, Balat	5
54. Saints Taxiarchs, İstinye	10
55. Saints Theodoroi, Langa	f
56. Koimesis Theotokou, Beşiktaş	2
57. St. Therapon, Sirkeci	23
58. Holy Trinity, Kadıköy	33
59. Holy Trinity, Taksim	a
60. Zoodochos Pege (monastery, cemetery, and church), Balıklı	44a-c

More detailed, and most significant, in terms of the actual process of rebuilding was the Greek *6-7 Eylül Hey'et* archive. Only a small part of this archive was accessible; nevertheless, it was more than sufficient to reconstruct the committee's structure, activities, and policies regarding the work on more than 100 churches and religious institutions. By and large, it operated on the basis of church files and most often without any protocol numbers. Thus, as in the case of documents from the *vakıflar* (many of which originated with the *6-7 Eylül Hey'et*), these documents, too, have been identified by the name of the church to which each refers, as well as by the date it carries, and the names of sender and recipient. Most also bear signatures of approval or rejection of the actions described in the document. These documents cover the entirety of procedures: assessments of damages; bidding on contracts; prices set annually by the ministry of public works for materials and labor; approval or disapproval of contractors' work at regular intervals; approval, rejection, or price-cutting by the *vakıflar*; notation of expense (mileage) of inspectors to and from sites; payments into the government retirement fund on behalf of workers; and even cost of cigarettes, soft drinks, and sweets given to workers on the job. The archives also include all the lesser contracts for subcontractors hired by the principal contractor, as well as bank statements regarding funds made available to the *6-7 Eylül Hey'et* by the Istanbul *vakıflar* and the payment of all interest to the *vakıflar* on these banked sums.

Name of Church	*File #*
1. St. Athanasios, Kurtuluş	Xc
2. Christos Soter, Galata	I, IX, and XIII
3. St. Demetrios, Kuruçeşme,	XIV
4. St. Demetrios, Sarmaşık, Edirnekapı	II, III, VI, and XXX
5. Prophet Elias, Arnavutköy	IVa and XXX
6. Prophet Elias, Üsküdar	XIX
7. Euangelismos (Annunciation), Yenişehir	XIVa, XXIV, XXV, and XXVI
8. St. George, Edirnekapı	XVIb and XVIe
9. St. George Potiras, Fener	XXX and XXXV
10. St. George, Heybeliada	XVIIb
11. St. George Kyparissas, Samatya	IVA, VIII, XVII, and XVIII
12. St. George, Yeldeğirmeni	XXI
13. St. George, Yeniköy	IXa and XXIX
14. St. Charalambos, Bebek	VIId
15. St. George, Fener	XXX
16. St. John of the Chians, Galata	I
17. St. John, Yeni Mahalle	V, XIVa, and XVIe
18. Saints Constantine and Helen, Beyoğlu	VIIa
19. Saints Constantine and Helen, Samatya	XVIIb
20. St. Kyriake, Kumkapı	XXIVa
21. St. Kyriake, *agiasma*, Paşabahçe	XXX
22. Metamorphosis, Şişli	V, VII, Xc, XX, XXV, XXVI, XXVII, XXVIIIa, and XXX
23. St. Menas, Samatya	XVIIb
24. St. Nicholas, Galata	I
25. St. Nicholas, Topkapı	XX, XXII, XXIII, and XXIV
26. St. Nicholas, Yeniköy	XXIIb
27. Panagia, Altı Mermer	XVIe
28. Panagia Balinos, Balat	XXX
29. Panagia, Belgratkapı	XVIe

30. Panagia Soudas, Eğrikapı   IVa and XXIVa
31. Panagia Elpis, Kumkapı   IVa
32. Panagia, Göksuyu   Xc and XXXV
33. Panagia, Salmatobruk   XVIb
34. Panagia, Tekfur Sarayı   Xc, XI, XII, and XIII
35. Panagia, Vefa Zeyrek   XV and XVIb
36. Panagia, Yeniköy   XXIII
37. St. Paraskeue, Büyükdere   Xa
38. St. Paraskeue, Hasköy   XVIb
39. St. Paraskeue, Tarabya   XXVIIIb
40. St. Phokas, Ortaköy   XVIe
41. Saints Taxiarchs, Arnavutköy   Xc and XXX
42. Saints Taxiarchs, Balat   XVIIa and XX
43. Saints Theodoroi, Langa (Vlanga)   Vb and VIId
44. Theological seminary, Heybeliada   XXXII
45. Koimesis Theotokou, Beşiktaş   XXXV
46. St. Therapon, *agiasma*, Sirkeci   IX
47. Holy Trinity, Kadıköy   VIId
48. Holy Trinity, Beyoğlu   VIIa
49. Vlacherna, Ayvansaray   IVa, V, VIb, VIIa, XVIb, and XXX
50. Zoodochos Pege, Balıklı   Vb, VIIa, VIId, and XVIe

II. Individual archives

A. Christoforos Chrêstidês archive

Deposited at the Center for Asia Minor Studies, Athens, this archive contains the 211-page manuscript of Chrêstidês's remarkable analysis of the pogrom, probably written in late 1957. It also includes a good deal on the Cyprus issue and the patriarchate. For the contents of this part of the archive, consult the catalogue and analysis written by Giannês Stefanidês.

B. Paulos Palaiologos archive

On this, much smaller but interesting, archive, see the Chrêstidês archive, as it has been absorbed into it. Of note is Palaiologos's own *Diagramma ektheseôs* on the pogrom, as well as his twelve articles written for *To Vêma* in January 1956.

C. *Anakefalaiôtikon sêmeiôma* of Vyrôn Theodôropoulos

Still in manuscript form, this invaluable analysis by Ambassador Theodôropoulos was written in the heat of the pogrom's aftermath in January 1956. It remains one of the most incisive analyses of the events and deserves publication.

D. Dêmêtrios Kaloumenos photographic archive

This archive of the pogrom is of great importance. Kaloumenos took hundreds of photographs of the destruction, starting on the morning of September 7. Consequently, they constitute the primary visual documentation of the massive devastation.

E. Demetrios Portokallis archive

This personal archive is also of great interest. Portokallis's jewelry store was in Beyoğlu, and he witnessed the violence. He has a considerable collection of photographs and has written extensively in the Greek American press on the pogrom. Most valuable are the letters—known as *Letters to Tatiana*—on the effects of the pogrom written by his mother, Despoina Portokallis, to a relative in Indiana. These, too, deserve to be published. Extensive use has been made of them in the present book, as they give a very clear picture of the economic havoc and destruction created by the riots.

F. Oral accounts

Fifty oral accounts of the events have been collected and published by Pênelopê Tsoukatou in her book. As difficult as it is to use oral accounts, they still contribute a personal understanding of the pogrom.

III. The press

A. Armenian
Har'ach (Paris)   09/9-12/1982; 09/14/1982

B. Belgium
Le Soir   09/7/1955

C. Great Britain
The Church of England newspaper   September-October 1955
Daily Mail   09/14/1955
Daily Telegraph   09/7/1955
Sunday Times   09/11/1955
The Economist   09/24/1955
Wellesley Cheshire   09/24/1955

D. Greece and Greek-language of Istanbul
Adamastos   09/3/1995
Anatolê (Istanbul)   01/1994; 06/1994; 08/1997; 04/2000;
                                     04/2003; 06/2003; 11/2004
Apogeumatinê (Istanbul)   09/1996
Dikaiôma   08/15-18/1994; 05/9/1995; 06/19/1995;
                                     September-October 1995; September-October

	1998
Eleutherê Fônê (Istanbul)	09/25/1955; 09/5/1994; and three Photostat issues after press was destroyed, the last one dated 09/15/55
Eleutherotypia	09/6/1993; 09/5-6/1995; 09/9/1999; 09/19/1999; 07/24/2001
Embros (Istanbul)	09/8/1955; 09/18/1955; 03/31/1957
Ethnos	09/7-10/1955; 09/12-16/1955
Kathimerini	09/13/1955; 09/12/1958; 04/16/1965; 09/14/1965; 09/6/1993; 09/4/1994; 09/4/1999; also *Epta Meres* Sunday magazine on 09/6/1995, 11/5/1995, and 08/16/98
Kyriakatika Nea	10/13/1955
Makedonia	09/8-11/1955; 09/13-18/1955; 09/20/1955
Nemesis	August 1998; August 1999; September 2000
Neos Kosmos	September, October, November 2000
O Chronos	09/9/1995; 09/20/1995; 10/20/1995; 12/15/1999; 09/5/2000; 09/11/2000
O Politês	September 1994; July, September 1995; November 1996; March 1998; September-October 1999; September 2001
Oikonomikos Tachydromos	09/7/1995
Pontiki	06/2/1994
Prôinê Kavalas	05/6/1998
Ta Nea	September 1955; 12/18/1961
The Athenian	03/1992; 04/1992
To Vêma	01/1/1956; 01/4/1956; 01/6/1956; 01/10-15/1956; 01/17-18/1956; 04/30/2000

E. GREEK PRESS OF NORTH AMERICA

Eleutheros Typos	09/4/1966
Ellênokanadika Chronika (Toronto)	09/13/1995
Ellênikos Typos (Chicago)	10/6/1995
Eseis (New York)	03/19-04/1/1994; 09/22-10/5/1990
Ethnikos Kêryx	10/20/1955; 10/27/1955; 07/7/1964; 05/20/1968; 09/6/1979; 10/11/1992; 8/27/1993; 10/1/1993; 09/15/1994; 10/11/1994; 09/2-3/1995; 09/6/1995
Kypriakatika Nea	10/13/1955; 10/17/1955; 10/20/1955; 10/27/1955
Paroikiakos Logos (Chicago)	06/16/1993; 09/2/1994
Prôinê	09/15/1986; February 1989; 09/6/91; 05/2-3/1992; 05/27-30/1993; 07/15/1993;

	10/1/1993; 08/16/1995; 09/9-11/1995
The Ahepan	Fall 1996
The GreekAmerican	09/28/1991; 07/23/1995; 09/23-29/1995
The Greek American Press	October-September 1955
The Greek Press (Chicago)	09/14/1966; 9/20/1985
The Hellenic Journal (San Francisco)	05/10/1996
The Hellenic News of America	September 1955
The Hellenic Review (Chicago)	October 1964

F. TURKEY

Akşam	09/8/1955; 09/10/1955; 06/30/1960;
	06/18/1960
Ayın Tarihi	#262, 1-30 Eylül (September), 1955,
	pp. 1-107
Cumhuriyet	09/6/1955; 09/22/1955; 06/5/1960;
	06/30/1960; 07/1/1960; 09/7/1996;
	01/18/1998; 09/6/1998
Cumhuriyet Dergisi	10/18/1998
Dünya	09/7-8/1955; 06/9/1960
Gökçeada	07/16/1968; 5/25/1990
Hayat	09/15/1961 (special issue on Yassıada trials)
Hürriyet	09/7-8/1955; 08/31/1964
İstanbul Ekspres	09/6/1955 (pogrom edition); 09/8/1955
Milliyet	09/6-9/1955; 09/18/1955; 09/20/1955;
	06/25/1960
Sabah Online	07/1/2000
Turkish Probe	09/13/1998
Vatan	09/7/1955; 06/25/1960; 07/3-4/1960
Yeni İstanbul	06/26/1960
Yeni Sabah	09/7-9/1955; 06/5/1960; 06/30/1960;
	07/1/1960; 06/24/1964

G. UNITED STATES

Chicago Tribune	09/8/1955
Newsweek	09/19/1955
Reader's Digest	May 1956
The New York Times	09/11-13/1955; 09/15-20/1955;
	09/24-25/1955; 12/6/1955; 12/22/1955;
	12/27/1955; 04/17/1957
Time and Tide	09/24/1955
Time magazine	09/16/1955; 09/19/1955
Washington Post & Time Herald	10/1/1955

For an excellent guide to international press reaction to the pogrom, see the *Ektakton*

Deltion #1 of Greece's Ypourgeion Proedrias Kyvernêseôs, Genike Dieuthynsis Typou (Exôterikon Tmêma), November 15, 1955. This is an extensive source with lengthy quotes from over 150 articles.

IV. Books and articles

Agaoğlu, Samet. *Arkadaşım Menderes*. Istanbul, 1967.

―――――――. *Demokrat Partinin doguş ve yukseliş sebebleri bir soru*. Istanbul, 1977.

―――――――. *Marmara'da bir ada*. Istanbul, 1972.

Agca, Mehmet Ali. *La mia verita*. Rome, 1996.

Ahmad, Feroz. *The Turkish Experiment in Democracy (1950-1975)*. Boulder, 1977.

Akar, Rıdvan. *Aşkale yolcuları. Varlık Vergisi ve çalişma kampları*. Istanbul, 2000.

―――――――. "Özür dileriz bay Nikolai." *Cumhuriyet Dergi*, sayi 650, September 6, 1998.

―――――――. *Varlık vergisi kanunun. Tek parti rejiminde azınlık karşıtı politika örnegi*. Istanbul, 1992.

Akçam, Taner. *From empire to republic: Turkish nationalism and the Armenian genocide*. London, 2004.

Aksoy, Muammer. *Partizan radyo ve D. P*. Ankara, 1960.

Akşit, Baha. *Kısaca Celal Bayar*. Istanbul, 1987.

Aktar, Ayhan. *Varlık Vergisi ve türkleştirme politikaları*. Istanbul, 2000.

Alavanos, Alexandros. *The Greeks of Constantinople: People without rights of succession*. Athens, 1994.

Alexandris, Alexis. *The Greek minority of Istanbul and Greek-Turkish relations 1918-1974*. Athens, 1983 (see also the second edition).

―――――――. "To meionotiko zêtêma 1951-1987." In Alexandris, Alexis, *et al.*, *Ellêno-tourkikes scheseis, 1923-1987*, Athens, 1987, pp. 495-522.

Alp, Tekin. *To tourkiko kai pantourkiko ideôdes*. Kasserian, J., translator, Athens, 1992.

"6-7 Eylül Olayları." In *Tarih ve Toplum*, 33:1986, pp. 139-154 and 178-180.

Anastos, Milton V. "Dumbarton Oaks and Byzantine Studies, A Personal Account." In Laiou, Angeliki, and Maguire, Henry, editors, *Byzantium: A World Civilization*, Washington, 1992, pp. 5-18.

Apostolidês, Nikos G. *Anamnêseis apo tên Kônstantinoupolê*. Athens, 1996.

Apuhan, Recep Şükrü. *Öteki Menderes: Eski D. P. milletvekili Giyaseddin Emre'den hatıralar ve 27 Mayıs Olayı*. Istanbul, 1996.

Arcayürek, Cuneyt. *Darbeler ve gizli servisler (1950-1988)*. Sixth edition, Ankara, 1995.

Arman, Furun, editor. *Türkiye arkeoloji haritasi, Kültur Bakanligi'nin atlas okuruna armagani*. Np,* nd.†

Armaoğlu, Fahir H. *Kıbrıs meselesi 1954-1959. Türk hükümeti ve kamu oyunun davranışları*. Ankara, 1963.

Arslanoglou, Leônidas S. *Tataula. Ekato chronia athlêtismos*. Athens, 1997.
Arzik, Nimet. *Menderesi ipe götürenle*. Ankara, 1960.
Association for the Protection of the National Heritage. *Opinions of Arabs about Turks*. Athens, nd.
Atalay, Mustafa. *Adnan Menderes ve hayatı*. Second edition, Ankara, 1959.
—————. *Celal Bayar ve hayatı*. Ankara, 1952.
Atzemoglou, Nikos. *Mnêmes + Theseis*. Athens, 1999.
—————. *T'agiasmata tês Polês*. Athens, 1990.
—————, editor. *Leukôma timês gia tê daskala-mana tês Kônstantinoupolês*. Athens, 2000.
Aydemir, Şevket Süreyya. *Ikinci Adam (İsmet İnönü). Üçüncü cilt, 1950-1964 (son)*. Volume III, Istanbul, 1968.
—————. *Menderes'in Dramı*. Istanbul, 1969.
Aydemir, Talat. *Talat Aydemir'in hatıraları*. Istanbul, 1968.
"Aziz Nesin'in Eylül (Hapishane) anıları." In *Tarih ve Toplum*, 34:1986, pp. 46-49.
Bagci, Huseyin. "Remembering 1955: A 'Black Day' in Turkish History." *Turkish Probe*, September 13, 1988.
Bahcheli, Tozun. *Greek-Turkish Relations Since 1955*. Boulder, 1990.
Balı, Rifat N. *Cumhuriyet yıllarında Türkiye Yahudileri. Bir türkleştirme serüveni (1923-1945)*. Np, nd.
Baraç, Fahri. *Demokrat Türkiye*. Istanbul, 1953.
Başar, Ahmet Hamdi. *Davalarımız*. Istanbul, 1943.
—————. *Degişen dünya*. Istanbul, 1941.
—————. *Demokrasi Buhranları*. Istanbul, 1956.
—————. *Iktisadi devletcilik*. Istanbul, 1931 and 1933.
—————. *Yaşadığımız devrin iç yüzü*. Istanbul, 1971.
Başgil, Ali Fuad. *27 Mayıs ihtilalı ve sebebler*. Istanbul, 1966 [see also the original French edition, *La révolution militaire de 1960 en Turquie (ses origines)*, Paris, 1963].
Batur, Muhsin. *Anılar ve görüşler. Üç dönemin perde Ankara*. Istanbul, 1985.
Bayar, Celal. *Celal Bayar diyor ki, 1920-1950*. In Segen, Nizami, editor, *Nutuk-Hitabe-Beyanat-Haabihal*, Istanbul 1951.
—————. *Celal Bayar, Präsident der türkischen republik*. Ankara, 1958.
—————. *Celal Bayar Vakfı*. Istanbul, 1970.
—————. *Cumhurbaşkanı Celal Bayar'ın Türkiye Büyuk Millet Meclisinin dokuzuncu döneminin ikinci toplantı yılını açıs nutukları*. Ankara, 1951.
—————. *Programme de la visite officielle de son Excellence le Président de la République de Turquie en Grèce*. Ankara, 1952.
—————. *Reiscumhur Celal Bayar'ın Türkiye Büyuk Meclisinin onbirinci döneminin üçüncü toplantı açış nutukları*. Ankara, 1959.
—————. *State visit: The story of the tour of the United States by President Celal Bayar of Turkey, January-March 1954*. Beirut, 1954.
Behramoglu, Namık. *Türkiye Amerikan ilişkileri (Demokrat Parti dönemi)*. Istanbul,

nd.

Bekata, Hıfzı Oguz. *Birinci cumhuriyet bitirken.* Ankara, 1960.

_____. *Türkiye'nin bugünkü görüşünü.* Ankara, 1969

Belen, Fahri. *Demokrasizim nereye gidiyor. Siyasi hatıralara dayanan tetkik ve tahliller.* Istanbul, 1959.

Beler, Belig. *1960 Yassıada 1990 İmralıada hatıraları.* Izmir, 1990.

Berkes, Niyazi. *Turkish Nationalism And Western Civilization.* New York, 1959.

_____. *The Development of Secularism in Turkey.* With a new introduction by Feroz Ahmad, New York, 1988.

Beşikçi, İsmail. *The Turkish state terror in the eastern provinces of Turkey.* Ankara, 1992.

Bil, Hikmet. *Kıbrıs Olayı ve iç yüzü.* Istanbul, 1976.

Bilginer, Receb, and Yalçın, Ali M. *Türkiye Reiscumhuru Celal Bayar'ın Amerika Seyahatleri.* 1954.

Birand, Mehmet Ali. *Can Dundar—Bulent Çaplı, Demirkirat bir demokrasinin doguşu.* Istanbul, 1991.

_____. *Shirts of steel: An anatomy of the Turkish armed forces.* London, 1991.

_____. *The generals' coup in Turkey: An inside story of 12 September 1980.* London, 1987.

Boze, Soula. *O Ellênismos tês Kônstantinoupolês. Koinotêta Staurodromiou-Peran.* Athens, 2002.

Burçak, Rıfkı Salim. *On yıllın anıları (1950-1960).* Np, 1998.

_____. *Yassıada ve öncesi.* Ankara, 1976.

Bürün, Vecdi. *Hazırlayan, Türk ordusunun zaferi. Kansız ihtilal.* Np, 1960.

Caratzas, Aristide. "The Turkification of Imbros and Tenedos: The Destruction of Two Greek Communities in Turkey." *The GreekAmerican*, July 8, 1994.

Cenar, Mine E. *Labor Made Opportunities for Homeworking Women in Istanbul, Turkey.* Los Angeles, nd.

Cerrahoglu, Piraye B. *Demokrat Parti Masalı.* Istanbul, 1996.

Ceylan, Faruk Erhan. *September 6-7 incidents.* Istanbul, 1996 (not available to me).

Chrêstidês, Christoforos. *Kypriako kai ellênotourkika. Poreia mias ethnikês chreôkopias 1953-1967.* Athens, 1967.

_____. "Ta Septemvriana (Kônstantinoupolê kai Smyrnê, 1955)." Published version of his *Ekthesis* in Stefanidês, Giannês A., editor, *Ta Septemvriana (Kônstantinoupolê kai Smyrnê, 1955). Symvolê stên prosfatê istoria tôn ellênikôn koinotêtôn,* Athens, 2000.

Citizens' Association of Constantinople-Imvros-Tenedos-Eastern Thrace. *1923-1993: 70 Years of Turkish provocation and violations of the treaty of Lausanne. A chronicle of human rights violations. The struggle for justice.* Komotênê, 1997.

Clark, Edward. "The Turkish Varlik Vergisi Reconsidered." *Middle East Studies*, 8: 1972.

Close, David, editor. *The Greek Civil War, 1943-1950: Studies in polarization.*

London, 1993.

Constable, Giles. *Dumbarton Oaks and the Future of Byzantine Studies*. Washington, 1979.

_____. *Handbook of the Byzantine Collection*. Washington, 1967.

Council of Europe, Commission on Human Rights. *Atrocities committed by Turkish troops in Cyprus*. Strasbourg, 1977.

Crouzer, François. *Le conflit de Chypre, 1946-1959*. Brussels, 1973.

Cypriot ministry of the interior (press and information office). *Flagellum Dei: The Destruction of cultural heritage in the Turkish occupied part of Cyprus*. Nicosia, 1987.

Çöker, A. F. *Türk tarih Kurumu. Ana hatları. Kemalist yönetimin resmi Tarih Tezi*. Istanbul, 1930, reprinted 1996.

_____. *Türk tarihinin ana hatları. Kemalist yönetimin resmi Tarih Tezi*. Istanbul, 1938, reprinted 1996.

Çulçu, Sadettin. *Yassıadan geliyoruz*. Istanbul, 1960.

Dadrian, Vahakn N. *The History of the Armenian Genocide: Ethnic Conflict from the Balkans to Anatolia to the Caucasus*. Providence, 1995.

Damtsas, Nikolaos Emmanouêl. *Ê agônia tês Kônstantinoupolês*. Athens, 1982.

Demir, H. and Akar, R. *İstanbul'un son sürgünleri. 1964'te Rumların sınırdışı edilmesi*. Istanbul, 1994.

Demirer, Ahmet Arif. *6 Eylül 1955. Yassıada 6/7 Eylül davası baglam*. Istanbul, 1955.

Demokrat Parti. *Beyanname*. Np, 1946.

Demokrat Parti. *Program ve tüzük*. Ankara, 1946.

Demokrat Parti. *26 Mayıs seçimleri*. Istanbul, 1946.

Demokrat Parti Il Idare Kurulu. *Basın Bürosu. Partimizin İstanbul II Kongresi münasebetile*. Np, 1951.

Demokrat Parti Neşriyatından. *Kalkınan Türkiye*. Ankara, 1954.

Demokratlar Külübü Yayınları. *Yassıada'dan anıt mezra'a*. Ankara, 1991.

Deringil, Selim. *Turkish foreign policy during the Second World War and active neutrality*. Cambridge, 1989.

Dikerdem, Mahmut. *Ortadoğuda devrim yılları. Bir Büyükelçinin anıları*. Istanbul, 1977, reprinted 1990.

Dilipak, Abdurrahman. *Menderes dönemi*. Fourth edition, Istanbul, 1990.

Dilligil, Turhan. *İmralı'da üc mezar*. Istanbul, 1998.

Dinamo, Hasan İzzetin. *6-7 Eylül kasırgası*. Istanbul, 1971.

Dodd, C. H. *Politics and Government in Turkey*. Berkeley, 1969.

Dogan, Mustafa, editor. *Adnan Menderes'in konuşmaları*. Two volumes, Istanbul, 1957.

Dokos, T. N., and Prôtonotarios, N. A. *Ê stratiôtikê ischys tês Tourkias. Proklêsê gia tên ellênikên asfaleia*. Second edition, np, 1996.

Dosdoğru, Hulusi M. *6/7 Eylül olayları*. Istanbul, 1993.

Dundar, Fiat. *Meionotêtes. Oi meionotêtes stên Tourkia symfôna me tis episêmes apografes tês statistikês ypêresias tês Tourkias*. Kenteridês, Savvas, editor; Kontou,

Anna, translator; Athens, 2003.

Durmuş, Enver. *Yassıada'dan İmralı'ya*. Istanbul, 1990.

Eliadês, Manos. *Oi Tourkikes mystikes ypêresies kai ê MIT*. Athens, 1998.

Enôse Omogenôn ek Kônstantinoupoleôs Voreiou Ellados. *Ekdêlôsis mnêmês tês Enôsês Kônstantinoupolitôn Voreias Elladas gia ta Septemvriana gegonota tou 1955, ypo tên aigida tou Dêmou Thessalonikês*. Thessalonikê, 1994.

Erer, Tekin. *Yassıada ve sonrası*. Istanbul, 1965.

—————. *Türkiyede parti kavgalari*. Istanbul, 1966.

Ergil, Dogu. "The Minority Debate." *Turkish Daily News*, November 8, 2004.

Eroğul, Cem. *Demokrat Parti (tarih ve ideolojisi)*. Ankara, 1970.

—————. "The Establishment of Multi-Party Rule, 1945-1971." In Schick, I. G., and Tonak, E. A., editors, *Turkey in Transition: New Perspectives*, Oxford, 1987.

Ertugrul, Halit. *Azınlık ve yabancı okuları. Türk toplumuna etkisi*. Istanbul, 1998.

Esatoğlu, Salahattin Hakki. *Zulme karşi 1950-1960 arası siyasi davalarda yapılan savunmalar*. Istanbul, 1961.

Esmer, Şükrü. *Menderes diyor ki*. Istanbul, 1967.

Evliyazade, Mehmet Özdemir. *Onları anlatıyorum*. Istanbul, 1966.

Exertzoglou, Charês. *Ethnikê tautotêta stên Kônstantinoupolê ton dekato ennato aiôna. O Ellênikos Filologikos Syllogos Kônstantinoupoleôs 1861-1912*. Athens, 1996.

Eyewitness Travel Guide, Istanbul. New York, 1999.

Faik, Bedi. *Ihtilalciler arasında bir gazeteci*. Istanbul, 1967.

Fersoy, Cemal O. *Bir devre adını veren başbakan Adnan Menderes*. Istanbul, 1971.

—————. *Devlet ve hizmet adam Fatin Rüştü Zorlu*. Istanbul, 1979.

Fielding, John. "What secret report tells about Turk atrocities," *Sunday Times* (London), January 23, 1977.

Findley, Carter V. *Bureaucratic Reform in the Ottoman Empire: The Sublime Porte, 1789-1922*. Princeton, 1980.

Friedlander, Saul. *Nazi Germany and the Jews: The years of persecution, 1933-1939*. London, 1997.

Genç Demokratlar teşkilat ve esasları. *Gençlik ve sizasi egitim*. Ankara, 1954.

Gençer, Ali İsmet. *Hürriyet Savaşi*. Np, 1960.

Giallouridês, Christodoulos. *Ê Tourkia se metavasê*. Athens, 1997.

Giritli, İsmet. *27 Mayıstan ikinci Cumhuriyete*. Istanbul, 1961.

Goloğlu, Mehmet. *Demokrasiye geçir 1946-1959*. Istanbul, 1982.

—————. *Türkiye Cumhuriyeti Tarihi*. Volumes I-III, Ankara, 1972-1974.

Gökalp, Ziya. *The principles of Turkism*. R. Devereux, editor and translator, Leiden, 1968.

Gökdemir, Orhan. *Devletin din operasyonu öteki İslam*. Second edition, Istanbul, 1998.

Gökman, Muzaffer. *50 yılın tutanagı 1923-1973*. Istanbul, 1973.

Göktürk, İsmail. *Adnan Menderes siyası hayatı ve nutukları*. Np, nd.

Gölpınarlı, Abdülbaki. *Mevlanadan sonra mevlevilik*. Second edition, Istanbul, 1983.

Gönlübol, Mehmet. *Olaylarla Türk dış politikası.* Ankara, 1977.
Greek Information Service. *The Greek minority in Turkey and the Turkish minority in Greece. How two governments treat their minorities.* Athens, 1965.
Grivas-Digenês, Geôrgios. *Apomnêmoneumata agônos E.O.K.A 1955-1959.* Athens, 1961.
Günver, Semih. *Fatin Zorlu'unu Öyküsü. S, "Zorro" gibi.* Istanbul, 1985.
Hale, William. *Turkish foreign policy 1774-2000.* London, 2002.
_____. *Turkish Politics and the Military.* New York, 1994.
Halman, Talat. *Contemporary Turkish Literature: Fiction and Poetry.* Rutherford, 1982.
"Haluk Nihat Pepeyi." In *Büyük Larousse sözluk ve ansiklopedisi.* Istanbul, 1986.
Hatzivassiliou, E. "The Lausanne Treaty minorities in Greece and Turkey and the Cyprus question." *Balkan Studies,* 32:1991, pp. 145-161.
_____. "The riots in Turkey in September 1955: A British document," *Balkan Studies* 31:1990, pp. 165-176.
Hekimoğlu, Müserref. *27 Mayıs' in romanı, Ihtilalciler, olaylar, dönüşumla anılar,* Istanbul, 1975.
Helsinki Watch (now Human Rights Watch). *Prison Conditions in Turkey.* New York, 1989.
_____. *The Greeks of Turkey.* Written by Whitman, Lois, for "Denying Human Rights and Ethnic Identity" series, New York, 1992, pp. 51-54.
Heyd, Uriel. *Foundations of Turkish nationalism.* London, 1950.
Hidiroglu, Pavlos. *Charaktêristika gnôrismata tês tourkikês diplômatikês symperiforas enanti tês Ellados.* Thessalonikê, 1995.
_____. *Oi Ellênes Pomakoi kai ê schesê tous me tên Tourkia.* Third edition, np, 1989.
_____. "Symvolê eis tên tourkikên Kypriologian." *Kypriakai Spoudai,* 42: 1978, pp. 175-196.
_____. *Thrace in the light of the national ideal of the Turks 1985-1991.* Athens, 1991.
_____. *Tourkikê ellênografia.* Thessalonikê, 1980.
_____. *Turkish conceptions of the Greeks of Asia Minor.* Athens, 1993.
_____. "Vivliografikê symvolê eis tên ellênikên tourkologian (1788-1975)."
Epetêris Kentrou Epistêmonikôn Ereunôn, VIII:1975-77, pp. 253-405.
Hitchens, Christopher. *Hostage to history: Cyprus from the Ottomans to Kissinger.* London, 1999.
Hofstadter, Dan. *Goldberg's Angel.* New York, 1994.
Holland, Robert. *Britain and the revolt of Cyprus, 1954-1959,* Oxford, 1998.
_____. "Greek-Turkish relations, Istanbul and British rule in Cyprus 1954-59: Some excerpts from the British public archives." *Deltio Kentrou Mikrasiatikôn Spoudôn,* 10:1993-1994, pp. 328-365.
Human Rights Watch. *Violations of Free Speech in Turkey.* New York, 1999.

Hürriyet Partisi Meclis Grubu. *Görüşümüz*, Ankara, 1957.

Iba, Şaban. *Ordu devlet siyaset*. Kadıköy (Istanbul), 1998.

Ilıcak, Nazlı. *Salim Başol'u 16 yıl sonra yargılıyoruz*. Istanbul, 1977.

Inalcik, Halil. "Istanbul." *Encyclopedia of Islam*. Second edition, Leiden, 1997, pp. 224-248.

Iordanoglou, Anastasios K. *To ethnikon Iôakeimeion Parthenagôgeion Kônstantinoupoleôs 1882-1988*. Thessalonikê, 1989.

Isen, Can Kayo. *22 Şubat-21 Mayıs. Geliyorum diyen ihtilal*. Istanbul, 1964.

İleri, Rasih Nuri. *Örtülü ödenek, 27 Mayıs Menderes'in dramı*. Istanbul, 1996.

_____. *27 Mayıs Menderes'in dramı*. Istanbul, 1986.

İnönü, İsmet. *İnönü diyor ki. A. Menderes'e cevaplar*. Ankara, 1960.

"İstanbul dogası-tarihi-ekonomisi-kultur." In *Yurt Ansiklopedisi*, Istanbul, 1983.

Jansen, Michael. "Cyprus: The Loss of a Cultural Heritage." *Modern Greek Studies Yearbook*, II:1986, pp. 314-323.

Johnson, Chalmers. *The Sorrows of Empire: Militarism, Secrecy, and the End of the Republic*. New York, 2004.

Journalists' Union of the Athens Daily Newspapers. *The anti-Greek riots of September 6-7, 1955, at Constantinople and Smyrna*. Athens, 1956.

Kaçmazoğlu, Bayram H. *Demokrat Parti dönemi toplumsal tartışmaları*. Istanbul, 1988.

Kalmaz, Ali Ihsan. *27 Mayıs devriminde şehid düşen tegmen Ali Ihsan Kalmaz'ın hayatı, şiirleri, konuşmaları ve hakkında söylenenler*. Istanbul, 1960.

Kaloumenos, Dêmêtrios. *Ê staurôsis tou Christianismou. Ê istorikê alêtheia tôn gegonotôn tês 6ês-7ês Septemvriou 1955 eis tên Kônstantinoupolin*. Athens, 1966, and subsequent editions of 1978, 1991, and 2002.

_____. *Ê syrriknôsê tou ellênikou ethnous*. Athens, 1985.

_____. *Ê tragikê nychta tês Kônstantinoupoleôs*. Second edition, Komotênê, 1993.

_____. *Mikra Asia. O ypo tourkikês katochês ieros chôros tôn Ellênôn*. Athens, 1996.

Kanakaria Mosaics: The Trial. Nicosia, nd.

Karagiôrgas, Giôrgos. "Enas Septemvrios prin apo 26 chronia." In *Dêmosiografika. Epilegmena keimena pente dekaetiôn*, Volume I, Athens, 1991, pp. 540-544.

Karakonyulu, Yilmaz. *Fthinopôrikos ponos*. Mystakidou, Liana, translator, Athens, 1998.

Karakuş, Emin. *40 yıllık bu gazeteci gözü ile işte*. Ankara, Istanbul, 1977.

Karal, Enver Ziya. *27 Mayıs inkilabının sebebleri ve oluşu*. Istanbul, 1960.

Kardam, Nuket. *International Norms: The Turkish State and Women*, Los Angeles, nd.

Kariôtoglou, Alexandros, editor. *Chalkêdôn. Ê istorikê mêtropolê tês Vythinias*. Athens, 1986 (?).

_____. *Kônstantinoupolê. Oi panseptoi patriarchikoi vaoi*. Athens 1986 (?).

Kemal, Mehmed, *Celal Bayar efsanesi ve raftaki demokrasi*. Istanbul, 1980.

Kentro Kônstantinoupolitôn. *Synedrion diamartyrias kai psêfismata*. Athens, 1964.

Keller, Morton, and Keller, Phyllis. *Making Harvard modern: The rise of America's university*. Oxford, 2000.

Kerr, Clark, *et al. The Gold and the Blue: A Personal Memoir of the University of California, 1949-1967*. Two volumes, *Academic Triumphs* and *Political Turmoil*, Berkeley, 2001 and 2003.

Kesisoglou-Karystinou, Melpô. *Enoria tês Agias Kônstantinoupoleôs Tzimbali*. Athens, 1998.

Kirişçioglu, Nusret. *Kayseri cezaevinde bir yıl dönümü*. Istanbul, 1968.

_____. *Partilerimiz ve liderleri*. Istanbul, 1975.

_____. *Yassıada Kumandanına cevap*. Np, nd.

Kitromilides, Paschalis, and Alexandris, Alexis. "Ethnic survival, nationalism and forced migration: The historical demography in Asia Minor at the close of the Ottoman era." *Deltio Kentrou Mikrasiatikôn Spoudôn*, V:1984-1985, pp. 9-44.

Kıvılcımlı, Hikmet. *27 Mayıs devletcilik yön'ün yönü*. Ankara, 1977.

_____. *27 Mayıs ve yön hareketinin son fasil eleştirisi*. Istanbul, 1970.

Kocameni, Ayetullah. *DPnin muhteşem zaferi. Adnan Menderes'in 1957 seçim nutukları ile Paris NATO Konferansındaki tarihi hitabesi*. Np, 1958.

Kosmadopoulos, Dêmêtrios. *Odoiporiko enos presvê stên Ankyra, 1977-1976*. Athens, 1988.

Koumakês, Leônidas. *The miracle: A true story*. Athens, 1995.

Köprülü, Orhan. *Fuad Köprülü*. Ankara, 1987.

Kuniholm, Bruce R. *The Origins of the Cold War in the Near East: Great Power Conflict in Iran, Turkey, and Greece*. Princeton, 1994.

Kutay, Cemal. *Celal Bayar*. Np, nd.

Lambert, Richard D., *et al. Beyond Growth: The Next Stop in Language and Area Studies*. Washington, 1984.

Landau, J. M. *Pan-Turkism: From Irridentism to Cooperation*. Bloomington, 1995.

_____. *Radical politics in modern Turkey*. Leiden, 1974.

_____. *The politics of pan-Islam: Ideology and organization*. Oxford, 1994.

Laskaridou, Aikaterinê. *Dekapente chiliades meres stên Kônstantinoupolê, tên patrida mou*. Athens, 1987.

Levi, Avner. *Türkiye Cumhuriyeti'nde Yahudiler*. Istanbul, 1996.

Lewis, Bernard. *The emergence of modern Turkey*. Second edition, Oxford, 1968.

Lewis, Geoffrey. *The Turkish language reform: A catastrophic success*. Oxford, 2002.

Lourideion Idryma. *Mnêmes tês Polês*. Athens, 1982.

Mango, Andrew. *Atatürk: The Biography of the Founder of Modern Turkey*. Woodstock, 2000.

Mangriôtês, G. *O epektatismos stên Tourkikê poiêsê*. Athens, 1991.

Mardin, Sherif. *The Genesis of Young Ottoman Thought*. Princeton, 1962.

Margaritês, Giôrgos. *Istoria tou ellênikou emfyliou polemou, 1946-1949*. Athens, 2001.

Maurofrydê, Eleônora. "Ê nychta tôn krystallôn tou ellênismou tês

Kônstantinoupolês." *Nemesis*, August 1998, pp. 16-20.

May, Ernest, and Laiou, Angeliki, editors. *The Dumbarton Oaks Conversations and the United Nations, 1944-1994*. Washington, 1998.

Mazici, Nursen. *Celal Bayar (Başbakanlık dönemi 1937-1939)*. Istanbul, 1996.

McDowall, David. *A Modern History of the Kurds*. New York, 1996.

Mehmedin, Kitabı. *Güneydogu savaşunu anlatıyor*. Istanbul, 1999.

Metropolitan Êlioupoleôs Gennadios. *Istoria tou Megalou Reumatos*. Istanbul, 1949.

Mêllas, Akylas. *Pera. To Staurodromi tês Rômiosynês*. Athens, nd.

Michalopoulos, Dêmêtrios. *Ellada kai Tourkia 1950-1959. E chamenê prosengisê*. Athens, 1989.

Milli Birlik Komitesi İrtibat Bürosu. *Yassıada Broşürü*. Istanbul, 1960.

Minkari, Ali Esen. *Demirkarat belgesine dair*. Np, 1990 (?).

Mirkelamoglu, Necip. *Ecevit Eceviti anlatıyor*. Istanbul, 1977.

Moutsoglou, Vassilês V. *Oi Ellênes tês Kônstantinoupolês 1821-1922*. Athens, 1998.

Mumcu, Uğur. *Tarikat, Siyaset, Ticaret*. Ankara, 1999.

Mystakidou, Liana. *Oi Alevides stê synchronê Tourkia*. Athens, 1997.

Nesin, Aziz. *Salkım salkım asılacak adamlar*, Istanbul, 1987. Translated into Greek by Abatzês, Arês, and Tragotsês, Sôkratês, as *Kremaste tous san ta tsampia*, Athens, 1998.

Nutku (Utay), Emrullah. *Demokrat Parti neden çöktü ve politika'da yıtırdıgım yıllar 1946-1958 siyasi anılarım*. Istanbul, 1979.

Oçak, Ahmet Yaşar. *Türkler, Türkiyede İslam*. Istanbul, 1999.

Oikoumeniko Patriarcheio. *Maurê Vivlos diôgmôn kai martyriôn tou en Tourkia Ellênismou 1914-1918*. Istanbul, 1919, reprinted 1996.

O'Malley, Brandon, and Craig, Ian. *The Cyprus conspiracy: America, espionage and the Turkish invasion*. London, 2000.

Oran, Baskin. *Türk-Yunan ilişkilerinde Batı Trakya sorun*. Second edition, Ankara, 1991.

Ozel, Mustafa. *Refahlı Türkiye*. Istanbul, 1997.

Ozkan, Tuncay. *Bir gizli servisin tarihi. Milli Istihbarat Teşkilatı*. Istanbul, 1999.

Ökte, Faik. *Varlık vergisi faciası*, Istanbul, 1951. Translated into English by Cox, Geoffrey, as *The tragedy of the Turkish capital tax*, London, 1987.

Ömeroğlu, Ilhani, editor. *Yabancı gözü ile Demokrat Türkiye*. Ankara, 1959.

Önder, Necmettin. *Yassıada'da milli irade nasıl mahkum edildi*. Np, 1990.

Örtülü, Erdogan. *Üç ihtilalın hikayesi*. Second edition, Ankara, 1966.

Özbay, Melih, editor. *Sabıkların gizli dosyaları*. Istanbul, 1960.

Palaiopoulos, Nikos. *Imvros. To drama tou nêsiou opôs to ezêsa. Autoviografiko afêgêma*, Athens, 1993.

Panagiôtidês, Nathanaêl M. *Mousoulmanikê meionotêta kai ethnikê syneidêsê*. Alexandroupolis, 1995.

Panimvrian Society. *Violations of Rights of the Greek Minority of Imvros and Tenedos*. Addressed to Hans van den Broek, temporary chair of the EU council of foreign ministers, Brussels, October 3, 1991.

Papadopoulos, Stefanos. *Anamnêseis apo tên Polê.* Athens, 1978.

Papastratês, Thrasyvoulos O. *Eptalofou Vosporidos odoiporia. Ellênes, Armenioi, Tourkoi, Evraioi.* Athens, 1998.

_____. *Geitonies tês Kônstantinoupolês.* Athens, 2003.

Paraschos, M., editor. *Greece and the American Press: Observations, Implications, Strategies.* New York, 1986.

Papazian, A. A. *The Armenian genocide based on the documents of the legal trials of the Young Turks* (in Armenian). Yerevan, 1988.

Parlar, Suat. *Osmanlı'dan günümüze gizli devlet.* Istanbul, 1996.

Perin, Mithat. *Menderes'i kim astırdı?.* Istanbul, 1985.

_____. *Yassıada faciası. 27 Mayıs darbesinden damlara kadar işkence altından ezitenlerin drama.* Volume I, Istanbul, 1990.

_____. *Yassıada ve infazların içyüzü.* Istanbul, 1970.

Pneumatiko Kentro Kônstantinoupolitôn. *30 Chronia apo tis apelaseis 1964-1994.* Athens, 1994.

Philaretos (Archimandrite). *Maximos o E', o martyrikos Oikoumenikos Patriarchês Kônstantinoupolês.* Volume II, Athens, nd.

R., R. *Vyzantinoi naoi pou katestrafêkan to 1955.* In *Archeion tou Thrakikou Laografikou kai Glôssikou Thêsaurou,* 22:1957.

Rallês, G. A., and Potlês, M. *Syntagma tôn theiôn kai ierôn kanôn.* Athens, 1992, reprint.

Reumiôtês, Megas A (Soltaridês, E.). *Ê syrriknôsê tou ellênismou.* Volume I: *Septemvriana tou 1955; Apelaseis tou 1964; Dyo orosêma stên poreia tou neôterou ellênismou;* and *Synoptikê syngrisê tôn dyo meionotêtôn.* Volume II: *Meionotêta kai arthrographêmata.* Komotênê, 1984, 1985.

Rodokanakês, J. A. *The last of the Byzantines: The Black Book.* Second edition, Athens, 1994.

Rouleau, Eric. "Turkey: Beyond Ataturk." *Foreign Policy,* June 1996, pp. 70-75.

Rubin, Barry, and Heper, Metin, editors. *Political parties in Turkey.* London, 2002.

Sakellariou, Kôstas. *Oi teleutaioi Ellênes tês Polês.* Athens, 1995.

Salapasidês, Giannês. *Ti na thymêthô! Ti na xechasô! To 55 stên Kônstantinoupolê.* Athens, 1999.

Sari, Şevket. *(Adıyamanlı) Milli irade.* Ankara, 1959.

Sarisözen, Güner. *Yassıada'dan anıtmezar'a.* Ankara. 1991.

Sarol, Mükerrem. *Bilinmeyen Menderes.* Volume I, Istanbul, 1983.

Sarrês, Neoklês. *Ê allê pleura: Diplomatikê chronographia tou diamelismou tês Kyprou me vasê tourkikes pêges.* Two volumes, Athens, 1982.

Serhadoglu, Riza. *Zulme karşı koyma hakkı.* Istanbul, 1961.

Sezer, Duygu. *Kamu oyu ve diş politika.* Ankara, 1972.

Shaw, Stanford. *Jews of the Ottoman Empire and the Turkish Republic.* New York, 1991.

_____. *Turkey and the Holocaust: Turkey's Role in Rescuing Turkish and European Jewry from Nazi Persecution (1933-1945).* New York, 1992.

Sidêropoulos, Fôkion. *Ta ethnika filanthropika katastêmata stên Kônstantinoupolê.*

Nosokomeio Valouklê. Athens, 1999.

Sitembölükbaşı, Şaban. *Türkiyede İslam'ın yeniden inkişafı (1950-1960).* Ankara, 1955.

Soltaridês, E. *E dytikê Thrakê kai oi Mousoulmanoi. Ti akrivôs symvainei.* Athens, 1990.

Sondern, Frederic Jr. "Istanbul's Night of Terror: An Eyewitness Account of One of the Most Destructive Riots of Modern Times." *Reader's Digest,* May 1956.

Sousa, Nasim. *The Capitulary Regime of Turkey: History, Origin and Nature.* Baltimore, 1933.

Sözen, Suzan. *'In Menderes yazilmiş aşk mektupları.* Ankara, 1960 (?).

Sözmen, Asim Neset. *Hicviyeler arasında Yassıadaya kadar Panorama.* Np, 1960.

Stamatopoulos, Kôstas. *Ê teleutaia analampê: Ê kônstantinoupolitikê rômiosynê sta chronia 1948-1955.* Athens, 1996.

—————. *Vêmata sta patria Kônstantinoupoleôs.* Second edition, Athens, 1992.

—————and Mêllas, Akylas. *Kônstantinoupolê. Anazêtôntas tê Vasileuousa.* With photography by Liza Evert, Dora Minaïdê, and Maria Fakidê, Athens, 1990.

Stavrou, Patroklos. *The destruction of the cultural heritage of the occupied part of Cyprus.* Nicosia, 1994.

—————. *The plundering of the heritage and the falsification of the national identity of Cyprus by Turkey.* Lecture, National Gallery of Greece, Athens, May 11, 1984.

Stefanidês, Giannês A. "To archeio tou Christoforou Chrêstidê (1899-1982). Katagrafê." *Deltio Kentrou Mikrasiatikôn Spoudôn,* 11:1995-1996, pp. 321-346.

—————, editor. *Ta Septemvriana (Kônstantinoupolê kai Smyrnê, 1955). Symvolê stên prosfatê istoria tôn ellênikôn koinotêtôn,* Athens, 2000.

Stergellês, Aristeidês. "Apo tên istoria tôn filekpaideutikôn sômateiôn tês Kônstantinoupoleôs. Patriarcheio kai Ellênikos Filologikos Syllogos." *Deltio tou Kentrou Ereunês tês Istorias tou Neôterou Ellênismou,* Volume 1, "Mnêmê Eleutheriou Prevelakê," Athens, 1998, pp. 101-116.

Steuerwald, K. *Untersuchungen zur türkische Sprache der Gegenwart I-III. Die türkische Sprachpolitikzeit.* Np, 1928 (1963-1966).

Suskind, Ron. *The Price of Loyalty: George W. Bush, the White House, and the Education of Paul O'Neill.* New York, 2004.

Svôlopoulos, Kônstantinos. *Kônstantinoupolê 1856-1908: Ê akmê tou ellênismou.* Athens, 1994.

Syllogos Imvriôn-Kônstantinoupolitôn-Tenediôn and Anatôlikothrakôn Thrakês. *Oi paraviaseis tês Synthêkês tês Lôzanês.* Second edition, Komotênê, 1993, pp. 19-28.

—————. *Thrakê: Apo ton Omêro mechri tis meres mas.* Komotênê, 1994.

Syllogos Kônstantinoupolitôn. *66 chronia prosforas, 1928-1994.* Athens, nd.

Syndesmos tôn en Athenais Megaloscholitôn. *Ê parousia tôn ethnikôn meionotêtôn stên Kônstantinoupolê tou 19ou aiôna*. Athens, 1977.

Szyliowicz, J. *Religious Education and the Future of the Turkish State*. Los Angeles, nd.

Şahin, Süreyya M. *Fener Patrikhanesi ve Türkiye*. İstanbul, 1980.

Şahingiray, Ozel. *Celal Bayar'in söylev ve demeçleri 1946-1950. Demokrat Parti'in kuruluşundan iktidara kadar politik konuşmalar*. Ankara, 1956.

Şakir, Ziya. *Celal Bayar, Hayatı ve eserleri*. İstanbul, 1952.

_____, editor. *Türkiye cumhurbaşbakan Celal Bayar' ın Yunanistan seyahat hatıralar*. İstanbul, 1953.

Tanyeli, Halit, and Topsakdaglı, Adnan. *Izahli Demokrat Kronoloji*. Two volumes, 1945-1950 and 1950-1958, İstanbul, 1958, 1959.

Taylak, Muammer. *27 Mayıs ve Türkeş*. Ankara, 1976.

Tekil, Füruzan. *İnönü Menderes kavgası*. Ankara, 1976.

Tenedos: The forgotten island of Tenedos. Athens, 1997.

Tenekidês, Giôrgos. *Imvros kai Tenedos. Istoria/Nomiko kathestôs*. Thessalonikê, 1986.

Teoman, Zeki. *27 Mayıs devrimi niçin yapıldı*. İstanbul, 1960.

Tezcan, Gürsoy A. *Infant Mortality: A Turkish Puzzle*. Los Angeles, nd.

Toker, Metin. *Demokrasimizin İsmet Paşalı yılları 1944-1973. DP Yokuşu aşağı 1954-1957*. Ankara, 1991.

_____. *İsmet Paşalı 10 yıl 1954-1957*. Volume I, np, 1966.

Toprak, Zafer. "Altı-yedi Eylül olayları." In *Dünden bugüne İstanbul ansiklopedisi*, Volume I, İstanbul, 1993, pp. 213-216.

Trumpbour, John, editor. *How Harvard Rules: Reason in the Service of Empire*. Boston, 1989.

Tsaparas, Stefanos. *Ekato chronia polemos Elladas-Tourkias (1900-2000)*. Athens, 1999.

Tsormpatzikôstas, Stylianos K. *Istoria tês Kônstantinoupoleôs tês Aretsou (Rysiou) kai tôn allôn proastiôn tês Chartolimês, Panteichiou, Maltepê, Touzlôn kai Prinkiponêsôn*. Athens, 1973.

Tsoukatou, Pênelopê. *Septemvriana 1955. Ê "nychta tôn krystallôn" tou Ellênismou tês Polês*. Athens, 1998.

Tunaya, Tarık Zafer. *Türkiye'de siyasal partiler*. İstanbul, 1989.

Tunçkanat, Haydar. *27 Mayıs 1960 devrimi (Diktadan Demokrasiye)*. İstanbul, 1996.

Turan, Osman. *Selçuklular zamanında Türkiye. Siyasi Tarih Alp Arslandan Osman Gazi'ye (1071-1381)*. İstanbul, 1971.

Turgut, Hulusi. *Menderes/Zorlu/Polatkan'dan yaptırılmayan savunmalar: Yassıada Belgesi*. İstanbul, 1982.

Turkish embassy (office of press attaché). *The Turkish reform movement of May 27, 1960*. London, 1960.

Turkish ministry of finance. *Speech of the minister in connection with the presentation of the 1954 budget bills to the Grand National Assembly*. Ankara, 1954.

Tünay, Bekir. *Menderes devri anıları. Gördüklerim, bildiklerim, duyuduklarım*.

Istanbul, nd.

Türker, Orhan. *Osmanlı İstanbulun'ndan bir koşe Tataula.* Istanbul, 1998.

Türkiye ve Atlantik Paktı. *Demokrat Parti neşriyatından.* Ankara, 1954.

Türkiye nasıl ileriyor, 1950-1957. *Basın-yayın-ve Turizm umum mudurlugu.* Np, 1957.

Tzaferês, Solôn. *To Oikoumeniko Patriarcheio. E Megalê tou Chrêstou Ekklêsia.* Geneva, 1989.

Ural, Orhan. *Diktatörlerin Yassıada muhakemeleri.* Third edition, Istanbul, 1960.

Vafeiadês, Simos. *Enas Politês thymatai.* Athens, 1998.

van Wees, Nicole. *Ta Septemvriana. Oi apopseis ollandikôn diplomatikôn apostolôn stên Tourkia kai tên Ellada.* Groningen, 1996.

Vlanton Elias, "Tripartite: The First Cyprus Conference." *The GreekAmerican,* September 28, October 5,12, 19, 1991.

Vural, Haydar. *Hürriyet savaşımız olurum? Böyle olur mu? Kardeş kardeşi vururmu?.* Ankara, 1960.

Vryonis, Speros Jr. "American Foreign Policy in the Ongoing Greco-Turkish Crisis as a Contributing Factor to Destabilization." *UCLA Journal of International Law and Foreign Affairs,* 2:1997:1, pp. 69-89.

_____. "Byzantine Patriarchate and Turkish Islam." *Byzantinoslavica,* 57: 1966, pp. 83-84.

_____. *Cyprus between East and West, a political and moral dilemma: The past as prologue to the present.* Êrakleio, 1994.

_____. *Stanford J. Shaw,* History of the Ottoman Empire and Modern Turkey: *A critical analysis.* Thessalonikê, 1983.

_____. *The Decline of Hellenism in Asia Minor and the Process of Islamization From the Eleventh Through the Fifteenth Century.* Berkeley, 1971.

_____. *The Turkish state in history: Clio meets the Grey Wolf.* Thessalonikê, 1991.

Wasserstein, Bernard. Review of *Turkey and the Holocaust. Times Literary Supplement,* January 7, 1994, pp. 4-5.

Weber, Frank G. *The evasive neutral: Germany, Britain and the quest for a Turkish alliance in the Second World War.* London, 1979.

Weiker, Walter. *The Turkish Revolution 1960-1961: Aspects of Military Politics.* Washington, 1963.

Whitehill, Walter M. *Dumbarton Oaks: The History of a Georgetown House and Garden, 1800-1966.* Cambridge, 1967.

Yabancı gözü ile Demokrat Türkiye 1950-1959. Ankara, 1959.

Yahl, Leni. "Kristallnacht." In *Encyclopedia of the Holocaust,* Gutman, Israel, editor, Volume 2, New York, 1990, pp. 836-840.

Yalçin, Günel. *Seçkin devrim 1960. Milli inkilab'ın ilim ve sana yönünden izahi.* Ankara, 1960.

Yalman, Ahmet, E. *Yakın tarihte gördüklerim ve geçirdiklerim 1945-1970.* Volumes

I-IV, Istanbul, 1970.

Yavuz, Hakan M. *Islamic political identity in Turkey.* Oxford, 2003.

Yelda, *İstanbul'da Diyarbekirde azalırken.* Istanbul, 1996.

Yeni Iktidarim Çalışmaları. *22.5.1950-22.5.1952. Demokrat Parti hizmetinde bulundugu Türk milletine hesap veriyet.* Np, nd.

Yesin, Mehmet. "Perishing Cyprus." Translation of series first published in *Olay,* April 6, May 3, 10, and 17, 1982.

Zürcher, Erik J. *Turkey: A modern history.* Third edition, London, 2004.

*Np = no city of publication
†Nd = no year of publication

INDEX

INDEX: GREEK ORTHODOX CHURCHES

A NOTE ABOUT USAGE

We have used the Turkish alphabet to denote Turkish in most cases, except in some obvious ones, such as Istanbul or Izmir, as these cities are known universally to English-language readers through their transliteration (although Turkish script is used when either name is part of a Turkish phrase or title). We have also used Turkish toponymy for the regions of Istanbul (and Turkey generally), again for the self-evident reason that this volume addresses a historical event that occurred in modern Turkey. When quoting from original English-language sources, however, we did not intervene, so that, for example, if a document indicates Kurtulush instead of Kurtuluş—or Pera instead of Beyoğlu—we have left it as is in each case.

In transliterating Greek, our intention has been to convey the actual orthographic form as opposed to simply the phonetics of the language, and to reproduce Greek spelling. In doing so, we have, as much as possible, directly mapped the Greek alphabet according to letters pronounced similarly in English. There are, however, a few instances in which we felt that phonetic transcription rendered certain diphthongs in Greek more accurately: for example, *mu-pi*=b, *gamma-kappa*=ng, *gamma-chi*=nch (aspirate "ch"), *nu-tau*=d. In addition, references to Greek authors published in English follow the Library of Congress catalogue; we have also respected reality in regard to Greek publications with English-language editions (such as *Kathimerini*).

We also followed the standard practice of all Greeks in using both the demotic and *kathareuousa* forms of names interchangeably, as, for example, with Mesochôrion/Mesochôri or Palaion Banion/Palio Banio. Finally, we have kept the traditional denotation of Greek Orthodox ecclesiastical institutions: for example, St. Kyriake (as opposed to Agia Kyriakê), St. George (as opposed to Agios Geôrgios), and Saints Constantine and Helen (as opposed to Agioi Kônstantinos kai Elenê).

In all cases, we have tried to balance fidelity to the respective language—whether Turkish or Greek—with common sense and, above all, respect for the reader of the English text.

greekworks.com

Speros Vryonis, Jr., is one of the most eminent Byzantinists of his generation. After a distinguished career at UCLA, he became the founding director of the Alexander S. Onassis Center for Hellenic Studies at New York University, from which he retired as emeritus Alexander S. Onassis professor of Hellenic civilization. Prof. Vryonis's extensive work on the history and culture of the Greeks from Homer to the present, and on their relations with the Slavic, Islamic, and New Worlds, includes the seminal *The Decline of Medieval Hellenism in Asia Minor and the Process of Islamization from the Eleventh through the Fifteenth Century*; *Byzantium and Europe*; *Studies on Byzantium, Seljuks and Ottomans*; *Byzantium: Its Internal History and Relations with the Islamic World*; and *Studies in Byzantine Institutions and Society*. He has also edited, among other volumes, *Aspects of the Balkans: Continuity and Change* (with Henrik Birnbaum); *Essays on the Slavic World and the Eleventh Century*; *Islam and Cultural Change in the Middle Ages*; *Individualism and Conformity in Classical Islam* (with Amin Banani); and *Islam's Understanding of Itself* (with Richard G. Hovannisian).

Prof. Vryonis is a Guggenheim Fellow and Fulbright Scholar, as well as a fellow of the American Academy of Arts and Sciences, the Medieval Academy of America, and the American Philosophical Society.